COUNTING OUR BLESSINGS

Counting Our Blessings: New Orleans Stories 20 Years After Katrina
Copyright © 2025 by Carol Bebelle
All rights reserved.
ISBN: 978-1-60801-303-6

Cover illustration by Bryan Brown.
Cover design by Alex Dimeff.

Printed in the United States of America.
University of New Orleans Press
2000 Lakeshore Drive
New Orleans, Lousiana

COUNTING OUR BLESSINGS
New Orleans Stories 20 Years After Katrina

edited by
CAROL BEBELLE

This collection is dedicated to:

my brother, LaSalle M. Rattler Jr., who, as a member of the New Orleans Police Department, stayed to defend and protect our city when she was almost destroyed. Covid-19 took his life in 2020 due to national leaders who failed in their responsibility to protect and defend the people of the United States in the early stages of the pandemic;

Caldonia Staton, who took two evacuating friends who needed shelter and gave them a home and made them part of her family while theirs were scattered—to and for each other;

our fellow Americans who came through for us when our government failed us;

and to all the tender mercies and compassionate care shown to us.

This volume is a reminder to us of who we could be in times of trouble and who we can be every day.

ACKNOWLEDGEMENTS

The longer we live the more we learn that, as the proverb says, "many hands make light work." This project was created by the awesome team of generous, bright, and committed supporters and believers who were blessings to me and made it possible for me to undertake this project.

I thank the authors who opened the door on this distressing period of their lives to mine the bright spots to share. My editorial work was supported by Antwamesha Jenkins, Dr. Tia Smith, Lynn Suruma, and Dr. Pam Breaux.

And, finally, I thank Loyce Wright, who forever reminds me that "there are blessings in the midst of storms. And, God is." The hundreds of times I've heard her proclaim this helped the focus of this volume to emerge.

Without Abram Himelstein and the University of New Orleans Press, this would not have been possible.

Working together, we can do great things.

TABLE OF CONTENTS

Preface 13
   Carol Bebelle aka AKUA
Katrina: A Personal Odyssey 15
   Orissa Arend
Still, Tomorrow Comes 31
   Carol Bebelle aka AKUA
This is Not That Type of Storm 48
   Steven Bingler & Linda Usdin
Joy on the Horizon 59
   J. B. Borders
What New Orleans Has Taught Me 78
   Andrea Chen
Critical Imagination, Philanthropy, and Disaster: 87
   How Women on Stoops and Men on Milk Crates Changed the World
   Flozell Daniels Jr. with Pam Jenkins
Love After the Storm 102
   Jarvis & Kelly DeBerry
Happenstance 110
   Lloyd Dennis
The Calling 117
   Lucas Díaz
On Love and Leadership 126
   Lamar & Ashleigh Gardere
Right Time Right Place: Philanthropy Learns to Build Community 157
   Linetta Gilbert
Sankofa Journey Continuum 167
   Cherice Harrison-Nelson & Herreast Harrison
Buck It Up, Buttercup 181
   Sharon Howard
Holding the History of Those Who Died 187
   Pamela Jenkins
Charlie & Louise 200
   Charlie Johnson & Louise Mouton Johnson
Surviving Katrina with Frozine and Auggie Doggie 215
   Chakula cha Jua

From Tragedy to Transformation: 225
   Finding Purpose in the Aftermath of Katrina
   Damia Khanboubi
The Seeds of Strength, Courage, and Confidence 235
   Dwana Makeba
Jazzman in the Storm 240
   Ed Morris
The Brighter Side of the Storm: 246
   Stories of Compassion and Courage
   Minister Willie Muhammad
Federal Flood Precipitated by Hurricane Katrina 258
   Jamilah Peters-Muhammad
After the Storm: Moving Forward 267
   Valentine Pierce
Blessings in the Midst of the Storm and "God is . . ." 294
   Loyce Pierce Wright
Blessed 313
   Gregory Rattler Sr.
Transcending Storms: Creating Beauty from Uncertainty 331
   Asante Salaam
Go Biblical 344
   Mathew "Mat" Schwarzman
Acts of Kindness 357
   Julie Menhati Singleton
At the Water's Edge 362
   Nick Slie
The Blessing of Togetherness 375
   Karel Sloane-Boekbinder
Inside the Cone of Uncertainty: Between the Dark & the Light 392
   José Torres-Tama
Blessed by God's Grace and Families' Faith 423
   Dwight & Trudell Webster
From New Orleans to Birmingham: 434
   A Journey of Resilience After Hurricane Katrina
   Kyshun Webster Sr.
Reflections 445
   MK Wegmann

The Financial Part 453
   Lynnette White-Colin
My Silver Lining 462
   Freddi Williams Evans

CONTRIBUTORS 469

PREFACE
Counting Our Blessings

August 29, 2005:
Hurricane Katrina hit New Orleans leaving approximately 70 to 80 percent of the city underwater. The city was vacated except for the first line workers (police, fire, hospital, and critical members of the administration, etc.). It was six to eight weeks before New Orleanians started returning; 1,833 fellow New Orleanians and Louisianians had lost their lives. The New Orleans East and Ninth Ward were devastated.

Twenty years later, these realities are still dramatic reminders. Horrific stories of abandonment, desperate acts of rescue and protection; an estimated 160,000 children were separated from their families in an ultimate act of sacrifice; commercial activity was shut down and City Government and Civil Servants took residence on cruise ships.

In the personal lives of New Orleans residents, people were faced with loss of home possessions, personal power, jobs, privacy, independence, family memorabilia and, in extreme cases, human lives. The city wasn't destroyed, but it was in serious jeopardy of being too damaged to repair. The US Army Corps of Engineers had been charged with planning, building, and monitoring the levee system, but they had made critical errors in their assessment of the strength needed to withstand the pressure of raging water in the turmoil of the weather associated with Category Four and Five hurricanes.

Twenty years later, the city of New Orleans is still rebuilding. The city's near destruction created opportunities for developers and entrepreneurs and these opportunities were seen and often taken by those of who came from other parts of the nation and the world, first, because their lives were in order and those of New Orleanians were not. In fact, New Orleanians were returning home for years after Hurricane Katrina having to maintain an alternate residence elsewhere while rebuilding their lives. Lots of financial support was forthcoming to individuals, families, organizations, government, and the food industry. Jobs had big jumps in employees that were paid not only for work, but for showing up and accepting long overtime schedules. The school systems closed down and universities created agreements with other universities for their students to attend. Families were traumatized by separations, deaths, stress, and loss of control of their lives. The fragility of government resources was visible.

For Black people, this disaster picked the ancestral wound of the MAAFA (great tragedy associated with the slave trade): being snatched, separated, losing privacy and control with a dehumanizing circumstance and treatment, and having to count on others for food, clothes, shelter, and safety. Our lives were in a constant state of negotiation. Our access to resources, finances, and many other things were a daily challenge. We were overwhelmed, frightened, and scared to do much more than figure out how to avoid being in the "less than" existing reality longer than necessary. Looking for the light at the end of the tunnel and praying we would get there. This became our post-Katrina reality. Our memory of Katrina begins with an overwhelming sense of loss of power, possession, personhood, and regard. Most of us have this message embodied in our scars, our wounds, and our spirits. And, we don't easily return to this period of our lives unless asked to. This is a result of the overwhelming loss.

While living our post-Katrina life, thousands of small and large blessings, kindnesses and considerations became the nurturing elements, the hope and faith influences, in our lives. In the end, these minor and major moments of relief became critical parts of our capacity to persevere. This volume uplifts the many who came, contributed, tended to, assisted, and provided the lights that continue to lead us to recovery. The stories are told in the authentic voice of those who experienced it. Sometimes as a result of something very disturbing, sometimes in response to an unexpected surprise of help or assistance, sometimes as relief from distress that is almost too difficult to bear. So many moments, people, and circumstances that joined together to create next steps on a journey that we only had faith that we were going to be able to continue. Thousands didn't make it, but we are some of the ones who did.

KATRINA: A PERSONAL ODYSSEY
ORISSA AREND

When Hurricane Katrina suddenly roared into New Orleans, I was fifty-nine years old, a mediator and psychotherapist, married for the second time, and the mother of two wonderful children off in the Northeast learning to be doctors. My work schedule was fairly flexible with a small private practice. I organized local trainings for the People's Institute for Survival and Beyond on Undoing Racism, and I was in the process of writing a book about the New Orleans Black Panthers and the stand they had taken here in 1970. I was also in charge of a group of restorative justice AmeriCorps mediators. My husband, Richard, was teaching special education in an elementary school in Luling, just up the Mississippi River from here. Although I'm not a Catholic, Richard and I enjoyed a regular worship at St. Augustine Church in Tremé because we were so inspired by Fr. LeDoux and his parishioners, steeped as they were (and are) in the Holy Spirit and the Lord's work. Richard even received a full-immersion baptism in the church's font.

We lived (and still live) in a comfortable four-bedroom house near Tulane University on the "sliver by the river," which came close—a few blocks—to flooding but, by the grace of God, didn't flood. We fled, at the last possible moment, to Natchez, Mississippi, where a friend of a friend took us in. In mid-September, we managed to rent a house in Luling with another couple, Jeanie and Ross Lunz. They often shared our little getaway cabin on the Wolf River in Mississippi with us, and Jeanie taught at Luling Elementary with Richard. Richard and Jeanie were lucky to return to their teaching jobs just a few weeks after the storm.

So, my perspective on Katrina and its aftermath, though I was disoriented, traumatized, and fearful for my city and my friends, was one of luck, adequate resources, and white-skin privilege as I hoovered around the city, sneaked in, and made numerous forays over to the west bank of our city, a place called Algiers. I couldn't stay away from New Orleans for long. Even as I visited my friends and family in their gorgeous new limestone homes in Austin, where everything was clean and well run, I couldn't wait to get back to my moldy city where nothing worked and we stuffed rags and foam in the rafters to plug up holes in the roof when it rained.

I was born in Austin and grew up in Texas. I didn't get to New Orleans, a totally new and foreign place, until my last year in college. And though this is heresy for a Texan, I realized, in those forlorn months after Katrina, that I could never happily live anywhere but New Orleans, even as I wondered if our city could ever come back.

I'll divide my remembrance of blessings, surprises, and opportunities into two groups: the personal and the institutional. The two institutions I was most intimately involved with were St. Augustine Church and Common Ground Relief. The first had existed since before the Civil War, and the second sprang up in the wake of the hurricane, like wildflowers in spring, seemingly from nothing.

St. Augustine is a study of how the archdiocese tried to exploit disaster to kick out a beloved priest. In the process, it nearly destroyed one of the most venerable and valued community organizations in a devastated city. By contrast, Common Ground exemplified the way disaster provided fertile soil for a radically fresh approach to community health and medicine. Both St. Augustine and Common Ground fired up the community activism that ultimately prevailed, saving one institution and supercharging the other.

I would have thought, looking back, that the total collapse of all the systems that had worked so well for me would have created a fearful chaos, isolation, and a fear of others, especially given the realization that those same systems had betrayed and victimized huge portions of my fellow citizens and left them desperate even before the storm. The systems I'm talking about are the police, healthcare, education, electricity, water, phones, and on and on.

What I found was just the opposite. What rushed in to fill that fearful void was camaraderie, creativity, strange and interesting bedfellows, and, yes, at times, what I can only call miracles. I'll sprinkle the personal blessings and gifts into these larger institutional stories, not because they are important in and of themselves, but because they were my omens, my signposts, the small flickering candles that kept me going, prompted me to show up and pay attention anywhere that I might be needed.

* * *

I'll start with St. Augustine. It was built in 1842 in the historic community of Tremé. Tremé, just north of the French Quarter, is the oldest African American neighborhood in America. At St. Augustine Church, enslaved people, people who owned slaves, and free people of color all worshipped together. It's the oldest Black Catholic church in the United States and the first integrated church in the US. It was home to Homer Plessy and the Venerable Henriette DeLille. It serves as a spiritual and cultural hub for New Orleanians of many denominations and for visitors from abroad. The church is noted for its jazz masses and its showcasing of Black Masking Indians, local musicians, and Creole, Haitian, and European traditions of art. Outside sits a sculptural memorial to the Unknown Slave.

The church didn't flood in Katrina. Its food pantry and relief services were operating full tilt in the spring after the storm. Students from HBCUs were sleeping on cots in the sanctuary. Its beloved priest, Fr. Jerome LeDoux, took care of anyone suffering in Tremé, played the piano, worked on his memoir about the church and its history, and inspired his parishioners with sermons that soared elegantly—so elegantly, in fact, that I thought he might actually take wing himself. He soldiered on during Katrina and after—a man in his eighties sleeping on the floor, eating raw foods, as he always had, never missing a beat. Now more than ever, he was exactly what his community needed.

What happened next looked to many of us like a power grab, so common after Katrina. In early February 2006, the Archdiocese of New Orleans announced a plan, in response to storm-related financial losses, to combine parishes and close seven churches. Under this plan, our parish was declared dead. The church was to be taken over by a neighboring parish and its white priest. Given LeDoux's competence and popularity, the move smacked of jealousy tinged with resentment and racism because LeDoux wore African vestments and wasn't all that careful about record-keeping.

All of us were suffering. We had lost friends and neighbors in Katrina. We were afraid of losing our city. And now the threat of the loss of our church and our priest was too much. The St. Augustine congregation came together in shock, mourning, confusion, and anger to decide what to do—not an easy task for a diverse group of people who were young and old, Black and white, rich and poor, conservative and revolutionary. And all of us were reeling from the multiple recent traumas of loss and displacement after Hurricane Katrina. But we did agree that we had to do something.

Our first steps were to write letters, say prayers, contact the media, raise money, and launch a formal appeal. But even with friends in high places, none of it worked. Archbishop Alfred Hughes stood firm in his decision to close our parish. On the Ides of March 2006, it was a fait accompli.

That's when all hell—or all heaven, depending on your point of view—broke loose. An assortment of young people who had originally come to town from the Beneficent Elsewhere to help us gut houses and clean up seized the rectory at the request of parishioners. (More about this group later, in the section on Common Ground Relief.) They barricaded themselves inside and stayed for twenty days. Even our elders who had never questioned Catholic or white authority figured, *Well, what do we have to lose?*

Lawyers, strategists, and activists of all stripes set up a constant vigil on the sidewalk and in the courtyard next to the church dedicated to the Unknown Slave. Work and prayer were punctuated with food, song, poster art, and soulful jazz for an ever-expanding band of well-wishers. But when the new priest arrived to say mass with ten armed bodyguards, a spontaneous protest arose in the church. A cadre of young people had planned this direct action on their own, not bothering to consult us, their elders who were spending endless hours in strategy meetings. These young people carried signs into the sanctuary that said, "We shall not be moved" and "Thou shalt not steal."

The new priest, claiming that he feared for his safety, beat a hasty retreat. Indeed, his group was so scared that all it took was the silent march of children to get them to scurry out mid-service, knocking down one of their own parishioners in the street in their hurry to leave.

The choir burst into song: *"Shake, shake, shake the devil off."*

We danced in the aisles. With LeDoux already banished to Bay St. Louis by his superiors, Al Harris preached an impromptu sermon about how we are peaceable people.

Doubling down, the archbishop then declared the altar defiled and closed the church itself as well as the parish.

There were many angels during this period. One was a prominent French Quarter hotelier who prefers to remain nameless. He offered the archdiocese a donation of one million dollars to settle church dues that were in arrears, an offer that he rescinded after LeDoux was ousted. Sandra and Ben Gordon were primary organizers. They unloaded the huge trucks of food donations for the free food bank in the parish hall.

Other angels were the Golden Girls, as we called them, dignified Black elders who had never before dreamed of defying Catholic authority. Among them was Joyce Montana, widow of the late Black Masking Indian Big Chief Tootie Montana. These elders, dressed in church clothes, placed their chairs strategically in a semicircle at sunset to make sure the police and archdiocesan authorities didn't try to enter the boarded-up rectory.

Let me circle back to the boarded-up rectory. After the church was closed, Suncere Ali Shakur, a volunteer with the hurricane recovery collective Common Ground, mentored by the group's leader, Malik Rahim, a former Black Panther, took charge of the rectory along with some parishioners. The parishioners called the shots during the occupation. Common Grounders followed their lead. For twenty days, Suncere would lower a bucket from the second-floor window, and we would load it up with chicken and other edibles. The cadre who had boarded up the doors and stuffed the locks with epoxy after LeDoux's departure would lean out of the same window and give press conferences, prompting even Al Sharpton to come down from New York to express solidarity. The cloistered cadre spent their free time cleaning the place up. They felt a spiritual presence—one also described by LeDoux in his book *War of the Pews* (2011). Spirits abound at St. Augustine. Groups who visit St. Augustine's Tomb of the Unknown Slave feel the spirits of those early parishioners who were in bondage.

I had enlisted Suncere as an AmeriCorps mediator. Ted Quant, then director of Loyola University's Twomey Center for Peace through Justice, was Suncere's mentor. Quant was a St. Augustine strategist and experienced facilitator. Though we were looking for a face-saving solution to the impasse, the intransigence of the archdiocese, their guards with guns, and their absurd spin about outside agitators disrupting mass led me to give up all hope of a negotiated settlement. This was deep into Lent.

But nobody came to lock the church doors. Nobody carried the revolutionaries bodily out of the rectory. Al Sharpton, Jesse Jackson, and Marc Morial all stopped by to wish us well. Local and national media swarmed all over us. Suncere and his cadre ate well on hauled-in meals. They passed their days doing a little house-cleaning. Doretha, the church secretary with her perfect flip hairdo, climbed in and out of a window to get to her computer. A food and supply giveaway program for hurricane victims ran full tilt in the parish hall. We were far from dead. You can view all of this in real time because Swiss documentarian Peter Entell and his crew had taken up residence at the church and would go on to produce a spectacular film called *Shake the Devil Off*.

There were other angels: Jacques Morial, who helped avert an NOPD SWAT team that was preparing to swoop in on our prayer vigil on the last Friday of the occupation. Had they come, they would have found Rev. Al

Sharpton, Rev. Jesse Jackson, James Andrews, Trombone Shorty, Kermit Ruffins, Delfeayo Marsalis, John Boutté, Michael White, and hundreds of others. Jacques let NOPD know that Joyce Montana would proudly be the first to be arrested. The NOPD responded to Jacques's legal memo by deciding that this was a "civil matter."

Jacques was always there as our lead strategist. But he takes exception to my calling him an angel. In an email to me, he said, "I'm no angel, though, Orissa. Some of the things I said and did to the Archdiocese and Bishop Hughes might seem to some to be pretty diabolical, but certainly justified for the greater good. I'm not sure if I told you what my mom told me: She feared I would be excommunicated and couldn't be buried in the family tomb."

Another angel: Dyan French Cole, a community organizer better known as Mama D who took the vocalization of Black rage to the level of a high art form. Picture her on her knees (if you can), begging the interloping celebrant not to follow orders and betray the faithful. I remember Jerome Smith, the civil rights Pied Piper of children, making just such a plea.

It was during this struggle that I met Alison McCrary, when she was in her twenties, before she became a nun for twelve years, before she became a civil rights lawyer, before she became an advisor on death row, a tireless seeker, and a solid social justice activist. She organized the health fair and the food pantry. We are fast friends today, and she tells me that this experience helped shape her future path. She was a Katrina gift to me.

Ten days after the disrupted mass, Ted Quant got a call from the spokesperson for the archdiocese asking him to negotiate a resolution to the dismal stalemate. Quant pointed out that he was not neutral, that he sided with St. Augustine parishioners. The response was, "That's OK. We know you can be fair." Doretha fingered her rosary beads underneath the table the whole time the negotiations were going on.

Speculation abounded as to why the archbishop might change his mind, something that no one in New Orleans could recall happening here ever before. Some said it was pressure from on high resulting from all the bad publicity about hitting people when they were down. Me, I'll go with the oft-used Catholic "explanation," which is that some things are just a mystery.

Two days later, a settlement emerged. Both sides were pleased, but both had made significant compromises. The parish would remain open and independent. It got an administrator to help meet benchmarks over the next eighteen months.

The revolutionaries flung open the doors to the rectory. The archbishop held a reconciliation service to bring back the sacrament. It began in the dark. Amid incense and holy water and a sermon about the prodigal son, the lights came on. The next day, Palm Sunday, Father LeDoux, Archbishop Hughes, and the takeover priest celebrated mass together. Suncere and the archbishop hugged each other.

On Holy Thursday, the spokesperson for the archdiocese washed our feet. On Good Friday, pilgrims from all over town made our church the third stop as they walked the Stations of the Cross. At the fish fry that evening, stories of the successful mediation were spilling forth like points of light on a star that signifies a miracle.

It was a good Lent. It was a hard Lent. Each of us had participated personally and communally in a first-hand experience of death and resurrection. Easter, the first after Katrina, took on a new meaning as the St. Augustine parish came back to life.

What is Katrina's role in all of this? Because of the immediate and urgent need for solutions, and because of the wild diversity of helpers it brought together, Katrina set up a little social experiment that I would call Breaking the Rules. In ordinary times, who would have thought of seizing a rectory to forestall a parish closure? I read about teenagers confiscating a school bus to ferry people to safety.

Lance Hill, author and activist, stayed in New Orleans for the storm. He took time off from delivering water and supplies to desperate people downtown on his bicycle to check on my house and try to coax out the cats that a friend, who had sheltered in my house, had left behind. On September 15, he found time to travel to Jefferson Parish, a suburb of New Orleans, another world. He wandered into a Rite Aid. He had almost forgotten about money. He asked the guard, "Is the store open? Can I go in?"

"Yes."

"Can I take anything I want?"

Silence, a blank look. Then, "Yes."

Lance again: "Do I have to pay for it?"

Lance loved New Orleans after the storm. He could be helpful in concrete ways. He could see the stars at night.

From our perch in Luling, various of our friends would gather from the diaspora and plot ways to sneak into the city, bluff our way past the National Guard to check on our houses or those of our friends. No one was allowed in without special credentials. And National Guards from different states and territories were very protective of their turf. Heavily armed, they really didn't have that much to do in the deserted city. Lance, for instance, had a lot of explaining to do to the Texas guards about what he was doing at my house. He finally had to call in the Oklahoma National Guard (he had made friends with some) to vouch for him. They pulled out their guns and surrounded my house while Lance checked on the cats.

Trying to get to our houses, our ad hoc refugee group, which included a lawyer and an anthropologist, decided that if we were turned away at the parish line, we would just ditch our cars and run for it. But what we discovered was that any laminated explanation dangling from a lanyard around our necks would work. Breaking the stay-out rules, we snuck in often.

During one of our sneak-ins, Richard and I went to visit Mama D in the 7th Ward. We admired the small, clean oasis she had created in and around her house. When we arrived, she was actually Cloroxing the street. At the time, the spiritual benefits of that endeavor made perfect sense to me. She asked for a favor. A neighbor of hers needed medication. And every time he left his house, the National Guard harassed him. Could we drive him? No problem. A good chance to put our white-skin privilege to good use.

Breaking the rules—some of which applied only to Black people and some of which were just plain stupid. In ordinary times, breaking the rules would be associated with "getting over," trying to get something extra for personal gain. In Katrina time, breaking the rules was an adventure, empowering, liberating. Sometimes we felt like children again. I put anarchist revolutionaries on the clock doing their civil disobedience as part of my AmeriCorps program. I was breaking the rules. In Katrina time, you could get away with stuff like that.

During another sneak-in, we attended a Voodoo ceremony conducted by a Jewish Voodoo priestess and attended by her real estate-developer boyfriend and a few others clad in white. As we left the alley, with its strange, twisted metal markings, and drove onto the gray, unlit streets, we noticed that we were being pulled over by some version of the omnipresent military. We were out after curfew. It was 8:00 p.m. The official asked if we had been drinking. My husband said we wished we had. We all laughed, and he waved us on.

When we were in Luling, we took the first opportunity when there was enough gasoline and enough food to drive over to Mississippi and check on our Wolf River cabin. My heart sank when we got there. No sign of the driveway or a house. Just a huge pile of uprooted trees. But as we climbed and climbed over trees toward the river, our house suddenly appeared before us, mostly intact. A miracle.

Climbing back to our car, I noticed how different the country was from the city in its response to the storm. Instead of the awful smells in the city, the air here was perfumed with tree sap. Newly felled, the trees were still green, whereas all the trash in the city was gray and moldy. In the woods, there were already new habitats with birds and flowers and bees who had made a rapid pivot, and a delighted one, to post-storm conditions. A spider had woven a beautiful web, her home, between tree branches. She had done that overnight, whereas some of our homes in New Orleans would take us years to restore. What can we learn from Nature's response to disaster? For the trees and the birds and the spider, was Katrina even a disaster?

Ross, who was living with us in Luling, needed something physical to do while Jeanie taught school. So he came out to the Wolf River with a chainsaw and spent weeks clearing the road. It was a wonderful gift, because at that time, it was almost impossible to find anyone to do physical labor.

The other part of Katrina's role in my personal and institutional stories is the storm's effect as a great equalizer. I'm not saying that it wasn't much harder on some of us than others. It was. I'm just saying that since all of us were refugees, we were open to receive help wherever it came from: art, food, money, media, politics, hospitality, physical labor, the Holy Spirit. Because all of this was welcome, it all worked together, instead of splitting us off into the factions and personalities and rivalries so prevalent in ordinary time. I think it was that radical welcome that made the difference.

* * *

Now, back to the assortment of young people from the Beneficent Elsewhere who came to St. Augustine worship services in support of Father LeDoux. They did this a few times before they seized the rectory. A scruffy lot they were. And you couldn't really blame them because they were living in tents. I was touched that they took a bath, put on clean clothes, and showed up for worship. The self-proclaimed anarchists were mostly unfamiliar with Catholic ritual. They had come to town to be part of Common Ground Relief.

Common Ground is the second institutional miracle I witnessed firsthand. It didn't exist before the storm. It wasn't until this writing that I realized how closely the St. Augustine story and the Common Ground story fit together.

This is how I got involved: I was writing an opinion column for *The Louisiana Weekly*. At that time, the columns focused on the New Orleans Black Panthers standoff with the NOPD in 1970. They were collected in a booklet that I hoped would someday turn into a book. (It did in 2009.) In the process of reviving the Panthers' story in the columns, I had become good friends with Malik Rahim, the Panther in charge of security at their headquarters on Piety Street in 1970. I had also grown close to Robert King, then the only freed member of the Angola Three, a political prisoner held for decades in solitary confinement at the Louisiana State Penitentiary at Angola. Ted Quant, who mediated the agreement between St. Augustine and the archbishop, had mediated an even more startling agreement two years prior between the city officials of 1970 and the Panthers, in front of a huge audience at the Ashé Cultural Arts Center. Father LeDoux was also a central figure in the Panthers story.

The young anarchists who came here to help after Katrina were enthralled with Malik and King, with New Orleans history and culture, with the principles of self-determination espoused by the People's Institute for Survival and Beyond, by the ten-point program that had sustained the Panthers for decades, and even by my booklet. The booklet put some of New Orleans' revolutionary history in narrative form. An anarchist press in California pirated the booklet—breaking the rules—and it went viral. I was delighted.

The hardest part of Katrina for me was thinking that King might be dead. Two weeks after the storm, no one had heard from him. I asked Richard to consult his spirit power animals. They weren't optimistic. I put out a notice on Vincent Sylvain's lost person website. It got the attention of Davia Nelson, one of the NPR Kitchen Sisters who knew about King from a voicemail I'd left her several years back about King's Freelines (rhymes with "pralines"). He made his candy in a very hidden kitchen in Angola. You'll have to read my book for that story.

The Common Ground Health Clinic came into being in the Westbank community of Algiers in September of 2005, just a few days after the storm. There were as many idealistic, fantastic visions for the clinic's future as there were scruffy revolutionaries, doctors, nurses, and alternative healers who converged from the Beneficent Elsewhere. Their visions, fueled by endorphins of kindness and adrenalin of desperation, were a beautiful thing to behold. And though they sustained me at that terrible time, I gave somewhere between a zero and a negative one to the chances that any of these visions would endure. I'd wake up in two years, I figured, and this fairy tale collective of healers, who could do anything they set their minds to and who embraced justice as a part of health, would seem as distant a dream as the nightmare of Katrina.

It didn't turn out that way. Who would have imagined that *The New England Journal of Medicine*, *The Washington Post*, *Mother Jones*, and *The New York Times* (they called it "The Little Clinic that Could") would take notice? Who would have imagined that local physicians, organizers, and visionaries would take a keen interest and form a board to direct the clinic? Who would have thought that an immigrant from Cameroon, a public health specialist in maternal and child health, would step forward to channel the idealism of the volunteer founders into practical avenues?

In 2006, Antor Ndep Ola, the clinic's executive director, said that the Common Ground Health Clinic was here to stay and to provide free primary healthcare for all who walked through the door. "We remain true to the model that we are here in solidarity. We are not charity. We are in solidarity with the community," she said. Even though there was no blueprint out there, Antor acknowledged, she saw the clinic as a catalyst. "Yes, we are providing quality primary healthcare. But we are taking it a step further, and that further step is recognizing that racism does exist and it does influence health. We recognize that there are people out there who are hardworking people and still cannot afford healthcare and should be receiving healthcare."[1] The clinic is still thriving today.

Its origin story: When Katrina churned into the Gulf, Malik Rahim and his partner Sharon Johnson decided to hunker down in their Algiers bungalow. They had always ridden out hurricanes. And as a former deputy of security in the Black Panther Party, Malik knew quite a lot about making preparations for just about anything.

Three days after the storm, a techno-miracle occurred. Mary Ratcliff, editor of the *San Francisco Bay View*, reached Malik on his landline. He was incensed.

"This is criminal," he told her. "There are gangs of white vigilantes near here, riding around in pickup trucks, all of them armed.... People whose homes and families were not destroyed went into the city right away with boats to bring survivors out, but law enforcement told them they weren't needed. I'm in the Algiers neighborhood. The water is good. Our parks and schools could easily hold forty thousand people, and they're not using any of it.... This is criminal."

Ratcliff typed like crazy as he talked.

---

1   Orissa Arend, "Birth of the Common Ground Health Clinic," San Francisco Bay View, November 27, 2007, https://sfbayview.com/2007/11/birth-of-the-common-ground-health-clinic/.

* * *

Meanwhile, Scott Crow and Brandon Darby, white activists from Austin who had worked with Malik to publicize the plight of the Angola Three, felt drawn to New Orleans to help. The Angola Three were Black Panthers who spent decades in solitary confinement at the Louisiana State Penitentiary at Angola for their political beliefs. Scott and Brandon brought Malik some supplies and went to look for Robert King in flooded Mid-City in New Orleans proper. But they were turned away by the authorities.

They returned to Austin for more supplies and this time vowed to swim to King's house if they had to. Brandon insisted that some rescue workers go look for King. When they agreed to take King's dog, he got into the boat and met Brandon and Scott on higher ground. Brandon and King headed for Malik's. It had been a long two weeks for all of us, wondering if King was alive. (Brandon later went undercover with the FBI and wreaked all kinds of havoc with his former friends.)

Malik told Amy Goodman with *Democracy Now!*, "While we was together, we—every evening, we used to have these dialectical discussions, and one of our main discussions was on why progressive movements have always started with such a bang and then end in such a frizzle. And we kept coming up with that, we allowed our petty differences to stop us from working together. . . . King said that the thing that we need to find is the common ground, and so with that, we took that name . . . and Common Ground was founded. Sharon Johnson, my partner, put up thirty dollars. I put up twenty dollars. And with that fifty dollars, we founded Common Ground."

Prior to the storm, Sharon had no community organizing experience, and she and Malik were a newly established couple. But she chose to stay. And with enormous grace and spiritual radiance, she took on critical organizing roles and held together an odd, ever-expanding commune of people determined to help.

Ratcliff emailed her group the "This is Criminal" missive, and they forwarded it around the country. A few days later, activists began arriving in Algiers: Jamie "Bork" Laughner, an advocate for the homeless from Washington, DC; street medic Roger Benham from Connecticut; Noah Morris from Rhode Island; and twenty-year-old Scott Mechanic from Philadelphia (we called him Boy Scott to distinguish him from the two other Scotts). Two weeks later, Mo, a registered nurse and herbalist from Dillon, Montana, came. She and Bork had conceived the idea of an anarchist clinic in New Orleans before they met Malik.

When the self-identified white anarchists knocked on Malik's door, he directed them to the mosque he once attended, Masjid Bilal, where they emptied the refrigerator, put tarps on the floor in deference to the sacred Muslim space, and set out supplies. This was September 9, 2005, eleven days after the storm. Bork spray-painted "Solidarity not Charity," "First Aid," and "No Weapons, including Police and Military" on plywood outside of the mosque. Then the group began to think about how to get patients.

Their first ambassador was a local woman, Mama Souma, who took her daughters around the neighborhood knocking on doors. Malik was as interested in easing the racial tensions as he was in building a patient base. New Orleanians fleeing the flood had been turned away at gunpoint by authorities as they tried to walk across the Crescent City Connection to higher ground. The governor had issued a "shoot to kill" order, affirmed by New Orleans' mayor and police chief, on looters, many of whom were only securing survival rations. Algiers had been invaded by soldiers, federal police officers, and private paramilitary personnel, creating an atmosphere of tension and trepidation.

The newly arrived young white medics fanned out on bicycles, asking people if they needed water and telling them about the clinic. Malik knew that white skin had its privilege and its uses. He could see the real possibility of the whole African American community in Algiers being slaughtered.

When people asked the medics if they were Red Cross or FEMA, neither of which had made an appearance in Algiers, they said no, they were just volunteers who had come without authorization. They took blood pressure, offered first aid, and checked for diabetes, anxiety, and depression. "It was the street medics who really stopped this city from exploding into a race war, because they were white and serving the Black community at a time when Blacks were fed up. They are the real heroes of this thing," Malik said.

Boy Scott limited conversation with guardsmen to healthcare. But Bork saw fit to reveal her anarchist political context, causing one incredulous soldier to ask, "So you're the anarchists in the mosque brought in by the ex-Black Panther giving free healthcare?"

"Yeah. And we're environmentalists, too," Bork replied.

The medics were followed a few days later by a caravan of doctors, nurses, grief counselors, acupuncturists, and herbalists from San Francisco. On September 11, a French relief organization, Secours Populaire Français, arrived. When the French physicians accompanied Roger on house calls, they were amazed at people's poor health. "Chronic illnesses, old untreated injuries, and results of neglect had only been exacerbated by Katrina, not created by it," Roger wrote in *What Lies Beneath: Katrina, Race, and the State of the Nation*.[2] In this regard, New Orleans was merely a microcosm of a healthcare disaster happening nationwide.

Word spread, and almost overnight, health practitioners and political activists arrived in droves. On September 22, with Hurricane Rita threatening to make landfall who knew where, my son Jonathan called me from New York, where he was doing a community medicine residency. He was aching for his hometown. He said that FEMA and the Red Cross had not been responsive to his offers to help, and did I know of anything? I called Malik, and he told me about the first aid station. But he recommended that volunteers not come until we knew where Rita was heading.

Jonathan, who only had a week off, pondered the situation into the wee hours and then hopped a plane, figuring the worst that could happen is that he'd evacuate with me and his stepfather from our temporary digs in Luling. The next morning, I crossed the Mississippi River and picked him up at the New Orleans airport. It wasn't hard to find him. As far as I could see, we were the only people there.

Malik wanted rain gear. When we found ponchos at a dollar store, we felt like we had won the lottery. We made our way to the mosque, bullying through all the checkpoints and defying the mandatory evacuation order. The guards with guns made me nervous, but Jonathan's stethoscope worked like a charm—that, and the fact that we were white. I left him at the mosque and headed "home" (euphemism for our rented house in Luling), wondering to what great vortex of weather and social chaos I'd just sacrificed my firstborn son.

Later, my daughter Rebecca came down to volunteer. So, I got to see both of my children practicing the medical skills they were learning in socially relevant ways while working under enormous duress. I like to think that this experience helped shape them into the compassionate, brilliant, service-oriented physicians they are today.

Jed Horne notes in his excellent 2006 book *Breach of Faith*, "Six days after the clinic opened, some forty out-of-state activists were camped out in and

---

2   Roger Benham, "The Birth of the Clinic," in *What Lies Beneath: Katrina, Race, and the State of the Nation*, ed. South End Press Collective (Cambridge, MA: South End Press, 2007), 77.

around Rahim's home. By year's end, a total of 170 volunteers would have rotated through the clinic, including three dozen locals ... Common Ground's first aid station had become a full-service medical clinic, still a cash-free operation dependent on in-kind donations and volunteers." In addition to traditional medicine, it offered herbalism, massage therapy, and acupuncture.

By early October, the clinic was treating over a hundred drop-ins per day. It also spawned the Latino Health Outreach Project to help migrant workers with health and legal issues. They even made house calls for workers injured on the job.

Scott Weinstein, a tall, slender RN from Quebec who arrived soon after the clinic opened, quickly made strategic linkages with what was left of the New Orleans medical community. He says that the clinic reshaped the way he thinks about politics. "Most people think of direct action as taking a street during a demonstration," he says, "but big deal. So you got a street. This is not about taking the streets; it's about taking healthcare." "SOLIDARITY NOT CHARITY" became the clinic's motto.

During the week that Jonathan was there, the clinic never closed and volunteers slept wall-to-wall on the floor. Intake was thorough, and records were meticulously kept. The list of projects and tasks on the wall that needed volunteers included critical incident debriefing; medical legal support—or, covering our heinies; and infusing all we did with anti-oppression intentions.

Jonathan told Michelle Garcia of *The Washington Post* that locals such as Swampwater Jack, who lived across the street from the clinic, stayed away from the medical facilities with soldiers stationed out front. He "preferred to have his asthma checked at home, where he could show off photos of the gators he had shot down in the bayou."[3]

Two years after its founding, the clinic became a registered 501c3 organization providing primary healthcare, social work, acupuncture, herbalism, prescription assistance, health education, HIV testing, referrals for specialty care, and a mobile unit for Latino health outreach. The clinic moved out of the mosque and beyond "disaster mode."

There had been no reason to worry about King. Opting to ride out the storm on the second floor of his Mid-City house with his dog Kenya, subsisting on peanut butter, he made neighborhood rounds to care for the ani-

---

3   Michelle Garcia, "For a Former Panther, Solidarity Afer the Storm," *The Washington Post* (Washington, DC), Dec. 5, 2005, https://www.washingtonpost.com/archive/lifestyle/2005/12/04/for-a-former-panther-solidarity-after-the-storm/7383a28d-f72e-4e8f-8247-99374ee08719/.

mals. He cleaned oil off of a bird's wing. He waved away rescue boats because they wouldn't take Kenya. After three decades in solitary confinement and a prison escape break, everything Katrina could bring was no big deal for King.

After being at Malik's for a while, King flew out to California to meet Davia of The Kitchen Sisters. She confided in me later that she had been a little scared by the prospect of the encounter. How could a man be sane after all he had been through, she'd wondered. Davia recorded a tender and moving radio piece that included my voicemail, King's description of his time in flooded New Orleans, and the story of his candy, called Freelines. It aired on public radio stations nationally for months. Davia and King became good friends. She set him up with a first-rate kitchen, and his national candy business took off.

When the electricity came back on uptown, I think it was sometime in November, we moved back home from our place in Luling. King came back to New Orleans to collect his belongings, and he lived with Richard and me for a few months before he moved to Austin while he waited for New Orleans to recover. We sheltered a bunch of friends, including filmmaker Royce Osborne and his wife Dama Fountain. Royce and Dama had waded through the water with their possessions and their cat held above their heads. They escaped on a bus to Texas and then a plane to California. Royce became a Katrina celebrity because of his post-storm adventures and his documentary film *All on a Mardi Gras Day*.

We also sheltered a rotating variety of Common Ground volunteers who needed a bed and house for a while instead of a tent. My house became a glorious commune. People helped us with all sorts of things, even decorating my Christmas tree when I was too down and tired even to do that. My former policeman next-door neighbor, Bill, looked at me askance when I told him an ex-Angola inmate was moving in. King cooked Freelines in the backyard, sweetening up the neighborhood. And before long, King and Bill would sit out back and smoke and talk into the evening hours.

Katrina time was magical. I witnessed two institutional miracles and several personal ones as well. What made that magic? Maybe it was that we needed each other. Maybe it was because the question of what to do next was so unpredictable. We lived in the moment. That was all we knew we had. We met new people. We went to new places. We took chances. We defied the odds, which were daunting.

I would never ask for that kind of crucible again, and yet I would not trade my odyssey through it for anything.

STILL, TOMORROW COMES
CAROL BEBELLE AKA AKUA

In December of 1998, Douglas Redd, an incredible community artist, and I founded Ashé Cultural Arts Center (CAC), a community-based cultural arts center located in Central City, a center dedicated to a mission of culture and art as a strategy for community, cultural, human, and economic development. Renting a space was a point of excitement, but running the space became the challenge. Very soon I discovered that we had not just rented a space, but we had begun to birth an institution, an institution that was dedicated to culture, heritage, and art derived from the African diaspora. Though I had spent a previous career as a community-based human services planner in education, substance abuse prevention and treatment, and public health, choosing to build an institution dedicated to culture in New Orleans was no easy feat. The first few years were trying and would have convinced us to quit were it not for the cheerleading band of community, family, and friends who kept us aiming for a vision of something wonderful.

For the purposes of this story, I am sharing our journey between 2005 and 2010. The progression of the story here is not intended to be chronological, because re-experiencing a journey like this tends to operate from streams of consciousness, one thing provoking the thought of something else. During that time, much of my life and focus was on the Ashé Cultural Arts Center. Its evolution carries you from one moment to the next and is full of activity that I cannot describe by myself. So, for most of this narrative, I will speak in the first-person plural pronoun, "we."

Suffice it to say, times were hard. I had considered going back to work to ensure we preserved the Ashé space. In 2005, to encourage us, Ford Foundation program officer Linetta Gilbert had sponsored an extensive visit to South Africa to observe the many ways culture was organized for its communities and visitors, and she included our board chair president, Dr. Beverly

Andry, co-founder Douglas Redd, and me. I was cautiously shifting my sense of failure to the possibility of continuing.

We had hardly settled back in after our tour of South Africa when Douglas Redd was starting to look at the television, which, for him, was rather unusual. He had positioned a television in an arc that made it easy to check throughout the day. When I inquired what was up, he explained he was watching Mother Africa stir up another storm, the storm that would become Hurricane Katrina. This impelled him to begin strategizing how he was going to protect Ashé's exterior glass showcase. The result was a wooden shield that was fixed to the front of Ashé CAC. When, weeks later, we returned from evacuation, the Center was as we had left it. Artist Jeffrey Cook visited Ashé several times over the weeks we were away and convinced potential looters he encountered that the "imaginary" people inside of Ashé were prepared with fire power to protect themselves and the Center. Thank you, Jeffrey Cook (rest in peace), for your multi-creative gifts. The combination of Doug's wooden shield and Jeffrey Cook's role as guardian proved to be a real lifesaver for the Center. Once Doug and I had completed our respective hurricane prep assignments, we were off to Opelousas, Louisiana, to the home of our friend, Caldonia Staton (rest in peace), who had sheltered us the year before.

The traffic was frustrating and, to an extent, distracting. But as we got closer, I thought about being fifty years old, in the process of building a community institution, and being forced to recreate my life. Thinking this directly, as the thing that I would least like to do, is how I have always taken on scary things: I think about them deeply enough to imagine being in the circumstance, and then I let that fear chase me away with the determination not to get there. That drive allowed me to reckon with the possibility of a fretful future, and to close the door and lock that possibility away, not quite knowing how, but knowing that I would find a way to continue the life I was living before Katrina. In the next four hours, we were out of crisis, anxiety, and fear and went into normal life, which we shared for six weeks before we returned.

Once we'd settled in at Caldonia's, caught our breath, and had a moment to think, we realized we were a remote asset for our community still in New Orleans. We heard from my brother, LaSalle Rattler Jr., a member of the New Orleans Police Department (rest in peace), that Ashé and my home were in good shape after the storm. A call to Fred Johnson, a culture-bearer and leader with NDF (Neighborhood Development Foundation), informed us that he had remained in the city. Fred had become an operative with the sheriff's office and the key administration personnel for the city. Once his family had been secured, he made the decision to stay in the city. When the levees broke, he was invited to go to the Hyatt, where essential personnel and other key organizations were housed, and was accompanied by other men from the Black Men of Labor Social Aid and Pleasure Club, including Todd Higgins, Gralen Banks, and Paul Sylvester. They were security for the Hyatt, protecting the people; at other times, they were assisting with mobilizing and onboarding people from the Dome, or working with security officials on boats to check on people who had been left behind or had been running errands for friends and associates who were worried about their property, people, or homes in the city. We talked back and forth with him on several occasions as we checked on the safety of friends and heard about the status of the circumstances in the city.

In retrospect, sometimes we can recognize the moment when a choice became a major influence on our future. For me, it was in 2004, during the threat of Hurricane Ivan, when I heard Mayor Ray Nagin say, "For those of you who can evacuate, please go so our resources can be focused on attending to those who could not evacuate." It was then that Douglas Redd and I reached out to our friend, Caldonia Staton, to live with her as evacuees. Caldonia was an educator and an entrepreneur. She had lived in New Orleans for many years before deciding to return home to Opelousas, near her family. So, when Katrina was threatening, we reached out again. She laughingly said of course, mentioning how some others had called but she'd delayed answering because she waited to make sure Doug and I were taken care of.

So, Opelousas became our evacuation home. It made it possible for us to catch our breath, relax, and focus on how we could help contribute to our extended and cultural family in New Orleans. We began searching for artists, culture bearers, partners, and friends. I had family in New Orleans, and Doug's family was in Baton Rouge. My family was all accounted for: one brother was in Gonzales, and the other, a policeman, was in New Orleans after securing his family's safety in Houston.

Our financial circumstances at Ashé were dire. Before the hurricane threat, Linetta Gilbert indicated that she may have found a small grant that could be made available to Ashé in a short timeline. However, once we were settled, we heard from Linetta, who said all bets were off, the Ford Foundation was in deep thought about how it would respond to Hurricane Katrina, and that she would get back to us. Our assigned program officer at Ford, Miguel Garcia, called and said he was releasing the remaining funds in our existing grant for emergency use, which we divided in three ways: part for Douglas, part for me, and part for Lashaundal Moore, who was working with us.

We became a hub of sorts, hearing from our friends and community about their whereabouts and from others calling to arrange donations of money and other things. Caldonia gave us part of her kitchen to use as office space, and we started anticipating what a post-disaster existence was offering. When someone did something or contributed or provided an opportunity that served us unexpectedly, I became more aware of the phrase that goes, "Sometimes we encounter angels, unaware." Such was the case with Joycelyn Reynolds, grant officer for the Arts Council New Orleans, who, in early 2005, had advised us that the best opportunity for funding in the organizational category was one that provided some contribution of payment for Doug and me along with payment for insurance for both of us. She offered that an organization run by volunteers was not viewed as stable. It could cause other potential funders to be reluctant to fund us or make them willing to provide only smaller amounts. This advice, which we followed, would prove to be a tremendous blessing for us.

After two or three round trips from Oppelousas to New Orleans on the same day, returning home to the city became the best choice. Ashé was as we had left it. Doug's house had problems. My house was fine except that it was located in a part of the city that was not well lit and electricity was unreliable. At the same time, Kysha Brown Robinson, a resident of Tremé, was having similar feelings of vulnerability. Kysha was the CEO for the Central City Renaissance Alliance, which had offices in the apartments above Ashé. So, she and I worked during the day in our work spaces, and at night we slept on floor pallets in the office. Doug started off sharing this communal life with us but decided the space, with our constant chatter, was more than he could absorb and still do his work. He moved to sleeping in the upstairs balcony space of Ashé.

Post-Katrina New Orleans was, physically, a sick city. Life was listless, the communities empty. The vibrant green of life was absent, replaced by dull gray and brown. There was a heavy musk smell and a foul odor. The telltale smells of life were missing: the smell of flowers, cut grass, the escaped smells of cooking, the smell of rain in the air. All the aromas of life were dramatically absent. It was clear that New Orleans was a patient in need of healing—for the land and for the people. This theme of healing came to define our overall work at Ashé. Doug brought the spirit of the people forward with his 2000 installation *The Ties That Bind: Making Family New Orleans*

Style, which was funded by the Annie E. Casey Foundation. This installation provided three entrances: one each for biological family, spiritual family, and cultural family, with images of New Orleanians in the tradition of each style of family covering the walls of Ashé. With planning meetings and comeback events occurring, it was our way of bringing the pressure and spirit of our community to bear.

Doug and I began to realize that we were best committed to being nimble in what we did and how we did it and how we involved the community, both Central City and the cultural community. Ashé CAC became a space where many official (federal, state, city) meetings were held as well as community meetings and celebrations. Soon we were programming again. Linetta Gilbert was able to provide a sizable grant to put us in the position to be a ready resource to our community, our neighborhood, and our affinity community of cultural bearers and creatives. We built a team, inviting evacuated artists to return, including Luther Gray, Jamilah Peters-Muhammad, Frederick "Hollywood" Delahoussaye, Karel Sloane-Boekbinder, Drena Clay, Tammy Terell, Jerald White, Gwen Richardson, Lloyd Daly, and Dollie Rivas. My sister-in-law, Twyla Rattler, joined us to manage operations and provide leadership in organizing necessary administrative details, and Victor Robinson joined as our financial officer. As the team assembled, we began programming and being available to receive resources to distribute and to represent the interests of our communities in planning meetings. We realized that we were becoming an answer to our communities' needs, and being such a contribution was a welcome distraction and a nurturing inspiration.

I don't know if every cloud has a silver lining, but silver linings started appearing for us almost immediately. In December of 2005, we decided a Holiday on the Boulevard celebration was a good way to help people to find a little bit of joy. During the celebration, I experienced a most memorable moment in our after-Katrina story when a woman called and asked for me and said that her family in North Carolina decided at their Thanksgiving table to suspend their Christmas spending, combine it, and send it to New Orleans families. Ambassador (to South Africa, under President Bill Clinton) James Joseph and his wife Mary Braxton-Joseph had recommended that they contact me to accomplish their holiday gift-giving. And so, they forwarded a five thousand dollar check with the direction that it be certain to go to families with children. I contacted Olayeela Daste, who worked with Agenda for Children, to help to identify four families.

We delivered checks to these families, who were unaware we were coming. I will never forget this experience. It reminded me of a line in the song "Ordinary People" that says, "God uses ordinary people like you and me." This experience solidified its place in all my Katrina speaking engagements when I would say, "You came through for us when our government was delayed and scattered; our fellow Americans came through for us." In too many ways to count, individual people, families, organizations, churches, synagogues, mosques, and others took it upon themselves to be the change they wanted to see. But the best was yet to come.

Another warm spot in our journey was in July of 2006, when we were able to gather again in Congo Square for the annual MAAFA commemoration. This commemoration was a yearly community ritual for Ashé, and it served as an opportunity to come together and be reminded of the journey of our ancestors that made it possible for us to be here. With Katrina in our rearview mirror, the difficulties and the struggles of our ancestors had become more dramatically present to us as we were forced to leave our homes quickly, separated from family, living in less than perfect circumstances, and losing privacy and agency in our lives. This reconciliation of our recent life after the storm with the life of our ancestors became a point of clarity as we realized the progress that had been made since September of the previous year, compared to the hundreds of years that it took for our ancestors to progress out of enslavement. The motto for the MAAFA is "the past we inherit, the future we create." Hearing that and meditating on it inside of the journey we were on—rebuilding our lives, community, and city—became a point of inspiration for those in attendance.

We gathered in the early morning, all dressed in white. There was a quality of sacredness that was palpable as we stood together and walked through the streets to acknowledge the places where our ancestors had been sold. It's been said that context is everything; the context of 2006 helped us to generate a bit more spirit and a bit more inspiration to face the difficulties and challenges that were before us. Senator Diana Bajoie contacted us shortly after the storm to let us know she was moving our state capital request into priority status. As a result, our 1712 Oretha Castle Haley Boulevard location became our legal home when we were able to purchase it. Mayor Ray Nagin had made an election night promise in 2002 to do something good for Ashé before his term of office ended. In 2007, he presented a $2.2 million check to Efforts of Grace (the corporate sponsor for Ashé) for the purchase of the apartments above Ashé that helped us establish a community of creatives, culture-bearers, activists, and students in housing, half of which was subsidized. These are times when I think of what we would have missed if we had given up.

By 2006, Oretha Castle Haley Boulevard was seeing signs of returning life. Ashé was open six to seven days a week. Hope Credit Union was open due in large part to the efforts of Lynette White-Colin, the manager who staffed the credit union alone for a while to ensure that people could negotiate financial business at such a critical time. Greater Living Witness Sanctuary Church of God in Christ, pastored by Elder John Pierre, returned, offering The Men of Nehemiah recovery program, the participants of which acted as guardians for events and organizations on the street. The men also kept the street clean and generally helped to look out for those of us there. This helped us greatly, but it also helped them to make such a dramatic contribution to the caring and protection of all of us at a time when we felt so exposed and vulnerable. There were balls in the air everywhere and all kinds of opportunities being offered. We were able to encourage a giveaway program to add artists and culture bearers to the list of preferred recipients for loaded Visa giveaways, which were one-time financial contributions.

By the spring, we were operating on a banana peel and a skate, trying to keep up with all the things happening. We received a visit from one of our original board members, Ifama Arsan, who was in town handling business, having evacuated to her hometown in the Lafayette area. Doug was experiencing vertigo and nausea, possibly due to sinus allergy issues. This was a recurring spring malady for Doug, and with the environment quality being what it was, it was worse than usual. Ifama encouraged Doug to go to the hospital, and she would accompany us and help handle anything that came up. He said he needed to rest more than anything, so she left.

That evening, Doug returned to a makeshift sleeping area equipped with a barstool we had created in front of the stage at Ashé. I left a bell and told him we had to go to the hospital in the early morning, and it was agreed. I felt like we had a good plan. I returned to my desk to work, then napped for a few hours. I was awakened by a sharp noise and ran to find Doug had fallen on the floor, seizing, next to the fallen barstool and bell. After that, we were off to the emergency room with the paramedics. I called in support, and my sister-friend and Doug's nurse-confidant, Sheila Webb, arrived. Tests were taken, and we had been there about four hours when the emergency room doctor came in and told us that Doug had lung cancer with brain metastases. In a moment I realized that healing was now a very personal matter.

Doug's diagnosis came in March/April of 2006. And I became oh so grateful to Joycelyn Reynolds because Doug had insurance, and most importantly, he had a community. He needed a caretaker, and I was it. Immediately, John O'Neal, master theater artist, playwright, civil rights activist, and founder of Junebug Productions, offered us his and his wife's apartment above Ashé as a homebase for Doug. John traveled extensively, so the apartment was available for Doug when John and Bert were on tour and when they were gone. It was a solution to my anxiety about my two A priorities: Doug and Ashé.

Now I was right upstairs from Ashé, and that made a difference to Doug as well. When he was up to it, he could come downstairs and see for himself that things were well. Being upstairs at Ashé also made it easy for Doug's family and community to find him. He had regular visitors. Jerome Smith, civil rights icon and cultural advocate and culture-bearer, was a self-appointed coach for Doug, creating a nutritional supplement program, being present for nearly all his radiation treatments, and bringing the thunder of elder reasoning when he thought it was necessary.

As time progressed, it became apparent we were not going to win this fight. As Doug's health declined, the need for round-the-clock attention reared its head. Kalamu ya Salaam took the evening shift, coming four or five nights a week with companionship and cultural distraction: concerts, music, lectures, documentaries, and conversation. In time, we hired a gentle spirit named Christine Brown, who was a perfect caretaking companion for Doug. They were similar spirits: quiet and laid-back. His nursing team included his nursing confidants, Sheila and Jamilah Peters-Muhammad; caretakers, Christine, Kalamu, and myself; spiritual team, Nana Anoa Nantambu and Sula "Spirit" Evans; his brothers, Lenox Davis, Eric Waters, Luther Gray, Jeffrey Cook, Matt "Flukey" Suarez, Fred Johnson, and Carl Boloney; the many cooks and field trip assistants; and, last but not least, his Baton Rouge family and friends, including Brenda Williams and Chuck Siler.

Importantly, New Orleans artist Jeffrey Cook, who also resided in the apartments, had become his co-conspirator in imagining and creating the creative environment that Doug wanted to have at Ashé. As Doug became less able to do that on his own, Jeffrey willingly and generously became his representative. He also assumed a greater role as a protector for Ashé. This role was one that would become stronger and more definitive in our future.

In mid-June, Sheila assembled a team that included her sisters, Pam, Gilda, Beverly Ann, and Millie, along with Jeffrey Cook and Lloyd Daly to clean and prepare Redd House for Doug's arrival. Redd House was an in-community residence purchased by Efforts of Grace and renovated to be an artist residency in Central City. Doug was to be its inaugural resident. When Sheila called to say that it was time to go home, Doug moved to his new residence and his team followed. On July 17, 2007, Douglas Redd became an ancestor.

The outpouring of support and assistance was overwhelming. His wake was held at the Tremé Community Center and his funeral at his beloved Ashé Cultural Arts Center. The Black Men of Labor Social Aid and Pleasure Club, who had built the ramp for Doug at Redd House, planned his second-line procession from Tremé to Ashé with a horse-drawn carriage. Rev. Dwight Webster, an Efforts of Grace board member, provided leadership at the service at Ashé. The unimaginable had happened and was as unbelievable and devastating as it was sobering. Realizing that Ashé was a legacy gift Doug had left for the community, his life and sacrifice were now part of Ashé's institutional DNA. In a very dramatic way, I realized that this institution was for our community, culture-bearers, and for the ancestors. Ashé CAC was an actual presence, a legacy impulse of our ancestors, ensuring that the heritage, culture, and perspective of African Americans would be professed, promoted, and evolved into perpetuity. Douglas Redd, Baba Doug, was gone, but this spirit would live on and be encouraged in children, artists, elders, and culture-bearers into the future.

In retrospect, it is interesting that, at a time so sad, a bright light can just show up. For me, one of those bright lights was Viola Johnson, a friend and former coworker whom I had met at the first job I had with the school board in the early 1970s. When Viola heard about Doug's passing, she came by Redd House and said, "Carol Bebelle, I know that this is a really hard time for you and you could use some help, and so I am offering my assistance to help through this hump." That was 2007. A powerful source of connection with the media, promotions, and the community in her role as communications officer, Viola left Ashé when I retired in 2019, twelve years later. We continue as friends in our individual life journeys now. Along with Viola came a young artist named Frederick "Hollywood" Delahoussaye, who had begun to stay close to Ashé and started making Ashé his homebase. He was generous in offering his time for production and events, and he was a key feature in organizing young people, in particular young poets, a community with whom he was very involved.

Throughout this period, I remained aware that sometimes we encounter angels unaware. Jeffery also became a reliable member of the team that could be counted on to help us deliver what we needed to a community that was in great need of reminders that they were seen and that people were there that wanted to take care of them. The efforts of Jeffrey and Hollywood combined with those of John Grimsley, our theatre artist and set designer, gave us the capacity to turn the inside of Ashé into whatever we needed: anything from a theater production, music concert, training or workshop series, youth program, baby shower, wedding, or repast after a funeral. We were a place where people could celebrate important moments in their lives or be involved with or affected by art and culture that inspired them and celebrated who they were and how they lived.

In December of 2006, we welcomed a popular visitor, Eve Ensler (today known as V), who was on the ground looking for a way to help. After a couple of conversations, she welcomed the opportunity to partner with Ashé and collaborate with women artists in the creation of a theatrical work of stories of women in New Orleans living with the threat, experience, and aftermath of the storm. Her entrance into our life was a great gift, and I'm reminded again of "encountering angels unaware." For fourteen months, Eve came to New Orleans and met with sixteen women artists in a workshop where we created songs, monologues, poems, and story content that Eve then combined to create a work called *Swimming Upstream*. This opportunity for women creatives and cultural-bearers to gather monthly focused on rants, prayers, wishes, and dreams—insights that became a therapeutic outlet for us.

Creating the work was a fabulous gift, but this was only part of the experience. In the expanded landscape of New Orleans and the Gulf Coast, there were many organizations that were working on behalf of women. We were already connected to some and began to reach out to others as the idea emerged to create a grand return for women evacuees for a weekend of healing and support. Colette Pichon Battle with Moving Forward Gulf Coast, Denese Shervington with The Institute of Women and Ethnic Studies, the Tulane Center for Women's Health, Dr. Pam Breaux with the UNO Sociology Department, and Cherice Harrison-Nelson with Guardians of the Flame all became key partners in bringing to life a plan to return women to the city in 2008.

The tenth anniversary of V-Day, the movement that Eve created to promote equity and justice for women around the world, was in 2008. Using the renowned theatre work *The Vagina Monologues*, women around the world produce the work and raise funds for women's work in their communities. So, in true Eve fashion, she orchestrated the idea of returning evacuated women back home to New Orleans to participate in a reclamation of the Superdome, which she termed a symbolic vagina. Nearly forty thousand people came to New Orleans to participate. Over two thousand women returned to their community where they could be celebrated and have their bravery and resilience honored. The weekend was full of healing services. The premier of *Swimming Upstream* was held at the Superdome, and a celebrity cast performance of *The Vagina Monologues* was presented at the New Orleans Arena, now the Smoothie King Center. Eve also raised nearly seven hundred thousand dollars, which was distributed to various women leaders in New Orleans. I never saw this coming. This theater work toured the country, bringing throngs of women to audiences in Atlanta, New York (the Apollo Theater and Ford Foundation), Houston, and New Mexico. *Swimming Upstream* became a touring work like UPROOTED, another Katrina production featuring some of New Orleans' best and brightest. The authors of *Swimming Upstream* initially jumped into flood waters with the expressed desire to survive an admittedly terrible experience in their lives. Along the way, we all learned that life is not just about getting through the storms but also about learning to dance in the rain.

A recurring insight was the ongoing and deep need that our community had for healing. Various healing efforts were being generated in the community, with practitioners (massage therapists, acupuncturists, reiki practitioners) making their services available to churches and other organizations because the need for healing was so profound. Though people were returning to their city, they were often not returning to their homes. The sense of belonging was less available, and many people felt unrooted and estranged in their own city. In response to this need, Nana Anoa Nantambu brought Sobonfu Somé, a renowned Burkinabe teacher and writer specializing in African spirituality, to create a healing ceremony in New Orleans, and many came to receive the relief that the ceremony offered.

Because we were a familiar place where people found comfort, we joined the circle of healing efforts and established the Chill Zone. Our support for each other began with us being willing to listen and to help troubleshoot, share information and resources, and just be there to bear witness. The Chill Zone was a time to authorize folks to catch their breath and take it easy. Sessions began in January of 2007 and were held on Fridays. Attendees were encouraged to wear comfortable clothes. Food, tabletop games, and activities were provided, and healing practitioners were invited to share massages, acupuncture, healing, and touch. We owe special thanks for the efforts they offered to complete the Chill Zone: Dr. Denese Shervington, Menhati Singleton, Dr. Quang, Jamilah Peters-Muhammad, Nana Anoa Nantambu, and Diana Panara. We filled the atmosphere with healing sound, music, and poetry. A small and brief sanctuary from a world full of challenges. We give thanks for these tender mercies that fortified spirits, processed distress, and encouraged folks to see what tomorrow might bring. We were so glad that we had the perfect prescription for our community: cultural healing made of healing touches, fun, food, music, dance, and each other. We distracted our community for moments of release, reflection, and readying for the next thing.

Stirring up the culture and the spirit for our community became a spiritual healing and beaconing for us. We worked with other Central City efforts—Central City's own community mayor, Barbara Lacen-Keller, who rallied up the troops; Kysha Brown Robinson, with the Central City Renaissance Alliance; and Priscilla Edwards with the Central City EOC (Economic Opportunity Corporation)—all had put us ahead of the game in planning for recovery. Soon we became an on-the-ground contact for funders, donors, and media. We were very conscious of not wanting to be a gatekeeper. We held conversations with other on-the-ground contacts who had similar feelings: Dr. Sheila Webb (director of the city's Health Department and founder of the Center for Empowered Decision-Making) and Steven Bingler (principal of Concordia architects and longtime ally and friend). We came up with the idea to invite all the funders down to a Making It Happen (one of the definitions for the Yoruba word "ashé") Festival at Ashé and to invite the community to meet with them so that they could represent themselves.

We also provided guidance to community members on how to prepare grants for their organization. The grant to Ashé from Ford, in addition to providing funds, provided access to other organizations and personalities who became funders, contributors, and supporters to Ashé. I list their names to acknowledge them and to remind us that many people empowered with resources will find ways to use their power in effective ways to respond to great need and provide assistance. A particular support to me was Juana Guzman, then vice president of the National Museum of Mexican Art in Chicago; Roy Priest, executive director and CEO of Alexandria Redevelopment and Housing Authority (ARHA); and Linetta Gilbert, longtime mentor and grant officer, who provided support and counsel for decades.

Others who were part of our funding, who were supportive, encouraging, and otherwise provided us uplift, include: Tom Bailey, State Senator Diana

Bajoie, James Borders, Claudine Brown, William Buster, Dr. Gail Christopher, Flozell Daniels, Miguel Garcia, Jennifer Henderson, Gerri Hobdy, Maurine Knighton, Kathy Laborde, Spike Lee, Richard Martinez, Katherine McFate, Mayor Ray Nagin, Deborah Pollard, Judy Reese Morse, Judi-Lee Reid, Joycelyn Reynolds, Mary Rowe, Christy Slater, Regina Smith, Javier Torres, Roberto Uno, and MK Wegman. Listing names here does not represent the complete collection of people who made a difference in Ashé's, Doug's, or my making it. If every person who contributed were listed, the list would be as long as I am tall, and it would include everything from watching a door left open overnight to make sure no one entered, to giving us a check for $2.3 million, to the people who, out of nowhere, showed up, made sure we were made part of something bigger, thought about us, and carried that thought over to a phone call that arrived at a time when we needed to know that people we didn't know were thinking about us. It would also include celebrities stopping by to say "hi" and choosing to send us big checks, and every person that ever worked at Ashé, because nothing ever happened at Ashé without people working together. And so, as we say in the community, if your name was not listed, owe it to the head and not the heart.

Then there were the others who saw our need and organized to provide what became one-time funding or assistance, but, importantly, it helped us make it through. This funding circumstance was tricky. We were not an art center, and we were not a social program or education program. We were all of that and more. We were a community-based cultural arts center dedicated to celebrating, lifting, and continuing the cultural traditions of people of African descent and to respecting the same for people of other ethnic traditions. No one specifically funded this work as a priority. The people I've listed saw value in our efforts and aided us in navigating the demarcation lines of funders. In many ways, they demonstrated the very thing we were celebrating: the ability of the culture to adapt, if necessary, to ensure the benefit of its community. When I look back on the early days, when we returned home, and the many opportunities that surfaced, I am unable to just call this good fortune or luck. I think that the suffering of our people, the bravery of facing the challenges, the hopes and prayers of us, our fellow Americans and fellow Earth-dwellers, combined to become divine intention and ashé (the ability to make things happen).

Making something out of nothing is no small feat. Douglas saw this potential and made it a real enough possibility to me that I saw it too. And sharing the vision with others got them believing in it too until we were moving along, bringing more and more people into this empowered intention to count our blessings. This could be called cultural-rooting and -bearing, which leads us to bridge our culture with others and to create new cultural content and traditions that can serve us all.

When we partnered with the Contemporary Arts Center (CAC) to capture the moments of reckoning with race and racism in post-Katrina New Orleans, we created a project called Truth Be Told. We put representatives from Ashé together with representatives from the CAC in teams to handle various aspects of the project. We had two artistic directors: John O'Neal (rest in peace) and John Grimsley. Each organization's staff participated in story circles and attended the Undoing Racism training provided by the People's Institute for Survival and Beyond. After participating together in this consciousness-raising work, John Grimsley wrote a play that John O'Neal directed called *Story Circle*, which presented perspectives on race and racism from the viewpoint of white people and Black people. This was made possible by the story circle process, which is a practice evolved from civil rights activist and master theater officer John O'Neal and inspired by the Native American talking stick. Everybody tells their story and the others listen.

The production was presented at the CAC and Ashé. After each performance, a talkback was held. We saw people being vulnerable and considerate. And then the deeper work got harder, and the project slowly ended. The work that was done helped to put a dent in the race issue in the cultural community. It became easier to express and spotlight inequity and disparity for some of us. The glaring examples and experiences of inequity helped to fuel the dramatic voice of creatives and culture-bearers in their various undertakings. There was so much to spotlight and so many people who were too busy just working to survive.

It was 2008, a big year for us. The W. K. Kellogg Foundation started an effort called America Healing. Its board saw tackling racism as a major way to create better lives for children. Importantly, Ashé was selected to be a part of the initial cohort due to the Foundation selection team's recognition of the cultural influence in racism and racial bias. The good fortune of being in the initial cohort carried forward for over a decade as the Kellogg Foundation conjugated the America Healing project to the Truth, Racial Healing & Transformation (TRHT), an expansion led by Dr. Gail Christopher. Involvement in this effort has many residuals that continue to this day with the TRHT Wisdom Circle, composed of those of us involved from the beginning and younger racial healers involved over our last three cycles. Participating in these efforts situates Ashé and myself in a circle of allies representing Native American, African American, Asian, Latine, and European American perspectives. It also has expanded our capacity to collaborate and contribute at many levels.

With so much need at the local level, it was helpful becoming part of regional and national efforts that provide encouragement, support, and small-to-large financial investments. A similar opportunity that presented itself, provided by Dr. Amy Koritz, a professor at Tulane University, was to contribute to a volume called *Civic Engagement in the Wake of Katrina*, edited by Koritz and George J. Sánchez, University of Southern California professor of American Studies and Ethnicity and History. This team was supported by graduate students who assisted with the editing and afforded me the opportunity to meet Adam Bush, a PhD candidate at the time. Adam and I met when he introduced himself to me on one of his visits. We bonded over his work with an up-and-coming, non-traditional higher education project called College Unbound, where students created customized curriculums. This approach to education connected with my long history with Upward Bound, and an ally match was made that, over the years, has evolved into a long-term partnership and friendship.

In 2010, College Unbound partnered with Ashé CAC to demonstrate a remote model of College Unbound called Ashé College Unbound, with an initial cohort of eight students who were artists, culture-bearers, and activists. To date, we have four graduates from that cohort. One of our members, Késhia "Peaches" Caldwell, is deceased now, and two more are organizing to complete work before graduation. Adam went on to nominate me to the board of Imagining America, a collaborative of humanities scholars, artists, design professionals, and more. He has made Ashé, and me personally, a forever cheerleader and supporter. Today, College Unbound sponsors a Carol Bebelle scholarship for artists.

In the end...

It was very apparent that our community was hurting. Grief, loss, and anxiety were palpable. An easy *How are you?* could be responded to with a quick *Trying to make it* or with a thirty-minute story of trials and tribulations. When we are in the darkness, the smallest amount of light is appreciated. We recognized this and the power of family, friends, and community. So, our programming became an already/always feature of our post-Katrina existence. From 2005 until 2010, we recognized our ability to leverage coming together, ritual, being soothed by music, dance, poetry, and theater, and enjoying breaking bread together. But we also realized that maintaining our own cultural institution would be an ongoing challenge that would require adaptation of strategies and expansion of the community of people and institutions willing to invest. Entrepreneurship would have to be a part of the formula for support of the institution going forward. At a time when darkness and fog were everywhere, disappointment and distress were as present as the oxygen we breathed. We created a choreography of circling, huddling, hunkering down, dancing, singing, and laughing till we cried. We had seen days that looked like the end and had awakened to tomorrow, and the day after, and the day after that. Today's report was better than fair. The challenge for tomorrow would be met by a community stronger, smarter, and determined to ensure the influence of culture and heritage in the experience of life and the solving of problems for our people.

I am left believing to my soul the wisdom of this Patrick Overton poem:

When you walk to the edge of all the light you have
and take that first step into the darkness of the unknown,
you must believe that one of two things will happen:

> *There will be something solid for you to stand upon,*
> *or, you will be taught how to fly*[4]

Have faith!

Working in a collective mindset after Katrina, we came to appreciate that the work before us was:

- Instilling heritage

- Joint economic efforts

- Confidence and culture in children providing open-minded consideration to the challenges for young people and elders

- Creating forms

- Answering needs and problems

---

4   Patrick Miles Overton, "Faith," *The Leaning Tree* (St. Louis, MO: Bethany Press, 1975), 91.

- Creating new cultural traditions that emerge from the influence of our heritage meeting our present experience

- Creating opportunities for lifelong learning

- Being about humanity, beauty, and empathy

We moved forward with these lessons and guidelines. They were rooted in the radical commitment to hope and faith born from generations of our ancestors who believed in the light in the darkest of times. They believed that despite what a day brings, still, tomorrow comes. . . .

THIS IS NOT THAT TYPE OF STORM
STEVEN BINGLER & LINDA USDIN

Introduction

Hurricane Katrina touched every person living in New Orleans: some people lost family members, everything they owned, or at least much of what they most valued. Others were able to evade the immediate destruction, evacuate, and choose whether they wanted to return to rebuild their lives. Some never returned, either by choice or necessity. As the impacts of Katrina and the levee failures overcame the city, we realized how lucky we were to have the resources and networks that would protect us from many of the tragedies that so many others were experiencing.

But, we realize that "lucky" isn't really the right word. We were operating with the mobility of a car, resources for a hotel in Houston and rental apartments in New York, and an amazing social network that sprang into action to provide temporary shelter and emotional support when we needed it the most. We were well positioned to weather this storm.

So, when we think about the blessings of this time, we must see them through the lens of the immense runway of suffering that surrounded us for years when, after the storm hit and the levees broke, people were abandoned, left behind, lost everything, and then slowly reconstructed their new lives. That shared grief is the wash that covers any canvas on which we tell our stories.

Many moments nurtured us through the grief, giving us reason to laugh and feel grateful. There are stories of the luggage guy in the airport who refused a tip when he learned we were from New Orleans, the schools in New York City that offered us free tuition. Most powerfully, we remember stories of all the people from all the phases of our lives who reached out immediately and asked how they could help.

There are also less personal, more global positive elements that came through Katrina. Some were learned, some evolved, and some have been forgotten. A twentieth anniversary is a good time to raise them up.

Steven and Linda
Steven's story in New Orleans began when he graduated from the School of Architecture at the University of Virginia. He had grown up near the Appalachian Mountains, in a family where everyone stayed close by. His family traced its roots back four generations, and along the way, they were related to the famous bluegrass Carter family, which Linda says made them hillbilly nobility. Steven branched way out, was the first in the family to go to college, chose a career in architecture instead of auto mechanics, and moved to New Orleans, where he was lured by the beauty of its buildings and culture. When he and Linda met, he had just purchased an 1830 Creole cottage in the French Quarter.

Linda, on the other hand, could trace her roots in New Orleans back four generations on her mother's side. Her great-grandfather got his start sweeping out a coffee warehouse when coffee was traded at places like Maspero's Coffee Exchange. Hers was a civically involved Jewish family who knew the differences between being well connected in the Gentile versus Jewish spheres of the city. It was the restrictive, entrenched racial and social climate of the city that contributed to Linda leaving with no thought of ever making New Orleans her home again. She lived in New Mexico, North Carolina, California, and New York before she and Steven met, got married, and settled in together in New Orleans.

Moving back to New Orleans was a challenge for Linda, who didn't relish diving back into the world she had fled. But Steven had a new architecture firm at the time they married, so she agreed to come back home for five years or so.

Linda began working through the lens of her training in public health to help implement initiatives funded by national and local institutions and governmental entities that encouraged progressive community change. Some of the initiatives were neighborhood-based, and others were citywide. Through this work, she met and developed deep relationships with people like Saundra Reed, whose family had been in Central City for four generations, Linetta Gilbert, who would later become a trusted partner in the post-Katrina recovery, and Carol Bebelle and Petrice Sams-Abiodun, whose work has intertwined with hers for over thirty years. She also focused her work on lifelong learning related to anti-racist action.

Meanwhile, Steven was also working with Central City residents on developing a community-centered master plan for the neighborhood. Through a robust process of community engagement, he was able to work closely with some of the same local leaders, like Saundra Reed and Carol Bebelle, along with other neighborhood leaders like H. M. K. Amen, Audrey Browder, and many others. The result of the plan was a holistic set of guidelines addressing not only the physical but also the cultural, social, economic, organizational, and educational elements of community life in Central City.

Katrina Hits and the Levees Fail

In 2005, as the monster Hurricane Katrina headed for New Orleans, we were still living in the French Quarter and in the midst of building a new, environmentally sustainable home that Steven had designed in the Carrollton neighborhood. During the previous twenty years, we had welcomed two daughters, Anya and Josephine, who became the delight of their older brother, Dan. Steven's firm had grown in scope and size, and Linda was deeply involved with social justice projects throughout the city.

We had a lot of conversations as Hurricane Katrina was approaching. Linda remembered hurricanes that came through New Orleans when she was growing up. Steven hadn't grown up in New Orleans, but his work with civil and structural engineers on the redevelopment of the Jax Brewery, Aquarium of the Americas, and Woldenberg Park on the Mississippi riverfront gave him a unique perspective on the forces of nature.

Linda remembered Hurricane Betsy, when her father took her brothers, sister, and her out with football helmets on to experience the intensity of nature. She had grown up with hurricanes where people taped their windows and slept in the hallways—when a couple of days of no electricity and candles everywhere were exciting. So, as Katrina was approaching, Linda wanted to stay in New Orleans—in solidarity with her city and the people who couldn't leave.

"This isn't that kind of hurricane," Steven kept saying, it is what his engineering friends said could be the "perfect storm." It took him until the day before Katrina hit to convince Linda to leave.

We loaded up the car with our daughters, our dog, Ruby, and clothes for the weekend (except for our oldest, then teenaged daughter, who packed enough for months...). We headed out with a friend, a single mom with her daughter, in a caravan to Houston.

Houston, normally six hours away, ended up being a seventeen-hour drive, complete with a fender bender between the two cars in our caravan. We expected a few days away from home—which turned into nine months. We started in Houston, spent a week in Atlanta, and ended in New York City. Linda got a job consulting with The Ford Foundation, and Steven began his commute, managing his architecture firm, Concordia, with people spread throughout the country. The girls were given free tuition at two different schools. Through friends in New York, we lived in four different apartments over the nine-month period.

On the day before the storm, as we were leaving the city in our caravan, Linda had called Saundra Reed to ask what she and her family of more than a dozen people were planning to do to flee the storm. She offered for them to stay at the weekend place in Mississippi that we shared with our friends, Jane Wholey and Jed Horne. Saundra's family packed up and headed out to Poplarville. We didn't know until much later that their experience had terrifying moments, culminating in a harrowing account described in Jed Horne's book *Breach of Faith: Hurricane Katrina and the Near Death of a Great American City*.

It wasn't long before Steven returned to lend his support in urban design. At the time, Ray Nagin was moving forward with his Bring New Orleans Back (BNOB) plan for the city's recovery. To gather more authentic input from the community, Steven worked with Carol Bebelle and others from Central City to facilitate a Making it Happen Festival, with a series of impromptu meetings held at the Ashé Cultural Arts Center. This work built on the foundational planning that Concordia had done pre-Katrina in Central City. These meetings led to the development of a Funding Festival, involving a wide range of philanthropies working closely with Carol and Sheila Webb, among many others, including playwright Eve Ensler (now known as V), who later championed a citywide convening at the Superdome. Times were tough, but by working together, there was finally some hope on the horizon.

The work of Ray Nagin's BNOB planning process soon morphed into a parallel effort by the city council, called the New Orleans Neighborhoods Rebuilding Plan (NONRP), and finally into the Unified New Orleans Plan (UNOP), which built on lessons learned from the Central City planning process, BNOB, and NONRP to include more than nine thousand residents from all parts of the city, 64 percent of whom were African American. The process also reached out to people who were still dislocated, who were included in the process through virtual outreach that at one point included large, two-way television broadcast connections to Houston, Dallas, Baton Rouge, and Atlanta. Patricia Jones, a local organizer, claimed that at that moment, New Orleans surely had more citizen planners per capita than any other city in the country.

For Steven, the opportunity to participate in and contribute to this planning process would become one of the most memorable and meaningful experiences in his fifty-year career in architecture and urban design. The relationships formed and lessons learned during this time have been seminal for his work in community-centered planning, both in New Orleans and elsewhere.

Looking back with the perspective of twenty years, we recognize that the experiences that we raise up below are ones that we value, ones that speak to the past as well as to the future. They are lessons that require deep and continuous study; they are admonitions; they are guides for how we can help heal ourselves, our community, and ones we can offer to our country.

When we approached writing this chapter, the questions we asked ourselves were: What did the Katrina/levee failures teach us? How did it change how we thought about ourselves and our city? Could we talk about the positive changes that we experienced during the tragedies that we knew so profoundly?

The experiences of working on rebuilding the city after the storms and levee failures led to complicated realizations about how New Orleans saw itself, how outsiders saw the city, and how profoundly important it was to rebuild in a way that honored these new realizations and shifted how New Orleans operated. Through the process of working with others during the recovery, we also came to acknowledge that the forces aligned against making these changes were sometimes more powerful than the need to change.

We Saw New Truths

The truth of our country is that racism was baked in from its inception. It was not just there at the beginning, but it has persistently created the opportunities that are or aren't available to each person. New Orleans, as many other Southern cities, has its own brand of racism. The social classes are solidly set, and the roles are clear.

Traditionally, cross-racial relationships in New Orleans were often ruled by rigid social classes, where the white people defined the relationships and came from the place of power afforded to them.

We, in New Orleans, often see ourselves as more nuanced than other places. We love our culture, our music, our food—all provided to us through the African, Caribbean, Cajun, and Latinx people, who in many cases were brought in to serve the existing white power structure of New Orleans. The opportunities to enjoy these cultures are vast, and it can appear that we have more appreciation of communities of color than most places in our country.

Katrina clarified that mirage. What we saw from the moments before the hurricane hit, and straight through these many years after, is that our community was and is just as racist as others. The people who were left behind, on roofs and in the Superdome and at the Convention Center, were predominantly African Americans and other people of color.

The truth was laid bare. We could no longer claim our exceptionality. And this is good. This changes the narrative. This is a place from which changes can be made—by seeing things for what they really are. In the years since Katrina, over a thousand New Orleanians participated in Undoing Racism workshops organized by a cadre of young professionals that branded the effort as CENO (the Campaign for Equity in New Orleans). This work led to new relationships and helped develop shared vocabulary, but it is generational and muted by many countervailing pressures.

New Relationships Were Possible

CENO was one example. As the city began its slow recovery process, people from different neighborhoods reached across boundaries they had not crossed before. People talked to people in our city they had never talked to before, worked with more diverse people, and visited neighborhoods they had never seen. We learned to appreciate our culture and culture-bearers with new fervor. New organizations sprang up as existing neighborhood organizations grew stronger.

The Neighborhood Partnership Network (NPN) formed to promote neighborhood collaboration through forums and training sessions for neighborhood activists and to create an inclusive, citywide framework for neighborhood groups who wanted to become involved in post-Katrina planning.

Local musicians like Branford Marsalis and Harry Connick Jr., who had long since left New Orleans for bigger cities, came together with local and national leaders to build the Ellis Marsalis Center for Music and Musicians' Village in the Upper 9th Ward. The Center is now a major musical educational venue and a magnet for concerts, attracting people from all over the city and beyond.

Social Entrepreneurs of New Orleans (now Propeller) was formed to support residents who had entrepreneurial ideas to improve life in our city. This organization has supported over three hundred entrepreneurs who have created close to five hundred jobs in small businesses. Linda got involved with Propeller in its early days, mentoring the entrepreneurs who started The Roots of Music, a music and social support organization dedicated to providing opportunities for young people to keep our brass music tradition alive.

The Ashé Cultural Arts Center expanded its advocacy for African and Caribbean art in our community not only by increasing its program offerings but also by updating and renovating its headquarters on Oretha Castle Haley Boulevard, as well as expanding its footprint to the Powerhouse on Baronne Street. Steven led the design process for the Ashé renovation, which resulted in not only a rich cultural collaboration with Carol Bebelle but also a joyful collaboration with Luther Gray and others in the development of an architectonic Bamboula Wall to celebrate the undulating iconic bamboula rhythms that originated in West Africa and migrated to New Orleans, where they were performed in Congo Square. Luther Gray, with his colleague Jamilah Peters-Muhammad, also kept our musical traditions alive by hosting events in Congo Square that began attracting drummers from all over the city, including at Sunday drum circles.

With Ashé as the anchor organization, one of the oldest boulevards of New Orleans began to come alive. Once a center for Jewish commerce, Oretha Castle Haley (then called Dryades Street) had suffered from suburban flight and urban decline. In the years after Katrina, it became a new hub for cultural and culinary activities including the Southern Food and Beverage Museum, the New Orleans Jazz Orchestra, Café Reconcile, Casa Borrega, Good Work Network, the NET: Central City school, and the Youth Empowerment Project. In 2022, after ten years of renting, Steven and his business partner Bobbie Hill purchased a building at 1610 Oretha Castle Haley Boulevard, which, in addition to Concordia's offices, also houses three other like-minded community-centered organizations.

We Learned New Strengths and New Leaders Stepped Up

In the aftermath of Hurricane Katrina, New Orleans served as a hotbed for a new generation of community leaders to flourish. One of these leaders was Fr. Vien Nguyen, priest of the Mary Queen of Vietnam Church in New Orleans East. In the early days after the disaster, Father Vien helped his mostly Vietnamese community members share electricity, food, and shelter. Their

New Orleans East community was one of the first of the devastated communities to become functional again, and the strength of this community has continued to be manifest in groups such as Vietnamese American Young Leaders Association (VAYLA), the VEGGI Farmers Cooperative, and the Sông Community Development Corporation.

During the rebuilding process, a new organization, Puentes, was formed to meet the needs of youth in the rapidly growing Latine population in the greater New Orleans area. Another network called the Black-Brown Coalition formed to recognize and meld the common agendas of Black and Latine communities.

Both Puentes and VAYLA were partners in the NPN. The NPN, in turn, was a partner in the New Orleans Coalition on Open Governance (NOCOG), which was launched to shift the backroom decision-making that traditionally kept many New Orleanians from participating in critical civic decisions. Linda served as the first director of NOCOG, believing that opening up the process of decision-making and expanding those who could be involved was essential to institutionalizing the changes underway after Katrina. One powerful outcome of NOCOG was the birth of an award-winning, nonprofit investigative newsroom, The Lens, which has contributed to a more transparent news and information environment.

Another important organization called Sankofa was formed by Rashida Ferdinand in the Lower 9th Ward, where she and many of her family members had grown up. To date, they have created not only a fresh food market that helps people get food from local farmers and fishers, but also the Sankofa Wetlands Park & Nature Trail, where a team of wetland ecologists and landscape architects turned forty acres of wetlands along Florida Avenue into a space for environmental education, relaxation, and recreation.

The Lens, Sankofa, Puentes, NPN, NOCOG, VAYLA, Sông CDC, and many other nonprofits in the Greater New Orleans region came from a recognition that, after the disaster, changes were more likely to come from building upon our strengths than waiting for the realignment of powerful forces outside of New Orleans.

We Were Connected to Larger Communities

Although we recognized that change had to come from within our community, Katrina was also one of the first catastrophic disasters in our country's recent history. As a result, most of the major national philanthropic organizations, such as the Rockefeller, Ford, W. K. Kellogg, Walton Family,

Surdna, Conrad N. Hilton, Kresge, and Open Society Foundations, all established funds, and many hired local representatives to be their eyes and ears on the ground.

Through these national philanthropies, New Orleanians also became more connected internationally to other communities who were experiencing catastrophic disasters and to the experts who came in to help. National foundations supported intercontinental learning with communities in Japan and Thailand that had also experienced devastating climate-related disasters.

Steven's work in coordinating the Unified New Orleans Plan led to urban planning partnerships with international experts like Laurie Johnson and Rob Olshansky, whose work with the University of Kyoto and the Japan Foundation led to professional and cultural exchanges that contributed to our city's recovery. Other relationships led by architect David Waggonner and Congresswoman Mary Landrieu led to an extensive exchange with the Netherlands and a planning report called The Dutch Dialogues. This collaboration resulted in changes to the city's planning and building codes to improve resilience and long-term viability around the concept of living with water.

After Hurricane Katrina, artists in New Orleans were also led to focus on what their roles, and the role of the arts in general, could be in the rebuilding of the city. Among other things, this led, in 2007, to the first Prospect exhibition at venues throughout New Orleans. In the fall and winter of 2024, New Orleans hosted its sixth Prospect, with artists, collectors, and other art-lovers attending from around the world.

In 2015, the Joan Mitchell Foundation opened the Joan Mitchell Center in New Orleans, a national artistic residency center that has provided residencies for over three hundred artists on its two-acre campus. This Center has not only exposed many national artists to the culturally rich New Orleans environment but has also lifted New Orleans up as an important site for the visual arts in our country. The Joan Mitchell Center, in conjunction with the launch of Prospect, has had a profound impact in raising the profile of the visual arts in our community.

We Got Early Exposure to the Fundamental Challenge of Our Times: Climate Change

One of the most impactful learnings from Hurricane Katrina for Steven has been work in climate change planning. At the heart of this work has been the need for engaging a full range of stakeholders in planning for authentically shared outcomes. Through many professional collaborations, Concordia has continued to evolve its work in climate change planning with a focus on engaging communities in addressing the formidable challenges of race, equity, and other aspects of environmental justice. Learnings from the UNOP planning process have been expanded to the regional LA Safe climate change planning project that included the voices of more than 2,500 residents in Plaquemines, Jefferson, Terrebonne, Lafourche, St. John the Baptist, and St. Tammany Parishes. Concordia led the community engagement component of this initiative that resulted in a resilience plan for all six parishes. A related research project, funded by the Rockefeller Foundation, called the Global Transformation Roundtable included a diverse team of eighty national and international climate scholars and planners in extending this work into planning for a larger Gulf South Partnership. This partnership currently includes fifteen technical planning and grassroots partners from the states of Texas, Louisiana, Mississippi, Alabama, and Florida.

We Experienced Personal Transformations

The examples we give in this chapter are from our own experiences and are a sampling of others. Most important is that we are both committed to carrying these learnings forward, even when the most immediate peril is not another hurricane but the daily turbulence of inequity and injustice that we face as a community, even in the best of times.

While much of the growth we have discussed thus far has focused on lessons we learned from our involvement with efforts that impact New Orleans as a whole, other impacts were more personal. Our children were young when Katrina and the levee failures happened and their worlds were turned completely upside down. In the process of coming back, they learned that terrible things could happen and that we can work to define ourselves not by these terrible things but by how we react to the challenges. Hopefully, they also learned that the ability to react is influenced by factors that occurred long before the event, such as socioeconomic status, social networks, gender, and race.

For us, this work changed the trajectory of our careers. It defined our careers, imposed huge burdens, and offered many opportunities. Linda sees her involvement in the recovery process as a deep focusing-in. The most powerful work came from being amid the chaos and focusing on what was most essential to ameliorating some of the historical plagues of our city and country. Being able to focus work on these big issues was, in a strange way, centering.

For Steven, transformational conversations with family and friends from many faiths and backgrounds led to lessons on the meaning of life. One of these lessons came through a conversation with Carol Bebelle about the ancient West African tradition of ubuntu, which means, "I am because we are." We exist through our relationships and the lives of the people around us. In many ways, this concept reflects the most important outcome of our city's recovery, at least for those of us who were honored to celebrate conversations and experiences that were cross-cultural, defied racial boundaries, and reinforced lifelong bonds of love and friendship.

JOY ON THE HORIZON
J. B. BORDERS

Call me James B. Borders IV, if you want to be factual and precise. That's my full name, my government name. I'm the great-grandson of Rev. James Buchanan Borders, a Baptist preacher from Macon, Georgia, who was himself the son of a preacher, Rev. Purnell Buchanan Borders, also of Macon. My great-grandfather, known in the family as Big Daddy, graduated from Morehouse College before it was called Morehouse and married a Spelman graduate named Leila Birdsong, a country schoolteacher who had matriculated there when it was still known as the Atlanta Baptist Female Seminary. My great-grandparents had eight children, at least one of whom became a preacher. That was not J. B., my grandfather. Instead, it was one of his younger brothers, William Holmes Borders, who pastored Wheat Street Baptist Church in Atlanta for over five decades and was a proactive community builder and civil rights activist.

My grandfather followed a different professional calling than his father and grandfather. He worked in the insurance industry, moved his family to Florida, and speculated in real estate there before the Great Depression of the 1930s wiped him out. Despite being musically gifted and a resourceful inventor/tinkerer, he later became estranged from his wife and their five children. From what I have been told, he drank a bit and pontificated aplenty on a wide range of topics until his death in 1943 at age forty-seven. Mr. SeeDaPoint, his friends and critics alike used to call him. I do what I can to keep his name and spirit alive.

I was born in New Orleans, my mother's hometown. She was a second-generation Southern University grad who had married a Bethune-Cookman man in Daytona Beach, Florida, but had come home to Charity Hospital to have her first child the same year Louis Armstrong was the Zulu king, 1949. (That's the way I have been framing it in my old age: born during the reign of

Satchmo, New Orleans's greatest musical genius and its most embarrassing buffoon. To his credit, however, he nearly rehabilitated his reputation when he unexpectedly pulled off his coon mask for a moment in 1957 to protest the racist harassment of the Little Rock Nine, who were cursed at and spat upon daily in their efforts to integrate Central High School. Three years later, the New Orleans Four—Ruby Bridges, Leona Tate, Tessie Prevost, and Gail Etienne—would suffer the same abuse at the outset of their elementary school education.)

I was reared in the Catholic faith, not the Baptist church, though I don't consider myself a religious person in the formal sense. I always believed in a Supreme Intelligence/Creator presence, but I don't think I ever was a wide-eyed sectarian believer or fanatic; I just went along with the rituals and recited the catechism and the prayers because that was what we did in our family and neighborhood, especially after I became a full-time New Orleanian at age thirteen and most of my friends and neighbors were Catholic. Everywhere else I had lived, we were a distinct minority. In fact, in Daytona Beach, my brother and I were the only Black kids who made our first communion in the church there. I think I vaguely remember us being seated apart from the other children during the ceremony.

Not surprisingly, I stopped going to church almost as soon as I moved away from the city and got to college (Brown), where I pursued undergrad and graduate studies and evaded the military draft in the process. Throughout the 1960s, the draft was shoveling tens of thousands of young Americans like me into the armed services and onto the deadly front lines of the US's war of aggression in Southeast Asia.

After my careers as an editor and an arts administrator, from the early 1970s to the very end of the twentieth century, I became a full-time consultant in 2001, mostly undertaking strategic planning and grant writing for small nonprofit organizations. That's the kind of work I was doing when Hurricane Katrina struck: startups and turnarounds, trying to effect change and development on the micro level. And that's what I returned to after the storm, only with a much more New Orleans-centered focus and a broader range of clients from the small business sector to go along with the social service, affordable housing, and cultural nonprofits that formed my pre-storm base.

Having previously spent six years as a grantmaker, I knew firsthand how tiny and precarious Black-led, Black-serving nonprofits were in their respective fields. But I also felt the surest way to have sturdy, major Black organizations was to grow them ourselves. In the midst of the billions and billions of dollars that were pouring into New Orleans back then, I was certain we could establish footholds for organizations that were committed to serving their communities with integrity, and not just the naked opportunism and illicit scheming that had infected so many people at the time, including the good folk who had been buffeted about so badly by the storm, its aftermath, and dealings with corrupt individuals and entities that they just succumbed to the pressures and decided, *If you can't beat them, join them.* And that's how the rot kept spreading.

I know we all have stories to tell. I have heard lots of them. By comparison, mine are not especially tragic or slathered in suffering, misery, and the struggle to survive. You will find no disaster porn here, no deep violet, woe-is-me blues. Ditto for weeping accordions and bleeding violins. If you're looking for a body count, you will not get one here. Nothing to report.

In fact, in some way, I think my experiences before, during, and after Hurricane Katrina are more typical of the travails suffered by a majority of New Orleanians. No matter how unsensational, or even on the other end of the spectrum, how incredible, crazy, weird, heartbreaking, absurd, or miraculous some of our experiences were, we could generally be philosophical about them (in hindsight, at least) and say, "It could have been worse—a lot worse."

Like most of us, I was lucky. Not brave, just too insignificant, I suppose, for the Fates to dispense with me back then. That's all it could have been. Death was merely biding its time. Some people I knew, however, did not get by so easily.

I evacuated, of course, on Sunday, August 28. My checking account was low, but I had a car and three credit cards in my wallet, so I crawled my way up I-55 along with thousands of others intent on evading Kartrina's path. I had two passengers with me in my road-loving Jetta: Brenda Marie Osbey, my long-time companion, and her mother, Lois Emelda Hamilton.

My own mother, Florence Edwards Borders, was evacuating to Baton Rouge with my daughter Miaflor and my sister Thais and her daughter Julie. They had made arrangements to stay with a friend there.

Earlier, I had helped my son Che (James B. Borders V), a mechanical engineer, and his housemate Clark Beljean, a public defender attorney, secure Che's home—boarding up windows, bringing the lawn furniture indoors—before they drove out of town. Neither was engaged then to the women they would marry and start their families with, so it was just the two of them and Clark's dog to worry about. Their plan was to head west to Houston, but they only made it as far as Opelousas on the first day. They spent the night in the parking lot of a motel there when they couldn't get a room. The next day, they changed direction and drove north to Dallas, where they stayed for a week in a hotel. After that, they wound up in the Outer Banks of North Carolina, where a friend let them use a vacation rental for another week. When they had to move out of that space, Clark went on to stay with his sister in the Midwest, if I recall correctly, and Che drove down to Orlando, where his company, Siemens, has a presence. He operated out of Orlando and Atlanta temporarily for a few weeks. Eventually, both he and Clark made their way safely back to New Orleans.

My brother Van (Sylvanus, "god of the forest," he liked to boast, named after our maternal great-grandfather and grandfather) was a copy editor at the daily newspaper and would not evacuate. They had regular editions to put together and distribute. It was their collective duty, their professional obligation. The storm was The News!

Likewise, Brenda Marie's brother, Lawrence, opted to remain at his mother's apartment in Tremé. He knew it was high ground, and he knew that many of the elderly folks in the neighborhood would not be able to evacuate and would need someone looking out for them. Lawrence has street smarts. He figured he and a handful of buddies who had worked all over the French Quarter for decades would be able to scrounge enough resources from businesses there and elsewhere to help people in the neighborhood get through whatever was coming.

As for me and my traveling party, we had no idea where we were headed—just north until we could find safe harbor. It wasn't the first time I had taken such a gamble, venturing in some direction out of New Orleans without a specific destination in mind, just driving until I thought I would be out of harm's way, and then looking for a room to spend the night in—or however long it took to ride out the storm. (This was well before someone could search for lodging or get traffic reports on their cell phones.) I didn't expect to be gone for more than a couple of days and packed accordingly: a spare shirt, an extra pair of shorts, and my toiletries bag.

Because residents of the city had been under mandatory orders to evacuate, the interstate traffic was bumper-to-bumper and maddeningly slow for as far as I could see. After a couple of hours of that stagnation, I got the bright idea to get off the interstate and head west to Highway 61, which spliced right into the heart of the Mississippi Delta.

I didn't expect to find rooms in Natchez or farther north in Port Gibson, or Vicksburg, but I stopped in anyway and inquired at both fancy hotels and budget lodges, many of which had already taken to posting No Vacancy signs out front. In other words, *Don't waste our time or your breath asking about a place to sleep.*

So, we trudged on through the night until we reached Clarksdale and the intersection of Highway 49 sometime after midnight. Legend has it that that's the place where bluesman Robert Johnson sold his soul to the devil in exchange for success in his career. I wasn't looking for anything quite so monumental, just a room for the night. And we found one—in a dingy motel operated (and presumably owned) by South Asians. At the time, I felt fortunate to have it, to be out of the coming rains and wind, and to take a break from driving for ten hours.

The next morning our odyssey continued, still going in a northerly direction, still trying to evade the huge storm's winds and rain—ahead of us at first, but later in the rearview mirror (just barely). After a few twists and turns, we ended up at the Peabody Hotel in Little Rock, Arkansas, where we arrived in time to see live ducks walking, mostly single file, out an elevator and across the hotel lobby to a fountain pool in the atrium. The Peabody in Memphis is world-famous for this parade, but the one in Little Rock features its own daily show, too.

After leaving Little Rock on Tuesday under a clear sky, we headed for an excursion to Hot Springs. None of us had ever been there, and I wanted to see what all the hoopla was about. It has faded considerably from its twentieth-century heyday, but there is enough left to see why it was a hotsy-totsy resort for so many years, attracting the wealthy and powerful. The mineral baths are still open, the architecture is still impressive (e.g., the Spanish Colonial Revival Quapaw Bathhouse and the Italian and Spanish Revival Fordyce Bathhouse and Museum), but the Black-owned segregated spas and accommodations on Malvern Avenue, "Black Broadway," have largely been demolished. That's where the likes of Duke Ellington, Count Basie, Cab Calloway, and others recuperated from the grinds of show business and celebrityhood.

When our excursion to Hot Springs was over, I drove down to Shreveport and booked rooms in a casino hotel there. I was hoping to avoid much of the traffic from returning evacuees by steering wide of their expected paths as long as possible. But it was in Shreveport that we got the news on television about the increasing breaches and flooding throughout New Orleans. That was when I realized that the aftermath of this storm was going to be far more devastating and debilitating than probably anyone really wanted to imagine.

By now, there were horror stories popping up in the media's coverage of the storm. New Orleans had dodged a full-on direct hit, but there was significant wind damage. And the flooding didn't seem to be abating. And there were too many people crammed into the Superdome as a refuge of last resort. And it was hot.

In retrospect, I think I was still being a tad cavalier about the whole predicament, convinced everything would get back to "normal" in a couple of days. I generally don't think of myself as an optimist or a pessimist, just a non-dogmatic empiricist—I trust what my senses and mind experience, even though I realize humans can only see, feel, hear, touch, taste, or otherwise process just the tiniest sliver of what is actually going on in the universe. Nevertheless, I go with the little bit I think I know. That would not be enough, however, to get me through what was coming, even though in my case, it would turn out to be a lot milder and less consequential than some of the other stuff fellow Orleanians would suffer.

The truth is, I could have predicted some of these consequences if I had only bothered to look and think about it deeply enough in advance. But who isn't wracked by their own lack of foresight in the wake of catastrophic experiences?

I had been paying for this getaway, this storm-evasion excursion, with credit cards, which is what most people would have done. At the outset, I had fully expected to be able to pay off the expenditures when I got back to town and collected the funds that some of my New Orleans-based clients owed me. I had not bothered to pick up any payments the Friday or Saturday before I left the city. I figured people were trying to prepare for the storm and paying me could wait until next week. I wasn't in a hurry for the money—and that nonchalance cost me big time.

It turned out that I would not receive any mail at all for six months, and when I did, it had to be routed to an entirely different city in a different state. Needless to point out, my credit card debt mushroomed. Worse, even if I had contacted my creditors and negotiated repayment schedules, I didn't have the funds to pay back what I had charged six months previously. In fact, I never did collect on any of the receivables that were due me from New Orleans clients before Katrina. And I certainly never generated the projected income I was slated to earn from them through the end of 2005. I was in a bit of a pickle, and it would take some time and luck (in the form of a Small Business Administration low-interest loan) to climb out.

"You never know how strong you are," Bob Marley is thought to have said, "until being strong is your only choice."

At that moment, however, in Shreveport, I still wasn't overly worried. My home was on the Gentilly Ridge, relatively high ground. But it wasn't very large, and I was trying to figure out how many people I could house at my place until they could get back to theirs. That, too, was delusional thinking on my part, as I was soon to realize when I saw footage showing that the flooding of the elementary school in my neighborhood had reached its roof. That was three blocks away from where I lived. There was no way my place could have escaped the deluge. I would also be among those looking for a place to live for a while. New Orleans was uninhabitable, and there was no telling when residents would be allowed to return. (It turned out that Brenda Marie's place near Bayou St. John was the one that didn't flood, but we had no way of knowing this for another four or five weeks.)

In the meantime, while we tried to figure out our next move, we stayed at that casino hotel for another couple of days. But the weekend was approaching. They were going to be fully booked. We had to vacate the suite.

And then Brenda Marie got a call from an old friend in Baton Rouge, the esteemed literary scholar John Wharton Lowe, whose specialty was African American literature. He said he and his wife June would love to have us as houseguests until things got sorted out in New Orleans. So, we headed down to the Louisiana capital and were blessed to decamp to the extraordinarily hospitable Chez Lowe. The man loved to cook, and he prepared gourmet-level meals every evening, after which we retired to the living room or screened-off side porch for stimulating conversations.

The news about New Orleans continued to be more and more dire in the first weeks after the storm, nevertheless, and the city remained closed to all residents. My mother and daughter, who had evacuated to Baton Rouge, had since relocated to a nice mobile home community where my sister's husband Wayne had family who took them in. That was in Walker, Louisiana, about twenty minutes east of Baton Rouge. I drove out there one afternoon to visit them and was struck by the generosity of one of my brother-in-law's cousins, who had just turned over his tricked-out trailer to my folks carte blanche. Their eyes were glued to the TV and images of New Orleans. The realization that there would be no going home anytime soon had sunk into their consciousnesses as well. It was dispiriting, and even though that little idyllic Black compound of trailer homes nestled just off a major highway was comforting, soothing, nourishing even, it was also clear that it could not be a long-term housing option.

My sister, with her typical spunk, had bought a house in Baton Rouge after the storm. The owners had advertised it as "No Down Payment Required." She said, *I've got that*—and proceeded to acquire the property quickly and to move her family in since her home in New Orleans East would likely need a complete renovation.

I was still worried about what to do for my mother and daughter, however. My mother was eighty-one, with high blood pressure and diabetes. I needed to be sure she could get the medical care her condition required. Mia had just graduated from high school the previous spring but had been pushing for a gap year before starting college, a break from her studies and a chance to find out more about the world and herself. I had resisted the notion: *We plow through with our schooling. Always have, always will. You're too young to go off adventuring God-knows-where with God-knows-who.*

She begrudgingly accepted my argument. Then nature stepped in. There was no way she could think about going off to college now. There was no way she would abandon her grandma, her best bud. So, she got her gap year along with a modicum of personal growth and career focus in the process. But it wasn't exactly what she'd had in mind.

After I had gone out to Walker to visit with my mother and daughter, my cousin Tony Axam, a highly-regarded defense attorney from Atlanta who had been like another sibling to me since our childhood, called me out of the blue and said he had a two-bedroom apartment in downtown Atlanta near the courthouse that I could stay in until things got sorted out in New Orleans. He only used the place to prepare witnesses before trials at the Fulton County Court, but he didn't have any immediate need for it now.

I took him up on his offer, convinced my mother and daughter to come with me, and left Brenda Marie and her mother at the Lowes'. In the meantime, Tony and his wife Vicky generously got together some furnishings and supplies for the apartment and did everything humanly possible to make us comfortable once we arrived in Atlanta.

Professor Lowe had arranged for Brenda Marie to be hired by the English Department at LSU. Her former employer, Dillard University, had summarily dismissed the school faculty and staff after the storm. The entire school went on hiatus, I think, for a year. Her appointment at the state's flagship public university began just after the new fall semester had gotten under way. It was a fortuitous zag.

Earlier in 2005, Brenda Marie had been named poet laureate of Louisiana, an unsolicited and unexpected honor for her. She was the first person ever recommended to the governor for the position by a panel of literary experts (not politicians or financial donors).

As it turned out, she would spend nearly the entirety of her term as Louisiana Poet Laureate teaching at LSU on Mondays and Wednesdays and then travelling across the country on weekends doing readings, giving interviews, participating in panel discussions, and otherwise explaining the situation in New Orleans: who and what New Orleanians are as a people, our distinct culture, and our history of resistance and resilience.

But we did not know, and could not have predicted, any of that back then.

* * *

Hurácan is said by some to have been a word coined by the Maya, an advanced civilization that reached its peak from 250–900 A.D. and built cities made of stone in the Yucatán peninsula of present-day Mexico as well as across vast swaths of Central America. Other etymologists have reported that hurákan is a Taino word meaning "god of the storm." Since the Maya and Taino were both Indigenous people inhabiting nearby spaces in the Caribbean basin and southern Gulf of Mexico, it wouldn't be surprising if the word and its meaning were shared by both groups. When the Spanish arrived in the area in the sixteenth century as conquistadors (i.e., pillagers and genocidaires), they appropriated the word and applied it to the many devastating storms that periodically unleashed nature's punishing power. It's from Spanish that we get the English word hurricane.

Katrina is a form of Catriona, which is the Scottish and Irish form of Katherine, from the Greek katharos, meaning "pure." What Katrina brought to the Gulf Coast was pure—pure hell, including 1,500 lives lost, fifty billion dollars in property damage, and incalculable psychological damage.

* * *

My brother rode out the storm on the twenty-ninth, and the next day, or the day after, as he was preparing to head to work for his regular 3:00–11:00 p.m. shift, he noticed water rising quickly in his home in New Orleans East. The more he scrambled to move his belongings to tabletops and counters, the more the water kept outpacing his efforts. In short order, he was forced to whack a hole in the ceiling of his slab-on-grade, one-story, brick, ranch-style home and then make another escape hole from his attic to the roof. When the water reached that height, he decided to make a move and abandon his perch. He swam for roughly a quarter mile in the direction of Interstate 10, near Wright Road. The waters had not topped the road surface there, so he was able to swim to where he could stand up and walk in the direction of downtown. He never made it that far, but he did join a bunch of other people who had been pushed onto the highway in a bid for safety. After some time in the scorching heat, they were rounded up, put on a bus, and driven out of town. Van eventually ended up in San Antonio, where he was stranded for weeks.

When he returned, the newspaper had relocated its operations to Houma, Louisiana, roughly sixty miles south of New Orleans. He joined his colleagues there, rendezvoused with his long-time lady friend Ann, and began the process of commuting to the city and plowing through the rigmarole of securing insurance payments and other funds to repair his home and rental properties.

He was fortunate, too. His fate could have been far different if we hadn't spent so much time learning to swim as children. There was a stretch of years when we spent our summer afternoons swimming laps and diving and horsing around in the competition-sized natatorium on the campus of Grambling College, as it was known back then. A few years later, in the 1960s in New Orleans, we once lost a neighborhood friend to drowning when a bunch of us piled into a car and snuck off to the Point on Lake Pontchartrain in the middle of one of those lazy, sweltering Crescent City summer afternoons. Not content just to cool ourselves off by splashing around in the water, someone decided to issue a dare to everyone else in the group to swim from our side of the Point on Lakeshore Drive to the other side of the waterway, maybe a distance of fifty yards. We all swam across the channel just fine, the first time. After a short respite, we dove back into the water and swam back the other way. Unfortunately, the oldest boy in our group didn't make it. No one noticed at first that he was in serious trouble, not joking around.

When we did, it was too late. A handful of us had already reached our original starting point. But midway across, this dude went under and disappeared. He wasn't pranking us. We were dumbfounded, of course. It was sudden, unexpected. Everything had been upbeat and jovial with us, carefree even. And then something incomprehensibly tragic flipped the whole mood. Our laughter and joking stopped. We hung around for hours afterward while the officials dragged the lake for our friend's body and got information from us about how to contact his parents. My brother and I were probably thirteen and fourteen years old at the time. The fellow who drowned was a couple of years ahead of us in school. He had driven us to the lake in his family's car. I don't even remember now how we ever got back home, but I know for sure we never went swimming at the Point again.

I thought about that day again when my brother recounted later how he had to swim from the roof of his house to the interstate. That one little thing, the ability to swim, meant all the difference to his survival. Many other folks weren't as well prepared.

For those of us who made it through the storm, our collective memories are still crowded, probably, with images of bodies floating in filthy flood waters that lingered in the city for six weeks and stank up the place for months after that. We also will never forget the families of people stranded on the roofs of apartment buildings, waving at passing helicopters, begging for someone, anyone, to help them after three and four days in the heat without water or food. The situation at the Convention Center and the Superdome appeared to be even more dire for thousands of people, for an even longer period.

Many of us who evacuated before the storm were displaced from the city for months. In my case, it was eighteen months before I returned on a permanent basis. Everyone else in my family had returned to the city well before then. I was splitting my time between Atlanta and New Orleans when my schedule permitted—two weeks in one place, two weeks in the other. I was blessed back then to have some significant clients that were not based in New Orleans, so I was able to keep working through all the other turmoil. The drives to and from the ATL also gave me ample time to think, reflect, plan, relax, and be fortified by the great music I had stashed in my car right before the storm: David Murray Quartet + 1, *Fast Life*, the ideal traveling soundtrack; Cassandra Wilson, *New Moon Daughter*, an endlessly rewarding example of song interpretation and originality; the astounding Impulse Records compilation *Red Hot on Impulse!*; the wise and plaintive Abbey Lincoln, "*You can never lose a thing if it belongs to you*"[5]; the ever-grooving and politically committed Hugh Masekela; mellow Charles Lloyd; Betty Carter, *Feed the Fire*; and the master, Terry Callier, *Alive*.

There were moments, of course, when something would trigger some overwhelming, unexpected dolefulness about how the storm had upended my life. I still vividly recall the first time I was able to push open the swollen front

---

5   Abbey Lincoln, "Throw It Away," recorded May, August, November 1994, track 1 on *A Turtle's Dream*, Verve, Spotify, https://open.spotify.com/track/5b-0ZYe9B8jotKlAg44s3bc?si=9b912b4234bd4683.

door to my home and see how everything inside had been overturned or undercut by flood waters that left a four-foot-high watermark on all the walls of a structure that was already raised two feet off the ground. My baby grand piano had been thoroughly soaked. All my bookcases, too.

Brenda Marie, my ride or die, accompanied me on that first trip back to my place. Recently, she reminded me that when we were finally able to get inside, the framed photograph of my late father, curiously enough, was still upright on top of one of the tall bookcases that hadn't tumbled over. The presence of his image looking totally unaffected by the turmoil below might have had a subliminally calming effect on my psyche.

My father, whom people called Buchanan or, more commonly, Buke, had died suddenly, unexpectedly, in 1959, when I was ten years old. His death was caused by a cerebral hemorrhage, we were told. Apparently, there were no warning signs, just here one second and gone the next. Gone. Gone. Gone. For. Ever! Just like that. And he was just a few weeks shy of his thirty-third birthday.

Nothing had ever gut-punched me harder. Nothing would hurt me so deeply ever again. Nothing would catch me so emotionally off guard ever again.

Naturally, my father's death turned our family upside down. But once again, it could have been worse. We quickly moved from Nashville, where we had been living for the past year (while my father attended Meharry Medical College, one of several older students following the same dream), to Grambling, Louisiana (where my mother, suddenly a widow with three kids to raise, had gotten hired as a college librarian, thanks to the intercession of friends). During an interim between the moves, we spent a couple of months in New Orleans getting our bearings straight after my father's funeral and burial in Daytona Beach.

For many years afterward, I used to wonder if what killed my father was a congenital condition, and I steeled myself to be prepared to die young, too. I didn't, but perhaps that's why his photo survived the damage from Katrina the Pure: to remind me that it would eventually pass, too; that we would survive whatever the storm took from us; that life would change, sometimes drastically, but it would go on.

Though my father's confident, smiling image might have been standing tall after the storm, virtually everything else in my home was wrecked. The refrigerator was flipped over on its side, and the odor of rotten food stank up the whole space. Back then, all of New Orleans was odoriferous. It reeked like the first time I set foot in rural Morocco one midnight in 1974—like centuries of dung, urine, and sweat baked in a furnace that I was walking over, walking into. I hadn't realized that particular memory, that specific sensation, was still buried in me more than thirty years later. It just instantaneously sprang to mind the first few times I came back into the city.

One night after I had been in Atlanta for a few weeks, my cousin and his wife invited me to a social gathering. One of Vicky's friends, Hank Aaron's daughter, was married to a grandson of Dooky and Leah Chase, and a passel of their New Orleans kinfolk had evacuated and arrived at their place. When I walked in, I could hear lots of laughter and warmth seeping out from the den of the house, which overall was spacious and tastefully appointed, not nouveau gaudy or conspicuous like those Atlanta McMansions on television. Nick, the host, immediately offered me a cocktail—Crown Royal and Seven Up—that let me know I could close my eyes and hear authentic New Orleans soul in the accents emanating from the den.

For a while, I was really happy to meet him and to talk about "home." But when our small talk ended, I found a deep sense of melancholy creeping over me for the very first time post-Katrina. Worse, instead of following Nick into the den where his New Orleans kin were reveling, I found myself being drawn to his living room, where no one was, where the centerpiece was a beautiful black grand piano. I didn't utter a word, but it was as though I was communicating with that piano, apologizing to it for what I had let happen to one of its kind. That I hadn't appreciated enough, hadn't played enough, hadn't valued enough until it was lost to me. My rarest books, too. I knew I had kept them on the lowest shelf of one of my bookcases to prevent the sun from shining on them, but why didn't I just pack them away high on a closet shelf or somewhere else that was safer? And why hadn't I bought insurance to cover my most valuable contents? I probably could have gotten a policy for as much as I would spend some random weekend on dinner and a show.

Then, as I was really starting to admonish myself for the myriad moves I had not taken to protect my belongings, in walked Hank Aaron himself, the baseball god, along with his wife Billye. I quickly pivoted from ruminating about my own stupidity and fecklessness to being fully present in the company of these new arrivals. They were an elegant older couple and very warm when we were introduced. But they must have thought it quite odd to step into their daughter's home and find a strange man there all alone, staring in the direction of the piano with a cocktail in a red plastic cup.

Since my options were limited, Atlanta became my base of operations for eighteen months by default. But I didn't mind. In fact, it was helpful to my outlook for a couple of reasons. The first was that the rest of the world seemed to grasp for the first time that New Orleans was a really, really Black city and one that was very, very poor, too. This seemed to make it easier for powerful Washington politicians and all sorts of highfalutin urban planners to categorize it as a hopelessly failed space (perhaps deliberately, like Haiti or some intentionally impoverished African nation, in their minds) and to openly advocate that New Orleans not be rebuilt, that whole sections be left to return to nature, never to be peopled again (especially by Blacks).

At the same time, Atlanta was in the process of becoming the undisputed capital of Black America. Though it had and has its share of problems associated with poverty, homelessness, financial stability, racism, urban sprawl, and inner-city gentrification, there were still plenty of noteworthy positives in the ATL's built environment that I felt offered valuable lessons and examples for New Orleans.

So, I started dreaming out loud, fully cognizant that two years after the fact, more than one hundred thousand Afro-Orleanians still had not returned to the city, that all the former residents of the four big public housing projects had been summarily evicted, given five thousand dollars for their troubles, and barred under threat of arrest from ever returning to their apartments again. That all public school teachers had been fired. Healthcare workers, too. That the big public hospital was shuttered, along with public transportation services. That tourists—leisure visitors (except those taking disaster tours) and conventioneers—were staying away from local hotels, restaurants, and other visitor attractions. That the whole situation was dystopic, but that didn't mean things had to stay that way. Money was starting to roll out to rebuild homes and schools and hospitals and other essential infrastructure and services. With a lot of pushing, pulling, and a dollop of grace, we could end up with our own urban utopia.

My mantra back then was, "In the bowl, but off the grid." I was convinced that New Orleans could rebound and survive by fortifying its levee system. The only reason the situation had turned into such a cluster of catastrophes to begin with was because the levees the Corps of Engineers installed to protect the city were shoddy and collapsed in more than fifty locations. The poor city never had a chance. But now it had an opportunity to build back better than ever. That's what lots of us believed.

Louisiana has been the oil and gas industry's cash cow (and lap dog) for the past hundred years, but we had a compelling opportunity to develop solar capacity in the state and repower our comeback. Back then, I envisioned electric buses and streetcars taking passengers to destinations such as a man-made beach on Lake Pontchartrain; solar-powered, high-speed train service connecting New Orleans to the whole Gulf Coast and the Deep South; revamped retail centers with venues like an IKEA store at the intersection of Gentilly Boulevard and Elysian Fields; other shopping center and community shelter redesigns that didn't have massive parking lots fronting the street view; storm-resistant, energy-efficient homes, cars, and businesses (cooperatively owned and operated); smartly surfaced streets; New Urbanism-influenced neighborhood redesigns; and, most crucially, Black people making the decisions about matters most important to their lives. Some of these visions are being realized; others have seemingly been pushed to the back burners until, perhaps, there is greater grassroots support for them. Grassroots support on its own, or in the hands of timid, uncreative leadership, is no guarantor of exemplary, groundbreaking, equity-making results. But that's a discussion for another time.

There were and are, of course, wealthy whites in the city's old-guard establishment who have a different vision about who should inhabit and control the city. They want us scrubbed from the scene, relegated to the servants' (slave) quarters once again. There were at least two organizations whose primary mission was to recruit new prospective residents to the city, including teachers and administrators for the swiftly assembled and implemented decentralized charter school system that was touted as the salvation for young Black minds so grossly underserved by the previous public school system. But twenty years later, these know-it-alls have been unable to improve the educational infrastructure they finagled from Black control and are attempting to give it back to us, except for continuing to funnel boatloads of money into the pockets of non-unionized, inexperienced, non-Black "educators" and "school leaders" at both failing and passing schools.

The former Black healthcare workers who have returned to the city now work mostly for private hospital systems that nevertheless treat thousands of patients whose care is paid for by Medicare and Medicaid—like the old public hospital they replaced. Many city streets now have bike lanes and charging stations for electric vehicles to accommodate predominantly white residents and visitors. And the new Riverfront District development is shaping up to be New Orleans' version of Atlanta's billion-dollar, multi-use Atlantic Station development, with the standard public pledge to award significant contracts to qualified disadvantaged businesses—which end up so often being businesses set up by white men with white women as the figurehead CEOs. Blacks still dominate in elected politics, as they should, but white-owned firms continue to garner more than 95 percent of city contracts. The white community may not control the Black political and civic mouthpieces totally, but they still have the purse strings locked down tight.

Despite its widespread destruction, Hurricane Katrina's aftermath provided a major new boondoggle for outsiders and insiders alike. After the storm, there was a feeding frenzy here of grifters, con artists, and plain old crooks masquerading as developers, bankers, contractors, planners, researchers, program administrators and managers, nonprofit leaders, faith-based apostles, casual laborers, and/or community activists all angling to get their piece of the billions of dollars that would be invested in rebuilding New Orleans through the Federal Emergency Management Agency, the Road Home Program, other government departments, and various philanthropies. Cronies of then President George Bush the Younger from Texas and Florida "won" contracts to demolish the brick-faced public housing complexes that suffered no major damage during the storm and replace them with wooden mixed-use developments intended to lessen the concentration of the poor and their allegedly criminal behavior in those neighborhoods. They and a lot of outright hustlers lived high off the hog for a number of years. Many are still feasting today.

There were, to be sure, many decent altruistic people who also came to town from all over the globe and kicked in money and sweat to help people get back into their homes, places of worship, businesses, and the like. They were truly a blessing to the city and helped to demonstrate the best characteristics and potential of humanity. Nevertheless, despite all their good deeds and generosity, the foul, opportunistic, avaricious elements that descended on the city and emerged out of its own populace seemed to be everywhere you turned, working some sort of angle to line their pockets, to take full advantage of The Great Big Easy Boondoggle.

The city was ground zero for what author Naomi Klein dubbed disaster capitalism, the wanton and rapacious exploitation of unstable social, political, and economic situations by powerful forces seeking to snatch and control economic resources and money-making opportunities by whatever means necessary, including deregulating industries, privatizing public assets, and eliminating political opposition. What the environmental activist John D. MacDonald once decried as "instant Florida" could also have applied to the reconstructed, rejiggered New Orleans in those first years after Katrina. It was "tacky and stifling and full of ugly spurious energies."[6]

---

6   John D. MacDonald, *The Dreadful Lemon Sky* (Rochester, MN: Fawcett, 1982), 45.

The ugly, spurious energies that permeated the environment here and amped up our status as the Big Sleazy (where chicanery abounds) have superficially abated somewhat since the George Floyd murder in 2020 reawakened the national consciousness and fired up an intense insistence again on righting this country's racial wrongs. "I say it plain," Langston Hughes once declaimed, "America never was America to me / And yet I swear this oath—America will be!"[7]

This long-held insistence that Black Lives Matter has now blossomed into its own life-affirming corollary, Black Joy. It is the north star guiding the mobilization of hundreds of thousands of younger Black folks across this nation and the globe, especially in Africa, which is going to rise and shine through the intensifying struggle against white supremacy for the rest of this century before coming into its own in the twenty-second. And make no mistake, the death throes of white supremacy—as inevitable as rain—will grow more and more gruesome and desperate until it is wiped out. Black bodies will pay a heavy price once again in this crucial struggle. Just the same, the momentum for Black Joy is growing throughout our diaspora, and there is no place this blossoming mindset fits more comfortably, more naturally, than it does in New Orleans.

From the rooter to the tooter, we are the real bamboula. And post-Katrina, we are purer and more steadfast in our convictions than ever before. We know what the commitment to a celebratory, life-affirming culture has cost us already, and we know it will exact an even greater toll in the days ahead—if history is a reliable guide.

The formerly unthinkable is now commonplace; the previously unimaginable is now stark reality: mass shootings in any and every public space, persistent wildfires, prolonged droughts, unprecedented heatwaves, wicked tornadoes, lethal floods, raging hurricanes, unrelenting pandemics, and the like. In addition, Black people are confronting environmental poisoning, systemic racism, internalized racism, gender inequality, social reconstruction, and intractable economic inequity. Through it all, however, we have built up an unshakeable resolve to overcome every obstacle in our path, no matter how long it takes. And to do so with buoyancy and style.

"The mere existence of Black joy is an act of defiance, one that customarily withstands the onslaught of destruction, disinvestment, dispossession, and

---

7   Langston Hughes, "Let America Be America Again," Poets.org, Academy of American Poets, accessed June 4, 2025, https://poets.org/poem/let-america-be-america-again.

death," urban ecologist and Afrofuturist Christopher Schell has written. "In this way, Black joy serves as an elixir to rejuvenate communities and motivate the fight for the civil rights of all peoples. This radical inclusivity serves as the foundation of social and environmental justice movements, which stress the humanity of all peoples and the need for equitable access to healthy environments."

Later in that same essay, "Hope for the Wild in Afrofuturism," Schell goes on to assert

> [. . .] that we can authentically implement proposed solutions once we become fully liberated, emancipated, and decolonized. We can build resilience into our cities and towns, suburbs, and rural neighborhoods with the important start of understanding that we must change our relationship with nature by seeing how we are connected to nature through each other. Luckily the ancestors and elders from the diaspora and beyond have etched that path of compassion and empathy in our collective memory. We simply need to regain our power to hear those past lessons for a better future.[8]

As lucid and powerful as these observations are, I take exception to one of Schell's key arguments. I would argue that it is the process of devising and implementing solutions to our problems and challenges that actually liberates, emancipates, and decolonizes us. "We make the road by walking it," the old revolutionaries used to say. We can't wait to solve our problems until after we are liberated; we become liberated in actuality through waging the struggle, undertaking the work to implement our vision for a better world.

"I slept and dreamt / that life was joy," the South Asian sage Rabindranath Tagore once wrote. "I awoke and saw / that life was duty. / I worked—and behold, / duty was joy."

"Joy" is the current buzzword we use to define our aspirations. It has upstaged "resilient," which in turn superseded "militant" and "revolutionary" in progressive quarters. Whether it remains au courant, only time will tell.

---

8   Christopher J. Schell, "To Dream of Beauty: On the Possibility of Afrofuturism as a Solution to Climate Catastrophe," LitHub, August 15, 2024, https://lithub.com/to-dream-of-beauty-on-the-possibility-of-afrofuturism-as-a-solution-to-climate-catastrophe/.

As poet Aja Monet reminds us, however, "True joy has always been, and will always be, justice."[9] Until we secure that, our duty remains: to fight on all fronts, to find joy through struggle, and to take solace even in our inevitable, but never final, setbacks and defeats along the way.

Bring it on, our young'uns say. All of it. We ready.

---

9   Ilo Toerkell, "Freedom Dreaming Alongside Orishas In A Brownstone: aja monet's Blues Poetry," Off Key, NBHAP, July 16, 2023, https://nbhap.com/blog/freedom-dreaming-with-aja-monet.

WHAT NEW ORLEANS HAS TAUGHT ME
ANDREA CHEN

Before the Storm
The first week back at school at John McDonogh Sr. High School (affectionately known as "John Mac") arrived, and I was feeling pretty great about how this school year was going to go. The previous year had been tough, but my "reputation" as the tenth- and eleventh-grade English teacher had spread, and my former students, including the kids who often loved to challenge me in class, popped in their heads to let this year's students know that "*Ms. Chen don't play,*" which was hilarious news to me. I had made announcements in class that students who struggled to read could come in during lunchtime for help, they showed up, and we were starting the phonics curriculum training I had prepared over the summer.

Meanwhile, as a recent transplant from California, New Orleans had already started feeling like a place where I belonged. It didn't take long. The people I met were the free spirits I aspired to be, everyone greeted me on the street, some called me "shorty," every house was a different color of the rainbow, people dressed with stylish, coordinated ensembles and everyday flair, and someone was always available to hang out any hour of the day. I could be myself in a city where people always had time to hang out, to talk to neighbors from the porch, to stay up late at Le Bon Temps bar, to dance wild, to dress loud, and to carry our velvet couch to the sidewalk to watch the Mardi Gras parades. I learned that I would never be able to say that I was "from" New Orleans, but it felt like home. I loved it so much, I looked forward to summertime.

The Evacuation
Then we got the notice: "Storm's coming." Followed by, "OPSB [Orleans Parish School Board] schools are closing." Hurrication for the teachers! There

was a concert at Tipitina's on Saturday night—if we didn't leave town, maybe we'd go and enjoy a less packed house. Then came the evacuation order. *I guess we're leaving.* As long as we avoided taking I-10 West, I was feeling okay. The previous year's evacuation, I had spent twelve hours falling asleep at the wheel in middle-of-the-night bumper-to-bumper traffic to Baton Rouge.

I was living uptown on State Street with two teacher roommates, and all of my friends were teachers. We packed our vacation flip-flops and summer sundresses, we filled up on gas and water, I unplugged and moved my one "electronics" (a printer) to the top of a shelf, and we were on our way to Nashville to extend our summer vacation. Only later did I recognize how many New Orleans families could not get out, did not get out, were left behind, or barely made it out in time.

My parents, both immigrants from Taiwan who raised us in the San Gabriel Valley of Southern California, hadn't been too worried during my first hurricane or for Katrina. The first time, my mom told me that if I stayed, I just needed to fill my bathtub with clean water. She warned me that power might be out for a while, so stock up on candles, gas, and dry goods. She was more concerned about me driving out of town on my own and getting into a wreck. When my parents were growing up, typhoons on the tropical island of Taiwan came through several times a year, and she remembers the first floor of their house flooding almost every year, at least seven or eight times, and having to evacuate their whole family of five kids to their second floor. She was familiar with storm prep: they boarded up the windows, unplugged their electronics, took everything upstairs, and lived out of their second floor for a week while the first floor flooded. After every flood, it took weeks to dry out the house and make repairs. Only once, though, did the floodwaters get so high that the water almost came up to the second floor. That time, she saw lifeboats go by, and it wasn't until she saw drowned cockroaches and dead mice that she knew to be scared.

The Reality Sets In

In Nashville, my friends and I gathered around the television to watch the weather reporters getting pummeled by the sideways rain. And then something unusual happened. The levees broke. Flooding. Horror. Shock. Panic. Images of children and families carrying belongings above their heads through the water. Could these children be my students? Several of them had already told me they weren't planning to evacuate. And then the Superdome and helicopters. Twenty years later, the television footage blurs in my mind—stories, videos, and photos that came out much later versus what the broadcast actually was on August 29 and the days after.

The Aftermath

For the next year, sleep was hard to come by. And once I slept, I wouldn't wake up, sleeping ten to twelve hours at a time, finally waking up unable to open my jaw. With nowhere to go and the entire city under water, all of us OPSB teachers received our letter notice that we were being let go as teachers. *What am I to do now?* My caravan continued traveling up north to the East Coast, staying a few days with friends or friends of friends, buying us time to figure out what to do now that we were all unemployed and didn't know when we could come back to the city. Some of us ended up getting jobs working for FEMA.

I caravanned all the way to Albany, New York, and received the notice that graduate schools across the country were accepting displaced students. I applied to Harvard, having previously been enrolled in the University of New Orleans' education program, got accepted, and flew to Cambridge, Massachusetts, with a suitcase full of shorts and T-shirts and joined the snowy fall semester on scholarship with the regular students. This was an incredible privilege in the midst of others not even having a place to live, and I carried the obligation to do something useful heavily in my heart throughout that semester. Not being set up for an East Coast winter, my most vivid memory is of taking my rolling suitcase to the grocery store and packing it full of groceries and rolling it back through the snow over cobblestone and brick-lain streets. The university set up a faculty housing facility for all the displaced graduate students at no cost to any of us. But I felt a strong urge to go back to the city. I needed to know what happened, and I needed to be part of the recovery.

Return to New Orleans

As soon as the city reopened, I found a new high school English teaching job and rushed back in January to start the winter semester in the city's new charter school system. My sister flew to Albany to fetch my car and drove with me all the way from Upstate New York to New Orleans. My new colleagues had to clean the leaves out of their offices, and some were still living out of their cars those first few months post-hurricane. The city had a curfew in place, since we didn't have the majority of our streetlights. As someone who rarely eats at McDonald's, I remember feeling my heart lift with joy when the first McDonald's reopened. I remember cheering when Kinko's

Copy Center on Tchoupitoulas, which used to be my most frequent retail stop, opened again, and I went back to making my copies there.

A year or two after the storm, we had settled back into some kind of "new normal," but the city was still a complete mess. We had no street signs and were missing street lights, but artists had painted and nailed up new street signs. The neutral ground in most places was completely overgrown since city government and regular operations were nowhere to be found. But neighborhood groups started taking matters into their own hands and began mowing the neutral ground themselves. There were thousands of teenagers who didn't have any school to go to. Maybe only three public high schools had reopened citywide since the Recovery School District had taken over all of OPSB schools in November 2005; all reopened as charter schools. My own high school, John Mac, never reopened, and a decade later, it was converted into a K–8 charter school. For at least four years, the marquee sign still said, "Welcome back to school. August 18, 2005." In the Lower 9th Ward, you could still see cars upside down on top of two-story houses and plenty of staircases going nowhere that were all that remained of entire houses.

Community Response
It was clear that no one was going to save us. The government had failed us during the storm, and even a year, two years after the storm, the government still couldn't get our basic functions like schools and streets together. If anything was going to happen, we'd have to do it ourselves. We had all just gone through the shared experience of a gut-wrenching collective loss, and we had all been abandoned by the powers and systems that were supposed to protect us.

I was born in Canada and grew up in California, and my own loss was miniscule compared to what others lost. My shock was that our country and government betrayed New Orleans, my adopted home, in a way that I didn't think was possible in modern times. I was shocked that relief didn't come straight away. That, in the richest country in the world, we couldn't deploy more helicopters to rescue everyone from their roofs. That people were left to swelter and die in the Dome when we could have easily gotten supplies and generators. That, two years later, we couldn't open enough *schools* or even replace *street signs*.

As "recovery" progressed, I came to recognize that racial inequities were embedded in every aspect of the disaster response from housing to education. The Road Home program, which disbursed over ten billion dollars in federal funds, discriminated against Black homeowners by calculating grants based on pre-storm home values rather than actual rebuilding costs. This meant that homeowners in historically Black neighborhoods, such as the Lower 9th Ward, often did not receive enough to rebuild their homes and received significantly smaller grants despite identical storm damage, a practice later challenged in a federal lawsuit filed by the Greater New Orleans Fair Housing Action Center and the NAACP Legal Defense Fund.[10] The OPSB dismissed approximately 4,300 teachers after Katrina, 71 percent of whom were Black and made up the backbone of the Black middle class. Most of them never taught in Louisiana again.[11] The demographics of teachers shifted significantly to just under 50 percent Black in the years following.[12] As an Asian American educator with only one year of teaching experience, I was among the few initially rehired in the charter system while thousands of more skilled and experienced Black teachers were never hired back. Even FEMA's own National Advisory Council acknowledged that its disaster programs "provide an additional boost to wealthy homeowners and others with less need, while lower-income individuals and others sink further into poverty after disasters."[13]

---

10   Dwayne Fatherree, "New Orleans homeowners still in financial storm 18 years after Katrina," Southern Poverty Law Center, August 31, 2023, https://www.splcenter.org/resources/stories/
new-orleans-housing-crisis-18-years-hurricane-katrina/.
11   Emmanuel Felton, "What Happened to All of the New Orleans Teachers Fired After Hurricane Katrina?", Education Week, May 31, 2017, https://www.edweek.org/teaching-learning/
what-happened-to-all-of-the-new-orleans-teachers-fired-after-hurricane-katrina/2017/05.
12   Sarah Carr, "What Happened After New Orleans Fired All of Its Teachers—and Why It Still Matters to Diversity in the Classroom," Slate, June 18, 2015, https://www.slate.com/blogs/schooled/2015/06/18/
black_teachers_in_new_orleans_the_number_of_them_has_plummeted_since_hurricane.html; Education Research Alliance for New Orleans, *Did the Teachers Dismissed after Hurricane Katrina Return to Public Education?*, New Orleans: Tulane University, 2017, 5, https://educationresearchalliancenola.org/publications/did-the-teachers-dismissed-after-hurricane-katrina-return-to-public-education.
13   Thomas Frank, "Advisers Rebuke FEMA for Racial Disparities in Disaster Aid," Scientific American, February 20, 2021, https://www.scientificamerican.com/article/advisers-rebuke-fema-for-racial-disparities-in-disaster-aid/.

Building Something New
I saw what others were doing—what regular people were doing—real estate agents, former school teachers, stay-at-home moms, artists—to be a part of the grassroots recovery efforts. I saw how people were coming together, seeing what was needed and stepping up to deliver services for their neighbors and their communities. From watching those around me, I saw what was possible, and I felt inspired, energized, and encouraged. I wanted to contribute, to fight the structural forces that caused this in the first place, and I desperately wanted to stay and be a part of mending what had been broken. Teaching in the classroom taught me invaluable lessons about community building, relationship building, and work ethic, and it remains the hardest thing I've ever done in my life. It was difficult to leave the classroom, but teaching also became the foundation that prepared me for my current work.

One of my friends at the time, a native New Orleanian with deep family roots, had started a civic engagement group pre-hurricane called Social Entrepreneurs of New Orleans. My friend and I decided to restart this group to contribute to the collective energy of the time, to be part of the movement, to find resources to support the heroic efforts of people on the ground making change. We convened a group of volunteers in the back room of the Bridge Lounge (now called Barrel Proof on Magazine Street) to figure out how we would do this. Many of our original steering committee members have gone on to lead significant citywide racial justice efforts, successful racial discrimination lawsuits, and widely-recognized New Orleans brands.

This organization grew into my life's work, and I put my heart, energy, and focus into building the nonprofit organization now called Propeller. As volunteers, we began elevating the stories of longtime New Orleans social entrepreneurs like Cherice Harrison-Nelson from Guardians of the Flame, Carol Bebelle from Ashé Cultural Arts Center, and Craig Cuccia from Café Reconcile, all elders and innovators who had been strengthening our community and tackling injustices for decades. We wanted to provide examples of those who had come before to inspire those who were in the thick of the Katrina rebuilding. We then began hosting citywide pitch events to elevate new initiatives, to bring together new changemakers, and started an accelerator program for social entrepreneurs.

One of the first social entrepreneurs who participated in our volunteer-run Impact Accelerator was John "JT" Thompson, who had started Resurrection After Exoneration (RAE), the first exoneree-run re-entry program in the country. After having been falsely accused of committing a crime he did not commit and having spent eighteen years on death row in the Angola prison, JT was exonerated through DNA evidence that had been hidden and mishandled by the district attorney, and he dedicated his life to helping others transition from prison. We worked with JT to launch RAE's print shop and other earned-revenue businesses to help employ others.

The Work Continues

Propeller's mission today is to support and grow entrepreneurs to tackle social and environmental disparities. We deliberately focus on the word "disparities" because research consistently shows that inequities across every industry and sector break down along racial lines. We recognize that meaningfully addressing health, education, economic, and environmental challenges requires embedding racial equity into everything we do. This organizational commitment mirrors my own post-Katrina journey of race and racism re-education, which entailed unlearning and learning the history and analysis of race in the US through my mentors at the People's Institute for Survival and Beyond and the Racial Equity Institute.

Our work centers on capital access and contracts through programs such as our Impact Accelerator, hosted at our ten thousand-square-foot coworking facility at Washington Avenue and Broad Street. Our goal is to transform New Orleans' economic landscape by increasing Black-owned business receipts from less than 2 percent of total citywide revenue to one day reach demographic representation. The current data paints a stark picture: While Black residents comprise nearly 60 percent of New Orleans' population, Black-owned employer businesses generated less than $1 billion in total receipts, a mere 0.5 percent of the city's total $180 billion in business receipts, revealing a profound economic disparity.[14] We're addressing this disparity through a comprehensive strategy that works with BIPOC entrepreneurs to secure government and private-sector contracts, advocates with anchor institutions for procurement opportunities, provides much-needed equity capital, and facilitates access to debt financing through a collaborative, citywide coalition of organizations. This multi-pronged approach recognizes that closing the racial wealth gap requires structural interventions across all aspects of the business ecosystem.

---

14   "SEE CHANGE Business Database," SEE CHANGE Collective, Nonprofit Knowledge Works, accessed June 4 2025, https://www.datacenterresearch.org/seechange/.

The Spirit of New Orleans

What I learned from New Orleanians, the advocates, and the social entrepreneurs in the process of building and leading Propeller became the biggest gift of a lifetime. For all that I have been given and learned, and for all who have welcomed me, I stay motivated to continue strengthening the New Orleans community and fighting the inequitable systems that continue to pervade our city and country.

When the layers of New Orleans revealed themselves with time, what I discovered was the depth of the generosity, the love, the connectedness, the courage to fight and tell the truth, the commitment to belonging, forgiveness, and the obligations to family and community that I have not seen anywhere else. And, of course, all the other things that people see more readily: the fun, the creativity, the laughter, the self-expression, and the ability to make something magical and delightful out of essentially nothing.

The spirit of New Orleans became part of my spirit. I aspired to be more like the New Orleanians I knew. I became more present, more generous, more compassionate, more caring, more connected, and more courageous as a result. Seeing the incredible work of our entrepreneurs and the passion they have—all united by love and caring for our city—gives me the energy and hope to continue day to day.

Looking Forward

Since Katrina, New Orleans has faced other existential threats: the saltwater intrusion crisis threatening our drinking water, chronic flooding from failed pump systems, the mass exodus of private insurers after Hurricane Ida, causing skyrocketing property costs, the devastating impact of Covid-19, and crippling budget cuts to essential services. Each one of these things could have taken us out and would have maybe taken out another city, but we remain. In times when we could have turned against each other, we turned towards each other.

The level of care and compassion I've both observed and experienced, from the smallest of interactions to the grand gestures, defines this city. To remember how we came together in the aftermath of the storm, and to know that this care, love, acceptance, courage, and generosity is what makes New Orleans what it is and what makes us New Orleanians who we are—most of us know that what we have is too precious to give up and too precious to not fight for.

We don't know what disaster will strike us next, and people are stretched thin and have gone through more than anyone should have to go through, but I know that New Orleans will continue to turn towards each other as we have done. If it's in the last reserves that we hold, this is our best hope of making it through.

CRITICAL IMAGINATION, PHILANTHROPY, AND DISASTER:
How Women on Stoops and Men on Milk Crates Changed the World

FLOZELL DANIELS JR. WITH PAM JENKINS

"We decided justice was going to be at the center of the Foundation for Louisiana work. We were going to be courageous because it's the only thing that has ever saved anybody. It is the only thing that honors this life that we've been given. We have to have a universal understanding of the miracle of these atoms exploding in us. Being able to exist in form and then be with each other and shape a social context is a miracle. I do not know what you call it, and so you may as well honor it with some decency."
— Flozell Daniels Jr.

Over hours on Zoom, Flozell and I talked about his life, Hurricane Katrina and other disasters, philanthropy, and the future. Flozell and I have been friends for more than two decades. I had the pleasure of serving on the Foundation for Louisiana (FFL) board for nine years, eight of them as chair of the board. It was my honor to talk with him. The conversation was both inspiring and aspirational. This chapter provides a glimpse of Flozell forging policy, relationships, and action in the midst of disaster.

Life in Disaster
In the immediate aftermath of Hurricane Katrina and the mandatory evacuation of New Orleans, life changed drastically and overnight for all of us.

Pam: Flozell, talk about what your life was like during the year of Hurricane Katrina.

CRITICAL IMAGINATION, PHILANTHROPY, AND DISASTER: HOW WOMEN ON STOOPS AND MEN ON MILK CRATES CHANGED THE WORLD

Flozell: I was the executive director and assistant vice president of state policy affairs at Tulane University for six years. I had the opportunity to expand Tulane's vision for what that work looked like because I focused on building statewide networks that would support both research and community programming. I learned about what it meant in different corners of Louisiana to develop narratives and relationships that would build consensus on equity issues, even though, quite frankly, we were not calling them equity issues. If you think about our testing these concepts pre-Katrina, we certainly didn't go to Baton Rouge or to Shreveport to say, *We're going to sit down today and have an equity-centered discussion.* But I am reminded that the tools I acquired to navigate complex policy constructs in community spaces came out of some of those experiences.

Pam: Before Hurricane Katrina made landfall, Flozell was already at work on the issues of equity in disaster. Flozell's personal journey through Katrina and its aftermath is at once unique to him but happened to thousands of others.

Flozell: I was in Atlanta, Georgia, when Katrina hit. I was married with two kids, and we did what people always do. We made a commitment when the kids were super young that if there was a storm coming of any particular size, we would always leave. We were not going to negotiate or try to decipher for ourselves what that looked like. And we were fortunate, even though we were just average middle class. We had relatives in Atlanta, in Mississippi, family and friends in Houston. We had places to go. When Katrina happened, we got on the road, we thought, for maybe two or three days, just like the year before. And then we woke up, effectively, the morning of August 30, or in the middle of the night, once the phone started ringing and the news got out about the levees breaking. It didn't feel like a dreamscape, more like a nightmare.

Pam: And like us all, Flozell had family spread everywhere. I asked Flozell about his mom, who remains a force in Flozell's and many lives.

Flozell: My mom refused to come with us, because you know what a Taurus does, and so she went to Mississippi with her aunt and cousins. And even then, I thought, *Okay, that will be fine.* I was just glad that she had chosen to leave the house because she would not usually. And then at the last minute, she drove to Foxworth, Mississippi, about an hour and a half from here. She was OK there until she was not. Because, as you know, Katrina devastated Mississippi, well beyond the Gulf, the Gulf Coast, and the coastal areas. And so they had no energy, no water, no anything, and I had to get them.

Pam: As with many of us, Flozell's journey home was long and filled with the unexpected. Flozell and his former wife were able to play the important role of translators of aid for their family and friends.

Flozell: We didn't get home right away. We were in Atlanta for weeks until we could figure it out, like everyone else. We were in the FEMA line, trying to sign up for things, trying to figure out what to do. And we were fortunate because, between my wife and I, we had five degrees, we had laptops, we had access, we had the ability to navigate complex situations. We both had managed federal grants, and we knew how to read policy. We got called by others. *Can you help us with this? What do we do? What do we do?* And we were doing all that paperwork for all our family because so many people just couldn't navigate it. We were trying to calm ourselves down because the children were scared.

Pam: So, Flozell, how did you begin to think of your place in the disaster?

Flozell: Again, my story reflects my privilege. Tulane quickly developed a disaster recovery team, a tiger team of sorts. And because I oversaw all the state and local policy work, I was at the epicenter of that. And they brought me back. Tulane had an alum in Houma who owned an apartment complex that was brand new and undamaged, and so I was able to get a two-bedroom apartment in a place called Houma Highlands. I will never forget this. I moved my family to Houma, which by now included my mom, my mother-in-law, and, on occasion, a few other people. There were eight or nine of us in these two bedrooms. My wife started to work through the responsibility she had because, in addition to her job and family stuff, she was a school board member. From the moment we moved back, I was driving to Baton Rouge every day. Every day, back and forth from Houma to Baton Rouge, which is a more difficult drive than from New Orleans to Baton Rouge.

The drive was a disaster. It was a mess. It comes up time and time again. I am hearing it with [Hurricane] Helene. We didn't have any options. It was as Audre Lorde said: "Sometimes we are blessed with being able to choose the time, and the arena, and the manner of our revolution, but more usually we must do battle where we are standing."[15] There was a moment when you're just standing, you're going to have to do something. We did not have an option. And the good news, when there was good news to be found, was when we got to Houma, a community that I certainly knew politically and demographically, and understood what I thought I knew about it—they were delightful. They were loving and caring. Our children were brought into the schools and supported. They created community space for people and did this amazing thing to make us feel welcome in a space where I was uncertain whether I would be welcome just because of our understanding of the body politic.

Pam: I know how difficult it was during that time—not knowing and having no control of what is next. And the endless tasks that faced us. What brought you joy?

Flozell: The community making us feel welcome. It felt good to be able to bring our kids to school and know they would be taken care of. It felt good, in some ways, to have our moms living with us, and they were helping watch the kids. And it just felt like the way I grew up; we have gotten away from those practices and habits of living really near or with each other. I think it's fair to say, honestly, there weren't a lot of moments that brought us joy until we got home.

Pam: It is that feeling of feeling lost—you are safe and your family safe, but you are still not home.

Flozell: It took a year and a half, but we rebuilt that house and got scammed by a contractor. I was struggling to find materials and all the things that everyone else went through while working full-time. That whole time, every day I was driving to Baton Rouge. There were no days off. We did not have Zoom. You had to be present because it was happening, either to you or with you. We were just working nonstop, and it was taking a toll on us.

---

15   Audre Lorde, *A Burst of Light: Essays* (Ithaca, NY: Firebrand Books, 1988), 120.

Influences of Community, Background, and Theories of Life
There were many experiences in Flozell's life that led to this lifetime of work. In this section, he reflected on the many experiences that led him through the disasters and the rest of his work.

Flozell: I was taught frequently by the community that raised me right. If you think about this seventeen-year-old mom and me living across the street from Belmont Park—what some people call Roberts Park, the church of Greater Gethsemane, Church of God and Grace. Literally a hundred feet away from the church where my mom's second mom, the church mother, Beatrice Trish, was the pastor and first lady. She adopted us, as did the entire community. Women on porches and men on milk crates, who, every day, looked out for me. They would say: "Young man, make sure you do well in school. I made some extra food. You bring this home to your mama." "Oh, I know it's report card day, boy, let me see that. Come here. I got some candy, but don't tell your Mama."

Everything that I negotiate reflects the tension between radical imagination and life, a term I was taught years ago in the faith-based, progressive, organizing movement spaces. I was at a Samuel DeWitt Proctor Conference, which is this traditional, faith-based, policy organizing civil rights group. I was first taught by someone who spoke about radical imagination, and that is this idea that what has happened in our history is that there were people who decided that there was something better for us, even though there was no evidence that it was possible or achievable.

It means that you have the imagination, which liberates you to dream about what you deserve. If you have this radical imagination, you design the purpose of your life. And when I say, *People are doing the best they can with what they got*, it is a way to understand the work.

A person can barely take a step forward with me, and I must be OK with that, if my intention is to build community in a way that gets us to things that live inside of our radical imaginations. And if anybody says to you, because I've been told this before, *Here you go, talking about this stuff, all in your head. Look at the civil rights movement: They'll lynch you; they'll kill you; they'll take away your jobs.* They will. They absolutely will. *You're going to get on that bus with those Negroes, you Jewish people, they're going to burn you, they're going to beat you. Look at women's suffrage. Look at the women who were killed for daring to go against their husbands.* But look at the LGBTQ movement. At the labor movement. It is a powerful part of my origin story in the way it extends through as a constant thread in my life and my way of thinking, both in my work life as well as my personal life.

This thinking through the idea of radical imagination has been transformational for me in my ability to hold relationships, to get work done, and to have integrity. And so, in all of my years now, it's been seventeen years of running a philanthropy of one kind or another, three different ones, as it turns out now. In all those cases, I have had skirmishes and disagreements and headbutting with staff and with the board, and there is not a one of them that I'm not in a good relationship with, not a one. And I count that not because of any great thing on my part—other than my understanding that if you have some integrity, if you're willing to tell the truth, if you're willing to lean in and care about people, then difficult decisions land differently and are perceived different, not only between you and that person, but by the rest of the body who is watching close.

The Road to Foundation for Louisiana runs through the Louisiana Disaster Relief Fund

Pam: There is a through line of people and organizations that are constantly trying to bring the potential of philanthropy to a true and equitable power. And that's what you are doing. You started in 2007, and you're still doing it.

Flozell: I walked into LDRF and quickly understood that the design of that work was deeply aligned with my own way of seeing the world. What I found in LDRF, that was led by Charice West before I got there. It was this incredible team: Ashley Shelton, Landon Williams, Christy Slater, and Samantha Bickham. LDRF staff were already in partnership with PolicyLink, Brookings, local scholars, and other experts. The analysis began with the assumption that disaster policy was inequitable. It's not designed to even replace what people actually lost. And that, by itself, is not equity. Disaster policy is not intended by design or impact to improve the lives of people who were on the margins before the disaster. LDRF was trying to make investments that would create betterment and community to address the storms of inequity, injustice, racism, and gender bias that had already hit the shores of Louisiana decades before Katrina. They were trying to use plain language to say that the real opportunity for us was not just to get back to where we were but to create some critical infrastructure and practices and behavior and policy changes that would leave us better than we were before.

Pam: And how is that different from traditional philanthropy?

Flozell: I think there are a few things that were different, but we had the advantage at LDRF of wise counsel, including James Joseph. Ambassador Joseph was sitting on the LDRF board with his perspective from having been beaten when he was organizing civil rights movements in Mississippi and Alabama. He's sitting there with the experience of having been a chaplain at the Claremont Colleges. He's sitting there as the man who stood up at the Southeastern Council of Foundations and said, "We're no longer going to allow you to not put Black people on this board so that we can have a voice in the body philanthropy." And then he created the Association of Black Foundation Executives, which still literally guides us through this work and has recently been holding sessions and hearings on how to deal with these lawsuits against racial equity and nonprofits. We had as chair of the board someone who's not only from Opelousas, Louisiana, who went to Southern University and then to Yale for grad school, but someone who's put himself on the line and understands how to anticipate and to respond to things that might endanger the mission. And they have already established that this was about an equitable recovery and put it in writing.

Pam: The values of equity and justice, how do they appear in a disaster setting? Recovery is such a complicated term. How is it that you guided this organization to make criteria for what recovery spending would look like?

Flozell: Think about our folk down in the bayou areas, who we have funded. These were folks who just had never been resourced at any particular level, and all of a sudden, this money—this is the power of the money, by the way, the money matched with the purpose—gave power to groups of people who'd never had it. That power established an opportunity to at least defend themselves from some of the dangers that are inherent in any disaster recovery environment. People did not often equate disaster recovery with a justice conversation or an equity conversation. We knew full well and had the luxury of engaging experts who were justice-minded to develop complex policy that was matched with simple wisdom from the community so that we could establish complementary policy positions. We designed housing and small business programs that just gave people money without the red tape and without making them submit their spirits in exchange for this money. We called it high-dignity work.

CRITICAL IMAGINATION, PHILANTHROPY, AND DISASTER: HOW WOMEN ON STOOPS AND MEN ON MILK CRATES CHANGED THE WORLD

Pam: Talk a little more about this high-dignity work.

Flozell: When the Louisiana Disaster Recovery Foundation was created, it was explicitly designed as a spend-down entity. Whatever money was raised was going to be moved up and out the door as strategically and quickly as possible. And so that was the tension that we were managing when I got there in 2007. They had just gotten the twenty-five million dollars from the Bush Clinton fund earlier that year. Because that was a competitive process, they had been spending millions of dollars from other sources, private and individual and public sources from other countries. And I did ask, before the spend-down, wouldn't it make sense to carry some of this money over and create a permanent organization? I was told that that would violate the spirit and intent that was shared with donors at the time and that the board wouldn't do it. It was one of the rare times that I had a disagreement with Ambassador Joseph, Linetta Gilbert, and others. I could already tell that there was a need for a permanent social justice plan. This was our opportunity while we still had ten or fifteen million dollars to anchor it so that we could have the strength and the ability to do the justice work. However, we went through the process and did a great job of essentially spending down most of those resources.

We got a strong response from the community. When I say community, I mean grantee partners, policy partners, funders, and others who said, "Well, no, no, no, you cannot go away. We have never had anything like this. And we need this." We started asking around, started thinking about board members and others who were supportive, even though they were not supportive of doing it as a turnover to put these monies into an endowment. They were supportive of the idea, but everybody was clear. They said, "Well if it's going to happen, you're going to have to do it." And I said, "Well, what does that look like?" So, I did what I had been trained to do. I started testing ideas with national leaders who had some experience in this. We had enough support from the board to approve hiring a consultant to do an analysis about whether we should shut down or whether we should transition. For me, it made sense to know how much money do I have to raise, what does it look like, and what kind of money does it have to be, and what kind of programming will we offer? What is the design of the work? It was not going to be the Louisiana Disaster Recovery Foundation. We didn't transition; we created another organization in a way that shifted the mission and the design of the work.

Pam: LDRF's move to become the Foundation for Louisiana is the best, most creative example of an organization that began to understand how disasters such as Katrina clearly show the chronic disasters of inequality and oppression.

Flozell: By 2011, we went about the business of changing the documentation and the charter and then starting to put a narrative strategy together. It was framed in the context of what it means to acknowledge justice work as permanent work, and if it is permanent work, then it requires permanent resources to support the people who are courageous enough to do that work. We are creating something that we had not seen before: a permanent social justice philanthropy in Louisiana, one of the most oppressed and anti-justice states in the United States. It was really a great opportunity to tell a story about what was possible.

We were able to carry over less than two million dollars. It was very spare, especially because fundraising cycles typically take two to three years to fulfill. It ended up being about relationships and people trusting in me. I also got access to a fund development consultant who was really like a fundraising coach. I have been raising money at that point already for fifteen years. She came to New Orleans; we spent two days holed up in the Magazine Street office. By the time we got to the second day, we had all this stuff sketched out on paper, on the walls. She said, "You have all these amazing ideas, concepts, programs, funds, initiatives, and you have no sense of who your market is." I said, "My market is the community. My market is the people." She said, "The people have no money to invest in this. Your market is funders and donors, and if you do not know what they're buying, it doesn't matter a damn what you're selling." You must find out who is doing the work you want to do, who's funding the work you want to do, and how does your work match theirs? Then you might have a fighting chance to convince them that there is a connection.

During a looming crisis, I figured out what they were funding that was aligned with what we had the capacity to do exceptionally well. I matched it with a strategic plan that we had come out with to say, *Here's what FFL is going to do*, and then I started dialing for dollars: "We do this better than anyone in the country. We have the opportunity to learn some lessons together. You should fund me. When can I send a proposal?" And it was just that over and over and over again, and it was matchmaking with the talent that we had with the dollars they had. And within a year, we were off to the races. And then I had enough money to bring a fund development person on full-time, which helped with the volume.

Pam: Flozell, tell me, on a deeper level, while you are going through this remarkable transition, what are you thinking about policy and process?

Flozell: This transition was happening right at the edge-of-a-cliff moment. Five years after Katrina, the money disappeared. I mean, when I tell you it vanished, there were some who were doubling down, like the Kellogg Foundation and the Ford Foundation. People have no idea what it is like to actually get something done with almost nothing. People have no goddamn idea. None; we fight about it all the time.

Pam: But somehow you figured it out—and FFL is thriving.

Flozell: I think once we had enough work under our belt, it was a bit of a chicken-and-egg [thing]. We got some eggs, and we were able to get some chickens. We were able to show to the funders that this was not a Katrina conversation, because they were no longer responsive to that. This was a capacity-built environment with leaders and institutions that know how to do things that are both locally important and nationally relevant. There was a narrative that we were able to shape along those lines that really got funders, and then later donors understood that this was not charity work. This was strategic philanthropy. We knew how to put a community-benefits agreement together. We knew how to do these things as a philanthropy, and it put us on the map.

Pam: The creation of FFL is an essential part of your long-term life strategy.

Flozell: In high school at McDonogh 35, my favorite teacher was a woman named Aquanela Reese. At the time, she was Miss Mullen, but now she's Miss Reese. She taught us Black literature. She introduced us to Toni Morrison and Octavia Butler. She made sure that we were reading Zora Neale Hurston and W. E. B. Du Bois. And so, what, in fact, was supposed to be an English literature set of classes was a lesson in identity. It was a lesson in understanding my legacy and history in this country in a way that I did not understand or did not get to understand at home. It taught me, at a very fundamental level, that Black folk in America had decided from the time we got here that we were going to realize our full humanity and resist any and all efforts that were trying to diminish us. We did it during actual enslavement. We did it on the way over here, when folks were sacrificing their lives because they would rather be dead than be captured. We did it during the Civil War, when we showed up to fight for our own freedom. We did it in the context of Reconstruction and those challenges. We did it during Jim Crow. We did it by creating a civil rights movement that would free this country from itself. I do not know what you call it, but in many ways, Black-identified people have been the conscience of this country.

Pam: And how does inequality work?

Flozell: I am convinced that not only is justice work permanent work, but work that is required of us in places where the entire design of the power structure, a set of systems, is to oppress Black and other people, including white people. But to use anti-Blackness, which is so endemic, so powerfully threaded through our psyches, you can look at the Southern strategy, something that Nixon and those folks developed, which said, *Well, if you can convince a white man that he's better than a Black man, he will vote against his interests, his woman's interests, and his children's interests.*

Being Summoned
Pam: It strikes me that two phenomena emerged out of Katrina. I observed that the storm illustrated in the most graphic fashion possible the inequities of the system. It also brought out and allowed for what I refer to as the African American public intellectuals and activists—you, Carol Bebelle, Linetta Gilbert, and others—[because of Katrina,] these brilliant, innovative thinking people found a way to coalesce. Am I wrong in that analysis?

Flozell: Not wrong. We not only found a way to coalesce, but we were also summoned by the disaster and the recovery process. We were summoned to protect what we understood as this community and its identity and its culture and its ideas and its history. Because remember, to me, the instigating force was not the levees. But immediately thereafter, while water is still running in the streets, you have powerful people planting green dots on maps. They are designing strategies to take over systems that they had lost control of because of demographics and civil rights. And we understood explicitly and implicitly that we not only had to come back and recover our own lives:

we had to come back and regain control of a city because they were going to whitewash it, literally and figuratively.

And I tell people, this is not a conspiracy theory. No, it is not misrepresenting facts or the truth. We have the documentation. We have the witness of people who were on those calls, who were present when those conversations were being had, when the lawyers were being hired to execute the strategies, and then we saw the outcomes of some of those strategies come to fruition. How many times did I tell people this takeover of public schools would be a disaster? No, they powered it through with the more than three hundred million dollars of investments and just decided, *If you do not agree with us, we're just not going to fund you.* So, they choked out anyone who had a dissenting voice, and twenty years later, they are now trying to figure it out.

Pam: This idea of being summoned came with some risks.

Flozell: It was a calling. Anyone in their right mind would have moved somewhere else because it was, as it turns out, was so stressful. It killed people. The stress killed people. It destroyed neighborhoods all over the place, but it was a calling to this, this mysterious place. Once you love it, you cannot unlove it.

Pam: So one of the things that occurs to me about this, in listening to you and knowing Carol and other African American leaders who came back to this city and fought for this city and were betrayed by the city, in many ways—when you talk about your childhood, you talk about the love, and it seems to me that this love [for New Orleans] is born in the oppression in a way that I don't understand. Can you talk about that a little bit?

Flozell: It is interesting. I think about this a lot and have to revisit this with my therapist. Some years ago, there was a moment when she said, "Well, we are going to have to go back to your childhood." And I said, "What the hell for? Who wants to do that?" I was born in 1970, right on the softer side of the civil rights movement. The CRA [Civil Rights Act] had passed. Schools were integrated.

My mom is still being called the N-word and having to fight at school, and then she gets pregnant with this little boy in her senior year. And, surprising to her, her mama did not say, "Oh, you have to quit school, or you should get an abortion." But my mom is really concerned. She is like, "I thought my mom was going to kill me." And she did not. She says, "Oh, good, okay. Well, let's get ready." And so it starts there.

Before I'm born, my grandmother, having fled Mississippi to come to New Orleans to make a better life for her children, decides that my unborn life is a blessing for which we should get prepared and be ready to celebrate while they are living in a two-bedroom, a two-room apartment, a two-room apartment with four people. I mean, negative money—absolutely nothing. From birth to nineteen years old, I have this whole community around me who treats me like I'm theirs. Full stop. Never, never, never anything else. I had no idea what it looked or felt like that I should not be wanted or be desired by the community.

Pam: I see this community of care that you grew up in as profound. I don't have another word for it.

Flozell: It is. It is when people ask me now—I'm fifty-three, and I was just talking to some young professionals—"What's the secret sauce? Was it grad school? Was it this? Was it that?" It was these people who gave me the kernel of understanding that I deserve the best in life. They treated me that way. They would say to me: "You are so smart. You're the smartest boy that's ever lived. You're so good. Your heart is so good. You're such a good person. Come over here. Send this to your mama. I love her, she's such a good person. She's doing such a good job as your mom." This is what I learned from my community and my schoolteachers.

One of my teachers explained it this way: "Well, these teachers were missionaries who had come out of the civil rights movement." These women—mostly women and one male teacher in elementary—some were young, some were older, but all of them had come out of the 1960s as teenagers into this profession. When a teacher walked by, you treated them like a university president or like a church pastor or something. They were revered, and they behaved accordingly, and they did this beautiful work. These are the glory days. It's the 1970s, honey. We're free, and we get to be ourselves. It was something powerful about it, and because we were still living in this pro-Blackness, that would be a source of strength for me later on.

Hope

Hope and history provide good metaphors. When we look back, hope at first glance seems inadequate and unrealistic, particularly when we are still

CRITICAL IMAGINATION, PHILANTHROPY, AND DISASTER: HOW WOMEN ON STOOPS AND MEN ON MILK CRATES CHANGED THE WORLD

surrounded by so much evidence of human failure. But hope allows us to see beyond what is and to imagine what can and ought to be. This new hope takes imagination and courage.[16]

— Ambassador James Joseph

Pam: Flozell, I always close with a question of hope. Tell me some about hope.

Flozell: I am practicing hopefulness. I pause because you made me think about Ambassador Joseph, who, in those building-of-FFL days, I would call sometimes, and I would say to him, "I can't do this. I don't think I can do this." And he would listen. He would listen well and long and give me space. And then he would say to me, "You come from a legacy of people and places that are permanently anchored in hope. This is not optional." And so, you get to have hopeless moments. You get to experience hopeless situations, but you are whole. And then he said, "And if you need evidence, I have it." He said, "How did you get here? Where were your people from?" What does it take for a woman to pack her four children up and move to a city where she knows no one and has nothing, to build a life that then I would be born into, to get the advantages and opportunities that I have today? What did it look like for her parents, who had to leave Alabama because their family was being pursued by the Klan in the middle of the night? "Displacement," he said to me, and, "You don't even know the stories before that. No, but you have to trust that they are rife with examples of folks building a life on hope."

In church, we say the evidence of faith, faith being the evidence of things unseen. When I met with my team Wednesday morning at eight o'clock after the Tuesday of the national election, I had to figure out what was I saying. And it was James Baldwin that reminded me. I don't know the quote directly, but it basically says you don't have an option but to be hopeful because life is not an academic matter. It is a real thing, and to survive it and to thrive in it, you have to have hope to do what it is that you have been put here to do. And so I shared that quote with my team after a lot of love. It's OK to be enraged and sad and depressed. On the other side, you have to go pick up your whole bag and put one foot in front of the other.

---

16   Louisiana Disaster Recovery Foundation, "Chronicles of Resilience & Resolve, A Three Year Review: 2005–2008" (New Orleans: Louisiana Disaster Recovery Foundation, 2008), https://www.foundationforlouisiana.org/wp-content/uploads/2024/07/Louisiana-Disaster-Recovery-Foundation-2008-Annual-Report.pdf.

Flozell's experience with LDRF, FFL, and now the Mary Reynolds Babcock Foundation is justice work—work that has taken him all over the world. His practice of hope that began in a two-room apartment in New Orleans was nourished and deepened at every stage of his life so far. We end this interview with a quote from an annual report of LDRF.

"We will stand fast in our promise to play our role in ensuring this state never returns to business as usual. Instead, it will be government that listens to all residents, economic development that works for everyone, education that teaches all children, and housing that provides the foundation for healthy and prosperous communities. Working together, with focused intensity and heightened expectations, this promise is already taking shape." — Flozell Daniels Jr.

LOVE AFTER THE STORM
JARVIS & KELLY DEBERRY

There was a moment on August 29, 2005, that I will never forget. I was standing in the middle of an empty Interstate 10. Below the elevated interstate highway, I knew that people were fighting against drowning and that some of them had likely already drowned. In the distance, I could see fires burning. I pointed a fire out to a fireman who came by on a fire truck, and he said that the fire department was aware that things were on fire. But the water was too high for them to get close enough to put them out.

Given the depth of the water I saw all around me, I said out loud, "Okay, my house is probably gone." I said it in an attempt to stop worrying about what might have happened and to focus on my work, but it was gone. Though I'd only been living in it for eighteen months, I'd never live it in again. It would take weeks, though, before I'd return to see the X a search party in boats spray-painted near the roofline of my house, and months before the entire contents of my house were dumped out onto the curb.

On Sunday, September 4, six days after the storm, I went to a Baptist church in Baton Rouge with my cousins who lived in the city. The congregational song that morning was by Andraé Crouch & The Disciples, "Bless the Lord." I got through the words *"Bless the Lord, oh my soul, and all that is within me"* okay, but it was only through tears that I could sing, *"He has done great things. Bless His holy name."*

It was hard to see that anything great was being done at that moment. It was hard to appreciate—or even detect—any blessings. I was singing along with the choir, *"He has done great things. Bless His holy name,"* but it was hard to even conceive of any blessings that could come out of such tragedy.

I didn't know what life was going to look like post-Katrina. I'd not only lost my home, I'd lost my truck. My job was temporarily displaced to Baton Rouge, and it wasn't sure initially that the job would last. Less than a month after the storm, I turned thirty years old in Baton Rouge, one of the first landmark birthdays that can make you take a hard assessment of your life. I arrived at that age with my slate wiped clean. No wife, no children, and, now, no house, no car, and no real sense of where to go or what to do.

What I did know was that I was happy to survive. Happy to be alive. And open to whatever blessings might come.

And they came quickly. In fact, the seeds of my greatest blessings—my marriage to Kelly and the family we'd build together—had already been planted.

Two months before Hurricane Katrina, I'd met her at Cave Canem, a premier retreat for Black poets. It was a miracle we became a couple. She was living in Cleveland and living her best professional and artistic life. I was in New Orleans, working as an editorial writer for *The Times-Picayune*. There weren't a whole lot of things I was sure of immediately after Katrina, but one of them was that I didn't want to talk to anybody else about what I was going through as much as I wanted to talk to Kelly. When everything else felt rudderless and unmoored, she was clarity. From a distance, she became my friend and eventually my emotional anchor, and she blessed me by becoming my wife in 2008. Her addition to my life realigned how I would live and work as a New Orleanian. I now had to think about New Orleans in terms of having a wife and keeping us both safe. Four years later, we welcomed our daughter, Naomi.

If there was ever a child born to be a New Orleanian, it's Naomi. Known as a community baby, Naomi was welcomed into a village of artists, activists, and leaders. She immediately became an extension of us—but a better version of creativity, introspection, and kindness. She talks and reasons like a New Orleanian. She makes distinctions about what is and ain't New Orleans—all this by the time she was six years old.

Naomi's birth provided a new way of seeing and being for both of us. Having a daughter born and raised in New Orleans further legitimized our transplant status. Kalamu ya Salaam loves to quote Naomi: "My daddy is from Mississippi. My mama is from Cleveland, but me? I'm New Orleans."

Kelly and I had to learn what it meant to be parents in New Orleans post-Katrina. Whatever we wanted for Naomi's upbringing in New Orleans, we knew it would be a post-Katrina version of it. Although things weren't like they used to be, we found opportunities for Naomi to be in New Orleans. It was the people—the community, a community like no other in the world that not only taught Naomi but also myself and Kelly how to be self-determined and bold and vocal about our existence and art because it could all be taken away by water or oppressors. Oral history from elders like Jerome Big Duck Smith and Dean Millie Charles and dancing in Congo Square became vital parts of her upbringing and thus furthered our commitment to personal and spiritual resistance.

* * *

"Moving to New Orleans was difficult for me," Kelly says. "People think I escaped Cleveland, but I loved being from there, and I was thriving. Moving forced me to reset professionally and artistically in a new place while embracing a new identity as a wife. Ironically, I was moving to a place that was also resetting itself. I was navigating my own personal newness while embracing a New Orleans that was figuring itself out post-Katrina."

Our story isn't just Jarvis falling in love with Kelly or Kelly falling in love with Jarvis. It's also the story of us loving and being loved by a city and a people who'd lost close to everything but never lost that spirit of generosity and hospitality. Seeing New Orleanians pick themselves up after such devastation and moving forward inspired Kelly as a woman, as a poet, and eventually as a mother. "I don't know what it would have been like if I had moved to a New Orleans where Katrina had never happened. But arriving when I did meant that I got a chance to see and experience individual and collective stories of reinvention."

Co-founder of Ashé Cultural Arts Center Carol Bebelle often talks about the "power of we." New Orleans is its own philanthropy and has shown us what is possible when we all pull together. Kelly says the sense of community that she saw from people at Ashé Cultural Arts Center and places such as Christian Unity Baptist Church helped her to expand her definition of family. The "power of we" is not simply a notion of what can be if we are united, but it is a way of living in New Orleans. Whether it's in how we refer to one another as Baba or Mama, and so on, there is a real village of artists, healers, leaders, and caretakers in New Orleans that is unlike anywhere else.

We're writing this almost five years after a fundraiser was held in New Orleans at the Ashé Cultural Arts Center's Power House before my kidney transplant. That gathering was held more than fourteen years after Hurricane Katrina, but when we think about the question *What do we count as our blessings after Hurricane Katrina?*, we think about that night when we were surrounded by so many friends.

That night wasn't just a fundraiser to help us meet the medical costs of the upcoming transplant: it was also meant to be our goodbye to New Orleans. We'd decided against my staying at *The Times-Picayune* when the newspaper was sold, and our plan (that later got changed) was to move to Cleveland (Kelly's hometown) some time after I recovered. If, at any point before Katrina, you'd told me that so many people would show up to wish me well, I wouldn't have believed you. It wasn't until after the storm that I felt the full community's embrace of me beyond my professional title—first of me. Then of me and Kelly. Then of me, Kelly, and Naomi.

I was shocked at the number of people who showed their love and support because being a journalist, especially one who writes opinions, can mean having more foes than friends.

This gets to the heart of a lesson I learned, a lesson I'm still learning: There's often more love and support available to us than we initially perceive. This is a lesson we learned as a family and one we hope everyone can embrace.

Consider the Biblical story of the prophet Elisha praying that God would make his servant see that there were far more warriors with them than against them. This scripture has become our lived experience.

At the fundraiser, my eyes were opened to the number of warriors that had amassed on behalf of me and Kelly and our family in the years since Katrina.

Before Katrina, I was probably the youngest editorial writer at a major daily newspaper in the country. I also wrote a personal column that appeared once a week. That would be a big deal for anybody, but especially for a Black man. Even so, I didn't fully appreciate then how much I'd been blessed or fully comprehend the responsibility that came with my position.

And as much as Kelly worked as a professional and creative in New Orleans, she always felt she would never fully embrace or be given opportunities because she wasn't born and raised in New Orleans—and that even when shown love, it was limited by birthplace.

This was never a worry for Naomi because she was the true New Orleanian of the house.

But in putting together *I Feel to Believe*, a collection of my *Times-Picayune* columns, I revisited every column I'd written. Doing so helped me identify my best work, but, importantly, it also helped me see that some of the complaints my critics had made about me were valid. Some of my arguments were naive. Some columns showed my ignorance about the history (or even the present) of New Orleans. Some were self-centered. Some were proof that though I had found community inside Kalamu ya Salaam's NOMMO

Literary Society writing workshop and Christian Unity Baptist Church, I still hadn't fully become a part of the New Orleans community as a whole. Or maybe just hadn't fully matured.

I believe I wrote some great columns before Hurricane Katrina. Still, I had missed some opportunities to engage with and champion the people of New Orleans, particularly the Black people of New Orleans.

Post-Katrina, I was a columnist married to a writer—a new status for me. My wife would privately challenge me on some of my stances in my columns at home. Prior to marrying her, I didn't have someone so close to me saying things like, "I think you should reconsider that tone or perspective" or "You're coming off in a way you don't intend." Admittedly, it was frustrating at first. *She's never worked for a newspaper*, I thought. However, I came to understand that I needed someone to challenge my thinking and to care about not just my columns being published but about how they would live in other people's lives and in mine. I didn't have creative tension or a trusted sounding board until after Hurricane Katrina. Kelly was a big part of some of my shifts as a journalist.

I lost the friendship of a fellow journalist, then away from the city, who took offense at my argument that we should celebrate Mardi Gras six months after the city flooded. Looking back, I can see the part of the argument he probably found problematic. (It sounded more respectful in my head than it looked on paper.) Despite my attempt to mend things, that friendship died. And then he did.

But as soon as the storm was gone, it became clear that I had a new opportunity to embrace and be embraced by New Orleans. A week after the storm, I interviewed a Tremé man who was defying the city's order that everybody leave. "If I leave New Orleans," he told me, "where the hell I'm gon' be after that?" I believed then—and believe even more strongly now—that he wasn't asking where he'd be taken but how he could be expected to live, to thrive, without his community around him.

In my columns after Katrina, I fought back against anybody and everybody who saw the storm and everything that happened afterward as an occasion to shame and defame the people of New Orleans. I believe so many people showed up for us in 2019 for my kidney fundraiser because they saw me as a New Orleanian, a status I didn't have before Katrina. I was more than a journalist; I was family. I had a New Orleans family. What a blessing.

* * *

As the twenty-year anniversary of the storm approaches, I've generally resisted thinking of blessings, out of fear of dishonoring the memory of those who didn't survive and upsetting those who only experienced Katrina as a hardship.

An experience I had in May 2022 describing my Katrina experience to a documentary film crew made me realize the limitations of my perspective in talking about the storm, limitations I had even though I was in the city on August 29, 2005.

I'd reported to *The Times-Picayune* building at 3800 Howard Avenue, just a stone's throw from Xavier University, that Sunday, and that's where I was when the storm hit. I knew it had arrived when a window on the third floor shattered, and we were all ordered to move further into the interior of the building.

On a television operating on generator power, we watched the big red spot that was Katrina move from the Gulf of Mexico onto land and over our city. We heard the reports that a hole had been ripped in the roof of the Louisiana Superdome. We watched the wind sway a huge pine tree in front of the building, back and forth and back and forth, and at about 2:00 p.m., when that tree wasn't swaying quite as much, teams of us cautiously ventured outside.

Our plan was simple: We would climb up and into the newspaper's delivery trucks—we believed them to be high enough to navigate high water—fan out across the city, and report what Hurricane Katrina had done.

The truck I was in set out for New Orleans East about five minutes after a truck ahead of us left for St. Bernard Parish. But as we hit the I-10 curve right there at the Superdome, we saw the truck that was headed to St. Bernard coming back—on the same side of the interstate we were on.

When our two trucks met, the first driver said that the base of the high rise was underwater and that even our trucks weren't high enough to keep going.

"I wanted to check on my house in the East," our driver said.

The first man said, "Oh, man, all that's under water."

We kept going anyway. We drove past downtown, and somewhere around where the 6th Ward becomes the 7th Ward, our driver stopped the truck. Another reporter and I walked over to the riverside of the guardrail and looked down.

I saw Black people clinging to whatever they could grab to stay afloat. One older man had his arms draped over the kind of orange water cooler you see on the sidelines of football games. Two men in a boat with utility lines near their heads yelled up to ask for help at a house where they said multiple people were trapped, including a pregnant woman.

When people have asked me about the day Katrina hit, I have always told that story. But talking to that film crew on that day in 2022, my voice broke, and rather than fight my emotions and keep talking, I chose to sit there without saying anything. And let the tears fall.

I'd been describing that scene for nearly seventeen long years, but that day, it hit me that I didn't know—that I don't know, that I can't know—if the people I saw that August 29 are somewhere telling somebody how they survived—or if I, the journalist looking down on them from my perch on the interstate, had witnessed their final moments.

My hesitation to speak about the good things that happened to me after the storm comes out of a recognition of the limits of our perspective. Even though I was telling somebody my own experience of Katrina, I wasn't aware of how the story ended for the others involved. I don't even know the name of the man who drove the truck I was in that day, what part of the East he lived in, or if any of his loved ones died or what condition his property was in or when he was finally able to reach it.

My hesitation comes out of the realization that for so many people, there was no after-the-storm. In every situation, I think it is important to remember those who did not make it.

One of Kelly's favorite go-to books for social and cultural analysis is June Jordan's *Some Of Us Did Not Die: Selected Essays*. Jordan writes: "And what shall we do, we who did not die? What shall we do now? How shall we grieve, and cry out loud, and face down despair? Is there an honorable, non-violent means towards mourning and remembering who and what we loved?"[17]

We are embracing the notion that counting our blessings publicly is not a brag but proof that there is light on the other side of storms, and that even when you least expect it, you are loved more than you think.

And it's just as important twenty years after, I think, to count those blessings and to work through the guilt of having survived or doing well after Hurricane Katrina.

Mama Carol Bebelle said in 2014 at Ashé's MAAFA commemoration honoring those lost in the Middle Passage, held at Congo Square in New Orleans, that our ancestors who'd endured the Maafa, and who'd spent all or

---

17   June Jordan, *Some Of Us Did Not Die: Selected Essays* (New York: Basic/Civitas Books, 2003), 13.

most of their lives in slavery, didn't struggle to survive just so we would be suffering all these years later.

She said it dishonors them to situate ourselves in the pain and not work to free ourselves from it. "The past we inherit," she said. "The future we create."

Our future was created both by love and hardship. We measure our relationship by Hurricane Katrina because the storm is a part of our love story and family identity. We met right before the storm, and we aren't sure that our friendship would have progressed to a relationship and then marriage if the storm hadn't happened. One thing we do know is that New Orleans loves us, and we love New Orleans, and that is a blessing.

HAPPENSTANCE
LLOYD DENNIS

My name is Lloyd Dennis, now seventy-three, fifty-five times around the sun when the storm struck. My wife Anne, my Boo, and I established and operated a successful video and photography business in New Orleans for thirty years until the levees broke. Until then, we were the first call for many local businesses, social organizations, politicians, and, yes, brides and grooms. We raised three children who, by then, were grown and gone, with my eldest son, Fahamu, working with us in the business.

Marriage and family life were my primary aspirations. As a child, I witnessed the troubled relationship between my father, Lloyd Sr., and mother, Lorraine. The truth is that all I ever wanted to do in life was to be the best husband and father I could be. Everything else I managed to accomplish was happenstance. Formally trained as an electronic technician in the Air Force, I worked as a technician and then service manager for several companies, ten in twelve years, until I realized that I didn't fit into any corporate structures and wasn't very interested in just making more and more money.

An important happenstance in my life was a hobby photo lab on the naval base where I was stationed. I soon was reading everything about photography that I could get my hands on and soon had designed a portable darkroom setup in our bathroom. When our firstborn came into the world, it was my excuse to buy a 35mm camera. I had no idea that I would become a photographer. Photography offered me the opportunity to be a free Black man in America and partner with my Boo in a business that could sustain our family.

Life was good for us and our children, leading me to understand that if our people could get together, stay together, and raise their children to repeat the cycle, most of the ills would disappear.

My Boo and I married when I was twenty and she was eighteen, having been a couple since she was fourteen and I was sixteen. We shared this family vision from the beginning, and it worked. Widely known because we worked together in our family business, we were admired ... and people wanted to find their path to relationship success, so everyone told us their "business," and we shared how we did what we did.

A woman we knew from elementary school worked with *Data Weekly*, a New Orleans weekly newspaper, and after sharing some relationship insights, she challenged her brother, *Data's* owner, to give me a column. She had called me a "love doctor," and The Love Doctor column was born. For the next twenty-five years, I wrote The Love Doctor column, the first five anonymously because the owner didn't believe a photographer would be credible as a relationship advisor. It worked; by the time I posted my photo and announced who I really was, the readership was hooked.

One of my readers convinced her husband, who managed six radio stations, that I should be on the air. He knew me because I was the photographer for one of his flagship stations and had photographed their wedding. So, I was The Love Doctor on WODT and eventually became the only talk show on that blues station. Four years later, under different management, WODT went sports talk, and that was that.

While all the above was going on, I continued to engage in the community with a commitment to help make things better. I served on nonprofit boards, including that of the Ashé Cultural Arts Center. I worked in Urban League summer youth programs, volunteered as coach in our first neighborhood, was a Big Brother mentor and addressed young people whenever asked, and actually taught photography at L. E. Rabouin Vocational High School, using ancillary credentials from documenting that we had made our living for many years in photography.

* * *

I had driven two days from Milwaukee alone to get back to New Orleans after the storm. My wife, her aged aunt Tee, and my mother were staying with her sister Mimi, who had moved to Milwaukee several years earlier. I was finally alone as I drove, and tears streamed down my face as Hendrix blasted away that countenance I felt I had to maintain in front of people who depended on me.

It had been two weeks since we had loaded our van for a three-day evacuation to Jackson, Mississippi. We were going to stay at the casino, like the last time we evacuated. The girls had had a great time that time, but we didn't stop now because the storm was following us up the highway, and Jackson was in its path. Anne texted her sister Mimi that we were going to drive through to visit her and other family in Milwaukee. Mimi and cousin Stacey and her husband Marvin would have space for us.

We were tired but in good spirits as we pulled up some eight hours later. It's always good to see family, and we had been promising to visit for quite a while.

Then we watched the waters rise and our people being treated like looters and refugees as they scavenged. The city was filled with salt water. Things had changed. It wasn't going to be three days. There's nothing like family; we were accommodated and made comfortable, and we pitched in wherever and however we could as to not be dead weight. The old girls did some magic in the kitchen, cooking and cleaning. I pitched in and helped Marvin finish paneling the basement, where my Boo and I slept. We got our ten thousand dollars per household and pitched in for food.

After several days, reality began to sink in for me. Most of the city was destroyed, and so returning to my life as a professional photographer wasn't likely. But I had craft skills, ironically, because after Hurricane Betsy, my dad had taught my brother Don and I, as fourteen- and fifteen-year-olds, how to do all the repair work: plumbing, drywall, ceramic tile work, carpentry, electrical, painting, and even how to hang wallpaper. Since then, Don and I amplified and honed our skills as we purchased, then repaired and remodeled our own homes. We could help the city recover by contracting repairs or working as subs.

An aunt in Chicago offered to provide me with the money to acquire the equipment to move forward with Plan A; however, when I presented the budget, she withdrew the offer. Plan A died on the vine.

By that time, the 504 area code was reliable again, so I went through my contacts, checking on friends and looking for any leads where I could use my photo/video or craft skills. Perhaps my client, the New Orleans Sewerage and Water Board, needed documentation photography. They did, but couldn't afford to pay what I needed, nor anyone else. Plan B was done.

Then I got a phone call and recognized the number of a business for whom we had done video documentation work, Citywide Testing and Inspections, but the call had nothing to do with video or photography. Citywide had landed part of a contract to supply quality assurance (QA) people for the Army Corps of Engineers, who were managing the cleanup of all the mountains of debris. He told me that if my son Fahamu (also in Milwaukee) and I could get back to the city in a couple of days, we could make good money supervising the contractors who were doing the debris cleanup. We had a plan C.

We found ourselves policing cleanup crews in Algiers and New Orleans south of I-10 for safety and ensuring the correct handling of the different types of debris. It was seven days a week, twelve hours a day. I did pretty well, I guess, because after a week of being "seasoned," I was asked to go uptown to meet with the Corps' people. I walked into a room of QAs in safety gear and took my place along the wall with others until I found myself introduced as the lead QA, in charge of starting garbage operations between St. Charles Avenue and the river, that sliver of high ground along the river that didn't flood.

I had never been a lead anything, but things went well. Everyone was making more money than they had ever made in their lives . . . and I could fire them. I was fair and firm and applied all the rules . . . all the rules. I didn't have field duties, so I read the regs!

I was still working under Citywide's sub-contract and had complained about having management duties without additional compensation. I was asked to "hang in there," and I did, and I am glad I did.

A few weeks later, I received another call from Citywide to come into the office. When I came, I was informed that they had been awarded two one-year contracts to provide seventy-five QAs each to the Corps' lakefront headquarters for cleaning up the city north of I-10. I was offered to be the lead supervisor of the two authorized, one for each contract. I was to have an assistant supervisor and ten team leaders to manage 150 QAs over everything from demolitions, vegetation removal, removing dangerously leaning trees, and now managing the dumps.

Because I read the regs, and enforced them all, at first, I was the most hated guy on deck, by the Corps because I knew their boundaries, and by my people because I enforced the regs to the letter and had fired several people who endangered our ability to maintain the contracts to term. To this day, I believe that we had received two contracts (in a combination of three minority firms) because certain people were waiting in the wings for us to fail.

But then two things happened that changed my standing. First, when I was "directed" to fire one of our employees because of a contractor's complaint, I demanded an adjutant general hearing, which shocked the Corps into a different reality about dealing with my people. The hearing determined that the contractor had lied, and they lost their contract. The contractors knew better than to come at Citywide's people with bullshit, and my people knew that I had their backs.

HAPPENSTANCE

The second thing that happened was that first Mardi Gras after the storm. I had begged the Corps to give our people that day off but was told that if they did, the government would have to pay a penalty to the contractors, because Mardi Gras wasn't a federal holiday and without QAs, the work couldn't continue.

By that time, the deck was mine, and each day I gave a short message about safety, well-being, and personal motivation. The day before Mardi Gras, my message was: "In their infinite wisdom, the Army Corps of Engineering has decided that we have to work tomorrow, so tomorrow morning, I will be on deck at 5:00 a.m., and I expect that all who are scheduled to work will be here as well."

When I went into the office, my boss entreated that I not fire any no-shows, and I was taken aback because by now I didn't expect any. "My people are coming," I said, and they did. 150 out of 150 QAs showed up on time, ready to work ... but only half of the Corps' staff showed, and none of the contractors could field a work team. (Hell, it was Mardi Gras in New Orleans.)

The Corps' leadership approached me, saying, "There won't be any contractors working today, so you can give your people the day off."

I said, "No, sir, under the contract we are entitled to make twelve full hours today. We're here ready to work."

I then turned to my people and, with tears in my eyes, said: "I would walk through hell with you folk, and since no one else is working, if you want to take a few minutes to go home and grab some meat and your grill, I'll see you in a couple of hours at your stations for my official taste tests. If you must move away from your site, please take that safety gear off. Otherwise, I'll see y'all on deck at 5:00 p.m. for sign-out."

I learned that if I led with knowledge and integrity, people would follow.

I haven't done photography since.

I remember the stress my mother had about the prospect of returning to another destroyed home after having gone through Hurricane Betsy. I sensed it the minute we knew that the Lower 9th Ward was flooded again. My father had passed away several years ago, and Mom lived alone, peacefully, her sister renting next door in the double on Saint Maurice Street. They had moved there because that block of Saint Maurice Street hadn't flooded during Betsy. She had nervous habits with her hands. I could sense her dread.

Boo and I had moved into and rehabilitated a 3400-square-foot, 1920 family-style home on the west bank of the river, where it didn't flood.

I took Mom's hands and told her, "Momma, you don't have to go back to that house."

When we purchased the house, we had made it a point to show both our mothers "their rooms." Boo's Mom, Barbara, had spent several months living with us until she passed.

Mom looked up at me with relief.

"Yeah, Mom, Don and I will handle whatever needs to be done."

This turned out to be the beginning of fifteen years of good times for Mom, Boo, and me. In many ways, she got to share in our happiness, which her relationship with my dad hadn't provided since Betsy. She was so happy and felt so loved here. We took her on our road trips. She was always game. We had swapped roles; I was now her security and protection. Even now, I shed tears of joy at being able to be that and for her to have had that.

When it came time for us to evacuate in 2005, she had a calm demeanor. Mom had her money and felt good about carrying her weight. We put the insurance into her bank account and later sold the Saint Maurice Street house "as is." She never saw it again.

She lived with us until she passed away during home hospice during the Covid pandemic. Thankfully, her decline was quick and not painful, and we got to love on her when she couldn't do for herself. I could never have imagined how loving as a verb can make one feel. At a point, she couldn't hear or see, but she knew she was loved... and cared for. Boo and I have such joy and peace about Mom's stay and transition. Were it not for the destruction of her house, we may not have enjoyed that time as intimately as we did.

Two years after the storm, with our public schools in disarray after the summary firing of experienced Black teachers, Pastor Wardsworth and I volunteered to work with the boys at an elementary school at the request of a concerned principal. The Silverback Society Mentoring Program was born, ultimately growing to sixteen schools, supporting over one hundred volunteers, and becoming a well respected nonprofit. Thousands of young people have embraced hope with the motivation to make life better for their children.

Prior to the storm, I had served on the board, eventually as chairman, of the New Orleans Black Tourism Network, which we renamed the New Orleans Multicultural Tourism Network. The network's job was to engage Black and multicultural businesses to participate in New Orleans tourism as business owners.

Sixteen years after the storm, I've accepted the role of New Orleans Tourism and Culture Fund board chair from Mayor Cantrell, with the challenge to work with our board and next-generation leadership to uphold the New Orleans Tourism and Culture Fund. NOTCF reinvests hotel tax revenues into our culture, culture-bearers, and local events to ensure that New Orleans continues to be the most amazing and authentic cultural attraction in the United States.

But it was all happenstance. None of it was planned, and neither was the storm. All we can do is the best we can with what we have at the time.

So, now I teach:

Accumulate knowledge: Learn as much as you can about as much as you can ... and stop learning by mistakes.

Treat everyone like you will need them tomorrow.

Become an expert at one or a few things.

Life will happen better if you do the three above.

THE CALLING
LUCAS DÍAZ

I am an immigrant from the Dominican Republic who naturalized in New Orleans in 1996. I am not the same person today that I was then. I am also not the same person today who packed two days' worth of clothes and drove out with his mother, siblings, and their children to ride out Hurricane Katrina in a downtown Memphis hotel on August 28, 2005. Certainly, life has happened to me, just as it has happened to you, changing me in small ways, but this is not what I mean. My change was deep. My change was transformational. My change was unforeseen and furtively radical (compared to the me before the storm).

Today, I can be called a university professor, leadership educator, researcher, community organizer, public participation consultant, social justice advocate, academic author, university program manager, and more, but this list only paints a partial picture. These names may provide you with something you can visualize in your mind's eye. They may say something about me to you. To me, these titles represent a spectrum of the worlds I never imagined inhabiting before Katrina struck. To understand how any of this relates to the storm, I must take you with me to the life I led before the levees fell.

Immediately before the storm, I worked as a fundraiser for various organizations in New Orleans. If I can presume to serve as a type of semi-representation, then I would say I'm a member of the Latinx immigrants who came to southeastern Louisiana as part of a small wave of caribeños (mostly Dominicans) in the 1970s. They worked in the refinery fields dotted across the lower Mississippi and spread out in homes across Highway 90 in southeast Louisiana. In the Westbank town of Gretna, where I grew up in the 1970s and 1980s, there were few others like me. My interactions were with the local kids, so over time I grew up like them, losing my comfort with the Spanish language as I eased into the English that was all around me. I became a

Westbanker (as the local saying goes). Unlike most Westbankers, however, I left that side of the levees and made my way over to the big city across the river, slowly making my life in New Orleans as the years progressed. When Katrina came, I was back on the Westbank side of the Mississippi, but in Orleans Parish rather than the adjoining Jefferson Parish, where my family lives.

I had just wrapped up my MFA in creative writing in 2003, and as a single weekend dad, I tried to spend my free time working on my writing if I wasn't parenting. My priorities were clear: make a living so I could help raise my child, and work on my craft whenever life allowed. There was nothing else for me. I wasn't involved in anything beyond my mother's family. I didn't volunteer much. I didn't engage in any advocacy activities. I lived mostly in comfortable obscurity while I toiled away at making a life for myself.

To me, the week before Katrina landed, the world was challenging, full of suffering, including my own battles with depression, but it wasn't something I could change much. I was too preoccupied with personal struggles to give much more than a quick glance to problems in the world. My only play in the world was to tell stories that might help someone get to know a stranger, the same way Steinbeck helped me get to know Oklahomans looking for work in the Dust Bowl. The rest of me was focused on doing right by my son. He had just completed his first week of kindergarten in a New Orleans Catholic school when we evacuated. The photo I took of him on his first day in his uniform is one of the few mementos I have of the week when Katrina landed, which now stands as a bridge between a life that vanished in the blink of a night and the life that began thereafter.

Here's a question I have for you: After calamity strikes you, when you have been able to surface and take a breath, do you go back to the moments of difficulty to find a silver lining? At first, I didn't, but time can have a way of giving breath to what one needs to consider that was once ignored or overlooked.

My immediate family and I left New Orleans on August 28, around 12:00 p.m., in a caravan of five cars: my mother in her car and my siblings in theirs with their families. I drove alone (my son had evacuated with his mother's family). The disaster and tragedy that were to come were neither anticipated by us nor grasped in the moment. Our needs were immediate: get situated in our hotel rooms, watch the news, and try to have a normal day in Memphis while pretending not to worry about my sister's son who was not with us, but was instead back in New Orleans.

Katrina came through quickly in the early morning of August 29. When we awoke that morning in Memphis (the first night of our two-night reservation), we immediately turned on the news and began talking with each other. "It doesn't look too bad so far." "We might be able to go home when we check out tomorrow." "Did you see the news at 7:00 a.m.? Home looked okay."

We tried to call friends and neighbors who stayed behind to ask them how much damage they saw, and if it looked good enough to come back. Despite not being able to reach anyone, a false sense of hope filled us that if the pictures of New Orleans looked good that morning, then for certain our homes were ok, too, on the Westbank side of things. Our littlest family member, only weeks old, would be fine, we believed. We'd be back in no time to check on him, we assumed.

Unfortunately, we were wrong. We would not be back to New Orleans, or anywhere near it, on the thirtieth of August. As the images rolled into our hotel televisions throughout the day on the twenty-ninth, we began to realize (and, of course, learn) that our two-day trip would be extended. That short-lived relief we'd felt early that morning disappeared, replaced with a growing anxiety. By nightfall, we had no place to stay the next day after our hotel check-out. The hotel we'd evacuated to was booked solid the rest of the week. So were other hotels nearby. It didn't matter. We were short on cash. New apprehensions entered our lives. There were twelve of us. Where would we go?

The First Two Blessings

My sister had the worst time of it. Seeing the waters rise downtown and the images of stranded folks in flooded neighborhoods only served to create a sense of dread among us. Being unable to reach the hospital, we had no way of knowing how the newborn was doing. Yes, in retrospect, we were lucky—lucky to have gotten a hotel booked, lucky to have gotten out, lucky to have each other, lucky to have the resources to play at becoming nomads without work or home (for a minute), and lucky that our homes were not ten feet under water (we overconfidently believed). With the floodwaters rising across New Orleans and night falling on August 29, 2005, we didn't feel so lucky.

The newest member of our family, my nephew, who had been left behind intentionally at Tulane Hospital, fought for his little life at the neonatal intensive care unit. He'd been born August 3 with multiple congenital heart defects. When Katrina made landfall, he had completed his third week of life and was just days removed from open heart surgery. On our way out of town on the twenty-eighth, we all stopped at the hospital. We went in one at a time to lay eyes on him and pray. His skin was the color of ash, a gray so lifeless that when I first saw his diminutive body, I thought he had just coded. The sight of him like that hit me hard. I cried a while. But as in all difficult moments, we did what most people do: we put one foot in front of the other. We said goodbye to him, hoping with all faith that we would see him again in two days, right where we had left him. As night fell on the twenty-ninth in our hotel rooms in Memphis, we could sense despair creeping in, all sense of hope eroding away.

That night, Katrina rolled through Memphis with 40 mph winds. We had not escaped her after all. On the morning of the thirtieth, the news images on the TVs were beyond imagination—homes completely submerged across New Orleans. Meanwhile, we had no plans. It was clear we couldn't go home. We tried frantically to come up with a plan before our late morning checkout from our rooms. By the time we had packed our bags and loaded our cars, we had no place to go and had no news about our little one. Was he safe? Was he still at the hospital? If he was, were the generators holding? Did the hospital evacuate him? Having no information, we decided to just drive towards Louisiana generally. Something would come up. A prayer would be answered. Things would work out.

Within three hours driving, we learned that the baby was evacuated by helicopter early that morning to a hospital in Lafayette. And just as we learned this, my son's grandmother's partner's family opened their home in Elton, Louisiana, to all twelve of us. We checked our maps and made our way as directly as we could to the place we would call home for the next two weeks. Elton was less than an hour's drive from Lafayette. Our prayers had been answered. Our family had received its first two blessings.

Almost complete strangers took us in. The only connection we had to the folks who offered us a place to stay was Tookie. That was her nickname, my son's other grandmother, the partner of his biological grandmother on his mother's side. Tookie knew me, and she'd met my mother several times and enjoyed her company. She had no hesitation in saying "come on" when I asked if she could let all twelve of us spend the night while we figured things out. That evening we arrived, exhausted but in lifted spirits, and hugged the German immigrant and Cajun woman who said yes when their daughter asked if they could keep us. To me, it was just beyond words that we could land there, being so close to home, when just hours before we'd felt rudderless and ill-fated in Memphis.

We created a deeper bond in that time with Tookie and her family. She became more than my son's other grandmother. She became a family member, the kind you carry in your heart, the kind you know without a doubt is in your crew and you care about deeply, even if from a distance. From Elton, we made several trips to Lafayette to visit the little guy, who was making a positive recovery. Two blessings in one—a place to be and a chance to see our little miracle baby come through his post-op trials—underscored our immediate days after the storm. Whatever state our homes were in mattered a little less, knowing that other human beings could do so much to help us recover.

In time we would return to our homes (sooner than the flooded areas within the city proper) and begin to put the pieces back together. I continued in my pre–Katrina path as a fundraiser but changed jobs so that I could help an up-and-coming big band find the resources it needed to keep playing during the recovery. From 2005 to 2007, I did my part to help this big band make a name for itself, helping New Orleans musicians secure meaningful gigs during the uncertain recovery years after the storm. These two years were formative for me in a way I did not realize at the time. A part of me was awakening that had only ever existed as an occasional outburst: standing up for a friend in a fight, chasing down a drunk driver because he sped through our street when children were playing outside, or confronting my drunken father as a teenager when his behavior crossed the line. These moments were signals from a deeper part of me, a part I had never fully regarded until now.

The Third Blessing
In 2006, Latinx people across the United States marched in the streets to urge then President Bush to pass comprehensive immigration reform. Unlike what is taking place in the political landscape of the 2020s, there was a nationwide sense that comprehensive immigration reform was attainable, in part because President Bush shared his support for a reform bill in May 2006. The old me, the one who still did not participate in any form of political advocacy, listened to folks talk about their organizing efforts on the radio and wondered why they would even plan to march. My personal thoughts at the time were against such marches. I imagined that marching would only increase the anxieties of white people. Too many brown people in the streets demanding fair immigration reform, I thought, would create backlash and anti-immigrant sentiment by those who would and could take advantage of fear.

At the same time that this was happening, I was representing the big band organization at regular cultural committee meetings held by Mayor Nagin's Bring Back New Orleans Commission. This was my first-ever seat at the table, if you will, in which major questions about the future of a place were being discussed and ideas recommended for real decision-making. It began to open something inside me about the possibilities for change and what people from all walks of life could potentially do. In this space, more than any other, I began to realize that my defeatist views about change were perhaps inadequate, perhaps short-sighted. The artist-turned-fundraiser in me began to consider the idea (though not fully fleshed out yet) that change could happen from below, and that people not in power could perhaps succeed in making those in power make better decisions for all and not just for a few.

The storm stirred me out of my previous existence, not immediately, but definitively. Those signals that would occasionally pop out of me in bursts of protective or defensive action began to surface each day between 2006 and 2007 as the streets that were so familiar to me began to look different. At the end of 2006, the big band office was on Tulane University's campus. While there, I saw a growing population of Latinx people. It caught my attention. Across town, there were Latinx people gathering near hardware stores, at bus stops, moving about in places I would not have walked in before Katrina. They came in gradually, and at first, I barely noticed. Their presence grew, however, and no matter where one drove in New Orleans in late 2006 and early 2007, the newcomers were there.

As the number of Latinx people grew in New Orleans, so did the backlash to Latinx immigrants across the US after the 2006 marches. By the end of 2006, Congress failed to pass any immigration reform and states began their first salvo of anti-immigrant bills. I felt, for the first time as an immigrant in this country, a real sense of a threatening, unsafe world and knew that it would only be a matter of time before what was happening across the nation reached New Orleans. It began as a concern that would not go away. By January 2007, I was more concerned in my heart and mind with the newcomer Latinx community and what they may be facing than I was with trying to raise money for local musicians. An overwhelming urge to do something took hold, and before I could make sense of it all, I was unemployed in February 2007 and working on my own dime and time to start a new non-profit organization that could serve the Spanish-speaking community. But I didn't want to just do something service-oriented; I had in mind that New Orleanians should welcome the heavy influx of migrant workers from Latin America rather than vilify them, as other states were doing. I wanted these newcomers to feel the same welcoming spirit my family received back in the 1970s, when we landed here.

With little experience in starting a completely new organization from zero, I embarked on doing just that. By April 2007, I had connected with my co-founders, who would serve as the inaugural board members of Puentes New Orleans (the word "puentes" means "bridges"). In four years, we grew into an important mediator and convenor on Black-brown relations and worked on various social justice issues not just on behalf of Latinx people, but on behalf of anyone involved in social systems that unnecessarily punished people for no reason other than their being poor or non-white or foreign. I learned community organizing from both Dr. Michael Cowan, my newfound organizing mentor in the work, and from professional organizers with a long history of success across the US.

I shared what I learned with others, building leadership fellowships, homebuyer training programs, and cultural competency programs for the police. I built new relationships within the rich New Orleans tapestry of community leaders (whom I feel lucky and grateful to have been given the opportunity to work alongside). I joined various other groups and lent the concerns and voices of the Latinx community to those of other communities, creating alliances and inclusive change efforts. In these four years, I moved in and upon spaces I couldn't have ever imagined that morning on August 30, when my family and I found ourselves stranded in Memphis.

At the start, between February and December 2007, I moved quickly, almost without conscious planning, to get Puentes New Orleans off the ground. I had little time to reflect, feeling driven to just keep pushing. But by the end of 2008, I had come to perceive that I was answering an inner calling to act upon the world. Therein lies what I consider the deepest blessing of all that Hurricane Katrina brought to my life: I am convinced that had Katrina not damaged New Orleans the way it did, causing the levee failures and untold misery and devastation, I would not have undergone the personal transformation I experienced. For me to even have been in a position mentally, emotionally, psychologically, and spiritually to hear an inner call and then act upon it and move not just for myself, but for others—it's something I still find remarkable today. Would I have found this calling without Katrina's effects?

It's not lost on me that while Katrina destroyed community for many, permanently displacing thousands of families, it gave me the opposite: a new community. And what an amazing community it has been, with people from all walks of life, of all ages composing it—a collection of community-based leaders, organizational leaders, and more who have become friends, colleagues, allies. It was this community that stepped up to support me and Puentes New Orleans in 2010, when the first ugly depiction of Latinx immigrants in a political ad hit the airwaves in the metro area. It was an ad by then Senator David Vitter. The ad showed Latinx men crossing a border through a hole in a fence in ragged clothes only to be greeted on the US side by cash and a limousine.[18] The community leaders I worked with were outraged. No one had ever seen an ad like that at the time. Puentes was asked to comment. Puentes was asked to do something. I dared not.

Fearing that voicing any critique of a sitting senator would draw unwanted attention that I had no interest in bringing to Puentes, I tried my best to dissuade everyone. I was unsuccessful. The call to do anything became so deafening that we had to respond as an organization. I spoke to colleagues I had worked with over the last three years. I asked for their wisdom, and out of these conversations emerged an idea for a press event in which community leaders of various backgrounds would join Puentes in denouncing the Vitter ad. My mentor in community organizing, Dr. Cowan, suggested this approach. We would present a coalition of multicultural, multi-ethnic leaders who would openly call on Vitter to remove the ads. I drafted an invitation letter and sent it out. Now we needed a location and the participation of the local media.

Here's what I found out after four years of living a life completely antithetical to the life I lived before the storm. When you show up to help in the struggle for a better world, you find friends in arms, colleagues with whom you can interlock elbows. You learn very quickly that you are not alone. Within this community of new allies and friends was Carol Bebelle. Mama Carol (as she is affectionately and respectfully called these days) was among the group of community leaders I had the good fortune of meeting during a retreat sponsored by a foundation that brought folks from New Orleans together for a three-day stay on Mobile Bay in 2008. I called on Mama Carol and asked her if she would not only step in front on this issue with us but also host us. Without hesitation, she said yes to both. We had our location.

Our network of community leaders did the rest to bring in the local news channels. Although we didn't get great coverage on the airwaves, we did get all four local stations to show up. On October 18, 2010, I began our press

---

18   Elva Ramirez, "Attack Ad: David Vitter's 'Enter Here,'" The Wall Street Journal, Dow Jones & Company Inc., October 22, 2010, https://www.wsj.com/video/attack-ad-david-vitter-enter-here/BD4F9733-F051-4C09-BFF8-EADD-49BA53EC.

event by reading a statement, then introducing the next speaker from the more than ten community leaders who had something to add about the Vitter ads.

We had religious leaders of various faith traditions, immigration attorneys and advocates, and local leaders who organized on various issues, providing a glimpse of the true possibilities of a multicultural, pluralistic society, a picture far different than the one typically offered about these United States. We didn't succeed in getting that ad off the air, but on that day, I felt an inexpressible sense that no matter the rhetoric outside New Orleans, the leaders within the city would do their part to make newcomers feel welcomed, no matter where they came from or why they arrived.

This moment marked for me a sort of arrival, if you will, of what I had hoped for when I changed course in my life in 2007. I had no idea where it would lead, and I had no idea who I would become in the process. I only knew back then that I had to do something, similar to what the community asked of Puentes in the days leading up to the 2010 press event denouncing Vitter's attack ads. If I had any doubts before that moment, I knew afterward that I could no longer go back to the life I'd had, no matter how hard things would become moving forward. I had entered the public space in a significant way, and the journey since then continues to amaze and inspire. Katrina devastated hundreds of thousands of lives, but within it were also the seeds for rebirth, not just for the city, but for my own life as well.

ON LOVE AND LEADERSHIP
LAMAR & ASHLEIGH GARDERE

Lamar: I am, in my eyes, an unlikely leader: a natural introvert who would most often rather be solving some puzzle through coding, engineering, or just deep-thinking about new approaches to old problems. If not that, then enjoying some old sci-fi flick that I've seen so many times, I don't need the audio to know the dialog. Either way, not the person that delights in motivating staff to their highest potential or engaging crowds of people—strangers or otherwise. But introverted leadership seems to be having a moment, so I find myself leading one of the more influential organizations in New Orleans. As unlikely as it would seem to my younger self, I can't even say this is a new situation. I've led some organization for thirteen of the past seventeen years since moving back to New Orleans in 2007. Over the last twenty years, we've blamed many things on Hurricane Katrina and the levee failures, and I'm willing to blame this anxiety-producing reality on her as well!

My name is Lamar Gardere, and professionally, I am the executive director of The Data Center. The Data Center is a nonprofit, operating in southeast Louisiana, dedicated to democratizing data as a catalyst for informed decision-making, towards a vision of a prosperous, inclusive, and sustainable region with good quality of life for all. The Data Center works with countless decisionmakers, elected officials, and community, business, and nonprofit leaders every day to ensure they are armed with the best research, data, and insights about our community to make decisions that will impact systems and change the lives of New Orleanians in positive ways. The Data Center has been a critical component of New Orleans' development since 1997, but my connection and deep devotion to New Orleans started well before then and is one of many blessings from the storm.

Ashleigh: I am Ashleigh Gardere. Wife. Mother. President of PolicyLink, a national research and action institute committed to advancing racial and economic equity. I begin my story with these three identities because each of them are identities that emerged from Hurricane Katrina, blessings from the storm.

On August 29, 2005, I was three days from my twenty-fifth birthday. I'd returned home just one year before the storm, having landed a job in the Mayor's Office of Economic Development. By this time, my immediate family lived elsewhere. My parents were in New York City, as my mother had been recruited to the Ford Foundation. My brother was living and working there, too, soaking in New York's arts and theater scene, and my sister was pursuing graduate studies in Minnesota.

Technically, I arrived back home alone, but that could not have been further from the truth. Let me explain.

Extended Family (Ashleigh)
My mother, born Linetta Jones in Rochester, New York, was the youngest of four girls. Sixteen years younger than her oldest sister, with four years between each sibling, she was considered the baby of the family. My mother was a high achiever—the only one of her siblings to attend college. She graduated high school at age sixteen and moved to Washington, DC, on her own to attend Howard University on scholarship.

My father was the oldest of four children, born in Steubenville, Ohio, and raised in Buffalo, New York. One of the first Black students and graduates of Hutchinson Central Technical High School, my father moved to Washington, DC, to attend Howard University, where he met my mother. Before completing college, he was deployed by the US Army to fight in the Vietnam War. Upon returning to the United States, he honored my mother's staunch opposition to living as an "army wife" and accepted a three-year civilian post at the US Navy Base in New Orleans, Louisiana. What was intended to be a three-year assignment became a forty-year settlement. New Orleans became our home.

Soon after my parents settled in New Orleans, we joined Beacon Light Missionary Baptist Church. Through this community, I not only grew faith, I gained family. In-home Bible studies and after-church Sunday dinners grew deep family ties: aunts, uncles, siblings, cousins, and two New Orleans grandmothers. Through church family, I experienced deep love and abundance in a city that was wary of outsiders.

New Orleans is a community that often demands proof of lineage for at least four generations before you can declare yourself a New Orleanian. Consequently, the unofficial rules would deem me an outsider with no "Big Mama," no grandmother to anchor my New Orleans story. That means every school year, I should have submitted at least one school project untethered to the rich cultural traditions of a city like no other.

Instead of feeling like I had no grandmothers, I had four: two by birth and two by choice. And my grandmothers—all of them—like so many others, experienced the realities of oppression, which, at the very least, resulted in poor education, low-skilled work, and low incomes. Nevertheless, there was always a bottomless pot on the stove with enough red beans and rice or gumbo or pot roast to feed four of us or forty of us. Our blended family blended resources to ensure that all of us had what we needed or wanted. There was always enough food, love, wisdom, and encouragement for everyone.

And my parents, the same. There was an open-door policy at our house. Innumerable folks had keys to the front door. In fact, our two-sibling household became a three-sibling household when we welcomed my older brother, a church member whose mother succumbed to cancer when he was fifteen years old. Our church family was foundational.

So, even without my immediate family in New Orleans, I was not alone. I was surrounded by church family, still wrapped in the love of Sunday dinners, still making groceries and running errands for Big Mamas and aunties.

It is only with this understanding that my Katrina evacuation makes sense. I left New Orleans on Sunday, August 28 as part of a fourteen-person caravan, spanning ages six months to eighty years, across five cars. We were mothers, fathers, daughters, sons, uncles, aunties, and cousins—as many by choice as by blood. And we would stay together for the next thirty days. First, we landed at a motel in Galveston, Texas, our temporary shelter from the storm. Days later, we upgraded to a hotel in Houston, Texas, until we could find apartments to host our resettlement, only beginning to understand that our lives would be forever changed.

Proof of Lineage (Lamar)

I am, in fact, a native son of New Orleans, husband to Ashleigh Gardere, and father to our two boys, Jayden and Justin Gardere. Though my mom is from Portsmouth, Virginia, my father was born here, and as far as anyone can tell, our family has been here for many generations. In most other cities, a long family tree rooted in the same region simply means your family might be well established or respected in the community. But New Orleans has a long and unique history, and if your family roots run alongside its roots, whether you know it or not, New Orleans has made you into who it wants you to be.

From its beginning, New Orleans had its own character. Even though the city we know today was born in the American South, it wasn't of the same lineage as the rest of the region. Well before the French colonized and renamed it New Orleans in 1718, the region was already a busy trading post known to indigenous peoples as Bulbancha, or "place of many tongues." While indigenous people knew to live with and respect the seasonal flooding this deltaic region exhibited, French, Spanish, and, later, American engineers sought to control the land through the construction of levees and drainage canals, which made the successful long-term colonization of New Orleans possible.

The French and Spanish ruled New Orleans early on, which made it different in terms of the rights afforded to free people of color and to the enslaved. Free people of color were allowed to settle and own property in certain parts of the city and, for those who had the wherewithal and desire to do so, to start and grow their own businesses. It was also possible for an enslaved person to purchase their freedom and live as a free person of color. For sure, New Orleans did not escape the barbarity of slavery. In fact, some of New Orleans' early wealth was due to its huge role as a financial center for the slave trade. Still, New Orleans was one of the most diverse places in the country early in its three hundred-year history, and when the Haitian revolution began in the late 1700s, people left Haiti—Black and white, Creoles of all types—and came here largely because it was a relatively welcoming and prosperous place. By 1810, the city's population was approximately one third enslaved, one third free people of color, and one third white—a mix that was unheard of elsewhere in the South or anywhere else in the country. By 1840, the city boasted the nation's third-largest population.

To be a free person of color often meant that you were also of mixed race—of European and African descent—and, historically, enjoyed somewhat of an elevated status. In part due to the divisive effects of Jim Crow laws, these "light-skinned" Black New Orleanians, sometimes and somewhat controversially referred to as Creoles, tended to form more insular communities, giving rise to the particular brand of colorism that New Orleans still struggles with today. As far as genealogical records suggest, this is the context through which much of my patrilineal line developed. We were denizens of Creole New Orleans.

Pre-Katrina, if you grew up in New Orleans, you didn't venture too far from where you and your family lived. You could be a downtown, uptown, or Westbank kid, but you didn't spend too much time in the other areas. I was a downtown kid and spent my time mostly in the Gentilly and 7th Ward neighborhoods. The 7th Ward neighborhood has historically been one of the enclaves of light-skinned, middle-class Black New Orleanians, and unsurprisingly, this is where much of my family's history lies. Many educated and accomplished people of color lived there before the Civil War and throughout the time that Jim Crow laws were in effect. But after desegregation, the city built the I-10 interstate over the Claiborne Avenue neutral ground, destroying the 7th Ward's prosperous business district in the process. The 7th Ward of my adolescence was a shell of its former self, with more than a few dangerous, dark alleys of which one should be wary.

Though the 7th Ward was where most of my dad's family lived, I spent most of my formative years in Gentilly. There, my parents were able to give my sister and me a typical middle-class upbringing. Back then, Gentilly Woods, the specific Gentilly neighborhood we lived in, was nearly 70 percent Black, with only about 16 percent of people living in poverty, but you could find families up and down the income spectrum. Most people were either teachers, worked in healthcare, or worked a retail or hospitality job. Though suburban, Gentilly wasn't the bastion of roomy family houses and manicured yards. It's an inner-ring suburb and includes its fair share of California bungalow-style houses and small, single family rental properties.

When Hurricane Katrina struck and the levees failed, I was not in New Orleans. I was in graduate school in Atlanta, but it was both my immediate family and my lineage that were being washed away. For better or for worse, which only someone whose life was rooted in pre-Katrina New Orleans can say, few things would be the same after "The Storm."

Those were the times (Lamar)
My young sister and I were raised in a modest house on a busy street, literally a stone's throw from the interstate and across the street from a gas station. That is to say, we had a stable family life with plenty of love and safety, but it wasn't luxurious. Like many in the area, my mom was a teacher. My dad worked for the post office and off and on in the family business that my grandfather started in the 1970s. My grandfather was one of the many artisans New Orleans is well known for. He did plaster work in his younger days and eventually owned clubs and other small businesses before estab-

lishing a cultured marble manufacturing business that he ran through the late 1990s. My dad, who has a great and imaginative mind for building and artisanal activities, succeeded my grandfather in running the business until his retirement.

Like in many families, my mom was the nurturer. She always made sure we were well taken care of, emotionally supported, and had a balanced sense of right and wrong. While New Orleans' indomitable culture has its influence on everyone who lives here, my dad provided a great example of what faithfulness and loyalty in family life look like, but my mom probably shaped my values and worldview the most. I was her firstborn and seemingly inherited much of her patience and cautious eye in social situations. She ensured I would have the confidence and sensibility to reject colorism and the traditional patriarchal structures most of us in America are born into, and to operate within racist structures while still performing at my potential.

This is an area where not being from New Orleans advantaged her. My mom, not being from here and being darker skinned, could see the differentiations historically made based on complexion. She made sure that I understood very early on that because I had a lighter complexion, people might make certain assumptions about me, and that I might be tempted to make certain assumptions about myself, but that I should know right now that I'm no better, no worse, no different than anybody else based on the complexion of my skin. She would say: "You are Black. They are Black. We are all Black."

I went to a nearby Catholic school—St. James Major—for kindergarten through eighth grade. Going to a parochial school is another one of those common New Orleans experiences that arises out of its history, but this decision was largely due to my mom's experiences in the public school system. She started her teaching career in Portsmouth, Virginia, but transferred into the New Orleans public school system when she moved to New Orleans after marrying my dad. She immediately felt the difference between the two school systems. There were fewer resources in the classroom, fewer resources for the teachers, and fewer resources for the kids. For both the students and the teachers, it was a difficult environment to be successful in, and frankly, she didn't want her child to be in that lower-resourced situation. So, we went to St. James Major. I don't know that there were necessarily more resources at St. James, but the environment was perceived as one that was more protective.

Currently, New Orleans' education system is well known for being a fully charter school system, which, among other things, means there isn't a concept of neighborhood schools anymore. Now, students go to whatever school they choose and can get into regardless of where they live in the city, but in 1993, when I started high school, unless you went to a private school or Catholic school, kids generally went to the school in their neighborhood. There were several exceptions to this rule, and my high school, Benjamin Franklin Senior High School, was one of them.

Ben Franklin was then and still is a magnet school, meaning that kids from anywhere in the city can go there as long as their test scores are high enough and they aren't waitlisted. Locally, it's one of those schools whose reputation precedes it. I would ride the bus home after school, and whenever kids asked me what school I went to, they would always say, "Oh, you go to school with the smart kids." As uncomfortable as that would make me sometimes, it was also nice because it meant the environment fed my curiosity. In hindsight, one of the things that was special about Ben Franklin was that it allowed me to be as "smart" or to pursue whatever academic interests I wanted to with no judgement. There was no such thing as being a nerd at Ben Franklin—of course you were; we all were. That's why we were there. Everybody was free to perform as they wanted to, and that created a social environment that facilitated academic achievement.

Ben Franklin wasn't without its challenges, but I loved my high school experience. It was my first chance to experience the city for myself without so much of the cover family life provided. Franklin was a more racially mixed environment than I had been in before. While New Orleans was well over 60 percent Black at this time, Franklin was majority white and may have been the only majority-white school in the New Orleans public school system back then. While this wasn't a defining reality of my time in high school, it did allow me to experience groups of people and parts of the city I hadn't known before. Likewise, catching the bus home every afternoon allowed me to see more of the lower-income neighborhoods in New Orleans.

After my freshman year in high school, we moved back to the 7th Ward, into the area where most of my dad's family had lived throughout our history. My grandmother had lived there, two of my great-grandmothers, my great-grandfather, great aunt and uncle, cousins, they were all in that area. By the time we moved there, my grandmother had passed away and so had my great-grandmothers and great-grandfather, but that was where the family really had its roots. We knew the houses where they'd grown up, and we lived in some of those same houses.

It was quite a bit different from the Gentilly neighborhood where I'd spent my younger years. By this time, it was a much rougher neighborhood. The conditions people lived in seemed considerably worse, and families weren't necessarily middle-class anymore. Many were single-parent households and didn't always have all the resources they needed day-to-day, nor the time in a day to do all life demanded of them. Crimes of desperation were fairly common. Subsequently, I didn't spend much time hanging outside, and most of my interaction with the neighborhood was based on leaving and coming home.

While, developmentally, my preteen years might have been the most formative, these high school years are the ones I remember most. This is when I began to perceive that life was harder for some folks than others, but it's also when I met my closest friends, shaped my self-identity, and met my wife, Ashleigh Gilbert.

Though we knew each other for most of high school, we didn't start dating until the second half of my senior year. Better late than never! By then, I was well on my way to a career in technology, though at the time I had no idea how to turn my interests into a job, nor did I know anyone in technology. But Ashleigh somehow already knew she was going to work in and on behalf of the community, which was a career path that was a bit foreign to me. She also seemed to already know she would be a leader in some shape or form. I remember hanging out and talking about our futures one day (as young boyfriends and girlfriends do!) and saying explicitly that I would leave working on behalf of the community and fighting for others to her; that I didn't think such causes were for me, but that I didn't mind supporting them if I had the money to do so. I saw myself as a future software developer, and that probably meant some sort of corporate job somewhere out-of-state. And I think I believed that until New Orleans decided otherwise.

For Such a Time as This (Ashleigh)

When I was eight years old, the pastor of Beacon Light accepted a new post in Boston, Massachusetts. Tensions flared among church members over the selection of a new young pastor, Rev. Dwight Webster. A small group of elders did not approve of the church's new direction, rooted in Black liberation theology. After a contentious church business meeting one Friday night, we arrived at the church edifice on Sunday morning to discover the locks had been changed. We were locked out . . . of church.

That Sunday, we had church service on an unkempt, empty lot next door. Rather than engage in a public fight that could cause outside observers to question the fundamentals of our faith, we founded a new church, Christian Unity Baptist Church, where love and liberation were central.

The love that was nurtured among members of Beacon Light transferred and deepened through the establishment and growth of Christian Unity. Over the next year, we met and worshipped in members' homes, host churches, even a local university auditorium. We also tended to the business of founding a new church, together. We answered big questions: What core values would undergird our faith traditions? What new name would reflect these values? What kind of members did we aspire to be, and what culture did we want to create? What impact did we want to have on the broader New Orleans community?

At eight years old, I was a co-founder of a community institution. Out of the tragedy of a church split, the founding of Christian Unity Baptist Church taught me that crisis could offer an unexpected opportunity to rebuild, redefine, and transform. This first existential crisis in my life had birthed a new and different future, one that I could not have imagined.

My family—biological and church family alike—taught me love and abundance, fundamental building blocks of my value system. They also introduced me to the cause of justice. Every Sunday, the call to discipleship began with a powerful statement: "The doors of the church are open and swing on welcome hinges." It should come as no surprise that a church rooted in Black liberation theology would bind itself to the struggle for civil rights.

Jerome "Big Duck" Smith[19], a Freedom Rider and staunch advocate for civil rights, was a quiet member of our church. He would arrive late and sit in the very back, beyond the sanctuary in the fellowship area. However, Big Duck was not a quiet man. In fact, he was often the loudest and fiercest advocate for government and community investment in the city's youth. From city council meetings to private board meetings, Big Duck consistently interrupted standing agendas to demand that decision makers put children first.

Big Duck's actions reflected his words. He established Tambourine and Fan, a social justice camp designed to develop the next generation of young leaders committed to the cause of justice. At thirteen years old, I served as a camp counselor to five-year-olds. In order to teach my campers civil rights history, I had to learn it myself. We learned facts about Fannie Lou Hamer

---

19 Jerome Smith is lovingly referred to as "Big Duck" because he was always seen with children. Folks thought that he looked like a duck with little ducklings following behind him.

and Rosa Parks. We recited lyrics about Southern trees that bore strange fruit. We advocated and protested at City Hall for more funding for youth programming, drafting letters to elected officials and making public comments at city council meetings.

That summer, Maurice, one of my campers, had a nosebleed and was feeling ill. I ran across the campus to call his mother, knowing that she would come to his rescue immediately, as any mother would. After I had provided her with a fulsome update of her son's condition and offered guidance for easeful pick-up, Maurice's mother said she was not coming. *What?!* I was confused and devastated all at once.

In that moment, I understood in a very real way that the lessons we were taught at Tambourine and Fan were not theoretical. The systems that shaped our daily lives were failing us so significantly that this five-year-old child could not be assured that his most basic needs would be met. In this moment, I was forced to see how our educational, health, and workforce systems were failing him. This reality was unacceptable. That day, after many tears of my own and processing with Big Duck and my parents, I committed myself and my life's work to continuing the fight for social justice and transforming systems to work for all people.

Indeed, the turn of the century offered unthinkable opportunities to test my leadership training. In 2001, as a college student and resident assistant at New York University, I was responsible for ensuring the safety of dorm residents in Lower Manhattan as terrorists crashed planes into the World Trade Center buildings. In 2005, just one year after returning home following graduate studies, I was called into service to support the rebuilding of New Orleans after Hurricane Katrina. In 2006, I had a front-row seat to witness the tragic consequences of poverty, gun violence, and the failings of our criminal-legal system after a friend of mine became a shooting victim while leaving my post-Katrina residence.

Collectively, these tragic events reinforced an early lesson from the church-lockout turned church-founding: We have agency. Even in the most horrific and uncertain circumstances, we can build anew. And we can rebuild together.

Doing a New Thing (Lamar)

I should give credit where credit is due. While I am The Data Center's executive director and have been since 2017, I hadn't even heard of The Data Center, then the Greater New Orleans Community Data Center, when Hurricane Katrina hit. But it was out of the resulting devastation and subsequent rebuilding that The Data Center's prominence grew. The Data Center was inarguably an essential resource in New Orleans' rebuilding and, for a time, was the only place, locally or nationally, for reliable data on New Orleans' recovery. Supported by the Brookings Institution, The Data Center learned to apply its expertise in data and particular neighborhood-level focus to the enormous task of rebuilding a nearly three hundred-year-old American city. It was already part of its mission to democratize data, but now people needed specific guidance on what data mattered most for the task at hand, what that data meant within the current and historical context, and how that data could be used to make the best decisions possible.

What was needed was PhD-level research on disaster recovery but delivered in plain language so that folks on the ground could activate it. So, that's what The Data Center became—part data intermediary, part think tank—delivering regular guidance on the path to recovery through consistent engagement with community leaders and decision makers and through regular publication of *The New Orleans Index*. Early on, two themes arose:

1. While a glass-half-full view of disasters might identify them as hidden opportunities for change, the research was clear that, as a matter of course, they do not bring change. Instead, disasters only exacerbate or accelerate existing trends.

2. If what New Orleanians wanted was to rebuild New Orleans as they had always imagined it, instead of as what she had been, then what we needed was not to chart a pathway to recovery, but to chart a *new* pathway to prosperity.

This would become the mantra The Data Center would preach locally and nationally, in the media and in community meetings, and to elected officials and ordinary residents alike. If this was to be a moment of rebirth, we would need to be willing to rethink how our systems worked; come to terms with the effects that historical oppression and racism continued to have on the outcomes of real people in our city as well as New Orleans' relationship to both state government and the state in general; and figure out how to build a new economy and governance structures that valued and prioritized the well-being and prosperity of every person in the city, regardless of income, situation, or social standing.

New Orleans would have to acknowledge the harm it had done to Black communities over the generations even as those communities continued to imbue the city with their unmatched talent. From the unjustly obtained and exploited labor that cleared swampy lands to make way for New Orleans' expansion and continued existence, to jazz and other musical forms, to its world-class cuisine and Mardi Gras traditions, New Orleans prospered from the hands of its people of color and their vibrant, indefatigable Afro-Caribbean culture. It had largely built its former wealth, mystique, and global prominence on these riches, but now the city's future depended on doing something it hadn't done well for generations: bringing Black New Orleanians into the full economy in a way that it hadn't come close to since prior to the Civil War—but this time, for all Black New Orleanians.

The Data Center's primary tool for facilitating the necessary focus on economic inclusion for all New Orleanians was through democratizing and disseminating data and information on this reality, but it would need community, government, the private sector, and philanthropy to activate it for any progress to be made.

Rebuilding, Together (Ashleigh)
In October 2005, I would be called back into service to support the rebuilding of New Orleans, my home. Lest this sound glamorous, I'll remind you that power still had not been restored to a majority of the city. No streetlights. No grocery stores. No family. No home.

Like hundreds of other workers, a cruise ship would become my new home. That's right. Cruise ships provided emergency shelter for first responders of all kinds—police officers, firefighters, city workers, medical staff, schoolteachers, and administrators—as we worked to reopen the city.

My previous role as policy director in the Mayor's Office of Economic Development had no usefulness in this moment. My new job was to track and report business (re)openings daily and support business owners as they worked to provide essential amenities and services to New Orleanians trying to rebuild their lives. Likewise, my colleagues were clearing roads of debris, restoring power across the city grid, reopening hospitals and schools.

Hurricane Katrina's destruction was so complete that it required New Orleans to reimagine and rebuild every single system essential to modern civilization, from housing to healthcare, education to economics, criminal justice to transportation. Out of necessity, residents, businesses, and community leaders learned to collectively address the immediate needs of family and community while planning for and building toward our radical aspirations for a future New Orleans that was better than the one we'd lost. We were good stewards of the nation's $120 billion investment in New Orleans' recovery.

Working together, we invested in resident engagement to set priorities for rebuilding. We funded culture bearers to help reach and engage residents throughout the post-Katrina diaspora. We invested in community groups and resident leaders to fully participate in (and sometimes redirect) neighborhood plans. We adjusted voting requirements and polling sites to expand access to voting during the height of our exodus experience.

We reimagined systems to work better for people. We rebuilt neighborhoods, making affordable housing available to low-income families, with greater access to new community centers, hospitals, libraries, schools, and parks. We developed climate resilience plans, invested in coastal protection, and built one of the most advanced flood protection systems in the world. We built a new healthcare system with a network of community-based clinics that served patients in their neighborhoods. We established new policies to decrease the number of people in jail and increase transparency and accountability in the criminal-legal system.

New Orleans has been recognized nationally for its remarkable comeback. After years of all-in engagement by residents, community groups, philanthropy, government, and business leaders, New Orleans did recover. That alone is worth celebrating, as recovery seemed nearly impossible in the days immediately after Katrina hit and we were pummeled with imagery of Black people suffering and dying in what looked like a wasteland. Our recovery is a story of self-determination, even a new practice in partnership.

Here's just one example from my service in Mayor Mitch Landrieu's administration: Nearly ten years after Hurricane Katrina, with the city's educational, economic, health, and justice systems reestablished, the Landrieu administration set out to connect people to sorely needed economic opportunity. Specifically, we wanted to expand opportunities for working-age Black men.

We did all the things. First, we took a data-driven approach to our work. By disaggregating data, The Data Center found that 52 percent of working-age African American men were not working. We were missing the brilliance and creativity of 38,600 residents. And while the census data helped us to identify this population of folks being left out of our economy, census data could not tell us why.

So, we hired and trained unemployed Black men as surveyors, and they took to the streets of New Orleans, surveying their peers. The board chair of our economic development organization, a Black man and owner of our local McDonald's franchise, donated McDonald's gift cards as incentives for completing the survey. This incentive followed the advice of our surveyors to meet the most immediate need of out-of-work folks: food. We also hired Black men and women with lived experience as long-term staff of our initiative.

Our strategies engaged and supported government leaders, community advocates, and private-sector decision makers towards a shared result, meaningfully reducing unemployment rates among African American men. We hosted expert roundtables and focus groups for job seekers, workforce training providers, and human resources professionals to give voice to their perspectives, share their experiences, and articulate their needs. We interviewed major employers to identify pain points within their organizations so that our strategies effectively responded to existing needs of employers.

Then, we brought all participants together to share what we'd learned across those conversations, hosting collaborative design sessions where attendees—in hybrid groups—began to build prototypes that addressed employer pain points while creating more employment and ownership opportunities for neighborhood residents, especially Black men. One of my favorite memories is of a formerly incarcerated man collaborating with a vice president of human resources for one of our health systems. Together, they were crafting career pathways into one of our local hospitals.

We measured everything. We established a monthly performance accountability system called Opportunity STAT, where we tracked the performance of every program or initiative that was a part of our work. We were tough on ourselves. Off target, or in the red, meant that partners were more than 10 percent off our goal.

Our strategies included revamping the Workforce Development Board to engage major employers. Our goal was to make sure that we were maximizing federal dollars to address the employers' pain points. So, we built industry advisory boards with clear pathways to good jobs and advancement opportunities. We redesigned our career readiness curriculum to provide consistency and predictability to employers, and we created a whole new service delivery model that fully leveraged the best of our community resources. As these interventions began to deliver positive outcomes, we passed local legislation to bolster the city's contribution to a strong economy through local hire and living wage ordinances.

We celebrated huge results. The non-employment rate for African American men in New Orleans moved from 52 percent in 2013 to 43.9 percent in 2015! The fact that, in 2023, the non-employment rate for working-age Black men in New Orleans is still hovering around 42 percent is proof of the good and lasting systems-changing work that we did. With non-employment rates for white men at 19 percent, there's still so much more that needs to happen, but this at least proved that change was possible.

We delivered similar interventions to accelerate the growth of Black-owned businesses in the city. Our rationale: Because data showed that Black-owned businesses hire Black people at a higher rate, the growth of businesses would expand job opportunities for Black people, including Black men. Likewise, we prioritized business support in sectors with higher rates of male employment.

We established a small business training program coupled with a Mobilization Fund, which provided financing to contractors to cover costs incurred before the start of a project. At the City, we began proactive planning, identifying future projects and bid opportunities, and pairing the training program and Mobilization Fund to these opportunities.

We fully staffed the city's Office of Supplier Diversity and streamlined the Disadvantaged Business Enterprise (DBE) certification process from two years to fourteen days. We proactively monitored contracts with an online compliance monitoring system that helped project owners track spending, one of the pain points we surfaced earlier in the process. We published our performance to the city council annually. We not only met an already ambitious DBE policy goal of 35 percent but reached nearly 50 percent of city contracts going to DBE firms: $192 million in municipal government contracts and $450 million in awards from sister public agencies, like the Regional Transit Authority, international airport, and local water utility.

I learned many lessons from this experience that I still carry with me on my leadership journey.

The first lesson is that data is one of the most powerful tools we have to shine a light on unjust systems. Compelling data can be a rallying tool and point the way towards effective and equitable solutions. Second, I learned that worthwhile strategies are far bigger than any one institution or sector can achieve on its own. Third, I learned that social justice efforts must stem from the experiences and engagement of those directly affected. At every turn, we were careful to make sure that the voice of residents, job seekers, and business owners informed the development and evolution of strategies.

On Doing Things Differently (Ashleigh)
Five years later, I attended a conference designed to create an anti-displacement housing agenda in New Orleans. As a former public official who'd worked aggressively to expand economic opportunity for Black New Orleanians, tracked with discipline the impact of our well-researched efforts, and celebrated tangible outcomes with elected officials, business and civic leaders, pastors, neighbors, and families, I was deeply irritated as I sat in the audience while a national policy expert from out of town presented data that basically said our efforts were for naught.

How could that be? I had proof—quantitative and qualitative—that the citywide Economic Opportunity Strategy that I'd led as part of Mayor Mitch Landrieu's administration transformed lives and helped to grow the local economy. Didn't this academician know about the eight hundred people who were hired at a minimum wage of fifteen dollars per hour to help build our new, world-class airport? Hadn't he seen that New Orleans was one of the first cities in the American South to successfully pass and implement a local hire policy to expand living wage employment opportunities for local and disadvantaged residents? We carefully crafted the ordinance to help close the employment gap for working-age Black men.

Hadn't his research revealed that Louisiana's largest employer, Ochsner Health System, established a new minimum wage of $12 per hour—up from $7.25 per hour—for all its seventeen thousand employees across the state? Most importantly, had he not heard that we used the momentum from those successes to reimagine economic development, transforming our local economic development organization (EDO) into one of the first of its kind to prioritize inclusive growth? At the time of the conference, I served as the EDO's executive vice president and COO and was shepherding in a new, organization-wide results statement that prioritized—on purpose—eliminating racial economic disparity.

So, how in the world could a national policy expert stand in front of this audience and insinuate that none of these efforts mattered?

For all the well-researched, well-reasoned, and well-tracked efforts to "move the needle" on economic opportunity for Black New Orleanians, I was sitting in a conference about housing affordability. Despite our exacting efforts to expand economic opportunity, we had not taken a cross-systems approach. Despite the remarkable pace at which we made change happen, from a generational perspective, it still registered as incremental and siloed.

If I'm honest, the national policy expert at the anti-displacement conference was directly calling out what had been a nagging feeling throughout my work. My secret about the insufficiency of our efforts was being exposed. Dozens of cross-sector partners and I had been building within structures that were never designed to serve everyone, certainly not 38,600 unemployed Black men in New Orleans, nor the nearly one hundred million economically insecure people in the United States.

Policymakers, practitioners, advocates, and academicians across the country are working diligently to improve systems that impact our local economies. We are committed to solving problems in our local communities and are generous, in time and partnership, in sharing our progress with other cities. Nevertheless, we fail to acknowledge that all systems in America have been built based on a hierarchy of human value—the notion that some people matter more than others.

While technology has quickened the pace of information-sharing and created demand for immediate action and permanent solutions, our siloed approach to systems-change has proven insufficient to the community's demand for enduring change.

I'm Here, If You'll Have Me (Lamar)

When I went to bed on August 27, 2005, I knew there was a hurricane named Katrina out there, but it was originally forecasted to come across Florida from the eastern side, then move northward and eventually dissipate. It also appeared to be a relatively average hurricane in size and intensity. But on the morning of Sunday, August 28, my mom called and said they were evacuating to Tallahassee, Florida, where my sister was in college. I was a bit confused, because my parents don't normally evacuate, until I checked the latest weather report and saw a massive storm strengthening to a Category Five hurricane. I immediately knew evacuating was the right move. What happened next is well documented, but what might be less well documented are the incredibly mixed emotions New Orleanians who were not in New Orleans when Katrina struck and the levees failed experienced.

Maybe I was the only one who felt this way, but when New Orleans was devastated by disaster, I ping-ponged between a range of emotions: empathy for my compatriots; horror at the devastation, the lives lost, and the massive recovery task ahead; a certain amount of gratefulness for my personal safety and to be out of harm's way; sadness for the state and future of my hometown; and guilt that I had been spared from the adversity folks were dealing with and, likely, the worst of the incredibly difficult situation ahead.

Guilt was the emotion that was most unexpected. Up until that point, I had experienced all the joy and pain of living in New Orleans. No, I hadn't grown up in the worst of circumstances, but I still understood them, even if I was only adjacent to hardship. I could say I had both soaked up the vibrancy of New Orleans culture and survived the violence of the 1990s. I wasn't a Mardi Gras Indian, but I could appreciate a second line. I didn't go to the most famous of high schools, but when the question was presented, I could boast of going to a real New Orleans school. In other words, I was a bonafide New Orleanian. But now there was a new challenge causing heartache, but because I wasn't there to experience it, I didn't have the standing to talk about it with other New Orleanians.

This odd mix of gratefulness and guilt motivated the idea that I needed to find a way to give back what the city had given me. Don't tell the state of Georgia, but I never traded in my New Orleans license (yes, I know it's a Louisiana license) for a Georgia one, even though I had lived in the state for three years. Some part of me had never left the city, and if there was ever a time to come back, now was that time. When my dad mentioned wanting to retire from the family business, it presented a way back to New Orleans while also helping family. Even though cultured marble manufacturing wasn't my thing, I was still happy to jump in and contribute. I moved back to New Orleans in 2007, and in 2008, never having run anything before, but always being thought of as someone who would do a good job with whatever you gave him, I took over sole ownership of Centurion Marble. We used to call it "the shop." I ran the shop for several years, but post-Katrina recovery-related economic factors combined with the lingering difficulty brought on by the Great Recession made business very difficult, and by 2012, I had to close its door. Though I couldn't continue the business's long history, I did get good experience with what it meant to lead people, engage customers, and to run an organization.

By this time, I was realizing that in the chaos of widespread devastation emerged opportunities in New Orleans for people who wanted them, particularly high-potential but less experienced young people. When disaster strikes, outside help is great, but people will need some of their own to step up. So a young person whose sensibilities were born of New Orleans' own unique culture and idiosyncrasies was particularly endearing to many people working to restore the city. Because disasters accelerate existing trends, the conditions were right for young, talented native New Orleanians to be thrust into leadership positions at an earlier age than was likely possible in the past or in other parts of the country.

Prior to closing the shop, I had been recruited by the city government to be a part of the Landrieu administration by helping to run the revamped IT department, now renamed ITI: Information Technology and Innovation. I had never considered working for city government before, likely because the prevailing notion of local government had always been that it was plagued by dysfunction, unprofessionalism, and ineptitude. But when I got there, I found quite the opposite. The city's chief information officer, Allen Square, who recruited me, was smart, young, and determined to recruit the best talent from around the nation. The civil servants I met there were dedicated, knowledgeable, and far more interested in serving the public than I could have imagined.

The more time I spent at City Hall, the more I understood the value of public service. The IT department and city leadership had embraced the "open data" movement and its ability to contribute to transparency and operational efficiency. There, I saw difficult conversations between the city and the public go from confrontation to collaboration all because the city was willing to openly share high-quality data for all to see. When people saw their own situations in the data, it boosted confidence and public trust, making the task of working together to solve problems and deliver city services easier. Even if the city was having trouble with a particular issue, through the data the public could better understand the problem they were facing, see their good efforts to solve it, and join in where they could. This also had the effect of creating community advocates who could spread positive feelings about the role the government can play in the lives of ordinary people. Like so many things related to data post-Katrina, The Data Center had its hand in this development as well. In an interesting exchange of talent, a number of Data Center employees left the organization for city government. That's how I met Denice Ross, the former co-director of The Data Center. She helped me to realize how my technical skill set could be used to improve the lives of real people through the direct provision of technology services and by improving existing technology so that it worked better for all residents.

Ashleigh had started her position in the Landrieu administration in 2010. I wasn't far behind, starting in 2011. By 2014, I was being promoted to the city's chief information officer, one of the youngest CIOs of any major municipality in the country. Those years working with Ashleigh in city government and alongside colleagues who truly understood what it meant to be civil servants working tirelessly to improve government and recover New Orleans from the inside out changed my perception of my role in the world. No longer did I believe my fate was in corporate America as a stereotypical cog in the machine. Instead, I understood that my combination of background and talents put me in a one-of-a-kind position in New Orleans. I had a role on the front lines of helping my city that seemingly only I could fill.

Not only did I contribute to restoring public faith in city government from a department that had seen more than its fair share of leaders be arrested and jailed, but we also transformed the department into a high-functioning agency. We pushed for more open data, eventually operationalizing the concept through city policy by declaring that data should be considered open by default, not closed off from the public. We produced new services like NOLA-311 and made the resulting data open and freely available. We were one of the first cities in America to make its data on policing open and freely available to the public. We used data to solve tough problems, like blight eradication, and contributed to some of the city's most important efforts, like NOLA for Life, the city's murder-reduction strategy, and the Network for Economic Opportunity, the city's workforce and employment strategy designed to improve Black male employment outcomes.

The ITI department built or implemented new software applications to make delivery of city services easier, and we produced many informative and useful government websites that either provided insight on important things happening in neighborhoods, directly provided services, or made accessing them easier. Towards the end of my tenure in 2017, we were planning construction of a fiber optic network across the city that could simultaneously support city services and provide internet access for low-income residents, and implementing a digital equity program to improve digital literacy and close the digital divide.

New Orleans was now a nationally recognized leader in open data and respected for the heroic way in which we recovered towards something better than what we had before. I'm sure someone else in the world could have done the job, but by now, my self-image has been rewritten as a leader, laser-focused on how I can use my personal background and abilities to the benefit of the community. I have finally been wholly converted to the cause Ashleigh already knew would be her life's work more than twenty years ago.

A Love Story Within a Love Story (Both)

By now, you already know that Lamar and Ashleigh Gardere are husband and wife. Also, you may have observed our deep love for and commitment to New Orleans. In many ways, our love, commitment, and support for each other has helped to supercharge our work.

We met in French class in the fall of 1994, as students at Ben Franklin. Ashleigh had just begun her freshman year. Lamar was a sophomore. Friends first, we began dating near the end of Ashleigh's junior year, Lamar's senior year. As most young people do, we broke up, grew up.... Nevertheless, we remained in touch.

Like so many New Orleanians, Ashleigh tested the bounds of resilience and strength during the first twelve months of the rebuilding process. During one of the toughest moments of this testing, she needed to talk to someone who knew her well and understood her sense of loss, beyond property. Loss of community, tradition, grounding. Ashleigh called Lamar, and he answered.

During the call, Ashleigh mentioned that she needed to get away from New Orleans for a bit. Lamar quickly offered to pick her up on his way back to Atlanta (he'd been working remotely as a software developer while visiting friends in Chicago). He said that he'd planned a stop in New Orleans, and it was no problem for her to hitch a ride. Note: Ashleigh later discovered that Lamar had only tentatively planned said pit stop in New Orleans. It was by no means the solid plan he made it out to be. But, not one to miss a good opportunity, he firmed up his plans on the fly for the chance to spend time with her. He believed he could (re)capture her attention and her heart during the seven-hour drive to Atlanta. He was right.

Ashleigh, still working for the city of New Orleans, returned home after her respite. New Orleans was testing ways to make room for highly trained expatriates to bring their ideas, intellect, and creativity back home. Though her previous attempts to recruit friends, family, and former classmates back to New Orleans had come up short, her first successful recruit was Lamar.

In what now seems like an unlikely but inevitable series of events, Lamar initially stepped into his family business after moving back to New Orleans but was later recruited to the city of New Orleans' Information Technology and Innovation department, where he would advance from a functional director to chief information officer for the entirety of the municipal government, then ultimately become executive director of the Data Center. Likewise, Ashleigh's leadership would evolve from serving as policy director for the city of New Orleans, to vice president of community relations at JP-

Morgan Chase, to senior advisor to Mayor Mitch Landrieu, to executive vice president and chief operating officer at the New Orleans Business Alliance, to her present role as president of PolicyLink.

As you might imagine, the support that Lamar modeled at the start of our grown-up relationship would become a core element of our marriage commitment to each other later. Ashleigh was recruited to join Mayor Mitch Landrieu's administration first, in 2010. During the recruitment process, we had extensive conversations about how this new role could impact our family-planning decisions. We were newly married and suspected that a senior role in the mayor's office would be grueling. So, we decided to delay starting our family. However, after Ashleigh's first week on the job, we discovered we were already pregnant.

For eight years, we masterfully juggled the responsibilities of municipal government as working parents. Ashleigh worked all the way up to her due date. She stayed home with Baby Jayden for six weeks, then, with Virgo precision, staged her return to work over the remaining two weeks: one week working two days a week, then one week working three days a week, until her full-time return to the office. Lamar made (and maintained) a most noble commitment. Each night, after Ashleigh fed Jayden during the middle of the night, Lamar stayed up and rocked him back to sleep . . . for as long as it took, knowing he'd still have a full day's work ahead. Ashleigh pumped in her office between meetings and delivered breast milk to Jayden during her lunch hour as necessary. One year later, we had Baby Justin and did it all over again.

We managed a strict schedule, working until 5:15 p.m. on pick-up days, then leaving to pick up the boys from day care (we alternated pick-up and drop-off every other day and picked up each other's slack when the day ran longer than it was supposed to). We would play, have family dinner and bathtime, and put the kids to bed by 8:15 p.m. We often took naps for two to four hours, woke up, then worked during the middle of the night to make sure that we'd met all our responsibilities. As the boys got older, we leaned on our family supports to help us out. One grandmother picked up the boys religiously from school every Wednesday to ensure consistent quality time. The other stepped in, as necessary, when our calendars did not align with the boys' activities. Our family operated like a well-oiled machine until Covid emerged in 2020.

Two months before the onset of Covid-19, Ashleigh submitted her resignation with sixty days' notice to her then employer, New Orleans Business Alliance. After sixteen years of dedicated service, helping to rebuild New Orleans from every possible perch—city government, nonprofit organization, corporate philanthropy—she'd reached her limit. With Lamar's support and encouragement, Ashleigh planned to take a three-month sabbatical before figuring out her next move. Perhaps she could craft one of those fancy fellowships where folks get to read, reflect, and offer insights to the field.

About forty-five days into her sixty-day transition, Covid hit. Our sons' school announced that day as the last day of in-person learning. Parents were directed to pick up their children along with their books, laptops, and school supplies. The school system would transition to virtual classes. In short, Ashleigh was called into service as a homeschool teacher, something she never aspired to be, and Lamar, despite his full-time job, would become the homeschool principal, math and science tutor, school administrator and IT specialist, and aftercare lead. Over the weekend, Lamar and Ashleigh exchanged notes and proposed strategies with other parents. Our initial approach reflected how we'd managed the past several years: on a tight schedule. The boys would complete all their coursework by noon and have the rest of the day to relax. So would Ashleigh. Then, a family friend shared a sample homeschool schedule that would change our lives. The schedule started with physical activity, then some schoolwork, then art, then lunch, then schoolwork, then play. With some skepticism, we decided to try it out.

We had a blast for the remaining three months of the school year. We took turns starting every day with a walk with the boys, which grew longer and longer as we discovered new parts of our neighborhood, stopped to smell flowers, and gazed at insects. We dreamed about the future. We conducted science experiments and made craft projects. We slowed down and enjoyed precious time together. For years, Ashleigh had dreamed of becoming more physically active and resetting her schedule. She finally did. In the evenings, the boys practiced martial arts. Their karate dojo offered virtual classes to keep students engaged. During a virtual belt test, Ashleigh was inspired by their progress and discipline. At forty years old, she decided to follow in their footsteps and join the dojo once it reopened. That decision opened up another level of connection and bonding in our family, as Lamar would also join the dojo and renew his study of martial arts, having earned his second-degree black belt in his youth. All four of us studied martial arts together. For four years, we would take a journey of self-discovery and personal growth, together. We learned how to breathe, push ourselves, fall down, get back up, and make progress.

Ultimately, we learned balance.

We close our story with this peek into our current lives for a few reasons:

In accordance with this book's broader theme, there were unimaginable blessings in the storm. Lamar and Ashleigh found each other, supported each other, and established our very own family.

We also found our way. As Allison Plyer, The Data Center's chief demographer and former executive director, deduced from the first five years after Hurricane Katrina hit, disasters exacerbate or accelerate existing trends. That finding applies to racial stratification and unjust systems, but it also reflects our own love story and leadership journeys. The upheaval created by devastation also created opportunities for high-potential young professionals, especially ones whose sensibilities were shaped by New Orleans' unique culture. Outside help is great, but leadership from homegrown talent is welcome.

Living life on-schedule helped us balance our commitment to justice and liberation with our choice to have a family, but on-schedule is not the same as in-balance. Our family has always been a stabilizing force for us, a source of restoration. Creating more space for joy and connection with family—and community—makes us better leaders.

What Now? (Lamar)

Stepping into leadership at The Data Center turned out to be the unavoidable blessing from the storm that I couldn't have seen on my own. I didn't know about The Data Center at all until I met Denice Ross in city government. Denice encouraged me to apply for the promotion to CIO and the executive director's role at The Data Center. Years earlier, The Data Center had already made important contributions to Ashleigh's life as a neighborhood resource very early in her career and helped spark a new chapter in her career by surfacing a compelling data point about life in New Orleans for Black men at just the right moment. It was unlikely that I would have found my way to government if Ashleigh hadn't introduced me to Allen Square, and of course, she was the real driver for me returning to the city in 2007. All started by our early meeting in a high school French class.

When I applied to The Data Center, I had no idea how important of an organization it was to New Orleans. By the time I realized it, it was too late to turn back, but that didn't stop self-doubt from causing me to question whether I was ready for this. Then a friend of ours, who is also influential and well respected in local nonprofit and community spaces, told me, "You are exactly the person we need at The Data Center at this moment in time in New Orleans." From then on, I moved forward, trying to do the best job that I could in terms of not only advancing The Data Center's work, but also trying to get the value of its insights deeper into communities that needed data as a tool to fight for their needs, but who weren't aware of The Data Center as a resource or how to use it. I also believed it to be my job to push the envelope on what the data was telling us about New Orleans and what we needed to be a broadly more prosperous place.

Less than a year into my term as executive director, New Orleans celebrated its three-hundredth anniversary. To mark this occasion, we knew there would be celebrations about all the great things about our city, but that we might overlook the hardship that still existed here and miss the opportunity to commit to a better thirty years ahead than the three hundred years behind us. So, in the midst of celebration, The Data Center published *The New Orleans Prosperity Index*, a report focused on an oft overlooked dimension of prosperity in our region: inclusion.[20] At this point, not just in American culture but also in local culture, the idea that people are in poverty because of some set of wrong decisions they made—some individual set of failings—was still very common. This is opposed to understanding how the history of past decisions, policies, and behaviors and the broader collection of federal, state, and local policies that impact us all contribute to a person's present situation and outcomes in life. We knew that without this understanding, there was little chance that we would make decisions that would lead to the post-Katrina vision of a more prosperous city for all, not just recovery to the economically declining city we were before.

The Prosperity Index's primary research question was: "Have African Americans in New Orleans experienced increased economic inclusion since the end of the Civil Rights era?" It was a question that, as far as we knew, no one had ever tried to answer here in New Orleans, despite our high proportion of Black people in the city. Surely, as this large swath of the population goes, so goes New Orleans. We documented as many data points from 1980 up to about 2016 as we could, and overwhelmingly the data suggested Black people in New Orleans were either the same or, in some cases, worse off than in the years just after the civil rights movement. Despite all of our work, Black people had, at best, managed to just tread water while their white and Hispanic peers largely improved over the years.

---

20   The Data Center, *The New Orleans Prosperity Index: Tricentennial Edition*, New Orleans: Nonprofit Knowledge Works, 2018, https://www.datacenterresearch.org/reports_analysis/prosperity-index/.

These findings were met with resignation by some, validation by many, and anger by others. The people who were angry with The Data Center for publishing such a report were most surprising. Some felt this was bad timing, to publish a sobering report just as we were celebrating the splendor of our accomplishments. Others felt that we were just making the job of promoting the city unnecessarily hard. But a meaningful set of people felt despondent that they had worked their whole careers in pursuit of a better New Orleans, particularly for Black people, and all they had to show for it was the fact that we had treaded water for forty years. Being a New Orleans native and knowing people whose lives were reflected in the data, it pained me to experience these realizations as well. But it was a key moment for growth in the city. By showing data over time and across many systems, it made it painfully clear how we had failed our local brothers and sisters. We had focused too much effort on programs to fix individual bad circumstances and not enough doing the hard work to fix the underlying and hidden systems that influence everyday behavior and outcomes. Don't get me wrong—helping people out of bad situations, or helping one thousand people out of bad situations, is good work that we can all be proud of. But when your problem is, as with Ashleigh's earlier example, 38,600 people-big, you need more than good work: you need transformational work.

The Prosperity Index marked a moment in time to better understand what New Orleans needed for success, and it helped to change the way people think about the work they do, but it wasn't the only report that we've published since the tricentennial. By the time we arrived at post-Covid New Orleans, The Data Center had described the region and its strengths and weaknesses in just about every way that we could, and now people were asking, *Now that we know the problems, what do we do about them?* Fixing a problem is a much different exercise than simply pointing one out. Eventually we would land on the idea of wealth to both help concisely summarize the breadth of the issues and to lead the way to solutions. But for this work, when we referred to wealth, we would need to make it clear that we weren't talking about big cars and fancy houses or influence and affluence, or other typical things that come to mind when you hear the word.

Mechanically, wealth is the sum of all assets minus the sum of all debts. The related term "wealth gap" fundamentally describes differentiated access to the basic resources required to live and advance in today's economic context. But an expanded definition of wealth, based on what it enables and not merely its monetary properties, has the potential to better guide efforts to truly reduce the wealth gap. To realize this potential, we reframed wealth in New Orleans as a measure of one's ability to thrive—to weather emergencies and health shocks, to succeed through the foundation of stable housing and educational opportunities, to pursue investment and business opportunities as they arise, then to pass down resources and assets to future generations so that they, too, begin life with enough financial stability to thrive. In short, wealth is a quality-of-life measure that reflects one's ability to have viable choices and the agency to make reasonable decisions on behalf of one's family.

Whereas the data in *The Prosperity Index* could only broadly describe the different circumstances that groups of people live with, wealth is a powerful way to contextualize the problems communities face, clearing the path for data to better contribute to problem-solving. Indeed, many of the factors described above are readily quantifiable using existing data. Unfortunately, measuring how each of those elements contributes to overall individual or community success is hard. Wealth sidesteps this issue by condensing the social and economic successes and injustices of the past, uneven opportunities in the present, and hopes for a future of shared prosperity into a single calculation. From this perspective, wealth is a useful and easily understood way to sum up New Orleans' problems into a measurable construct. And because its components are well known, this data can point the way to specific actions that can be taken to solve wealth disparities. Importantly, it also provides clear guidance on the scale of problems and therefore the scale of required solutions. With this information, The Data Center is now providing the necessary tools for people to do transformational work, not just good work.

Conversations on the wealth gap often center on disparities by race, and for good reason, but our data suggests there is a significant element that goes beyond race. With the data we've produced, solutions can be better tailored to address specific circumstances that cause hardship for many in our region. As such, solving the wealth gap can be a unifying activity, bringing the shared prosperity necessary for all groups to perform at their utmost potential and fully participate in the economy. To be sure, the causes, solutions, and subsequent choices for solving social issues may differ across demographics, but the necessity of addressing them all remains the same. We need not be divided over ideas on improving lives in our region, but rather work together using tactics suggested by rigorous analysis of good data to the benefit of all.

Redesigning the Nation (Ashleigh)
I joined PolicyLink, a national research and action institute dedicated to advancing racial and economic equity, to learn how to deliver enduring change across systems, at scale. Founded and led by people of color, the organization has developed a clear understanding of what is required to build, launch, implement, and sustain successful racial equity policy initiatives through the delivery of over five billion dollars in racial equity policy wins over the last twenty-five years.

PolicyLink brings credibility across constituencies and deep expertise in the capacities needed to fuel policy change, including data and research, policy advocacy, communications and narrative change, movement-building, and implementation. Our local, state, and federal policy initiatives bridge innovations and ideas from social movements, government agencies, and influential corporations.

That said, I entered PolicyLink when the organization, like me, was acknowledging that its efforts were not achieving the scale, pace, or impact necessary to realize equity in this country. The people most impacted by inequity—people of color and the one hundred million folks who cannot make ends meet—were not experiencing substantial, increasing, and sustained benefits because of the organization's efforts. This was not due to a lack of inspired ideas or hard work. Instead, PolicyLink was confronting the reality that success at the scale of one hundred million people requires that we lift our gaze from incremental policy wins alone to the structures that undergird our democracy and economy.

Even before the United States became a nation, race and racial stratification were constructed to fuel the economy of the land. This hierarchy of human value shapes American democracy and capitalism. Consequently, racial disparities cannot be closed until systems and structures are redesigned to support everyone's flourishing. Because our democracy and economy were designed to value some lives more than others, I believe this generation's leadership charge is to redesign legal and regulatory structures to work for all.

This quest towards becoming a more effective leader in service to a more equitable nation has caused me to ask a new set of questions, not unlike those we asked when founding Christian Unity Baptist Church. What if the founding of this nation is an ongoing practice, not a one-time effort? What if it is our job to build on the original design? What core values are necessary to realize a flourishing multiracial democracy and equitable economy? What mindsets and skills are necessary? What kind of laws and regulations would be required? What must our institutions become?

These questions have called me to reconsider my role in the ecosystem. In the first twenty years of my career, I have cultivated skills as an institution builder. One of my strengths is establishing new organizations and transforming existing ones to drive systems change. If we get locked out of our church, let's found a new one. If we aspire to build new, community-led models for redevelopment in post-Katrina New Orleans, let's invest in the leadership skills of residents and meaningfully fund community organizations to drive redevelopment. If Black men are being excluded from good jobs and ownership opportunities, let's remake career and entrepreneurship pathways that prioritize family-sustaining wages and wealth for Black men. If we need a permanent institution to continue the work of economic inclusion, let's transform the local economic development organization to house the work.

I understand now that we not only need builders in the equity ecosystem but also planners and architects focused on the core values and governing infrastructure necessary to deliver a nation that works for all. These crucial roles are a gap in our movement. Without them, our program and policy interventions will not hold. New Orleans' post-Katrina recovery demonstrated the transformative power of people working together through organized networks to rebuild and redesign essential institutions. The persistent disparities across all systems—housing, health, education, transportation, and criminal-legal systems—serve as proof that we must also redesign the logic of our governing institutions to deliver for all. An evolution of our national and local identity calls for new values concerning the responsibilities of our governing institutions.

How would different values and new governing standards have changed post-Katrina decision-making and human-centered outcomes?

New values. Despite the promises made in this nation's founding documents—liberty and justice for all, for example—we advance and reward the values of individualism, scarcity, and competition. But imagine if we valued our collective flourishing. Instead of accepting the notion that there must be winners and losers, we would demand policies that support everyone's thriving. In fact, fundamental fairness, an expression of collective flourishing, is a constitutional requirement of the Fourteenth Amendment. If we were living up to this requirement, we would see our governing institutions at every level designing recovery investments that center people rather than negotiating market trade-offs, with a seemingly singular goal to limit profit losses to corporate entities.

My Katrina evacuation experience models this important distinction. Just imagine if the Johnson family considered the financial consequences of evacuating with more than just the five members of their biological family and decided to leave the rest of us to fend for ourselves? How would my experience of Katrina have changed? What physical, psychological, and emotional losses would I have suffered? Would I have been able to contribute to the rebuilding of my city, my community, our cultural institutions?

New governing standards. New values of collective flourishing and governmental compliance with a fundamental fairness requirement would not simply change how we relate to each other; this new way of being would change post-disaster outcomes, too. For example, the Federal Emergency Management Agency (FEMA), a unit within the US Department of Homeland Security, would be held accountable for making equitable investments across all affected neighborhoods. Instead, wealthier neighborhoods get more resources while poorer neighborhoods get less resources. Likewise, insurance companies would not be permitted to prioritize properties of the highest value.

Another example is reflected in the government's post-disaster valuation of property. After each disaster, the government sets compensation based on the historic value of the property rather than on the cost of rebuilding. How many times did we see homeowners receive $60,000 in compensation, based on the pre-disaster assessed value of their home, rather than the $180,000 that would be required to rebuild the same house on the same lot? Never mind the fact that the neighborhood where the house is located did not receive climate mitigation investments that were made in higher valued neighborhoods. We prioritize finance and banking industry profits over people and the protection of all communities.

Now imagine what New Orleans—one of the most creative cities in the world—could become if our governing institutions simply provided essential tools to all residents? A city rich with culture, with a thriving economy that works for everyone. Proud parents with good jobs and successful businesses that afford time with children and joyful connection with community. Healthy, happy children that experience the pleasure of learning and the comfort of supportive family, teachers, and friends. Communities with safe and affordable housing and reliable transit so plentiful that everyone can choose where and with whom they wanted to live.

One of the most frustrating realities of costly emergency response is that it proves that making substantial investments in core infrastructure is practical and financially feasible—if we truly wanted everyone in the city, in our nation, to be healthy and safe, to participate fully and succeed. If there's one key takeaway from our individual and shared journeys over the past twenty years, it's that love is enough. In fact, it's more than enough to rekindle a childhood relationship and raise a family, rebuild a city, and reimagine a world that delivers for all. Underneath rich data analyses and inclusive policies is a simple truth. The city we know New Orleans can be, the nation we know the United States can become is directly tied to our choice to love. That simple choice makes room for young leaders, new ideas, and communities that demand the best for all of us.

RIGHT TIME RIGHT PLACE:
Philanthropy Learns to Build Community

LINETTA GILBERT

The Premonition of a Storm
It was a crisp November day in 2004 when I sat in my office at the Ford Foundation in New York, a coffee cup cooling on my desk and my computer humming faintly beside me. I was supposed to be preparing for a meeting, but my attention was riveted to the TV in the corner of the room. The images on the screen were mesmerizing and horrifying: a wall of water, relentless and unyielding, surging over villages and cities in Southeast Asia. The sheer power of the tsunami that had struck Indonesia and other neighboring countries was devastating. Entire communities were erased in an instant. Families separated. Lives lost.

I couldn't look away. The video feed, grainy but raw with emotion, showed people running, shouting, crying. The sound of rushing water seemed almost louder than the voice of the reporter narrating the disaster. I could almost feel the heaviness in the air, the choking humidity of that tropical region disrupted by the chaotic roar of destruction. The faces on the screen—young, old, mothers clutching their children, fathers desperately searching for safety—burned themselves into my mind.

As I watched, something inside me stirred. I knew this devastation was thousands of miles away, yet it felt uncomfortably familiar. At that moment, seated in my office chair, staring at the screen, I had a chilling premonition: This could be New Orleans. This could be my hometown.

The thought sent shivers down my spine. I could almost picture it, as if the images from Southeast Asia were superimposing themselves onto the streets I knew so well. The French Quarter submerged, the old oak trees of City Park bowing under the weight of floodwaters, the vibrant shotgun houses of the 9th Ward reduced to debris. I tried to push the thought away, but it clung to me.

New Orleans had always been precariously perched, vulnerable to the whims of water. Growing up there, you learned to live with that ever-present threat. But this—this nightmare on the screen—was different. It wasn't just the water that scared me; it was the utter helplessness of it all. No number of levees, and no amount of preparation, seemed sufficient in the face of a force that could swallow entire cities.

The tsunami was a call to action for me. My portfolio at the Ford Foundation was entitled Community Philanthropy and Civic Culture. My first question to myself was, *What can I do for those communities?* My immediate response to myself was, *You can mobilize giving globally for those communities.* Within minutes, I was calling colleagues with interests in Southeast Asia and Eastern Africa, soliciting funding for those communities. One colleague, who headed the International Community Foundation based near San Diego, told me that the United Nations would match three dollars for every dollar raised for the region. So, I shared that information with Ford staff and other global foundations.

As I went through the motions of meetings and phone calls, the potential vision of New Orleans being hit by a Category Four or Five hurricane stayed with me. I didn't speak of it aloud, not even to my colleagues, but it haunted me. That night, as I walked back to my apartment in the city's brisk November air, the lights of Manhattan twinkling around me, I couldn't shake the feeling of foreboding.

Nine months later, my premonition became a reality. Hurricane Katrina made landfall, and the nightmare unfolded just as I had imagined—and worse. Watching it unfold from afar, and later being in the middle of it, felt surreal, like living in a déjà vu.

On the morning of August 29, 2005, I was at home in my apartment in Brooklyn. The day felt eerily quiet, but I was anything but calm. My husband and I had decided not to travel during my vacation time—I'd been on the road too much already. Instead, I had planned to rest and recharge. But rest was impossible that morning.

The night before, I'd heard the storm was heading straight for the Gulf Coast. My thoughts immediately turned to my daughter, living in New Orleans, and to close friends who felt more like family. I called them frantically, asking, "Are you leaving? Have you left? What's happening? Where are you going? How can I help?" Their voices, filled with uncertainty and urgency, stayed with me as I tried to sleep.

The next morning, as the news began to unfold, my heart sank. The storm had come, and it was worse than we'd feared. Sitting in my living room, glued to the television, I gripped the arms of my chair so tightly that my fingernails left marks in the fabric. I could do nothing but watch as the waters rose, submerging the place I called home—the streets, the neighborhoods, the lives intertwined with mine.

I couldn't ignore the bitter irony. Less than a year earlier, I'd sat in another chair in another room, watching the tsunami that devastated Indonesia and Southeast Asia. The waters were different, but the destruction and despair felt heartbreakingly familiar.

New Orleans, my community, was being washed away before my eyes. And from so far away, all I could do was sit and grieve for the soul of the city I loved. The images of my beloved city mirrored what I had seen in November 2004: desperate families, water consuming entire neighborhoods, chaos, and cries for help. It was as if the universe had warned me, and I hadn't known what to do with the warning.

How I came to love New Orleans and the Deep South

When we moved to New Orleans in the early 1980s, I was prepared for a lot of things: a new job for my husband Paul, new schools for our kids, and a fresh start for our family of four. What I wasn't prepared for was New Orleans itself. Don't get me wrong; I knew we were heading south. But coming from Washington, DC, I thought I already had a handle on Southern living; after all, DC sits below the Mason–Dixon line. Turns out, I didn't have the faintest idea of what the Deep South was really like, especially New Orleans. The city greeted me with its heat, its accents, its cuisine, and its culture, all so vibrant yet so different from what I'd known. I had to learn to navigate not just the streets and services of our new neighborhood, but the layers of history, tradition, and community that defined this city.

Paul's new role as personnel director for the civilian Navy office brought us to the Algiers section of the city, just across the Mississippi River from the famous French Quarter. We were outsiders, but from the moment we arrived, we were enveloped by a kind of warmth and hospitality I hadn't quite experienced before. Our neighbors welcomed us as though we were long-lost cousins. They offered us everything from red beans and rice to crawfish étouffée, dishes I couldn't even pronounce, let alone cook. I tried to make a pot of gumbo once and was gently told by a neighbor, "Bless your heart, sugar. Just buy some Zatarain's."

RIGHT TIME RIGHT PLACE:
PHILANTHROPY LEARNS TO BUILD COMMUNITY

The food was just the beginning of my initiation. Then there were the accents. In DC, people spoke with a kind of clipped precision, but in New Orleans, words stretched and bent like river reeds in the wind. I'd never heard "baby" used so generously. "How ya mama and dem?" wasn't just a casual question; it was a philosophy of life. I was fascinated and a little bewildered.

And let's talk about the culture for a moment—specifically the layers of Creole identity and colorism. Growing up, I thought I understood race in America, but New Orleans introduced me to a world of nuance. People proudly identified as Creole and seemed to have endless debates about ancestry, skin tone, and hair texture. "You're not just Black; you're Creole Black," someone explained to me one day. I nodded along, still trying to figure out the difference between a po' boy and a muffuletta.

But despite all the quirks and complexities, New Orleans began to grow on me. As we settled into our neighborhood, I threw myself into civic life. I joined the PTO and quickly became "that mom" who was at every bake sale and school meeting. My involvement didn't stop at the school gates. I saw how the community faced real challenges, from poverty to housing instability, and I wanted to be part of the solution.

Eventually, I took a position at the Housing Authority of New Orleans. That job opened my eyes to both the city's struggles and its resilience. I met families who had lived in New Orleans for generations, their roots as deep as those of the cypress trees in City Park. They shared their stories, their hopes, and sometimes their frustrations, but always with a sense of pride in their city.

And then there was Carnival. Oh, how I resisted Mardi Gras at first. I thought it was just a big, rowdy party for tourists. But during our first year in New Orleans, we joined our neighbors on a parade route, and I finally got it. Mardi Gras wasn't just a party; it was a celebration of survival, community, and joy. Beads, king cake, second lines—they were all part of the magic.

Looking back, I didn't realize I was falling in love with New Orleans as I stumbled through those early years. This city, with its gumbo of cultures, its contradictions, and its unyielding spirit, had quietly claimed me. New Orleans has a way of doing that—it lets you think you're just passing through, but before you know it, you're home.

My Evolution as a Community Activist in New Orleans

When we moved to New Orleans in the early 1980s, I could never have predicted how deeply I would become intertwined with the city's community and civic life. My journey as a community activist began almost by accident. Early on, I connected with a group of passionate early childhood education advocates. Together, we shared a vision for improving the lives of children across Louisiana, and our collaboration led to the founding of a state child advocacy organization called Agenda for Children. It was a bold name, but it reflected our collective commitment to giving every child a fair start.

That experience ignited something in me: a drive to be part of shaping a better future for New Orleans, not just for my family, but for everyone. My work with Agenda for Children caught the attention of others in the community, and I was honored to be appointed to the fledgling board of directors for what would eventually become the Louisiana Children's Museum. It was an exciting time, filled with ideas about how to create spaces where all children and families could come together to learn, play, and grow.

My activism expanded further when I took on the role of director of social and tenant services at the Housing Authority of New Orleans. For five years, I worked with families facing significant challenges who lived in public housing. My role was to understand their needs, amplify their voices, and help improve their communities. I also engaged with local leaders—those who held the power and resources to create change. Bridging these worlds, I learned how much each group could bring to the table when reimagining a city that worked for everyone, from those on the margins to those at the center of influence. That information was critical to the work that I did as a program officer and, later, as vice president for programs at the Greater New Orleans Foundation, our community foundation.

In these roles, I met people from every walk of life, cutting across socioeconomic, racial, and ethnic lines. Those interactions revealed the heart of New Orleans: a city rich in diversity, complexity, and resilience. It wasn't just the people; it was their shared determination and creativity that defined the soul of this place.

By the time Katrina and Rita struck, I had come to truly understand New Orleans—not just as a city, but as a collective spirit that refuses to be broken, no matter what the storm.

My Jolt into Action while at the Ford Foundation

When Hurricane Katrina struck the Gulf Coast, it exposed not only the physical vulnerabilities of the region but also the deep inequities that had long plagued communities in the Deep South. On August 30, 2005, as I sat in my Brooklyn apartment fielding calls from colleagues, family, and friends,

RIGHT TIME RIGHT PLACE:
PHILANTHROPY LEARNS TO BUILD COMMUNITY

I was tasked with a monumental responsibility by the president of the Ford Foundation: to help design a comprehensive philanthropic investment strategy for rebuilding and recovery. It was a question I had never faced before: how to serve and uplift not just New Orleans but the entire Gulf Coast, spanning more than one thousand miles of devastation.

I spent years as a program officer at the Ford Foundation, focusing on communities in the Deep South. My work was grounded in the belief that community was capable of extraordinary things when people came together with a shared purpose. This belief had driven my research, my investments, and my strategy for working in Southern communities, especially in Louisiana. I had worked to amplify voices that had been marginalized for too long, always guided by a humble understanding of what it means to serve. My roots in New Orleans and my understanding of its people made me uniquely equipped to take on this daunting role, even if I didn't feel fully prepared at that moment.

Katrina was a violent and decisive force, but it was also a turning point. In the aftermath, the community itself became a rallying cry, a force of resilience and reimagination. Howard Gardner's words about democracy and community echoed in my mind: that community is not just a physical place but a space where ordinary people come together to achieve the extraordinary.[21] That philosophy became my guiding principle as I worked to design a recovery strategy rooted in the strength and potential of the people themselves.

At the Ford Foundation, my job was to connect resources to needs, but it was also to see beyond the immediate disaster. The work wasn't just about rebuilding homes and businesses; it was about reclaiming the spirit of the Gulf Coast. This meant preserving culture, relationships, and values—elements that might not appear in a funding proposal but were vital to the soul of the region. I knew the people of New Orleans and Louisiana deeply, and I understood their resilience. They had endured centuries of inequities, yet they held fast to a culture that was as rich as any in the world. That spirit became the foundation for recovery efforts.

I also understood the stark inequalities that Katrina laid bare. The storm did not discriminate, but its impact was felt differently depending on who you were and what resources you had. For some, survival was a matter of having a credit card or cash to evacuate. For others, it meant navigating shelters and displacement in unfamiliar states. Those who lived in wealthier areas, often farther uptown, escaped the worst of the flooding. Meanwhile, those

---

21 J. W. Gardner, *On Leadership* (New York: The Free Press, 1990).

in poorer neighborhoods, like the Lower 9th Ward, lost everything. These disparities couldn't be ignored, and addressing them became central to the recovery work.

Investing in Young Leaders of the South During the Recovery

As a funder, I have always believed in the transformative power of community-based leadership, particularly among young people who possess the vision, drive, and lived experience to bring about meaningful change. After Hurricane Katrina, as the Gulf Coast began the long, arduous process of recovery, I saw a historic opportunity to invest in the very people who would shape its future: young leaders from the South, living and working below the Mason–Dixon line. These were leaders who had been historically overlooked and underinvested in, not because of any lack of talent or determination, but because of the entrenched divisions and biases that have long defined our nation's history. I embraced the idea of moving beyond recovery to transformation.

The North–South divide, rooted in the economic legacy of cotton wealth and the ideological battles of the abolitionist era, had left a deep cultural and economic chasm. For too long, Southern nonprofit leaders were dismissed or underestimated by national funders and institutions. The South was seen as a place to endure, not a place to innovate. But I knew differently. I knew the brilliance and resilience of the people in this region, and I understood that the key to a truly equitable recovery lay in trusting them to lead.

Katrina was a devastating equalizer, but it also offered a unique chance to reimagine the South. The storm had uprooted lives and revealed stark inequalities, but it had also cleared space for new and innovative ideas to emerge. The young leaders I met—visionaries working in local government, grassroots organizations, education, environmental justice, and community development—were not just rebuilding homes and businesses. They were rethinking what it meant to live and thrive in the Gulf Coast. Their ideas were bold, their approaches were creative, and their commitment to their communities was unshakable. These were not people looking for saviors; they were leaders waiting for investment.

It was humbling to be in a position to help resource these leaders. I was honored by the trust they placed in me—not just as a funder, but as someone who listened, who believed in their potential, and who could offer counsel when needed. I didn't see my role as one of directing their efforts but rather amplifying their voices, elevating their line of sight while leveraging private and public investments, enabling them to bring their visions to life.

In funding some of these newer, young leaders, I saw the opportunity to rewrite a narrative that had long diminished the South. This was about more than rebuilding—it was about creating a new foundation of equity, innovation, and self-determination. These leaders weren't just restoring what had been lost; they were building something entirely new, something that reflected the true spirit of the Gulf Coast. And I was deeply humbled to be a part of that journey. It reminded me, every day, of the resilience and brilliance of people who, given the chance, could transform not just their communities, but the very perception of the South itself.

Spiritually, I felt called to this role. I believed I was in the right place at the right time, not by coincidence but by a higher purpose. My deep connection to the region, my understanding of its struggles and strengths, and my role at the Ford Foundation aligned in a way that allowed me to be of service during one of the most critical moments in its history. It wasn't about me—it was about what I could offer to the community and its steps toward new community development.

Katrina and Rita forced people to confront the systems that had held them back and to imagine a future where those systems could be transformed. Recovery was not just about rebuilding what was lost but reimagining what could be. For many, this meant exploring new ways of living without losing the essence of their culture. For others, it meant forging connections across lines of class, race, and geography in ways they hadn't before.

The work was humbling, grueling, and deeply fulfilling. I witnessed the worst of what nature could do and the best of what people could be. The Ford Foundation's support became a bridge between those with resources and those who needed them most, and I was honored to help design that bridge. The Ford Foundation used its mission and philanthropic relationships to encourage philanthropy to re-consider investments in the American South.

The experience taught me that even in devastation, there is hope, and even in chaos, there is the possibility for transformation. For me, Katrina was not just a disaster; it was a call to action, and I was grateful to answer it.

Looking back, I think of that day in my office often. It taught me something profound about the interconnectedness of humanity. Watching a disaster on the other side of the world opened my eyes to the vulnerabilities of my own home. It reminded me that while the contexts may differ, the pain and resilience of people in the face of disaster are universal.

New Orleans, with all its quirks and contradictions, had quietly claimed a part of my heart. It wasn't a love born in an instant, but one that grew over time—a love for its people, its music, its food, and its unshakable spirit. Now, whenever I see communities devastated by storms, tsunamis, or any force of nature, I'm reminded of that August day and of Katrina's aftermath. The world is smaller than we think, and the waters that rise in one place will inevitably ripple across the globe, touching us all.

Lessons Learned from the Field

As I reflect on the role philanthropy has played in the South, particularly in New Orleans, I am filled with a sense of gratitude, hope, and possibility. The investments made in this region over the years—investments in people, ideas, and communities—have offered invaluable lessons about what it truly means to build for the future. Philanthropy, as a collective field, has often been criticized for moving too slowly or failing to take risks. But in the aftermath of disasters like Hurricane Katrina, we were forced to act boldly. And in doing so, we discovered that the South, so often dismissed or misunderstood, holds within it a reservoir of creativity, resolve, and vision that can reshape not only the region but the nation.

One of the most profound lessons has been the importance of investing in young leaders of color. These individuals, deeply rooted in their communities and committed to justice, are driving a new narrative for the South. For decades, young leaders in the Deep South were overlooked, their voices drowned out by historic inequities and systemic barriers. The South's legacy of racism, segregation, and economic exclusion often kept these leaders from accessing the resources and platforms they needed. Yet they remained steadfast, envisioning a better future for their communities.

When philanthropy began to center social justice and racial equity in its Southern strategies, the results were transformative. Supporting these young leaders has not only created the next generation of leaders but has also provided a powerful testament to what is possible when resources are aligned with vision. These investments are not just about money; they are about trust—trusting leaders to define their needs, to drive their own solutions, and to speak to the unique challenges and opportunities of the South.

The insights gained from this work are clear. First, investing in young leaders of color builds the capacity for a new generation of leadership that is bold, innovative, and unapologetically committed to equity. These leaders are rewriting the narrative of the South, challenging outdated stereotypes, and articulating a vision for what their communities can become. Second, philanthropy has learned that transformation happens not in isolation but through relationships—when funders step back and allow communities to lead. Finally, this work has shown that the South, and particularly New Orleans, is not just a region of need but a region of solutions.

As I worked in the Gulf Coast region, I learned that the resources I had leveraged for communities in Southeast Asia and East Africa went to the big nongovernmental organizations such as the Red Cross, the Red Crescent, and other European-based organizations, not to small, community-based organizations. There were few such organizations that were considered capable of handling the investments. That also meant that people who worked to rebuild their communities were rarely able to develop consistent community leadership with resources to manage the next challenge that their community might face.

The implications are profound. By investing in these leaders, we are not only addressing the injustices of the past but also laying the groundwork for a future that is more equitable and inclusive. These young leaders have something to say about the South, and their voices are reshaping how philanthropy engages with this region. They remind us that leadership is not about proximity to power but about proximity to people—and the courage to serve them.

For me, these lessons are deeply personal. I have seen what happens when leaders are given the tools to succeed, when their visions are supported rather than stifled. It is a reminder that philanthropy's greatest role is not to lead but to follow—to listen, to invest, and to believe in the extraordinary potential of people and communities. In the American South, particularly in New Orleans, we are witnessing that potential come to life. And it is nothing short of inspiring.

SANKOFA JOURNEY CONTINUUM
CHERICE HARRISON-NELSON & HERREAST HARRISON

Cherice: No need to close my eyes to remember hearing the urgent knocking at my door on August 26, 2005. It was my brother, Donald, who'd come to stress the importance of evacuating—not with his normal cool and debonair demeanor, but rather a look of fear of what was headed our way; it almost, to me, seemed like a horror movie scene. Although I lived in his upstairs house, he stressed it wasn't safe for me to stay. He wanted to know if I'd made arrangements for our mother and sister. Brian, my son, who'd urged us to leave earlier, had flown out the day before to the Dallas–Fort Worth area.

I was dating Teohosa "Dada" Idahosa from Benin City, Nigeria. He kept encouraging me to make reservations at the Hyatt Hotel in Houston, Texas, a hotel he was certain would accommodate dogs just in case we would need to evacuate with my sister and her fur baby, Pookie. I had, but I was still undecided. After all, I lived in an upstairs house, and my sisters, nephews, and parents had waited out a previous Hurricane Andrew threat. My son evacuated with his father, Dalton Nelson, to a hotel in downtown New Orleans. He'd survived his home flooding as a teenager during Hurricane Betsy in 1965 and did not want to chance his son's safety. The Hurricane Andrew shelter-in-place event hadn't been so bad; the power went out, we cooked up the food in the refrigerator, and we laughed at my dad's adamant remarks about being safe and not afraid before we convinced him to leave the home he purchased in September of 1965, the date of act-of-sale. The house, located in the Upper 9th Ward, flooded, and our family was not able to move until December of 1965.

The approaching Hurricane Katrina was different. We were blessed to have a new vehicle, courtesy of my son, to evacuate in. He'd won a Lincoln Navigator in an online contest for the movie *Are We There Yet?* in February of 2005, presented by the star of the movie, Ice Cube, in Los Angeles, California. My personal car was inadequate to accommodate my mother, Dada, sister, Michele, and her large Labrador Retriever. Michele would have been reluctant to leave her fur baby, my mom would have stayed with her, and I would have stayed with my mom if it were not for Brian's blessing of a new, full-sized SUV.

We left midday on August 27, 2005. I do not remember who, but someone called to check on me and informed me to take Jefferson Highway rather than the interstate to North Louisiana and then a junction over to another highway to I-10. I missed the junction, and we ended up in Jasper, Texas, almost out of gas and 124 miles off course. Jasper was the location of the brutal death of James Byrd Jr., who was terrorized and murdered by three men by being tied to the back of a pickup truck and driven around until he died of dismemberment. We finally arrived, due to my sister generously driving miles to Houston after almost a full day of traveling.

After bathing and getting settled into our rooms, we watched the television to keep abreast of the situation in New Orleans. It was not good! The anxiety of witnessing wind and sheets of rain pounding the city, the Superdome's ceiling being compromised, reports of residents being trapped in their homes, and an overall feeling of helplessness. The next morning, as news crews were surveying the damage, reports of citizens assisting each other were caught on camera. I remember one of a young man in a white T-shirt rolling an elder woman in a shopping cart to safety. Those young men in white T-shirts were, and continue to be, unheralded on-the-ground soldiers and heroes.

Later reports showed aerial views of familiar locations, such as the Circle Food Store in the 7th Ward, and of what seemed like the whole city submerged under water. It was difficult to hear reports of residents trapped in their homes and on rooftops. The United States Coast Guard carried out, in my opinion, some of the most efficient rescues of families on rooftops and other elevated locations by helicopter. We spent days watching the devastation in awe—and the failure of the federal government to first have a proactive plan in place for the evacuation of New Orleans residents (this includes pets); further, the lack of an efficient, humane after-event plan to provide basic human needs of food and shelter was catastrophic. Later in the year, I worked with children who witnessed death, endured lack of food, and had no usable restroom facilities at the Louisiana Superdome, New Orleans Convention Center, and elevated portions of the I-10 Interstate. Their trauma was real!

One morning, when I could not endure watching television news reports, I went to the hotel coffee shop to chill by myself, hoping to clear my mind and muster the strength to be the family coordinator of our own survival mission as we all hemorrhaged money on our fifth day in Houston at the Hyatt Hotel. The hotel served as a base camp for search and rescue crews from California, who were trained for wildfire disasters. One remark by a firefighter with a beautiful golden Labrador Retriever lying at his feet that I overheard made me really realize the devaluing of the lives of human citizens of New Orleans: "I don't want to be here sipping coffee at the Hyatt! We are sitting here watching a search and rescue mission turn into a search and recovery mission. The government is not for the people!"

Amidst the loss of human life, ways of life, homes, and property, I thought of our cultural artifacts. We packed my dad's last suit and those of other family members in suitcases, evacuated with some, and left others in family cars at a parking lot across the street from City Hall. Those cultural items were important to us as a family, to my family's legacy and our collective memory of my father, Big Chief Donald of the Guardians of the Flame. Members of the Harrison family have participated in the Carnival Day cultural tradition referred to by some as masking Indian. Our group embraces the identifier of a "maroon society." My father said the tradition began as an homage to the mutual kinship and quest for freedom in America by the people who were here when America was "discovered" and the people were stolen from their ancestral home of Africa, sold, and held as property to work on forced labor camps (plantations) and in other jobs of servitude as enslaved human beings. The tradition metamorphosizes the hypocrisy of a country built on the ideals of freedom, yet so willing to institutionalize taking the freedom of some away by limiting their freedom of movement, spiritual practices, language, grieving rituals, foodways and by asserting domain over their bodies and reproductive choices—among other dehumanizing practices—into a self-actualizing expression of celebratory and joyous beauty, one that includes hand-beaded original ceremonial attire, featherwork, ritual, community-based interactive processions, sacred call-and-response chants, percussive rhythms, and theater.

I met Catherine Flowers, who worked in then Lt. Governor Mitch Landrieu's office prior to August 29, 2005. She had given me her card and told me, as the curator and co-founder of the Mardi Gras Indian Hall of Fame, if I ever needed anything, to simply call her. Well, I called and explained that we had several suits (original art, Carnival Day attire) parked in cars and stored in our homes that we wanted to retrieve if possible, due to their historical and cultural value. She quickly arranged a Louisiana State Police escort from Baton Rouge to New Orleans for us. It was affirming to have our culture respected and deemed worthy of saving. When we met with Louisiana State Police Captain Clarence Landrum, who directed our escort into the city, one of the officers warned us, "Your car may have been stolen by someone after the storm." My immediate response was, "Not stolen, but seized to ensure survival, which, if that is the case, I'm elated. Life over things every day, all day."

As we approached the city, the new normal smell of New Orleans gently permeated the car and increased until it was almost unbearable. It was a smell like no other—the smell of death, human excrement, rotting garbage, and what then seemed like hopelessness. The city was quiet—quiet, quiet! Streets were void of cars, the sky was birdless, no movement of anything as we approached the public parking lot near City Hall. Our cars were parked on the third floor, and when we got out, we hit the key fobs and heard the familiar sound of the doors of the cars unlocking. Both cars were parked where we'd left them, and the suits and other family items of historical value were still in the trunks. Praises to the Creator. We were then led in a caravan to my house uptown in the Broadmoor area. On the way, we passed the Superdome. The street was strewn with the remnants of survival and young National Guardsmen with rifles who looked like they were barely old enough to vote.

As we approached my house, my heart began to beat faster. There were occasional visual reminders of the devastation, of what was not salvageable. It was a sad sight indeed. Being a teacher of young children, I was actually elated to see refrigerators taped shut with rows of duct tape. Some had the words "Do Not Open" spray-painted on them. I naively thought this was solely a safety precaution for children. I later learned refrigerators contained two-week-old food that had sat in hot, humid conditions, not something one wanted to see or smell.

My house is a few feet off of the ground; the watermark was waist-high on me. When I turned the key, we had to push the door to enter the living room. It was unrecognizable: furniture had floated throughout the first floor, the refrigerator was on its side, and the God-awful Katrina smell was inescapable. We gathered what we could from upstairs, packed the cars, and headed back to Houston for the next chapters of this thing called life.

Collectively, my mother and I have experienced the gamut of human emotions: joy, calmness, sadness, grief, despair, anger, fear, disgust, relief, and, I reluctantly admit, pride in achievement. Our journey to recovery continues, but along the way, we have had several events that are notable. Here is a list of highlights:

- When Katrina hit, my son, Brian, was in his last semester of college at the University of New Orleans. He completed one week of the fall 2005 semester. He vividly recalls the announcement by Mayor Ray Nagin: "This is not a drill, this is the real one, and if you don't leave, you probably won't survive." Well aware of the potential danger from a science class the previous semester, which detailed what would happen to the city in the event of the direct hit of a Category Four or Five hurricane, Brian warned us, bought a ticket that night, and left the following day. He was able to enroll in the HBCU Texas Southern University, complete the requirements for a degree in communication, and graduate with his parents, grandmother, and brother in attendance in a ballroom at the Hilton Hotel. He went on to earn an MFA in cinematic arts from the University of Southern California. His industry mentor was the late Jonathan Demme, Academy Award–winning director of *The Silence of the Lambs*.

- I was invited by the late John O'Neal to join the People's Hurricane Relief Fund and Oversight Committee, an activist group dedicated to getting resources directly into the hands of New Orleanians. Being a member provided me with valuable resources, beginning with training at the Penn Center by civil rights activists from throughout the Gulf South and country, including the late Chokwe Lumumba, who would become a mentor and hero to me. He later was elected the mayor of Jackson, Mississippi. The group included Malcolm Suber, Shana griffin, Curtis Muhammad, and others.

- At the invitation of Jewel Bienville Jackson, fourth-grade teacher at Joseph Maggiore Elementary, my mother and I worked to develop an arts project collectively with the Newcomb Network, the People's Hurricane Relief Fund and Oversight Committee, the Women's Reconstruction Network, based in Oakland, California, and other groups. The result was a quilt with children's drawings, beadwork-embellished patches by my mother, and a book of writings based on the Language Experience Approach, which teaches that children enhance their writing skills through creating narratives from their life experiences. The children wrote and drew pictures ranging from their lives before August 29, 2005, to their experiences during the event, to the world they envisioned for themselves in the future. The project concluded with a celebratory unveiling and was featured in a June 11, 2006 *Times-Pica-*

yune East Jefferson Bureau article titled "Work of Art," by Christine L. Bordelon. In 2007, the quilt was acquired by the Louisiana State Museum system and held in its permanent collection. Each child received a personal letter of thanks, as requested by my mother.

- In 2006, my mother established the Donald Harrison Sr. Book Club in memory of my father, who read over forty books a year and gave books as gifts. The book program started with community events and at Albert Wicker, the school where I temporarily worked as a Art Teacher. It included an indigenous cultural arts presentation, a celebrity reader (Clarke Peters of HBO's *Treme*, Adella Gautier, NBA basketball players, and local actors Chakula cha Jua and Donald Lewis), and the gift of a new book to each student in the school. The program expanded to sixteen partner schools at one time. Now, my mother and I are both older and have reduced the scope of the program to children enrolled in our youth programs. These children serve as Donald Harrison Sr. museum ambassadors of culture and literature. Each child is given a budget to purchase books for their classmates and select an artist from our faculty roster to co-present a cultural program. It is our goal to enhance their leadership and artistic expression as well as plant seeds of activism for literacy and philanthropy by modeling giving. They co-present books to their peers with my mom.

- Rebecca Mark, the interim director of the Newcomb Institute at Tulane University, developed an initiative to bring queens from the Black masking Carnival tradition together by providing space for panels, celebratory gatherings, resources, and information-sharing in 2006. The initiative included assisting me with ghostwriting grants and the development of a network of supporters. This also led to a *Times-Picayune* feature story by Alison Fenderstock on the queens, along with profiles on five queens, including youth participant Malon McGee and myself.[22]

---

22   Alison Fensterstock, "Malon McGee, Little Queen of the Young Guardians of the Flame Mardi Gras Indians, sews after school," NOLA.com (New Orleans, LA), Feb. 28, 2014, https://www.nola.com/entertainment_life/music/malon-mcgee-little-queen-of-the-young-guardians-of-the-flame-mardi-gras-indians-sews/article_0fc8b2a3-cfe1-5dff-a2a1-52a9e399f063.html.

- The Louisiana Cultural Economy was established to assist artists with their diverse needs after Katrina; grants were available to artists in the impacted areas of the state. After ghostwriting grants for a few elder Indians, news of the grants spread throughout the Black Masking Indian community. The sudden surge in requests for assistance with submitting an application was overwhelming! At the time, I lived in an apartment over Ashé Cultural Arts Center, and it became common practice for Indians to appear in the parking lot, call, and ask me to write a grant on their behalf. Rebecca Mark was my lifeline! She encouraged me to make a check-off template and spaces for standard biographical responses, which streamlined the grant-writing process to about forty-five minutes per application. By the end of the grant period, over ninety artists had received grants, and each had a basic resumé for future applications—a one hundred percent success rate. It was a grueling task; everything else in my life was put on hold. I developed pneumonia, was bedridden after the process and physically and mentally exhausted. The project ended my pursuit of a PhD in cultural anthropology from UNO. "What happens to a dream deferred?" Yes, mine did "dry up like a raisin in the sun...."[23] In addition to the Louisiana Cultural Economy Foundation, grants were also ghostwritten to the Contemporary Arts Center, New Orleans, the Arts Council of New Orleans, and the New Orleans Jazz & Heritage Foundation Community Partnership Grants program, with a better than 95 percent funding rate.

- In times of tragedy, there are individuals who engage in unscrupulous business practices for the sole purpose of defrauding the most vulnerable out of the insurance funds allocated to repair their homes. Post–August 29, 2005 was no different. My mother was the victim of contractor fraud. She trusted a local contractor who began his deception by sharing stories about his family's work ethic and dedication to improving the lives of citizens of the region by providing low-cost, quality repairs as well as service through elected positions at the state and federal levels. She was defrauded of $57,000.[24]

---

23 Langston Hughes, "Harlem," Poets.org, Academy of American Poets, accessed June 11, 2025, https://poets.org/poem/harlem-0.
24 Becky Bohrer, "Contractors ruin the ruined in Katrina's wake," *The Seattle Times* (Seattle, WA), Aug. 26, 2008, https://www.seattletimes.com/nation-world/contractors-ruin-the-ruined-in-katrinas-wake/.

- In 2006, we made plans to bring the Young Guardians of the Flame group out on Carnival Day at the urging of Dana Roy, mother of Little Chief Kevin, who had dressed for the first time in 2004 at the age of two. That year, Kevin was featured on the front page of *The Wall Street Journal* and, along with Little Queen Nadia, the metro section of the local *Times-Picayune*. Other children joined the family group, and by 2010, we had a membership of ten children. Within two years, they were being requested to perform all over the city of New Orleans as well as at the University of North Carolina. A highlight for the children and their parents was an invitation to close out the Super Love Festival at the Superdome. My babies, in my absence, received a standing ovation. Their participation was solely due to V [then Eve Ensler] and Carol Bebelle having faith in them as representatives of our future, a bright one, one that must be focused on the legacy we guard and pass on to our precious children. The Young Guardians continue to enjoy community support. They have been featured in numerous print and television reports as well as documentaries and books. They were filmed for an upcoming Netflix documentary and are prominently featured in the award-winning documentary *Guardians of the Flame*, filmed by Daniel Wolff and the late Jonathan Demme and produced by Brooklyn Demme, Brian Nelson, and Marta Renzi.

- Along with Little Queen Malon McGee, I participated in a procession for the V-Day performance at the New Orleans Arena. Malon experienced the aftermath of "the event" first at a hotel in New Orleans East, then at the New Orleans Convention Center, on I-10, and finally in relocation to Houston. When she first entered the Young Guardians program at the age of seven, she was a reluctant participant, often holding her head down and rarely making direct eye contact. During her tenure as a Young Guardian of the Flame, Malon grew in confidence, public speaking, and leadership. She proudly tells the story of the day she had a life-changing moment at seven or eight years old: "I used to be shy until I got my makeup done at V-Day with Eve Ensler [sic] and Jane Fonda. It was so much fun. They put Miss Nelson out the room because only three people could be in the room at a time." This is true, but when my mother came backstage and saw me waiting outside of the door, she went in anyway to check on our little queen and found her laughing with Eve and Jane as though they were best buddies.

• It was common for people to want to see the devastation caused by "the event." Some were truly concerned and wanted to spread light and do good. Others were opportunists who sought to enrich themselves off of the suffering of the survivors. Still others were voyeurs, trauma-porn observers: "show me your trauma, suffering, and life devastation."

• The Young Guardians of the Flame, under the direction of Big Chief Brian Nelson, were fortunate to engage individuals who were truly concerned about the well-being of children. Visitors included renowned photographer and then clinical professor at The University of Texas at Austin School of Journalism Eli Reed, world-renowned musical artists and relatives Donald Harrison Jr. and Chief Xian aTunde Adjuah [then Christian Scott], filmmaker Jonathan Demme, Alvin Ailey artistic director Judith Jamison, and actor Cameron Diaz, to name a few. Each of the aforementioned in their own way extended acts of kindness and generosity to children in our group and the city, acts unknown to the public, at their request. The first to approach me was the late Clyde Woods of the University of California. He organized a book drive and collected over sixteen thousand dollars to purchase books that were given to children in partnership with my mother, through the Donald Harrison Sr. Book Program.

• Shifting paradigms of power and mutual respect from hierarchical models to models that are lateral, mutual, and collaborative is something I've advocated for based on my civil rights and artist-activist training, lead in part by John O'Neal, and my home training by my parents, Herreast and Donald Harrison Sr. This shift continued when Clyde Woods, PhD, listed me as a co-writer of the article "Upholding Community Traditions: An Interview with Cherice Harrison-Nelson" in the September 2009 edition of the academic journal *American Quarterly*. His actions were based solely on our conversations around appropriation, the co-opting of "everything basically" for other folks' projects: "my book," "my article," "my script," "my picture," "my documentary," "my TV show"—you get the picture. Where was the space for the subjects to have ownership of themselves, their bodies, their stories, their artistic expressions, their lived experiences? When was the modern-day colonial practice of owning the fruits of people's trauma, grief, and terror metamorphosed into joy going to end?

Dr. Woods' actions began a movement with future projects for me. Some entities were willing to be co-producers. It benefits established institutions to partner with small, community-based ones and with artists in the creation of works and projects. Larger institutions truly can provide the sharing of resources, both human and financial. Smaller institutions receive ancillary benefits that can be leveraged for future support, opportunities to be in spaces and positions of leadership with well-respected institutions. An example of a collaboration that has worked well is the one with WWOZ 90.7 FM that formally began when the late David Freeman was the general manager. Dee Lindsey, artist liaison and manager of special projects, proposed a calendar featuring queens. Dave Ankers, director of content at the station, agreed to a partnership with the Mardi Gras Indian Hall of Fame as a co-producer, rather than simply a thanked organization. Since then, the station has collaborated on archiving projects and produced several mini documentaries and memorial tributes on members of the Black Masking Indian tradition.

As an artist, I am currently working on more than one project with the New Orleans African American Museum. Executive director Gia Hamilton is guiding projects that include me as a full-fledged partner with institutional support and financial resources. I have been humbled and honored and look forward with great anticipation to this being truly life-changing for me as an activist-artist. Chief Equity & Executive Officer Asali Eccesiastes, of Efforts of Grace/Ashé Cultural Arts Center, is creating a model for true collaboration with the newly established A.C.E. (Alliance for Cultural Equity) by creating a coalition of small community arts organizations to leverage funding opportunities, professional development, and collaborations.

- The Donald Harrison Sr. Museum is located in the Upper 9th Ward area of the city. It is a testament to my mother's sense of hope, determination, and sheer tenacity to do something to, to quote her, "make a footprint." She calls the museum an "eyeball" one: "you can eyeball the collection in its totality while standing in the doorway." The museum, designed by Scott Ruff, has a square footage of only eight hundred feet, but it is the epicenter of good work that spreads far and wide. Built with a one hundred thousand dollar grant from the Tulane City Center and constructed under the leadership of Emilie Taylor Welty, it sits on two lots owned by my mother behind her home. On any given Sunday afternoon, the day our children's programs are held, the spaced is filled with the laughter of children, bounce-inspired chants led by my son, Big Chief Brian Nelson of the Guardians of the Flame, call-and-response chants in Kikongo led by Papa Titos, jazz riffs by my brother Donald Harrison Jr., or stretch music by my nephew, Chief Xian aTunde Adjuah. The museum is home to the Donald Harrison Sr. Book Program, Throwback Thursday programs for neighborhood elders, featuring music from the 1960s with a communal meal, and ice cream sundae parties and book readings for children. It is a destination for intergenerational fun and happiness. It is also a place of history that honors the memory of my mother's late husband, Donald Harrison Sr., and our collective family history. In addition to the ceremonial attire on exhibit, my mom has documents of historical merit neatly archived in presentation binders for visitors to peruse.

- In November of 2005, my son, Big Chief Brian Nelson, led a delegation of Carnival Day dress artists along with percussionist Luther Gray on a Jazz at Lincoln Center coordinated "thank you" tour to India, United Arab Emirates, and Sri Lanka. The tour made stops in countries that offered financial assistance to the Greater New Orleans area after August 29, 2005 by providing area musicians an income-earning opportunity and a chance to break the mental and physical effects of life after the "event." It was indeed a healing and stress-free experience thanks to our tour manager, Jackie Harris.

This was not the only event that had a focus on reaching out to survivors. Others included the International Festival in New Haven, Connecticut, a tour and exhibition for me at the Marie and Louis Pasteur University in Besançon, France, and a ride on the specially created Magic of Mardi Gras float in the Rose Parade, as well as speaking engagements at Columbia and Georgetown Universities, to name some. We remain grateful to the individuals who had the vision and compassion to reach out to artists from New Orleans with opportunities to earn income and enjoy wellness breaks.

I use quotes, adages, and sayings regularly. I quote my grandmother, parents, Mr. Ike, Chief Joseph Jenkins, and myself. "Go with what you know"—Donald Harrison Sr. "Don't trouble trouble, and trouble won't trouble you"—Grandmother Mattie, from a Br'er Rabbit tale. "That's a fact, Jack"—Chief Joseph Jenkins. And my cancer journey take-away: "Don't sweat the small stuff, and when you're fighting for your life, it's all small stuff."

My cancer journey was life-changing and, in an unorthodox manner, a blessing, in that it caused me to reevaluate my life priorities and conceptualize how I wanted to live my remaining years. I am grateful for every day that the Creator blesses me with the ability to open my eyes. However, I am focusing on finding personal joy. Joy cannot be given by others, but it can be a road map provided by well-meaning friends or family.

Throughout my African studies at Southern University in New Orleans, I encountered the phrase "the Door of No Return." I did not have the mental framework to truly understand the literal meaning. Somehow, I thought it was a collective metaphor used to describe the door from which my ancestors were stolen, forcibly taken from their homes and savagely transported to the so-called New World as chattel for the inhumane practice of human trafficking for wealth accumulation. In a preparatory session with Dr. Phanuel Egejuru for the 1994 Fulbright study group whose research she facilitated in Ghana and Senegal, she gave group members a historical map with castles (in my world, also known as torture chambers, prisons, places of unrest, and purgatory) and forts that dotted the West African coastline, often appearing to overlap one another. It was only then that I understood the magnitude of the inhumane foundation of the building of America and other geographic locations dependent on the forced labor of Black bodies.

The Door of No Return is both literal and metaphorical and, for me, the personification of Èṣù/Elegua/Papa Legba. This Orisha guides the crossroads of destiny. For me, once you have passed through the door of no return, you will never go back to the way it was—it is impossible, everything is changed: the trajectory of your life path, your confidence in tomorrows, your faith in humanity, the air you breathe, what sustains your life, spiritual practices, the list goes on and on and on.

When I left my home on August 27, 2005, the school where I taught, Oretha Castle Haley Elementary School, the Harrison family home, the grocery where I shopped, and even my vehicle—nothing would be the same when I returned. The first floor of my home was compromised with waist-high water; the watermark at our family home was a few inches from the ceiling. The corner grocery where the butcher cut chickens and made sausage was flood-damaged as well. The school took on a minimal amount of flood water and served as a shelter of refuge for neighborhood residents. My neighborhood normally had a soundscape of young children playing, teenagers' hearty laughter, and church bells tolling. Now, there were no smells of foods cooking from Latin American neighbors, Creole dishes, or the ever-present garlic-stuffed roast on Sundays. We all have scents that may seem odd but offer familiarity and comfort. Mine: the scent of the laundromat around the corner. I looked forward to the warmth of Tide-, Gain-, Bounce-, and Downy-filled air on the corner of Elba and S. Salcedo Streets.

New Orleans seemed dead when I returned with a special Louisiana State Museum police escort to retrieve sacred Carnival Day dress attire. There were no birds flying, no green grass, insects, or any other forms of life once you left the epicenter of New Orleans, the French Quarter and CBD. There, it was like a party! Contractors and their crews in hotels with coolers on the sidewalks drinking beer, barbequing, with loud laughing and Gomer Pyle looks of joy. A *tale*gate party of sorts, full of tales of all of the federal dollars being racked up in their coffers.

As I looked at the children in Congo Kids and the Young Guardians of the Flame Maroon Society at the nineteenth annual Katrina Commemoration, I felt both joy and overwhelming sadness. My babies, ranging in age from four to twelve years old, were honoring the lives of citizens who perished in an event that occurred before they were born. Yet, almost by osmosis, their young, innocent bodies moved in reverence to the lives loss and simultaneously with joy as they sang a sacred Kongolese chant, under the direction of Papa Titos Sompa, and "This Little Light of Mine" as a congregational song, one they learned from Wendi Moore-O'Neal.

On November 16, 2024, they appeared as Steampunks inspired by Engineering NOT (STEAM) education, with the "punk" representing Perpetual Universal New Knowledge Stars. Just as steampunks represent what is sometimes referred to as neo-Victorian, the children are simultaneously embracing the past and their future as luminaries.

Looking forward—
"[E]verybody can be great, because everybody can serve."[25]
— Dr. Martin Luther King Jr.

---

25   Martin Luther King Jr., "The Drum Major Instinct," in *A Knock at Midnight: Inspiration from the Great Sermons of Reverend Martin Luther King, Jr.*, ed. Clayborne Carson and Peter Holloran (New York: Warner Books, 2000), 182.

Herreast: New days bring new hope. As I look forward to the future, at eighty-seven years old, I am certain there are others like me who want to leave a mark, make a path of ease for individuals desirous of being in service to others, and navigate the world as a vessel of possibility. The Donald Harrison Sr. Museum is located on land behind my home. The Young Guardians of the Flame and Congo Kids meet weekly on Sunday afternoons. It gives me immense joy to watch them learn from my family, continental Africans, and artists of local and national merit. The children come from diverse backgrounds, but play, learn, and work together effortlessly on cultural expressions from the African and American diasporas to present to audiences at local and national events.

Their most recent appearance was at LUNA Fête, a community light festival hosted by Arts New Orleans in downtown New Orleans. The children studied futurism and time-traveling based on STEAM (Science Technology, Engineering, Art and Math) principles. The children worked collaboratively with their parents to add elements of light to their attire to make a grand entrance at the festival as Steampunks and Yemaya mermaids. They were joined by adults in their procession, but they led and lit the way.

Their presentation was symbolic of what we, as a community of elders, in my opinion, must do. We are obligated to pour into young people what we know about how to advance equity and justice for all people, to be rooted in "something"—in other words, knowing you come from something and being obligated to guard, carry, and pass it, the flame, on to those coming behind you with intentionality and love.

Children are our future. May it be filled with joy and hope for all.

BUCK IT UP, BUTTERCUP
SHARON HOWARD

"Ms. Howard, can you come down to the receptionist desk? We have a worker under your supervision who reported to work with a crochet top and a crochet skirt (basically a see-through outfit) wearing no undergarments."

"Ms. Howard, can you come down to the receptionist desk? A large black funeral wreath was delivered and addressed to one of your employees with the following message on the card: 'Stop messing with my husband or else.'"

"Ms. Howard, can you report to interview room number one? We have an applicant for disability assistance who refuses to complete his redetermination of eligibility interview without his support animal: a live, multicolored snake that's around his neck and draping over his shoulders."

My career as a BA, MSW social worker has been a treasure trove of challenges. So it is no surprise to me that on the morning of August 29, 2005, I found myself in the Office of Public Health (OPH) Emergency Operation Center (EOC) in Baton Rouge, Louisiana, as the assistant secretary responsible for protecting the public health of all Louisiana citizens. My husband, Wayne, was also working in the OPH EOC in his capacity as an information technology officer.

August 29, 2005 was the day that Hurricane Katrina made landfall. August 29 was also our thirty-fifth wedding anniversary. I remember leaning over to Wayne while he worked on OPH computers and asking him if he knew what day it was. He quickly replied, "No," to which I responded, "It's our anniversary," to which he replied in his direct, loving, and irreverent way: "Shit, Sharon. Happy anniversary."

"Coincidence is God's way of remaining anonymous" is a quote often attributed to Albert Einstein. Coincidence, to me, is God's way of showing up and showing out to help us navigate difficult times.

Wayne, my mother, and my father being in close proximity to me, plus my two adult daughters not living in New Orleans, allowed me to focus, navigate, and exercise OPH's response to and recovery from Hurricane Katrina.

My family's safety was a coincidence (God working) and my North Star and haven in the darkness and despair of Hurricane Katrina.

So, let me back up to August 27, 2005 to start the timeline that landed me smack dab in the middle of the OPH EOC on August 29, 2005.

The morning of August 27, 2005, I was in the hair salon with my fellow Breakfast Club ladies getting my hair done.

I have always called my weekly salon visit my mental health therapy session: talking with my friends about what was going on in the world and in our community. Placing my head in my stylist's sink . . . feeling the caress of the warm water along with a firm but gentle massaging of my scalp, literally and figuratively washing the troubles of the week away . . . preparing me to embrace the upcoming week with a replenished spirit.

It was around 8:00 a.m., and I was under the dryer with my conditioner when I got a call from Dr. Jimmy Guidry, the state health officer. I stepped outside in the parking lot (with my conditioner cap on my head) and joined the statewide conference call.

I was told that the OPH EOC had been activated. I was instructed to pack a go-bag for three days and report to the EOC in Baton Rouge as soon as possible because New Orleans was in the path of a Category Three to Five hurricane: Katrina.

I went back into the salon and advised all present to evacuate if possible because the approaching Hurricane Katrina was going to be catastrophic.

My stylist finished my hair, and I rushed home to pack and deploy. Once packed, I remember stopping to check on my elderly neighbor and her special needs daughter while on another statewide conference call, to ascertain if they had an evacuation plan. Dr. Guidry gently told me to mute my phone. I was prepared to have Ms. Lucille and her daughter accompany me to Baton Rouge. Ms. Lucile declined my offer.

I proceeded to the Office of State Buildings in New Orleans and joined up with the OPH medical director, and we headed to Baton Rouge in a state vehicle. It took us six hours to get to Baton Rouge (normally an hour-and-a-half commute) because thousands of NOLA residents were evacuating the city.

On my drive up to Baton Rouge, I was concerned about my elderly parents, who were refusing to evacuate. The plan was for my parents to evacuate with my husband, who was also required to report to the OPH EOC in Baton Rouge for duty.

After several hours talking to them without any agreement to evacuate, I made my final argument. I told my mother that I would not let them stay in the city alone and that I would ask Wayne, their favorite son-in-love to stay with them . . . and then I asked my mother, "Do you want to see Wayne die?", because I was certain that lives would be lost in Hurricane Katrina.

My bluntness and my parents' love of Wayne convinced them to evacuate with Wayne as their chauffeur. And just like that, they were on their way to Baton Rouge. It took them eight hours.

Once in Baton Rouge, my mother, father, Wayne, and I had bunk beds in a Jimmy Swaggart Bible College dormitory room across the street from the OPH EOC. The dormitory was designated emergency housing for OPH employees deployed from New Orleans. As OPH assistant secretary (a title equivalent to CEO in the private sector), I was tasked with developing and implementing a response and recovery plan that would protect Louisiana residents' public health before and after the hurricane.

Coincidentally (God working), OPH had had a hurricane emergency drill two weeks before Hurricane Katrina and developed a response and recovery plan to a Category Five hurricane making a direct hit on New Orleans traveling up the mouth of the Mississippi.

Some elements of the response plan, not listed in priority order, were: statewide staff deployment and waiver reviews, designated special needs shelters, evacuation of special needs citizens below I-10, triage and healthcare of special needs citizens, and hospital and nursing home evacuations, with the Superdome designated as a shelter of last resort.

Some elements of the recovery plan, not listed in priority order, were: immunization strike teams, public service announcements, testing drinking water, and sanitation inspections.

OPH's response and recovery plans were a roadmap touched by coincidence (God working) that was essential to our mission and task of mitigating the public health damage caused by Hurricane Katrina.

Right before and soon after Hurricane Katrina made landfall, my adult daughters, Kelley (finishing her residency in Chicago) and Krystal (beginning her career as a nurse practitioner in Memphis), started to call me insistently. I didn't have time to talk to them, so I rushed through their calls because I was busy resolving some mini and/or maxi crisis. I remember Kelley saying to me, "You busier than the president," (President George Bush at the time) to which I replied, "I am.... Goodbye."

I witnessed many public health heroes and she-roes during OPH's response and recovery plan for Hurricane Katrina. A shining example of a public health she-roe is Avis Gray, RN, MSN, and OPH regional administrator.

Avis was responsible for triaging the special needs patients in the Superdome and arranging transportation to special needs shelters in Baton Rouge and/or above Baton Rouge, as capacity allowed.

I had to "order" Avis to get on the last ambulance leaving the Superdome with special needs residents. She saw the deterioration of the Superdome and the chaos that was ensuing. Avis was committed to do all that she could do as a nurse to lessen the suffering she saw.

I was determined to have Avis in Baton Rouge utilizing her healthcare delivery skills for the greater good, with the citizens in the Baton Rouge special needs shelter, as well as triaging incoming patients to other special needs shelters north of Baton Rouge.

Once in Baton Rouge, after receiving the bulk of the New Orleans special needs residents, Avis joined forces with several RTA bus drivers who had evacuated New Orleans in their buses with their families. They became her evacuation squad, and they did plenty evacuation missions to New Orleans and back to Baton Rouge. Avis and her evacuation squad rescued hundreds of New Orleans residents.

Avis also worked herself into a state of mental and physical exhaustion.... For her safety, I ordered her to cease and desist rescue missions, barred her from the EOC, and asked her to rest in a friend's apartment in Baton Rouge.

Avis ignored my orders. We laugh to this day about how, in all the organized chaos of the EOC, I stood up in my glass-front office and spotted her crawling around the floor, gathering Wayne and her RTA rescue squad for one final rescue mission at one in the morning. Avis Gray is a she-roe extraordinaire, and I am forever grateful for her unrelenting service to the citizens of Louisiana and her friendship.

After Hurricane Katrina landfall and the subsequent levee breaches, rescuing residents from New Orleans was marked by confusion. Families were being separated. I was walking in the EOC, and I saw a female employee crying hysterically, so I went over to her to see if I could help or console her. The employee told me about three children from New Orleans who were brought to our EOC, a four-year-old and two toddlers. The children were alone, and the public health employee was crying because she thought the mother had abandoned her children and left them to fend for themselves.

As coincidence (God working) would have it, the four-year-old was quite verbal and knew his mother's name, his home address, and the names of the two toddlers, who were not his siblings.

We pushed this information out in our statewide public health network and discovered that the parents were looking for their children because they were put on two different buses headed to Baton Rouge. We were able to reunite the mothers with their children, and the public health worker's faith in humanity was restored.

On Monday night, August 29, I got a call on my personal cell phone from the distraught parent of a Xavier University student. To this day, I don't know how this mother got my cell phone number. The mother had lost contact with her daughter, and she was emotionally overwhelmed and concerned about her daughter's safety.

After a couple of hours, I was able to confirm to this mother that her daughter and other Xavier students were safe in the campus dorm and that the flood waters were receding and that she and the other students would be okay. As a coincidence (God working), I knew someone who knew someone who knew someone who was affiliated with Xavier University.

So, what had happened was, my three-day deployment to Baton Rouge ended up being three months. My administrative assistant, Wilfred, secured housing for Wayne and me and my parents. Wilfred's niece, her husband, and their baby daughter moved into her mother's home, and the Casa de Howard and the Casa de Gayden moved into their home.

We paid their expenses (mortgage, energy, water, cable, and newspaper delivery bills) for the three months we lived in their home. It was a win-win situation: we felt like we were helping a young couple, and they were graciously allowing us to live in their home, which was in Brusly, a couple of miles outside of Baton Rouge. Brusly was giving *Andy Griffith*, Mayberry vibes—a sweet, rural town a little too laid-back for the Casa de Howard.

By coincidence (God working), I got my hands on a little blue book that detailed potential federal disaster aid to public health departments and potential federal disaster aid to individuals. I discovered via the little blue book that the public health lab that was destroyed by Hurricane Katrina could be rebuilt with federal disaster funds, and that Wayne and I qualified for a SBA loan to mitigate the damages that we experienced as a result of Hurricane Katrina.

During the recovery phase of Hurricane Katrina, I particularly enjoyed that all of the major players in New Orleans' healthcare delivery system were of one accord: We were all Team Recovery.

Our home in New Orleans was one of the 80 percent of homes in New Orleans that flooded. We had six feet of flood water in our New Orleans East home. Our home and our worldly possessions were gone.

Now I had time to talk to our daughters. I was feeling sorry for myself. I was fifty-seven, and Wayne was fifty-nine. Our home would have been paid in full in 2008, but now we had to start all over again.

My daughters and I almost always talk three-way to each other. So I got on the call with a defeated demeanor, and Kelley and Krystal both said in unison, "We ain't having no pity party. . . . Buck it up, buttercup, and get busy on your comeback." So that was the grand opening and grand closing of my feeling sorry for us.

The series of coincidences, God working anonymously to help me through difficult Hurricane Katrina times, is profound:

My mother and father being safe and secure across the street from the EOC; Wayne working with me in the EOC; and my daughters not living in New Orleans all allowed me to be laser-focused on response and recovery.

The emergency preparedness drill (Category Five hurricane landfall at the mouth of the Mississippi River hitting New Orleans) two weeks before Katrina landfall prepared me to implement the plans outlined in the drill.

Having a four-year-old, articulate child able to assist in the reunification with his mother and the toddlers' mother was uplifting for all staff involved.

Assuring the parent of the Xavier student of her safety by using my social network was a boost to my spirit.

Identifying a funding source to rebuild the public health laboratory and learning how the SBA loan could mitigate our personal losses was God-sent. God was working with me and through me to address the public health needs of my community and my own personal needs.

The biggest affirmation I learned from Hurricane Katrina was that Wayne and I had raised two good-to-the-bone women, who were now practicing what we'd preached to them for years: "No one wants to be invited to a pity party. . . . Buck it up, buttercup, and get busy on your comeback."

HOLDING THE HISTORY OF THOSE WHO DIED
PAMELA JENKINS

Introduction
Hurricane Katrina changed us all. It left the community with an enduring unease about storms and catastrophe. As important, living through Hurricane Katrina left me with a profound sense of gratitude—for friends, family, acquaintances, strangers, and, to some extent, the government response.

To be clear, I stood in privilege throughout the years-long recovery from Hurricane Katrina. My husband and I both had jobs. My husband, Ed, had a small law practice that was interrupted in the wake of the disaster. He almost immediately went to work with FEMA in grants administration. While my university, the University of New Orleans, was shuttered for the fall semester, it came back for the spring but continued to pay faculty and staff through the devastating fall.

We both knew how to work complex systems. Ed could fill out any form, and I could be on the phone for hours, following up. What held us together, though, is that we had people from near and far who stepped up, stood up, and held us together while we worked through gutting our house to the studs, hauling our wet, soaked, ruined stuff to the sidewalk, and negotiating our way through multiple levels of bureaucracy. There has not been a day that goes by that I do not remember the kindness that we received. Fred Rogers wrote that every day, he worked to practice kindness—an intentionality I learned in the months and years following Katrina.

There has not been a year since Hurricane Katrina that I have not written about it, spoken about it, or thought about its impacts. In this essay, I tell three related stories: one is personal, the second is professional, and the third is my experience with the community. I explore my own personal reflections of gratitude, joy, and thoughtfulness that occurred during and after this traumatic event, but also how this event led to moments that changed my beloved and tragic city.

FEMA has a model that describes the four phases of disaster management: response, recovery, mitigation, and preparedness. In each of these phases, individuals and communities make choices as best they can. I use these phases in this essay to mark time, remembering that they ebb and flow with each new storm.

While most of us in New Orleans lived through multiple storms and became familiar with the roller coaster of watching the tracking maps, the wind, the rain, the lack of electricity, and on and on, nothing prepared us for the devastation of Katrina and the additional traumatic process of recovery. However, there were places and times at each phase of the FEMA model where our friends, neighbors, and community stood back up with care and joy.

Response: How much water did you get? Where are you staying?
The storm created a great disconnect among folk. Some stayed and got lost, others left and got lost as well. When we found each other, something changed. Not only did we hug and cry; we felt different. I remember when we were in Baton Rouge, and we finally saw three of our closest friends in a small café off the LSU campus. We were all thankful to be alive. We gathered each other in our arms and in our hearts. That joy is not replaceable—under the most trying of experiences, we found our community.

Like many, we lived in nine places before we got back to our home. We tried our best to create home wherever we were. In Baton Rouge, we lived in a friend's two-bedroom, one-bath apartment with five other people. Extraordinarily, she stayed with another friend to create more room for us. Other friends bought houses in Baton Rouge or knew someone with a vacant rental property that they made available. Each night, we would cook for everyone, including stray folk who would just show up. Each morning, we would get up early to listen to the news, trying to figure out what to do. It was crazy and wonderful at the same time—feeling that we were not alone, but not knowing how we were going to get through it all.

My friend and colleague Vern Baxter wrote that the storm tore the veneer off the structure of our lives, leaving us to view inequality and injustice in stark relief. When that happened, as we saw the bodies, the Superdome, the New Orleans Center (now the Smoothie King Center), something altered with us all. We might have been safe where we evacuated, but we were connected to those who were lost, and those folks trapped in the Superdome. We began to make phone calls to see what we could do, talk to the press about the issues of equity, challenge the notion about looting, and think about what a more equitable response might look like. One of the most important activists of that time was Greta Gladney. She said to me on the phone one night, "The water knocked us down, but we stood back up." In an interview, famous New Orleans musician Allen Toussaint, lamenting the loss of his instruments, recording equipment, and other accoutrements of his craft, said, "The spirit didn't drown."[26] Those two phrases sum up our recovery.

As social scientists, we began to collect stories of rescue and recovery. We would interview people wherever we could find them. Nearly everyone I spoke to in those initial days and months after the storm took the story deeper. The courage that individuals and community members showed still gives me pause. There was an older gentleman in Hollygrove named Beau. At the time of the storm, he had recently been diagnosed with lung cancer. He told the story of his own response to the storm. A boat appeared in his neighborhood, so he took it and began getting people from their flooded homes to the island (a bit of high ground). He did not know how many folks he rescued. Talking with him several years later, before he passed, he said the storm had given his life purpose.

Another piece of this story focuses on the survivors of domestic violence and sexual assault. The only battered women's shelter in the city, Crescent House, flooded and then burned down. But before that happened, the director, Mary Claire Landry, commandeered a school bus and drove the women to safety to Baton Rouge. She did not ask permission; she just drove with the survivors.

A nurse I interviewed worked in a neonatal unit in a hospital that was running out of supplies. She looked around, gathered her colleagues, and they drove their own cars with these babies to Baton Rouge. An ambulance driver I got to know drove her ambulance with as many as ten people in it, repeatedly rescuing those in need.

A woman bus driver told a story that haunts to this day. She was driving people out of the area, often without being able to tell passengers where they were going. No one had luggage or any possessions. One young woman came to her and said, "Please let me out in Baton Rouge. I need to bury my baby." The young woman was holding the now dead child in her arms. The bus

---

26   Larry Blumenfeld, "Yes, Now We Know Exactly What It Means to Miss New Orleans," Daily Beast, Feb. 16, 2021, https://www.thedailybeast.com/yes-now-we-know-exactly-what-it-means-to-miss-new-orleans/.

driver thought and said, "None of the passengers have any luggage. We will put the child in the baggage compartment." She let the mother and child get off in Baton Rouge.

The concept that my friends and I (Steve Kroll-Smith and Vern Baxter) used to describe this behavior was "the bricoleur." This signifies making do with what is at hand. Individuals and community members took what was at hand, imagined something that would work, and did it. We heard story after story of courage, hope, and compassion. A friend of mine, a police officer, had boats in storage around the city. He got them out and went to Gentilly and the East and pulled people out of their homes. Social scientists write about prosocial behavior that occurs after a disaster, when community members help each other. It does not quite describe what ordinary people did. Many stories we heard or observed for ourselves involved ordinary people being extraordinary—the moment came, and they stood up.

These moments of the immediate response are invisible in most of the public narrative about Katrina. These are stories of individuals and groups standing up in new and innovative ways of thinking and doing. These moments would follow all these actors through the rest of their Katrina experiences.

Recovery: Sunday at Pam and Ed's

Recovery is often categorized as being both short- and long-term, an eventual return to normal. The concept of recovery did not have much meaning to those of us on the ground. We saw recovery as one obstacle after another. As a community, recovery had as many dimensions as individuals and organizations could imagine.

The third week after the storm, several friends drove up to Baton Rouge, where we were staying, to visit. They told us, "Don't hire people to gut your house. We will do it with you." We had yet, like many, to receive our insurance money, had gotten exorbitant repair bids from contractors, and were hesitant to begin. Gutting a house is no small feat. Their help began an eighteen-month journey back home.

Over the next eight months, every Sunday, friends, acquaintances, and strangers would stop by and help us with the lengthy process of throwing away nearly all of our possessions and tearing up walls and floors. What this meant is that people would go through our belongings and we would decide whether to keep them or not, and then carry what was unwanted to the curb. Flood insurance adjusters instructed us to document all our damaged possessions because flood insurance only paid depreciated values.

We created a word for the ever-present smell—we called it "ook." A smell of dirty water, sewage, and anything else left around. Mold was omnipresent throughout. The ook did not matter; some would come and carry things. Others would bring food. When you are masked up, knee-deep in ook odor, touching your stuff that stinks and is falling apart, the bonds you build with your friends and strangers are different.

Friends would send their students over to help. Our biggest day, we had students from Oklahoma State University, Louisiana State University, and the University of New Orleans. On that day, we carried out the piano, the refrigerator, and the stove. Those students showed an appreciation for the work that we faced. They came with joy at being able to help. Our volunteers were not unique. All over the city, people showed up to help.

After a day of cleaning, my friend Barbara and I would drive around and take photos. We would talk to whomever was out, learn their stories of survival and how they were doing. We brought water in our car that I had gotten from the Salvation Army and handed out what we had. We still cherish those moments when we saw the best of human beings trying to return to their lives.

Two sociologists of some note, Kai Erikson and Brenda Phillips, both walked through our house on separate occasions. They each said to themselves, *They won't bring this back*. Because they are our friends, they kept their thoughts to themselves. They only told us what they had thought once the house was rebuilt. It is from these dregs that we rebuilt our home and community.

Recovery for scholars took different paths. As social scientists, local scholars were in a liminal space—were both subjects and objects of the experience. We would work on our houses and then document the storm. We found ourselves interviewing folks in all manner of places. One of our favorite stories took place at a dark bar where we could hardly see to take notes, interviewing a police officer who was clearly not all right yet with what he had seen. What was to come for this officer would be yet another disaster. Yet, he spoke of his job and the people that were saved with respect and care.

Kai Erickson (Yale University, emeritus) put together funding, forming the Social Science Research Council taskforce on Hurricane Katrina, and allowed local and other scholars to work collaboratively to document the aftermath of the storm. This funding allowed scholars to author single stories or wider descriptions of the impact of the storm. (See the Further Notes section for the work completed.)

Community organizations also began the process of rebuilding. The story of organizations nearly parallels the story of individuals recovering—an unevenness of fits and starts. Some organizations received national and international donations that provided monies for them that they had rarely had; others continued to struggle, and some shut their doors. Some of the organizations that received money immediately hired more staff, bought new buildings, and found themselves some years later unable to maintain that same capacity.

Katrina also caused some organizations to change direction. They viewed the tasks of recovery—housing, employment, and other issues related to recovery from the disaster—as a new or enhanced part of their mission. This change could be seen from smaller agencies to bigger organizations and began a creative period where individuals and organizations thought differently about their purpose.

The development of the New Orleans Family Justice Center is an excellent example. Family Justice Centers are defined as one-stop shops for survivors of domestic violence, sexual assault, and, in some places, elder and child abuse. There are more than one hundred family justice centers in the United States now. As stated, the only battered women's shelter in New Orleans when Katrina hit flooded and then burned—actually, not only did the shelter burn, but the courts closed, and many of the measures to provide safety to women disappeared.

As soon as water receded and people were able to cobble their way home, the Mayor's Domestic Violence Advisory Committee reconvened. This committee had been formed by Mayor Marc Morial six weeks into his first term years earlier; it would go on to change the landscape for survivors. The committee looked at the impact of disasters on domestic violence. Disasters tend to result in two things: isolation and living in crowded, stressful conditions. As a result of the intense flooding and destruction, livable housing was scarce. Women were at risk when the housing was very crowded and when they were living in a house that had no neighbors (the jack-o'-lantern effect). All this contributes to the risk of violence, coercion, and control.

Here is where the notion of bricoleur takes on additional meaning. Mary Claire Landry, then director of Crescent House, went to Washington, DC, without an invitation and met with Department of Justice personnel. She came back with a promise to fund a Family Justice Center. It usually takes eighteen months for funding to be put in place to open a center. In New Orleans during recovery, the Center opened in six months.

From my perspective, recovery is the most treacherous of all the stages. It is the longest stage and the most complicated: trying to rebuild in an environment that is familiar yet unknown. The communities I came to know were willing to leap into that future.

Christmas Eve 2005

We were living with a friend who went away for Christmas. We were invited to the Ashé Cultural Center for Christmas Eve for a program featuring Danny Glover. It was a small circle of people, twenty or so. Mr. Glover had worked with The Algebra Project, and he knew people from around the city. He spoke about our loss and our survival. And then he read the Langston Hughes poem "The Negro Speaks of Rivers." When I am traumatized by events, this poem comforts me:

> I've known rivers:
> I've known rivers ancient as the world and older than the flow of
>   human blood in human veins.
> My soul has grown deep like the river.
> I bathed in the Euphrates when dawns were young.
> I built my hut near the Congo and it lulled me to sleep.
> I looked upon the Nile and raised the pyramids above it.
> I heard the singing of the Mississippi when Abe Lincoln went
>   down to New Orleans, and I've seen its muddy bosom turn all
>   golden in the sunset.
> I've known rivers:
> Ancient, dusky rivers.
> My soul has grown deep like the rivers.[27]

Next Moment of Joy

New Year's Eve in the early years of recovery: it was so foggy that night that we could barely see. We heard that there was a New Year's Eve party at the Make It Right Foundation homes in the Lower 9th Ward. We drove over the Claiborne Avenue bridge, where you could hardly see in front of you. We arrived in the Lower 9th and took the left toward the sites of the houses that were dummied out with pink tarps. It was eerie and yet surprisingly

---

27 Langston Hughes, "The Negro Speaks of Rivers," Poetry Foundation, accessed June 5, 2025, https://www.poetryfoundation.org/poems/44428/the-negro-speaks-of-rivers.

hopeful. These pink shimmering structures were visible through the fog and gave us hope.

Third Moment of Joy
Mardi Gras, February 2006. The first Mardi Gras after the storm was epic. It was as if the whole community came together to say, *We're back*. They left their FEMA trailers, their gutted homes, or drove in from where they had evacuated. It was the first of many years that we would walk with the Krewe of Kosmic Debris, founded by Deborah and Alan Langhoff. There are so many walking parades in any Mardi Gras, but this year, people were everywhere. The Krewe of the Blind Levee Inspectors. The Krewe of the Katrina Debristants (women in their debutante dresses with obvious waterlines). We walked from the Blue Nile in the Marigny to the Mississippi River. I began my own tradition that year by walking as close to the musicians as I could. We walked through Decatur Street and sang "Down by the Riverside": *"I am going to lay down my sword and shield down by the riverside / not going to study war no more."* When we got to the river, as with other walking krewes, we called out the names of people who'd died that year. It was the perfect New Orleans moment: sadness, joy, laughter, community.

Mitigation: Is this really going to work?
Mitigation means lessening the effects of disaster. Mitigation has become the buzzword for all kinds of actions. There can be structural mitigation, such as levees, and non-structural, such as elevation.

In our lives, mitigation took on a variety of meanings. In many ways, it meant the slog of decision-making about everything—from the pulls on the cabinets to elevating the house. Would the house survive? Would we? There are photos of us at every stage, pulling the tiny nails out of ruined floors. With each nail, we began to see hope.

The story of our house reflects what worked in the aftermath of Katrina. We have a better house—a different home than before the storm. As I said in the introduction, we stood in privilege from the storm. We were welcomed everywhere, had places to stay that did not cost us, food to eat we did not buy, and friends who loved us. We have a better home because it was built with the love and sweat of our friends. We mitigated not only the structure of our home but of our lives. It is something when I witnessed our home down to the studs. And now we have this small cottage, a warm and welcoming place. It has new windows, new floors, new furniture, new everything but its occupants.

For the scholars, mitigation took many forms. We finished our books and articles. We began to sort through all the stuff we had. The storm became the most documented in the United States. We saw when we went to conferences that Katrina was the touchstone for all future conversations about disaster. Hurricane Katrina and its aftermath are the ways by which we measure storms and recovery now.

For some nonprofits in the area, a transformation occurred. The Family Justice Center of New Orleans opened its doors in 2007. It has since grown to meet the needs of a community, their former director a national spokesperson for how Centers can thrive. Today, almost two decades later, it is the local leader of the response for safety from interpersonal violence.

KID smART, Trinity Christian Community Center, and Goodwork Network all are examples of organizations that looked at themselves differently. Every successful organization had to pivot from one thing to another. Those that could do that did more than survive; they thrived.

We also learned about everyday mitigation. When the rain comes now, we look for the highest ground for our cars; we fill our bathtubs with water; we fill a cooler with ice. We mitigate what we can; the state and the federal government have larger mitigation plans, but ordinary citizens do what we can.

Preparedness: Now what?

The way the FEMA disaster management model is designed suggests that there is a response, a recovery that includes mitigation for the next storm, and, finally, preparedness that changes from one disaster to the next. The problem in an area such as Louisiana or Florida is that they have never quite recovered from one storm when the next one hits. We had a little time between the double hit of Katrina-Rita and the next set of storms. And lately, the major storms are coming faster and stronger. The levees in New Orleans have held since they were rebuilt after Katrina, yet doubts linger.

Louisiana has elevated numerous homes across the state and increased the ability of parishes to communicate with each other, and individuals and families are more likely to evacuate than ever before. We are, in a sense, prepared.

For us personally, we have made some decisions. We look for a place to be during hurricane season out of New Orleans. Many have moved altogether. It is a dilemma for everyone living in New Orleans, and in coastal areas. It breaks our hearts, but the city and the state have not taken full advantage of the great renaissance that occurred in the city. The spirit of our renewal allowed the community to ask different questions and expect different answers.

No disaster scholar was the same after Katrina. All of us, even our most senior members, knew that Katrina had shifted the paradigm. The question of equity in response and recovery is now at the center of any disaster story. There is still much more work to do, but the narrative can no longer shift back to an essentialist view of disaster.

It also changed how scholars do their work. Much prior disaster work was done from a ten thousand-foot view. While this view is valuable, the use of qualitative work explores how we began to understand the experience from the ground. From this perspective, scholars saw the entire story, from response to preparedness. We saw residents right after the flood, in their FEMA trailers, and then in their new homes. We saw life emerge from the death and destruction. We saw people have agency and take control of their lives during destruction.

The community is stronger in many ways than it was prior to Katrina. The leadership that emerged from the storm included people whose voices were known but not heard as often. The cry for equity in recovery remains persistent.

What to do next?

My family and friends were but one group among thousands of people who rebuilt their lives after Hurricane Katrina. And while government help finally came, it was not always equitably accessible. We need to build a proactive culture around recovery. The state can now evacuate areas in a more effective manner. They have built an infrastructure for response to storms. What needs more attention is the process of building a sense of what recovery looks like going forward. How soon will the mitigation monies be available? How do we prevent future storms? We can get people out of the city, but can we get them back and whole again? There are bigger questions at the forefront now.

Standing on the history of those who did not survive.

Now, when there is a disaster, I look first for the death count. Since 2005, no death count has come close to the 1,400 souls lost in Katrina. In some way, those folks we lost in Katrina helped to firm up policy and safety for future storm victims. The death toll in Katrina convinced people to leave for the next storm who were usually reluctant. These deaths meant that parishes and states coordinated more closely with each other. These deaths saved future lives. I think of our former department secretary and her husband (both disabled), who could not leave and perished. I think of her smile and what her life meant.

We can do better. We can remember that for a community to be safe from disasters, everyone needs to be safe. The diversity of a community, as we discovered in the aftermath of Hurricane Katrina, is its strength. Our knowledge about storms has grown exponentially. We can understand that lives that were lost could have been saved. We can save those lives and more homes even as the storms grow stronger.

Further Reading
To read *The Katrina Bookshelf* series of eight volumes, go to the University of Texas Press. https://utpress.utexas.edu/

To view the entire bibliography created by National Hurricane Taskforce, see https://www.preventionweb.net/files/2751_KatrinaBibliography.pdf

Other books and articles discussed here include:
Brown, Bethany L., Pamela Jenkins, and Tricia Wachtendorf. "Shelter in the Storm: A Battered Women's Shelter and Catastrophe." *International Journal of Mass Emergencies and Disaster* 28, no. 2 (2010): 226–245.
Jenkins, Pam and Brenda Phillips. "When Catastrophe Strikes Battered Women: Domestic Violence in the Context of Disaster." *National Women's Studies Journal Special Issue on Katrina* 20, no. 3 (2008): 49–68.
Jenkins, Pamela and Bethany Van Brown. "Ten Years Later: Domestic Violence and Hurricane Katrina." In *Rethinking Disaster Recovery: A Hurricane Katrina Retrospective*, edited by Jeanne Haubert, 39–52. New York: Bloomsbury, 2015.
Jenkins, Pamela. "Before and After Katrina: Gender and the Landscape of Community Work." In *Women of Katrina: The Gendered Dimensions of Disaster Recovery*, edited by Emmanuel David and Elaine Enarson, 169–179. Nashville: Vanderbilt University Press, 2011.
Jenkins, Pamela. "Faith, Disasters, and Communities." In *Disaster's Impact on Livelihood and Cultural Survival: Losses, Opportunities, and Mitigation*, edited by Michèle Companion, 281–292. Boca Raton, FL: CRC Press, 2015.
Jenkins, Pamela. "When Resilience is not Enough: Recovery, Privilege, and Hurricane Katrina." In *Sociologists in Action on Inequalities: Race, Class, Gender, and Sexuality*, third ed., edited by Kathleen Odell Korgen, Jonathan M. White and Shelley K. White, 18–22. Thousand Oaks, CA: Sage Publications, 2014.

Jenkins, Pamela and Branda Nowell. "Humanistic Perspectives on the Policy and Praxis of Disaster Management: Reflections on Freire and Recovery Post Katrina." *Administrative Theory and Praxis* 32, no. 3 (2010): 431–437.

Jenkins, Pamela, John Kiefer and Shirley Laska. "Integration of a Social Responsibility Paradigm Into Evacuation Planning." In *The Practice of Strategic Collaboration: From Silos to Action*, edited by Dorothy Norris-Tirell, 99–121. Washington, DC: Taylor & Francis, 2010.

Jenkins, Pamela, John Renne, and John Keifer. "Gender Differences in Self-Reported Evacuation Experiences: An Analysis of the City Assisted Evacuation Program During Hurricane Gustav." *Women's Issues in Transportation* 2 (2011): 127–133.

Jenkins, Pamela, Shirley Laska, and Gretchen Williamson. "Connecting Future Evacuation to Current Recovery: Saving the Lives of Older People in the Next Catastrophe." *Generations: Journal of American Society on Aging* 31, no. 4. (2007–2008): 49–52.

Kroll-Smith, Steve, Pamela Jenkins and Vern Baxter. "The Bricoleur and the Possibility of Rescue: First Responders to the Flooding of New Orleans." *Journal of Public Management and Social Policy* 13, no 2 (2007): 5–21.

Kroll-Smith, Steven, Vern Baxter, and Pam Jenkins. *Left to Chance: Hurricane Katrina and the recovery of two neighborhoods*. Austin: University of Texas Press, 2015.

Phillips, Brenda, and Pamela Jenkins. 2016. "Gender-based violence and diasters: South Asia in comparative perspective." In *Women and Diasters in South Asia: Survival, security and development*, edited by Linda Racioppi and Swarna Rajagopalan, 225–250. London: Routledge India, 2016.

Phillips, Brenda and Pamela Jenkins. "Violence and Disaster Vulnerability." In *Social Vulnerability to Disasters*, second ed., edited by Brenda Phillips, Deborah Thomas, Alice Fothergill and Lynn Blinn-Pike, 311–341. Boca Raton, FL: CRC Press, 2013.

Phillips, Brenda and Pamela Jenkins. "Faith Based Efforts for Hurricane Katrina Response and Recovery." In *Meeting the Needs of Children, Families, and Communities Post-Disaster: Lessons Learned from Hurricane Katrina and Its Aftermath*, edited by Ryan P. Kilmer, Virginia Gil-Rivas, Richard G. Tedeschi, and Lawrence G. Calhoun, 215–238. Washington, DC: American Psychological Association, 2010.

Phillips, Brenda, Pamela Jenkins, and Elaine Enarson. "Violence and Disaster Vulnerability." In *Social Vulnerability to Disasters*, edited by Brenda Phillips, Deborah Thomas, Alice Fothergill and Lynn Blinn-Pike, 279–306. Boca Raton, FL: CRC Press, 2010.

Renne, John, Thomas Sanchez, Pamela Jenkins and Robert Peterson. "The Challenge of Evacuating the Carless in Five Major US Cities: Identifying the Key Issues Being Faced." *Transportation Research Record: Journal of the Transportation Research Board* 2119 (2009): 38–45.

CHARLIE & LOUISE
CHARLIE JOHNSON & LOUISE MOUTON JOHNSON

This is our narrative about blessings, and many, though not all, of our blessings came during our evacuation, relocation, and return home resulting from Hurricane Katrina, even if we didn't see them as such at the time. Somehow, in retrospect after all these years, we can appreciate them as the gifts that they were. But let us start from the beginning.

Charlie: At first, we did not take Hurricane Katrina seriously because 2005 was a relatively quiet year for hurricanes. The few previous hurricanes that year were insignificant, and we evacuated only to return without noteworthy incidents. So, we waited until the last minute, after the mayor ordered all New Orleanians to leave the city.

Louise: As the weather forecasts seemed more foreboding, I and my husband Charlie expressed our feelings that this one felt different. Of course, we and our family had evacuated before for several hurricanes in the past two or three years, but Katrina felt different. Maybe because of its size and strength, or maybe because it was headed straight to New Orleans. There was just this eerie feeling we couldn't explain that prompted us to pay more attention to the details of preparing our household as we assisted other family members with preparing theirs before we left the city.

Charlie: We called family and friends to encourage them to evacuate. My mother Helena, a foster grandparent, asked if I could take three of our nieces, like in past evacuations. Unfortunately, we couldn't take them because we had our son and Louise's mother and brother traveling with us.

My mother said my brother, who was on National Guard duty in the Superdome, wanted to keep two of his older children with him in the Superdome. I explained that those high school children could not be left in the Superdome if my brother had duties to perform and convinced my mother to take those children with her. We set out around midday Sunday, August 28, 2005—my mother from her house and Louise and I from our house—en route to my sisters' homes in New Boston, Texas.

Louise: When we'd evacuated from the previous hurricanes, it was usually me, Charlie, and our daughter, Isis. Occasionally we included two or three of our nieces, who were close to our daughter's age, and my mother, Mrs. Jessie Mouton. The destination, however, was always the same: New Boston, Texas, a city near Texarkana that is about a one-hour drive from Shreveport, Louisiana. Altogether, on a normal trip, it takes about six hours to drive from New Orleans. Charlie had two sisters who lived there with their husbands and children, and we frequently traveled there for Thanksgivings, graduations, and other family gatherings, so it was not only a practical, but a warm and welcoming, destination.

I am currently enjoying retirement after a thirty-three-year career teaching visual art in Orleans Parish public schools, but at the time of the storm, I was teaching at the New Orleans Center for the Creative Arts (NOCCA) Academy, a middle school on Constance Street originally named Live Oak. The school was in the uptown Irish Channel, a part of the city that did not flood because of its proximity to the Mississippi River levee. As usual for evacuations, teachers were directed to unplug all electrical devices and cover computers and other materials and supplies with plastic in the event that windows were broken and water came in. I prepared my class and assured my students that we would catch up on classwork when we all came back sometime the following week. Our daughter was in seventh grade at NOCCA Academy. Isis and I left school together that Friday, and I was able to keep my 3:30 p.m. dental appointment before going home to make our final preparations to evacuate.

Charlie and I consulted with family members on both sides to coordinate our plans to make sure everyone had a way out of the city and to figure out who was traveling with whom and when they were leaving. For the rest of the evening that Friday and all day Saturday, we continued the conversations while securing everything (we knew the drill) inside and outside our home, moving everything in our walk-out basement to about four feet off the floor. We based that on our experience from the previous flood event, when we had three feet of water come in that had receded in a few hours. Extremely long-standing water was never a problem during past floods, whether from a hurricane or any other heavy rain event. Evacuations never lasted more than three days, which is why everyone packed no more than what was needed for that amount of time and was prepared for a quick clean-up once we were able to return home.

On Sunday morning, my mother made the extremely unusual decision not to go to her usual ten o'clock Mass at St. Raymond Catholic Church on Paris Avenue, which she, my brother, and I attended from the time we moved into the 7th Ward neighborhood on Buchanan Street. My mother was anxious and felt the urgency to leave before traveling conditions worsened, once she felt that her other relatives had a safe escape. Contraflow, making all traffic on the interstate highway travel in one direction, was already in effect, and traffic on I-10 headed west was getting heavier when we began our journey.

After securing my mother's home and moving everything we could onto higher surfaces and gathering what she needed, we went to my brother's home and helped him do the same. We finally gathered everyone together, travelling in our van, which may have comfortably seated the six of us physically, but mentally and emotionally, this evacuation was anything but comfortable. It was noon when we finally got on the road. We were my mother, my brother, our son, our daughter, Charlie, and me. We said a prayer before leaving.

Charlie: The six-hour trip was more than twice as long and had us arriving in New Boston around two or three the next morning. Rather than wake up the family, we checked into the Best Western hotel. We just wanted to sleep. They gave us the honeymoon suite that cost us three hundred dollars a night. We were told by the hotel staff that we had to pay another three hundred dollars or check out at 10:00 a.m. The hotel wasn't the same quality as the last time we'd stayed there. We decided to check out of that filthy, price-gouging dump of a hotel and go to my sister Charlean's house. She welcomed us and found out that my mother was a long distance away. Something like six or more hours away.

Louise: Around the middle of Monday morning, August 29, 2005, we watched television as we prepared for check-out. We saw that the storm had passed through, and people who'd stayed in New Orleans were venturing out, assessing the initial damage. The news changed so suddenly that I didn't even comprehend the impact at first. It was just too surreal. What seemed like no time at all had passed, and the news was announcing that two levees had breached, and the city was beginning to flood. Eventually, it turned out that 80 percent of New Orleans was underwater.

Charlie: I asked my sister Charlean and her husband Larry to look for a place for us to stay to wait out the storm. You see, I knew that my mother was coming with a party of nine. My daughter Tamika was coming with a group of two or four from New Orleans, and my nephew was on his way from Jackson, Mississippi. The closest place was Hot Springs Village, Arkansas, in a forested, gated retirement village that had all the amenities of a small town. We settled into a three-bedroom, two-bath house, with the closest neighbor about half a mile down the road. Things were going well until we saw on TV that in New Orleans, some levees had broken, and the city was flooded. We concluded that we would be in Hot Springs for a while.

Louise: They found us a timeshare/vacation house in Hot Springs Village, Arkansas, about two-and-a-half hours from New Boston. Charlie had family in Hot Springs Village, also. While the reservations were being made, we had a chance to spend several hours with family. It was early Monday afternoon when we left, and I felt a little anxious at first, since we really did not know exactly where we were going. We were still using road atlases and maps to travel, so getting there was an adventure.

The drive to Hot Springs Village was easy at first as we continued to travel on the Interstate 30 Highway. However, about thirty minutes out, it was quite nerve-wracking. Charlie was driving while I read the road map. Driving on the roads that wound up and down and around the Ouachita Mountains was something I was not used to. Exits from the interstate highway transitioned into a state highway, into two-way traffic streets, then unlined roads, with each turn off the previous road getting narrower and more rural—less road, denser forest. I could hear the theme song "Dueling Banjos" from the movie *Deliverance* playing inside my head! Hot Springs Village was a gated community, eighteen miles from one end to the other, with a combination of mixed-income family homes, mostly retired seniors. It also included many amenities: banks, pharmacies, dentists and eye doctors, veterinarians, libraries, a natatorium, tennis courts, churches of many denominations, and lots of golf courses.

In a way, once we settled in, this adventure turned out to be one of the first blessings when we looked at the endless depressing and heartbreaking news stories on television, and when I realized we were in a naturally peaceful area. Sometimes I felt guilty, knowing the chaos that our city was in, but I have always appreciated the blessing of being in that setting. Living in a house while displaced was a blessing. I could not imagine my mother, who was in her mid-eighties at the time, being in a hotel or shelter or any other overly crowded space. The rental house was a fully-furnished, one-story cottage with three bedrooms, two bathrooms, a kitchen, an open living/dining room, and a small, attached sunroom which opened to the backyard, which was essentially nothing but an endless wooded area with lakes, natural and man-made. My mother and I spent many hours in that space sorting through items, drying photographs and other important papers, and washing garments, fabric, dishes, and other small things that Charlie and my brother Girard salvaged and brought back to Hot Springs Village in the weeks, then months before we all returned to New Orleans.

Charlie: We heard an announcement on local TV stations our first weekend in Hot Springs Village asking those of us who were displaced to go to the Hot Springs Civic Center to register with the Federal Emergency Management Agency (FEMA) for relief services. What was remarkable and a blessing was that we saw several church members, friends, coworkers, and associates from New Orleans in the Civic Center. One day while standing in line, a volunteer who identified himself as Sarge pulled me aside and said we were different and didn't act like people from New Orleans. I guess we did not fit the stereotype that much of the media portrayed. Sarge said, "You know, I'm Cherokee Indian, and what will happen to your people is what happened to my people. You all will be displaced, and no one will know where other people are, and the government will not share the information to let you know where your family and friends are." Sarge's prophetic message is exactly what happened. The federal government did not let us, or local leaders, have data about our relocation. Reflecting on the experience, I think about the African Middle Passage, Indigenous people's relocations, and the Jewish holocaust.

Louise: The following is one of those surprises that illustrates the concept that "necessity is the mother of all invention." Even though cell phones were not a new invention in 2005, it was only about three months before Katrina that I'd purchased my first one. I used it only to make and receive calls, but during the early part of our evacuation, our 504 area code was not consistently receptive. It became an absolute necessity that I learn how to send and receive texts on my cell phone, which only had buttons with numbers, and not the QWERTY keyboard that is the standard now. It was a very time-consuming process just to type a few words, and if you're reading this and have no idea what I'm describing, please ask someone or look it up! Texting was the main form of communicating with family, friends, and others for whom we only had a phone number. The value of true friendship and strong family ties became so apparent when those who contacted us were not living in or from New Orleans. We were contacted by people whom we hadn't seen or heard of for ten years or more but who made the effort to find us through the Red Cross database for displaced persons and families. Our hearts are eternally grateful for their true love and friendship.

Another much appreciated blessing came to us on the second or third Sunday we were there. My mother, who I mentioned earlier never missed a Sunday of going to church, felt the urgency to go to mass. We looked through the Hot Springs Village directory for Catholic churches and found Sacred Heart of Jesus Catholic Church. The congregation was representative of the Village demographics: mostly older white individuals, with a few younger families. When we walked into the nave of the church, searching for a pew with enough space to seat the six of us, we spotted one other Black family. As we got closer, we recognized them as a family from my very own St. Raymond's Church! We all greeted each other with tears of sadness for what brought us there in the first place and tears of joy for seeing other members of our church home so far away from New Orleans. Our reunion at first turned a few heads, but the congregation quietly approved once they realized our bond. Then we all settled into solemn worship. The priest said a special blessing for our two families, and when the mass was over, we were warmly greeted by many of the members, even invited to dinner and offered home-cooked meals as well as clothing and other items that they collect on a regular basis for families in need.

The other family left to live with relatives who had evacuated to Baton Rouge, Louisiana, after about three weeks. Even though it wasn't home, and we were now the only Black family there, my mother found solace just being able to socialize with members of a church, enjoying the fellowship and breakfast after Mass, and even participating in the parish's Christmas dinner and programs just before she left.

One couple, Jim and Nancy, invited us to have dinner with them after Mass one Sunday. The backyard to their home overlooked a golf course complete with several man-made ponds. They were very kind to us and introduced us to a few other families in the Village, listening to our experience and informing us of other helpful resources in addition to the governmental ones. I remember some of their favorite pastimes were going to high school football games, riding motorcycles, and (of course) playing golf.

Charlie: Being displaced and having a comfortable house for all of us and meeting friends from home was a blessing. A miracle of a blessing happened when I received a call from a stranger trying to assist Virginia Johnson Bijol, my Auntie Sister—my father's oldest sister. This airline stewardess "saw a beautiful old lady sitting in a nursing home in Georgia and walked up to her." As they talked, Auntie Sister told the lady that her brother, Charlie Thomas Johnson Sr., had recently celebrated his birthday and recently died. I remember my Auntie Sister visiting my father on his last birthday. They sat side by side in his living room for hours. They said very little to anyone and each had a pleasant look on their faces.

My dad also died near his birthday in June 2005. Somehow, the kind stewardess was able to locate me, Charlie Jr., by researching my father's obituary. She found my phone number through the database, established by the Red Cross, of displaced New Orleanians. I contacted Auntie Sister's daughter, Jean, when the lady told me where health officers had relocated my aunt. Jean said her mother's medical caregivers had failed to let her know where they evacuated my aunt, as promised. Jean immediately went to pick up her mother once she knew her location. I don't know what would have happened to my elderly aunt if not for the kindness of a God-sent stranger.

Louise: After about two weeks, Charlie and I enrolled our daughter Isis at the nearest school, Jessieville Middle School, which was several miles away. A school bus picked her up around 6:30 a.m. and brought her back around 4:30 p.m. The first time the bus broke down, and she was hours late getting back to the house, so, in order to relieve the extreme anxiety brought about by that situation, we celebrated her twelfth birthday in October by purchasing her first cell phone. Again, born of necessity, it was a nice gift and a way for us to stay in contact with her in case there were any other emergencies, and it made her very happy!

Charlie: Louise and other New Orleans Public School personnel were fired shortly after New Orleans was flooded. But I was blessed to have my job with Southern University at New Orleans, but had to report to the Baton

Rouge branch of the Southern University System. Our son Ian enrolled at Southern University at Baton Rouge in September 2005, the same time I began working there. Ian lived in the dormitory and took the same courses he had while enrolled in Southern University at New Orleans, but with Baton Rouge university faculty. I drove back and forth from Hot Springs Village to Baton Rouge. I left home before sunrise and returned after dark because I could not find accommodations in Baton Rouge. Eventually I got a bed-and-breakfast room in New Orleans thanks to the city's mayor, Ray Nagin. Then, I taught at Southern University at Baton Rouge and cleaned my house in New Orleans during weekdays. I traveled from New Orleans or Baton Rouge to Hot Springs Village on weekends to be with family until Louise and Isis moved back home.

My first visit to New Orleans after Katrina was like a scene from an apocalyptic movie. Practically all vegetation was dead, windows in high-rise buildings were blown out, homes were branded with Xs and symbols, and everything was covered with gray dust. I drove around the east bank of New Orleans, first to check on family properties, then neighborhoods. The craziest thing is, I love to take photographs, but for some unknown reason, I didn't take a single photo of the devastation. I don't know why that happened; I had my camera with me all the time, but I just could not bring myself to take a single photograph of all of the things I saw, the damaged buildings, the waterlines, the devastation. I just did not document what happened to New Orleans—the devastation. Fortunately, other people did!

Louise: Opportunities came in several forms, often arriving after much frustration and distress. I was one of the approximately six thousand New Orleans Public Schools teachers who were fired immediately after Katrina. I think I received only two full paychecks before getting my pink slip. I had also applied for the National Board Teacher Certification (NBTC) and had already gone to several training meetings, writing sessions, and other preparations. When I contacted the National Board for Professional Teaching Standards (NBPTS), they had already formulated a plan and informed me that I could continue in the program if I found a school that participated in the programs, and possibly worked with a teacher who had received National Board Certification. Most states created a reciprocity opportunity for teachers who were evacuated and had a valid teaching certificate.

The rude awakening came when I contacted the Arkansas State Board of Education and explained my situation to see if I could add my name to the list of teachers seeking full- or part-time employment. Evidently, my ancillary certificate to teach art in Louisiana was not recognized as a valid teaching certificate in Arkansas, nor by the NBPTS, even though that was the one big question that I had asked of them and the Louisiana Department of Education more than once before embarking on that endeavor. Even though I had a master's in fine arts, had been teaching since 1980, and renewed my ancillary certification every year, I could not take advantage of the reciprocity opportunity. I had to withdraw from the NBTC program without getting a refund for my application fees. This was very frustrating.

My mother, a retired elementary school teacher, and Charlie, still teaching at the time, strongly encouraged me to do something they had been telling me to do for years: get teacher certification. It made perfect sense, even more so now considering the hiring practices of the "new" New Orleans school system. With a bachelor's degree in education, I could become more marketable. I enrolled in the alternative teacher certification program at Southern University at New Orleans and started classes in January 2006. I took all of my classes online, reading, studying, taking tests and exams online during the day while Isis was at school. Charlie was furloughed from his university teaching job at the end of the fall semester. Fortunately, he got a job teaching art at the Audubon Charter School in New Orleans that started in January.

Also in January, my mother finally returned to New Orleans. I remember my mom quietly crying that last time I drove her back home. Even though she was no longer driving, her presence was comforting, and she knew I would be making the long drive back to Arkansas alone with Isis. My mother moved in with Girard in a house on Lapeyrouse Street that he had rented when he returned in early December 2005 for a job opportunity.

I remained in Hot Springs Village with our daughter Isis, waiting for Charlie to renovate our home good enough for us to move in. She and I were now the only two left in Hot Springs Village, occasionally making the eight-plus hour drive home and back. This was a period when I learned how to power through a particularly challenging time, because the weather became increasingly hard to drive in. I remember one Friday the prediction was a snowstorm moving south toward us. I was so anxious to get on the road back to New Orleans that I packed everything Isis and I needed for the weekend so that the moment the bus dropped her off, all we had time to do was use the bathroom and get in the car. The snow had already started to fall as we drove ahead of the storm, making it safely back home. But the drive back up to Hot Springs was a real test of nerves. It was a slower drive from Shreveport to Texarkana, since many of the bridges and overpasses were icy, then a large stretch of interstate between Texarkana and Hot Springs was closed off because of the dangerous driving conditions. I had to take detours onto roads that I was unfamiliar with, all the while making sure I was going in the right direction. I could sense that Isis was anxious also as we travelled mostly in the dark. The trip back to Hot Springs this time was about two hours longer than usual. This was our last drive to Arkansas.

The principal at Jessieville Middle School asked if we would allow Isis to stay until she took her third-quarter assessments before coming back. Charlie had already arranged for her to be enrolled in a school here as soon as we got back, so fortunately there was no lag in her education. In March 2006, Charlie was there to help with all the packing, then the three of us finally got on the road for one last time headed back home to New Orleans.

Charlie: We are fortunate to live on the second floor of our house with a walk-out basement. My home's living area was just as we'd left it. Only the refrigerators were damaged in our living area. I went into my basement, and it looked like someone had just lifted everything, thrown it all in the washer, and agitated it. Equipment that was standing had been toppled over. I mean heavy cabinets. All of my paintings and other supplies were scattered all throughout the basement—that was the space that I used as my art studio—and now destroyed. Although she lost some materials and supplies also, Louise's studio was on the second floor and was intact after the storm. She is blessed to have art materials and a head start that many creatives did not.

Louise: After going through two disappointing school placements with Isis once we were settled for good, Charlie was able to enroll her at Edna Karr High School for her sophomore year. This was a huge blessing for her because she was able to be in school once again with many of her friends from her elementary school whom she had not seen since sixth grade. She was very happy about that joyous reunion, and so were we, because it seemed that her life was beginning to be a little closer to normal again.

Charlie: One constant for me was the Ashé Cultural Arts Center. The building had electrical power and it was open. It had spiritual power. It had healing power and was a gathering place for us. You know, folks from all over would go there to find out what was going on. I would go to Ashé if I had free time from work and cleaning my house to sit around and talk with Carol,

Doug, and others. I just hung out for a little while. It was good to be around friends like family, let them know what I was doing, find out who was back in town, and then go about my business.

We were constantly fighting battles trying to rebuild the city the first years after Hurricane Katrina. I had the privilege of working with many people and organizations to bring back New Orleans. I reestablished the New Orleans chapter of the National Conference of Artists and served on the board of the New Orleans African American Museum. We had to rebuild Southern University at New Orleans and had to fight to prevent powers from shutting down the institution.

Louise: On December 27, 2007, Girard and I lost our mother. I have always felt that post-Katrina stress had much to do with it—not being able to move back into her home; losing family and friends; having family move out-of-state that were no longer part of the Sunday ritual where she would visit after church; having her own church not open back up. She decided to sell her house (the same house that Girard and I grew up in) to the Road Home program. I think it was because she had a sense that she would not live long enough to rebuild and move back into it. I feel her soul is happy that a small businessman from her neighborhood purchased it for his daughter and her family, where they still live today. Our mother's house became a home for a young, growing family. Her home is now in heaven.

Charlie: Although the flood waters from Hurricane Katrina destroyed most of the art we owned or created, I was determined to figure out a way to keep some of it. I spread out the artworks on paper in my yard, on the porch, in the driveway, and everywhere else to dry. Then I treated them to remove mold. I was able to save many of them even though they were submerged for weeks—they were damaged, they had water stains, and they had signs of mold growth. The dried and sanitized art was reclaimed when mounted on more stable paper before I combined them in a multimedia composition. The inspiration came from feelings related to Hurricane Katrina—the rain, wind, water, destruction, obstacles, and resilience. This was combined with African textiles, textures, and patterns observed in Senegal in 1985 and subsequent trips to Africa. Nearly two hundred works on paper were saved, and more than a hundred reclaimed works have been part of a transformative redesign.

Louise and Isis came home once the house was habitable with utilities and appliances. We were the first on our block to move back into our house.

The city was not the healthiest place, but Louise was determined to make our house as normal, safe, and germ-free as possible. We monitored which people returned and those who decided not to return to New Orleans. We heard numerous stories about the trials and tribulations encountered by culture bearers who returned to rebuild New Orleans, so Louise and I set out to record some of their stories in a book. The book's title is *Didn't Wash Us Away: Transformative Stories of Post-Katrina Cultural Resilience*. The book shared Katrina experiences through essays, personal stories, poetry, and hundreds of pictures.

Louise: I continued with my studies on campus at SUNO and earned education certification in art on all levels (K–12) and in elementary education in 2009. In the meantime, I replaced Charlie as the art teacher at Audubon Charter School. It was also there that I reconnected with a friend from Xavier University. We were both in the art department in the mid-1970s. We reunited not only as coworkers but also as active members in the National Conference of Artists, New Orleans Chapter. Most importantly, though, we remained dear friends and spent uninterrupted time together until she passed, way too soon, in March of 2024. As I reflect upon our relationship and how it developed after Katrina, I'm not sure if we would have crossed the same paths again if it had not been for the way our lives and careers were rearranged after the storm. I miss her dearly, but I smile when I think of her.

Also, my coworkers from the school that I worked in before Katrina all relocated to different schools or other professions, as NOCCA Academy did not reopen after the storm. However, I remained in close contact with three of the teachers, and we made a commitment to share a meal together at least once a year, usually during the Thanksgiving or Christmas break, to catch up on life and its ups and downs. During the pandemic, we were not deterred, as we had cocktails via Zoom, toasting each other in gratitude of just being able to celebrate together!

Charlie: My maternal grandmother and mother placed a high priority on education, and I guess it rubbed off on me. I attended a reading and math summer camp at Xavier University when I was eleven years old. I would sneak away to visit Xavier's Art Department and secretly sit in on Dr. Rousseve's art class either during a break or after the day's activities ended. This was my first exposure to a university, and I knew then that I wanted to go to college and study visual arts. When I was fifteen years old, I learned that the Doctor of Philosophy was the highest educational degree one could achieve and made earning a PhD one of my life goals. I even had a deadline to acquire it.

Obligations and unexpected circumstances meant taking a serpentine route to achieve that mandate. Post-Katrina activities created major disruptions, but I would not trade those obligations. I was president of the New Orleans Chapter of the National Conference of Artists and was obligated to help fellow artists prosper after returning home. There was a major undertaking to save Southern University at New Orleans from forces that wanted to shut it down. The New Orleans African American Museum was badly damaged, with limited operating funds. I feel blessed to have had the opportunity to assist with measures that prevented the closing of those institutions.

So, life changes and events took priority over my PhD aspiration for decades, but the desire always burned bright. It wasn't until retirement in 2019, when the climate around me was less turbulent, that I was able to begin a program, and I eventually achieved a Doctor of Philosophy in Urban Studies at the University of New Orleans in May 2022. At this time, I am working to revitalize the National Conference of Artists, coordinating the annual NCA MLK Commemorative Exhibition, and totally engaging in visual arts. Katrina destroyed most of my artwork, but like the phoenix, I have arisen, found ways to take damaged artwork to reach new creative heights.

Louise: Our nuclear family was very fortunate in that we all stayed well during the pandemic and are here to talk about it. We did lose a brother-in-law in New Boston to Covid-19 but have remained in close contact with everyone on all sides of the family. Charlie's family actually celebrated their first family reunion here in New Orleans in 2016 and again in New Orleans after the pandemic in July 2024, with Charlie chairing both reunions.

As I reflect upon the purpose of this writing, I can recall a very long list of other fortunate events that I will touch on briefly but feel that I have already detailed some of the more important ones. In the summer of 2010, I participated in a professional development program called the Greater New Orleans Writing Project. While there, I wrote a Katrina poem called "In My Mother's Kitchen" that was included in the anthology of Katrina stories that Charlie and I edited in 2015. Later that summer, Charlie, Isis, and I took a road trip to Las Vegas, including several days exploring the splendid Grand Canyon. We traveled different routes going and coming back, visiting family and friends whom we hadn't seen in a while, or ever before. A highlight for me was spending the day with one of my mother's elderly cousins in Flagstaff, Arizona. We spent hours going through photo albums, sharing stories, and observing similar physical features and mannerisms. She told me that my mother made her wedding dress! In the summer of 2017, I received certification as a Louisiana Master Gardener and am currently active as a volunteer with the Master Gardeners of Greater New Orleans.

In the spring of 2018, I was an artist-in-residence at the Joan Mitchell Center here in New Orleans. While there, I created new artwork that was a continuation of a series I started in 2007 entitled *Unfinished Business*. This concept was actually inspired by my practices as both a quiltmaker and a printmaker. Instead of discarding paper from a print that didn't come out right, I repurposed it by cutting the print into smaller shapes and stitching the paper as you would do with fabric to make another work of art. The concept of unfinished business was inspired by Katrina. It was a way for me to reclaim what may have been lost or ruined, instead of mourning its destruction. I also made connections that allowed me to collaborate with other artists and participate in two major art exhibitions at the Newcomb Art Museum. In 2019, the New Orleans Chapter of the National Conference of Artists hosted the national convention, where one of its most respected co-founders, Dr. David Driskell, gave what turned out to be his last presentation at an NCA convention; he passed away in April 2020.

Our oldest child, Tamika, remained in Texarkana, Texas, graduated from Texas A&M University with a master's degree, and is currently pursuing her doctorate in religious studies—a natural path for her, as she has always been a caregiver and spiritual counselor. Our son, Ian, talented and skilled in the visual arts, has struggled with dependency most of his adult life. His challenges have led me to become not only more sensitive to his situation but also more aware of a growing population that faces this disease every day and the importance of seeking help and not hiding. I also have developed empathy for other families who strive to balance being lovingly supportive without becoming enablers. Our youngest child, Isis, graduated from Edna Karr in 2011, spent her freshman year at Jackson State in Mississippi, then decided to return to New Orleans. While working in retail, she also attended the school of social work at SUNO, earning her bachelor's degree, then her masters in May 2018. In August 2018, she gave birth to her adorable daughter, Naomi. The opportunity to assist in raising our granddaughter, now six years old, has been an absolute joy!

Charlie: Louise and I are fortunate to have relationships with innumerable family and friends we met before and since Katrina. Family and the teachers in my life are a special blessing. Our children Tamika, Ian, and Isis and granddaughter Naomi have given me the blessing of being parts of my own development and maturation. Our mothers, uncles and aunts, mentors, and close friends who transitioned after Katrina are dearly missed, but memories of them are joyous, uplifting occasions. Our quality of life is good even despite setbacks like Hurricane Katrina.

I enjoyed living in Arkansas, California, Minnesota, Virginia, and Washington, DC, but the muses' call always lures me back home to New Orleans because there is no place like New Orleans. Its people, culture, and my family let me know love, keep me grounded and creatively inspired. Coming home to rebuild New Orleans after the city's devastation in 2005 is a source of personal pride. For me, there was not one single moment that I thought New Orleanians could not rebuild the city.

These are just a few of our Katrina experiences of finding blessings and light among the stress and darkness. I cannot imagine what our lives would be like if New Orleans had not flooded in 2005. Seeing how my family has grown closer and spiritually is truly a joyous blessing. These experiences accentuate our appreciation of the environment we live in and our grateful love for the people, past and present, in our lives.

SURVIVING KATRINA WITH FROZINE AND AUGGIE DOGGIE
CHAKULA CHA JUA

Chakula cha Jua is the name most people know me by. It's my Free African Name, which I gave to myself back in the early 1970s during the first Kwanzaa celebration ever presented in New Orleans. It is of the Swahili language. Swahili, also known as Kiswahili, is a Bantu language originally spoken by the Swahili people in Tanzania, Kenya, and Mozambique. Chakula cha Jua literally means "food of the sun."

The organization conducting the celebration was called BLKART-SOUTH, a writer's workshop that came out of the Free Southern Theater. The Free Southern Theater, which was started in Tugaloo, Mississippi, and moved to New Orleans around the late 1960s, was a Black community theater company that came out of the civil rights movement of the South. Anybody who knew me before that time would still call me McNeal Cayette, which is my legal name. I never changed it legally. I still use it to sign (and receive) checks. So if you are thinking about sending me some money, make sure it is made out to McNeal Cayette. I still use both names interchangeably because, as I used to tell my kids in the classroom, they are both historically and sociologically significant.

I'm an actor, playwright, theater director, educator, poet, storyteller, and retired comedian. I only mention the retired comedian part because at one time I was one half of Chakula and Chink, New Orleans' Only Professional Black Comedy Team. We performed in just about every major Black night club in the city (not to mention schools, community centers, churches, etc.). But New Orleans wasn't ready for us, so we disbanded. I joined the Free Southern Theater after spending four years in the United States Air Force, which I had signed up for immediately after I graduated from high school (Booker T. Washington, class of '64). I joined the Air Force to give myself some time to decide what I wanted to do with my life. After four years of competing in the annual Air Force Worldwide Talent Search, singing with the Anchorage Concert Chorus, performing in plays with Alaska Pacific University, and producing, writing, and directing various variety shows and stage productions at Elmendorf Air Force Base, I decided the Air Force was not for me. Returning home in time to join the Free Southern Theater was just what the doctor ordered because I had decided I wanted to do theater, but I wanted to do something relevant. The Free Southern Theater, with its productions of change and social significance, answered that need.

When Katrina hit New Orleans, I was gainfully employed by the Orleans Parish School Board as a drama instructor for the Talented in the Arts theater program. When I wasn't teaching or doing theater workshops somewhere, I was usually directing or performing in some theatrical production with some local theater company or my own Chakula cha Jua Theater Company. The Chakula cha Jua Theater Company (named after myself, as you have probably noticed by now) was formed in 1978 as part of the Alliance for Community Theaters, Inc. (ACT I) annual New Orleans Black Theater Festival. At the time, I was living in the house on Wales Street in New Orleans East that I had purchased back in 1999 and which I am back in today. I lived there alone with my faithful dog, Auggie Doggie (also known as Duchess), the name her mother, my lady friend Frozine, called her by. Auggie was actually a gift to Frozine and I from her brother, but I ended up keeping her with me. Auggie was happy with the arrangement.

Katrina came out of nowhere. It was like it all happened in one weekend. By the time we realized it was upon us, it was a Category Five. I hadn't planned on going anywhere anyway because my car would probably not have made it to Slidell and I had just about enough money to order a burger and fries. So, I packed up my overnight kit and Auggie Doggie and headed over to Frozine's. I had already decided to ride out the storm with her, as I had done so many times in the past . . . and I figured this one would be no different.

Frozine's house sat on the corner of Pauger and N. Roman, a raised shotgun double that had been converted to a single. I parked my car in an empty lot across the street from her house where I could see it from her front door. There wasn't too much we could do in preparation for the storm except sit tight, pray, and hope for the best. I don't remember too much activity when Katrina actually passed through. Heavy, howling wind and sweeping rain . . . but it didn't seem to last too long. I remember Garland Robinette on the radio saying that the worst of the storm had passed through. (I can't remember if we still had power or a battery-operated radio.)

Feeling a little relieved, I opened the front door only to see that the water was to the top of the four steps leading into the house and just above the tires on my car. Even with that, I felt that we had been spared the worst and that this water would recede in a couple of hours. I kept returning to the door every few minutes or so until I suddenly realized that the water wasn't going down; it was rising. In fact, it was slowly beginning to cover the floor inside the house. Almost before we realized what was happening, the phone rang. It was a call from Frozine's neighbor, who was living across the street in an apartment located on the second floor, above the corner grocery store. He told her he was sending a couple of people to help her get over to his apartment because, from what he could see, the water was steadily rising and it wasn't about to go down any time soon. The three of us, Frozine, Auggie, and me, grabbed whatever we could and headed toward the door. When we moved down the steps to ground level, the water was just above our waists. I didn't know Auggie Doggie could swim, but she waded right across with no problem.

We remained with this neighbor, his wife or girlfriend, three or four teenagers, and about four others for the next day and a half. All were relatives or close friends to the neighbor, who hadn't hesitated to invite us over when he saw the water rising. The neighbor couldn't have been more generous. What he had, he shared with us, and we were thankful. This was the first of many acts of kindness I was to witness before this Katrina incident ended. Later that night as we sat on the upstairs porch, we could hear gunshots in the distance and actually witnessed people wading in the water, attempting to break into houses.

The next day brought lots of sunshine, with the water in the streets settling but not going down. People were sitting on their porches while children played in the filthy water in the streets, now filled with gasoline, garbage, dirt, and grime. A couple of the men and myself decided to walk to the intersection of N. Claiborne and Saint Bernard Avenues to see what we could see from the ongoing ramp heading to I-10 West. Circle Food Store was completely underwater, along with every business and house on that stretch. Every store or business on the block had been broken into, and shelves were empty. We even witnessed a couple of guys carrying computers they had stolen from a nearby school, which had also been broken into. Despite stories we heard of shootings at the Superdome (which were never proven to be true), we managed to get through our first day or two with enough food and drink, thanks to our good neighbor. It wasn't until the third day, when the city finally cut the water off, that we realized we were in serious trouble. I realize now that if I had to choose between having electricity or having water, I would have to say, *Give me my running water*. With no power, you will always get sunlight eventually, but when you lose that running water and can't flush that toilet, you are going to have some big problems.

That's when the boats arrived (police boats, I guess), going from door to door, telling people to pack whatever personals they could throw together and get ready to be taken to the airport. The city was being evacuated, and everybody had to leave. This was not good news for everybody. Some of the residents on the block did not want to leave. They were actually running and hiding. Our little group hurriedly got our gear together, excited about leaving, although we had no idea where we were going.

And I was concerned about Auggie Doggie. Would she be allowed on the plane? "She would not," I was told by one of the officers. "You'll have to leave her."

What was I going to do? We had never been separated before. How could I leave her in a city filled with streets of contaminated water, where the only part of the ground visible was the neutral grounds, and that was only on the main streets? At first, I wanted to leave her in the apartment, where she would not have to worry about the flood water, since it was on the second floor... but all others present agreed that was not a good idea, that she would do better outside. So, with the few minutes remaining before the boats returned, I put Auggie on her leash and walked her the three long blocks from Pauger and N. Roman to Elysian Fields and N. Roman, which was the nearest intersection where the grass was actually visible. For me, the water was waist-deep all along N. Roman; for Auggie, that meant she literally had to swim those three blocks, keeping her body afloat. How she managed to do it, I will never know. But the exhaustion from the swim made our departure much easier. I knew she wouldn't let me just walk away from her, but she was so tired, she just plopped on the ground. I whispered a soft goodbye and headed back to the apartment, not knowing if she would live or die or if I would ever see her again.

The boats arrived a few minutes later and took us to the on-going I-10 East ramp at Saint Bernard and N. Claiborne Avenues. Several helicopters were lined up, coming and going. This was my very first helicopter ride, so I was a little bit excited. But any joy I may have felt for a brief moment was soon taken away as I gazed down at the city below. New Orleans was underwater. The entire city was underwater. It was hitting me for the first time—this was a natural disaster. All we could see were the tops of the roofs of houses for miles and miles. Cars and trucks were underwater. No land was visible except for major streets and intersections. We were being taken to the airport, where we were being sent to a shelter in Houston. People were scattered all over the place, some in wheelchairs and some on crutches, just looking lost. Water was being distributed to everyone, so it really saddened my heart to see some half-filled bottles thrown on the ground after one or two sips were taken, despite the fact that many of these folks had been without food or water for the past two days.

Before long, we were all boarding a plane for not Houston but San Antonio, Texas. The first thing I noticed as we boarded the plane was a woman with her dog. And I'd been told I could not bring my Auggie Doggie with me. The ride to San Antonio was short and sweet. We were taken to a school gymnasium, which was made into a shelter, lined with cots. From a distance, my eye captured a massive, front-page newspaper headline that read "NEW ORLEANS UNDER WATER," with photos of several Black people wading through waist-deep water. For the second time it hit me: *This was for real. . . . This was not a movie. This was actually happening.* And I couldn't begin to imagine how it would all turn out.

From the moment we stepped into the shelter in San Antonio, we were treated like royalty. The volunteers were genuinely happy to be at our service. Tables were lined with snacks, personal items like toothpaste and deodorant, and clothes of all sorts: underwear, shirts, pants, coats and hats; you name it, it was there. We were told that if we didn't see anything we needed, just ask for it, and every effort would be made to get it to us. Showers were provided and, at last, telephone and cell hookups (our phones had been out for two days). I immediately got in touch with a few family members who had already relocated to Houston. Once they knew where I was, they said, "Don't move, we're on our way to get you." Frozine hooked up with her daughter, who more or less said the same thing.

Since it was late evening when we arrived in San Antonio, we did have to spend one night at the shelter, which turned out to be quite nice. I kind of hated to leave the next morning; I was enjoying being the one waited on for a change. My coffee and doughnuts and a copy of the daily newspaper (which I had requested the night before) were waiting for me when I woke up. The volunteers at the shelter were just super nice. Whoever they were and wherever they may be now, I want to give them a great, big, overdue thank you. They helped make this horrible ordeal bearable for us all.

I said goodbye to our New Orleans crew (all of whom had people on the way to take them to wherever) as my niece, Marcia, who had been living and working in Houston, arrived to take me to her apartment. At her apartment, she was already housing from New Orleans her mother, my oldest sister, and her youngest daughter and son. Houston was almost like a second home for the next year or so. My immediate family who remained in Houston were Joyce, my oldest sister, with her two youngest children, Bernita and Leo Jr., sister Jeanie and her husband George, sister Bernice, sister Dolores, and sister Christine and her husband Ralph. We all eventually found separate apartments and all remained there from anywhere from a year to a year and a half, all eventually returning to New Orleans. I was the last one to leave Marcia's apartment. I took my good time finding something I liked, and Marcia was such a gracious host, I really was in no hurry to leave. I eventually found a very nice place in Southwest Houston, where I stayed for a year and a half until I was ready to return to New Orleans.

I settled in an apartment complex on the southwest side of Houston called Meadow's Place Senior Village. This was my first time living in an apartment, so all of this was new to me. In fact, the whole complex was new, sparkling brand new. The place was beautiful, and I had a pleasant stay there before I returned to New Orleans. I called myself the teenager of the complex, since I was a bit younger than most of the other residents but still old enough to be considered a senior citizen. It was finally working to my advantage to be older. But with it came a price. Because I had a car, I spent a lot of time helping some of the older residents get to their doctor's appointments or do their shopping. I really didn't mind, since most of the folks were wonderful to be around and always had great stories to tell.

Houston, on the other hand, was quite an interesting place compared to small-town New Orleans. Lots of people and lots of traffic and lots of places to spend your money. One thing I loved about the city was its availability of goods and services. Every apartment complex or housing development came equipped with its own shopping mall and restaurants. And there was always something for everyone. I personally loved the variety of dollar stores. You could find just about anything in most of the dollar stores in Houston. (Bad news report: I read recently that most of them have closed down or are in the process of closing. What a shame). I also found a couple of theater companies that were quite good. I never got involved in any stage shows while there, but I did thoroughly enjoy those that I got to attend. One problem I did have was trying to find a good, solid Black restaurant. With all the restaurants in the city of Houston (I know I'm going to get into trouble for saying this), I could not find a good, solid, sit-down, classy Black restaurant in the city. I did find a couple of buffets or barbeque joints or take-out joints, but no classy, upscale Black restaurant. And, unfortunately for Houston, I was there the year they did the Essence Fest there. Houston had to realize the hard way that Essence Fest is more of a fashion show than anything else, and without Poydras Street and the French Quarter to parade up and down, as in New Orleans, half of the festival was missing.

Although I had very few worries while in Houston, it was no vacation. The reality of Katrina lingered over my head like a big question mark: *What do I do next? Do I want to stay in Houston? How do I apply for this? How do I apply for that? What about my job? Since the teachers in New Orleans were forced to resign, will I be able to find work?* These questions were working on me mentally and physically. I found myself visiting the hospital for ailments I had never had before (all of which miraculously disappeared once I returned to New Orleans).

I made several trips back and forth to New Orleans to get the house together. My first visit revealed that everything was gone. Water had risen to the window seals. As with most people, the refrigerator lay flat on its side. Believe it or not, I was able to save my computer because I had unplugged it and sat it on top of the cabinet, where it did not get wet. Lucky, also, was the fact that I was able to save all my play scripts because I had removed them from the file cabinet. The files in my four-drawer file cabinets were only wet in the two bottom drawers, but by the time I returned a month or so later, the water had seeped to the top drawers, turning everything into ashes. It took some time getting the house back together. Since relief money was coming in pieces, I had to rebuild in pieces. But through the grace of God, it happened, and I have been happily back in my house in New Orleans East since 2007.

Each time I visited New Orleans, I spent time trying to find Auggie Doggie. People in the neighborhood of Pauger and N. Roman had seen her several times. They said she would come and sit on the steps of Frozine's house, just staring at my car as if waiting for me to return. They said she would leave at sunset every day and return the next morning, that she did this for so long, and then she suddenly just stopped coming. At least I knew she was still alive. I hung up signs with her picture, and several people in the surrounding areas reported seeing her from time to time, but she wouldn't allow herself to get too attached to anyone. Not being in New Orleans every day made it difficult to follow any leads.

But finally, a breakthrough. While visiting one weekend (almost ten months or so after the storm), there was a note left on the door of my house in the East. It was from some animal rescue people who'd spotted a dog who looked like Auggie living under the I-10 bridge at Saint Bernard and N. Claiborne. Saint Bernard and N. Claiborne was the very spot where we had boarded the helicopter that took us to the airport. Auggie had probably traced my smell to the area and was going back and forth from there to the house on Pauger Street, hoping for my return. The animal rescue people explained how they had made several attempts to capture her by setting food traps, but she would not fall for them.

When I got to the area under the interstate, Auggie was nowhere to be found. I returned to the area every day while I was still in town, but she was not there. I returned to Houston at least knowing that she was still alive. It wasn't until three or four months later, on another visit to New Orleans, that I got a call from Frozine, who was also in town that weekend. *She had found Auggie.* She had gotten a call from a neighbor telling her that he had spotted Auggie on N. Claiborne Avenue, close to Ernie K-Doe's Mother-in-Law Lounge. Auggie was there when she arrived. She put the phone to Auggie's ear, and when she heard the sound of my voice, she started licking the phone.

At long last, a little more than eleven months after we had parted, *Auggie Doggie was found*, alive and well. Auggie's story was included in a book by the animal rescue group, but I don't know if it was ever released. The chapter was called "Allen's Story"; the group had named Auggie Allen because Allen was the street where Auggie was living underneath the interstate.

The next morning she was in the back seat of my car headed for Houston. It took her a while adjusting to apartment living (as it did me), but she blended right in and became the sweetheart of the Meadow's Place apartment complex. The complex was animal friendly, but your dog had to weigh twenty pounds or less. I think Auggie weighed around sixty pounds. But since I had been there for so long and was loved by all, all dog fees were waived, and no one ever mentioned her weight.

It seems everyone else in my family made it back to New Orleans before me. Before long, the New Orleans East house, fully renovated, was ready. Auggie and I packed our bags and returned home. To what? New Orleans East was already on the decline even before Katrina, and now it had become worse. None of the big, name-brand stores had returned and weren't making any plans to do so any time soon. Supermarkets were few and far between. A new Walmart did open on Chef Menteur Highway a couple of years later, which was very popular only because there was simply nowhere else to go. Before the Walmart opened, I had to go to Metairie or the Westbank just to find an ink cartridge for my printer. Dollar stores were plentiful only because no one else wanted to come to the East. As I write this, most of the dollar stores are closing.

So, what did Katrina teach me? Without sounding corny, I would say: *It's all material.* What made Katrina different from other storms we'd seen in the past, and some we are still witnessing today, is that the water didn't just come; it came and it stayed. It stayed for a very long time. And that long stay just caused everything in your house to rot and turn into ashes. I lost it all. Everything was totally destroyed. The hardest part was starting all over again. But then I have to stop and ask myself, *What did I lose?* I didn't own any crystal chandeliers or Persian rugs. But it wasn't about how expensive my belongings were. It's all material. It can be replaced. I can't. I still have my good health (and my good looks, as I jokingly tell folks all the time). That cannot be replaced. *It's all material.* You can't take it with you. The bright side of it all is that I ended up with a newly renovated house that I eventually was able to pay off. That was the bright side. As for my valued treasures that I lost, personal and sacred as they were to me, as I said before, it's all material.

Another major lesson learned from Katrina is that *people* are amazing. I am a firm believer in the song lyrics *"People who need people are the luckiest people in the world."*[28] This was best exemplified by the people who came together and who seem to continue to come together whenever there is a major storm or disaster. From Frozine's generous neighbors to the volunteers we came across in San Antonio, they were super amazing. They were so genuinely honest about wanting to help. Maybe they had their own motives, but I detected honesty in their efforts, and I was moved.

In closing, I would like to comment on FEMA and insurance as related to Katrina. One of my policies paid off in full; the other gave me hell. It makes you wonder even further how you can spend a lifetime paying insurance and never see a penny of it, or have to go through holy hell to collect on it. Makes you wonder. As for FEMA, it received much criticism on the way people were paid (most of it deserved, some of it not). Also, a lot of Katrina

---

28   Barbra Streisand, "People," track 7 on *Funny Girl*, Columbia, Spotify, https://open.spotify.com/track/0AfseROXCjDFXudJKAH0Zc?si=df22c-09b913e4a1d.

victims were criticized for abusing FEMA funds. I only have this to say on the matter: For the first time in my life, I felt the US government giving me something back. We pay to be citizens in the land of the free. Although there are many freedoms we enjoy by being good citizens, it was good having something come back to me from my government that I could see and feel and know was well deserved.

After many trials and tribulations, Katrina provided time to step back and refocus. A time to determine what is really important in life: family and friends and the trust of God. We've come this far by faith, and that can only mean that better times are yet to come.

FROM TRAGEDY TO TRANSFORMATION:
Finding Purpose in the Aftermath of Katrina

DAMIA KHANBOUBI

In August 2005, I was just starting my sophomore year at Louisiana State University (LSU) in Baton Rouge, Louisiana. I had just moved into my first apartment with three of my best friends from high school. It was a cute, four-bedroom apartment in an apartment complex just a few minutes' walk from campus. I'd been looking forward to living in my own apartment for so long, and it felt like I'd finally arrived. I was nineteen years old, and after being sheltered my whole life as the eldest and only daughter in a patriarchal Moroccan household, I felt like I was finally free.... I could do what I wanted, when I wanted, and no one could tell me anything.

And I took full advantage of my newfound freedom. I was the quintessential college party kid, going out to bars and clubs in Baton Rouge almost every night, meeting new people at house parties, and just generally indulging in all the fun I could. I was also very privileged in that I didn't have to worry about money. Scholarships and loans paid for school and my rent; calls to my mom paid for everything else. But the extra money that my parents so generously provided came with an unspoken condition: I was expected to excel academically and pursue a degree that promised financial success. And as someone who had always done well at school, there was no doubt in my mind that I would continue to do so, even as partying became more and more of a priority.

On the morning of Sunday, August 28, 2005, I was woken up after a night of being out with friends to a call from my mom letting me know that New Orleans had just received a mandatory evacuation order—its first in history—and that she, my father, and my three younger brothers were evacuating. My three roommates had already left with their families, who'd decided to

FROM TRAGEDY TO TRANSFORMATION: FINDING PURPOSE IN THE AFTERMATH OF KATRINA

evacuate before it was made mandatory and gone west from New Orleans, passing through Baton Rouge on their way. My family had decided to go east, and because traffic was horrific on all roads leading out of New Orleans and Baton Rouge was far enough inland for my family to feel confident I'd be safe from the impact of the storm, they left me in Baton Rouge.

For those who don't experience regular evacuations, let me share some insight on what it's like. When a hurricane is approaching, residents in its path are often given the option to evacuate or stay in their homes. Deciding whether or not to evacuate is not easy. There's so much to consider: the strength of the hurricane, access to transportation, and the ability to pay for evacuation expenses like lodging. For some, there is no choice at all because a lack of resources makes it impossible to evacuate.

My parents emigrated to New Orleans from Casablanca, Morocco, in 1985. My uncle, my mother's brother, was already here and established as a vendor selling leather belts in the city's historic French Market. In a few short years, my parents worked their way to establishing their own booth, selling souvenir items like T-shirts and tote bags. They would also go on to have various shops in the French Quarter that sold Moroccan imports, but it was their booth in the French Market that offered the most stable support for their growing family. I say "the most stable" because though their booth in the French Market provided a privileged childhood for me and my brothers, it was also subject to the ebbs and flows of the tourism industry. And summer is a notoriously slow season for my parents.

This meant that, since a large part of hurricane season takes place in the summertime, our ability to evacuate varied greatly from storm to storm. But when times were good and we were able to make that decision easily, we'd drive to places like Houston or Memphis or Destin and make a fun trip out of it. We'd spend our time like tourists, swimming in the hotel pool, eating out, and visiting local attractions. There's a word for this experience: we call it a "hurrication," a vacation spurred by an incoming hurricane. These hurrications, like regular vacations, cost hundreds to thousands of dollars depending on how long we'd stay. And in our experience, the hurricane would often end up missing New Orleans altogether or causing minimal damage, and we'd return home and resume our lives just like it was a regular vacation. Even in the best of circumstances, however, evacuating is always a source of anxiety and stress. Until the storm passed, we'd spend time in these other cities in a constant state of worry about the safety of our homes and belongings. Or the extra schoolwork we'd have to do when we got back (if the hurrication occurred after the school year had started up again).

And sometimes, we didn't evacuate at all. We'd stock up on water, snacks, candles, and flashlights and ride out the storm. For those of us in hurricane- and flood-prone areas, power outages and disruptive flooding really do become a mundane part of our lives. We learn to live with it and so it can be really easy, when considering all the effort and money it takes to evacuate, to decide to stay. Which is exactly what my family had been planning to do before then mayor Ray Nagin issued a mandatory evacuation order the day before Hurricane Katrina made landfall. And even then, my parents only decided to leave because they'd just gotten a car rental because our family van had broken down. With the new rental, they were able to take my brothers out to a beach in Florida for a few days.

Back in Baton Rouge, I was already experiencing the early impacts of Hurricane Katrina. I walked to the gas station down the street and was stunned to see it was packed with people and cars in lines for blocks. Then, friends in Baton Rouge started calling me to ask if their friends who were evacuating could stay at my apartment. There were three empty bedrooms in my apartment, and without hesitation, I opened my apartment to those who needed a place to stay. Looking back on my decision now, I'd like to think it was wholly compassion and generosity that led me to invite strangers to live in my apartment with me, but I think there was also a healthy amount of youthful spontaneity and disregard for consequences mixed in. I never stopped to think, what if my roommates objected to having a bunch of strangers living in their apartment? Would it be dangerous for me to be there with a group of people I didn't know?

But nevertheless, that decision would shape the next few days of my life in ways I could never have imagined. As Hurricane Katrina made landfall as a Category Three hurricane, my apartment transformed into a makeshift shelter for college kids. At any given time, there were between eight and fifteen people there cooking for each other, sharing stories, partying all night, and trying to make the best of a scary situation. As I think back on this time, what remains with me is the strange mix of camaraderie and chaos in the air that held me as I watched the devastating footage of my city underwater on the news. Almost twenty years later, I can't remember the names or faces of the strangers who stayed with me, but I remember their kindness. Some even left me money to help cover the costs of food and drinks. Those few days were truly a testament to the power of human

FROM TRAGEDY TO TRANSFORMATION:
FINDING PURPOSE IN THE AFTERMATH OF KATRINA

connection and the ability of ordinary people to come together and support one another in times of crisis.

It's important to note, always, that the eye of Hurricane Katrina passed east of New Orleans, sparing us from the worst of its impact. It was the failure of our city's levee and flood walls in over fifty locations that led to New Orleans and its people being submerged in flood waters for days.

My family's trip to Florida turned into a twelve-hour trip to Mobile, Alabama, a city we can drive to in two hours on any other day. Hurricane Katrina shifted east after they left the city, and a majority of their twelve-hour trip was spent in back-to-back traffic in the midst of severe storming and tornado warnings. After being the last car to fill up their tank before the gas station they stopped at ran out, they drove to Tuscaloosa and got a motel, where they watched the devastation that rained upon New Orleans as a result of our failed levee system. My parents quickly realized that this would be no short trip to the Florida shore and decided to continue driving north to Indianapolis to stay with my uncle. They would be gone until December 2005, marking the first time in my life when I was apart from my family for such an extended period.

While in Indiana, a church group donated a house in Plainfield, a car, and clothing to my family. This is an example of the incredible kindness some Katrina evacuees would experience across the country, though it does not diminish the discrimination and xenophobia many of the people escaping the devastation after Katrina experienced. And while our home in New Orleans experienced minimal damage, my parents lost their livelihood. The destruction of the city was widespread, and the tourism industry appropriately came to a screeching halt. My mother, who had been self-employed for decades, now had to seek employment. Ironically, she ended up working at the airport in Indianapolis selling souvenir shirts, mirroring her own business selling souvenirs in New Orleans. My father was unable to find a job.

And for the first time in my life, I had to get a job to support myself. Overnight, I was responsible for paying for my own living expenses. I had no savings to fall back on and no understanding of how to budget. The combination of financial stress and the grief I felt seeing my hometown destroyed made it difficult to focus on school and maintain my mental health. Despite the challenges and my initial attempts to run away from it all and join my family in Indiana, I eventually found a job that allowed me to support myself.

My three younger brothers also struggled with the changes that Katrina brought. The separation from their daily routine and friends weighed heavily on my brothers. The oldest of them called me every day to express the depression he was feeling. I didn't understand the depth of his pain at the time, and he was communicating it clearly. It wasn't until I saw *Katrina Babies* last year that I finally realized the emotional toll Katrina had taken on my brothers. Because he was already eighteen, he made the decision to return to New Orleans first, followed by my father, who came back to take care of the house and start rebuilding my parents' business. The middle of my three younger brothers had the opportunity to attend a high school in North Carolina where another of my uncles lived, so he moved there. The youngest of my brothers stayed with my mom in Indiana.

We all struggled to adapt to our new normal; a family that was very rarely apart now found themselves involuntarily spread across the country. The experience taught us the true meaning of emotional fortitude and the importance of our family bonds. We learned to appreciate the little things we'd often taken for granted, like having a roof over our heads and food on the table. Eventually, the day came when my mom and my younger brothers finally returned to New Orleans. While our city still bore the scars of the hurricane, they were so happy to be home.

By 2007, we would all be back home, reunited by another tragedy and one of the first major blessings to come out of Hurricane Katrina. The devastation following Hurricane Katrina shut down Charity Hospital, New Orleans' largest public hospital, leaving St. Thomas Community Health Center as one of the few clinics in the city providing care for uninsured patients. Around the same time, the Susan G. Komen Foundation partnered with the LSU School of Public Health to provide mobile mammography and, later, a state-of-the-art breast imaging center at St. Thomas Community Health Center. It was here that my mother was diagnosed with breast cancer in early 2007.

I got this news during the first few weeks of what would have been the second semester of my junior year at LSU. In what I can only describe as divine intervention now, I'd decided not to go back to school after my winter break. I didn't know it then, but I was experiencing a deep depression that would only get worse over the years. I was less and less concerned with my future and more and more focused on numbing the pain with alcohol. So, when it was time to go back to school in January 2007, I just didn't, and I planned on keeping the fact that I wasn't in school from my parents for as long as possible. But when my mom called me to tell me she'd just been diagnosed with breast cancer, she asked me to come back home and help my dad with

FROM TRAGEDY TO TRANSFORMATION:
FINDING PURPOSE IN THE AFTERMATH OF KATRINA

their business since I was no longer in school. I was stunned that she knew; it'd only been a few weeks. But like she told me on that phone call, she ain't dumb and I'd made it quite obvious by not mentioning school once, when I used to talk about it all the time.

I say it was divine intervention that I'd quit school weeks before my mother got diagnosed with cancer because my mother would have put my education before her health, and because I'd already made the decision to not go back, it was easier for her to ask me to come back home. And I did. I took a duffle bag of clothes, left all my things in my apartment in Baton Rouge, got someone to take over my half of the rent, and never looked back. In a lot of ways, my mother's breast cancer diagnosis saved me from the path of self-destruction I was on.

After a hard year of brutal chemo, we received the joyous news that she was cancer-free in 2008. There are no words for the immense gratitude and relief we felt. The unwavering support and exceptional care provided by St. Thomas Community Health Center played a pivotal role in my mother's triumphant journey towards recovery, and I am forever thankful. To this day, even with our good insurance, St. Thomas is still our healthcare provider. Their unwavering dedication to their patients regardless of insurance, coupled with the exceptional services they offer, has made them an integral part of our family's well-being. However, what I didn't realize until I told my mom I was writing this chapter is that the very existence of St. Thomas's breast cancer center was a direct result of the substantial investment made in New Orleans' healthcare system in the aftermath of Hurricane Katrina. This investment turned out to be a true Katrina Blessing, it not only provided my mother with the life-saving diagnosis and care she so desperately needed but also provided the same for so many who needed accessible healthcare in the community.

From 2007 to 2009, I worked alongside my parents at their booth in the French Market. Little did we know that the devastation of Hurricane Katrina would play a pivotal role in revitalizing their business. The wholesale T-shirt companies my parents bought from began to create souvenir T-shirts adorned with Katrina-related content. These T-shirts bore slogans such as "Chocolate City," a reference to Ray Nagin's 2006 Martin Luther King Jr. Day speech in which he said, "It's time for us to rebuild a New Orleans, the one that should be, a chocolate New Orleans. And I don't care what people are saying uptown or wherever they are, this city will be chocolate at the end of the day."[29] These T-shirts became incredibly popular with tourists and visitors alike, and so did the books we sold that documented the aftermath of Katrina. People were eager to purchase a piece of history, a tangible reminder of the resilience and spirit of New Orleans. It was our first experience with the double-edged sword that is disaster tourism. On the one hand, we were grateful for the increased business and the chance for my parents to rebuild their livelihood. On the other hand, we couldn't help but feel a sense of unease at profiting from a tragedy that had caused so much pain and suffering. Working at my parents' booth during that time taught me valuable lessons about entrepreneurship, the power of resilience, and the complexities of profiting from tragedy. Most importantly, it made me really clear on the fact that if one is going to profit from tragedy, it matters who and how.

That depression that I talked about earlier certainly hadn't disappeared. And though I say coming back home saved me from certain self-destruction, my lifestyle remained far from healthy. I was still partying almost every day and still struggling to find meaning beyond the moment. In 2009, our family friend who would later become my boss and mentor, Carol Bebelle (affectionately known as Mama Carol), suggested I seek therapy. She was alarmed by all of the weight I'd lost to depression and suggested I see Dr. Denese Shervington. Dr. Denese guided me toward finding suitable therapy options, and in a few weeks, I was in therapy for the first time. A few months later, in January 2010, Mama Carol temporarily hired me to replace her then assistant while she spent a month abroad. This month-long contract eventually turned into five and a half years as Mama Carol's executive assistant at Ashé Cultural Arts Center. But more on that later.

In the years after Hurricane Katrina, the city of New Orleans struggled to regain its footing. Businesses had been destroyed, homes had been gutted, and the spirit of the city had been dampened. But in February of 2010, a glimmer of hope emerged. The New Orleans Saints, the city's beloved football team and quintessential underdog, made it to and won the Super Bowl. For my mother and the rest of the city, that moment was more than just a game. It was a symbol of triumph, a sign that the city and its people were starting to heal. My mother still points to that Super Bowl as the time when business finally started to feel the way it did pre-Katrina. The city was slowly but surely coming back to life, and the Saints going to the Super Bowl was a

---

29   "2006: Ray Nagin's 'chocolate city' remark," posted January 18, 2013, by CNN, YouTube, 1 min., 29 sec., https://www.youtube.com/watch?v=QEH9u-26Vlhk.

symbol of that rebirth. For my mother, it was the moment when she finally felt like we were going to be OK again. It was a moment of unity and pride, a time when everyone in New Orleans could come together and celebrate. It was a reminder that even in the darkest of times, there is always hope.

Now, back to Ashé Cultural Arts Center and how it changed my life. At the time that Mama Carol offered me the temporary position, I was working at a po' boy shop and struggling to discover what a meaningful career would look like for me. I thought working at Ashé would expose me to professional possibilities, and I was absolutely right. I discovered a place where my passion for equity and my love for the arts could be translated into a job that paid my bills and taught me so much along the way. I immersed myself in the richness of African history, art, and music and in all of the ways it shows up in New Orleans culture. As Mama Carol's executive assistant, each day brought new challenges and opportunities. I coordinated events, managed projects, and assisted Mama Carol in her tireless efforts to collaborate with artists, educators, and community leaders to create impactful programs that celebrated the beauty and diversity of the African diaspora. The experience transformed me both personally and professionally. Mama Carol's mentorship shaped my work ethic, taught me the power of art to inspire change, and instilled in me a deep appreciation for the cultural heritage I was fortunate enough to be a part of. It opened doors to incredible opportunities, fueled my passion for cultural preservation, and connected me with an inspiring community of artists, activists, and scholars.

Through this learning and these connections, I found my own voice in the movement for equity and liberation. I developed a deep sense of purpose to ensure that the artists and culture-bearers of this city—the ones who hold the stories, the songs, and the soul of New Orleans —had the resources, recognition, and support they needed to continue their work of reflecting and shaping our world. Their contributions are an invaluable gift to the city, a vital part of our shared history, and the key to a brighter future.

Ashé is also where I truly developed and deepened my analysis of race in America and the intricate web of systemic racism that permeates our society. Though I was very aware, through lived experience and otherwise, of the ways racism manifests in everyday life, my time at Ashé taught me about its origins and design. It is through this lens that I was able to see what was really happening in New Orleans during post-Katrina "recovery." It was already painfully clear that New Orleans' predominantly Black communities were disproportionately affected by the storm and its subsequent flooding, revealing stark disparities in infrastructure, emergency response, and access to the resources needed to evacuate and then return. And now I saw more clearly that the systemic failures that led to these disparities were not simply the result of negligence or oversight; they were the direct consequence of a long history of intentional discriminatory policies and practices that had marginalized and disadvantaged Black communities for generations. Understanding and acknowledging how systemic racism operated during a crisis like Katrina allows us to advocate for policies that lead to a radical transformation of the systems and structures that perpetuate racial injustice—not just in New Orleans but across the nation.

The legacy of Hurricane Katrina continues to ripple through our neighborhoods, cultural traditions, and displaced diaspora. While the floodwaters receded long ago, the waterline of trauma they left behind remains etched into our hearts. Contrary to some prevailing narratives that suggest the city has "recovered," many of us who lived through it, and especially those who returned to rebuild, know that true recovery isn't just about rebuilding homes, being able to go back to business as usual, or adding amenities without care to who gets to access them—it's about healing hearts, minds, and communities.

Over the past two decades, as I've navigated my own healing journey alongside the city's, I've come to understand that recovery involves addressing not just the symptoms but the root causes. The flood and the ensuing horrors that occurred as a result of it weren't an inevitable result of Hurricane Katrina. It was a failure centuries in the making—one shaped by neglect and disinvestment in Black and low-income communities, the same neglect and disinvestment that we continue to experience in "recovery efforts" that don't include prioritizing the needs of the most negatively impacted people who were here before Katrina.

And so we come to another one of the biggest blessings I've experienced since Katrina: being able to be a part of a community that is focused on building a better future for this city by actively confronting injustice and creating lasting, positive change—a community of artists and activists who are working to debunk the myth of a racial hierarchy and shining a light on the truth that our racist systems have been deliberately designed and can be deliberately replaced by systems that ensure we all have equal access to the ability to thrive. Today, as I stand alongside incredible people fighting for justice in New Orleans, I am constantly inspired by the strength of our community. Together, we are not only healing from the wounds of the past but also forging a future in which we can all thrive. And though we have and continue to face daunting challenges, through our unwavering commitment to our shared vision, we honor the revolutionary spirits of those who came before us and continue their work to create a New Orleans that is truly just and equitable—for everyone who has the honor of calling this city home.

THE SEEDS OF STRENGTH, COURAGE, AND CONFIDENCE
DWANA MAKEBA

The Arrival of the Storm
It was an ordinary day, one that began with an unexpected shift in the sky. Thick, dark clouds rolled in from the horizon, swallowing the soft morning light and turning the world a muted gray. Back then, I was thirty-four years old. Now I am fifty-four years old, a two-time homeowner with a flourishing business and a master's degree.

I stood by the window of my new home on Humanity Street, nestled in the historic Gentilly neighborhood of New Orleans. It was a house I had saved for, dreamt of—a symbol of the life I had worked hard to build. But now, as the first drops of rain splattered against the window, a sense of unease washed over me.

The rain started gently, as if testing the ground, but within moments, the winds picked up, and the drizzle became a torrent. It was as if the heavens had opened up, releasing a force that would not be denied. The storm was here.

As I watched the fury outside, I felt a familiar sense of chaos stirring within me. For years, I had been at war with myself, my confidence worn thin by life's endless challenges. But something about this storm was different. The more I observed its intensity, the more I felt it mirror my own inner turmoil. And in that reflection, something began to shift. I was watching the news, and Margaret Orr was advising that we immediately start to evacuate. Margaret Orr was the chief meteorologist for our local news channel, WDSU. A friend of mine was coming in from New York to assist me in driving to California for a new job position. He arrived late in the night, and the storm was going on. We decided to leave immediately and began driving in the middle of the night. By the time we made it to Texas, it was early morning, and the phone was ringing off the hook with a number of concerned family members asking me if I had gotten out. We only stopped for gas and drove straight through. We arrived in California on Sunday evening. The twenty-eight-hour drive out of the storm and into a new beginning created an opportunity for me to reflect about the power of Katrina, the storm, and the internal storm within me, Dwana.

Roots of Resilience
Since my friend had offered to do most of the driving, I was left with the flurry of thoughts that ran through my head. My deep thinking and reflections helped me make sense, in some way, of the uncertainty of nature and the courage to walk in faith.

I thought about strength. Strength, I realized, isn't something we are born with. It's something that grows inside us, often in the harshest of conditions. I thought back to my childhood, growing up with parents who worked tirelessly to provide for me and my siblings. Life wasn't easy then. But their perseverance, their refusal to give up, had planted the first seeds of resilience in me.

I found myself rooted in memories of their strength. My parents' lessons were my foundation—my roots. They had taught me how to weather life's storms, and now, as we were making our way toward California, I recalled how I had leaned on that foundation to weather Hurricane Katrina.

When I was back in New Orleans, in the midst of the storm, I knew I would not break. Like the trees outside, swaying but standing tall, I would bend, but I wouldn't be uprooted. I recalled the wind howling and the rain thrashing against my windows. I felt fear begin to gnaw at me. The fear wasn't just about the storm outside. It was also about my internal storm. It was a familiar, deeper fear—the fear of failing, of not being good enough, of not being strong enough to withstand life's challenges. But something flickered inside me, a determination I hadn't felt in a long time. Courage isn't about not being afraid. It's about acting in spite of fear. I thought about the people I admired—ordinary people who had shown extraordinary courage. They had faced their personal storms and emerged stronger.

I reflected on being in Katrina and stepping out into the rain. My heart was pounding as I invited the storm to engulf me. I could feel the cold wind whipping through my hair, the rain pelting my skin. But with each step I took, I felt a sense of defiance rising. I wasn't just standing up to the storm outside—I was standing up to the storm within. As I stood in the storm, I did not know what my next steps were.

Facing this storm felt like the next step in a journey I had already begun. For years, my confidence had been eroded by a thousand tiny failures, setbacks, and rejections. It had withered, trampled beneath the weight of disappointment. But as Katrina continued to thrash against the world outside, I felt something changing. I was no longer the person I had been before this storm—unsure, hesitant, afraid. I was growing.

As my friend and I continued to drive toward California, I reflected on what I had left behind, my old life, for what I hoped would be a dream job in Hollywood. It was terrifying to leave everything familiar behind, but deep down, I knew it was time to take control of my life.

Confidence, I realized, doesn't come all at once. It's built, little by little, like a flower that blooms after being battered by the wind. I started to see every small victory as proof of my strength—like getting through another day, or accomplishing a goal I once thought was impossible.

I silenced the doubts that had held me back for so long. Hurricane Katrina became my reminder that life's chaos is not something to fear, but something to embrace.

The Power of Perspective

I had spent so many years focusing on my failures that I had lost sight of my strengths. When I faced Hurricane Katrina, in its destructive beauty, I was forced to stop and reevaluate. It stripped away the illusions, leaving me exposed. And in that vulnerability, I found something precious: perspective.

I began to see myself not as a victim of circumstance but as a warrior. I had faced challenges before and survived. Now, I could do more than survive. I could thrive. Each setback was a lesson, each failure a stepping stone.

Katrina had changed me. I was no longer afraid of what lay ahead. I had found strength in embracing the uncertainty, just like my daddy had modeled for me.

Embracing Change

Change is often terrifying, something we resist. But when I faced Katrina, as it howled around me, I realized that it wasn't something to fear—it was something to welcome. The winds had torn through the landscape, leaving a path of destruction but also of possibility.

As I settled into my new career in California, I thought about the changes in my own life—stepping into the unknown. I was afraid, but I chose to embrace it. I put my faith into action, trusting that whatever challenges lay ahead, I would have the strength to face them. I made a choice: I would no longer cling to what was safe. I would embrace the new. It wasn't easy—change rarely is. But I knew I was strong enough to handle whatever came next.

The Role of Community

Strength is often thought of as a solitary thing, but Katrina showed me the power of community. In times of crisis, there's a bond that forms, a shared resilience that pulls you through. My godmom Linda Merritt was a very close bond. She made me know that I could face anything. She made me know my strength. Her life was a huge example for me. She was a loving, caring, hardworking woman. She loved life and people. In my darkest moments, it was the people around me who reminded me of my strength. Their encouragement became the foundation for my courage. Together, we faced the storm, and together, we emerged stronger.

California was fine, but I longed for New Orleans. I missed my community and decided to move back to New Orleans. That is when I opened the salon Beauty on de Bayou. I was one of four women who opened up shop on Bayou Road after Katrina. It was a strong bond of four women: Vera Warren Williams of Community Book Center, Yashica Jordan and her daycare, Mother Nature of the Coco Hut Restaurant, and me. We shared our resources and began building the business corridor on Bayou Road. The significance of community extends across various aspects of human life, influencing individuals and societies at emotional, social, cultural, and economic levels. A sense of community provides individuals with a sense of belonging, purpose, and security, which are fundamental to psychological well-being and social stability.

Finding Purpose

Hurricane Katrina wasn't just an external force—it was a catalyst for finding purpose. In the chaos, I began to question what really mattered to me. What did I want out of life? What was my true goal?

I realized my purpose wasn't just about success. It was about making an impact. Helping others, being part of something bigger than myself. That's where I found my strength. It was what my father, Ricardo Stevenson, had long instilled in me. My father still helps others to this day by volunteering in his community and church.

With this new sense of purpose, I felt a renewed confidence. The challenges ahead didn't seem as daunting because I had a reason to face them. I knew who I was and what I wanted to do.

The Journey of Self-Discovery

The storm was more than just an event—it was a journey. It forced me to look within, to discover things about myself that I had buried long ago. I learned I was stronger than I had ever realized. I faced fears I had tried to ignore for years, and each time I did, I grew.

Self-discovery is not an easy path, but it's necessary. Through Katrina, I found new strengths, confronted old weaknesses, and learned to appreciate both. I began to see myself not just as someone who had survived struggles but as someone who had thrived because of them.

Moving Forward with Confidence

Looking back to my experience during Katrina, when the storm finally subsided and the skies cleared, I felt a deep sense of calm. I had been through the storm and come out stronger. My confidence had been rebuilt, not in an instant, but through every challenge I had faced.

The lessons I learned in the storm stayed with me. I no longer feared failure or the unknown. I knew now that I had the strength to face whatever came next.

And with that knowledge, I moved forward—not just surviving, but thriving.

JAZZMAN IN THE STORM
ED MORRIS

Part 1: Jazzman in the Storm

Jazz has been described as a broad style of music characterized by complex harmony, syncopated rhythms, and a heavy emphasis on improvisation. Wynton Marsalis teaches that it encourages the expression of personality and individuality while teaching one how to listen to others—sort of like democracy.

My dad, Leonard Morris Sr., was a jazzman—a jazz trumpeter. As a little boy growing up in New Orleans in the early 1940s, he fell in love with the sounds of Satchmo's horn. His dad bought him a trumpet, and there was no looking back. His aptitude and adeptness on the trumpet were such that he soon became known as Lil Clifford (after jazz great Clifford Brown). He enlisted in the Army at seventeen years old, was honorably discharged in 1952, and married his high school sweetheart. Nine children came from their union. I am number three. Dad said that children gave purpose and direction to his life. In fact, he turned down opportunities to travel with some of NOLA's great musicians because of the negative impact a traveling musician's life could have on a family.

Now, be patient and bear with me as I provide the mise-en-scène to a loving and dynamic father-son relationship. To say that Dad was my hero is a colossal understatement. Unlike most kids growing up, I had no need for heroes, sports or otherwise. Dad was my hero! This GED-holding, blue-collar welder, mailman, and jazzman was who I admired, idealized, and wanted to emulate! Dad was one of the smartest people I knew. He could talk history, politics, religion, and astronomy (yep, including "black holes") with the best of them! He could intellectually challenge you, enrage you, and make you laugh—all in one living room discussion (or, should I say, debate). But his greatest attribute was his love—the love he spoke and demonstrated through deed. He was also a fierce warrior, in spirit and deed.

So, imagine my upset and confusion in October of 2002 when Dad and I had our first, and very major, falling out. I'll spare you the details of the argument, but my "un-inviting" Dad to my daughter's (his granddaughter's) wedding should give you an idea of the magnitude of the disagreement. Now, you may ask, what does an argument in 2002 have to do with Hurricane Katrina in 2005? Well, Dad and I had not spoken since that disagreement in 2002.

Against that backdrop, this is how Katrina unfolded for my family.

Eva, my wife, and I are native New Orleanians and have never evacuated for a storm. But, because we'd just had our first grandchild (a granddaughter in Memphis, Tennessee), we thought we would take a road trip to Memphis to see her for the first time. Like everyone else, we never expected the devastation caused by Katrina. When the scale of Katrina's devastation began to unfold, we began getting a head count of everyone's whereabouts. The only person we could not account for was Dad.

We were told that Dad and Mom had left their home in Pontchartrain Park with Karen, the baby of the family, to evacuate New Orleans. But, a half-block away from home, Dad got out of Karen's evacuating car, decided he would ride out Katrina, and walked back home. His quote: "Can't be no worse than Hurricane Betsy!" Well, Dad (like everyone else) found out that it would be far worse than Hurricane Betsy. However, in the tradition of the Boy Scouts—"Be prepared!"—Dad was always ready for what life might bring . . . and could improvise for the unexpected like any great jazzman.

Now, mind you, the rest of the family had no idea of Dad's heroics unfolding in New Orleans. The last image we all had of Dad was him getting out of Karen's car and returning home before Katrina made landfall. So, when pictures of New Orleans began to flood (pun intended) the TV airwaves (pictures of water almost covering the iconic Circle Food Store), we didn't know if Dad was dead or alive. Had Katrina taken our dad—my hero? I was heartbroken, angry and confused. Angry that he had decided to get out of Karen's evacuating car, and confused because he and I had not reconciled.

Well, after much agonizing phone-searching with the Red Cross and others, a number of family members decide to organize a search posse and try to return to New Orleans (although no one was being allowed back into the city) to search for Dad. As the search posse neared New Orleans, they began stopping at Red Cross Evacuation Centers to see if Dad's name was on any of the lists. On their third stop at a center near Baton Rouge, although Dad's name was not on the list, my nephew Zack had to use the restroom. Upon entering the restroom, there was Dad, returning from the restroom with his folded newspaper under his arm—as was his custom. Also in the shelter were all the neighborhood people rescued by Dad in his boat.

CNN, the National Association of Letter Carriers, and others proclaimed Dad a hero. They told the story of how Dad, in his boat, rescued two neighbors from around the corner (women he had promised that if things got bad, he would come and get them). A promise made and a promise kept. Just like Dad! But as things got worse, three women and a toddler who lived across the street from Dad's home found themselves in a life-or-death situation. In the pitch-black of the night, he (and the two women already rescued) could hear the cries for help from the women across the street. Dad promised that he would come and get them at daylight because the boat engine had malfunctioned and, also, Dad didn't want to risk dangerous downed electrical power lines in the dark. The stranded women cried back that they would be dead by morning: flood waters were already above their waists as they stood on their beds. Dad determined that he had to improvise a way to rescue these three women and their baby. Seventy-four-year-old Dad (with a busted back) tossed the anchor and pulled the boat (an eighteen-foot boat with two women and their family dog already on board), tossed the anchor and pulled the boat, again and again (in the darkness of night) until they were across the street, where he could make the rescue. Improvisation—a part of a jazzman's trade and repertoire!

Reconciliation: Mom and Dad's home in Pontchartrain Park (their very first home bought in 1956) and thirty years of family memories were destroyed by Katrina. In fact, when Dad got into his boat after the catastrophic failure of the levees, flood waters were already up to the roof at their home. Dad and Mom spent the next, post-Katrina year in Atlanta. Everybody began to realize Dad's need to return to his beloved New Orleans and the sense of familiarity—food, street sounds, the sense of neighborhood, the sense of "small town"—that New Orleans offered.

Well, mine and Eva's home had sustained only minor damage. And Eva was working in Atlanta, and I was doing church work in Phoenix, Arizona. So, Eva and I agreed to make our home in NOLA available to my parents. Dad called to express his gratitude—the first breakthrough in repairing the fracture in our relationship! In that first month, Dad called frequently to thank me for making our home available to him and Mom. On the third call, I stopped him mid-sentence to remind him that I'd lived under his roof for twenty-one years (with all provisions) at no cost. And, he better not call me one mo' time to thank me for this one instance when a child had an opportunity to thank his parents for all they had given him. They lived in our home until their home was rebuilt.

Part 2: Expect the Unexpected (A Blessing in the Desert)

Against the backdrop of the devastation of Hurricane Katrina, my wife and I were in Memphis, Tennessee, at the home of our younger daughter. And, like every other displaced New Orleanian, we are attempting to plan our next move—no access to our city, no home, no jobs... basically starting over. Our hurried plan was to go to Atlanta, where there was the prospect of work for both of us.

With that in mind, I made my way over to the mall in Memphis to purchase clothing suitable for a lawyer starting a new career in Atlanta. I was alone. As I parked the car, I was suddenly stopped in my tracks by the sound of nearby church bells ringing out a familiar song, "It Is Well With My Soul." As an aside: this lawyer was also a Baptist preacher (since 2003) after being raised Catholic and being away from the church as an institution since my late teenage years. This spiritual journey is a whole 'nother story!

Back to the church bells! So, I stopped in my tracks and began to apologize to God for making all of my post-Katrina plans without consulting Him. I asked God, "What is it You, God, would have me do at this juncture in my life?" Right there, in a still, small voice, came the word *"Phoenix."* It took a few minutes for me to gather some context for "Phoenix." Well, a couple of years earlier, I had read about a church in Phoenix, Arizona, doing extraordinary work through its numerous ministries. In fact, the church (Phoenix First Assembly, or PFA) had taken over an abandoned major hospital complex in Los Angeles, California, out of which it operated its Dream Center. The Dream Center was, among many other things, a drug rehabilitation ministry that operated 24/7, 365 days a year. Its success at transforming addicts and downtown LA was so dramatic that the mayor and LAPD asked the Center's leadership for the "magic formula." I had a passion for "servant leadership" and the work of the church in transforming lives as well as saving souls. So, I made a mental note (trust me, nothing more than that) of planning one day to visit PFA. So, there I was, post-Katrina, in the parking lot of a Memphis shopping mall, with God reminding me that He had some immediate plans for my life.

Sooo, now I had to return to my daughter's home (without new business attire) and explain to my wife and extended family that instead of Atlanta,

God was sending me to Phoenix, Arizona. After answering all of the obvious questions—"Do you know anyone there?" No. "What do you know about the church?" Nothing—my family released me to go to Phoenix (all was not joyful, to say the least). The next day, I began my 1,400 mile drive from Memphis to Phoenix. My wife left for Atlanta that same week.

I drove during the day and rested at night. The scenery was breathtaking, and the drive was cathartic. All along the way, I was questioning my own sanity. My conversations with God went something like this: "God, I've read in the Bible about a lot of strange things happening in the desert. I hope you have prepared some hearts in Phoenix to receive me."

Well, I finally reached the PFA campus (and I do mean campus—it's a megachurch). I knew nothing about the Assemblies of God denomination, nor anything about the "diversity" (or lack thereof) of the church's membership. I walked into the administration building and told the receptionist that I'd like to speak with a minister, if there was one available. A Hispanic gentleman came out to greet me. I told him my story, all of it—at the risk of sounding absolutely insane. And that I didn't know why I was in Phoenix, Arizona. After listening intently to me, he smiled and asked me to take a quick walk outside with him. We walked a few hundred yards, until we were positioned before the vast sanctuary building. He asked me to look up. Draped across the front of the church was a banner that read "Expect the Unexpected!" He said that their pastor (Pastor Tommy Barnett) had preached that message the Sunday before my arrival. He gave me a great big hug and said, "We've been waiting for you, my brother!" I met Pastor Barnett—a great, humble man with a heart for "the least of these my brethren."

The Church immediately put me to work as a lawyer and a minister. They helped me find a nearby apartment, and one day I returned from work to find my entire apartment fully furnished—dishes and all.

The Church sent me to LA to spend a couple of weeks at the Dream Center. Their ambition was to open and operate a Dream Center in Phoenix, and they wanted me to assist with the effort. And we did in fact open the Phoenix Dream Center in downtown Phoenix.

I spent a year at PFA. During that time, I witnessed an incredible love for the Lord and the people of God, especially the "least of these." I saw and heard testimonies from former addicts, prostitutes, motorcycle gang leaders, and homeless folks who had lived for years under the interstate—all transformed by the loving ministries of PFA. The transforming love of God was palpable at PFA. Being part of such a ministry for that season blessed me immensely—even in the wake of the devastation of Hurricane Katrina.[30]

Part 3: Postscript

Dad passed away on May 6, 2012 (seven years post-Katrina). Dad was eighty-one years young. He died at his home surrounded by the sounds of Miles and Coltrane and the presence of a loving and proud family. When Charbonnet Funeral Home came to retrieve his body, we told them to be careful with it—they were handling royalty! I was asked to write his eulogy and speak at Dad's funeral. It wasn't an emotionally agonizing task to undertake because 1. Dad and I had reconciled, and 2. how difficult can it be to talk about your hero?[31]

Not a day goes by that something Dad said or did doesn't visit my spirit. I miss him dearly, but I never feel void of his presence. His presence is eternal!

As for my spiritual journey, it continued in post-Katrina New Orleans. Pastor Dwight Webster of Christian Unity Baptist Church continued to speak into my life, and Pastor Dean Hinton of City of Refuge encouraged my spiritual growth. For a brief moment, I thought the Lord was calling me to pastor a church. Obviously this was more my longing at the time than God's charge. I'm so glad I didn't get ahead of God!

Spiritually, I'm currently in a very good space. I'm not "churched." I have no problems with the church as an institution. But the Lord has not impressed upon me the need to join any particular local body of believers. My "theology" is evolving and expanding. My spiritual journey continues. And I believe Jesus and I would enjoy each other's company at evening supper! I tell my preacher friends not to be concerned—Jesus and I are doing well!

---

30   I cannot vouch for the spiritual reputation of PFA once leadership was transferred from Pastor Tommy Barnett.

31   Sidenote: A friend asked me whether Dad had ever "apologized" to me for the argument in 2002 that caused our great falling-out. My response: There was no need for him to. First, there was a "great body of work" that defined mine and Dad's relationship. And that incident in 2002 was an aberration, although significant. I am the man that I am today because of all that Dad poured into me. Second, I could not predict what the response of that crazy jazzman would have been had I gone to him and demanded an apology. I was not willing to test his improvisational response!

THE BRIGHTER SIDE OF THE STORM:
Stories of Compassion and Courage

MINISTER WILLIE MUHAMMAD

New Orleans is all I know when it comes to living in a city. Despite its challenges, there are very few other cities I would want to live in. I grew up in the uptown area of New Orleans known as the Irish Channel. I was born to the parents of Willie and Clara Beal. I can vividly remember, as if it were yesterday, when my father walked out. My mother cried and begged my father not to leave her and her three sons. Her crying and her begging were to no avail. My father took his tools, clothing, and some furniture, never telling his oldest son (me) that he was leaving or explaining the reason why.

Later that day, my uncle, who has really been like a father to me, and the backbone of the family, said, "You have to be the man of the house now." I said, "I will," inwardly knowing that I had no real idea of what it was to be a man. I have always been one who believes that if I observe and analyze my surroundings, I can learn and adapt. In my quest to become a man, I talked to other males in my family and neighborhood. Thus, the streets and television became my instructors in what I thought was Manhood 101.

Listening to countless stories told to me by my older cousins about their experiences and consuming images portraying men on television led me down a path of mistreatment of women, numerous participations in neighborhood fights, and dabbling in minor drug dealing. Looking back, I realized that I was trying to fulfill a false vision of what it was to be a man. Even though I lived my daily life trying to capture this persona, inwardly I still felt a void and did not believe that I was really becoming a man. This doubt further increased after hearing a man, while flipping through the television channels, who would give meaning to my life one day.

I saw the Honorable Minister Louis Farrakhan speaking at Southern University at New Orleans. The part that I happened to catch was the Honorable Minister Louis Farrakhan talking about how he would respond to someone who would offer him one million dollars to sleep with Farrakhan's wife. This was when the movie *Indecent Proposal* was released. The minister said that the fool who would approach him with such an offer would be "picking his teeth up off the floor!" After hearing those words, I thought to myself, *That's a man.*

Time went on, and I found myself at Walter L. Cohen Sr. High School, one of the roughest high schools in the city of New Orleans. During my junior year, I was enrolled in an American history class being taught by a teacher who was considered to be the meanest and hardest teacher in the school, Mrs. Jeff. She tried her best to teach us some form of Black history by having a Black History Multiple Choice question that many of us did not pay attention to. I would later find out that she was the wife of one of New Orleans' great Black social workers, Morris F. X. Jeff. Many students were either flunking her class or transferring out of her class. For some reason, I refused to do so and decided after getting a D during the first quarter to start reading the chapters while in class.

As I began reading, I learned about how the Native Americans were slaughtered by white settlers. This made me want to learn about the experiences of Black people in America. I began reading more and more books about our people's past accomplishments and struggles. I came across *The Autobiography of Malcolm X* and became so attached to the book, I used to read it at night with a flashlight after my mother had made me turn off the lights and go to bed. However, I never completed the book because a girlfriend lost it. The majority of what I read dealt with Malcolm's early life and his work in the Nation. By then, I wanted to learn more about the Nation of Islam (NOI) and the Most Honorable Elijah Muhammad.

I decided to do my research paper on the NOI. I remember using the book *When the Word is Given* as my primary source. I was attracted to the discipline and the teachings of the NOI. I remember reading what the Most Honorable Elijah Muhammad said about the so-called "UFOs" and thinking to myself, *Man! That is what those things are. That makes so much sense!* Public Enemy was hot at that time, and I kept hearing them say, "*The follower of Farrakhan / Don't tell me that you / understand until you / hear the man!*"[32] This increased my desire to learn more about the Minister.

---

32   Public Enemy, "Don't Believe the Hype," track 3 on *It Takes a Nation of Millions to Hold Us Back*, recorded 1987–88, Def Jam Recordings and Columbia Records, Spotify, https://open.spotify.com/track/5k8dJvnLKfv1YN9W3bO79x?si=30acb308b817470c.

THE BRIGHTER SIDE OF THE STORM:
STORIES OF COMPASSION AND COURAGE

I was in high school the first time I saw the book *Message to the Blackman in America*. A motivational speaker came to the school and lined up a bunch of books on the chalkboard, one of them being the book written by the Messenger. When I saw the book, I thought, *I'm Black, I am a man, and he has a message. I need to read that book.* I decided that I was going to steal it while the speaker was distracted by students talking to him after his speech. As soon as that thought crossed my mind, the speaker said, "Don't ask to see my books because some people have been stealing them." I scrapped that mission, and it would be almost two years before I had the chance to read the book. What's funny about that situation is that the motivational speaker is a registered member of the Nation of Islam, Brother Stan Scofield.

Even though I never got the chance to read the book at that time, I did become acquainted with *The Final Call* newspaper. A friend of one of my older cousins would always purchase *The Final Call*. I used to go by his home just to ask him if I could have the paper after he finished reading it. He would give it to me, and I would take it home and read it over and over. He also let me borrow a videotape of the Honorable Minister Louis Farrakhan on *Donahue*. I was blown away from watching that video. I was so touched that I began speaking to a teacher about it so much that she asked me to bring the tape to school. I did, and she allowed our class to watch it. She was so blown away that she allowed all of her classes to watch it also.

My senior year, I wrote a play during Black History Month titled *A Black Tragedy*, which was about the struggles faced by a young Black male. At various intervals in the play, historical figures such as Rosa Parks, Malcolm X, and Dr. King would appear and comment on the young man's life. I played Malcolm X. The play was so powerful that the local school board paid for us to travel to perform at different schools throughout the city. That same year, the movie *Malcolm X* came out. Our school organized a field trip for the students to go and see the movie. Years later, one of my classmates who'd attended the movie saw me out with *The Final Call*. When he saw me, he said, "Man, I knew you would become a Muslim the day we had that field trip to go see the Malcolm X movie. You came out of that theater in deep thought."

After my senior graduation, I began co-hosting a local cable access show geared toward the youth. Through this television show, I had the opportunity to interview Brother Khalid Muhammad. A year or so later, after joining the Nation, I found an old *Final Call* lying around the mosque that had a picture of the interview. While in high school I wanted to join, but I never knew anyone who was a member. In fact, in high school, I decided I wanted to become a teacher of history. I wanted to do so because I wanted to teach our people the truth of what I had been learning. I remember hearing a voice in my head saying, *You will not be successful as a teacher unless you become a Muslim.*

After interviewing Brother Khalid, I got the mosque's telephone number and called, constantly leaving messages that were never returned. Not far from where I lived, there was a building that had the star and crescent on the door across from the now popular Ashé Cultural Arts Center. I thought that was the mosque. I went there with my mother on a Sunday and did not see any cars out front. I knocked on the door anyway.

A brother answered, slightly opening the door not more than a crack. He talked to us in a very cold manner. "What do you want?"

I said, "We are here for the service."

"We don't have a service."

My mother and I left, but I later learned that it was not a mosque under the leadership of the Honorable Minister Louis Farrakhan.

My time to fully become acquainted with the NOI came during my freshman year in college. I used to hang out with two brothers from up north. One was from Detroit and the other was from Chicago. The brother from Chicago used to strongly believe that America was a melting pot, and he would always talk about how racism was a result of Black people overreacting. He was basically a Negro. One day after a heated debate, I wanted him to see the truth so bad that I brought him to the Black studies professor. She tried to talk to him and was not able to penetrate his thinking. After an hour or so in her office, I realized that she was not reaching him. I remember saying to myself, *He needs to speak to a Muslim.*

After leaving the office, we went to have a seat on the yard. Once there, we continued to debate our viewpoints. While debating, I saw a student walking across the yard coming our way, who I know today as Brother Jason Muhammad; he was X back then. I'd seen Brother Jason once before, and something about him made me believe that he was a member of the Nation of Islam. I had never seen him in a suit and bowtie at all. I had never heard him talk before, nor had I ever talked to him. I signaled for him to come over to where we were.

Once he came over, I asked, "Hey man, you are a Muslim, huh?"

He said, "Yes, sir, brother."

I explained to him the issues my friend and I had been debating and asked him to shed some light. The brother just started dropping bombs. Everything he talked about, I visually saw flash in my mind as if I was sitting in a movie theater watching it happen. He talked about the genocidal plot to kill our people, the government's plan to place us in concentration camps, and much more. My brain became so heavy that all I wanted to do was sit down. After talking to us, he took our numbers and invited us to the mosque. When he left, the brothers from Detroit and Chicago wanted to go walk the yard to chase females. I told them I needed to sit down until my head felt lighter. Eventually, all three of us accepted the Teachings. However, I was the only one to remain.

My journey in Islam led me to meet my wife, Michelle Muhammad, the best bean pie maker in the entire Nation of Islam to me (that might cause an argument in some circles, but I stand by that). This coming December, we will be married for twenty-four years. She is the mother of my two daughters, Nandi (biological daughter) and Azire (our adopted daughter). Our marriage and life, for the most part, have been good. Together, we have been able to provide our children with experiences that both of us only dreamed of, growing up in poverty-stricken New Orleans. My wife has been by my side from my time in the mosque as just a regular believer to, now, as the student minister of our mosque. I married her when I was twenty-five years of age, after a six-month courtship.

Prior to Katrina, we lived in a home in eastern New Orleans. I am *so thankful* we moved to the Westbank a year before Katrina. I say that because that home was flooded, and if we were living there, we would have lost everything, specifically the several shoeboxes filled with photographs of my childhood, family, friends, and memorable moments. Those photographs mean so much to me, partly because I am a visual person who likes to see things, but also because photographs help me to remember those moments and those loved ones who are not here. That would have been devastating to lose. I know many did; I am grateful I did not have to experience that impact of Katrina.

I can honestly say I was caught by surprise by the seriousness of Hurricane Katrina. That week, I was involved in so many activities—community protests, ministerial responsibilities, and family responsibilities—that I was not checking the news. When I sat down in the barber chair to get my haircut, the barbers started talking about their potential plans. The more I listened, the more I realized this was serious. I came home and spoke to my wife about the possibility of leaving. I told her I would monitor it and decide later. Well, we ended up making that decision and evacuated around 1:00 a.m. that Sunday morning, prior to the hurricane making landfall. A large portion of that day was also spent trying to convince my mother, who lived with my disabled brother, to leave. She did not want to go. My wife was able to persuade her. It's a blessing she did because the area where she lived was soon to be underwater. If they had not left, I do not think they would be here today.

We were on the road for what seemed like an eternity. It normally takes an hour to get to Baton Rouge, but I think it took us about two hours. We had to drive through Baton Rouge to get to my brother-in-law's apartment in Lake Charles. He provided shelter for my family (my wife and young daughter, my mother, and my brother) along with several other family members who also sought refuge there. We stayed there for a few weeks, and at times I found myself mediating tensions between family members: my wife and her niece, and my mother and my wife. (My mom was just being rude. I love her, but I have to tell the truth.) All the while, I still had to keep abreast of the well-being of members of our local religious community. I also need to add that I had no contact with my father, who had decided to stay.

All of this weighed heavily on me. My mom's behavior caused me to make a hard decision, but it was needed to keep the peace: I had to find another place for her to go. I remember wanting to talk with my uncle, who is one of the men I greatly admire and respect and whose insight I value. I can't say enough about my Uncle Lawrence. Ever since I have known him, he has been smooth, charismatic, industrious, and more. Most of my cousins and I grew up without our fathers in the home, but my Uncle Lawrence filled that gap for all of us. I can remember him gathering all of us, along with his own children, at his shotgun apartment on Second Street for the weekends. He would cook us breakfast in the morning and take us to the park or the movies. I even remember my uncle sewing summer short sets for two of his sons.

A Cadillac was always his car of choice. It wasn't until years later that he began to drive different kinds of cars. He was also a sharp dresser. When I look at older pictures of him, I see he has always been smooth and cool. Growing up, my uncle's first set of children were my cousins Fat (Lawrence Keys Jr.), Marland (who was around my age, so we hung out a lot), and their baby sister Tenisha, whom we called Tee (she was much younger than Marland and me). I thought that Tee was my uncle's biological daughter. It wasn't until my late thirties that I found out she wasn't. He raised her in such a way that anyone would have thought the same.

My uncle has always been good with his hands. He built what we now call an entertainment center, which held his radio system, VCR, reel-to-reel, and more, long before such a thing existed. He organized all of his albums and movies in a system he designed. I later found out that he is dyslexic. He was raised during a time when such a diagnosis was not well known. After an older cousin of mine, who shared the symptoms, was diagnosed with dyslexia, my uncle confided in him that he experienced the same. He found his own ways to navigate through life.

He is one of the best chess players I have ever met. His motto is, "The game will end in two ways—either I win, or it's a draw!" I have seen him play, and he is not lying. I trust my uncle so much that when I was contemplating marrying my wife, I went to him for advice and his opinion. I did not do the same with my father. Whenever my mother fell short on funds for food, utilities, etc., my uncle was right there covering the difference, even though he had his own children to take care of. To me, my uncle is one of the best examples of a man I have known. It is very hard for anyone to tell me something negative about him. So, when I needed insight regarding how to deal with my mother during the aftermath of Katrina, he was the first person that came to mind.

He gave me advice that confirmed the decision I knew I had to make. One of the funny things about talking to him was that it provided me with an opportunity to laugh amongst all that I was dealing with, and I sure needed it. I had been trying to reach him for days but was not able to because the line was busy. When I finally reached him, I was excited. I asked him if he was alright, did he have food, how was he managing? My uncle has always been cool; I have never seen him angry.

He said, "I am good. I am a survivor. Plus, Walmart is open."

Then I went on to share with him the dilemma I was facing. He gave me some advice, and the call ended. I shared with my wife that he was doing well despite the city being flooded, etc. I shared with her what he'd said about Walmart. I thought that was strange. It wasn't until sometime later that I burst out laughing when I realized he was telling me that, like others still trapped in the city, he was going into Walmart and getting the items he needed.

More days passed, and my family and I went to Houston, Texas, where my wife and daughter stayed with Brother Eric (now Abdul Aleem Ansari Muhammad) and his family. Brother Eric made us feel like his home was our home. I never felt unwelcome. It was there in Houston, Texas, that, for the first time in my life, I stood in a line to get food stamps. That experience further taught me to never say never. It was also there in Houston, Texas, that I first met the Honorable Minister Louis Farrakhan in person. He and a delegation were traveling to various cities to participate in town hall meetings to add his voice to the fight for evacuees to return to New Orleans, and to check on evacuees in shelters to ensure they were being treated right, because there were complaints by evacuees that they were not, due to the negative popular images of people from New Orleans. The Minister walked around the shelter in Houston giving words of hope to those there, hugging many, and praying for them as well. I don't think many realize how deeply this man loves our people and even humanity.

My family and I would finally end up in Baton Rouge, where we stayed with Brother Andrew and his then wife, Sister Dusty. Initially, in addition to my family, Brother Andrew and Sister Dusty also opened their home to another family from our mosque. What I remember about those days is the strong sense of family we experienced. Everyone contributed to the daily household duties: cooking, cleaning, and laundry. We would also gather to watch movies together and have discussions about marriage and family. Eventually, the other family left, and I found a job at a local middle school. It was supposed to be one of the worst in the city, but compared to what I'd experienced when I taught in New Orleans, it was manageable. I bought my daughter her first bicycle for her birthday while in Baton Rouge. She was so happy. I don't think she really understood the magnitude of what we were experiencing.

My wife landed a job with FEMA and moved back. Our personal home was on the Westbank, so it was not damaged. She and my daughter returned home, and she worked while our niece homeschooled my daughter. I would drive home on the weekends to be with my family, to begin working to restore properties we owned, and to start seeing how to repair our mosque so our believers would have something to return to and to engage in the fight for the right to return for our people. Many of the areas populated by our people were re-designated as green spaces by those who did not want to see us return. It was said they would not be habitable. If our community accepted that, they would not be back in New Orleans again.

I would look forward to driving from Baton Rouge to New Orleans on Fridays after work to see my daughter and my wife. When I think of what to compare seeing my wife every weekend to, what comes to mind is two teenage lovers who have talked on the phone for weeks finally getting to see each other. Sometimes, as married couples, quality time can be impacted by arguments over silly things or unfulfilled expectations that were not expressed or not expressed clearly. During those weekends, it was clear to me that those encounters were not worthy of taking away from the limited time we had together before I had to get back on the road and be away for another week.

I also remember the joy on my daughter's face (we only had Nandi at that time). She would meet me at the door or run to hug me. My daughter has always made me feel like the most important man in the world. I have met men who feel incomplete because they have not had a son. I don't feel that way. A large reason why is because of the love and admiration I have experienced and continue to experience from my daughters.

Prior to Katrina, our religious community would hold most of our meetings at our mosque on Downman. After Katrina, due to our building being down, we held meetings in our homes on Fridays and then on Sundays. The meetings were more intimate and really felt like family. Being that there were only a few of us in the city, I think we appreciated one another more. When I reflect back on my experiences with Katrina, my heart is warmed when I think about how happy past tenants were when we informed them that they could rent properties we owned. Many of them shared stories about how difficult it was to find rental units. Being able to offer them a place to return to helped them fulfill their dream of coming back and beginning to rebuild. I am thankful to God that my family and I were able to help.

One of the most heartwarming, memorable things I experienced upon returning occurred at S. Claiborne and Toledano while I was out with *The Final Call* newspaper. This was some months after Katrina. Some FOI (Fruit of Islam, male members of the Nation of Islam) were back in the city working, rebuilding their homes, and contributing to the rebuilding of the city. We wanted our people to know that we (Mosque No. 46, i.e., the Nation of Islam) had not abandoned them. The joy I saw on people's faces and the expressions of gratitude they shared about seeing us out there really warmed my heart! We heard and saw this from people who did not give a donation nor want a paper. Because of a lot of negative propaganda that has been put out about the Nation of Islam, the Honorable Elijah Muhammad, the Honorable Minister Louis Farrakhan, etc., not all of our experiences out distributing *The Final Call* are pleasant. But hearing people express how seeing us made them smile, encouraged them, and made them happy made our presence and years of work in the city feel not in vain. I am not saying that we never heard that before, because we have. But to hear such from people after one of the greatest natural disasters to hit New Orleans, while they were trying to rebuild their lives, touched me, made my sacrifice feel worth it, and fueled my desire to return to the city.

I found a picture of myself outside of an event in New Orleans post-Katrina that reminded me of what I was experiencing at that time, something that I was in denial about and no one but me knew. I realized I was depressed. I was depressed because of the condition of our city and, in particular, the circumstances our people were facing. I think a larger part of the depression stemmed from the religious community I was (and am) a part of, that had nurtured me from my early twenties into adulthood, being disbanded. People with whom I had dined, people whose life milestones I'd witnessed, and with whom I'd shared my own, were all over the country. I did not know if they all were returning. My depression manifested in the hairstyle I sported at that time. I cut my hair down to a Caesar cut (a low cut where all the hair is the same length all over). Since my teenage years, I'd sported a faded haircut. I never missed getting such a cut, but after Katrina, I did not allow my hair to grow high enough to fade. This all taught me more about my inner strength.

I was able to deal with those feelings and work through them in order to work with others to help rebuild our mosque and help our people return. This experience made me more aware of the importance of mental health. My love and appreciation for our people also increased as I began to hear about more and more acts of kindness and heroism that had taken place during and after the storm—for example, the twenty-year-old named Jabbar Gibson who commandeered a school bus and helped drive many from his project to safety. What a great demonstration of bravery. Do you know that his name, Jabbar, actually means strength, might, and great power? I heard stories from elderly people who talked about how the young boys who would be hanging out participating in criminal activities prior to Katrina were the ones protecting them, bringing them food, medicine, insect repellent, and more. These stories affirm what I have been taught from the theological teachings that I believe in, which is that by nature, our people are good, and by circumstances, we have been conditioned to act otherwise.

This anthology has really given me an opportunity to reflect on many examples of courage, resilience, acts of kindness, and charity that I know of but have never really had the chance to talk about. Like him or not, former Mayor Ray Nagin's controversial statement—"This city will be a chocolate city in the end"—was an act of courage and a message to those rich white businessmen who were trying to prevent New Orleans from being a majority-Black city again.[33] I personally believe he paid politically for that remark. Our people were determined to rebuild their neighborhoods despite the disparities they faced from the Road Home program and more. I handed out checks to

---

33   "2006: Ray Nagin's 'chocolate city' remark," posted January 18, 2013, by CNN, YouTube, 1 min., 29 sec., https://www.youtube.com/watch?v=QEH9u26Vlhk.

families from the Honorable Minister Louis Farrakhan that helped them rebuild, and years later, a popular violinist in the city shared with me how the minister had paid for his rent for a year while he lived in Houston after Katrina. I saw activists and clergy who did not get along pre-Katrina work together to combat police brutality, renters' rights, and more. We were able to renovate our mosque building in the most beautiful way yet since we'd first acquired the property.

Eighty percent of our community members returned, and we welcomed many new members. I was able to rekindle many relationships that I had prior to Katrina.

Reflecting on those turbulent days in the aftermath of Hurricane Katrina, I am struck by the resilience not only within myself but within the entire community that surrounded me. Despite the overwhelming challenges, the tensions, and the moments of uncertainty, what stands out most are the acts of kindness, the strength of family bonds, and the unwavering support from both familiar faces and unexpected allies. Whether it was the warmth of Brother Aleem's home, the courage of young men protecting the elderly, or the determination of our people to reclaim and rebuild their city, these experiences reaffirmed my belief in the inherent goodness and strength of our community. In the face of one of the greatest natural disasters, we did not just survive; we emerged stronger, more united, and more determined to ensure that New Orleans remained a place where we could continue to thrive and uplift one another. The journey was difficult, but it was in those moments of struggle that our true character was revealed, and for that, I am deeply grateful.

Going through the challenges of Hurricane Katrina taught me the importance of resilience. I had to adapt quickly to a new and unfamiliar environment, and in doing so, I learned that resilience isn't just about surviving tough times—it's about finding the strength to grow from them. The storm tested me in ways I never imagined, but it also showed me that I have the inner strength to bounce back from even the most difficult situations. One of the most significant lessons I learned from Katrina was the value of community. During the aftermath, it became clear that in times of crisis, we need each other more than ever. The support and unity of my family, neighbors, and even strangers played a crucial role in getting through those tough days. This experience reinforced my belief that there is incredible power in coming together, and that unity is essential for overcoming any challenge. Despite the devastation, Katrina taught me that there's always a brighter side, even in the darkest of times. I learned how to find positivity and growth in the midst of chaos. This experience helped me see that every difficult situation presents an opportunity to learn and grow. It wasn't easy, but I emerged from this experience with a renewed sense of purpose and a deeper appreciation for life.

FEDERAL FLOOD PRECIPITATED BY HURRICANE KATRINA
JAMILAH PETERS-MUHAMMAD

Before the Storm

Blessings. In the midst of a great tragedy, I have to first reflect on the grace of God and the peace in trusting in His Word and purpose for my and our lives. Sometimes it is almost too much, with my earthly eyes and thoughts, but throughout this journey, the one thing that was always evident was that blessings abounded. I grew up thinking my mother, Wilhelmina, was a bit crazy, but I saw over and over how God showed up for her. My name, Jamilah Yejide, means "beautiful image of her mother." I thank her for passing on that crazy gene called faith so that I too can know where my blessings come from. Thank you, also, to all the angels who helped.

About five years before the storm and the ensuing disaster, I had been diagnosed with a chronic progressive lung disease. The first blessing was that had this diagnosis occurred one year earlier, I would have been in the hospital, unable to care for my four grandchildren and ensure their safety. I'm a lifelong New Orleanian. I say I was born, bred, and deep-fried here, and New Orleans is my choice for a forever home. In all of those years, I had never evacuated, but looking out into the gulf, I knew this was a storm unlike any before in my lifetime. The whole gulf was white, and a Category Five storm was predicted. We had to go, but go where, and how?

As a result of my illness, I was no longer able to work as a healthcare consultant for the company I had been with for many years, which caused a big dip in my income. I also worked as a performing culture-bearer at the Ashé Cultural Arts Center, with the New Orleans Musicians' Clinic and Assistance Foundation and with Bamboula 2000, my band. I also worked with several other performers and was engaged in independent cultural work. Much of my time was spent teaching cultural arts of the African diaspora and traveling.

As an independent contractor, my boss (*me!*) could not pay me or offer me any benefits. Essentially, we were living off some savings and the blessings that continually flowed from my family and my church, Christian Unity Baptist Church, where I led the health ministry and our dance ministry, Mawasi. I had quite an active and rewarding life doing all the things I loved. But I had nada, nothing to evacuate with but prayers and trust in God. My sister, Jodice, had returned to the city the day before the storm and had given me an unexpected five thousand dollars. Now my family and I had a way to leave, to get out of harm's way. Not only did we have enough money to leave but also to catch up on our mortgage. We could sigh a breath of relief and focus on the daunting task at hand.

One day before the storm, tragedy had also struck one of my best friends, whom I call my Mama Sister because she is all of that to me. I had spent most of the day and night trying to help, console, and then persuade her to leave. Finally, I was able to persuade her and her daughter, whom I call my daughter, the baby her mother had for me, to leave town with us.

Three vehicles formed a caravan out of the city. My van carried seven other people: my Mama Sister and our daughter; three of my grandchildren, the twins, Craig Jr. and Tevis, who were nine years old, and ten-year-old Ashley Nzinga, whom we called Nzinga (my oldest grandson decided to stay with his parents); and my beloved elders, CeCe and Aberdeen, my aunt and uncle. Jodice's vehicle was packed, and my brother, Ricky, and his family were in the third vehicle. Off we went.

Originally, we intended to go to Houston, but after a twelve-hour drive to Baton Rouge, a drive that, normally, would take only one hour, we were too exhausted to go on. My sister and brother went to a relative's apartment that was being renovated, my friend and her daughter went to a relative in the city, and I went to the home of Gerri, whom I had met in college and who had become my sister and a member of our Peters clan. We arrived at her apartment with three children, two elders, and me. She opened her arms and her heart to us. We were at last safe and able to rest, as much as one could, considering all that was going on around us, comforted that most of my immediate family was safe and accounted for.

Living in Limbo

My niece stopped by a few days later on her way to St. Francisville, which is about a sixty-minute drive northeast of Baton Rouge, where her in-laws were. She invited me to take the ride with her. When I got there, her in-laws said, "Auntie, you don't have a place, let's get you a room here." "Here" was a local Best Western where many other evacuee families were staying. I got two rooms, one for the elders, CeCe and her husband Aberdeen, and one for me and the children, the twins and my granddaughter. We became part of a newly aligned band that formed an alliance around the common cause of survival and beyond.

What now?

St. Francisville is home to historic plantations and self-appointed "bluebloods." Even in this divided and unequal community, we found an abundance of love and support. The hotel manager was very helpful and caring, and she would ignore me cooking in the room to feed my family. Local churches joined in the efforts to provide for our needs. Faith, Hope & Love Worship Center, under the pastorship of Pastors Ronald and Robin Hardy, began visiting the hotel, door to door, to find out what we needed and, more than that, to attend to our spiritual needs.

The local restaurants were getting FEMA money, so they were bringing food to the hotel three times a day. Before they started doing that, other local churches stepped in and brought meals to the hotel. The hotel was located on a lake with a beautiful green space that the children could play on. There was also a pool that they could swim in until safety concerns around the absence of a lifeguard forced it to close.

Time and more time. Clothes, gift cards, monetary donations poured in from across the nation. We were all helping each other at the hotel. FEMA was hard to pin down, so if one of us was able to get FEMA on the phone, we kept them on the line so everyone could have access to make that all-important call for assistance to help us to go *home*. If one person found out about a resource, we told everyone else. We started a phone chain to expedite passing along any information we thought might help.

My family thought I had absolutely lost the last of my fragile mind when a local animal rescue came by to offer pets to us. Several of us jumped at the opportunity. I have had dogs for all my conscious life, and so have my children and elders. We chose a beautiful brown Rhodesian Ridgeback we named Buck Wild, and we all loved him so much. We had left our chocolate lab, Romeo (my chocolate lover), Satin, a handsome black tomcat, and Mr. Bunny, our furry forest friend, back in our devastated city, and we were really concerned about their fate. Uncle Aberdeen had been a boxer, and he loved taking Buck Wild for long walks around the property. He also loved to box with the dog, trading shoulder blows and punches. The children would run and let the dog catch them as they rolled in the grass together. Crazy, maybe, but joyful: normalcy, and the blessed space to forget, too. Time and more time.

My sister Jodice, my elders, Jodice's daughter, Trina, and her husband and two children left for Orlando, Florida, when Trina's husband, Leonidas, was offered a job and housing by the company he had worked for prior to the storm. They took my elders with them. This was a tough time for me. It was just me and the children—put on a happy face and keep dancing! — and that's what I did. I started an exercise and meditation class five nights a week at the hotel. Our little community responded and would faithfully come. In the beginning, some said, "I can't come, my children won't keep still long enough for me to do anything." I said, "Come. Bring the children, and I promise you they will get what they need."

Come with the children, they did. In the beginning, I had to gain their trust, prove that I would and could handle the children. After about forty-five to sixty minutes of movement and stretching, we would form two circles. The adults formed the outermost circle. The children formed the inner circle, and I sat in the middle of the circles. We lowered the light, played some soft meditation music, and channeled our collective breath to a place of inner peace that we had not found in a long time. Our circles grew as participants encouraged others to come. The children responded, and many nights, parents carried sleeping children and children relaxed and ready to go to bed back to their rooms.

We looked forward to this time together. I needed this for my mental health and well-being more than they knew. Our lives had always been surrounded by and grounded in the cultures of the African diaspora, so my grandchildren were a wonderful support system in making all of this happen. Again, normalcy for all of us. Dance has always been a refuge for me; I had found *peace*.

Eventually, more people began to leave the hotel, but our community was still standing, stronger together. This was a racist town, but even in that place, there were those who opened to us and truly wanted to help us. I found out the residents and city leaders were having meetings to discuss the needs of the "refugees," so I began going to those meetings and became the spokesperson for our groups.

The hotel was not the only place where there were evacuees. Many were living with relatives. Through word-of-mouth, others found us, and our community grew outside of the hotel. Other churches came into our community to share resources and information. Mama Carol and Baba Doug (co-founders of Ashé Cultural Arts Center in New Orleans) sent me a shipment of leotards, tights, and dance shoes to share with the children who wanted to study. My sister-friend, Emi Gittleman, sent me money donated by a group of her friends in Upstate New York. She also sent me cases of Putumayo Kids' *World Playground* CD, along with passports to teach about the different cultures and children around the world. Donations came from everywhere to help us adjust as much as possible.

We began to seek a church home and visited several local churches: Faith, Hope & Love, Star Hill Baptist Church, and Magnolia Full Gospel Baptist Church. The day we visited Magnolia, we had found a home. It was youth day there, and it mirrored our home church's youth days: the singing, the message, and the same Sunday school book we had studied from. My children and I felt spiritually covered. Before we could leave the church, Pastor Coates told his wife to go to the office to get that blessing that had been left for a family and gave us an envelope filled with cash. Glory. We left with hearts filled with gratitude and discussed what church we would join. We all agreed that Magnolia would become our home in St. Francisville.

Time and more time. Thanksgiving was approaching, and through many blessings, we were going to be able to visit with our family in Orlando. A wonderful, compassionate woman, who owned a local restaurant and was now bringing us the most appetizing and delicious meals many of us had had since we had left home, had made a complete Thanksgiving dinner with decorations for everyone at the hotel. Blessings keep coming.

While in Orlando, my family had landed in a lovely, supportive community. My nephew, Leonidas, worked at one of the Hyatt Hotels. They heard we were coming, and it was my sister's birthday on Thanksgiving Day, so they helped us with a deeply discounted suite in a local hotel and catered a full Thanksgiving meal for us all at the hotel. Blessings.

And what Orlando trip would be complete without a trip to Disney World? Many friends of my family worked at Disney, and they pooled their resources for tickets so me and my family could spend a magical day in the Magic Kingdom. Blessings.

Christmas? There was still no home-going for many of us as others began to leave daily. What to do for Christmas for the children? We gathered, we talked. The community was very safe and walkable, with safe streets and areas that were also inviting for riding bikes. So, in one month, we garnered all our supporters, including local businesses, the Bank of St. Francisville, the churches, and a local Walmart, and we began to plan Christmas gifts for every evacuee child aged eighteen and under in the community. We gave the older kids (fifteen- to eighteen-year-olds) electronic gifts and age-appropriate presents to infants and children under age six. Every child aged seven to fourteen received a brand-new bicycle, and we even had enough money to buy some small, token gifts for the kids to give to their mothers.

We went to Houston for Christmas to see my son, Craig Sr., the kids' mother, Tamiko, and their two other siblings, Emilio and Letecia, who had evacuated with their parents. Oh, happy day! Lots of fun, food, laughter, and sweet memories. Then back to the reality that they were staying and we had to go back to a hotel in St. Francisville.

Time and more time. The children had landed well in the Louisiana State of miseducation—the schools in St. Francisville had the highest educational scores across the state. We had to fight a *good* fight to get their multiple special needs accommodated. They were all in gifted math, visual arts, music, and English classes. They got what they needed!

More families had left. We had kinda normalized a life of hotel, school, church, and newly found friends, including Adrema Carter Vessel and her *large*, happy family, the Carters, led by her mother, Mama Nell, and her seven sisters and I don't remember how many brothers. They embraced us as their own with Sunday dinners and many "come on over" moments—and could that family cook! We felt love and remain connected to them to this day. We have lost Adrema and Mama Nell, but Carlon, Aldrema's daughter, and a few of her sisters are still in frequent conversation. Ken and Barbara Dawson had two sons who were about the same age as my grandsons. Ken was on the local council, but he was also an amazing all-around coach. My children played on the local football, basketball, and baseball teams. Nzinga, my granddaughter, has always loved to swim and joined the local swim team. New life, running from game to game and meet to meet. We loved it. We also continued to dance and drum and joined the dance and drama ministries at our church.

And, we found a great healer. Dr. Nnamdi Nwabueze not only skillfully cared for our healthcare needs, but he, his wife, Stacie, and their beautiful family of a boy and three girls also became family. All these wonderful people and so many others did everything they could to make us feel at home. They even encouraged us to stay, to make St. Francisville our home, but my heart belonged in New Orleans.

I started traveling a little to perform again. The community wrapped around me and took care of my children so that I could do this. It felt good to be back on the stage doing what I love, being with my band, capturing the love of an audience that appreciates the joy we bring to one another. I did several performances in St. Francisville at local events and for the library. My first major gig was for a festival in Shreveport that I had done for years. We went up on a Sunday and spent the week doing six workshops a day, Monday through Friday, sharing our cultural journey through the African diaspora with every fourth grader in the parish. At night we would perform at the festival grounds. My happy place is the stage! I love entertaining, and it's especially rewarding watching the kids turn on and just turn loose. It was a joyful moment to be able to get back to that again. Blessings.

Time and more time. On multiple occasions, FEMA had said they were going to stop paying for our lodgings. The meals had long been discontinued. We were living by the precious grace of God and the loving care of our family and community. And I was still unable to work and unable to get anything from FEMA or the Road Home, one of the subsidies available to evacuees who were homeowners. What to do? My insurance company used every tactic to avoid making a settlement. Nowhere to go. What now?

Finally, FEMA stopped paying for the hotel. Many of the people had started to leave, but they had no place to go. My pastor told me not to come back because of my lung condition; New Orleans was still a very toxic place. There were no birds for a long time, but there were rats, armadillos, and possums, lots of them. A couple of days before we had to leave, I got a knock on my door. We were one of the last families left in the hotel. There stood a man I had never met before, Mr. Edward Samuels.

Mr. Samuels said, "I heard about you and your children, and I'd like to offer you all a place to stay."

I gave him my appreciation but told him we couldn't pay for a place right now. I was living on my social security disability, which didn't total enough to pay the mortgage on a home we couldn't live in and all the other day-to-day expenses. How could I now add rent?

Blessings. Mr. Samuels said, "I'd like to show you what I have, and if you want it, there is no rent or utilities, it's yours as long as you need it, and one day, if you ever get something for rent, you can then take care of me in any way that you can."

Blessings. Mr. Samuels' property was a forty-acre, pristine piece of land where he often hosted family reunions and picnics. Above the downstairs, which was the public section, he had built a one-bedroom studio, partially furnished.

Blessings. And like the "refugees" we were beginning to feel like, we packed up our hotel room and moved into a wooded paradise in the trees. We had three roll-up beds. The school, which was next door, even offered to build a path to make it easier for the kids to walk to school. We had a stream that we could walk to from multiple trails. We were told that occasionally hunters would come during deer season, and they did. But there were birds of too many species to count, including hummingbirds that literally would come right up in your face. One thing we looked forward to was twice a day, by the sun, a huge buck would come onto a small hill on the property. He would gaze off into the distance, raise his majestic head, stay for a spell, and then disappear into the woods. Uninterrupted by glaring city lights and noises, we could have evenings sitting on our raised porch and watching sunsets and a real night sky. Mr. Samuels was a lifesaver for me and my family. I am forever grateful to him.

Blessings.

Time more time. We had to consider a longer-term solution, and the Dawson's offered us a home in St. Francisville with three bedrooms, a living room, two baths, a kitchen, access to a garage, and outdoor space in a lovely neighborhood. All utilities were included, but it was at a cost. I didn't know how we were going to pay for it, but we took it and finally had a home again.

Blessings and lessons learned. As I said, I had very limited funds, but I learned to totally trust and depend on God. In my moments of crying and distress, God clearly said to me, "What part of 'I'm going to take care of you' don't you understand?" And take care of me He *did*! Everything would fall into place. We ate. The kids had everything they needed; I had a peaceful refuge at last.

Then, my son took the children to Houston. I was so distressed and depressed. I didn't want them to go, but I had no control over this decision. It was time to go home, so I started packing up, and my brothers Greg, Ricky, and James loaded up a truck to put things in storage until I could find a landing spot.

Home

I knew it was time to go Home. My cousin, Janice, had a home in New Orleans that had an extra bedroom. She let me stay in her beautiful warm, loving home. Just before I left St. Francisville, I started having major car trouble. The car couldn't be repaired. One day, my family drove up to St. Francisville with a van that they had bought for me and handed me the keys. Blessings.

FEMA kept asking for the same paperwork, but they weren't sending any money. My insurance company wouldn't come through, they kept moving, and I couldn't get them on the phone. My friend, Kimberly Richardson, told me the Unitarian Church on Claiborne Avenue was rebuilding homes for similarly situated people, but by that time, I was so depressed and discouraged, I didn't inquire. So Kimberly did it for me, and the person she contacted made an appointment to go through my house to see what needed to be done. A team of people from Kentucky, led by Henry Austin, was the first to come. He asked me what I needed now to get back into my home. They cleaned and got me a functional bathroom, a space to put an air mattress, and a space to add a microwave and a small refrigerator at no cost to me.

Other teams came from across the country. Boston sent a powerful crew of teens, mostly girls. They did a lot of removal of damaged materials, but the most amazing thing they did for me was to get my hot water restored. *Yeah,* no more boiling water for baths! The Wisconsin team was composed of three elders: Margaret, Sandy, and Sandy's wife. They micro-cleaned every inch of my home, down to bathing my granddaughter's Barbie dolls that they had recovered. I was starting to feel like I was home. Furniture and donations of household items were constantly pouring in. One of the last teams to come was from California's Bay Area. This awesome team beautified my home; they painted and gave me my bedroom back. This team was led by Deedra and Raymond. Deedra's hobby was doing beautiful ceramic tile art. She and Raymond took on tiling my shower in beautiful tiles as their personal project. I still enjoy their work today.

After multiple requests, much paperwork, and multiple trips to the Road Home Program, they granted me funds. It was enough to pay off my mortgage and buy myself a new bedroom set. Blessings.

I am so overwhelmed by the many acts of love and kindness shown to me during this very difficult time in our lives. I saw the kindness and compassion of family, friends, and strangers repeatedly.

Blessings ... blessings ... *blessings.* I saw the Grace of God being bestowed upon me. My faith abounds in the word of God. What part of "God promised to take care of us" don't you understand? *His* Promises *are real.*

AFTER THE STORM:
Moving Forward

VALENTINE PIERCE

> *This is not the quiet tap of civilized literature;*
> *this is the loud, raw truth of life.* © 2000

Being the laughter-loving, tongue-in-cheek, perpetually sarcastic poet and writer that I am, I decided to open with a "who I am now" poem I wrote early this year before I go chapter and verse on my journey. You'll find poems and scribblings splattered on these pages because most of my life story is in the poems.

Super Hero

Half a lifetime ago I was Superwoman,
Slinging bookcases from room to room on my shoulders
Like feather boas.
She-Ra, flipping mattresses like pancakes.
Miss America, jump-starting cars like electric scooters.
Wonder Woman, standing on the kitchen table replacing lighted
ceilings fans.
Half a lifetime ago I was tough as a Mack truck.
If something needed to be done, I did it, by myself, because I could.
I was bad, my own superhero.
Now, just the thought of lifting a couch cushion is Kryptonite.

Poems might seem like a disconnect from the chapter, but poetry is how I re-connected. It is my first form of spiritual healing. When I went through a six-year disconnect due to personal devastation greater than the flood, there was initially no poetry. I could not write a single thing. I am getting back to it. It's a slow trip. Let's use the following poem to launch this story.

Apology

I never meant to be a poet
never meant to put these words here
to say something, to expound, to explain
never meant to revolutionize your thinking
make you question your convictions
make you look again at that
truth you know so well
could tell in your sleep
never meant to open your sleeping eyes
make you see, it just happened
See, I never meant to be
that
was my mother
birth a girl child blue
damn near dead baby
prayed I'd live long enough to write
gave me this poet's name
I never claimed poetry
never meant to be a poet
the poetry claimed me
it is determined to live
doesn't care who it uses to survive
as long as it remains alive
I never meant to be a poet
It's the poetry that's meant to be
it's only using me to get to you

I'd hoped to keep this in chronological order, but as I work through the drafts, it now seems unrealistic. Innumerable branches and tributaries connect to the rivers, lakes, streams, and bayous of our lives.

To begin this story, I opened the 2006 journal I'd written to help recount the multiplicity of work that came about during and after the Federal Flood of 2005. Journaling is one form of writing I don't routinely do, but this was such a rare and powerful time for my city and the country that I tried to write it all down. Some things, however, are missing, and others don't have enough detail. Ah, well.

I also decided to review my résumé to help me remember, but before I could do that, I had to assemble them from the varied edges of my computer. Some years ago, a crashed drive forced me to rescue my files. It created a tangled mess. A few days ago, I realized I could divide the drive into volumes, drop all the résumés in one folder, sort from there. I had to delete the duplicates and triplicates first, though. When I finished, I had seventy-seven versions of my résumés because I have three, one for each line of work: journalism/writing, graphics, and performance. I've honed it to forty-six raw pages and perused it, but that's work for a different day. I can't include the manifold things that came about in the last twenty years, so I'll have to figure out what's more important to share and just stop when I reach the limit. Here's my journey.

Thursday afternoon, August 25, 2005. Focused on my work at a small weekly newspaper. The paper went to the printer Friday and was distributed Saturday. We were in the throes of our deadline when our IT person came through and asked if we'd seen Katrina.

I looked up at him. "Katrina who?"

Generally, I chart major hurricanes. I don't care about Category Ones because they are merely heavy-handed tropical storms. I didn't own a television (by choice), so I really wasn't keeping up with the news, but after his question, I went online. Good grief! This thing was potentially catastrophic. We finished the paper midday Friday and went home to prepare for evacuation.

Saturday, August 26, I laid out everything in my house that I wanted to take. Then put 90 percent of it back; it wouldn't fit in my compact sedan. I shoved my books and writings into the tiny closet in the upstairs loft. It offered the most protection, but it's hard to squeeze almost a half-century into one small closet. I spent the day walking around my apartment, looking at everything, creating different piles, trying to figure out how to pack it, how to take it with me. I'd need a moving van. This was the last weekend of the month; vehicle rental sites did not have trucks because that's when most people move. Instead, I resigned myself to the possibility of loss and took what I could. I filled my trunk and every spot in my car. The only space left was the driver's seat. I took my Mac computer tower but not the monitor or printer. That turned into a huge issue when I couldn't get back home.

Midday, I went out to top my tank. Every gas station was packed. I was delighted. People were taking this storm seriously. I chose to get gas when I was heading out instead, since I had more than half a tank and could get to my destination in Jackson, Mississippi, and halfway back on that. I got home, and there was a message on my phone: "See y'all Tuesday."

I left at two in the morning. I always leave between 2:00 a.m. and 4:00 a.m. because there is less traffic and I want the contraflow to be smoothed out. Topped my tank; hit the road. Got to Jackson in three hours, the same amount of time it usually takes. A few days later, I attempted to get back into the city. I couldn't because I didn't have anything with my zip code on it (I'd recently moved), and I'd taken the interstate rather than a back road. I wasn't an adventurous, back-road person, then.

Between Tuesday, August 23 and Thursday, August 25, the storm went from Tropical Depression Ten to a Tropical Storm Katrina to Hurricane Katrina and sat on the Everglades for six hours. I still wasn't that concerned; it was downgraded to a tropical storm again before reaching the Gulf of Mexico Friday, the 26th and becoming a Category One. By Saturday, the 27th, it was a Cat Three. Time to go. This beast had a banquet to feast on. It was massive and dangerous. The barometric pressure was steadily dropping; the gulf waters were hotter than they'd ever been; at one point, its eye closed. Closed! I'd never heard of that in my life. I made copious notes. By Sunday, the 28th, it was a monster Cat Five, 250 miles wide.

I had so many notes because I had decided in June to write that novel I'd planned to write most of my life. I'd read a book as a teen about a boy and a sheriff who had the power to bring the storms. Even though it was a great book, I don't remember anything else but that. I consumed books as a teenager and young adult. I thought to myself, *No one has ever written about a massive hurricane, so I will.* Hurricanes fascinate me. I had done research for years. Their intensity, their power, their necessity to the forests and woodlands. I even worked on it at lunchtime, sitting in my car in City Park. I had 55,000-plus words when I stopped. The book sat fallow over and over again. This year, I started working on it again in earnest. I currently have 40,000-plus words, after some serious pulling apart of most of the existing chapters.

In Jackson, I called a radio station to get the hurricane's exact location. The woman gave me some information but not what I wanted. I told her, "Miss, I'm from New Orleans; I need longitude and latitude."

At first, she wasn't sure what I meant or whether she could get that, but then, with the kindest voice, she said, "I'll check." She got me the information I sought.

While in the kitchen cooking, I heard Norman Robinson's voice on the tiny, static-filled television in the front room. Meteorologist Dan Milham was there, too. I initially breathed a sigh of relief. Now we'll get the news the way we know it. Then I realized: This must be the most dangerous storm in history if one of our news stations was co-anchoring in another state! I remember, as the hours went on, the station's regular anchor started to get a snippy attitude, as though he felt Norman Robinson was getting too much of the spotlight. He began interrupting Robinson. Humans and their hurt feelings. Forgive me; I laughed. What else could I do? Call him up and tell him not to be mad and that we were all going home as fast as the flood water dissipated? It took longer, much longer than we expected and caused absolute ruin to 80 percent of our city. Mentally I could hear the *In Living Color* sketch "Men on Film," and one man saying to the other, in his sweetest accent, "Oh, Twan. Don't get mad."[34]

Monday, August 29, Katrina landed as a Cat Three near Buras about twenty-five minutes before sunrise. It turned dead north and hit Alabama and Mississippi. It bypassed New Orleans. Everyone thought we were safe—until the levees broke.

The power went out in 97 percent of Jackson. I was in the 3 percent. The lights didn't even flicker.

Jackson's mayor raised Cain when the gas ran out. That held me back from seeing my daughter's final design presentation because I didn't know if I was going to be able to get gas during the drive to Natchitoches.

The mayor did eventually get gas into the city. I made it to my daughter's school and brought her back to Jackson.

Later, in December 2005, I called her university asking what they were doing about Rita. A lady said, "They'll be in the hallways, and these storms never come up here."

My voice rising, I said, "Lady, Rita is a major hurricane, and it is riding up the Texas–Louisiana border!"

She said I could come pick up my daughter if I wanted to. Voice even higher, I told her I was hours away.

---

34   "Men On Films II *** In Living Color," posted August 10, 2013, by GreatestShowsOnEarth, YouTube, 5 min., 19 sec., https://www.youtube.com/watch?v=B4ojGuA33X4.

AFTER THE STORM: MOVING FORWARD

The 2005 season had a record-breaking number of named storms, the most I'd ever experienced. Arlene to Zeta ran from early June until late December.

Somehow, somewhere, in the grand scheme of things, I ended up in a trailer in Kenner. If you are thinking, *Somehow? Don't you know?*, consider this: *Everything* was a blur. Many, many people were like me. We lost track of the days, weeks, jumbled events because our minds were scrambled. I gained thirty-three pounds in that trailer, twiddling my thumbs in the depth of depression, grief, sorrow. Any time I left that trailer, I took my computer and important stuff; that thin, aluminum box could be opened with a dime-store can opener. At night, I worried that one of the many bullets being fired in the area would come through one wall and exit the other because the bullets were more powerful than the shell of that trailer was strong. This did not delight me, and I was so glad to get out.

I went home to move my things and put them in storage, but I literally don't remember the when or how. What I do remember is a song I heard on the radio. I called to find out the artist and the title, but they didn't know what they had played! I found that odd but acceptable, given our states of mind and the circumstances. I eventually learned the song was "Long Way from Home" by Roi "Chip" Anthony. I play it and "New Orleans Girl" often.

Knowing I could not go back home to stay, I headed to Phoenix, Arizona, my safe haven. My life-long friends, Carol and Bob, had a room for me. They called it my room. I never did, but I could have shown up in the dead of night without calling, children in tow, and they would have welcomed us, fed us, made a pot of coffee, given me a shot of cognac, and gotten us some clean linen. I was free to do whatever I wanted because this was my home. They took care of my children for six weeks when my daughter could still walk under their dining table.

I was assigned to a military school for training. Carol flew to San Diego, picked up my kids, and took them back to Arizona. When I returned to Phoenix, it took an entire day to get my daughter to recognize me. Until I blew raspberries on her belly, she would run crying to Carol. And my son was a miniature Bob. All his shirts had to be tucked in, even if they were rib-bottomed. Whew! How many memories are linked by little things.

* * *

En route to Phoenix, my companion and I stopped at a motel. It was the wee hours, and we were too tired to drive anymore. And hungry. My companion told the clerk we were from New Orleans and asked if he had any food. The clerk looked out the window, saw the license plates and the overstuffed vehicles. I could see the compassion in his face. He opened up the room where the morning buffet food was. I don't remember what we took. Not much, enough to ease the hunger. We then went to the room and fell asleep.

I stayed in Phoenix for a year and a half, reaping benefits I never envisioned. I took a graphic design/art class. I was already a full-time designer and a logo diva with a mouse, which stuns some designers who use art boards and styluses. Still, there was always something to learn, so I was glad for the class.

I brought in a drawing. (Yep, I sought encouragement.) The instructor thought it was quite good and asked how long I had been drawing. He didn't believe me when I told him the last art class I'd had was in elementary school. Though I dabble, I don't know anything about how to draw, don't know the techniques or tools. I was delighted. This confirmed I would probably succeed if I took some courses. Currently, the only reason my drawing resembled art is because Carol, a skilled painter, had given me a how-to-draw class. Told me to look at the shapes, draw the shapes instead of the lamp or the flower or whatever. Just the shape.

The class was an emotional high for me because of the way things panned out. I brought in a design I'd created that said, "Design is the Yoga of Visual Art." My teacher copied it (with permission) and hung it on the wall.

One assignment was to cut up photos and create cold and warm postcards. The instructor went through them and hung them on the walls, then the students voted. He hung up all three of my cards (yeah), and they got the most votes (double yeah). I told him about that later. He was like, "Really?" Of course, he verified it, then gave my grade a bump.

Next, we created art from our imagination. Since I couldn't draw, he let me do my work in Photoshop. Every time I submitted something, he would critique it and offer suggestions. When I brought it back, he praised it and eventually told me how pleased he was that I always got it right the second time. I think it was because once I had a starting point, his guidance helped me find just what I needed to make it work. He explained everything so well.

I felt free creating art, all sorts of images that looked like three or four different things, depending on the perspective.

Later in the year, I submitted my play, *Orleanne the Refugee*, to the school magazine's writing contest. I thought it was good, but I really didn't know much about writing plays either. I hoped I'd figured out enough that others might think it was good, because I thought it was. I submitted it on the off-chance that maybe... Well, I won second place at Glendale Community College and first place in the Maricopa Community College system.

I know mentioning all these things might seem like bragging, but it's not; I'm describing the lifelines that kept me from falling into the abyss. New Orleanians were going through so much trauma that any little thing could give a boost for a while. Maybe long enough for something else to come along and give us another boost until we were finally lifted up high. It was an arduous journey, but I was determined to survive and thrive.

A lot of unexpected things happened while I was in exile. Friends from my last job in California sent me eighty dollars in cash in the mail. I received monetary awards from arts organizations, including Ashé Cultural Arts Center's Efforts of Grace and the CAC's SweetArts grants. Forgive me; the names of the others are lost in the bins and boxes I still haven't gone through and in the trauma section of my brain. The key to that room is still missing.

I participated in *UPROOTED: The Katrina Project*, a multidisciplinary collaboration that took us to several cities and states. This was a creative time for me, and it was thrilling to travel to places like Texas, Virginia, Arizona, Connecticut, New York. I was not ready for the bitter New York cold and almost got frostbite on my fingers because I lost one of my gloves. I quickly bought another pair.

Mona Lisa Saloy's book *Red Beans and Ricely Yours* came out about the same time the Army Corps of Engineers failed us. Despite barely having funds, it was essential to my being, like medicine when one is ill. I read it from end to end immediately. That's not the way to read poetry, but I was hungry for poetry and New Orleans. Even though I was broke as a dropped mirror, I was never physically hungry or unsheltered. At Carol and Bob's, I didn't need money for those things. I am family.

In Phoenix, I made a friend, a running buddy—not that we ran around much. I don't remember how we became friends; we just did. I do remember that she showed me a few interesting places, like the red rocks of Sedona and devil's claw seeds, which look like huge, brown, wooden okra with long, curved spikes. I still have several. She painted a picture of me from a photo in *The Times-Picayune* that ran with the story about my residency at A Studio in the Woods. She is a painter and an airbrush artist. I was her assistant a couple of times, once for a bar mitzvah. I'd never been to a bar mitzvah, and if you ask me about it, I wouldn't be able to tell you anything more than that I was her assistant.

Everything can't be sweet and pretty. There was plenty of ugly handed out. I have this one story I want to tell. My friend and I had some of the same classes. In one class, the instructor, who seemed to instantly dislike me (I probably gave off some bad energy, honestly), made a comment about protected people such as white males over forty and "Blacks—I don't know what they call you now." Maybe she'd caught wind that I'd said her books were trash before I knew that she wrote them and that I was in her class. Books cost money, and I didn't want to waste it on something that should have been ripped apart and rewritten by someone who knew how. Before I even met her, the books told me she couldn't teach me a thing; I could teach her class better than she ever could. I had thirty-five years' experience; she had two. Her only credential was that she ran a small business. She was vain and egotistical without any ability. Pu-leeze.

I was the only one of that ilk—Black, I don't know what they call you now—in the class. The students were stunned and turned to look at me. My friend got so pissed, she thought I should report it. I told her that if I reported it, they would say I was playing the race card, and that she should report it (being the right color and all), but I knew she couldn't. She really wasn't that kind of person. She couldn't bring her shy, introverted self to report it, to challenge anyone about anything. I chose not to waste my time on a woman who had absolutely no degrees—not even an associate's degree (how had she gotten this job?)—printed information from the Internet, and forced us to write it down by hand while she read it from the paper. Sadly, the class was required, so I sat there repeatedly falling asleep, lines of lead squiggling down my notebook pages.

Spring 2006, I was back in New Orleans for a hot minute. Don't know where or how, but there I was, probably for something related to UPROOT-ED. Got an email from the host of the Thursday nights 17 Poets! reading series at The Gold Mine Saloon. Several artists who frequently read or presented art or music at 17 Poets! were invited to participate in a PBS program in New Orleans. I still have a grainy picture of that night, me at the podium in my all-time favorite jacket. Sadly, that jacket disappeared in the travails of surviving.

PBS was going to film a live documentary, *New Orleans After the Hurricane*, for the *PBS News Hour* with Jim Lehrer. Portions would be broadcast coast-to-coast via all PBS affiliates. Featuring twenty-four New Orleans poets, it would also include a narrative about how New Orleans poets had responded in their community over the days and months following the storm.

I did an excerpt of "Reluctant Migrants." Here's an abbreviated excerpt, if there is such a thing.

> We are reluctant migrants, living where we can until we can get back home. We don't know when that will be, but we keep hoping. We search the internet, call friends who returned, follow national broadcasts, dash off emails, listen in on others' conversations if they make any mention of our home. We want to go home and live our quirky, creative, urban metropolitan lifestyles in our own neighborhoods with old friends who know our idiosyncrasies and welcome us anyway.
>
> We know how to fend for ourselves. How to make do, because sometimes that is the best we can do as we try to get through the day or the week or, sometimes, the whole damn year on what resources we can scrape up. Yes, we beg, borrow, and steal to survive.
>
> We are Louisianians, New Orleanians, co-workers, communities, families, friends, artists, musicians, poets, street performers, palm readers, ne'er-do-wells, door poppers, masked marauders, free-loaders, and food lovers. Denizens of Uptown, Downtown, the 9th Ward, the Lower Nine, the 7th Ward, above Canal, below Canal, in the Cut, Pontchartrain Park, Tremé, New Orleans East, Carrollton, Gentilly, the Garden District, the Irish Channel, Gert Town, Pigeon Town, Back of Town, Desire, Calliope, Melpomene, Magnolia, St. Thomas, the projects, Bywater, Algiers, the French Quarter, Faubourg Marigny, Mid-City. Our skin is blue-black, black-brown, caramel, cocoa, cream, blue-veined, beige, albino, pecan, tan, redbone, melon, pomegranate, cinnamon, honey, high-yellow, light-bright-damn-near-white, and white. We are passionate, emotional, loving, warm, friendly, cold-hearted, evil, cheeky, hardheaded, and siddity. We are everything America has to offer—the bad and the good.

New Orleans Poets: After The Storm aired on April 4, 2006. Don't remember which poets were included in the final cut, but invited artists were: Dave Brinks, Kysha Brown, Megan Burns, Paul Chasse, Chris Champagne, Kip

Cairo, Thaddeus Conti, Gina Ferrara, Dennis Formento, Elizabeth Garcia, Quo Vadis Gex-Breaux, Lee Meitzen Grue, Felice Guimont, R. Moose Jackson, Saddi Khali, Jonathan Kline, Bill Lavender, Bill Myers, Niyi Osundare, Valentine Pierce, Jimmy Ross, Kalamu ya Salaam, Starlyte, Jerry W. Ward Jr., and Andy Young (poets); Robin Durand, Michael Fedor, R. Moose Jackson, Herbert Kearney, and Romano Zamprioli (painters); and flautist Eluard Burt and guitarist Harry Sterling (musicians).[35]

I looked forward to being in New Orleans and among artists. Not much (poetry) culture in Phoenix. But, it has beautiful geography and is a lovely landscape, which is how these two poems were born.

Phoenix Rises

It's chamber of commerce weather

    here in Phoenix:
Skies clear as music; days bright as
    heaven.
It's almost December
I long for September in New Orleans
When morning glories blossom.
Heaven is just an open window away.

Tortilla Moon

Tortilla moon sits flat, bright, high
in the desert sky
where purple mountains
rise in majestic splendor
to silently guard all four points
on the compass,
protecting the valley of the sun
where Phoenix rises.

---

35   At least four of the folks in these lists have transitioned.

I had twelve notebooks for this period (I lost one of them on an airplane), containing a series titled, *Come Hell and High Water: America's International Disgrace*, subtitled, *The Federal Flood of 2005—How the Army Corps of Engineers Failed New Orleans and Got Away with It*. I haven't brought myself to work on it yet, but I say my goal is to turn it into a book. I wrote so many things during this time: poems, a play, and a one-woman show, *Fanatical Fanny and the Cozy Cottages and Beatific Bungalows*, about living in a trailer. Later, the National Performance Network created the opportunity for me to present *Cozy Cottages* at Ashé Cultural Arts Center as well as an excerpt of *Landscape of Our Lives* at the National Performance Network annual meeting. Poetry is my go-to. I've been writing since elementary school. Almost everything in my life is captured in some poem or other. Yet there I was, doing a one-woman show. In reality, however, I don't limit or label what I write.

Having lost my job, I'd accumulated eighty thousand dollars in debt by living off my credit card—food, auto insurance, car note, whatever was due went on the credit card. I didn't know when or how I would pay this off, but since I dislike debt, I knew I would. Eventually, I did and got rid of the car. I believe in living within my means. If I don't have the money, I can't buy it—well, except for a car. Who has a pocket full of money for that? During the federal flood, however, I had no means, so the credit card was desperation financing.

I returned to New Orleans about eighteen months after the Flood. When I told people I was going back, they were surprised. "Already?" they said.

"Already?" I responded. "I've been gone eighteen months. The powers that be think they can turn our neighborhoods into green space. Are you kidding? If I don't get back to claim my city, who will? They will."

I'd previously left New Orleans in January 2000 and come back in January 2004. New Orleans and I have always had a tempestuous relationship that occasionally requires one of us (me) to leave. I had been a host of the WRBH *The Writer's Forum* in the late 1990s and was fortunate to host it again when I came back in 2004.

I freelanced for a year. However, the circumstances were such that I got enough work to survive but not to thrive. I sent out dozens of résumés during the second half of 2004. Early January 2005, I took unpaid training to be a tax preparer. I can't think of anything I'd rather do less than prepare peoples' taxes. I came home, flopped down in my big chair in tears, and said out loud, "Please, God, let somebody call me with a job." My phone rang in that instant.

It was the secretary from the newspaper. I'd gone for an interview but hadn't heard back. She asked if I was still looking for work and did I want the job. It was incredible! I know. I wouldn't believe it either if I hadn't experienced it.

New Orleans is where we have jazz funerals for the death of democracy (January 2005, November 2024) and second lines to celebrate the journey home. Like this one:

St. Antoine

All Saints' Day we honored St. Antoine of the Lower Nine
Gone to get his thrill on another Blueberry Hill
Hundreds of mourners flooded Bywater streets
Celebrating his "canonization"
Horns, drums, barbecue, cold-drinks
Wacky weed, handkerchiefs, umbrellas,
Baby Dolls, street folk . . .

Second-liners danced across the St. Claude bridge
Sang over the Industrial Canal
Strolled to that yellow and black house
On Caffin* at Marias
'Cause he been "out dat nine" all his life
Katrina drowned the house, the piano too
History washed downriver by broken levees
Left Fats for the Coast Guard to carry to safety

Today a brass band walked him home
* *Renamed Fats Domino Avenue*

Naturally, I didn't have any place to live when I got home. I spent my first night at "the boys'" place, two young men who were part of UPROOTED. Then another person from UPROOTED invited me to stay at her house as long as I needed. That was Christmas 2006. I remember it distinctly because James Brown died Christmas Day. I quickly found a place. Someone I knew had a duplex on Humanity Street. The gas line still hadn't recovered, so the gas kept going out—sometimes immediately after we lit it. The landlady eventually had to call for service. There was air in the pipe. They bled it, and finally, no more gas outages.

I recently came across a note I wrote around this time: "I can't ignore the irony of it as I drive through Gentilly to my half a duplex. I thought to myself, in this location, I have the chance, finally, to get to know the city intimately. I am perfectly situated. I live on Humanity Street, at the corner of Republic. I drive through devastation with street names like Treasure, Pleasure, Benefit, Abundance. I think of the nine muses. How devastated are they?"

Although I lapsed for a few years, I keep a copy of every event or publication I participate in. They are very useful during those times when you feel useless. Maybe you've never experienced feeling useless; I have. These collections remind me that I am not. In 2010, I was published in the hardcover anthology *New Orleans: What Can't Be Lost*. April 1998 was my first time in a hardcover anthology, *From a Bend in the River*. I teased my daughter because she was published in hardcover before me, with *Kentecloth* in January 1998.

* * *

In 2007, I visited my mom in Shreveport, Louisiana. She had lost everything, all her sewing items, including the sewing table she taught me to sew on when I was a child. She had been sewing all her life. It kept her nerves calm. Now, living in a hotel room (or small apartment; I just don't remember), all she had were electronic games and some word puzzle books. She piddled around, couldn't get settled, was filled with anxiety, her nerves rattled.

I showed up with a big ole box of goodies, including a sewing machine, fabric, thread, notions, and varied accoutrements from my own sewing items.

She reached in and pulled out a book of crochet patterns. "This looks like my book."

I laughed, "It is your book." I had borrowed it in an attempt to finally learn the pineapple stitch. I did learn it, but now I'd need the book again to re-learn it. She reached in again and pulled out an oversized scarf. She held it to her chest, and it was the first time I'd seen my mother almost cry. Before all of this came about, I'd had two big scarves. I'd kept one and given her one for her birthday the February before the Flood. She'd loved it; the storm took it; now, I'd brought her mine.

My hardheaded mom, not understanding the damage humans had done to the wetlands and the coastline, had refused to leave. My son called her at 12:30 a.m.

"Grandma," he'd said, "you need to leave."

After the storm, it had taken us four days to find her. My son was the one who finally got in touch because his cell phone has a different area code.

on the fourth day

> ...and on the fourth day the sun rose
> and my son called
> and my mother was alive
> my mother is a hardheaded woman, doesn't listen
> they tell me I am hardheaded too and my daughter, my son;
> we joke—where did we get it from?
> that old woman pissed me off
> told her to leave;
> my son called her after midnight,
> grandma, he said, you need to leave
> but she is a stubborn old woman—
> lived through Camille, through Betsy,
> through all the ones that came in the days
> when the wetlands protected us,
> before the swamps were swallowed up by progress,
> before fema.
> that old woman scared her grandchildren—
> my daughter most of all,
> who said she didn't want to know until we knew.
> and when we knew my daughter said it was good
> because she was starting to get upset about it,
> starting to have problems with it.
> finally, we knew and we were happy,
> lo so exceedingly happy, and angry
> with her in Arkansas and us everywhere but home.
> she said she was okay, being taken care of,
> didn't want for anything.
> I thought, how funny:
> for the first time in her life
> my mother doesn't want for anything.
> I guess, at that moment, hearing her voice,
> I didn't want for anything either.

This poem was published in my debut book, *Geometry of the Heart*, and in the *Callaloo* special issue *American Tragedy: New Orleans Under Water*.

I got situated in New Orleans and started attending Sisters Making a Change, exercising twice a week. I finally got my weight back down to my average. I also got my job back in January 2007.

Though I hadn't been to a parade since the late 1990s, I went to a parade and asked for a plush toy. The woman said they were for the children. I said it was my first parade since the storm. She gave me a plushy thing that eventually disappeared.

Tuesday

Tuesday everywhere else is a
week day work day worry day
here it's throw-your-cares-away day
throw-me-something-mister day
can-I-have-that-lady day
dance-in-the-street day
paint-your-face-and-body day
dress-fabulously-silly day.
Today is just Tuesday everywhere else
in the world

but here it's Mardi Gras Day
Al-"Carnival Time"-Johnson day
today in New Orleans
is the only day of its kind
in this country—Fat Tuesday
but tomorrow, tomorrow is still
Ash Wednesday

I watched my third-ever football game in 2010 at a friend's house. The first was an uninformed, insignificantly financed bet with my older brother when we were in high school. The Oakland Raiders and whomever. The second was my high school homecoming game. In 2010, I was compelled to watch the Saints. They were going to the Super Bowl; amazing. I was happy to be home. I even put the XLIV on a whole bunch of things. Crazy, huh?

Truce

Poetry comes in the midst of this constant war that is life.
It is a truce, a little space where I am safe from the enemy and artillery.
It is my anti-armor shielding, my home-base, my foxhole.
I am free for a moment or two—even three
Poetry is my DMZ.*

DMZ – demilitarized zone

The first Sunday I was back in New Orleans, I went to the open mic at the Maple Leaf Bar—because I could. I couldn't do that in Phoenix. I was starved for poetry, craved it.

A few months after returning home, John Travis, of Portals Press, called me about publishing my book. He said it was time; I'd paid my dues. Every day he included more and more poems. It ended up being 142 pages. Then, of course, we needed a title. We went round and round on several different titles, including *Geometry of Life*, which is the title of one of my poems. We ended up right where we'd started with the first title I'd suggested, *Geometry of the Heart*. We had the book launch at the Maple Leaf. The article Susan Larson had written was posted on the door. I barely glimpsed it, then turned around.

"Hey, that's my line," I said. That's when I realized it was the newspaper article. I laughed at myself.

In 2022, Lee Meitzen Grue started New Laurel Review Press. My book, *Up Decatur*, was the first and last book the press published because Lee passed away.

* * *

This little story was born in late December 2005. I was in New Orleans for a bit, standing in line at an auto parts store:

How Ya Momma'n'em

As I stand in the auto parts store in New Orleans a couple of weeks ago, a man keeps staring at me. I nod. He nods back and asks, "How ya momma and them?"

I squint, trying to see him more clearly without my glasses, and ask, "You know my momma?" There is every likelihood he knows my mother; after all, my mother knows a lot of people, I mean, a lot. And she has the habit, when we are together, of introducing me to people I never remember. "This is my big girl," she would say, as though she had any little girls. I never object, since I know it comes from years of having an older daughter separated by two boys from her four younger daughters. These days, however, most of her daughters' daughters have children.

"Yeah," he says. "And your brothers, Stanley . . ." At this point I stop listening and start shaking my head. "You don't have a brother named Stanley?" I continue shaking my head. He tells me where they live, but I'm not listening to the description. "Your name's not Lisa?" I shake my head again. "You look like Lisa."

I smile. "I look like a lot of people." In my head, a snippet of a song spins: *"I'm not Lisa [. . .] / Lisa left you . . ."*[36] He apologizes, and we go back to waiting in our separate lines.

Just then, the man in front of me finishes his transaction. As I walk up to the counter, he comments, "There you go, Lisa."

New Orleanians are quick to open a conversation in a store, standing in line, at the gas station, on the bus, while sweet-talking people for plant clippings. My mom is a master. I learned from the best.

Roux in Your Blood

"You gotta have the roux in your blood," he said.
New Orleanians understand.
It's an addiction—like alcohol or drugs or food
It's Jazz Fest, Mardi Gras, Essence Fest, Super Sunday.
Crawfish, August heat, summer showers.
It's neighbors on their porches, children in the street,
Chicory coffee at midnight,
Mommas in the kitchen, Daddies at the juke joints,
New Orleans—it's in the blood.

---

36 Jessi Colter, "I'm Not Lisa," track 6 on *I'm Jessi Colter*, Capitol Records, Spotify, https://open.spotify.com/track/2WQCzRvHubJxMIeCf2Y-hYG?si=016ee61ff92c4fb2.

January 2, 2006, my mom called me in Phoenix to tell me she had found my graduation photo. She and my oldest brother had gone down to New Orleans and rescued a few things from her house the week before. The day before, she'd dug through one of the containers, where she found my high school graduation picture along with a picture of me and my "little white girlfriend" from the military. She meant my bootcamp bunkmate, later roommate, and then friend of more than forty years.

Speaking of white, the cops or whoever patrols the streets of Arlington, Texas, measuring blades of grass, woke my mother on Mother's Day afternoon to tell her that her grass was too high. When I saw her again, I looked at the ticket and said, "Mom, this isn't your ticket. This says 5'3" white woman." We laughed.

A couple of days later, I received $507 of my Pell Grant. Thank whatever powers that be. I went to Wells Fargo to cash it, stood in a loooong line, then had to provide two forms of photo ID and my right thumbprint. I guess that's the price of a city ranking highest in the nation for identity theft.

I was at Estrella Mountain Community College, Avondale, Arizona, for a Katrina panel discussion on Thursday, February 16, 2006. I zoned out for a few minutes and got caught up in the week that'd just passed. It was a good week. I got birthday presents from my children: a wonderful card from my daughter that said, "Thanks for teaching me to color outside the lines" and a Brazilian amethyst stone from my son. As always, I had a quip. He has that same habit, and his sister has a dry wit, so he knew I was going to say something.

"You gave me a rock for my birthday?"

He sucked his teeth. "Mom, you know it's not a rock. It's a stone." A stone the size of my fist. My birthday stone. I also had chicken and dumplings that Carol cooked, a card from Bob, and a cake 'cause Carol could bake.

Tuesday, February 21, 2006, I was invited to read at The Gold Mine for a PBS filming on March 6, which meant I would have to fly, so I didn't miss too many classes. How'd I manage that? Don't remember. It's as though a part of your brain actually disappears when you go through such devastating trauma.

Little things make the most difference when you are a world away from your world.

About a month before the Goldmine reading, I'd fallen in love with the library all over again when I walked into a Phoenix branch. It was my second time in a week, but I'd been so overwhelmed by the newness and by trying to get a library card the first time that I hadn't noticed. Or maybe this branch was just so shockingly different.

I remember, years ago, bitterly complaining when the new technology took over. I wanted to keep the tactile joy of the card catalog system, the ancient smell of old books and the acrid scent of new ink. The new ones were so antiseptic, so sterile, that I hadn't dotted a library door in years.

Now that I was in school, however, and in need of books I could not afford, I was forced to give it a try. When I walked in, the guard sitting at the counter and the metal detectors were not exciting, and when I asked for the item I had on hold, I was not impressed that the man directed me to a red counter where I was to scan the shelves for my last name. I turned, and there before me was a counter whose walls were lit up and neon red, oxygenated, new-blood red. I found my item, a set of twelve CDs, an audio novel, *The Stonebreaker*. Then, as I turned back, I saw shelves and shelves of CDs, DVDs, and videocassettes. At first, I gave it a cursory glance but was quickly pulled in by a *Star Trek* DVD. I then began to understand the numbering system: alphabetical order. Of course, scanning so many shelves reaps little reward, so I looked around for the "catalog" system. Of course, I knew it would be a computer. I typed in names of things I'd recently thought I wanted to hear or read, and voila! Their details appeared on the screen.

Most weren't available, and typing in a fourteen-digit card number is so displeasing to me. Still, I typed them, placing the items on hold.

When I was done, I didn't know whether I could just leave or whether the dag-blasted metal detector/theft-prevention device would go off. I waited until someone else showed up at the desk. She explained I still had to check the books out. I looked at her and at where she directed. More machines, barcode scanners.

"Have you ever used one of these she asked?"

No. She didn't hesitate to show me how simply they worked. You scan your card, your books, and the printer gives you a receipt, of sorts, telling you what you have checked out and when it is due back.

Looks like I could give up searching for cheaply priced DVDs and CDs and just borrow them from the library. Heck, I didn't have room to own all of them, so I might as well borrow and return.

May 1, 2006, and so far, no word on the residency in New Orleans.

Wednesday, May 3. I bought *Fahrenheit 9/11*, a movie my then twenty-five-year-old son recommended. My children and I have a lot of things in common: dispositions, wry senses of humor, attitudes (sometimes), and, when they were younger, movies. We hated what Jim Carrey did to

The Grinch. We loved *The Rich Man's Wife*. But as children get older and begin their own lives, the twenty-odd years' difference begins to show. My son has surprised me with his choice of old-school music, but these days, I have no clue as to his taste in movies. Thus, I didn't rush to buy *Fahrenheit 9/11*.

One day, however, I needed a movie, an inexpensive one, on sale, and there it was. I popped it in the DVD player (times have surely changed; once, that was the VCR) and sat back for the 122 minutes it would take to watch it. It started slow, like a documentary; it continued slow, like a documentary, the themes from old movies popping up here and there. Slow, but intriguing. Some I already knew. As I sat watching, I kept thinking, *Is this what young adults are watching these days?* My son is cool, hip, up-to-date, and intelligent. Perhaps *Fahrenheit 9/11* helped him understand why I'd begged him not to join the military just to get a college education. As it turns out, he didn't need the military. (He is now on the cutting edge of technology as a biomedical engineer.) If the youth of America are watching *Fahrenheit 9/11*, there may be hope for this country after all. My hope is that Michael Moore does one on the hurricanes.

Thursday, May 4, 1:00 a.m., I was too excited to sleep. A Studio in the Woods (ASITW) employee had called earlier. I'd gotten the residency! ASITW said they'd been about to give up. They had been trying to get in touch for a long time. This was a good day. I did well on my two-dimensional final work; it looked like I might get my unemployment. I was going to Connecticut for *UPROOTED*. Just the day before, I'd been thinking I might have to quit school and go to work. I'd taken a sleeping tablet at 10:30 p.m., but I was nowhere near sleep. Plus, my classmates had said my work was bitchin'! How could I sleep after that?

During my Restoration Residency for summer 2006, all I had to do each day was write. For the first time in my life, I had no other obligations. The first week, I went to the store to get cream for my coffee. The stewards of ASITW were there. Lucianne threatened to spank me, told me to go back and write; she would get whatever I needed. I told her no one had threatened to spank me since I'd left my mother's house. I found it delightful, funny, old-fashioned, and comforting. It was such a familiar phrase. I had no plans to get spanked. Lucianne made me a Greek salad. It was my first ever; I fell in love with it. After that, the only salad I wanted in any restaurant was a Greek one.

There are moments in our lives when things could not seem more perfect. At those moments, we are ecstatically happy, convinced that no matter what complications come with those moments, nothing could mar them. As writers, we sometimes let those moments slip by unrecorded. Solitary, nocturnal creatures, we're often so busy wallowing in our own misery, and putting that misery on paper, that we fail to write about the great moments. Truly great moments when our lives—for however brief a time it might be—are joyous beyond belief.

This was such a moment for me. It had been so wearily hard those last few months as I fought government red tape, suffered a lack of income, struggled to stay in school, that I had worn a hole in my brain from all those brain cells rubbing against each other, like fingers rubbing a worry stone. Night upon night I'd worried, cried, hoped, doubted. I'd spent months mindlessly staring at a television that, primarily, gave me nothing. It was a newly developed habit. I had never let television babysit me. Never let it take the few precious hours I had. At one point during those years, my daughter had asked, "Isn't your brain turning to mush?" because I had never let television babysit her or her brother, either. My reward for that choice has been beyond measure.

New Orleanians take many things for granted, like red beans. Red beans are like the sun rising. We never question where or even whether we can get them any day of the week, any time of the day, but most especially on Monday. At least, we once didn't. During my visit to my home city at the end of May 2006, I'd found out just how many things had changed. It had taken me two weeks to get those red beans, because outside of the French Quarter, no one knew which restaurants were open, which had full menus, which had staff.

From my journal:

> Today is the sixth day of the sixth month of the sixth year of this century—060606. Don't ask me why it sticks in my head, but since the century turned over, I see the oddness and connectivity of numbers every day. It is too much to explain here.
>
> Today is Wednesday, June 7, 2006. I imagine what it might be like for someone fifty years from now trying to make heads or tails of all the pieces I've written, how the trajectory of my life was the same and different. Or even five years from now, looking back and thinking on the truth or falsity of each of these bits of information. Writing and poetry remain part of my essence, but I feel I am on an entirely different journey, on a trail with no markers or guides.

Even now, I can only shake my head at some, laugh at others. It is June 2006, and I am typing notes from September 2005. I begin to wonder how I will make sense of it all.

Sometimes it is just absolutely unbearable to go over this information—all the fact, fiction, and folklore surrounding New Orleans and the Federal Flood. Going through it, though, helps remind me of the many good things that slip in between the rough moments.

Wednesday, June 21, 2006: In a newspaper article, Chris Rose says, "We love Southern Louisiana with a ferocity that borders on pathological." True. "Dear America, [. . .] when you strip away all the craziness and bars and parades and music and architecture and all that hooey, really, the best thing about where we come from is us." Yes, indeed. Thanks, Chris.

In 2020, I participated in the National Veterans Creative Arts Festival. It was the twentieth anniversary of an event I didn't even know existed. I only participated once because there was no category for what I wanted to submit. The local coordinator did all he could to make a way, but it didn't happen. Based on what I observed during the festival, I felt I did not fit in this competition. However, I won four awards: two first-place and two second-place. Honestly, it seems an eternity ago rather than only four years, while some of the trauma events are as clear as if they'd happened this morning.

One of the things I missed while in Phoenix was New Orleans patois and front-step conversations. Even when the patois changes—and it does throughout the city—*pó-lice* never changes. Quirky New Orleans remarks: People put on their outside clothes as opposed to their house clothes or their good clothes. *We straight?* Seems I hadn't heard that in years, and I have heard it twice in the last two weeks. One man commented on a man who had been put out. Said he had "matching luggage"—Schwegmann's groceries bags. And he had on his outside clothes. *Shedded*—the past tense of shed. *Liked to drown.* New Orleanians have a unique twist to the spoken word because we come from so many cultures and languages.

October 16, 2007. Sitting by the window in the McDonald's nearest the interstate, awaiting fresh-brewed coffee before setting out on my three-hour journey back to New Orleans, having one of my rare public cell phone conversations. A "vagrant" fell soundlessly to the pavement at the gas station across the street. At least, it seemed soundless through the plate glass window. He then tucked his cap under his head and lay there. I exclaimed to my friend, but then I felt confused. Maybe he meant to fall there, to lie there. But no one falls that easily, that simply—like water from a faucet.

A little boy in the corner noticed too. Told his father. I confirmed it, told the counter folk that maybe they should call 911. As they picked up the phone, he sat up. Stood up. What was this man doing? My friend said it could be a medical problem. The police were there instantly. An ambulance's siren wailed on the main street, and the police officer hailed it. Never seen ambulances respond that immediately in New Orleans. I am ashamed that my first thought was "vagrant," not human, not man, not person. Vagrant. Someone living in and on the excess garbage of urban America.

In 2009, I brought my mother home from Arlington, Texas. Except for a brief stint living with me in Oceanside, California, she'd lived in New Orleans all her life. I don't think she even crossed the Mississippi River Bridge—as we called it back then—until the first time she took me to the airport in 1977.

Anywho, I drove eight hours to get there. My oldest brother and I packed up everything then loaded the truck. We stopped by my mom's friend's house before we left, and all the sudden, a fierce storm was brewing. Her friend said we had to spend the night. A lingering argument flared up between me and my brother. I angrily went out to the truck to get something. I tripped over the hitch, started falling backward. I was falling hard, and the back of my head would have slammed right on the edge of the curb. Instead, I felt something catch me and lay me softly down in slow motion. That lives with me, and I think of the many times I could have been shunted from this earth.

Morning came. My brother went his own way, and my mom and I took off. We got back, and several of her fourteen grandnieces and -nephews helped unpack. I was so glad because I was so exhausted. I bought us pizza and cold-drinks.

Christmas season. When my daughter was young, she and my mother loved Christmas. I would drop my daughter off at her grandmother's about three days in a row so they could decorate the house.

They also loved the Christmas lights in City Park. I don't like the cold, so it did not thrill me, but it lit up my mother's heart. By that time, she couldn't do a lot of walking. One of my sisters had a wheelchair from a deceased sister, so my daughter and I pushed her through the entire display. I can't express the joy I saw in my mother's eyes.

One of the most wonderful times I spent with my mother was when I learned to tat. A librarian had taught me. When my mom saw me tatting, she said she'd always wanted to learn that. So I taught her. I thought it was so cool, teaching my mom, the master. The hardest part was remembering not to hold the shuttle like a crochet hook. She was enthralled, so that Christmas, she also got tatting supplies.

"Mom, I have to get the thread from Turkey. I have one hundred dollars, including shipping, so choose with that in mind." She chose seventeen balls, half of them variegated or what she called multicolored. I also taught her two new crochet techniques. Imagine that.

I'm using my mother's personality, attitude, and quips in my novel *Dead North*. I don't think I've touched that novel in fifteen years, but now I am deep into it once again. The jump from poet to novelist is like taking a canoe over Victoria Falls or riding a bike up Mount Kilimanjaro. I suppose it could be done, but can it be done well and to great effect? And, why?

I still remember how terrible the first pages were. My son said, "Mom, writing is a perishable skill."

Writing, I thought, *is such a part of me, I could never lose the ability.* Perhaps the difference is that poetry pours from my pores like a mountain stream flows into a valley. It sinks and rises in seasons but lives always. Novels, however, are raging rapids, a dangerous haul. Not all of us can ride those waves, avoid those rocks jutting up into whitewater rushes. Some are even ocean journeys, long, large ships trying to avoid the ravages of weather and dangers of geography, trying not to founder or even flip bow to stern on the ocean floor. Water is one of life's metaphors.

Someday, this novel might make it to print. Even if it never gets beyond my little black-and-white laser printer, the journey is worth the effort.

Should it end up published, we'll be able to say that even though it was born before the storm, it was embraced at ASITW, where I had the time to have deep conversations with the folks in the story. Even though their lives are complicated, requiring my full attention, their futures, at this moment, are uncertain. Still, the journey is worth the effort. What if someday my writing is a legacy? Won't it be exciting to have some young writer poring over the first scrawled lines of something the way I pore over the works of writers I admire?

In early August 2005, I was invited to present an excerpt of *Landscape of Our Lives* for critical response at the Alternate ROOTS annual meeting. I had such a positive response that I asked someone to be my director. I was all set. Then the Federal Flood washed away all the opportunities and advancements I'd made. I was crushed. Little did I know the universe had a different journey for me.

In 2012, I was the lead character, Door Popper, whom I channeled from my mother, and a core writer of the play *A-Musing*. The Monday before the Saturday night presentation, the director came in with an entirely rewritten script. That Tuesday during my rehearsal, an American Association of Community Theatre representative commented that I needed to learn my script. He had no idea I had just gotten the script. The Saturday morning dry run was a disaster for every cast member. We didn't even get a full run-through. I went home in a panic. My daughter, who stood by me the whole day, calmed me down and walked me through the entire script while I cooked us lunch and for the rest of the afternoon.

That night, I flubbed one word, and I played that off. We won the local competition and went on to the regional in Texas. My awards were for Outstanding Actor and People's Choice Actor—after starting the week in a full-blown panic.

When I reviewed my résumé, I was surprised by the multitude of things I've done and organizations I've been involved with since the Federal Flood: UPROOTED, *State of the Nation*, ASITW residency, MAAFA, National Performance Network, Essence Festival, debut poetry book, book signings, Redd Linen Night, Tom Dent Festival, Playback Theatre, Dillard University, Tennessee Williams & New Orleans Literary Festival, Louisiana Book Festival, published works, "Womb Poem" airing on Dolphin Radio, "Bated Breath" airing online/published, along with other pieces, by Rigorous, book reviews. . . . No room to put them all here, no matter how much they mean to me. I searched my résumé for published works and came up with more than fifty! I am stunned at the amount of my writing that's been published and performances that have filled these twenty years, despite my six years of being a hermit. I didn't think in those terms. I was always simply moving forward.

I'll close with:

The Last Poem

When the day comes
Let the last poem
Sing praises
Of all who stood by me
Of all who tried me
Let it be grief and gladness
Joy and sadness

For it is all of these
That have molded me
You may be heartbroken to lose me
I will be heartbroken to leave you
But only the shell will be gone
With these words
I live to stand by you
When others try you
When grief bends you
When joy sends you
I will be there
In specks of dust
In pouring rain
In sleepless nights
In hurricanes
In September blossoms
In summer heat
In winter cold
And the pattering
Of children's feet
I will be there in unbearable strife
With these words, on this page
For words are the breath of life.

Live consciously, joyously, and the universe will provide. © 2009

BLESSINGS IN THE MIDST OF THE STORM AND "GOD IS..."
LOYCE PIERCE WRIGHT

2005 ushered in a new beginning in my life. My heart was finally thawing from the frozeness that sorrow and grief usher in when one experiences a significant death. It took six years for the pain to subside from the loss of ten close family members, including my parents, Frank and Victoria Pierce, and the love of my life, my husband, Louis Clifton "Roy Lee" Wright Jr. These were devastating losses. My parents and my husband played a pivotal role in shaping the person I became and am today, as they always supported and cheered for me as I sought to fulfill my destiny.

My father was born in 1901 in Port Allen, a town outside of Baton Rouge, Louisiana, the state capital. His mother died when he was an infant, so his father and an aunt assumed the responsibility of raising him, his brother, and his sister. In his late teens, having a thirst for adventure, he traveled around the country by rail, "hoboeing," as he relayed to us, performing odd jobs. He settled in New Orleans and became a foreman for a major construction company, supervising the construction of many of the Catholic schools, churches, and other buildings in the city. My father was a proud man with a vibrant personality. It is from my father I learned to be resilient and confident.

My mother was born in 1911 in the Creole-speaking town of New Roads, Louisiana. Her mother, Annette Victorin, made the decision to move to New Orleans with her two daughters and baby boy, hoping to provide a better life for them. My mother was soft-spoken, had a quest for learning, and was a devout Catholic. Her devotion to faith, family, and caring for others defined her life. It is from my mother I learned about faith, compassion, and the thirst for knowledge.

It was in New Orleans that my parents met. My mother said that my father was quite a handsome man and finely built. She often reminisced that she went looking for a fish and caught a whale. As a whale sometimes rides high, there are times it dives quite low. They were perfect for each other, as their contrasting personalities strengthened their marriage. Together they built a beautiful family that included a son, Leonard, and twin daughters, Loyce and Joyce. They showered their children with love and provided them with an excellent quality of life. They instilled in their children that they were descendents of kings and queens; that they were capable of achieving their hearts desires and to never limit their dreams and aspirations. I was so blessed to have been born into such a loving, kind family that affirmed the value and specialness of each of their children.

My husband, Roy Lee, as he was known by all who knew him, was a very handsome, dashing man with a cool demeanor. An accomplished athlete in high school, he embraced athleticism in his college studies and became a physical education teacher and coach in the New Orleans public schools. He loved his students and was a father figure to many young men. Known for his debonair fashion style, he chose his wardrobe with intentionality. He wanted to be a role model for his students. He believed that if his students saw him, a teacher, dressing in a manner that they admired, they would be encouraged to make the right choices, work hard, and believe in themselves in the pursuit of their dreams. To me, my husband was Mr. Wright. He always supported me, lifted me up, cared and provided for me and our daughter, Kiana, in countless ways. I would always say to anyone who would listen, "Everyone is looking for Mr. Right—I found him." From my husband, I learned devotion.

Rather than dwelling on my losses, I reflected on the countless happy moments we shared. To dim the sorrow from my loved ones' absence, I covered my heart with the memory of their unconditional love. It was following the loss of these important people in my life that "blessings in the midst of the storm" became my personal mantra.

So, what was so special about 2005? It was a happy and exciting time because the construction of my new dream house was completed. The impetus for building a house resulted from what I call a "God is . . ." moment. A God is . . . moment is a thought or feeling that one acts upon that leads to an outcome that alters the course of one's life or changes an anticipated outcome. The God is . . . moment that would lead to my dream house occurred in 2004, when I was returning home from a business trip. I was sitting in the Dallas airport, waiting to board my connecting flight to New Orleans. While waiting, I received two telephone calls, one from a staff member informing me that after multiple years of requesting an increase in the office's budget, it had finally been approved. The other call was from a family member, notifying me that test results had revealed that my brother did not have cancer. As I sat in that airport with thankfulness in my heart, reflecting on those two calls, a voice in my head said, *Build the house.* Upon returning home, I began to pursue the dream that my husband and I had had, which was to build our dream home.

Roy and I had purchased the property several years prior to his transitioning. We spent countless hours discussing the elements of our dream house as we looked at plans and color schemes. Of course, a large closet for his extensive wardrobe was a necessity. As the property was in a guarded community, I would joke with him about the many laughs he would enjoy when he would one day playfully deny permission for his friends to enter the subdivision. The anticipated reaction of their responses when they were denied admission brought him much laughter. His one request was to have a room for his music collection, for he was a lover of many genres of music. He was my personal DJ, and music reverberated throughout the house daily. Roy enjoyed spending countless hours recording music, meticulously labeling his recordings while filing them by genre. He was so happy as he looked forward to his personal space for his collection in our new home.

However, all of our planning was abruptly halted. In the middle of joyously planning for the construction of our dream house, without any forewarning, my husband was diagnosed with colon cancer—two words that were difficult for me to say for a very long time. It was such a shock to both of us because he looked perfectly healthy. He didn't smoke and was physically fit, for, as a physical education teacher and coach, he exercised regularly and always managed his weight. To hear the word cancer was a dagger in our hearts. Stunned by the news, we left the doctor's office, not knowing what to do or even where to go. We decided to go to the restaurant in the subdivision where we'd purchased the lot for our dream home. It was a quiet place overlooking a golf course, a picture that was serene and peaceful and totally opposite from the thoughts and emotions we were experiencing.

After sitting in silence, we began to plan our next steps. There was hope that surgery could remove the tumor and all would be well. We decided to share the news with a few family members as we asked for prayers. However, we did not tell our daughter Kiana, as she was at school in Atlanta, attending Spelman College. Our thinking was to wait until after the surgery, for there was no need to worry her if things worked out well. However, the surgeon's report shattered our world, as the tumor had grown into the aorta and could not be removed. Roy was so very strong and calm throughout the entire ordeal. He personified the famous quote attributed to Martin Luther King Jr.: "The ultimate measure of a man is not where he stands in moments of convenience and comfort, but where he stands at times of challenge and controversy."

We faced the inevitable with an outpouring of love unimaginable. Daily, our home was filled with family and friends providing distractions, extending comfort, and offering support. As we navigated through our new normal, they were our "blessings in the midst of the storm." My husband transitioned a year after his diagnosis. I grieved his loss in the home we'd shared with little thought to moving forward with building a new home without him. So, when it came, the message to build the house was astonishing. Yet I moved forward with the planning process.

Initially, I worked with a draftsman to design the house; however, he did not capture what I desired. I wanted a custom-designed house with the elements my husband and I had dreamed of. In my heart, I thought it would be nice to work with a Black female architect, for I was certain that she would be able to capture the details we wanted. A dear friend, Mary Ann, told me she knew of a female architect whom I should contact. I received her name and number and called twice. My calls were not returned. Subsequently, I received a phone call from the receptionist informing me that the person I was trying to reach was not available, but there was another person that could perhaps work with me. She asked if I wanted to meet with that person. I said yes, I would love to do so.

As I was now a widow, I wasn't comfortable meeting someone I didn't know at my home. I suggested we meet at a coffee house. We described the colors we were wearing for recognition. I eagerly awaited the arrival. When the door opened and our eyes connected, I couldn't believe the person walking toward me. It was a Black female! And I thought, *This is another God is . . . moment.* After introductions, I began explaining to her what my husband and I had envisioned in our dream home. She immediately retrieved a sheet of paper and began sketching. I was overjoyed as I knew she was the one.

The construction of our dream house was completed in December 2004. However, I did not move into it. I was having difficulty separating from the home that had been a place of refuge for my family—a place of comfort and celebrations. It was difficult to leave the home where my husband and I had built a life together and where we'd brought our daughter after she was born. And it was so very difficult to leave the place where the memory of the presence of Roy was in every room. The home held so many joyous memories; from it, I did not want to separate. My new home became a "showhouse." I would "show" it to those who wanted to see it. All marveled at how beautiful and well appointed it was and at the gorgeous view through the windows. Upon completion of the tour, I would return to the house with my memories.

Eventually, I began packing a box each night in anticipation of a move at some time. A few weeks before Mardi Gras 2005, my nephew Neal asked me, "Have you packed yet?"

I told him I had packed most of the items. Without a discussion, he came with a crew that weekend and moved me from my home filled with memories into my new house. I learned that family members had been discussing the fact that my emotional connection to the house was prohibiting me from making the move. Out of their love and concern for me, they boldly made a decision that it was time for me to move so I could begin the healing process in new surroundings. In time, I came to realize that the move was the right decision, for I truly enjoyed my new environment.

My home immediately became the place for gatherings. As my mother's home had been open and welcoming to all, so was mine. My family and friends loved the atmosphere and comfortability. We celebrated my Uncle Lawrence's seventy-fifth birthday in March, Easter in April, and Mother's Day in May. For the Fourth of July weekend, which is also when the Essence Music Festival is held in New Orleans, Kiana wanted to host a crawfish boil, as she had friends visiting for Essence. My brother-in-law Charles labored over the boiling of one hundred pounds of crawfish, as well as potatoes, sausage, corn, and even oranges. Every item was well seasoned and flavored deliciously. The house was filled with family members and friends. Chatter, laughter, and music permeated the air. Then, on August 12, 2005, we celebrated the birthdays of two family members. No one could fathom that in a few days, the joyous feelings, the laughter, the camaraderie that reverberated through the house on that day would change drastically and the home and city we knew would be shattered.

Within days, unbeknownst to me, news began circulating about a disturbance forming in the gulf that would potentially impact New Orleans. My job at the time was as executive director of the Louisiana Commission on Human Rights in the Office of the Governor. My office was located in Baton Rouge, the state capital. I would drive the one hundred or so miles to and from my office, returning late in the evening, routinely arriving home after the evening news broadcast. Therefore, I was unaware of the formation of the huge tropical cyclone named Katrina heading toward New Orleans.

Even though my family members were leaving the city, I didn't have a sense of urgency. However, I thought maybe this was a good time to visit Kiana in Kennesaw, a suburb of Atlanta, Georgia. I packed a small suitcase and decided to get a prescription filled at the nearby pharmacist. Interestingly, on my drive to the pharmacy, I didn't see a line of individuals at the gas stations filling tanks, which usually is a sign of families evacuating. Seeing that would have alerted me to indeed leave the city. Upon entering the pharmacy, however, I saw a long line. I couldn't imagine why so many people were there waiting. It didn't dawn on me that this was part of the evacuation preparation. Not wanting to stand in line, I decided I would pick up the prescription the next day and then drive to Atlanta. As I drove out of the parking lot heading home, I suddenly turned left, away from my home, entered the interstate, and began the drive to Kennesaw. To this day, I don't know why I abruptly turned the car. I later learned that that decision prevented me from being caught the next day in what would be the worst evacuation for the city of New Orleans—another God is ... moment!

Due to the severity of the storm and the trajectory of its path, New Orleans was expected to experience life-threatening conditions. The next day, I learned that Mayor Ray Nagin had issued an order for the entire city to evacuate, and the contraflow system directing traffic out of the city was initiated. The late notice to evacuate resulted in thousands of New Orleanians getting stranded for many hours on the interstate in bottleneck traffic. The abrupt decision I made on Saturday, to drive to Georgia rather than drive home, saved me from experiencing the stress and discomfort of hours in the standstill traffic of the contraflow. *A blessing in the midst of the storm.*

I arrived at my daughter's house in Kennesaw in the early morning hours. Shortly thereafter, her twin friends and their dog also arrived from New Orleans. We were glued to the television, eager to receive any information we could find about the hurricane barreling toward New Orleans. The news was very bleak. It was projected to create significant damage to the entire area and beyond. Our lives were at a standstill as we waited for Hurricane Katrina to hit landfall. And as it did, its impact was devastating. Anxious to get specific information about the devastation, I called the chief of staff in the governor's office. His response was that it was "very bad." I then specifically asked about the area where I lived, New Orleans East. His answer was, "Oh, my God," and my heart sank. I began searching the Internet to look at the aerial views of New Orleans, especially my neighborhood, to determine the damage. I was stunned to see the high level of the water. I knew then that my new home was destroyed, and a feeling of deep sorrow engulfed me.

In my mind I calculated six months—the length of time I'd lived in my dream home: six months of enjoying the results of years of dreaming, planning, and saving; six months of hosting dinners, parties, and family gatherings; and six months of experiencing the joy of living in the tranquil space of my dream home. The sense of loss and grief weighed heavily on my heart as my city and I faced an uncertain future. Compounding that misery was seeing the suffering of those left behind that the world saw through the television screen, people begging for help from rooftops and wading in waist-deep water, seeking higher grounds. It was heartbreaking, to say the least. It would be days before help arrived. To make matters worse, we learned that the severe damages to the city were due largely to the failure of the levee systems. If not for the levee breaches, a levee system that was the responsibility of the federal government to manage, the city of New Orleans would not have experienced the water intrusion that caused the major flooding of thousands of homes and businesses and the loss of hundreds of lives. It was a failure of major proportions.

The news channels in Atlanta provided significant coverage of the inhumane conditions those left behind were experiencing due to a lack of housing, utilities, and safe drinking water. I was extremely annoyed that during the coverage, reporters and commentators referred to displaced New Orleanians as refugees. I was so outraged that we, citizens of the United States, contributing members of our community, were being referred to as "refugees." Never being shy to stand up against an injustice, I called CNN in Atlanta. I requested to speak to the director or assignment editor to voice my displeasure at the narrative of their coverage. The response was, "That is the term that is being used." I insisted that they refrain from doing so, informing them we were citizens, not refugees. I was so elated a few days later when the Congressional Black Caucus held a press conference and demanded the media cease referring to those displaced due to Hurricane Katrina as refugees—and the reference ceased.... *Blessings in the midst of the storm.*

I soon learned that a number of friends had evacuated to the Atlanta area, including my embraced son Wayne, who had thoughtfully slipped me an envelope containing money, stating, "You are going to need this." He was correct, for I could not access funds from my bank in New Orleans. I decided that we should all come together for a Labor Day gathering at Kiana's house. It was a special afternoon. About twenty-five of us huddled together, seeking comfort in our shared grief. There also was a joyousness of being together and connected through the commonality of our indescribable loss. We happily reminisced, recounting moments of joy about our city, our home, the culture and eclecticism of our citizens. Suddenly, Philip, with his melodious voice, began singing a song reminiscent of Our City. In that moment, tears began to flow, and in our collective sorrow, as the words of the song enveloped us, a sense of hope permeated the space.... *Blessings in the midst of the storm.*

Another blessing in the midst of the storm occurred when I learned that the talented violinist Michael Ward would be performing with another violinist, Ken Ford of Atlanta, at a venue in downtown Atlanta. Michael and I had developed a personal relationship when he was a student at Southern University in Baton Rouge. He would frequently travel to New Orleans to play at venues, and I was always in attendance for support and to enjoy his electrifying performance. I was filled with joy as I looked forward to seeing him. It was a wonderful set featuring a battle of the violinists. At the conclusion of the set, Michael announced that he was playing a number that would have a special meaning to anyone in the audience from New Orleans. It wasn't apparent who in attendance was from New Orleans until he began playing a well-known second-line song. Immediately, the napkins started going up, the handkerchiefs came out, and a traditional second line began. It was a joyous moment reminding us what it means to miss New Orleans.... *Blessings in the midst of the storm.*

Several of my family members had evacuated to Memphis, Tennessee, including my embraced sister, Geraldine, her son Edward and his family, and and my goddaughter, Arlinda, and her family, who asked me to join them in Memphis. Arlinda encouraged me to do so, suggesting that there were wonderful stores to shop in, especially as I would need to replace furniture destroyed by the hurricane. I boarded a train in Atlanta and traveled to Memphis. It was wonderful connecting with family members and to hear of the outpouring of generosity extended to them by that community. The many acts of generosity extended to New Orleanians who had evacuated were replicated throughout the United States and beyond. These acts of kindness extended in the midst of loss and suffering revealed the true humanity of many.... *Blessings in the midst of the storm.*

But my Memphis visit was cut short. My twin sister, Joyce, and my niece, Yolanda, had traveled to Arkansas to assist a family member who had evacuated from New Orleans and was now hospitalized after becoming seriously ill. They were leaving Arkansas to return to their home in the California Bay Area. They convinced me to travel with them, and I agreed to do so. The plan was for me to meet them at the Tennessee–Arkansas border. With my little suitcase that contained my possessions, Arlinda's husband, Toikus, drove me to meet them on Saturday, September 18, 2005. As we were early, I told Toikus he could leave me. Standing there all alone on the side of the street with a small suitcase, I suddenly realized I was homeless. A wave of sadness engulfed me as I held back tears. Shortly thereafter, Joyce and Yolanda arrived and retrieved me, and we began the drive to California.

What a joy it was to be with my twin and to hear of her and Yolanda's experiences in Arkansas. There, they encountered many evacuees, men, women, and children from New Orleans who had been left behind. They recounted that after hearing the horror of their evacuation experiences, they wanted to do something to uplift them. In the true spirit of New Orleanians, they prepared a traditional New Orleans meal consisting of red beans, rice, and barbecue chicken topped off with rum cake and ice cream for the kids. Sounds of New Orleans music blared from the stereo. This generosity of spirit brought joy to the recipients, but not more so than to my sister and niece. *A blessing in the midst of the storm.*

Our drive was filled with chatter and laughter as we caught up on each other's lives and reminisced over the many adventures we had experienced throughout the years. I drove initially to allow them to rest, as it was a long drive. As night fell, my sister and niece dozed off, and I enjoyed listening to the sounds of some of my favorite artists. Suddenly, I was driving through heavy rain. The cascading rain limited my visibility so much that I could not see clearly, yet I did not pull over. I kept driving and praying. I don't know why I made such a foolish decision. When I came out on the other side of the storm, I was so relieved and thankful. I later learned that I had driven through the torrential downpour of Hurricane Rita. How fortunate was I to survive driving through a hurricane and come out on the other side safely.... *Blessings in the midst of the storm.* My sister and niece were horrified to learn that I did so and did not wake them up throughout the ordeal.

Yolanda relieved me from driving as we continued through Texas. We were looking forward to driving the historic Route 66. Suddenly, we noticed a large white cross projecting toward the sky. We were amazed and inspired by it and decided to drive to the location of the cross. We learned that the 190-foot-tall cross is located in Groom, Texas, and can be seen from twenty miles away. The cross led us to an outdoor display of life-sized bronze figures depicting the Stations of the Cross. To the left of the Stations of the Cross sat a grotto on a small hill. We climbed the hill and looked into the grotto. There, we saw the replica of "the empty tomb" with a life-sized figure of a kneeling angel next to it. We marveled at the experience, especially as it was on a Sunday morning, when we'd normally attend church.

We felt so blessed to have been led to the Cross. To emerge safely after driving through a hurricane and then experience the recreation of the crucifixion and resurrection on that Sunday morning was amazing and miraculous. *A blessing in the midst of the storm.* The drive on Route 66 was underwhelming yet nostalgic. Hours later, we arrived in Los Angeles. It was there that we spent the night. We concluded our trip the next day, arriving at my sister's house.

Joyce's beautiful home is situated on a hill above Contra Costa College. It has a stunning view of the Bay Area. As I looked around at her beautiful furniture, collectibles, and artwork, I immediately thought of my own home. Noticing my pensiveness, my sister began playing music. We sang and danced, enjoying the moment of being together, and the nostalgia faded. It felt good to be in an area where the devastation of Hurricane Katrina was not dominating the news. I was lulled into a sense of "all is well." As in Memphis, Joyce's friends showered me with gifts and food. She and her sister-friend, Cheryl, established a donation thread, collecting money from their friends. I was asked to provide names of family members and friends who had been displaced. Yolanda and Joyce's son, Melvin, wired money across the country to all whom I could contact. The gifts ranged in amounts from one hundred dollars to one thousand dollars, depending on the size of the family. It was a wonderful gesture of generosity and love.... *Blessings in the midst of the storm.*

My sister's home is always filled with music, laughter, dancing, and the aroma of New Orleans food, as she is an excellent cook—a chef, as she always reminds us. In the middle of this joyous moment, I looked out her expansive windows, enjoying the view of the Bay. It was a peaceful moment. Then, a song began to play that touched me profoundly—"Home," by Stephanie Mills. Suddenly, I felt a deep sense of loss as I thought about Home. Home, New Orleans—New Orleans, with its rich history, culture, food, music, and sense of community. All the emotions I had been holding were released in a torrential downpour of tears. When the tears subsided, I then thought about my house.

I said to God, *Why did you have me build the house just to have it taken away by a massive hurricane?* The answer that came to me was, *I put you in a better place*. It was true. For I was in a better place. As a widow living alone, I felt very secure. Looking out of my windows, I could see ducks and rabbits, egrets and turtles, and trees dancing in the wind. It was serene and safe. At that moment, as I was grieving the loss of my city and my home, I realized there was no doubt that I would eventually return home.

Shortly thereafter, the mayor announced that the city was open and residents could return home. I flew back to Georgia and prepared to return home. However, once again, the entire city was ordered to evacuate due to contamination.

In October, Governor Kathleen Blanco requested that employees in her administration return to work to offer support and information to the displaced citizens who were located throughout the state. I prepared to return to Baton Rouge. However, I didn't know where I would live. A dear friend and fellow displaced New Orleanian, Patricia, knew I was seeking housing. She called to tell me of a possible apartment available from a person who served in the military and had been called to duty. She said the apartment was mine if I wanted it. I was so happy to learn of this good fortune. Nony, a dear friend who lives in Atlanta, said he would drive me to Baton Rouge to see the apartment and that we could first stop in New Orleans so I could see my house.

Returning to New Orleans was difficult, emotionally. I had seen the images on the television of people walking in waist-deep water; at the convention center, pleading for help; stuck on rooftops, waving or carrying signs asking for help—yet nothing prepared me for the destruction I saw. It was overwhelming. What was very noticeable was the silence. There were no sounds of life—no birds chirping, no dogs barking. It was very strange and highlighted the fact that the vibrancy of our community had ceased to exist. It was as though the entire city was in a cemetery. We drove directly to my house, and I was stunned by what I saw. There was a gray pall over everything. Shrubbery and trees were dead. My beautiful new home, for which I had spent countless hours selecting the brick, the design, the colors, and the flooring, was destroyed. Someone had entered my home, searched through it, and taken shoes, clothing, and other items. I had no words. Despite what I saw, I knew I had to rebuild for this place. This city was home.

As I assessed the damage, I noticed something else. During construction, I had asked the contractor not to close the walls because I wanted to do something special: I wanted to tape scriptures to the insulation throughout the house. What I noticed was that the waterline in the house, which marked the height of the flooding, was at three feet, and the mold did not rise beyond that point! I smiled and offered a prayer of thankfulness, as I knew the damage to the house had been contained—*blessings in the midst of the storm*.

Such was not the case for the family home that I'd lived in with Roy and Kiana. Upon entering that home, I was devastated. The walls of the entire house were covered with mildew and mold; the waterline was to the ceiling. The resolve I felt previously about rebuilding dissipated, and the sight of the destruction of this house brought me to tears. I wondered what the future held for me and for the city I loved.

Leaving New Orleans, we drove to Baton Rouge and picked up the key to the apartment. I had mixed feelings. I was happy to have a place to live, enabling me to maintain employment. Yet I wanted to be home. Interestingly, according to the address, the apartment complex was a few blocks from my office. However, when I saw the complex, I had some trepidation, as it was not what I expected. The grounds were littered with trash, including discarded needles. Upon entering the apartment, I saw that it was in total shambles. The carpeting was filthy, and the place was littered with discarded items. I was so disappointed, and Nony saw it in my face. He said, "Don't worry, it can be fixed."

I suppose I should have been happy that I had a place to live, as so many people did not. Yet the thought of having to do so much to clean it up left me feeling overwhelmed. I returned the keys and declined to take the apartment, hoping I was not making a decision I would later regret.

Nony had made arrangements to spend the night with a friend. My plan was to rent a hotel room. To my dismay, the doors to every hotel I approached were locked. A sign posted on the door indicated that only hotel guests presenting keys were allowed to enter. I realized that policy was targeted at me and all of us who were displaced and seeking refuge. It was a painful reflection of the fact that we who were displaced were not desired, and were perhaps a burden. I experienced the same feeling of sadness I'd felt when standing on the roadside with my one suitcase as I realized, again, that I was homeless. I didn't know where I could spend the night. I thought about sleeping in my car. Then I realized I could go to my office. The building was secure, as there was round-the-clock security, and I had access to a bathroom. I was so relieved that I had recourse because the thought of sleeping in the car was frightening. I spent the night in my office chair instead.

The next morning, I freshened up in the bathroom, eager to continue my search for an apartment. Every apartment complex I went to had a sign reading No Vacancy. Then I experienced a God is . . . moment. I had an urge to check the availability of an apartment at Siegen Lane. For months, when driving from New Orleans to my office in Baton Rouge, I'd observed the construction of an apartment complex in close proximity to three crosses.

Upon approaching the office of the complex, I saw the sign on the door: No Vacancy, No Waiting List. Entering the lobby area, I immediately said to the person at the desk, "I apologize, as I am not disrespecting your sign. I just want to know when availability may occur."

She told me she did not know. I asked her if it was possible for me to see a unit. She responded that she could show me pictures of an apartment. Sharing the pictures, she pointed out special features of the apartment, including chair rails, which she began to explain to me. I told her I was aware of chair rails, and proceeded to share with her that six months before, I had completed building my dream home with its many appointments, which had been destroyed by Hurricane Katrina and the failure of the levee system. Listening to my experience, tears appeared in her eyes.

I said, "Please don't," as I too was on the verge of tears, and I knew that this was not where I wanted to give in to my sorrow.

She excused herself and left the room. Upon returning, I was astonished when she stated, "I have an apartment available for you. You can choose the first or the third floor, and you can move in today."

What! I thought about the sign—No Vacancy, No Waiting List—and I smiled. . . . *Blessings in the midst of the storm.*

After thanking her, I indicated I would return later to sign the lease. I wanted time to call my embraced cousin, Brenda, who was a consultant to the New Orleans Sewerage and Water Board. She was sleeping on the floor in an office building along with other employees and officials feverishly working to get the city opened. I shared with her the news of the availability of a two-bedroom apartment and asked if she was interested in sharing. She immediately said yes and explained that her colleague also needed housing. I chose the apartment on the first floor overlooking a lake, which reminded me of the lake behind my home. Her colleague was able to rent the apartment I did not choose. He, too, received a *blessing in the storm.*

That evening, as Nony and I drove back to Georgia, I reflected on the trip to New Orleans and Baton Rouge. I was so thankful that Nony had willingly adjusted his busy schedule to drive and accompany me, as his presence was comforting when I saw my home for the first time, as well as when we viewed the apartment. His optimism in both situations and the confidence he expressed that everything was going to be well replayed in my thoughts. Perhaps he was right after all. I had achieved a major accomplishment: securing a place to live. Realizing that lifted my spirits, and for the first time, I exhaled.

Having a place to live brought a sense of relief. It was a perfect location, as it was near my office and in close proximity to New Orleans. I made plans to move in after Thanksgiving. As the Thanksgiving holiday approached, my niece, Monique, who had evacuated to Houston, Texas, suggested that we should travel there for the holiday. She said it would be a family reunion. Uncle Lawrence, my mother's brother, the patriarch of our family, and his son, Lawrence Jr.; Monique's father and my brother, Leonard; Monique's husband, Neal, and their son, Neal III; and Monique's mother, Dorothy, all of whom had evacuated from New Orleans, were also in Houston. My nephew, Leonard, planned to drive in from Austin. Being away from family for such a long period of time was unusual, as we were always spending time together at our various homes. The anticipation of being together was exhilarating.

When Kiana and I arrived, it was truly a family reunion. We were so happy to see everyone, to enjoy New Orleans food, play a game of spades, sing along with the music, laugh at jokes, and, above all, feel the love. We ended the evening playing and rocking to the song that has become our family anthem: "Family Reunion." It was an emotional, joyful time. We were reminded of how much we had to be thankful for.... *A blessing in the midst of the storm.*

Upon returning to Georgia, I informed Kiana that it was time for me to return to Louisiana. Immediately, I saw a look of disappointment in her face. I shared her feeling. My heart ached at the thought of leaving my sweet, kind, generous daughter. We had not lived together since her departure for college. The opportunity to spend time together, despite the circumstances, was so very special. As her mother's and grandmother's homes had been welcoming to all, so was her home. During my stay, she cared so well for me. Not wanting me to dwell on my circumstances, she sought to entertain me in many ways. She and my embraced cousin, Sayonara, planned shopping trips, luncheons, dinner with friends, and whist card games, which I loved, since I am a great whist player. Yet I knew that I had to leave her, my *blessing in the midst of the storm.*

In early December, I moved into the apartment and returned to my job as executive director of the Louisiana Commission on Human Rights, Office of the Governor. My staff was traveling throughout the state, bringing messages of comfort from the governor to those displaced, as well as maintaining our primary responsibility of investigating complaints of discrimination in employment, banking and lending practices, and public accommodations. Complaints to the office increased during this period. Many of the calls related to denial of housing and refusal of services at various establishments. I empathized with those experiencing such treatment, as I recalled how I'd felt when I could not enter a hotel. With a sense of urgency, we sought to resolve all complaints expeditiously. I recalled one such call from a civil rights icon. After evacuating, she moved in with her daughter. Her niece's landlord was going to evict her because the number of people living in the apartment violated the lease. I immediately referred the complaint to the attorney general's office, and it was resolved. The eviction could not occur as we were in a state of emergency. For her, that was a *blessing in the midst of the storm.*

In spring 2007, I decided it was time for me to rebuild my home. I contacted my contractor, Kirk, to obtain the cost for rebuilding. During the discussion, he informed me that flood insurance should cover the cost. I told him I did not have flood coverage and that I would have to seek government funding. To my amazement, he informed me that he had obtained flood insurance after the slab was poured, as is a requirement. The cost for insurance was factored into the quoted price to build my home, and he had paid the premium. What a surprise! I was extremely elated to know that there was money available to restore my dream home. Even though I did not have insurance to cover the contents, I knew I had received a *blessing in the midst of the storm.*

Rebuilding proved to be very challenging. Thousands of homes were destroyed by Hurricane Katrina and the levee breaches, making it difficult to obtain materials and supplies. Additionally, I had to wait in the queue for tradesmen who were engaged in other jobs. It would take several months for the restoration of my home to be complete. Happily, it was partially completed as we approached the Fourth of July 2007 weekend. Kiana asked if we were going to have our annual crawfish boil.

I hesitated in my response because even though we had water and electricity, we did not have any furniture and the kitchen area wasn't complete. Despite my reluctance, I was convinced to do so when Kiana said it is important for us to embrace our present as we look forward to the future. We accommodated family and friends, utilizing folding chairs and tables. The crawfish boil was just what those of us who had returned home needed: a celebration. Once again, the house reverberated with laughter, music, and an aura of happiness that filled our partially renovated home, *a blessing in the midst of the storm.*

Since things were progressing with the rebuilding of my home, I turned my attention to the rebuilding of our previous home. I was fortunate to locate a contractor to restore it. The damages from the hurricane and intrusion of the flood waters required replacing the roof, walls, floors, and air conditioning system. Thankfully, I did have homeowners and flood insurance to cover the cost. I was eager to complete the renovation because my family friend, Euclid, was living there prior to the hurricane and he was anxious to return to his home. It was completed in time for him to enjoy Christmas at home.... *Blessings in the midst of the storm.*

I finally moved out of the apartment in Baton Rouge. It was good being home, yet it was different. So many had not returned. Also, there was still so much work that needed to be done on thousands of homes; the street and interstate lights were not working, casting a complete darkness at nightime, and the spirit, the joie de vivre of the city, was missing. Yet, there was a determination by city leaders, returning citizens, and others to rediscover, rebuild, and reclaim the city.

During this same time, I was contacted by Ava Simmons, president of the board of directors of the YWCA of Greater New Orleans. I have a long history of involvement with the YWCA, having previously served as president of the board of directors of the YWCA New Orleans and held leadership roles on the national level. I was elected to the YWCA USA Nominating Committee and to the board of directors, serving as vice president during my last term. The mission of the YWCA is to "eliminate racism, empower women and promote peace, justice, freedom and dignity for all."[37] That mission aligns with my personal views and the work that I have been involved in within my community for my entire adult life. As a result of my involvement on the local and national levels, the New Orleans YWCA bestowed upon me the title of honorary board member.

As an honorary board member, I was invited to an upcoming meeting of the board of directors. The meeting was to discuss the impact of the hurricane and levee failure on the operations of the organization, and the report was very bleak. All of the facilities were totally destroyed, including the daycare and administration building, the education building, and the transitional housing unit, along with all contents. Moreover, due to an oversight, the flood insurance had not been renewed, hence, there weren't any funds to aid in the rebuilding. A decision had to be made: cease to exist, or rebuild.

---

37   "What We Do," YWCA, YWCA USA, accessed June 9, 2025, https://www.ywca.org/what-we-do.

As we pondered the decision, I reflected on the fact that, for nearly one hundred years, the YWCA had provided services for women and girls in the New Orleans area. The services included childcare; after-school, summer education, and recreation programs; violence-against-women programs, including support groups; and services for the elderly. Understanding the importance of the work and what the YWCA meant to women and girls in our community, I told the board members that I would help anyone desiring to rebuild. Neither the president nor board members felt they could provide the leadership. I understood their reluctance, as they too had homes and lives to rebuild, with many of them living in other cities.

I was then asked, "Why don't you do it?"

I was initially stunned by the ask. With some hesitancy, I agreed to do so. In 2006, I was elected president of the board of directors. With fellow board members Shelia Webb, Arlinda Westbrook, Shawne Favre, Tamara Jacobson, Valerie Sholes, and Tracie Boutte, we embarked on a journey to rebuild an institution.

The task of rebuilding the YWCA Greater New Orleans has been hard to achieve. There have been so many challenges to overcome. One such challenge was obtaining public assistance from the Federal Emergency Management Agency (FEMA). It was important to receive FEMA assistance, as approval of an application would provide much needed funds to rebuild. Initially, we were told that an application had not been submitted. After providing evidence to the contrary, we received approval. We were so elated! *A blessing in the midst of the storm.* Two lessons we learned after receiving approval of FEMA funding: there is a penalty clause for not having insurance, and FEMA funds do not provide for enhancements unless mandated by city code. Our penalty of $500,000 was the maximum. Despite these regulations, we moved forward with optimism, confident that we would obtain the gap funding. After an open bid process, we engaged Landmark Consulting for project management and Trapolin-Peer Architects for design services, with Gabriel Virdure and Paula Peer as the lead architects.

Throughout the design process, we became keenly aware of the funding gap, which was projected to be in excess of one million dollars. Our efforts to secure new market tax credits and private funding failed. A breakthrough occurred when developer Zach Kupperman identified a funding source administered by the state of Louisiana Office of Community Development. It was an attractive loan, with an interest rate of 3 percent, with 33 percent forgivable upon achieving a hiring requirement. After submission of the application and a successful site visit, approval was granted. However, there were other hurdles to overcome. While the loan covered the $500,000 penalty, it did not cover funding to meet city codes, enhancements included in the design, nor the owner equity, a requirement of the loan. Through the sale of donated property, support from Mayor LaToya Cantrell, the YWCA of the Mid-Peninsula Fund in California, the YWCA USA, and other donations, the funding deficit was met: *blessings in the midst of the storm.*

On a beautiful fall morning, in the presence of board members, donors, former staff members, funders, elected officials, and volunteers, Gail Glapion, the longtime executive director of the YWCA Greater New Orleans, eloquently shared the history of the YWCA Greater New Orleans and its impact on the Greater New Orleans community. Thereafter, I shared our journey of persistence, perseverance, and faith. Standing in that moment, I reflected on all who had traveled on the journey with us in our unrelenting determination and tenacity to succeed, which mirrored that of fellow New Orleanians who sought to rebuild their homes after the hurricane. I concluded by thanking the volunteers, especially Marlene Bercy Dupuy, Legacy Circle members, donors, and board members, for their generous contributions and support.

Thereafter, we broke ground on the construction of a seventeen-thousand-square-foot building to house the much needed programs provided by the YWCA Greater New Orleans. It was an exhilarating moment. However, our enthusiasm was short-lived, as the construction was halted due to the unearthing of an additional foundation that needed to be removed. The cost for removal was not covered by the initial ten million-dollar bid. We were stunned by this new discovery. Confronted with a work stoppage coupled with an increased cost of hundreds of thousands of dollars, the project was at a standstill for several months.

Then, a God is... moment prompted me to call Congressman Troy Carter. I recalled the many conversations I'd had with Congressman Carter about the work of the YWCA and our efforts to rebuild. He always seemed genuinely interested in our progress and expressed his support. Encouraged by his genuineness, I gave him a call.

He listened attentively, and before I could finish, he said, "I really want to help because the work the YWCA has done in the community is well known and definitely needed."

With the help of Paula, Gabriel, and Shelia, a request was submitted for federal funding. Thanks to Congressman Troy Carter, we received congressional funding in the amount of one million dollars. It was enough to cover the deficit and provide funds for some enhancements.... *Blessings in the midst of the storm.*

However, the blessings did not stop there. Every year since 2015, with the assistance of Dr. Shanta Proctor-Harrison, I've submitted a request to the state of Louisiana for capital outlay funding to support our rebuilding efforts. In 2025—ten years later—thanks to the leadership and determination of Senator Royce Duplessis and support from Representative Matthew Willard and other legislators, our request for one million dollars was approved! *Blessings in the midst of the storm.*

As we prepare to restart the project, the anticipated start date is August 2025, which coincides with the twentieth anniversary of Hurricane Katrina. I am certain the activities around the twenty-year anniversary of Katrina will include reflections on the devastation, the losses of life and property, and the mistakes that caused so much suffering. Yet there will also be jubilation and celebration because a city that many thought would not rebuild, and whose culture would be silenced and whose people would not return, is thriving. The words that will resonate in messages and news stories will be determination, resilience, and fortitude. The celebration will undoubtedly include the sounds of the drums, the tubas, the trumpets, the trombones, and the tambourines in the many second lines, for in New Orleans, every celebration includes a second line.

For me personally, it will be a reminder to always listen to that inner voice—those God is ... moments—for doing so can prevent one from making a mistake, can cause one to move in a direction not previously contemplated, thereby changing the path for the better, or move one to act boldly in pursuit of something consequential. I will lament the losses, yet I will embrace the memories that I hold deeply in the crevices of my heart. I will remember that for every obstacle I faced trying to rebuild my homes and the YWCA Greater New Orleans, I was privileged to have angels, known and unknown, who provided assistance, support, shelter, gifts, and, above all, love. I will remember the heartbreak of being homeless, the feeling of rejection, and those difficult situations that seemed impossible to resolve, yet to be courageous when facing adversities and to always be compassionate. I will remember a city that once seemed to be dead but now is full of life, with its festivals, music, and joie de vivre. Yes, I will remember those things, but above all, I will remember and never forget that there are *blessings in the midst of the storm.* So, when the storms of life come, I will not look at the storm—I will look for the blessings.

BLESSED
GREGORY RATTLER SR.

Introduction

I'm told that from an incredibly young age (further back than I can remember), I somehow developed and displayed an interest in currency, money, dollars, capital, etc.

Being raised in a very "modest" working-class Black New Orleans community in the 1960s, I have no idea what could have inspired this inclination. I do, however, recall "lending money" to close friends and family members—with an expectation of receiving back more money than I'd originally loaned. I guess, in the context of this story, that, too, was an early blessing, for this childhood "quirk" has served me well across all aspects of my life. And thanks to the environment of love, boundless support, and encouragement that our parents provided for myself and my siblings, their enormous sacrifices that created the framework for my education and, by extension, my career, I never veered far from what has been part of my being since my formative days. I have had the privilege and good fortune of working in the highest levels of local and state government. And, as the following Katrina story reveals, I also spent the twenty years prior to the storm working for an international financial services institution that had become increasingly active in using its vast resources and expertise in ways that I never knew existed.

As we approach the twentieth anniversary marking the catastrophic 2005 weather event Hurricane Katrina, when approached, I welcomed the opportunity to reflect on the personal events that occurred within my immediate family that fateful late August in New Orleans. Thank you, Carol Bebelle, for giving me the nudge to commit some of these remembrances to paper. In the rearview mirror, some of those affected by this tragic event might be tempted to credit serendipity, chance, or plain ole luck. Given all of the myriads of possible deadly outcomes, I most assuredly attribute my family's overall outcomes to divine intervention or, said another way, my many Katrina blessings."

Keep Your Head to the Sky

My seven-year-old son, the youngest of four, was a very ordinary but socially engaging little boy making his way through his young life and trying his hand at full-contact recreational park football (mostly because his dad—me—never got around to that when he was that age). As fate would have it, we were just starting to see him take a liking to the sport after having spent the prior two seasons mostly playing in the dirt and/or with bugs as the rest of his team played what could best be described as little toddlers bumping into each other—ball or no ball!

On Saturday, August 27, around nine in the morning, I watched with growing excitement as all of the little boys actually competed and played somewhat organized football against another team within the New Orleans Recreation Department biddy football league. The game was held on a field two blocks away from Lake Pontchartrain, and the weather was Chamber of Commerce–perfect: blue skies with a breeze off the lake, which helped with the typical August heat of New Orleans. In addition to my wife, I was joined at the game by an older son, who was excited to watch his youngest brother play but even more excited about the upcoming week, when he would be starting high school at the world-renowned St. Augustine High School in New Orleans.

In the days leading up to the game, there had been local media reports of an upper-level tropical depression (TD #10) that had formed south of The Bahamas. For locals, a tropical depression is usually just a rain event with the possibility of a few power outages and perhaps some heavy rain. And, of course, in New Orleans, that could always mean some localized street flooding, but nothing more. I, like so many others, was somewhat dismissive of any "storm" that wasn't classified by weather and public safety authorities as a Category Three hurricane or above. Nevertheless, I kept a watchful eye on the beautiful skies of New Orleans as we went about celebrating my young football star.

As the game ended and we started to look forward to the next game, I could hardly contain my excitement that my seven-year-old son had played exceptionally well, to the point where I'd asked my wife several times as we watched the game, "Who is that kid?" and "Is that our son?" As I had done so many times before with all of my sons and their various performances, I needed to call my dad with the embellished play-by-play assessment of his grandson's performance.

At the time, Dad was in his mid-eighties and of sound mind, body, and spirit. Affectionately known as PawPaw and having been born in Woodville, Mississippi, in the 1920s, he'd served his country in the Korean War and had endured the brutality of the Deep South in the 1940s. He had been denied the opportunity to pursue a formal education and had witnessed the aftermath of the killing of one of his contemporaries at the hands of the people he referred to as "sheriffs by day, Klan by night." As it turned out, he became for me one of the smartest men I've ever known.

After our mother's passing in 1977, my dad had, almost overnight, become a completely different person at all levels and, for the rest of his life, the unmistakable, true patriarch of my family. Nothing of consequence happened to me, my siblings, his daughters-in-law, or especially his grandkids that he was not present for physically, spiritually, financially, or in some other capacity. Fiercely independent, when I challenged his decision to purchase a used vehicle for my older son, who was headed to college (as he didn't need nor was he able to park one on campus as a college freshman), my dad sternly said to me, "Don't ever tell me what I can or can't do for my grandchildren."

He attributed his incredible health to growing up at a different time and was always God-fearing and spiritual. He would often offer very short expressions and illustrations of how, no matter how many college degrees and credentials a man could accumulate, we are nothing without a divine force. "Wisdom can only be bestowed on those who are blessed to live long enough to experience and embrace God's handiwork," he would say. This has always proved to be true for me, even in the most unlikely places, and often under the toughest circumstances.

As he gracefully aged into his eighties, he decided on his own that it was time to sell his home of forty-plus years, his arsenal of hunting rifles, and his sixteen-foot, aluminum hull, side-console boat that had carried his son and grandsons into the surrounding saltwater fishing holes. It was there that we watched my dad put on a fishing clinic. Without anybody's awareness or involvement, he had quietly conducted his own research and, in 2003, decided to move into an independent senior living center not far from our Uptown home. Along with several other senior facilities, Chateau de Notre Dame is owned and operated under the auspices of the Catholic Archdiocese of New Orleans. I thought this was a little odd, as for his entire life my dad had been a devout and continually active Southern Baptist, serving as a church deacon for decades.

On that August Saturday morning, I felt that it was somewhat unusual for him not to answer the two or three cell phone calls that I made from my car so he could hear about his grandson's football game. As we made our way home early on that afternoon, I recall that the city did not seem any different from any other warm, Saturday afternoon in August. There were no cars lining up for gas, no plywood being nailed to windows, no sense of concern or panic at all. The radio carried a weather update that mentioned that Hurricane Katrina had come ashore in the southern tip of Florida the day before and was now expected to re-form in the Gulf of Mexico.

After arriving home, I started to passively watch the local news, which was now carrying nonstop weather updates regarding the possible paths of the storm, which was now re-strengthening over the warm waters of the gulf. On maybe the fifth or sixth call to my dad's cell phone, around two in the afternoon, he answered.

Just a simple inquiry of, "Dad, I've been trying to call you, where have you been?" was met with the response, "I've been on the road since before dawn." Not processing what that could possibly mean, given that he had never mentioned taking a trip, it took another minute or two of conversation for me to simply ask, "Where are you?"

Very casually—as if I was supposed to know—his response was, "New Iberia, Louisiana," which is a small town 135 miles west of New Orleans and approximately fifty inland from the Gulf of Mexico—a reasonable distance from any potential storm surge.

Apparently, in the wee hours of Saturday morning, the two hundred-plus residents and staff of the senior apartment complex had been evacuated by bus to New Iberia for what seemed, to me at the time, like some unknown reason. It was at that moment of realization (of why Dad had not answered) that the notion of paying more attention to the news became a bit more evident. I was still struggling with how my dad would so freely restrain his independence and "allow" people—Catholic people, no less—to take him away from his family with no notice whatsoever. Depending on who you talk to, I have been told that I have been blessed/cursed with quite a bit of that stubbornness gene. . . .

Dreaming?
And speaking of people who know me best, I also recall a brief, mid-afternoon call with my wonderful sister (who, long ago, had become the matriarch of our family). She had managed to create an incredible life of purpose after having served many years in social service roles within the city of New Orleans government. Blessed with boundless creativity, compassion for mankind, and a vast, international network of people who were drawn to her energy, she had decided to leave New Orleans and head to Opelousas, which is a small city just north of Lafayette, Louisiana, and 125 northwest of the city. In an abundance of caution, she had apparently decided to leave, I assumed to catch up with some close friends who were family-like. At that point, I still didn't sense imminent danger.

After talking to my sister about her R & R trip to Opelousas, and after hearing that PawPaw was on an excursion with his fellow residents of the senior apartments complex, it was around three in the afternoon. My youngest son, the football star, had been cleaned up, and we all turned our attention to the routines of a typical late-summer, Saturday afternoon. As my wife began gathering items for a meal, I was watching the news, and for reasons I cannot possibly explain, I then did something I can honestly say I have done less than a handful of times in my entire life: I fell asleep in the middle of the day. I don't recall being ill, being under doctor's care, or being tired at all, and there I was, dozing off while a threat was bulking up in the gulf.

I'm told by my wife that I didn't snore, didn't toss and turn, but simply fell asleep on the sofa as time passed. There was no dream that I recall, but I remember waking up (having no idea of how much time had passed) and screaming to my wife and two sons, "We need to leave!" Within a matter of minutes, we decided we would grab a single change of clothes and contact our families to get a sense of their storm plans.

By six that evening, then Mayor Ray Nagin was calling for a "mandatory" evacuation of the city, as the new storm path suggested Katrina might actually clip the eastern edge of the city or, worse, come straight up the mouth of the Mississippi River from the gulf. We were not sure exactly what would happen, but I found myself outside just to see what the situation was. I called my biological brother, a twenty-nine-year veteran of the NOPD and a seasoned veteran of countless weather emergencies, and he too suggested it would be wise to consider leaving, especially now that we knew our dad and sister had already left the city.

Within the ninety-plus minutes of returning home from the game, taking that unexpected nap, and checking in with family, there was now considerable activity throughout the neighborhood. For example, I saw the neighbor just across the street from us who was contemplating whether he and his aging mother would evacuate or stay. We had essentially the same house, a two-story California bungalow built in the 1950s, initially with open parking on the first floor and living quarters above, on the second story. Like mine and so many others in the Broadmoor area, the first floors of the vast majority of these houses had been closed in and converted to additional living space.

My neighbor was a sixty-plus-year-old, heavy-set gentleman who always had a positive energy and aura about him when you saw him. He was a widowed Baptist minister, and he mentioned to me that he was leaning towards staying, as he felt he could survive a "Cat Three" storm, and he was concerned about traveling too far with his mother, given her age and medical issues. We chatted briefly, and I shared with him that we would be leaving—still not sure exactly of why, or where we would be going, for that matter. We wished each other well and said we would see each other in "a couple of days."

Help Me Find the Road

Once the decision was made to leave, the next decision was to join my wife's other family members at our brother-in-law's family home in Alexandria, Louisiana, which is approximately three-and-a-half hours away, in the middle of Louisiana. Assuming we would be returning home soon, a day or two in Alexandria didn't seem so bad. We left New Orleans late on that Saturday evening, around nine, thinking the daytime exodus would have already dissipated by then. But despite the state's contraflow strategy to convert all lanes of the interstate system to outbound-only traffic, the westward interstate was essentially a parking lot. This trip by interstate is usually a four-hour drive. Twelve hours later, through a spiderweb of long-forgotten state roads, my wife, two sons, and I arrived in Alexandria, Louisiana, around noon on Sunday, August 28. We were joined there by several other branches of my wife's family. In total, there were at least seventeen people hunkering down in a small, three-room house in Alexandria, intending to ride out the storm. Of that number, at least six were children. Despite limited space, the proximity of loved ones was very comforting and gave an opportunity for kids and adults to entertain each other as Sunday night approached.

Given the accommodations and the news reports coming out of New Orleans, most of the adults, especially yours truly, could not sleep and instead made sure the children were well fed, bathed, and put to bed. Besides, we all fully intended to be back on the road headed home in just a few short hours. The hurricane had other intentions.

Sometime around 6:00 a.m., as we were watching CNN and The Weather Channel, it was announced that Hurricane Katrina had wobbled westward and made landfall in Plaquemines Parish, Louisiana, about two hours southeast of New Orleans, packing sustained 125 mph winds. Even at this moment, there was still optimism that the storm's strength would quickly diminish and the all-clear would be given for people to start returning home. The family members with cell service (which was by now very sporadic) were listening in to live reports of media and public safety personnel reporting from different locations in Southeast Louisiana and especially New Orleans. Text and cell phone service was beginning to become increasingly patchy. Fortunately for me, after numerous tries, I was able to get a cell phone call in to my brother (who, along with his NOPD colleagues, was deployed in downtown New Orleans). This call took place sometime between 7:00 and 9:00 a.m. as I stood in the middle of the street, hoping to get better reception. There are very few safety-type decisions of this magnitude that I would make without my brother's input, so my intention was to get his thoughts on me getting an early jump on returning to the city, to hopefully avoid the traffic nightmare we'd experienced driving out of the city the day before.

My brother was a very well-known and respected NOPD officer and was very serious about his chosen profession. Everyone knew he could be counted on to always be matter-of-fact and informative but, just like my sister, to never veer from his fundamental duty to be of service to others. He was always passionate and animated in how he explained important matters as he processed them from his perspective. Publicly, it was always done in a way that disarmed people and diffused tension. To us, he was just Junior, but on this day and at this moment, I was detecting a different side of him, from his vocal inflection and delivery.

Our connection was very weak, but I clearly recall him saying: "Well, the sun is up, and there is debris everywhere, and the city is eerily quiet." To which I started to say, "Good, so can I get on the road to head home?"

He didn't let me finish the sentence. "But something is wrong—there is water rising here on Basin and Canal Street." I had tons of questions, but before we lost the call, he said, "We have been told that a levee has failed," and, in his usual matter-of-fact style, "You probably won't be coming home anytime soon." We lost the cell call connection at that point. Not fully processing what that meant, I calmly walked back inside the house to share with the family what I had been told.

I was immediately shushed when I got inside, as everyone was gathered around the one television that we had in the house. It was around mid-morning Monday when CNN showed live footage of the rising water from a westward-pointed camera located at the intersection of Broad Street and Tulane Avenue in Mid-City, New Orleans. The camera was pointed towards the Broad Street overpass, which carries traffic over Interstate I-10 below. As my dad would have said, you could have heard a mouse piss on cotton as the reality of what was happening began to settle in on all of us. This emergency Alexandria family house would now need to become our home for "a while."

What's Going On?

Watching the CNN footage made it abundantly clear to me that if the Broad Street overpass was surrounded on all sides by water as far as the camera lens could cover, our New Orleans home, which was just an eighth of a mile on the other side—and at a lower elevation—was now sitting in water. Only later did we learn that the flood water level had actually reached nine feet in our neighborhood.

For the better part of Monday evening, I was really at a loss and can't remember exactly what I sensed, felt, or thought other than *Now what?* All of my immediate family members were accounted for, and we were safe, but what about our city and the people who didn't make it out? Ironically, the media's new attention on the unfortunate people who were stranded on rooftops and now finding their way to either the New Orleans Superdome or the Morial Convention Center reassured me that, once again, we had been blessed and were allowed to be with family and have resources that so many others obviously didn't have. Like everybody else who had evacuated, I just needed to know what the heck was going on at home.

Night two was another night of no sleep as the news reports, intermittent text messages, and sporadic cell calls got worse as the night went on. Media footage of floating bodies, people trapped on rooftops, recognizable structures ablaze, police suicides, stories of looting, and the flood waters continuing to rise all combined to numb my senses and forced me to start focusing on figuring out what I needed to do to take care of my family.

Order My Steps!
Early Tuesday morning, not having slept or bathed, I was, like everyone else, trying to figure out what I should do first . . . or next. As people were trying to reconnect to check on family members and friends, I got a text message from my manager at the time. The text was very simple: "I hope you and your family are safe. Text me who is in your family party and your whereabouts."

At the time of the hurricane, I worked for a global financial services company that employed over three hundred thousand worldwide and had operations in eighty-seven countries. Initially I was somewhat dismissive of the text, as I recall, thinking that somehow he was being insensitive by just asking me about my whereabouts. *Of course*, I thought, *this is to be expected of a "cold and impersonal" firm of this size and complexity.* Through the fog of everything else, I came around to thinking that despite the firm itself, my manager was a former US Air Force Intelligence officer whom I had always trusted and admired, so maybe now was not the time to be doubtful of his intentions. And with cell service still spotty, I responded via text that we were all OK and that we were sharing a house in Alexandria, Louisiana.

Within minutes of me sending my text, my manager texted me back. As was his style, his text was very simple: "Bring yourself and your family to this address in Gonzales, Louisiana, tomorrow morning at 9:00, and someone from the firm will meet you there." Now—like always—I had one thousand questions, but had limited access to my work colleagues and failing text service. However, I was able to text another colleague who I knew lived in a part of the city that by now was also completely devastated by the flood waters. She texted that she had also been instructed by her manager to report to the same location in two days, as she and her family had evacuated to Houston. Still somewhat suspicious, I was thinking that this was some attempt by the firm to corral the impacted employees in one place so that determinations could be made as to whose jobs might be affected. Again, my suspicions were proven to be grossly inaccurate and unwarranted.

Having told the other three members of my immediate family (especially my wife) that we were leaving the comfort of our family's evacuation haven, we packed up our overnight bags and set out from Alexandria on Thursday morning to an unfamiliar address in Gonzales. As I recall, the car trip was very peaceful other than the occasional, ". . . And where are we going again?" With no credible answer, I just responded again that I was told to report to this location, almost as a condition of retaining my job.

God Is . . .

Around noon, we arrived at the address just off Exit 73 in Gonzales, Louisiana. It was an apartment complex that, as we approached the front gate, we could see was in some stage of construction. I could see through the gates as we approached men in hard hats, several bucket trucks, material delivery trucks, and all sorts of other workers scurrying around the grounds. I thought I had taken down the wrong address and was looking at my cell phone to make sure I was indeed at the correct location.

Just as I was looking at the cell phone, a familiar face emerged from the rear side of my vehicle. A colleague from the firm came up to my window—which I could not roll down fast enough. There stood a guy I had known for a few years and with whom I had previously had countless conversations about everything from raising kids to politics to LSU football.

He lowered his head, looked in the window, and said politely, "Greg, I am so happy to see you. Are you and your family okay?"

I responded, "Yes, we're fine, but why have we been told to report here?"

Realizing that the stress level for me was still high, he looked over to my wife and said, "Ma'am, I am Robert, and I can't imagine what it must be like to be married to this dude, but nevertheless, you can trust me, and I am here to help you and your kids." Looking back, it was precisely the right thing to say at the absolute best moment.

I noticed he had a clipboard in his hand. He scribbled something and then handed me a key and said, "You are in unit 106. Take down my cell phone number and call me when you get inside. It's on the left-hand side. Just drive toward the first building to the left of the pool."

Thank You, Lord

Feeling somewhat better but still wondering, I proceeded to drive inside once the security gate was opened. We pulled up to one of several new buildings where construction workers were hanging light fixtures, and I found the brass 106 on the first floor of this three-story apartment building. We said absolutely nothing as we made our way to the front door, not knowing what was waiting on the other side. I recall sensing at that moment what an extensive and growing list of tasks we had that were yet to be done, but at least we had a roof over our heads.

I opened the door with the two kids between me and my wife. God is good all the time . . . and all the time God is good. The three-bedroom apartment was completely furnished with new furniture (most still in shrink-wrapped packaging). The bedrooms all had new mattresses, complete with unopened linen and pillows. The massive living room had new furniture and a new color TV. The living room opened into a kitchen, which also had all new appliances. The utility closet had a new washer–dryer combo complete with laundry detergent, dryer sheets, an ironing board, and a new iron. On the counter were so many new appliances and gadgets that you could barely see the counter itself. On top of one of the appliances was an envelope I immediately recognized as being a letterhead envelope used by the firm for official business. I was actually dreading a loss of employment. As my wife and kids stared silently at what we were all taking in, I went over and opened the envelope. It contained a simple note—"We're thinking of you and your family"—and $1,200 in cash. I stood frozen!

I remember I really didn't understand where I was or why I had been led there, but I knew I needed to reach out to my manager and/or Robert to find out what was up with these wonderful accommodations. Later that afternoon, still reeling from a multitude of different emotions and still gathering information about relatives, friends, and of course the city itself, I settled into trying to find out what the circumstances were around these sent-from-heaven accommodations. I learned in a phone call with my manager late that night that the firm had basically leased out a soon-to-be-opened apartment development for its entire impacted workforce and that over thirty families (like mine) would be moving into the complex just as the certificate of occupancy was being hurriedly issued by the parish building inspector. I also learned that a dedicated hotline and resource center had been set up for impacted employees to address a wide range of emergency family and personal issues created by the hurricane.

Over the ensuing few days, the employer-provided initiative assisted us with getting my dad back from New Iberia (to live with us in one of those three bedrooms), enrolling the two kids in nearby schools, facilitating the purchase of a new vehicle (to replace the almost new one we'd left in New Orleans), connecting us with various religious and charitable organizations, and a variety of medical access issues. I also learned that the firm had raised much of the money for this response from colleagues around the world and had pledged to match the donated funds four to one. The firm even set up a temporary office for me to use in Baton Rouge, Louisiana, for as long as I needed it. That, for all practical purposes, ended all of my conspiracy theories and the notion that there was no capacity for a firm to care that much about its employees, even in the face of a biblical disaster such as Hurricane Katrina.

I'll Always Love My Mama

As the immediate days of Katrina's aftermath played out nationally and internationally (complete with all levels of government failing, and the blame-gaming finger-pointing in full effect), we were very mindful of the many who were still trapped inside of New Orleans with very little support and assistance . . . from anybody. We were feverishly trying to contact and locate loved ones and friends whom we had not heard from. My immediate family were all confirmed okay. But it suddenly occurred to my wife and I that in our incredible moment of relief, as more connections were being made, we had completely overlooked someone.

A profound sense of dread and fear was now beginning to be very visible on the face of my thirteen-year-old son. His mother (my first wife) and his grandmother had last been seen the Saturday before the hurricane, and they lived in New Orleans East, which was one of the most devastated parts of now flooded New Orleans. Being in eastern New Orleans meant that your exodus from New Orleans would've been much more challenging than our departure from uptown New Orleans had been. My son's fear became our fear as media reports continuously increased the fatality count, which was by now only exceeded by the number of New Orleans residents being reported as "missing." Knowing how much my son loved his mother (and recalling how I felt when I'd lost my mother when I was sixteen years old), our collective priority became finding her.

As each day came and went with no word on his mother, his hopes sank, and the sadness and fear visible in my child became almost overwhelming and unbearable. At some point, I sensed that he had given in to the notion that he had indeed lost his mother. We used every tool and resource available to us, but it occurred to me that with zero cell service inside of New Orleans, his mother and grandmother could be near either of the two mass evacuation centers, the Superdome or the Morial Convention Center. Being at both of these venues was now a hellish experience, especially the Superdome, where confirmed reports were being released of documented murders and rapes taking place in a damaged building surrounded by contaminated water with no utilities, no food, and twenty thousand increasingly desperate citizens.

I was now using my temporary Baton Rouge office to handle the affairs of recovery as well as the official responsibilities and duties associated with the firm's clients—many impacted and directly involved in providing essential public services. While at work and as I prepared to deal with the challenge of walking my son through what seemed inevitable, a Louisiana state trooper, whom I had come to know over many years of working previously in state government, called me on my cell phone and asked me if I had any relatives (given our rather unique last name) who'd evacuated from the city and were staying at a nearby shelter. With everyone in my immediate family accounted for (including my brother's wife), I didn't make any connection whatsoever. He said he had seen some of the names that the state of Louisiana was compiling of people who were scattered literally all across the state in various evacuee shelters. He thought he'd seen a Rattler listed.

Then, late one evening, as my son was crying himself to sleep, an evacuation center, located approximately twenty miles from our apartment, called on behalf of one of the evacuees. It was my son's mother. I gathered him up, put him in my car, and blazed the twenty miles to a religious facility that had taken in people who'd fled the city. Seeing my son reunited with his mother was yet another meaningful example of a mother's determination to see her only child. We later learned that she had decided to wait until the very last minute (after ensuring the safety of her own mother) to leave New Orleans on a city-provided bus, as she felt her vehicle and mother would not survive a long road trip on a congested interstate. On the long journey, she said her cell service had failed, and then later she'd actually lost her cell phone, which was her only connection to the "outside" world.

Way Back Home
As the early weeks of September came and went, time began to illuminate the devastation and total extent of the death, destruction, and governmental ineptitude that followed this tragedy. As only limited access to the city was granted under the still existing curfew and evacuation order, I was able to leverage my not-for-profit and community connections to gain access to the city approximately three weeks after Katrina. My brother warned me, but, me being me, I had to go home. I reassured him that I would go alone so as to not traumatize the rest of my family.

Up to that point, what I had read, seen on TV, or heard about via phone calls and text messages did not at all prepare me for what I actually saw when I arrived in New Orleans. I had been born during peacetime and therefore only had a Hollywood frame of reference for what a war zone could be like. Growing up, I had heard my elders speak of the devastation and trauma they experienced in 1965's Hurricane Betsy, which took over one hundred lives and scarred New Orleans for generations to come. With that being my only frame of reference, I knew that this would somehow be far worse. The smell, the eerie silence, and the unique markings signifying where bodies had been found on structures were all surreal. As I drove through debris and downed power lines, I could not believe this was actually the city I'd called home just a few weeks earlier.

As I finally made my way to our home, I felt like I was the only living organism left on the planet. Death in every dimension was everywhere as I approached the house and saw the waterline, which was on the second-from-the-top step leading to our second-story porch. The orange spray-paint on the front of the house, the first responders' quadrangle, indicated that the house had been searched, the date it had been searched, and how many survivors or bodies had been found inside. Prayerfully, the number for the latter two was zero. As I had promised my brother, I quickly went inside the second story and found it was essentially unchanged from how we had left it weeks earlier. I didn't dare open the refrigerator door, as the overall scent in the air was almost unbearable already, and I knew there had been no utility service in the city for almost a month. As I was leaving, I walked around the first floor of the house and arrived at the rear only to see that the water pressure had taken the rear door off its hinges, leaving the inside of the house looking like a bomb had detonated. Everything was out of place and saturated with a pungent water that would likely remain another few weeks.

Back in my car and preparing to head back to Gonzales, I glanced over at my neighbor's home across the street, the home of the pastor who I remembered had decided to stay. His home, like mine and all the others, had apparently been searched and displayed the orange-painted quadrangle on the front, street-facing side, on his second-story porch. I couldn't help but notice that in one quadrant, there was a very visible number one.

Epilogue

Over 1,200 souls were lost during Hurricane Katrina and its aftermath, but all of my immediate family members were healthy and accounted for. Over 150 victims were never found and over two hundred bodies never identified. Unfortunately, we later learned that we'd lost one second cousin who drowned in his home, which was located in the Lower 9th Ward of New Orleans, the mostly African American neighborhood destroyed during Katrina when a barge broke loose from its mooring and gashed open an Industrial Canal levee.

My courageous brother and I were reunited in Baton Rouge around three weeks after Hurricane Katrina. This, after the city experienced two shocking suicides of police officers who had endured the unspeakable trauma of having witnessed many people drowning (due to many man-made failures) while being unable to render any assistance. When hundreds of New Orleans first responders were relieved by General Russel Honoré's troops, my brother and his colleagues were dispatched to Baton Rouge to begin reuniting with their loved ones after almost a month of separation. I met them as they exited the city-chartered buses and was immediately struck by the "thousand-mile stare" on their unshaven and unwashed faces. I phoned my manager and shared with him my joy and relief in seeing my brother and so many of his NOPD colleagues. He "instructed" me to take them all out for a meal, which I was more than happy to do.

I sat for five-plus hours and heard first-hand accounts of real heroism and sacrifice that these people made on behalf of people who will never know their names. One police officer related to me that he'd been on top of a gabled roof, surrounded by ten feet of putrid, contaminated, snake-infested waters, attempting to save a woman and her child in total darkness. He stared almost like he was in a trance as he said he couldn't hold onto both, as it would have risked him falling into the water to join the people he'd sought to rescue. The woman apparently told him to let her go so he could save the child. The child was eventually saved, but the mother's body was never found. To this day, I still wonder if that officer ever found a way to get that woman's face (from that very moment) out of his mind.

- My sister was prompt in mobilizing forces, just days after Katrina, to ensure the protection and sustaining of our cultural authenticity and conscientiousness as individuals and as a resilient community. The therapeutic impact of this effort shaped so many aspects of what the "post-Katrina" New Orleans ultimately became, in terms of repopulation patterns, resource allocation, and neighborhood planning designed to combat and minimize the rampant and obvious exploitation of the primarily Black working class of the service and hospitality industry.

- My dad, "PawPaw," remained faithful to his fundamental belief that God would continue to have the last say in this epic disaster. But he remained until his death the independent giant we had known and loved as the patriarch of our family. In the aftermath of Katrina, he was true-to-form. He eventually was allowed to visit his senior living apartment in uptown New Orleans and, on one trip, simply decided he would not be leaving. Fortunately, a genuinely nice and well-composed uniformed soldier guarding the building at time was able to convince him that going back to our Gonzales apartment was "in his best interest." It took some time, and I am still not sure if it was ultimately his respect for the soldier or the loaded M4 carbine rifle, but he was not pleased at all to have to ride back with me to our apartment.

- In the very early days of the city's recovery, hundreds of yellow, brown, and Black transient relief works and volunteers combed the city to clear out thousands of tons of debris, dead animals, and flooded vehicles from businesses, public streets and buildings, and personal residences. These people worked in horrific conditions in a city still with no consistent utility services, scarce police protection, virtually no cell tower transmissions, and very limited food options—all this against the national politician backdrop that had somehow changed us from "evacuees" to "refugees" and, at the same time, quickly changed them from "desperately needed recovery workers" to "illegal immigrants."

- My sons eventually adjusted somewhat to "life in exile," with both enrolling in Baton Rouge and Gonzales schools as the fall of 2005 approached. After reuniting my older son with his mom and having exceptionally nice living quarters secured via my employer, it was time to reflect on a full accounting of the countless, abundant blessings that had put us in that position. Our church, of which I had been a member for just about all of my life, began to offer Catholic masses once a week. Returning to that building even while living in Gonzales was very therapeutic and comforting. As a result, we were able to celebrate all of the 2005 holidays as a family unit. Having the ability to reunite with family and friends gave that holiday season a deeper meaning and provided a time for honest introspection.

- As the 2005 holiday season came to a close, 2006 ushered in a steady repopulation of the city, and another iconic cultural experience was upon us. After much spirited discussion (and other encounters not to be mentioned here), the Zulu Social Aid & Pleasure Club made the bold decision to stage a scaled-down Mardi Gras parade, despite the tragic loss of so many of its members and the diaspora of its many impacted members and their families. Opinions varied widely as to the appropriateness and perceived lack of sensitivity, but "with time, all things are revealed." Given the well-documented tactics, schemes, strategies, and behavior of the privileged and powerful elites of the city, it is clear to me and many others that had Zulu not paraded on February 28, 2006, it very likely would not have ever paraded on Mardi Gras Day again.

- My wife was absolutely the glue that held me together throughout the Katrina saga, even at times when I wasn't 10 percent confident in my own decisions. If/when to leave New Orleans, which road to take, how to comfort the kids, whom to trust, how to process the looming stress were all matters that I was simply ill-equipped to handle alone. Comfortably owning my shortcomings and flaws, I can be very stubborn and hardheaded. I often publicly acknowledge this by saying, "I am not always right, but rarely am I wrong." Usually I just get eye rolls from my wife, but the Katrina journey was very different and humbling. Just her being there through that moment was a large part of my validation about being a provider and being responsible for others whom I loved deeply and to whom I had made a personal pledge. As we were riding home one Sunday from mass at our church, I could sense that something better would happen for us, as we had been blessed to come through the Katrina journey much better than so many others. She was still devastated, but calm and upbeat, having moved back into the upstairs floor of our home just ten months after the storm.

- After returning to New Orleans, we learned that our neighbor from across the street had lost his mother a few days after the storm, having been trapped on his second story. Our neighborhood was inundated with Katrina's flood waters for twelve days at eight to ten feet, which prevented him from leaving immediately after the hurricane. Almost two weeks later (while his mother's body remained in his home), rescuers arrived at his home and recovered his mother's body and rendered medical aid to him. Just weeks later, he himself passed away from an infection he contracted from venturing out into the flood water to seek help immediately after his mother had passed. Regrettably, we were not made aware of their funeral services until much later, and so we were not able to pay our respects.

- Just over two years after Katrina, as we left a Sunday morning mass, we somehow found ourselves on a local street that I can honestly say I had been on maybe once in my entire life—until that moment. As we were driving and talking about our future plans, we passed a house where a young man was planting a for-sale by owner sign in his front yard. On a whim, we stopped at the corner stop sign, which was just one house away from the young man's home. I put the car in reverse and asked him how he was doing. Just being neighborly. He explained that he was an engineer, and after being very busy immediately after Katrina, his employer had offered to move him to Houston. Three weeks later, we put in an offer on that very house and have been living there ever since.

As for me and my family, we thank an almighty and ever-present God for all of our blessings, but especially for the following:

LaSalle Rattler Sr.
Château de Notre Dame
Carol Bebelle
Twyla Rattler
My four sons (collectively, the absolute most important accomplishment of my life)
My employer (and my fellow colleagues and employees)
Blessed Sacrament/St. Joan of Arc Church
The Zulu Social Aid & Pleasure Club
LaSalle Rattler Jr.

TRANSCENDING STORMS:
Creating Beauty from Uncertainty

ASANTE SALAAM

Artist Statement: Grounded in Spirit and Soil
Art, for me, is a living spiritual practice—a bridge between the material and the metaphysical, a journey of healing and transformation. My work is rooted in liberation and experimentation, inspired by my New Orleans upbringing, African ancestry, and Black cultural arts activism. Through my practice, I seek to transcend limitations, celebrate perseverance, and create a sense of wholeness that reflects the beauty and complexity of our shared humanity.

Being about beauty: in thought, word, action, and environment.

May my feet be grounded in earth, stable and solid in soil.

May my hands be connected to bark, leaves, fronds, petals, roots, seeds, pods, fruit, and all healthy plant life.

May my environment be drawn from natural materials—metals, glass, wood, fibers, textiles, papers, pigments, and beyond.

May my life be in harmony with nature and the elements of land, air, fire, and water.

May my being be holistic and whole, evolving for my highest good.

May my spirit be aligned with the divine infinite, life cycles, and creative processes.

May my path unfold before me like a dirt road, charting my journey, divinely guiding me on my way.

Prelude: Roots in Artistry
I've been an artist since birth. My mother, a meticulous keeper of art, saved several of my early drawings—simple yet brimming with life. The first was signed at the age of six. I also remember an early unsaved creation, my first

assemblage piece, a portrait of a little girl jumping rope. She was drawn on a scrap plank of plywood, her long bouncing braids crafted from woven yarn. Her bangs were formed by two or three large wooden beads salvaged from adorning macramé creations in the 1970s. Her dress was a collaged cutout of fabric, remnants from my mother's home-sewn garments or curtains. Her jump rope was made from woven strands of fine rope. She leapt across the grainy, open expanse of the wood panel—an early embodiment of my imagination rooted in the textures of daily life.

An Artist's Journey: Evolving Through Spaces

My early forays into art education began in childhood art classes and workshops, where we drew life-sized portraits by tracing our body silhouettes on butcher paper in the basement of the New Orleans Museum of Art (NOMA). In high school, I continued my path at the New Orleans Center for Creative Arts (NOCCA), which eventually led me to the School of the Art Institute of Chicago (SAIC) for college. I entered SAIC with aspirations of fashion design, inspired by my highschool successes designing outfits, hairstyles, and ball gowns for a few friends and teachers.

However, as I navigated the art and fashion worlds, I began yearning for deeper authenticity and connection. The environments I encountered often felt dissonant—superficial, rigid, impersonal—where the art products mattered more than the artist's being. Later, printmaking classes with John Scott in Xavier University's art department in New Orleans further shaped my artistic journey, offering new mediums and practices to explore. Even as I participated in exhibits and contests and sold my art, I perpetually sensed an undercurrent of resistance, a tension between my boundless, imaginative approach and the stifling institutional frameworks I encountered.

I was gifted and deeply passionate about creating, fully aware of my talent and love for the creative process. However, for decades, I resisted making art my career, unwilling to be and create in spaces that felt alien, limiting. Still, I kept seeking and finding ways to cultivate my artistry, trusting my innate capacity to create regardless of external constraints. Eventually, the cumulative weight of navigating these environments and conflicts led me to pause my artmaking altogether. This hiatus, though unsettling, evolved into a pivotal metamorphosis. This new stage of my artistic life began with a seemingly impulsive move to New Mexico, drawn by a long-held fascination with Georgia O'Keeffe and the Southwest's expansive landscapes. There, I faced a health crisis with a significant ovarian mass requiring hospitalization. This experience forced me to confront my well-being on every level. This period of reflection and renewal reconnected me with my intuition and creativity as I embraced holistic healing modalities, spiritual practices, and self-development. This transformative period ultimately restored my health and reignited my artistry.

Along the way, I found insightful moments of encouragement. Willie Birch's response to my drawings, writings, and mixed-media creations inspired me to expand freely beyond the confines of the hardbound sketchbook pages in my journals, leading me to experiment with assemblages and artists books. Raine Bedsole's early exhibit in Delgado Community College's Issac Delgado Fine Arts Gallery validated my exploration of three-dimensional assemblages as a meaningful, exhibit-worthy medium. My love of fashion and style led me to take a trip to San Francisco to visit a Vivienne Westwood retrospective. This transformative experience reinforced my commitment to charting my own path, grounded in the self-determination instilled by my Upbringing. A serendipitous encounter with Whitfield Lovell's portrait assemblages brought me full circle, back to one of my earliest creations: the little girl jumping rope on a plywood scrap. In early 2005, while living in New York for a couple years or so on a dear writer friend's couch, I had a crucial moment of clarity. I realized that if I died without fully committing to my art, it would be my deepest regret. That revelation set everything in motion. Within months, I returned to New Orleans, ready to begin again, with a renewed sense of purpose. I trusted in both my need and ability to create and thrive. I knew I couldn't let external circumstances stop me—or, at the very least, I knew I couldn't allow myself to give up. I had to keep going for it.

The Storm and Its Aftermath: Displacement and Perseverance

On August 29, 2005, Hurricane Katrina and the resulting levee-break failures surged through New Orleans, leaving lives and homes in ruins. My family and I, like countless others, faced the dual challenges of displacement and rebuilding. The concept of "home" fractured and evolved, becoming more fluid. The disaster was both a personal and collective rupture, an indelible moment of transformation etched in memory and history. For those of us who endured the devastation, both natural and man-made, the deep yearning to return home was ever-present, even as "home" shifted and remained in flux.

Yet, amidst the upheaval, there were glimmers of light. My art became a refuge and a lifeline. Two major art projects—*Five Doorways* and *Deeply Rooted*—emerged from the disruption and uncertainty, each comprising five pieces that reflected my journey through displacement and perseverance. These art pieces wove together themes of loss, connection, and transformation, grounding my practice in the visceral, dynamic relationship between humanity and the earth. Through these works, I explored disruption, loss, and perseverance while also honoring the transformative power of art to bridge past and future, history and possibility. Through these projects, I sought to evoke a sense of rootedness and reverence, bridging the natural and cultural ecosystems that sustain us. My art became a way to navigate the storm's aftermath, to find beauty and meaning in the fragments of a shattered world.

Evacuation and Disruption

On Sunday, August 28, 2005, my family and I joined the mass exodus out of New Orleans. We thought we were fleeing Hurricane Katrina and would be back home within days. Little did we know that a monumental, life-changing disaster was forthcoming. Our slow-moving, arduous mini-caravan brought us to a modest, nondescript hotel in Pell City, Alabama, where we spent the next few days glued to the television, watching nonstop with mounting horror as our city succumbed to levee breaks and flood waters. The scenes of devastation felt surreal—New Orleans, our beloved home, and so many of our people, flooding, suffering, and drowning.

After a family meeting, we dispersed in three different directions. My older brother, nephew, and I set out for Southern California, a journey punctuated by a long, roundabout trip back to Louisiana to pick up my ex-sister-in-law, and desperate attempts to stay connected with loved ones despite patchy cell service. Text messages and emails became lifelines, connecting us with family updates, out-of-town loved ones, and pit stop resources along the way as we zigzagged westward before finally arriving in Los Angeles. Though Los Angeles offered schooling opportunities for my nephew, jobs for us adults, and housing for us all, that city's seemingly frenetic pace wasn't what we needed. Seeking solace, we relocated to San Diego, where life felt quieter, slower, and more conducive to our healing. As we rebuilt our lives—finding housing, schools, jobs, cars, and other such basics relatively easily—we recognized how fortunate we were compared to many other displaced New Orleanians facing even greater challenges.

In 2006, while relocated in San Diego, I collaborated with ArtSpot Productions in New Orleans on an artist residency at A Studio in the Woods. These visits home brought mixed emotions: the joy of creating despite and amidst the ruins contrasted with the palpable heartbreak of our disrupted home. By April 2007, I was ready to return, restoring and cultivating my home base in New Orleans.

Salaam Family Writings

I come from a family of writers. My father's experience is recorded, and my sister Kiini, who was living in Oaxaca, Mexico, at the time, also recorded her reflections. For those interested, the reflections of my father and sister are accessible through the links below:

http://www.kalamu.com/bol/evacuating-new-orleans/
https://kibura.com/2005/09/20/vol-51-new-orleans-underwater/

Katrina Fever

The stories of Hurricane Katrina are endless, as are the memories. For many of us, they are etched into our minds and hearts, woven into our identities. Yet revisiting them often feels like reopening an old wound, raw and unhealed. Even nineteen years later, as I wrote these words in 2024, culling memories and compiling details regarding my experiences and perspectives of Hurricane Katrina and the flooding disasters, visceral surges of anger, frustration, trauma, fear, sadness, fatigue, and general disgust course through my body, mind, and soul. The inequities laid bare by Katrina remain glaring. Neighborhoods like Lakeview, predominantly white and financially comfortable, that were majorly ravaged have rebounded in bountiful resurgence and thriving overflow even better than before the Katrina disaster, while predominantly Black areas like the 6th and 7th Wards, the Lower 9th Ward, and New Orleans East are still damaged, scarcely rebuilt, and struggling to recover. It's a bitter pill to swallow, a reminder of systemic inequities that persist.

A decade after the storm-disaster, in 2015, city government leaders declared the "rebuilding" phase to be over. For many, this proclamation felt like an abandonment. Those still displaced or living in damaged homes were effectively pushed into the demographics of the underserved and forgotten, their recovery deemed "complete" by those in power. The lingering effects of Katrina aren't just physical—they're emotional, mental, spiritual, and psychological. The devastation illuminates a broader truth: we live in an interconnected world grappling with shared predicaments that demand collective action, enduring hope, and a commitment to equity for all.

Meanwhile, for government politics and the privileged beneficiary residents of New New Orleans, Katrina 10—August 29, 2015—meant the end of rebuilding. For those who remain missing, for those whose homes remain damaged and unlivable, for those who got swindled by predatory contractors, for those who are still yearning to come home, the story remains incomplete. If "rebuilding" is declared to be over, if it's time to "move on," I suppose those with lingering effects become added to the already overwhelming number of disenfranchised, under-resourced, under-served folks in need. It reminds me of standing for hours in a San Diego welfare office, when I first arrived in town after evacuating and relocating and was still job-hunting. One could be waiting and waiting and waiting in a line, and when that clerk closes the window, everyone in that closed line has to get to the back of another long, existing line. So it seems folks still awaiting emergency recovery may be obliged to join preexisting socioeconomic hardship status in our beloved city. To quote the late empowerment activist Fannie Lou Hamer, I am, as so many of us are, "sick and tired of being sick and tired."

The effects seem to indicate that a headache may be developing; however, I know it's simply a case of lingering and recurring, raging Katrina fever. For me, Katrina fever ebbs and flows. I straddle an unhappy medium of letting myself feel the yuck of it all and avoiding delving into it much, if at all, so as not to have distress build up unhealthily inside, nor have it burst out in ugly and unproductive ways. I strive to balance feeling the weight of it all with self-preservation, refusing to let these emotions consume me as I cultivate my faith in liberation and thriving for us all.

A Larger Lens

As a native New Orleanian, the lessons of Katrina are with me always. They inform my work, shape my worldview, and fuel my commitment to facilitating equity and empowerment, both in my communities and beyond. My story is just one among countless others. Together, we weave the complex, painful, and ultimately hopeful tapestry of life after Katrina.

While Katrina was uniquely devastating to New Orleans, it also mirrors global crises. Across the Gulf Coast, the nation, and the globe, humans and all living organisms face the compounded effects of global warming, environmental degradation, natural disasters, government neglect, economic upheavals, low wages, rising living costs, spreading gentrification, unequal education, cultural infringement, systemic injustice, capitalist greed, and general inhumanity. Layered onto these are the enduring oppressions of racism, classism, sexism, and countless other prejudices—persistent reminders of historical patterns that remain entrenched. The reality is harsh for way too many of us, and the challenges persist. In 2015, as a member of the City of New Orleans

Mayor's Office of Cultural Economy, I spoke with early-career philanthropists about how Katrina's legacy highlights our interconnected challenges and the urgent need for equity, justice, and sustainability on a global scale.

Five Doorways: Art Story

In fall 2005, I found myself displaced, relocated, expatriated, in the City Heights neighborhood of San Diego. There, I lived in a vibrant, bustling, multicultural, immigrant-rich community teetering between working-class roots, creeping gentrification, and burgeoning beautification. From the couch overlooking the deck of my temporary home, I often saw hummingbirds sporadically visiting hanging plants. I also gazed across a nearby finger canyon, where coyotes occasionally wandered through.

My brother and roommate, Mtume, spent his time off from work immersed in music and writing reviews at his desk. Our shared space was peaceful and orderly, yet my life was in transitional flux from Katrina displacement. Before the storm, I had recently returned to New Orleans from New York the spring before the disaster hit, in April 2005, full of optimism and actively job hunting. The disaster upended everything, leaving me navigating uncertainty and longing for stability.

Amid this upheaval, my friend and fellow artist Kathy Randels of ArtSpot Productions invited me to collaborate on their artist residency at A Studio in the Woods. Their interdisciplinary project, *Beyond the Strata/Disappearing*, sought to examine New Orleans' cultural and historical legacies through storytelling performances staged across the studio's grounds.

During the first phase of the residency, we ideated, masterminded, shared, and planned. I envisioned the site as a metaphorical house, with each performance area as a symbolic room and a realm of time. This concept birthed the *Five Doorways*, a collection of mixed-media sculptures I created using architectural doorway elements salvaged from houses damaged in the Katrina levee-break flood disaster. I then combined the elements into assemblages with repurposed tree branches and various mixed-media materials. These five themed doorways became thresholds—bridges between past, present, and future—embodying transitions and Transformations.

I designed natural element medallions, then worked with Ms. Herreast Harrison, who taught participating performing artists how to bead and sew the medallions in the Black Masking tradition (also known as Mardi Gras Indians), further grounding the work in New Orleans' cultural heritage. Collaborating with the studio's ecologist and environmental curator, David Baker, I learned about the site's environment and native plants, which informed the materials and symbolism of my sculptural pieces. During the second phase of the residency, I fabricated and installed the *Five Doorways*.

While completing these pieces, I stayed in Algiers Point, on New Orleans' west bank of the Mississippi River, living in a small apartment my mother rented while she temporarily relocated with my sister in Oaxaca, Mexico. The installation debuted as part of ArtSpot's collaborative interdisciplinary, outdoor performances, where audiences journeyed through the grounds, moving from one storytelling "room" to the next. The experience began with an opening piece at the levee-facing entrance to A Studio in the Woods and continued as audiences toured the grounds, following each performative story. Each doorway marked a portal, inviting reflection and connection as participants engaged with the layered narratives of the site and the performers.

After the residency concluded, I again returned to New Orleans from San Diego, dismantling the installation, deconstructing the Five Doorways sculptural pieces, carrying with me the profound sense of healing and learning it had cultivated. Nearly two decades later, I am honored to return to A Studio in the Woods as an artist-in-residence in spring 2025, ready to revisit and deepen the themes of transition, perseverance, and renewal.

Five Doorways: Art Description

Five Doorways was a site-specific, mixed-media assemblage installation created as part of *Beneath the Strata/Disappearing*, a multidisciplinary artist residency produced by ArtSpot

Productions in October 2006 at A Studio in the Woods along the Mississippi River. The installation's sculptural pieces incorporated salvaged materials such as door frames, bedsheets, household curtains, woven baskets, windowpane shards, soil, ashes, and other found objects, each imbued with the energy of its previous life. I created with reclaimed wood, earth pigments, fabric remnants, and natural fibers carefully selected and incorporated to echo themes of sustainability, renewal, and the cyclical nature of life. The series drew inspiration from the rich traditions of African diaspora art, jazz improvisation, and the dynamic rhythms of the New Orleans cultural landscape.

Each doorway was distinctly crafted and designed to be freestanding, allowing for surrounding views. Embedded in the ground, the sculptures appeared rooted in the earth, with branches found in storm debris attached like root tendrils, encircling their bases above the land's surface. This design evoked the image of tree trunks with exposed roots, emphasizing and highlighting organic growth. The front faces were constructed using architectural door sill materials, while the rear structures were surfaced with salvaged elements, including jacquard textiles from furniture upholstery and drapery, bedsheets, rough-textured soil concoctions, and raw wood. One doorway featured bark segments meticulously assembled to resemble a tree trunk.

Nestled among the roots were woven baskets and repurposed vessels holding collected altar-like treasures, further grounding the work in reverence for cultural and natural heritage. Brass wall hooks adorned the doorways, enabling performing artists to drape garments and hang altar-like artifacts, enhancing the installation's interactive and sacred qualities. The doorways were conceptualized as thresholds representing life's transitions: from birth through lived experiences, then through death. Each doorway embodied the present moment, bridging history and possibility, between what was and what will be. They urged awareness, self-determination, and forward movement. These art pieces emphasized the power of living in the now and choosing consistent action infused with positive energy.

In collaboration with the Black Masking tradition, Louisiana's disappearing coastal landscapes, oral histories, African drumming, and cultural mythologies, the installation honored the cultural roots of New Orleans and Louisiana. It also reflected profound dislocation and perseverance experienced in the aftermath of Hurricane Katrina and the levee breaches, drawing strength from resilience while mourning loss. This installation stood as a meditation on renewal, an homage to cultural legacies, and a call to action for the preservation of memory, culture, and future possibilities.

Deeply Rooted—Originally Uprooted: Art Story

The journey of *Deeply Rooted* began as a response to displacement—both personal and collective. Growing up in a city shaped by convergence of cultures, histories, and disparities, I witnessed and experienced the devastating impact of Hurricane Katrina and the levee-break-floods, which uprooted lives, traditions, and communities. This series reflects a reclamation of identity, belonging, and legacy amidst such upheaval. Each piece in this collection embodies a dialogue with the past and present, interweaving the pain of uprootedness with the beauty of perseverance and regeneration.

My art is steeped in the cultural narratives of New Orleans and influenced by decades of personal development, universal spirituality, and holistic healing practices. *Deeply Rooted* transforms grief into growth, fragmentation into flourishing creativity, and isolation into interconnectedness.

TRANSCENDING STORMS:
CREATING BEAUTY FROM UNCERTAINTY

In the two years following Hurricane Katrina, while relocated in San Diego, I found myself reconnecting with home in an unexpected way. Walking along a street, I noticed a banner promoting a fundraiser for Katrina relief. Something about the language or phrasing felt uniquely familiar to me as a native New Orleanian. I stepped into the business, Davis Marketing, and met the owners, who turned out to also be from New Orleans. That serendipitous encounter led to an invitation to exhibit during their annual holiday event. Inspired, I created a collection of new artwork. At the time, I called it *Uprooted*. The pieces, textured and translucent, hung from the ceilings near the walls as though suspended in memory, much like the homes they honored. Later, I captured images of the pieces as high-resolution photographs to reproduce them as fine art prints and greeting cards.

Over time, the collection evolved and took on a new name: *Deeply Rooted*.

Through these pieces, I reimagined the homes that held stories of my life in New Orleans.

Though I have lived and created art in many places beyond the Crescent City, my roots remain firmly planted in the soil of my birthplace. This collection stands as a testament to that connection—one that withstands distance, time, and even monumental disaster.

Deeply Rooted—Originally Uprooted: Collection Description

Deeply Rooted is a series of mixed-media assemblages, merging found objects, organic materials, subtle color palettes, layered three-dimensional textures, and bold symbolism. Each piece invites viewers to reflect on the intertwined stories and connections embedded within them. The *Deeply Rooted* collection reimagines four cherished New Orleans homes from my life, crafted with materials gathered both in my birthplace of New Orleans as well as during my post-Katrina evacuation and relocation to various places that I called home in different parts of the country. These pieces honor homes damaged or lost during the 2005 levee breaches, embodying themes of love, loss, perseverance, and hope. These pieces commemorate the collective experience of New Orleanians—our shared grief, enduring memories, and unwavering determination to thrive despite centuries of longstanding socioeconomic and cultural challenges. Each piece is a symbol of renewal and perseverance, like a seedling uprooted yet ready for replanting.

Medium: Mixed-media Assemblage (2007)
Materials: Recycled cardboard boxes, brown paper bags, coarse sea salt, glue, matte gel medium, rice paper, tissue paper, dead plant soil, shed tree bark, fallen branches, dead plant roots, vine tendrils, incense saturated Spanish moss.

Deeply Rooted—Originally Uprooted: Art Pieces

Touro ~ 7th Ward
A wooden clapboard shotgun double house converted into a single family home on Touro Street in the 7th Ward, a neighborhood traditionally home to generations of working-class Creole families. This house was where my mother was raised in the 1950s and early 1960s, a gathering place for numerous aunts, uncles, in-laws, cousins, grandchildren, and loved ones. Many of the homes, schools, and small businesses in the neighborhood remain abandoned and blighted since the 2005 flooding.

Deslonde ~ Lower 9th Ward
A small white clapboard house on Deslonde Street at the corner of Tonti, located across the Industrial Canal in the Lower 9th Ward. This house sheltered my first school, Ahidiana—an independent, community-based institution founded and operated by my parents and their colleagues in the 1970s. Ahidiana provided children with education, cultural identity, social Guidance, and self-development. The Lower Nine was a predominantly African American neighborhood of working-class homeowners. One of the areas most severely damaged by the levee-breach flooding disaster, the neighborhood has undergone minimal rebuilding in the years since.

St. Maurice ~ Lower 9th Ward
A warm-ivory brick residence built by my paternal grandfather deep in the Lower 9th Ward—way back o' town, as the locals used to say. My father was raised in this house, in a neighborhood rich with backyard gardens, chickens, and horses, as well as fig and pecan trees and a familial sense of community, mere blocks from the line between Orleans Parish, which is geographically synonymous with New Orleans, and the neighboring St. Bernard Parish. Like so many material possessions lost through disaster, any quality images of this piece remain unavailable.

TRANSCENDING STORMS: CREATING BEAUTY FROM UNCERTAINTY

Tennessee ~ Lower 9th Ward
My childhood home, a small white house with aluminum siding and a smaller separate structure in the backyard that was a garage-turned-studio apartment. Like the Deslonde house and the St. Maurice house, the Tennessee house was located in the Lower 9th Ward. I grew up there in the 1970s and 1980s with four siblings and multiple cousins nearby. Throughout most of the twentieth century, the neighborhood was a thriving residential area for working-class African American homeowners, small businesses, and families. Progressive economic downturns since the early 1900s, followed by 1990s surges in drugs and crime, diminished residents' quality of life. Then the neighborhood was completely devastated by the Katrina-related flooding disaster and has since experienced minimal rebuilding. When a barge broke through the levee two blocks away, surging water from the Industrial Canal pushed the house off its foundation into a diagonally adjacent lot. Many other houses in the neighborhood were washed away, yet the little house on Tennessee Street, though displaced and waterlogged, still stood erect after the flooding passed.

Solomon ~ Mid-City
A shotgun double with a treasured porch on Solomon Street near Banks in Mid-City, this was my favorite home. It was where I developed my creative career, hosted gatherings, exhibited art, and coached dreamers through life transformations in the late 1990s. Before the flooding disaster, Mid-City was one of the most diverse residential neighborhoods in New Orleans. It has since been exploding with rebuilding and gentrification. I also lived in homes on nearby Palmyra and Bienville Streets in this cherished area.

Creative Process
The house silhouettes are collaged from cardboard boxes used to ship salvaged belongings from New Orleans to San Diego. These were soaked in sea salt and water, mimicking the polluted saturation of Katrina's floodwaters. Materials such as soil, bark, roots, and branches were collected from my surroundings in San Diego, while Spanish moss came from surviving oak trees in New Orleans' City Park. Like a pot of jambalaya, these assemblages combine remnants and ingredients from the places I've called home. Each piece represents resilience and the enduring capacity to adapt and regenerate, even after profound loss.

Blessings Amid the Storm

The 2005 New Orleans levee-break disaster was a cataclysm, but it also brought unexpected blessings. It forced me to confront my fears, to reevaluate my priorities, and to reclaim my identity as an artist. Through displacement, I found connection—with other artists, with my heritage, and with myself. Reflecting on those years, I see the storm not only as a force of destruction but also as a catalyst for growth. It reinforced my faith in the power of perseverance, the treasure of family, the importance of community, and the necessity of creating spaces for healing and self-expression.

Looking Forward: A Legacy of Creativity and Care

As we approach the 2025 twentieth anniversary of Hurricane Katrina, I am reminded of the lessons we carry from that time. We must continue to advocate for better evacuation plans, equitable recovery efforts, and systems that center the needs of the most vulnerable. Also, beyond the logistics, we must also nurture the creative and cultural ecosystems that sustain us. Through art, we have the power to heal, to connect, and to imagine new possibilities. My hope is that my artwork serves as a testament to this truth—a reminder that even in the darkest storms, there is light to be found and shared.

GO BIBLICAL
MATHEW "MAT" SCHWARZMAN

> In the worst moments, the best of humanity shows up.[38]
> — Chef José Andrés, World Central Kitchen

The Hurricane Katrina story I'm sharing is more personal than political, more reflective than prescriptive, although it has some elements of all four. I did not suffer very much; I did not come out of my experiences with any new strategy or policy ideas for use during natural disasters, but I think, somehow, I might have gained some insights by virtue of being a good observer of human behavior, including my own. Under capitalism, many of us, especially in New Orleans, are forced by poverty to live our lives every day like there is a natural disaster. If you have more than the means to survive, it seems to me it is up to you to take what you experience during a disaster and use that as a new reference point for understanding the meaning of your own life and the lives of people around you.

In August 2005, I had already lived in New Orleans for four years. During the six months leading up to the Storm, several things were going on in my life that are important to know. Economically, we were okay. We were both employed and owned our home (along with our friends at the bank), but our 1998 Honda CR-V had just died of a lengthy and expensive illness, and by August, we were carless and short on cash. I was preparing for publication of my book *Beginner's Guide to Community-Based Arts*, after five years of work with my collaborator Keith Knight. In fact, my first box of books as an author arrived at our house just three days ahead of the Storm, on Friday, August 26, 2005—oddly, just a day ahead of us.

---

38   José Andrés, "The Best of Humanity," Longer Tables with José Andrés, José Andrés, April 29, 2024, https://joseandres.substack.com/p/the-best-of-humanity.

Part I: The Storm

Saturday, August 27: Up until forty-eight hours before Katrina made landfall near Bay St. Louis, Mississippi, Mimi and I were unaware of the seriousness of the coming storm, vacationing in Cape Cod with her family. It's hard to remember now, but right up until the storm, New Orleanians were being told to expect strong winds and rain but not a direct hit. Mimi and I had unplugged in Cape Cod, and it was only because I had made an early morning call to a theater collaborator back home that I learned how many people were leaving. I'd called about cancelling an upcoming rehearsal because of the storm, and he said: "Oh, no, things are a lot more serious than that. A lot more. Are you sure you want to come back?"

By 2:00 p.m. that afternoon, we were on a plane back to New Orleans to snatch up our beloved dog Lundi from our dog-sitting neighbors and secure our home.

When we landed in New Orleans late on Saturday night (about thirty-two hours before Katrina made landfall), we did not know whether we were going to leave immediately, the next morning, or at all. Remember, we did not have a car. By this time, things had gotten serious enough that no more planes were allowed in, the highways were switching to contraflow (i.e., both sides heading out of the city, to facilitate evacuation), and the president had declared a state of emergency. I remember the cab driver on the way back to our house from the airport droning on about all the preparations he and his family had made (where they were going to stay, how they were going to get there, etc.), and it was clear Mimi and I were not in a good place: We had no plan or place to go, we had no car, and we had a dog (Lundi Gras, named for the New Orleans holiday, a Louisiana swamp dog).

It's not like we didn't try to get out. We had reached out to maybe half a dozen friends while we were still in Cape Cod. Several offered spaces for us, but not Lundi, so by the time late Sunday morning came around (about nineteen hours before Katrina landfall), Mimi and I were still without a plan other than "riding it out" with a few immediate neighbors. These were folks who were fine to live next to but definitely weren't on our "wanna be on a desert island with you" list. Frankly, we were scared, but we were not going to give up our dog.

At about 11:00 a.m., we decided to take out the dog and ourselves for one last long walk to decide what we were going to do. By now, the neighborhood was eerily empty. The weather was uncharacteristically dry and sunny. We both remember thinking how beautiful and peaceful the world seemed at that moment. It felt a bit crazy to maintain the level of urgency that was needed to figure out what to do. We crossed over into the next neighborhood, and then it hit us: *Let's ask Kenneth and Melba.*

That beautiful thought—to ask Kenneth and Melba Ferdinand what their plans were—was the first blessing from Hurricane Katrina that I want to count. Without that, Mimi and I would have had a very, very different experience. At that point, we didn't know them very well at all. Kenneth and Melba were friends of friends, and they'd grown up in the Lower 9th Ward. Now, they lived a few blocks away. They had lived through major hurricanes since they were children. They were thoughtful, pragmatic people. *Yes, we'll ask them!*

Mimi, Lundi, and I took a small detour and walked by their house, fully expecting them to have been long gone, like most of our neighbors. Very, very fortunately for us, they were outside in the driveway, not quite finished packing their car yet.

"We'll be fine if we stay, right?", we asked them after hearing about their plans to evacuate in fifteen minutes. They were going to meet up with their two daughters, two granddaughters, and their dog Mocha, driving in their car, just outside of New Orleans, and together, they were going to head together to St. Francisville, a small town north of Baton Rouge, where they'd heard there was an unusually nice evacuation center. Standing and talking in Kenneth and Melba's driveway as they went back and forth, bringing out their essential belongings to their 2003 Acura SUV, Mimi and I pretended we could handle any other answer than *Sure, you'll be fine.*

We did not get what we wanted. That was our second blessing.

Instead, the two of them went silent and went inside the house for a minute or two. They emerged, noticeably more serious and without items in their hands this time. Melba said, "You're coming with us," and proceeded to take some things out of the fully packed SUV.

I know those were her exact words because I remember thinking how ominous they would sound in any other context. As it was, they were like a warm blanket. Mimi, Lundi, and I ran home and, as instructed, immediately packed three bags and returned to their house twenty minutes later. Fifteen minutes after that, the five of us (four people, one dog) were on the road.

Sitting at my writing table almost twenty years later, it is challenging to remember all the feelings I had at that moment, sitting in the back seat of their SUV with my wife, dog, and luggage all in hand. The first was an overwhelming sense of relief because we were not going to be left behind. It's true that even at our moment of exodus (just eighteen hours before landfall), forecasters were still predicting that the storm would go by but not hit New Orleans head on. But we learned from Kenneth and Melba that lifelong New Orleanians know it doesn't matter, because we all live in a topographical bowl below sea level—so, even if a storm is not a direct hit, if the surge created by the storm overtops the delicate perimeter of levees, we are still lost. If that were to happen, you did not (and still do not) want to be stuck here, regardless of what part of the bowl you live in.

What do I mean by that last sentence? This: While I love my city and state, we do not invest nearly enough in public programs or infrastructure. As a result, New Orleans and Louisiana are consistently at the bottom of national indicators for health and well-being and at the top when it comes to the antiquated nature of our utilities, sewers, and phone and Internet service provision. This is not a place that can bounce back from natural disasters quickly, in terms of people or built environment. Even if the storm didn't hit us straight on, the aftermath was going to be hard. We were happy to be leaving New Orleans at that moment, but we knew we would be back as soon as we could.

The second feeling was an almost overwhelming sense of guilt for having such privilege. So many people did not have the option to leave, either because they had a home, business, pet, or relative that needed tending through the storm, or they just didn't have enough money. We didn't have enough money to suddenly find and buy a car at this moment (we'd later hear of someone who did!), but we had access to people with the means to enable our safe departure. We were so incredibly lucky. I think it was only our sense of incredible luck and the obligation to use it wisely that kept Mimi and me from being overwhelmed.

The third feeling was, surprisingly, feeling exposed as Jewish. All the tropes were in place: We were leaving our home under duress, there was a flood coming, our belongings were in our hands, and we were escaping at the mercy of lovely, generous, non-Jewish people. There's a scene in the movie *Annie Hall"* when, under the gaze of his WASPy girlfriend's grandmother, Woody Allen suddenly sprouts the outfit, sideburns, and manner of an Orthodox Jew in response. That's how I felt. Mimi and I giggled nervously in the back seat about this for hours.

We slowly drove up the Great River Road of Louisiana that snakes up to Baton Rouge, a few hundred yards from the levee of the western bank of the Mississippi River. On normal days, this is a tourist road filled with attractions and restaurants—not a great route for entering or exiting the area quickly. On this day, as the clouds gathered above us, it was much worse: solid bumper-to-bumper traffic. It took us six hours to make it to St. Francisville when it should have taken ninety minutes. It was grueling. Even so, Kenneth had spoken with friends who had left town earlier and through them surmised that all the other possible escape routes were going to be even worse, which turned out to be true.

When we finally arrived at the St. Francisville High School auditorium (twelve hours ahead of landfall), yes, I think Mimi and I actually got out and kissed the asphalt of the parking lot. We were 150 miles inland from where Katrina was going to make land and were safe, and we didn't have to give up our beloved dog to be so.

Unfortunately, we hit a snag. When we tried to enter the auditorium to sleep for the night, we were told they could not allow dogs inside. We accepted that restriction as necessary, and even if we hadn't, we would not have complained, out of an abundance of concern for the awesome folks who got us there. All six of them were inside the auditorium, so Mimi and I decided instead to sleep in the SUV in the parking lot with Lundi. It was not a big deal, given how far inland we were.

This was when the third blessing came into being. Mimi, Lundi, and I had just bedded down for the night in the back seat when a car pulled up in front of us and a woman got out. Her name was Stephanie, she said as she stood outside Mimi's side of the car window. She lived nearby, and her girlfriend in the car, named Domino, had just taken possession of a house a few days before with plumbing and power, but nothing else.

"Do you need a place to stay?" she asked us. "It might be better than sleeping in a car."

It took us a minute or two to decide, but we said yes. The two women seemed genuine enough, and if nothing else, it was going to feel good to have a building around us for when the storm really hit in about eight hours. Apparently, Stephanie and Domino had been driving slowly around the parking lot for a while, looking for folks sleeping in cars who needed a place to stay. They had recruited another couple—Bill and Donna from nearby Hammond, Louisiana, also with dogs—who, like us, were a little anxious about following these very nice women to an empty house, but even more nervous about sleeping in the car during a major storm, even if it was not going to be life-threatening. Having another nervous couple to go through this with made it much, much easier for Mimi and me to say yes. Just to be sure, before we left in their car, we introduced Stephanie and Domino to Kenneth and Melba, made sure they knew where we were going to be staying, and everyone traded (pre-smartphone) cell phone numbers.

Just as Stephanie had said, the house was only two minutes away, and it was perfectly quiet and indistinguishable from the other quiet, small to mid-size mid-century tract homes around it. Still, by 11:00 p.m. (seven hours before Katrina made landfall), without power, people, or furniture in it, the house was spooky. We waited in the car outside with Lundi while Bill, Donna, and their two miniature poodles went into the house and then their bedroom for the night. We wanted to make sure our dogs did not interact and most likely start barking and attacking one another—this would be something "extra" that we knew we could not handle emotionally at that moment. So, once Mimi, Lundi and I got into our assigned bedroom, we closed the door and did not open it again until morning. Also spooky. Mimi and I slept on the bare wood floors, using some old shirts and pants that we had just acquired at the shelter wrapped up together as pillows.

We slept fitfully through the storm. By mid-morning, it had passed, but power was out in our area, so Mimi, Lundi, and I walked around our "new" neighborhood to survey the local damage and to look for someone with a battery-operated television (unsuccessfully).[39] We were safe, but now we were desperate to find out how our neighborhood fared: Did our home even exist, and if it did, how much damage was there? Would our lives ever be the same? That afternoon we spent in a surrealistic daze, sitting by the empty pool in the backyard of the empty house, alternating between severe bouts of anxiety and waves of profound appreciation. The power had come back on, and word had gotten out to all these friends and neighbors of Stephanie and Domino that there were these two "refugee" couples and their dogs staying at the empty house. Over the course of about four hours, about twenty people visited in different configurations (individuals, couples, families), bringing us food, clothing, and even appliances, including a television from which we could receive a broadcast signal. It finally sunk in: Mimi and I had no idea how long we would be there.

---

39   Mimi and I were living in San Francisco's Western Addition neighborhood in 1989 when the Loma Prieta 6.9 earthquake hit, and from that experience, we learned the inestimable value (prior to smart mobile devices) of a battery-operated television when trying to survive after a disaster. Thanks to the wealth and power of folks in San Francisco, we also learned what it's like to go through a rapid recovery.

At around 6:00 p.m., the fourth blessing came into being. Kina, Melba's younger daughter and the mother of Saida (age five) texted Mimi to say she was coming by the empty house to talk to us about something. When she arrived, Kina told us that a local landowner they'd met while staying in the auditorium had invited her and the rest of their family to live in his hunting cabin about ten miles away in the woods. She said it had A/C, full plumbing, basic appliances, and enough room for all ten of us (eight humans, two dogs) to live together. There were drawbacks, including poor TV and cellphone reception and a ten-minute drive each way over unpaved roads. But, were we interested?

Out of respect and (by this point) love for Stephanie, Domino, and their empty house, Mimi and I made a performance of weighing the options for a few minutes while Kina waited for us. But by then, we knew a blessing when we heard one.

The next morning, we woke up, said our goodbyes and thank yous to Stephanie and Domino, and got back in Kenneth and Melba's SUV one more time to move from the empty house to the hunting cabin. Before we separated, Bill and Donna pulled Mimi and me aside to tell us something important and (based on body language) awkward: On the one hand, they were ecstatic. They were headed back to their home, about thirty miles away, in a few hours. Miraculously, the house had been spared, even though many others in their suburban neighborhood had been damaged. They felt incredibly lucky and at the same time very sorry for us, because Mimi and I knew so little about the state of our home and even less about when we might return to find out. They made us promise to stay in touch, and here was some money, and if we needed to borrow their extra 1990s Buick, it was available. Mimi and I looked at each other, stunned: a car! This was Blessing Number Five, which would turn out to be the controversial one.

The local businessman and his wife who were going to host us came from an old Southern family and lived on the outskirts of town on a multi-acre estate. As I remember it (I haven't gone back to check), the businessman had built a small hunting cabin using modern materials, but then encased it in unmilled lumber to resemble a traditional log cabin construction. He and his buddies would go for long weekends to hunt deer and other small game. It was this small, one-story building (maybe eight hundred square feet) at the top of a ridge, surrounded by forests and meadows, about two miles on unpaved, backcountry roads to the closest store. This was where Mimi, Lundi, and I lived together with our eight friends and their dog for the next ten days and where we waited for news of our home, neighborhood, and city.

To say it was a bizarre experience is putting it very mildly. On the one hand, it was an epic fantasy. Our basic needs were taken care of, and we were bonding with this multi-generational family in an amazing natural setting worthy of a proverbial Louisiana Family Robinson. The beauty, the peace, and the tranquility all around us constantly took my breath away while I was there. Not to mention, we now had a powerful host who seemed intent, maybe even obsessed, with helping us make it through this tough period. At the same time, we were stuck in a kind of hell, far from where things were happening, receiving just enough information from intermittent texts with family in other places and intermittent reception from the cabin's small black-and-white television to be in a constant state of anxiety. *Do we have a home to go back to or not?*

For the first seven days in the hunting cabin, we had no idea what the state of our home was or what was in store for us. For all we knew, we would be living there together with the Ferdinand family for several more weeks, if not months. Each day was like a self-contained universe, filled with both logistics like shopping, cleaning the house, managing money, and entertaining children, and with intense, usually debilitating conversations about the future of New Orleans. We were not ignoring the reality, but neither were we letting it define our daily life completely. Maisha, Melba's older daughter, and her daughter Nyela led yoga at sunrise together on the cabin porch, for God's sake! Honestly, we had so many blessings come to us that it cheapens the concept to keep assigning them numbers. So instead, here some of the highlights:

- Day #1: All of us watched, laughing and in awe, as Lundi and Mocha bonded over hanging out with the donkeys and horses that grazed in the meadow next to the cabin.[40] I am not sure what would have happened if that had not worked out.

- Day #3: Through the generosity of someone we met in a store, Mimi and I were able to hitch a ride into Baton Rouge for cash cards from FEMA. While in line, we connected with some friends from New Orleans who helped me apply for a job.

---

40   Our host bred burros for use in pulling French Quarter carriages for tourists one hundred miles away in New Orleans. It was a small side business he inherited from his father. As a result, there were horses and donkeys cavorting in the meadows throughout our stay. Note: I could not make this stuff up!

- Day #4: Mimi and I arranged to meet Bill and Donna, our friends from the empty house, in the parking lot of a Baton Rouge mall so that they could loan us their old car. No questions were asked or future commitments made other than to stay in touch with each other. We felt truly blessed; we were mobile!

- Day #6: All eight of us were invited to our host's mansion for brunch. After we ate, he walked us through his family history on the walls of his home—photos, paintings, maps, newspaper stories—and his personal journey as the inheritor of his family's slaveholding legacy. He invited us to stay in the cabin permanently if we found out our homes were destroyed. He promised to use his contacts in New Orleans to keep us informed about our neighborhoods.

- Days #7–8: In the span of just two days, things fell into place for us. We learned that our home was OK from a friend who'd stayed through the storm.[41] Old friends in Berkeley, California, called up to offer their backyard cottage for us to live in as long as we needed it, free of charge. And Keith Knight, my book collaborator, invited me to tag along on his two-week Midwest tour and sell our book.

- Day #9: Woohoo! We suddenly had a plan. Only one drawback: thousands of miles of driving. I called Bill and Donna for permission to use their car to drive to California and back again to New Orleans through the Midwest. They said yes.[42]

---

41   Mimi and I were one of a few families for whom our friend was riding around on his bike, carrying a pistol, looking to see what he could learn about the state of their homes from the street view. He didn't dare break in, as he could easily been shot by one of our stay-at-home neighbors, but he could tell us how things looked from the outside.

42   Given we already had their car in our possession, Mimi tells me (even today, twenty years later) that she thinks I was pushy and rude by essentially telling them we were doing this and there was not anything they could do about it. I say that it was my clear understanding that the car was lent to us to enable us to keep going in our lives, and a cross-country drive was going to accomplish that. Besides, it was an old car, and it was just sitting in their yard anyway, waiting for their daughter to claim it one day.

- Day #10: We packed, made hotel reservations along the way for our three-day drive to Berkeley, and alerted our friends in the Bay Area that we were coming. The eight of us had our final dinner together. And for the first night since before we'd left Cape Cod, Mimi and I both slept through the night.

The next morning, as we left for California, Mimi wrote in her diary: "I am filled with emotions. This is my last day at the cabin. We hope the bonds created here don't ever get loosened. I love these people—all different and vibrant human beings who have enriched my life immeasurably."

Part II: The Aftermath

If I had chosen to be literal in how I split up the sections of this article, I would have begun this "Aftermath" section on August 30, 2005, the day after Katrina made landfall. But the experiences I have related so far, from the days shortly before the Storm to the day we left for California, will always represent a single chapter in my life, a complete process unto itself. It was only once Mimi and I left St. Francisville and the hunting cabin in Bill and Donna's Buick for Berkeley on Friday, September 9, 2005, at 8:00 a.m., that we resumed life on our own, and it was as if the clock started to move forward again.

If you are hoping to hear about all the awful things that happened to us next to balance out all the awesome things as a kind of karmic antidote, I am going to disappoint you. Berkeley was a blast, and as "Katrina refugees" we had a special status that got us extra attention, free drinks, and invitations to places we never would have been invited to previously. My ten-day Midwestern book tour in October with Keith Knight was a great success, and as his official wingman, I got to meet superhero-level activists and artists like Grace Lee Boggs, Harvey Pekar, and Phoebe Gloeckner. In early November, I drove back home to make sure everything in our home was okay, and it was, at least as far as I could tell. For one final blessing, my friends Bill and Sean helped me muck out my maggot-infested refrigerator.

Mimi and I got back home to New Orleans on December 20, 2005 (113 days after Katrina made landfall), having left Berkeley with a new (old) car and a party to celebrate our time there. We did have some immediate, measurable problems to address when we got home: disposal and replacement of our empty refrigerator, some roof damage, and a host of mold-related allergy symptoms that surfaced almost immediately.

The next eight months were a blur. We had a small electrical fire that was almost certainly the result of storm-related stress on the wires outside our house. I had a new job as the director of a musical theater company made up of teens. And we rode a wave of post-Katrina support from around the country to rebuild our lives.

Part III: The Reflections

Katrina was hard, but for me, the next few years were much harder. After about a year of excitement and intensity following the immediate danger and its aftermath, the glacially slow, grinding daily pace of recovery began. Over the next few years, we all became accustomed to the legacy of the storm. Empty "Katrina fridges," "Katrina cars," and "Katrina houses" and businesses were everywhere you looked. Ghostly "Katrina comeback" recovery projects launched with great fanfare sat unfinished and vacant, and thousands of "Katrina kids" were finding it hard to adjust to post-apocalyptic life.

When your life is under threat, your life-horizons shrinks to the size of a street, a building, or whatever mound of earth you could claim, and that is hard. But once your life is no longer threatened and you enter the recovery phase, your life-horizon actually starts moving backward, and that is much harder. Deadlines for improvement were constantly being set back, expectations were always being lowered, and many, many people were moving away. From my perspective, it was as if time had stopped again, and it took a solid ten years for the city's clock to start moving forward, and those were probably the hardest ten years of my life. This Recovery was the karmic payback.

I found myself wondering what had been different during and shortly after the storm that, despite all of the pain and suffering, made so many blessings possible. What made Kenneth and Melba, their children and grandchildren, Stephanie and Domino, their neighbors, Bill and Donna, the guy who gave us a ride to Baton Rouge, our hosts at the log cabin, our friends in Berkeley, all of them and more, offer these many blessings? I've had a lot of time (twenty years!) to think about it, and I think I may have an answer. Yes, a big piece of it was our privilege, no doubt. But I believe there was something else as well.

As Mimi and I were going through our "blessings period," I tried to make it a habit to ask people why they were going out of their way to help us. Everyone said the same thing: some variation of "I am treating you the way I would like to be treated—some variation of the proverbial Golden Rule, essentially. What if that was it? What if, under the stress of survival, that quaint old

Biblical saying became, in fact, the only logical approach to the transactions of life? *I will do it this way if you will.* What if, for a moment, we had unintentionally reverted to a more basic, a more natural, a more sustainable approach to life in general?

As I said when I began this article, I did not end up with any great answers to share from my experiences, only questions. But I did do a bit of research to test my theory, and I came up with two interesting facts. First, what Christians call the Golden Rule is the first, or one of the first, principles of every major religion worldwide:

- Islam: "None of you believes until he wishes for his brother what he wishes for himself." (An-Nawawi's Forty Hadith 13)

- Christianity: "Do to others what you want them to do to you." (Matthew 7:21)

- Judaism: "That which is hateful to you, do not do to your fellow. That is the whole Torah; the rest is commentary." (Talmud, Shabbat 31a)

- Buddhism: "Do not hurt others in ways you yourself would find hurtful." (Udanavarga 5:18)

- Hinduism: "This is the sum of duty: do nothing to others that would cause you pain if done to you." (Mahabharata 5:117)[43]

Second, many scientists who study the connections between human behavior, biology, and violence say something like this: Through millions of years of evolution, we human beings have been bred to respond in certain fixed ways (such as violence) to stress. This goes all the way from hitting those closest to us after having a bad day, to hanging our neighbors in front of laughing crowds because we think they are taking our jobs, to invading entire countries because we are afraid they will do the same to us. These behaviors come from deep within us and are very difficult to change.

---

[43] Islamic Networks Group (ING) Staff, "First Principles of Religion: Treat Others As You Would Like To Be Treated (The Golden Rule)," Islamic Networks Group, accessed June 10, 2025, https://ing.org/first-principles-religion-the-golden-rule/.

The common element in each case is social identity: Do I consider the other person part of my group ("us") or not ("them")? If I believe we share an identity, I am more likely to treat that person well, seek to know them as an individual, and avoid violence, like I would with close friends or family. If I do not believe we share an identity, I am more likely to question their motivations, accept popular stereotypes about them, and use violence towards them in the event of conflict.

Our only real hope to snap ourselves out of this, says Dr. Robert Sapolsky, is greater empathy and individuation: "Distrust essentialism. Keep in mind that what seems like rationality is often just rationalization, playing catch-up with subterranean forces that we never suspect. Focus on the larger, shared goals. Practice perspective-taking. Individuate, individuate, individuate."[44]

---

44   Robert M. Sapolsky, *Behave: The Biology of Humans at Our Best and Worst* (New York: Penguin Press, 2017), 423–4.

ACTS OF KINDNESS
JULIE MENHATI SINGLETON

Greetings, my name is Julie Menhati Singleton. My friends call me Menhati ("she who masters the breath in the grips of emotion").

On August 28, 2005, I turned fifty years old, lost my job with New Orleans Public Schools after fifteen years of service, had my divorce finalized, lost three family members, including my son, Tracy Girod Bridges, and became homeless—and, of course, on August 28, 2005, there was Hurricane Katrina. I am a mother of two children, Tantira and Tracy, two grandsons, Tre and Trevor, and two great-grandsons. I own The Breath Is Life Spa, LLC, where we practice several healing modalities and bodywork. While employed by New Orleans Public Schools for fifteen years, I planned to eventually retire and become a full-time owner and therapist at The Breath is Life Spa, licensed by the state of Louisiana.

On August 27, 2005, I was paying close attention to the weather forecast. Hurricane Katrina was projected to hit my city as a Category Five. I was finishing up with my last client, an elder of seventy-five who would schedule her massage after swimming eleven laps at Tulane University in New Orleans. (Mrs. Eileen St. Julian, may she rest in peace.) Truthfully, my daughter and I were not planning to leave the city; we would hunker down or go to the Superdome if necessary.

Before I continue, I must say it's very challenging reliving this story. I will try not to ping-pong and to stay grounded while sharing my story. Saturday afternoon, after finishing with my last client, my phone rang. On the other end was a hysterical woman saying, "Come to the barber shop, Tre has been shot."

I called my daughter, who was with my youngest grandson. I got in my automobile. I drove to Charity Hospital's emergency room. None of the employees had a clue what I was talking about. They could only say no one was there with my son's name.

I then drove to the barber shop on St. Claude. While driving, I called a girlfriend working at NOPD 911 dispatch to see if I could get more information. She instructed me to go to the hospital. When I arrived at the barber shop, I was met with a sea of hysterical people. I looked around in shock as the train slowly crossed the St. Claude train track, only a few feet away. Heru Khuti, a Kemetic deity that governs trains and guns, was an omen for what I was experiencing.

I looked up in shock, and my sister-friend, Jamilah Muhammad (Angel #1), was there to care for me.

We left the scene, grabbed a few clothing items and toiletries. Jamilah said my daughter and I needed to come with her. We could not stay in the city. We should come with her family to Houston, Texas, for a few days. After thirteen hours of driving, we only got to Baton Rouge. We decided that we could not all go any further. We split up. I called an old friend, Gerri Ellis (Angel #2). She said we could stay with her a few days until we could figure out what the city of New Orleans would do. Gerri agreed, so we stayed with Gerri E. for three months.

Rev. Charlie Moses (Angel #3), my cousin, generously loaned us his extra vehicle for as long as we needed it. This kindness allowed my daughter and me to travel to New Orleans to check on our home, and it allowed Tantira to continue working at Regions Bank in Baton Rouge, which was our only source of income.

My son was murdered on a Saturday, just a day before we were asked to evacuate from New Orleans. We were informed that all bodies had been moved from the city's morgue, but this turned out to be untrue. We were then asked to come to a hotel in Baton Rouge, Louisiana, to provide a DNA swab in case they found a body without identification. Later, we discovered that the bodies in the morgue had remained there throughout the flooding.

While staying with my cousin Teomakia V. (Angel #4) for a few months, we learned she had been searching for a home to buy. She made an offer on a new house, which was accepted, making her a first-time homeowner. At this point, I was presented with another offer. Since I would still need a place to live after Teomakia moved, we had a family meeting. Teomakia and Tantira suggested I ask the owner if he would rent the house to me and my daughter after my cousin moved. The owner agreed to rent it to us for the same amount of rent.

Taking care of my personal hygiene and grooming was important. It was the mental boost I needed. Gerri Ellis recommended Natural Mystic owner

Vanessa Williams. Meanwhile, Ms. Vanessa (Angel #5) offered me a small room in her salon to give massages to her clients, rent-free.

I began getting phone calls from old clients asking when I would be returning home. I was still uncertain where I would land. They said their bodies and spirit needed healing hands, and they really needed to see me. Somehow, I knew I needed something to hold on to to survive the storm. I understood my clients were going through a lot, just like me. They were looking for some comfort too. Somewhere in my head, I heard a voice saying, *Giving up is not an option*. That thought stayed with me.

So, once a week, I would put my massage table and chair in my van and drive to New Orleans to service my clients. I still did not have a place to live in New Orleans, so I would sleep at what I called my sofa-sisters' houses. After sleeping several weeks on the couch of Angel #6, sofa-sister Majeeda S., I did not want to wear out my welcome, so I bounced around. Next, it was sister Ausettua Amor Amenkhun, Angel #7, on N. Miro, and then a few weeks at Sister Saronne S.'s, Angel #8. I was so grateful for their kindness and love. Sarone made a black wreath to hang on the door of my son's barbershop. I always found a place of peace to rest my head. It was safer than sleeping in my van.

In the early morning when driving to New Orleans, I would sometimes watch the sunrise while sitting on the banks of the Mississippi River, having coffee near Café du Monde. I would watch the French Quarter wake up. I then found a little studio in New Orleans (Mid-City) near City Park, which I would rent and where I would sometimes sleep over the weekend while servicing my clients who were coming home to repair their homes.

My studio was located next to a workout studio called Studio 13, owned by Deanne Feaster (Angel #9). She would refer clients to me for massages after their workouts, including a woman who ran a family-owned funeral home with locations in Baton Rouge and in New Orleans. This client asked me if I would be interested in working for their funeral home in Baton Rouge. She gave me a name and contact number for HR, K. Astorga R. (Angel #10). I was still uncertain if I wanted to move back home or stay in Baton Rouge. I lost the HR person's information. So, the next time I saw my client, she asked me again.

I said, "Okay, the least I can do is call the HR department and find out a little more about the job." I scheduled the interview with Kathleenn. At this time in my life, I was fifty years old and had just lost my job after fifteen years.

I interviewed and was hired to work part-time. I could now keep my massage clients and work part-time at the funeral home.

I worked in Baton Rouge Monday through Thursday and drove to New Orleans for massages clients, staying Friday through Sunday. I was eventually hired to audit cases that came through the funeral home's Washington Avenue location. The funeral home was finished with its renovation in New Orleans and would be moving back in 2009.

My office was located on the upper floor, where I witnessed families grieve over babies and other family members. I witnessed mothers losing their babies unexpectedly.

Meanwhile, I was still grieving my own son's death, my firstborn. On October 13, 2005, we were notified that his body had been found at the morgue in New Orleans. It just so happened that Tracy Girod Bridges was born on October 13, 1972, at Charity Hospital, New Orleans. The funeral home strongly suggested I not go to identify my son's body. Instead, his father, Walter B., did. It was now time to bring closure.

I made my big move back home in 2009. Finding a place so quickly was difficult, but I did, a newly renovated house in Mid-City. Well, the house was in a seemingly safe neighborhood. The only problem was I being stalked by my neighbor's mentally challenged son. After six months, I broke my lease and got out of dodge.

There were many times I heard screams and crying sounds from the chapel below my office. I was forced to revisit my situation each time I heard a scream, remembering my own loss and grief through the eyes of others. I also worked as a massage instructor two days a week in Houma, Louisiana, and in Baton Rouge, for Blue Cliff College. I worked in the evening from 6:00 to 9:00 p.m. I soon understood that the experiences at the funeral home were to help me through my own grieving process as well as to help others through theirs.

I now have a component added to my business called Acts of Kindness. This is where I help navigate families through their grieving process after losing a baby or toddler.

I received my first doula certification in 2010 (Naziya Doula Collective) and the second in 2018 with Sista Midwives Production, Nicole Diggins. I am a Healing Touch App Practitioner, HTAP, Doula, Companion, and LMT Licensed Massage Therapist (2715-01) in the state of Louisiana.

Fast forward thirteen years later. Spirit began speaking loudly: *Start packing your bags.* I did not have a place in mind. I just felt I would get an answer if I obeyed the voice of my ancestors.

I continued packing and began looking for a house to purchase. Something simple, safe, and affordable. The only thing I knew for certain was I needed to get a house with a rental property attached to support my income.

During one of my drives with the realtor, I looked over my right shoulder and saw a For Sale sign. I said, "I like that one."

It was not on the list of houses to view. We did the research, and I patiently waited.

The house at 1662 and 1664 became my new home. I moved in March and had a hip replacement in April. Crazy, huh? I now rent the upstairs apartment to my two grandsons, who have returned to my life after nineteen years.

Just in case you are wondering where my lovely daughter Tantira Ausut disappeared to, she said it was time for her to move on, and would I be OK if she went to Atlanta, Georgia, which had been her plan prior to Katrina? I said yes, and she moved on to a new chapter in her life.

My Katrina story is more about my ancestors, angels, and spiritual guides that were sent to me on this journey. I am grateful it was more about the acts of kindness extended to me from my friends, extended community, and family.

AT THE WATER'S EDGE
NICK SLIE

Introduction

If you have ever driven from New Orleans to Gramercy down Airline Highway at night, you know the feeling in the pit of your stomach when you pass the refineries near Norco, Louisiana. I was doing that drive at 3:00 a.m. on August 27, 2005, and every molecule in my body was on full alert. Living through storms my whole life, the checklist of preparations was familiar to me. But there was something about the weariness of Norco on that particular night that allowed me to trust what my molecules were whispering: This storm was different.

My father is from New Orleans. My mother grew up in Gramercy, Louisiana. I sheltered in place with friends in Gramercy during Katrina because my mother was the CEO of St. James Parish Hospital and was required to be present at the hospital during the storm. I came to Gramercy because of the instinct of my mother, who had long discouraged me from staying in New Orleans for big storms. When I arrived in Gramercy, I returned to my checklist, boarding up the windows and preparing the home for the storm's arrival. This part of the process always felt good to me, an answer to the sweeping anxiety that emerges when a storm is in the gulf.

Walking through the house that evening, I remembered the feeling of terror that had pulsed through me when Hurricane Andrew whipped over our home on a similar date in August 1992. It is the first memory I have of being stone-cold terrified as a child. We spent an entire night as a family taking in the piercing howls of the wind as it threatened to lift the roof from the building for six straight hours. Through the swirls of Hurricane Andrew memories, I slowly completed my checklist: Windows boarded. Flashlight batteries replaced. First aid kit identified. Bathtubs filled with drinking water. Hurricane candle in place. Beer on ice. Wine, well, opened.

By the time Katrina was heading toward the fragile coast of Louisiana, I had been back in New Orleans for about three years. I'd returned from a two-year stint in Ireland to reunite with two friends, Beau Harrison and Bruce France, to form an arts production company called Mondo Bizarro. We were fulfilling a dream of producing our own work and opening a multi-disciplinary art space in New Orleans, our home. When the storm hit, we were just finding our footing, having produced one festival, a few films, and some theatrical productions.

We all scattered for the storm and vowed to be in touch after the winds and rains swept through. The night of Katrina in Gramercy felt more frightening than I had expected. There were the usual heavy rain and strong winds. But there was also this prescient feeling about what was happening back home in the city. We lost power pretty early. Once the power went, we were without any means to communicate with the outside world or find out what was happening in New Orleans. The fear during the storm was real, and our minds were preoccupied with imagining what the storm could do to our city. I remember falling asleep sometime in the early hours of the morning, just as the wild heat of summer began to remind us of what the next day would feel like.

We awoke physically unscathed. There were branches down and debris to clean up. But the house was intact, and most importantly, everyone staying there was safe. The anxiety to know more about what was going on in the city was urgent. I can't remember how we figured it out, but I have this vague recollection that we managed to get a small hurricane radio tuned into some station in the area. We were relieved that the reports out of New Orleans confirmed that our worst fears had been averted. The storm had veered right at the last minute toward Biloxi, and our beloved New Orleans had been spared. News that New Orleans was damaged but not destroyed was a welcome balm to our over-fried nervous systems.

Sometime around mid-morning, as the day's heat intensified, things changed for the worse. My mother came by the house and told us about news reporting a breach in the 17th Street Canal. Throughout that day, all of the reporting about New Orleans changed. And while we did not witness the over-sensationalized, often false barrage of reports streaming across the national media, we did begin to piece together the facts: New Orleans was slowly filling with water, the damage was beyond anything we could comprehend, and the road to recovery was going to be very long.

Amidst the sullenness that was lathering my body and spirit as reality sunk in, one of the first blessings quickly emerged. St. James Parish Hospital was one of the first places that began to receive people who had made it out of the storm in New Orleans. Throughout the day, many people began to land in the small town of Gramercy. Before you knew it, there was a triage station in the parking lot of Winn-Dixie, where a group of ordinary people began the process of collecting and distributing necessary supplies, finding people shelter, and, of course, serving hot plates of food. I remember the light that went off in my body when I witnessed how beautiful it was for a group of concerned citizens—many of whom had just experienced a pretty traumatic storm—to create the conditions of care for people in need. Here was the best of us during one of our worst moments.

The triage station at the Winn-Dixie emerged on Monday, August 30. The next day, I was concocting a plan with my creative partner Bruce France to make fake press passes and head back into the city. We had no idea what we would do or how we would get it done. But like those folks in the parking lot of the Winn-Dixie in Gramercy, we were alight with the need to do something. Days later, we meandered down Airline Highway, making our way to River Road, where we met a National Guard checkpoint for the first time. I wish you could see how ridiculous our fake press passes were. Thank God for Bruce France, who reminded me to act official, flash the badge, and pretend like I knew what I was doing. I remember rolling down the window, barely looking at the National Guard troops, flashing the badges, and moving through the checkpoint. That was one of the thousands of surreal moments that would permeate the next five to ten years in New Orleans. While everything that happened from that point on is simultaneously crystal clear and mentally foggy, one truth remains: There have been many blessings.

Writing this chapter has not been easy. While I show up here as an individual artist recounting my experiences of the storm, the majority of my work is created collaboratively with Mondo Bizarro. Throughout my writing, I have leaned into the collectively shaped wisdom of present and former Mondo Bizarro company members Bruce France, Dan Pruksarnukul, Joanna Russo, Hannah Pepper-Cunningham, and Melisa Cardona. Our work together across decades has inspired a way for me to see this territory of Katrina memories anew.

I underestimated how difficult it would be to re-enter this emotional landscape. As an artist who often begins creating performance material with a deep dive into the memories in my body, I should have known better. However, I was not prepared for the amount of trauma that would emerge when recounting the storm and its aftermath. When I met resistance in this writing, I tried to release from solid ground and float between what began to feel like islands of remembrance, an archipelago of sorts. When I arrived on an island of remembrance—small or large—I tried to absorb the various layers and textures of the memories therein. Slowly traversing this archipelago of memory allowed the gifts, blessings, and lessons of Katrina to emerge with a permeating softness. When the softness had permeated me, I would allow myself to write.

I have found it enormously difficult to organize these experiences into a coherent account. Some days, the lessons that surfaced in me were so clear, arriving as full, complete thoughts. Other times, the blessings of my Katrina experience emerged as fragments of potent memories that appeared and evaporated in the mist of my mind. The blessings that I have metabolized do not always fit into a rational, linear narrative. So, I've decided to share them in fragments, small anecdotes, and poetic phrases as a means to honor the power of their teachings and the ways they continue to pulse in me. Let's float.

Weaving the Dramaturgy of Rebuilding

It feels like it was mid-September when Bruce France and I walked into Ashé Cultural Arts Center to witness a stage filled with cleaning supplies. In the weeks before that, we'd spent our mornings meeting with other performance makers, artists, cultural workers, and organizers in our apartment on Second Street, which had power and internet restored very quickly. It felt good to bring people together, to listen to what everyone was doing, and to attempt to synergize our burgeoning recovery plans. Our afternoons were spent fulfilling any mission request we received. Someone's cat might still be alive in Gentilly. A precious heirloom may have avoided the floodwaters in Mid-City. The downstairs of a house near Franklin Avenue needed to be gutted in a day. All of this work had to be done before sundown, as there was still a curfew after dark, during which the National Guard could stop you if you were roaming without a purpose. It was all so surreal. There was a pack of wild dogs in Central City. Everywhere you turned, there were mountains of debris, duct-taped refrigerators, the smell of mold, and centuries of memories strewn about the streets.

Art and storytelling were a big part of how we all got through the poststorm era. We returned from our missions each day with stories to tell, and the meaning of it all began to emerge, piece by piece. But it was not until we saw that stage at Ashé that the true nature of our work as artists in the early recovery days became clear. Rebuilding was the performance. Taking care of our people was the show. Each day, we were staging the act of making ourselves whole again, creating the space to honor our loss, our immense grief, and the emergent sense that together, we were everything. Suddenly, the tenets of ensemble performance practice—collaborative creation, deep listening, coordinated movement, storytelling—revealed themselves as tools deeply ingrained in our bodies and useful to this emergent dramaturgy of rebuilding.

As artists, we were very much at the beginning of developing our values, and Katrina provided the big blessing of revealing these to us in practice. We witnessed the necessity of culture in rebuilding and sustaining vibrant places like New Orleans. One of the nation's most unique cultures was visibly threatened, on the verge of extinction. Like the plants that immediately bloomed after the storm as a means of survival, our job was to flower into action. Being an artist in this context meant braiding together aesthetic rigor, mutual aid, imagination, and collective purpose. Katrina confirmed the value of asking big questions, aligning your work with purpose, and the power of people from different disciplines and walks of life working together toward a common, creative goal. We were devising choreographies of change, and amidst all the destruction, there was intention, beauty, and hope.

A School as a Sanctuary

When I walked into the auditorium at Nunez Community College after the storm, there were dead fish on the stage. I was sweating and crying in a hazmat suit, and everything felt hopeless. I remember trudging through the mud with a barely working flashlight, making my way out of the entrance onto the grass near the front lawn. The afternoon sun was softening, and to my right, I caught a whiff of our gardenia bush bursting with its third bloom of the year. What was likely a minute felt like an hour. I turned left to watch the sunset over Bayou Bienvenue, took a deep breath, and said the words, "Day by day."

As an actor, I have been trained in the art of presence, of taking things one moment at a time. I can confirm that nothing helps you to slow down and appreciate the moment like witnessing everything you know turned upside down by the force of water. It is awe-inspiring and terrifying at the same time. It will stop you. It will fill you with inertia. And it will draw the best of you from places you did not know existed.

In the post-storm era, there were heroes and visionaries everywhere you turned. There was a lot of deferring your own pain to attend to someone else's. Maybe your house had four feet of water, but someone else got nine feet. You would often witness someone completely downplaying their circumstances to show empathy for what seemed like something worse. Witnessing the care in these currents between different people, and the visions that people held for each other, was amazing. I learned early on to allow myself to be swept into these moments, to trust the various calls of inspiration around me. Such was the case with what the waters of Katrina inspired in Chancellor Tommy Warner and the many employees of Nunez Community College.

Dr. Warner was the chancellor of Nunez Community College when the storm hit. Like everyone in St. Bernard Parish, Dr. Warner lost everything, as the storm waters reached the bottom of his home's roof. He rode out the hurricane on the second floor of Nunez with a team of dedicated employees, witnessing the seventeen-foot storm surge that rushed in off the banks of the Mississippi River Gulf Outlet (MRGO), inundating the college with water. Days after the water receded, without any official decree or permission, Dr. Warner led the process of gutting all the flooded buildings on campus. He was from St. Bernard and knew that, given the extent of the damage to the parish and the school, there was a chance that someone would make the call to shut the doors permanently. Dr. Warner had other ideas.

He set a goal of opening the doors to the public on January 1. He did not wait for permission or funding. He led with a bombastic vision that Nunez could be a sanctuary in a completely destroyed St. Bernard Parish. He knew that for people to trust that a place could return, they had to witness evidence of radical imagination. The small facilities staff and dedicated employees of Nunez—all of whom had sustained profound personal losses—gutted, cleaned, and remediated the first floors of all buildings by December 2005.

School started again in January 2006. All classes took place on the second floor of the Arts and Humanities Building, one of the few places in St. Bernard Parish that Katrina's waters had not touched. I barely remember teaching. I do recall a lot of crying, laughing, and storytelling, and persistent reminders of how remarkable it was to have a gathering place, a sanctuary from the heaviness of recovery life. By November 2006, the Nunez theater department, along with several community partners, staged a multidisciplinary arts festival in the gutted auditorium on the first floor, the same one that had been covered in fish. We had camping chairs and a few lights in the air. And we had the blessing of a space to gather, to sing, and to tell stories. We did so much with so little.

Years later, the dream of sanctuary that Dr. Warner began is being continued by another visionary leader, Dr. Tina Tinney. Today, Nunez is a thriving institution serving students from seven parishes and is at the leading edge of creating a better future for Southeast Louisiana.

Let the Listening Lead
It was the first few days after Katrina made landfall, and I was volunteering in a shelter at the Lamar Dixon Expo Center in Gonzales, Louisiana, sixty miles west of New Orleans, near Baton Rouge. Hundreds of our people were strewn about on the floor in row after row of cots. The image of my fellow citizens carrying everything they owned in a bag or two was devastating. There were a lot of tears and many thousand-yard stares. I remember humbly listening with my whole body each day as I visited the shelter. Hearing the kindness, care, and resolve in these stories was an antidote to the grossly exaggerated portrayals of New Orleanians as looting savages who took advantage of a disaster to benefit themselves. Leaving the shelter that day, I remember saying to my Mondo Bizarro colleagues Beau Harrison and Bruce France, "I just want to listen."

Our friend and mentor Joe Lambert from StoryCenter (then the Center for Digital Storytelling) got word of this desire and sent us our first recording device. In less than a week, the I-10 Witness Project was born. The idea was simple. With their consent, we would listen to and record people's Katrina stories. The person who shared a story would receive a copy, we would archive the recording, and a portion of it would be shared on our project website. The hope was that every story recorded with care could counter the careless narratives that were permeating the public imagination.

Artists possess many gifts that are valuable in the moments following a natural disaster. We train many skills, and none is more important than the art of listening. Sitting with people after Katrina, listening to hours upon hours of stories, taught me the valuable lesson that there is a way to listen that helps someone understand something about themselves they could have never known without your attention. And there is a way that listening to someone's story can help you understand the past, present, and future of the world you want to see. When you lean in and listen with your whole body, your molecules shake, and you open the possibility—even if for an hour—of a palpable reframing.

Everywhere in New Orleans, there were visible and invisible crops of memories calling to the surface. The stories were prismatic, reflecting the rich diversity of our people. The tales we heard were heavy and cathartic, unbelievable and filled with wonder. There were harrowing stories of death and drowning. There were stories of boat rescues and airlifts from rooftops. Almost always, there was a reminder of the innumerable moments of care that took place before, during, and after the storm. There were iconic stories about the failure of our governmental structures during Katrina. While important, those stories were played back to us ad nauseam. I was more interested in the stories of the thousands of people who'd made it to a shelter of last resort after the floodwaters inundated our city. I wanted us to remember the tales of kindness and heroism that inspired people to move together, through the most unimaginable circumstances, to safety.

The blessings of the plurality of stories here were twofold. First, the systems I've observed to have the deepest impact on my home—racism, unchecked capitalism, and wholesale environmental destruction—thrive on a singular narrative wherein they are the inevitable solution. In place of a singular narrative, we must create space for a plurality of narratives. As artists in the post-Katrina landscape, we were learning how to investigate the relationship between the systemic, the collective, and the intimate, and stories helped us to do so on an embodied level. Second, listening with others helped us understand the necessity of an interdisciplinary approach to art and recovery. We learned that our practice should include a multiplicity of forms so that we could draw connections for a diversity of people who experienced our emerging projects. Using a multiplicity of forms, we could create intimate and expansive spaces to share stories, journey through often hidden territories of experience, and expand what we could imagine. In these ways, stories helped us learn to use our artistic practices to encourage systematic shifts towards a more just and humane world.

We began to learn that if people cannot see themselves reflected in the process and product of the work being done, then they will have no need to become participants in that work. We found that the best way to bring people in was to involve them in all aspects of the work: planning, design, and execution. We created multiple entry points for people who wanted to participate in our efforts, including but not limited to planning meetings with community stakeholders, open rehearsals, live music, food, site-responsive performances, public dances, story circles, visual art installations, digital storytelling, salons, and public policy meetings.

Forward-Facing Nostalgia

In early November of 2005, I was lucky to be immersed in the development of UPROOTED: *The Katrina Project*. UPROOTED: *The Katrina Project* was a theatrical response to the human-made disaster that befell our region. It was a multidisciplinary collaboration between Gulf Coast artists: myself, Bruce France, Carlton Turner, John O'Neal, Kathy Randels, Maurice Turner, Millicent Johnnie, Roscoe Reddix, Saddi Khali, Stephanie McKee, Webo O'Neal, and Valentine Pierce (all members of Alternate ROOTS). The production and accompanying community dialogue traveled to numerous cities around the country and brought together displaced Gulf Coast residents and concerned citizens who wanted to help. Participants discussed conditions in their communities that could lead to the same tragic breakdown that happened in New Orleans and other cities destroyed by Hurricane Katrina.

I had known John O'Neal for a couple of years by then, but we had never collaborated on a project until we began to create *UPROOTED*. It was one of the storm's greatest blessings to be in the presence of that beautiful man for weeks on end. John was a teacher to many people. He taught me so much about slowing down and being direct. His analysis was incisive. He could get straight to the point with precision and care. His empathy made him a great actor. His listening made him a wonderful writer. His heart made him a great artist and organizer.

Through our time together, John imparted the wisdom that memory is a great innovator. Looking back is not always nostalgic. If it is sometimes nostalgic, it can be a forward-facing nostalgia. He would always remind me that it is possible to look back while simultaneously building and envisioning a better future.

Too often, our expectations of the work we must do are derived from the limitations of the present. John helped me imagine a world where our impact as artists is measured by how effectively we link our collaborative efforts to the endless triumphs of the people and movements that came before us. He helped me ask big questions: What if the resources applied to reward the myth of genius were used to strengthen the art of social coordination? How can we revive the dual possibilities within the word "original"—meaning both "something that has never happened before" and "something connected to its origin"? How much space would be freed in us as individuals, as a field, if we understood that our efforts were part of a continuum of impact, the arms of which stretch across time and borders? John taught those of us lucky enough to work with him to root our work in a clear image of what came before, to recognize how impact persists through our veins over time, to shape our work as a corridor between the timely and the timeless.

Flow

Katrina welcomed me into a more intimate knowledge of the fact that Louisiana is disappearing. In the last forty years alone, we have seen more of our shoreline fall prey to the waters lapping at our banks than any other region in the world. This is happening in part because the leveeing of the river all across Southeast Louisiana shut off the flow of sediment that nourished and built this land, resulting in the erosion of almost two thousand square miles of wetlands since the 1930s. The overengineering of the Mississippi has historically been embraced as positive due to the wildness and lack of security that characterized life before levees and the job opportunities afforded by flood-control structures. But it has led us to the point of environmental crisis: There is now water where houses once sat. Without sediment from the river replenishing it, our land washes away. We now face the necessity of re-engaging a relationship with the tumultuous, powerful, and capricious river that is the unfettered Mississippi—a relationship that we abandoned nearly one hundred years ago.

I have observed how the systems of oil and gas extraction and the structures of flood control—which, together, are responsible for much of the catastrophic land loss in Louisiana—have embedded themselves in the experience of the people and shielded us from a most necessary tool of adaptation: grief. We are so busy scrambling to survive these disasters with our culture and communities intact that we have been unable to pause and fully experience the range of emotions that accompany living through one ecological crisis after another. I believe that our ability to respond adequately to the climate crisis in Louisiana is seriously hampered by our failure to acknowledge this grief. I know that this deep, wide sense of all that we have lost and all we are losing must flow as wildly as the river diversions we are currently using to try to save our home. If we must rewild the river and the land, we must also rewild ourselves. So far, attempts to address climate change in Louisiana have failed to acknowledge this. Just as Katrina invited me into a reckoning with all we are losing, it also taught me that we must stop, listen, and dream about how to live with fluctuation, to live with uncertainty, to live in symbiosis with our increasingly watery world, both inside and out.

At the Water's Edge
My family has loved and listened to the mysteries of Southeast Louisiana for ten generations. This ephemeral locale of ancestry, nested in the physical locale of place, is the source of my inspiration. My home is a treasure trove of joyous art forms—fiddling, dancing, cooking, storytelling—that have been carefully passed down to help me survive and thrive. My people wield celebration as a weapon. We remain unforgetful of our origins. We view the imagination as a way to build things. Art and survival are one.

My grandmother Rita Zeringue grew up in a squatted house in Convent, Louisiana, with very little money. But you would not know it from the way she talked about the abundance of the land and the communities that enveloped her. She especially loved the ritual of the boucherie, when families from the community would come together to share in the labor of collectively harvesting and breaking down the life-giving nourishment of a pig. Toward the end of her life, I'd listen in amazement as she figured out that all this talk about "going green" was just what her family had been doing their whole lives out of necessity. When you don't have much, you use everything. Your waste is regenerative compost. You look out for your neighbors. What's mine is yours. Mutual aid is part of the fabric of life.

One of the greatest blessings of Katrina was the deep and abiding remembrance of the practice of mutual aid. I have found that the training we received during Katrina endures to this day. So, when Covid-19 descended upon New Orleans, I was not the least bit surprised by the incredible generosity and synergies that pulsed through our creative community. Within a month, I watched with great pride as Antenna, Ashé Cultural Arts Center, Junebug Productions, and Punctuate distributed the start of what would become nearly $1.2 million in emergency relief grants, making approximately 1,610 awards to artists in the Greater New Orleans metro area. This was all part of the Creative Response Network (CRN), an emergent and collaborative effort led by a consortium of local arts leaders representing diverse, critical, and justice-focused arts-organizing efforts in New Orleans. We met during the pandemic and beyond, developing a resource and advocacy hub for the cultural community. The lessons and blessings of our Katrina days permeated the sophisticated and heart-centered organizing that happened as part of the CRN.

When Hurricane Ida struck, Mondo Bizarro—thanks to Another Gulf Is Possible and The Land Memory Bank and Seed Exchange—was part of a coalition of nearly thirty-five organizations that distributed over two million dollars to the artists, organizers, and culture-bearers in our region. The organizations distributing this vital mutual aid varied in size, scope, and mission. But they all shared some common traits. They were trusted by the individuals in their communities. They were rooted in powerful values. They were nimble and rarely burdened by the trappings of institutional baggage. They all moved at the speed and needs of the people on the ground doing the real work of recovery when disaster strikes.

The more we've worked together, the more we have realized that the people most disproportionately impacted by land loss and hurricanes in Southeast Louisiana are frequently absent from the dialogue about how we address these things. Despite the astonishing amount of legislative and scientific responses to climate change occurring in our region, there are shockingly few opportunities for people on the front lines to have a voice in discussions about the future. As such, there is simply no space for the profound emotions of loss and grief we are currently experiencing. Our work needs to invite people to imagine in the language of lived experience and to bring their entire selves to the equation. This is how culture is necessary in any larger movement to sustain vibrant places. When we, as artists and cultural workers, collaborate in broader coalitions, we can create not only space for action but also for inspiration—an essential ingredient in an area that has experienced one devastating ecological catastrophe after another.

The experience of Hurricane Ida further demonstrated something I've always known in my bones: artists and culture-bearers don't need marching orders. What we need is sustained support for our visions. By the time most institutions and government officials have thought about an idea, artists and culture-bearers have created it. Culture is like water: it always finds the low ground first. If we want to meet culture in its true beauty and splendor, we have to find a way for institutions to be wide, flexible, and open enough to accommodate the currents of change that will continue to shape this place. There is a tension between what we are asked to do by institutions to keep our work alive and thriving and what we need to do to listen to culture and people, to listen to where the water is going. We have to be brave enough to pivot and cede institutional power in order to heed the integrity of our vision, but the decisions have to include the wisdom and vision of the people on the ground, living the culture every day.

In 2015, a $14.5 billion project that improved levees, gates, and floodwalls was completed, designed to protect New Orleans and the surrounding area from a one hundred-year storm. This is itself a mighty blessing. We can and should give thanks for the surrounding levees that protect us from the ever-increasing storm surges emerging from the gulf. We should also mind the ways that these levees create a psychological barrier, fabricating a false sense of safety for the people who live here and cutting us off from the experience of one of our most miraculous collaborators: the water.

Most stories about the future of this place begin at the water's edge. If we are going to survive here, we need to develop strategies that do not simply name the problems but ones that, in intentional and beautiful ways, become a part of the solutions. One such solution is a broader and more nuanced listening to the waters that surround us. Our ancestors in Louisiana created floating adaptations for generations, living as they did along the banks of a wildly moving Mississippi. These floating boats/barges/homes/villages demonstrated a symbiotic relationship between land and water that has been disregarded and overengineered in the past century. Katrina was a reminder that we either move with the water or the water moves us. We must spend more time within and amidst the mystical waterways that pulse through New Orleans and Southeast Louisiana. We have to witness the water seeking its own level, escaping from our ideas about what it wants and showing us what true freedom looks like. We have to listen more intimately to the lessons of impermanence that the water carries. We have to remember what Katrina taught us: We can fully grieve and fully enact a more promising future at the same time.

I know in my heart that if we can spend more time with the water, it will create an opening for people to understand—in an embodied as well as an intellectual way—where we are, how we got here, and dream together about where we want to go. As Jo Carson says, "We are standing on the edge of a story." We are the water's edge. One hundred years from now, what will our story be? Can we learn to float again, releasing fully into the complexities of moving between what we need and what the water wants to do? With everything in me, I can imagine it.

THE BLESSING OF TOGETHERNESS
KAREL SLOANE-BOEKBINDER

There is a ragged crack, a gap where one section of Sheetrock ends and another begins. The crack runs from the ceiling to the floor. It is half an inch wide. The gap between the sections of Sheetrock started out as a sliver, then a slit; over the past two years, it has steadily and slowly gotten wider. The floor next to these separating walls is slanting. The linoleum crests and falls in a permanent wave. This is my home, an efficiency apartment at the back of a house in the oak-lined Mid-City neighborhood of New Orleans. There is one large room, a small kitchen, and a closet-sized bathroom. The separating walls and wavy floor are in the kitchen. There are three stone steps leading to the entrance. The steps wobble. The doorframe of the entrance, like the kitchen floor, slants. A small pecan tree grows next to the steps. At the edge of the backyard there is a small, gray shed. A cement slab extends from the left side of the shed. There is a roof above the slab—the perfect outdoor spot for painting.

At ten in the evening on July 6, Hurricane Cindy makes landfall in Grande Isle. It's a little over one hundred miles from New Orleans. The wind and rain last for hours. The wind doesn't shriek. It whooshes. Under my sheet and blanket, my cat Taylor and I feel each whoosh as the wind gusts through the apartment. The next morning, I am grateful the gap between the kitchen wall doesn't seem to be any bigger.

At the end of August, another hurricane, a Category One, is headed for Florida. A friend and I listen to a local weathercaster on the radio describe the storm as it cuts across the Florida panhandle. A day later, the storm turns. It is now heading for New Orleans.

I don't want to evacuate. The past several years, riding with friends, I've spent hours and hours bumper to bumper in unmoving, contraflow traffic. Then, after nothing happens, we turn around and return to the city. I don't trust the shape-shifting, half-inch-wide crack in my kitchen walls, either. I ask a friend if Taylor and I can stay at her house. I tell her I am worried about what the wind will do to my separating kitchen walls.

She is a social worker at a psychiatric hospital. She is evacuating with her patients to a sister hospital in Memphis. Her husband is staying; they live in River Ridge, a suburb of New Orleans. Their home is on a cul-de-sac that ends at the edges of the Jefferson Parish levee. They agree, and we make plans for her husband to pick us up Sunday morning.

I've filled a cloth backpack with a few changes of clothes, toothbrush, toothpaste, shampoo, my hair brush. Taylor is in her cat carrier. Her litter box and cat food are packed too. When my friend's husband arrives, he says he doesn't like the latest news about the storm. We're leaving.

I decide to pack a few more things: my passport, a photo album filled with images from a student trip to Europe I chaperoned, and two small medical textbooks that had belonged to my great uncle. I still think we'll be back in a couple of days. My friend's husband's decision to leave is a blessing. This blessing may be what saves Taylor and me from drowning. Life without a permanent address is beginning. In the week that follows, I start counting the temporary ones. Between Monday and Friday there are three, a motel and two hotels.

These are the days before Cortana, Alexa, Siri. Thanks to Expedia, while we are on the road, the first temporary address we find is a motel. We make it to Memphis in the wee hours of Monday morning. We pull in off the highway and see the motel comes complete with a strip club in the front yard and young women in tube tops and bikini shorts patrolling back and forth along the road. In our motel room, Taylor jumps back and forth from bed to bed, investigating her new surroundings. I turn the TV on.

A newscaster says, "New Orleans has dodged a bullet again." Katrina has passed. I wonder about the newscaster's word choice. And about storm surge.

The next morning, there is a robbery at the motel. A man with a gun jumps over the front desk, grabs all the cash he can carry, jumps back, and walks out the front door. The police stop us for questioning as we go out on errands. Impermanence is relative. We decide it is time to find a new address.

We go back to Expedia and discover a hotel with vacancies. They also take pets. We arrive to find the pet policy has been disbanded until further notice. I smuggle Taylor and her litter box in on a luggage cart, and for three days, we keep the Do Not Disturb sign on the door and don't allow anyone in to clean the room. Once Taylor has been smuggled into temporary address number two, we start settling in. My friend's husband turns on the hotel TV. Most of New Orleans is going underwater.

The levees are breaking.

That evening, as we drive on the elevated highway that circumnavigates Memphis, large raindrops splatter the windshield. The sky is bright green. It is the remnants of the storm. Hurricane Katrina has followed us to Memphis, bringing the possibility of tornadoes. We return to the hotel without seeing any and watch more updates about New Orleans. Emptiness doesn't focus on walls, what is filled already, or what has fallen away. Emptiness is abyss, the spoon yet to be full. I focus on this to try and fill the fraying edges of my life, a life falling away. I focus on this because I have no place to put myself right now. I don't have a new way to frame anything, only a small cloth backpack. So many names are being thrown at me: victim, evacuee, refugee, fortunate, homeless, untouched, survivor, rebuilder. I stand in a sentence, a space where I'm having a hard time completing things. The more I watch the news, the more I am at a loss for words. Like me, all my rituals are being displaced. It is odd not to have an address, odd not to have my favorite radio station wake me up, odd not to make breakfast in my kitchen, odd not to ride the streetcar to work. I look at the hotel phone and think about how I would call home for messages. Old habits have their own pulse. They die hard.

We shuffle from diner to restaurant, station to station, hotel TV to my friend's husband's laptop and Internet café. We shuffle until watching becomes impossible. Then we turn everything off and go for walks outside around the hotel. The fifth day, we switch addresses again; we are finally able to move into my friend's hotel, where hospital staff are staying, and share her suite.

The psychiatric hospital in Memphis, sister hospital to the one in River Ridge, has temporarily designated a section for the evacuated patients. My friend and her colleagues go to work at the hospital and then return to the hotel. Her shift is in the morning, 9:00 a.m. to 5:00 p.m. She joins us after her shift, and with Taylor sprawling across my lap, we all watch the news together.

I have a psychology degree with a concentration in art therapy. I also have experience working with unhoused people. Many of my former clients in the shelters where I worked had a psychiatric diagnosis. My friend suggests I go with her in the morning and volunteer at the hospital. Her suggestion is a blessing.

The next morning after breakfast, we go to the hospital, and I get acquainted with her coworkers and the patients. The New Orleans hospital staff are from many neighborhoods: the Lower Nine, Lakeview, the 7th Ward, Uptown, Gert Town, New Orleans East. So are some of the patients. Some of the other patients are from other parts of Louisiana. It is now clear that what was to be a brief evacuation is going to be longer. A lot longer.

Every morning, I eat breakfast with my friend and the other hospital staff staying at the hotel, and then we head to the hospital. I answer the phone, direct calls, and take messages. I make coffee. I empty garbage cans. And I listen. Most stories are about the broken levees and our homes that are now underwater. The Lower Nine, Lakeview, the 7th Ward, Uptown, Gert Town, New Orleans East, Mid-City. And we talk about the other people who live in our neighborhoods. Did they get out in time? We don't have a television on at the hospital. We watch the news when we get back to the hotel. Or before we go to the hospital. Every morning, I am grateful. I have a place to go, things to do. And I am not alone.

This is a time of discovery, an opportunity for me to figure out what I value most. This is life after New Orleans, Lou-ze-anna, life beyond the levee breaks and all the water that is rushing into the city. This is life in Tennessee.

Buddhists call it the "vast expanse." In Buddhism, the vast expanse involves traveling a life that flows eternally, even in furious times. These are furious times. And here I am, traveling the vast expanse. This expanding vastness isn't nothing; it's being totally open, without being attached to "up till now," or "later on." This is teaching me that I have been too attached to my presuppositions. This expanding vastness is emptying everything out, and emptiness allows for passage. Emptiness is the "after words;" it is full without having anything in it. This is lost time, and I try to focus on time and not on being lost.

One of the hospital staff hears about two local churches. One is offering dinner to anyone who is evacuated. Another is offering dinner and has converted part of their parish hall into a makeshift donation center. Several of us decide to go as a group for dinner and to see what the donation center looks like. The hospital staff and its volunteers, individuals from different New Orleans neighborhoods, are becoming a tiny community, a "we" and an "us."

The dinner is salad, pasta, thick slabs of Italian bread with butter. The room is full of people. We all have fuzzy looks, our faces different degrees of shell-shocked. After we eat, we investigate the donation area: long folding tables piled with clothing, shoes, purses, belts, neckties. A few tables are stacked with baby items, bibs, small clothes, diapers, containers of formula, wipes. The dinner and the donations are small miracles.

I evacuated with one pair of shoes, the flip-flops on my feet. I find a pair of sneakers that fit, three pairs of pants, a couple of shirts, and a hand-knit red, black, and white sweater. Twenty years later, I still have the hand-made sweater. I call it my EvacuSweater.

The local news says that ten thousand people from all over the Gulf South have evacuated to Memphis. More are coming every day. In New Orleans, water continues to gush over and through the broken levees. At the hospital, I learn everyone's name, the doctors, the administrators, the therapists, the social workers, the music therapist, and the patients. The patients sometimes tell me what happened before they ended up at the hospital. Sometimes they don't. Always, I offer a smile and a greeting to whoever may be passing by the desk.

At night, I use the hotel computers to email coworkers and friends. I am grateful. Everyone has made it out. Their stories are miracles.

Dinner at the church becomes a regular thing. We go, sit with strangers, folks from Alabama, Mississippi, other parts of Louisiana, share a meal, stories about our neighborhoods, our families, our jobs. There is grief. There is confusion. There is anger. There is laughter too. We are together.

Some tech genius develops an online water-level tracker to measure flooding in the city of New Orleans and the surrounding area. The water level can be tracked by address. Using one of the computers at the hospital, visiting the website to check the water level becomes something we all do.

There is no water on the cul-de-sac at the edge of the levee where my friend and her husband's home is. My home is under eleven feet of water. Some of us have homes under twenty-two feet of water.

Each day at the hospital, there are things to do, ways to help.

I don't just brew the coffee. I am learning the intimacy and intracity of a cup of coffee. I learn who likes it black. Who wants two sugars and a little of the powdered stuff. Who wants the real-deal Stonyfield milk. Or better yet, half-and-half. Who likes their coffee really sweet. Who wants pink packets instead of sugar, or yellow ones, and how many. Who can't stand it unless there's two drops of milk and a quarter-teaspoon of sugar only. And, who wants to drink coffee all day, or just a cup in the morning. Learning about how people like their coffee goes for everyone, medical staff and patients alike.

FEMA becomes a way to find some relief. And a challenge to navigate. We share information with each other. The best time to call is late at night. At the church dinners, we tell others so that they too can get through, talk to an actual person, and be able to file a claim.

Music is its own kind of medicine. The hospital's music therapist is in a band. Another hospital staff member plays guitar and sings. Several of us start going to B. B. King's Blues Club on Beale Street. The music is a gift. We dance. We sing. Our voices rise, fall, and rise again. Music transforms us in these moments. We are released from everything, from sorrow, from frustration, from rage, from powerlessness. And we are together.

In these moments of lostness, my mind is a room always moving, and the wind is a pen writing stories. The wind's stories fill the room of my mind until my breath pens a version of these stories from my lips back out onto the pages of the air. Do we tear at the dark, or dance in it? Flowing is the ability to maintain in the midst of movement. Maintaining in the flow is to be full while empty, full of beauty, and where it leads, and beauty leads to jubilation. It has taken me years to make sense of this bit of wisdom, make it more than just something I have read somewhere. These little insights are fleeting, pieces in the flow of forever, little insights I focus on while I try to get my bearings.

Beauty, to be full while falling away, is like fruit; it has to be full to fall. There would be no falling if things didn't ripen. When something is ripest, when it is its most delicious, the branch becomes empty in the fall. We are like the empty branch, and to live a ripe life is to constantly let go. The full fruit falls off because it is full of beauty. The empty space is the big mark that questions—what's next?

I consider this question with my new friends as we sit in Memphis under a full moon. We have come to see the hospital's music therapist and his band play. Closing my eyes for a moment on Beale Street, it could be New Orleans in November. The music. The breeze. Instead, it is mid-September in Tennessee. Someone in our group starts a second line. A main-line is a parade's core. It's made of elaborately decorated floats and riders, or Carnival krewes. Social aid & pleasure clubs, or krewes, sponsor each parade. Krewe members often are from the neighborhoods where their particular parade rolls. The revelers that go to these parades are called the second line. The second line is also a traditional jazz dance, and what happens on the way back from the cemetery, joy in the middle of a funeral.

We second line around the bar, weaving in and out of customers, waving napkins and bar towels. We swing our hips, step and slide our feet; these moments are ripening in the vast expanse that is now. Even the fountain in the middle of the bar's courtyard joins the celebration; it sprays us with water each time our second line passes. We can be lost in the brokenness of the flood, or we can find a way to swim.

We orbit again, the breeze sprinkles me, and I think about us. The broken levees have brought us here. This second line says New Orleans has been spread—its traditions sparkle in every shimmy and sliding step. New Orleans is alive and well and living somewhere else, just for now. Each of these new moments is a ripened fruit we are collecting and saving for later. Noise and movement and people, we have all been scattered here, and like fruit, what we carry inside us, the memories, the stories, the dance, the music will land in the next moment; it will sprout, and bloom, bloom like this second line. Catharsis can come with tears or laughter. Dancing is a way to carry laughter throughout the body and bring it to the feet. There is so much beauty in dancing, in being able to laugh. Laughter is the pathway to release. Second-lining is a New Orleans lesson in rejuvenation; this second line in a Memphis bar is a way to make life out of death. Time continues to churn, carrying us along with all the moments we have collected. Tonight, we dance; we are small orbiting colors, scattering little bits of the city that we still call home.

September 24, Hurricane Rita crashes into the coast. The levees are still broken. Water surges over, around, and through the breaks. New Orleans stays underwater.

At the hospital, routines continue. There is a technique to emptying the hospital trash cans in the place where we are, the temporarily designated section for the evacuated patients. The trash can by the desk is a small wastebasket. It fills up fastest. Mostly paper. It might need to be emptied twice a day. Just dumped. The bag doesn't need to be changed. The one in the other room, near the coffee maker, is messy. And bigger. The whole bag has to be pulled out at least twice a day. Someone from the main hospital comes by during the day with a gray cart and takes the full trash bags away. I keep spare trash bags in the garbage can near the coffeemaker. They're stored at the bottom of the can, under the one being used. After I pull out the full bag, I grab another from the bottom of the can, shake it open, and put it in. It makes the process go a little faster.

When I was a child, I believed there were things to hold on to—hands, tire swings, monkey bars, steering wheels—things to reach out for and grab hold of. These were the things I thought would guide me. I didn't know it was the leaping into empty space, not the grabbing hold afterward, that would teach me the most. The things I am learning to reach for are the hands of the compass, the internal one and the one outside. Both point to travel. The internal one isn't tangible; it's the small voice that tells me which way to go. The outside one contains points in all directions and changes depending on which way I turn. Taking hold of both of them is like reaching for the leap itself.

At the hospital, we also reach for each other, hands, hugs, a shoulder to cry on; being together is a gift. Someone donates tickets for the annual Mid-South Fair to the hospital staff. Chaka Khan is the headliner at an outdoor concert that is part of the fair. Several of us go.

It is glorious. The air is cooler. The sky is tinted with gold. Chaka Khan and her band fill the evening air with beauty. Song and music flow over and around us. We sing along. We dance on the grass. And we are not alone.

One of the hospital staff learns about the emergency financial assistance the Red Cross is providing. Another person learns about assistance being offered by The Salvation Army. A plan is made for us to go together in groups.

I have only the money I evacuated with, which is down to a few dollars and some change. And there is no possibility of work. This assistance is another blessing. We carpool. At the Salvation Army and the Red Cross, we each sit with a worker one at a time, answer questions, fill out and sign paperwork. In addition to financial assistance, The Salvation Army also has vouchers for furniture. As we complete our own paperwork, we are also there if anyone in our group needs help.

All of the patients that have evacuated to Memphis have to be placed. Some are admitted to other hospitals. Some return to their families. I field phone calls between hospitals, connect staff, pass messages along, greet people when they come to pick someone up, and wish the patients well when they leave. Soon all the patients that evacuated to Memphis have been discharged. The hospital staff begin to go their separate ways. One of the therapists and her husband want to give me a gift. It is their second car, an older Honda with two hundred thousand miles. This gift is totally unexpected; receiving it is another moment of beauty in furious times. There is a ragged crack that runs all the way across the Honda's windshield. The upholstery is worn away in places. The tint is peeling off the back windows.

I love this gift. I name her Pearl after the Janis Joplin album and because she is a shade of pearlescent green. I now have independence, a way to navigate Memphis on my own. And I can drive back to New Orleans.

As we go through the process of discharging the patients, several of us choose to have a FEMA apartment in Memphis. FEMA will also cover the cost of utilities and a phone. We ride together looking at apartments, houses for rent, signing leases, getting gas, lights and water turned on.

The highway in Memphis, I-40 to I-240, is a big loop around the city. Memphis itself is very spread out. My apartment is in a small subdivision on a wooded street, one of the exits off 240.

It will take a month to turn on my landline. I don't want to be away from everything and unable to call people if I need to. I finally break down and get a cell phone, something I've been resisting. Twenty years later, I still have the same cell number.

I use the vouchers from The Salvation Army to get furniture: a mattress and box spring, a small couch, a chair, a TV. I also get housewares, plates, glasses, coffee cups. I use the cash assistance for silverware, a cast-iron frying pan, dish rags, pillows, bedding, a few more clothes, the everyday details of life.

One of my jobs emails me. They offer nine hours a week. I take it. I want to return to New Orleans, to help put things back together however I can. I begin to work remotely. I use a computer in the public library. This technology is a gift, and I am grateful.

One of my new friends from the hospital uses his FEMA assistance to rent a small house. He has decided to transfer hospitals and stay in Memphis. He used to live in New Orleans East. He feels like there is nothing there to go back to now.

He has his eight-year-old daughter with him. They evacuated together. I go over to their new home to eat dinner, watch TV, check email on the computer. Sometimes I take them out to dinner or spend the day with his daughter while he's at work. There is a herd of buffalo a short way from my apartment. We like to go walking there.

It is a gradual get-to-know-you process between us and the buffalo. At first, they stand far away in their enclosure, looking at us. Over time, they come closer. Eventually they let us touch their large, wooly bodies through the wire fence. Then, often, when they see us, they come up to the fence and rub against it. Neither she nor I had ever seen a buffalo in real life before. They are gentle and beautiful, another blessing.

One evening, while I'm at their home checking email, I get one from Carol Bebelle, executive director of Ashé Cultural Arts Center. She is reaching out to every artist who has ever worked with Ashé. She wants to find out if we are alright, what we are doing now.

I call Carol on my new cell phone. She has evacuated to upstate Louisiana. When I tell her about my employment situation, she offers me a job part-time. I am grateful; she is giving me a major blessing, a blessing that will last for years. And I now have even more ability to return.

In October, another hospital friend and I travel to Mississippi. We visit the crossroads. Growing season has come and gone. On either side of the road, as far as the eye can see, are empty, brown fields.

Clarksdale, Route 61 and Route 49. Ground zero for the beginning of the blues. We go to a bar with the same name to hear music. It is jam night. The bar is packed. In the crowd, we sing along and dance. It is a night filled with joy.

In Memphis, once I am moved in, other friends come to visit me in my FEMA apartment. These friends have also evacuated. We are navigating the temporary together.

Nanette has a brother who lives in Memphis with his family. She has been staying with them. She helps me make arrangements so I can return to New Orleans to see what is left of my apartment and clean it out. And she takes me to buy garbage bags, the heavy duty kind.

My friend and his daughter agree to babysit Taylor. Nanette drives us to New Orleans. The plan is a day to drive down, a day to clean out what is left, and a day to drive back. It is the first time either one of us have been back since the levees broke.

Nanette has a musician friend who lives four blocks from my New Orleans efficiency. Bienville Ridge saved that side of the neighborhood. The south streets, where I lived, went under water. The north streets are higher and dry.

The first night we are back, Nanette's friend shares sleeping bags, lets us crash on his living room floor. Nanette brings gloves and a special mask for me to wear, one with eye protection and a respirator. The following day, driving from one side of the neighborhood to the other is another story in separating.

The November morning is bright and clear. The streets where Nanette's musician friend lives have houses with plants out front, porch swings, blooming flowers, bright colors. Once we cross Bienville Ridge, everything is gray. The houses, the trees, what is left of the plants. Nothing is growing on this side.

My apartment with its split open kitchen walls is still standing. Everything inside it is not. The refrigerator is lying on its back. There are several sludgy pools of water spanning what used to be my living room carpet. Everything is topsy turvy. And gray.

There is a technique to emptying my apartment, to filling the trash bags. Softer things go in first. I wrap broken things with sharp edges. I don't want anyone who may pick up the bags to be injured. Once a trash bag is full, I tie the ends together in a double knot. Then I carry it down the wobbly stone steps and put it outside.

When I empty out the bathroom, I look at my reflection. The respirator covers the lower half of my face. In the mask, I resemble someone in the trenches of World War I.

I spend hours filling trash bags. What was once a pillow, sheets, blankets, photographs and albums I did not take, cassette tapes, three portfolios of artwork, theatrical costumes, makeup, scripts, books, clothes, is now sludge. The photos are melted. So is anything paper.

Miraculously, a few magnets on the refrigerator survive. Angels. One of them has a broken wing. I carefully collect them and put them in the handbag I got from the donation table in the Memphis church.

A friend's artwork has also survived. It is above the water line and, like the angels on the refrigerator, untouched by the mold. I carefully collect it too.

It is dusk when I finish. Two by two, I carry the trash bags to the front of the house and place them on the sidewalk. When I am done, there is a large pile. I take off my gloves, throw them on top of one of the garbage bags. I take off my special mask with the eye protection and the respirator. I sit on the stone front steps.

Within moments, a garbage truck turns onto my street. A man jumps down. I watch him pick up the trash bags and toss them into the back of the truck. There is a sense of emptying, of endings, of timing, and the everything that is now trash. There is also gratitude. I am able to witness this, the finality of falling off the branch. I am able to be part of the ending, the emptying of my wrecked Mid-City, New Orleans, efficiency apartment.

A few minutes after the garbage truck drives off, I hear someone in the distance announcing on a loudspeaker that they have water. The announcer gets closer; the vehicle they're driving turns on my street. It is a Red Cross truck. I thank them and take several of the water bottles they offer.

There is no electricity, no traffic lights, no street lights. As dusk turns to dark, stars become visible. Nanette pulls up and drives me back to her musician friend's home, where there is a shower, clean clothes, flashlights, a meal, and a sleeping bag. I share the water bottles. I am grateful we are together.

When we return to Memphis, I begin to look for work. Places in Memphis are reluctant to hire anyone who has evacuated. There is concern that we won't stay. I understand. Many of us are longing to go back where we came from, to go back home.

I am among the very fortunate. I have interviews for two part-time jobs teaching for the spring semester, one for a local theater company and the other at a local community center. One job is in Germantown. The other is in Collierville. Both jobs hire me. The jobs will start in January.

My best friend Juliet visits too. She has her own version of a temporary address. She's been staying with relatives, traveling from couch to couch in different parts of the country. Her New Orleans home was damaged and is undergoing repairs. She wants to see for herself.

I reach out to friends who live uptown. When the levees broke, their home got no water. They are grateful—they want us to stay there so someone will be present on the property.

Juliet and I drive to New Orleans in Pearl. After a good night's rest on the couches in the living room of my friend's Uptown home, I drop her off at her apartment and head to Ashé Cultural Arts Center for my first day of work. Ashé is very fortunate—there was only some wind damage to the roof, which means the doors can open to the community; we can be a place of refuge in many different ways.

One of the things we work on is recovery. There are grants available to help artists and culture-bearers replace materials that were damaged or destroyed. We sit individually with each artist or culture-bearer and assist them with the completion and submission of a grant application.

Time is still upended, and this is a blessing. Writing an individual grant can take hours. Before we can talk about how to replace something, we must talk about what was lost. I understand the challenge of having everything emptied. It is hard to put things in categories. It is hard to think of each thing that used to be transformed into beauty as an itemized object with a dollar value. So we sit and talk. And we figure it out together.

After work, Pearl and I pick Juliet up. We drive to the French Quarter, park, and walk to find a spot to eat. We run into Leo, one of her coworkers. He stayed in the city. He has his own stories of what happened after the levees broke. Juliet asks him if I can stay at his apartment the next time I am in New Orleans. He generously agrees. It is a blessing that will change our lives forever.

The next week, Pearl and I drive to New Orleans, and I am grateful for a new temporary place to stay. I don't want to wear out my welcome anywhere. I am grateful for Leo's couch. At different times, two different friends who didn't know each other both introduced me to Leo.

The first, Merry, introduced us at a party she was hosting in her home. My then-boyfriend and I were in her kitchen, standing next to her refrigerator. We all chatted for a few moments. A few years later, Juliet introduced us.

After that, I see him at their workplace from time to time when I stop in to visit her or pick her up.

Leo has several couches in his apartment. The next week, I arrive late in the evening, exhausted. We talk briefly and then I curl up on a couch.

The following evening after work, we have time to sit and talk. We do, for hours. Our first date is December 18.

A new type of temporary is beginning, a new routine. Each week I spend four days in Memphis and three days in New Orleans. Sometimes, it's four days in New Orleans and three in Memphis. I am traveling; navigating the vast expanse of open road is what's next.

I also begin to explore places in New Orleans I can rent. I want to have my own temporary place to return to in the city. A friend offers me a room in his home at a reasonable price. It becomes a blessing I can share with others. It will be a place of refuge I offer to Nanette and then later Merry, a room so that they have a way to move back to New Orleans.

Nanette watches over Taylor when I travel back and forth. It is a blessing for both of them. Nanette loves cats. And Taylor, my cream- and brown-furred, blue-eyed Diva Kitty, loves being pampered.

I don't always drive Pearl. Occasionally I rent a car. Once, I ride a train called The City of New Orleans. It is early morning when I board the train. There is fog. Droplets of water dapple the train's windows. The fog is so thick, it's all we can see. No trees. No buildings. No streets. Just fog.

Slowly, as we roll along the ribbon of train tracks, things become visible. First colors, then shapes, as if the world is gradually coming into focus. The sun rises. This train ride is revelation, reminder, emergence, uncertainty into clarity, what is hidden shifting to what can be seen.

I don't always drive back and forth alone. Occasionally Juliet rides with me. She is flowing with her own temporary couch to couch.

Sometimes Pearl's radio works. And sometimes it doesn't. Sometimes Pearl's engine overheats. And sometimes it doesn't. When she overheats, sometimes Pearl stalls out and sometimes she doesn't. On the weekly trek over the roads that branch between Memphis and New Orleans, new habits emerge. I am a person who loves to drive. I get behind the wheel and then go, go, go, only stopping to refuel. Pearl's engine insists that motion also means making time for rest, for staying put. Pearl insists we have moments to pause, to get out and stretch, to get a bite to eat.

Pearl is a lesson about cycles. With time, overheating passes. Her engine cools. We can get back on the road again.

It snows in Memphis in the winter. I am grateful again for the makeshift donation center in the Memphis church. Another thing I find on one of the folding tables is a three-quarter-length purple coat. It's filled with downy feathers. It keeps me warm throughout this Memphis winter.

When seasons change, I learn another new ritual. It is springtime in Memphis. In the spring, there are tornadoes.

One afternoon, I arrive at the elementary school where I teach for the theater company. It is the end of the school day. I walk into the classroom where I teach. In the classroom, there are individual desks that I usually ask the students to pull to the side to give us an open floor space to move. All the children are under these desks. So is the classroom teacher. The school is finishing a tornado drill. As the drill concludes, they all emerge; it's like plants emerging above the ground.

Gratitude helps to reveal possibility within the circumstances of a situation. Opportunities can emerge. Even when one is out in the open, in seemingly impossible spaces.

Another spring day, there is a banshee raging outside Pearl the Honda's window. The banshee, a siren perched atop a metal tower, extends its long scream as I drive to my Memphis FEMA apartment, an address a little further away from temporary and a little closer to permanent. The sirens will scream for hours when there are tornadoes around. The announcer on Pearl's tiny radio tells me that, if I am driving, I should pull over and seek shelter in a ditch.

The sky distracts me as I drive. The moving wind is writing its own messages on the clouds. Lying still on the ground is the only thing that can be done if you are caught outside when a tornado takes over the air.

Not too long after, I have an encounter with a snake. I am walking a trail that connects my subdivision to the rest of the complex. The snake stretches like a green, striped ribbon across the trail's muddy slope. As I descend, it lays perfectly still. I began to think it is dead. Evidence that others have followed this same path is everywhere. Empty plastic soda bottles, a basketball hoop on wheels, and shards of what might have, at one time, been a child's large dump truck are scattered in the middle, and along the trail's edges. I begin to imagine that the bearers of these objects also encountered the snake, when its head moves. Carefully, I walk around the snake's full length while it remains motionless. A turn of the head is the only indication it is still alive. When I return minutes later, it is gone.

Some see snakes as the ever-turning circle of beginning to end to beginning again.

Like Pearl's engine, this snake is part of the "vast expanse" and the balance between motion and stillness. Stretched out on the trail, the snake is in its moment of temporary, too.

What alerts a snake to danger? What do their eyes witness as they roam the woods? What radar detected the echoes of my feet?

After the encounter, I begin investigating the eastern ribbon snake. They are flexible and quick. They are not known for sitting still, or for living in Tennessee. Normally, they are ready to run away or, if they feel cornered, bite. Maybe this snake was in search of a southern chorus Frog or a southern spring peeper when I interrupted it. The snake's eyes gave away nothing. I have heard frog song in the evening when I walk the trail. I don't know their tunes well enough to distinguish different frogs from one another, and I have never been able to get close enough to see them when they sing. I passed within inches of its body. Why didn't this snake run, or strike? And, what was it doing in Memphis?

I feel camaraderie with this particular eastern ribbon snake. Both of us are out of our element. Both of us have no choice but to flatten ourselves down in the face of the coming storm. The safest spot in a tornado is a cellar. Snakes sequester themselves below soil by borrowing someone else's basement. It could be an anthill or an abandoned mouse den; either will work.

I, too, am in need of borrowing something below ground. My apartment in this subdivision is on the second floor. The spot farthest from all the windows is the bathroom. I chose this particular apartment partly as a reaction; I desired elevation. Single stories, like my New Orleans Mid-City apartment, tend to flood more easily. I lived near City Park, one of the lowest points in the city. The lower they are, the more vulnerable. In Memphis, the reverse is true: the higher up something is, the more dangerous. I am like the eastern ribbon snake, caught on the trail, exposed, and in full view of the impending sky.

Like the eastern ribbon snake, the sky, too, keeps secrets. Tornadoes defy prediction. They keep their size and speed and the path they will travel to themselves. The Fujita scale measures the aftermath, not the actual rate of the wind's rotation. There is nothing that measures their movement. Like the snake, radar measures the rate and direction of an echo's return to determine a tornado's foot steps. This tracking measurement is still just an educated guess.

This sky is something alien, cleanly divided between dark and light. It is a foreign object. The clouds move of their own accord. The snake's skin is a series of cleanly defined stripes; they, too, section distinctly into light and dark. The snake and I share something: we are both powerless in the face of this storm. The snake and the sky share something: their tremulous natures are both of the unknown.

This snake is another reminder about the opened branch, the empty place that is part of learning, making do in the moment to moment in furious times.

This snake is a message about flexibility, stillness and perseverance, the inherent right of all living things to exist.

This eastern ribbon snake and I are travelers. The sky has brought us to this spot. This is not the first time wind and rain have brought strangers to Memphis. On January 15, 1877, after a particularly violent storm, snakes were found everywhere. Hundreds of them covered the ground for a two-block radius, like fish out of water. No one knows how they got there. It was not the first or the last time visitors accompanied the rain.

Many papers and journals, including *Symons's' Monthly Meteorological Magazine*, *Scientific American*, the *London Daily News*, *The Zoologist*, *The London Times*, *The Journal of the Asiatic Society of Bengal*, the *Philadelphia Public Ledger*, *La science pour tous*, *Nature*, and *The New York Times*, have reported strange groups of things found clustered together—snakes, fish, toads, and frogs, all materializing in abundance around the time of fierce storms. Humans, it seems, are not the only creatures who favor mass evacuation and togetherness.

Tornadoes and hurricanes are kin, their turning winds on kissing terms with humidity. Tornadoes are more about taking cover. Hurricanes are more about getting out of the way.

I am getting tired of this wind and its constant interruptions. Maybe I am not paying close enough attention to echoes. Maybe I should be more like the eastern ribbon snake.

Gratitude also means giving grace to myself. I take a moment to breathe. Inhale. Exhale. Sometimes, the only wise choice is to stay put.

And sometimes, the only wise choice is to move.

Across the world, many cultures see snakes as a representation of the connection between destruction and creation. Transformation leads to healing. Hope and fear are both part of considering what is beyond, the "what's next?" after the emptying.

Who listens when the wind is weeping? When the air comes whooshing through and the world rumbles, who wonders about where the air came from and why it is so rough? What does the wind retain, and what does it release? The in and out of breath, the holding a breath in place can mirror, can be a companion to the language of the wind.

The wind looks open, but it can be cluttered with ideas, conversations, collections of waves, electronic transmissions, little bits of coded nomials traversing from Earth to satellites, then back to computers and cell phones. The wind can be cluttered with fine particulate, tiny pieces of what was burned in petrochemical factories and coal plants. The wind's back and forth travel knows no boundaries, state lines, borders, or walls. The wind is full while appearing empty. Little impedes its trajectory or what it transports. Who has the keys to read what is encrypted?

Things I think about while Pearl and I drive around Memphis. Things I think about while Pearl and I cross intersections, enter or exit highways, roll past speed limits and route markers. Things I think about while I wait for Pearl to cool enough so that her engine can start again.

On March 4th, in the wee hours of the morning, I arrive back in New Orleans. Leo has been waiting for me. I call to let him know where I am parking. He comes to meet me, and we walk back to his apartment. He has a home-cooked meal waiting.

After we eat, he asks me to sit next to him. He is nervous and resolute at the same time. He takes my hand, looks into my eyes, and asks me to marry him. I say yes. It is a gift emerging from the emptied, from the broken and scattered, the beginning of a brand-new journey, one that will last for decades. And I am grateful.

INSIDE THE CONE OF UNCERTAINTY:
Between the Dark & the Light

JOSÉ TORRES-TAMA

> More and more I feel that the people of ill will have used time much more effectively than have the people of good will. We will have to repent in this generation not merely for the hateful words and actions of the bad people, but for the appalling silence of the good people.
> — Martin Luther King Jr., "Letter from Birmingham Jail"[45]

1. *Escape on a Stolen School Bus Three Days After the Levees Breached*
New Orleans has been my muse and adopted home since 1984, and three days after Hurricane Katrina exposed the weakness of poorly built and underfunded federal levees that breached easily in her crosshairs, I escaped my beloved "Babylon by the Bayou" on a stolen school bus—operated by a yin-yang duo of heroic buccaneers rescuing African American families.

Like thousands who did not evacuate, I was trapped in my darlin' New Orleans, but the fates intervened to offer an improbable escape from the "apocalyptic abandonment" of our drowning town by "Dubya" and the incompetent cronies of his corrupt Republican administration. Let's not forget Bush Jr. sold us a war in Iraq built on lies and "weapons of mass distraction." We, melanated people of power, we must dare to remember. As a poet, it's best for me to share some verse that addresses my post-storm trauma and what I observed from a despicable government response that killed a thousand-plus people in New Orleans.

---

45   Martin Luther King Jr., *Why We Can't Wait* (New York: Signet Books, 1964), 86.

I wrote to remember

in the immediate days after Katrina
our people were dying in the toxic floodwaters
Let's not forget Bush was on vacation
visited Arizona Senator McCain for his birthday
played air guitar with country singer Mark Wills
and our people were dying in our darlin' New Orleans
I wrote to remember
Let's not forget
Dick Cheney was fly-fishing on holiday
and our people were dying in our darlin' New Orleans
I wrote to remember
Let's not forget
Secretary of State Condoleezza Rice
at a Broadway play called *Spamalot*
and New Yorkers collectively booed from their seats
because our people were dying in our darlin' New Orleans
I wrote to remember
later she went shopping for Ferragamo thousand-dollar shoes
and a saleswoman chastised her for criminal negligence
because our people were dying in our darlin' New Orleans
I wrote to remember
that Chertoff, head of Homeland Security, declared
"We are extremely pleased with the response
that every element of the federal government,
all of our federal partners, have made to this terrible tragedy"
But our people were dying in our darlin' New Orleans
I wrote to remember
he lied without warrant while body count mounted
Let's not forget
nefarious spin-master Karl Rove
pimped media blame of city government
and Louisiana for disastrous federal fallout
because our people were dying
in the flooded streets of our darlin' New Orleans
I wrote to remember

INSIDE THE CONE OF UNCERTAINTY:
BETWEEN THE DARK & THE LIGHT

To add more insult to our serious injury, Dubya was quoted as stating, "Brownie, you're doing a heck of a job!" while our people drowned and the cadaver casualties mounted.[46] His callous and clueless statement was in reference to Michael Brown, who had no business being positioned as the head of FEMA and was exposed as another incompetent political crony. However, the "United States of AMNESIA" seduces you to embrace forgetting. We, the real people, must dare to remember.

As a performance artist, published playwright, and interdisciplinary troublemaker, "I channel my intrinsic immigrant courage and dare to remember," and twenty years ago, I remember escaping on the same bus as the iconic composer, singer, and native musical-genius son Allen Toussaint, who rode out of the social storm that followed the natural tempest. The Jefferson Parish School bus our good pirates commandeered delivered us to an illuminated and dry Baton Rouge Airport—as midnight merged into the very early morning of Thursday, September 1, 2005. We were catapulted into a dream reality with lights and electricity from a world that had become a living nightmare only eighty miles away. I had to flee a US city in peril—not via the efforts of "authorized personnel" or the many invisible "FEMA armies of compassion," who were AWOL, absent without leave five days after Katrina hit—but via a pirated vehicle operating the kind of rescue mission only imagined in a Hollywood South film version of *Hotel Rwanda*.

When recalling what happened, it plays out like a contrived screenplay, but we were delivered to the welcoming arms of Laura and Andrei Codrescu. Andrei has been a compatriot of the "sacred word," *un amigo poeta*, for decades now, and at the time, he was still teaching poetry at LSU in Baton Rouge. In another *Mission Impossible*–like scenario, I had saved one cell phone bar when the electricity had gone down three days before on that fateful Monday, August 29, 2005, and turned it off for any possible future use. I remember thinking to have some charge left on that antiquated silver flip phone in case of an even greater emergency need—not knowing when it would be of any use because "Ms. Bad Thing Katrina" had knocked out all the power grids in her wake.

We were without electricity a full three days before our liberating bus ride. As our rescue vehicle hit Gonzalez, Louisiana, with lights illuminating the 1-10 highway out of hell, I figured the cell towers were also working. The roads were finally lit, and we literally rode out of the darkness, which had

---

46 "KATRINA/AL BUSH/BROWN," posted July 21, 2016, by CNN, YouTube, 1 min, 1 sec., https://www.youtube.com/watch?v=x0TFv70v1uQ.

consumed the highway some fifty miles to that west-Louisiana point of our most unimaginable school bus escape. I turned my Motorola phone on, and its frame came to life—lighting up like some little robot awakened from a dreadful slumber. I scrolled for his number, and it was fortuitous that it started with an A. I called Codrescu, the famous Romanian poet, writer, and NPR commentator, with the iconic Eastern-European accent of his Transylvania-peppered English. I've known Andrei for some thirty years now.

I managed to reach him and blurted out, "We're on a bus that will drop us off at midnight at the Baton Rouge Airport." Then, the cell phone immediately died. In their petite vehicle, Laura and Andrei ushered our traumatized bodies to the safety of their home. They offered us priceless refuge, scrambled eggs with tomatoes, strong coffee, much needed compassion, and Internet access. I escaped with my then partner, Claudia Copeland, my writer friend Jimmy Nolan, who is a fifth-generation native born in the middle of an unnamed hurricane, and his neighbor, Kip, who was on his third day of survival without access to the dialysis machine that kept him alive.

2. We, the Ones Who Do Not Evacuate

We, the ones who stubbornly stay from one hurricane to another that places us in the "cone of uncertainty," do so because we understand that our human resilience after the natural storm will help rebuild and weather whatever Mother Nature decides to throw at us. We know how to live with hurricanes and their aftermath, but we were not prepared for the official sequestering that unleashed an even more furious storm of urban desperation that festered like an untreated wound in an August summer. Also, it's important to note that evacuation is a privilege, and a costly one at that. Not everyone can afford it, and the term "hurrication" has evolved from that privilege. I'm a working-class interdisciplinary immigrant artist and can rarely afford to just leave. Also, at this time, I had no vehicle to evacuate with.

Yes, Katrina was a force to be reckoned with, and her damage was more catastrophic than Hurricane Andrew, which hit west of New Orleans in the early 1990s. Yes, there was flooding in New Orleans East, the 9th Ward, the Lakeview area, and 80 percent of our darlin' New Orleans was underwater. However, it was never immediately reported that most of the Old Quarter and parts of the historic neighborhood called Faubourg Marigny, which borders the Vieux Carré, were mostly above water. Actually, we were very dry only hours after the Category Three pounding of Katrina. Having no TV access, we were unaware of the dire flooded conditions of the rest of the city. I believe we were recipients of all the prayers and rituals that keep New Orleans from total destruction because the Virgin Mary, Yemaya, and the river goddesses always protect us at the last possible minute—even Katrina did not hit us directly with her unrelenting winds and water. This city that knows respect for the ancient ones, this city of ghosts and ancestors, is ultimately protected by the magic chants, offerings, and incantations of the local priestesses and practitioners of Voodoo, who are at work every hurricane season to make their voices heard so that Mother Nature veers her force just enough to allow us another year of life at the Mississippi River's edge. I have more faith in the Voodoo practitioners and their prayers for the city than the officials of local government, whose initial perplexing propositions plunged us into greater chaos after the storm.

    Our City Hall is located at 1300 Perdido Street, and in Spanish, "*perdido*" means lost. It's a precarious address name and number combination for our mayoral seat of power, but it could be the more esoteric reason why leadership there is generally a mess and severely lacking coherent direction. When the storm hit, I lived in the 2300 block of Dauphine Street in the Marigny neighborhood, which extends downriver, east of the Quarter. We were mostly dry, and the camelback house I rented had some damage, with its cheap vinyl siding blown along the side yard. I am a pantheist, meaning that I respect many religious beliefs, and like other New Orleanians, I have many altars in my shotgun apartments. I am in big belief that the one altar to La Virgen María inspired the large fig tree in my backyard to fall towards the spacious open green space and away from the back porch. In fact, I had a gray cement statue of the Virgin Mary that had been positioned in a grassy cove between the two backyard trees, and before Katrina arrived, I placed her in the safety of the kitchen hallway. The large fig tree that fell would have crushed her, and had it fallen in the opposite direction, it would have crushed half of the house. Gabriel García Márquez, the godfather of magical realism, referred to la Nueva Orleáns as the northernmost point of the Caribbean, and it serves as my own personal Macondo, the fabled town of his masterpiece novel *One Hundred Years of Solitude*. Magic happens here, and so does tragedy.

    New Orleans occupies a rather precarious territory geographically and geopolitically, and it's inside and outside of the US simultaneously. Across the universe, it resides in the collective imaginations of people as the mythic birthplace of jazz. I find its swamp topography and the unique historical Spanish colonial architecture of the old city streets, where ghosts linger from one century to another, a fantastic setting that can transport you through a time warp and land you in another era. Its Catholic pagan hedonism; Yoruba-infused practices and Voodoo rituals; general inclination to debauchery; and the raucous celebratory spirit of its people offer a much more agreeable social landscape to inhabit, and it's Deep South enough to escape the puritanical tentacles that haunt and control the rest of this Anglican stronghold.

Ours was a miraculous escape through a wormhole that led us from one difficult dimension to a saner matrix with electricity and measures of civility still in place. Our bus rumbled down the highway with piercing headlights that cut two cone beams towards an infinite darkness for the first fifty miles before Gonzales, but we were in transit towards the light at sixty miles per hour. It was a stunning sight to pull up to the Baton Rouge Airport—lit like an elongated Christmas tree with fluorescent radiance. With his then wife Laura, Andrei greeted us with celebratory hugs of great relief, and the three of us, Claudia, Jimmy, and I, squeezed into the back passenger seats of their compact car. Kip did not join us, but I believe he took a flight elsewhere to meet family.

From the safety of their home, I scripted my first post-Katrina essay, titled "Hurricane Katrina and the Chaos of New Orleans in Her Aftermath." This piece was distributed widely and published on various sites and, with the support of well-known writer friends, Ariel Dorfman, playwright of the famous *Death and the Maiden*, and Guillermo Gómez-Peña, iconic, legendary performance artist and MacArthur Fellowship winner, was shared internationally. Also, it was published in numerous hard copy magazines, and it was the first account by a Latino writer who had survived the storm. I was a real-life, media-branded "storm refugee." I had not witnessed the raging hurricane on TV but had lived through it and actually escaped my beloved city submerged in social chaos and misery on a pirated school bus. This essay was also distributed widely through the support of the National Performance Network (NPN) and its presenting partners.

Shortly thereafter, Leo Garcia, then the artistic director of Highways Performance Space and Gallery in Santa Monica, California, extended an invitation to me—based on reading this account. I became an "artist in exile," and he encouraged me to transform that first cyber essay and others that followed into a new performance piece. Every week, I was scripting a new essay and sending it out via cyberspace through various networks and my own growing listserv and newsletter. When Leo made the initial heartfelt offer, I asked him to give me twenty-four hours to respond. I was deeply traumatized and was not sure I could script a "show" and memorize the twenty-plus pages that my solo performance texts normally run. However, the next day, I agreed, and it turned out to be the perfect creative strategy to address and release the storm trauma trapped in my body.

3. SPIC: I Am Brown Therefore I am Suspect / Transforming Trauma Into Performance

Performance art, my visual art practices, and the crafting of bilingual verse are all creative strategies to exorcise the many derogatory demons and expletives launched at me because of my "permanent suntan" during my challenging immigrant journey in "GrinGoLandia." I am a *Mestizo*, Ecuadorian-born, Brown immigrant of Quechua indigenous descent. "*Mestizo*" is the term used to describe someone of mixed European and indigenous heritage in the Spanish empire. The term codifies me as a bastard progeny of the Spanish raping of our indigenous mothers in Latin America, and wherever the Spanish conquered. Also, note that I will refrain from referring to the US as "America." I will refer to it as "GrinGoLandia" and remind you all that in geographical, three-dimensional reality, there is actually South America and Central America as well. The United States is in "North America." Even Mexico is in North America. I'm just saying.

Above all, I consider myself a bilingual citizen of the hemispheric Americas. Also, my writings are inspired by my conceptual mentor, Eduardo Galeano, the South American journalist, intellectual historian, and genre-bending writer from Uruguay, who believed in chronicling a people's history as more truthful narratives to counter the "official lies" forged by governments and their accomplices in the controlled spheres of historical accounts—where colonizers advantageously distort truth to benefit their crimes.

Galeano states that we, too, in Latin America "dream," and that we cannot allow the United States to take hostage the moniker of "America" for itself— as all that is good and noble. I add that we are well aware that the "United States of North America" has had a tough time living up to its press release identity as the "beacon of democracy" in the free world. Galeano's *Open Veins of Latin America: Five Centuries of the Pillage of a Continent* should be required reading for anyone trying to understand the historical subjugation of the South American continent where I was born. It's an oppression first spearheaded by Spanish conquistadors, who established the premiere template for conquering by framing genocidal practices as "discovery." Also, Galeano addresses the many other European colonizers and nations that took turns from one century to another to rape and pillage Latin American and Caribbean countries, and it includes the Portuguese, French, Dutch, and English. All these current "democracies"—and, of course, the "captains of capitalism" in the US—exploited our human and natural resources. This self-proclaimed "beacon of democracy" not only engaged in pillaging our Latin American nations, but has also supported numerous barbaric dictatorships and death squads from Nicaragua to Chile to the Dominican Republic—to name just a few—for corporate and political plundering.

As part of my artist statement, I often express that I dare to speak truth to the perverse abuse of power in the "United States of AMNESIA," which seduces its people to embrace forgetting. I dare to remember! Already, this may be too much truth for some of you to consider further reading. If so, I understand. Ironically enough, I am writing to you from my adopted home that applauds "freedom of speech" as one its most cherished tenets, yet encourages its citizens to indulge in mindless consumerism as a truer expression of individual "purchase freedom." Across the land, it inspires the burning of books that challenge its many original sins. ¡Ay, caramba!

While the n-word is employed to disparage African Americans, I was often called a "SPIC" in the so-called "liberal" northeast of the New York–New Jersey tribal cultural labyrinth—where I was raised before migrating to the Deep South. This is a common derogatory term thrown at Latin American, Cuban, Mexican, and Puerto Rican people to diminish us—make us feel inferior. The teen sons and daughters of Irish, Italian, and Polish immigrant parents hurled "SPIC" at me daily, and I saw red-fire yellow when this hateful term landed on my body like the violent curse word it was meant to be. That we were all Catholics mattered little. Even the worship of the same God was not enough to eradicate such learned hatred from their working-class parents. We were all fighting for space and the real estate of things in the cramped, working-class Jersey City neighborhoods under the shadow of Big Apple Gotham. Such immigrants of European descent easily migrated towards "whiteness," and it offered them an Anglican umbrella to "discriminate" against others. Such is the hierarchical racism that I experienced in the "liberal" Northeast, where previously diminished European immigrants learned to easily hate others. Black and Brown people were the main targets and recipients of their adopted racism.

Making art in a variety of genres keeps me sane and allows me to address the trauma immigrants like myself face in this hypocritical system, and maybe—just maybe—it will contribute to a more expansive human narrative on the storm for this twentieth-anniversary remembrance. My creative locuras dare to expose the underbelly of the American Dream mythology that too often transforms into a nightmare for immigrants in a system still submerged in white supremacist beliefs and a "plantation paradigm."

I am Brown therefore I am suspect

I am Latino therefore I am spicy
I am a poet therefore I am lonely
I studied art in college therefore I am unemployed
I am a performance artist therefore I am w e i r d
I am a c o n c e p t u a l a r t i s t therefore I am v e r y w e i r d
I speak my mind therefore I am un-patriotic
I am an immigrant therefore I am an alien
I am an intellectual therefore I am un-American
I am critical therefore I am dangerous
I am a shaman therefore I am a showman and a shyster too
I don't work nine to five therefore I am a rebel without applause
I speak Spanish to confuse my gringo audiences
therefore I am a pain in the conceptual derrière
of monolingual gatekeepers
hegemonic cultural paradigms
and nepotistic epistemologies
I often use big words therefore I am superfluous
¡Ay, caramba!

When I began this chapter, we were knee-deep in National Hispanic Heritage Month 2024 during another election year, which has spawned unprecedented "anti-immigrant hysteria." It's a reminder that I am still an immigrant. I am still a "SPIC"—even during this festive time of year where all things "Latin" and "Hispanic" are celebrated. It's a calendar time to shine with our people's food, and our cultural contributions are actually acknowledged by many institutions trying to do the right thing. We must dare to remember in a media-obsessed culture drowning in cyber misinformation and official government lies.

Such lies were abundant and evident during the "great flood" of New Orleans. I've always been intrigued by the hurricane weather term "the cone of uncertainty." It's intrinsically poetic, and Hurricane Katrina had her storm eye on us in that radar-like sphere of red graphic danger on all the weather news channels. Consequently, I titled the new performance solo *The Cone of Uncertainty: New Orleans after Katrina*, and with an NPN residency grant for exiled artists and Leo Garcia's unwavering support, I debuted *The Cone* on November 3, 2005, at Highways Performance Space, outside of Los Angeles in California.

We staged four performances exactly two months after the release date of my first essay chronicling that harrowing escape. *The Cone* was the first piece actually staged across the country that was written, performed, and conceived by a "storm refugee." Also, it was the first stage show that spoke of Latin American immigrants and their vital reconstruction contributions. I honor my immigrant people in all my post-storm performances. Honestly speaking, I was terrified for the staging of *The Cone* at Highways and was consumed by the "fear of failure." I did not have enough time to rehearse, memorize, and properly prepare this newly scripted performance for a professional staging. I was composing the piece while on the road and touring as an exiled artist and storm refugee, but I threw myself into the fire—as is my bad habit.

I cannot emphasize enough how essential the support of the National Performance Network was to this staging and how vital it's been to my professional career as a performance artist. The NPN helped to launch me into the national theater arena, and in December of 1994, I was selected to showcase my first performance solo for their first annual meeting held in New Orleans. Then, the NPN was stationed in its founding city of New York. With the technical support of John Grimsley, I threw down a twenty-minute excerpt of "We Are Patriots with Dark Faces," and the full house at the Contemporary Arts Center's Black Box Theater was moved to their feet. By the fall of 1995, I was touring nationally and internationally from that NPN showcase. It helped that a veteran NPN theater artist, such as the indomitable John O'Neal, was recommending my performance to NPN presenters. John brought people to that showcase, and my life was transformed.

From 1984 to 1994, I had performed on the streets of the New Orleans Vieux Carré and supported my bad habit of creating politically provocative performance art solos by doing a commedia dell'arte street theater show, which included a fire-juggling routine and comedic sketches engaging the audience. I was fortunate to have established a relationship with O'Neal's renowned Junebug Productions company and with its then managing director James Borders, who mentored me into the NPN. For five years, I was preparing to make a leap with my performance work onto the stage, and I had begun developing some touring projects. This fall of 2025 marks thirty years that I've toured through the NPN, and they have offered me three NPN Creation Fund Awards to develop new performance projects. As such, the NPN has been very good to me, and I have cultivated a national profile with presenting partners from San Diego to Minneapolis, from Tulsa to Anchorage to Washington, DC, featuring my hybrid, genre-bending performances.

For that Highways *Cone* performance, the NPN supported my invaluable touring assistant, Sara Jane Johnson, in accompanying me in staging the four Santa Monica post-Katrina productions. It was an intrinsic part of the NPN support strategy to make sure each touring artist was able to bring a tech assistant to develop their shows. Sara Jane traveled with me on touring projects to Anchorage, DC, Tulsa, Knoxville, and a number of other cities across the country. At Highways, we pulled off four successful shows of *The Cone of Uncertainty*, and it was a minor miracle that could not have happened without Sara Jane and Leo Garcia's support.

4. Returning to Threats of Evictions from Post-Storm Property Piranhas

But before *The Cone of Uncertainty* debut at Highways, we had driven back to New Orleans and had had to sneak back to my Marigny apartment home. Concentrating on the creative aspects of staging a new performance had kept me sane and in a creative bubble that was about to burst. I was still an artist living in exile, and the city was not open for us to return. Then Mayor Ray Nagin had instituted an ill-fated "zip code re-entry plan." His fumbling and dropping the ball on supporting his desperate people and displaced constituency began to show even more. I first returned on October 1, 2005, a month after the bus escape. It was the first Saturday in October, and it marked the cultural calendar event called Art for Art's Sake, which normally was anchored by the Contemporary Arts Center, the Ogden Museum, and all the galleries in the Warehouse/Arts District. None of them opened, and their administrative people were still evacuated and taking refuge in various parts of the country.

Barrister's Gallery in Central City on O. C. Haley was the only arts venue open, and it was by the heroic efforts of its owner, Andy Antippas. Then, Barrister's occupied the space next door to the original Ashé Cultural Arts Center, on the same avenue renamed for the local civil rights icon. Oretha Castle Haley was a force to reckon with and challenged the segregated, plantation paradigm that submerged New Orleans—its people and culture. Rightfully so, Ashé was founded on the boulevard that honors her legacy, and Central City was beset by many urban challenges then. I must take a moment here to offer my kudos and thousand thanks for the support of the Ashé Cultural Arts Center. They have been an arts home for me, and I began developing cultural projects with them back in the year 2004. In many ways, I owe my cultural ascent in this city to Carol Bebelle and the honorable Doug Redd—its co-founders.

Claudia and I had driven back from my exile on a goat farm in Gainesville, Florida. She had moved there in June of 2005 to begin a postdoctoral position at the USDA offices associated with the University of Florida, home of the famous Gators football team. We flew from the Baton Rouge Airport to Gainesville after a few days of refuge at Andrei Codrescu's house. It's a near eight-hour's drive from Gainesville to New Orleans, and I made that trip numerous times in those immediate post-storm months. Back in New Orleans and after our visit with Andy at Barrister's Gallery, we slowly negotiated our way back to my apartment in the Marigny. It was a ghostly city in a post-apocalyptic landscape from some sci-fi noir epic, with cars still overturned and a plethora of abandoned and damaged houses left in Katrina's wake. Her evil twin sister, Hurricane Rita, had hit west of New Orleans by mid-September and added to the great floods of 2005. On a personal level, my biggest concern was the fifteen-plus years of artwork still hanging on the walls of that camelback shotgun, my then Marigny home.

As soon as we got to the apartment, we began addressing some of the storm damage. Our upstairs bedroom had been exposed to the rains after the vinyl siding was ripped by storm winds, and our queen-size bed was soaked with water. Much water had trickled down the Sheetrock to the downstairs walls, where my home studio was positioned, and some works-on-paper were affected but not badly damaged. I was one of the fortunate ones because other artists lost much more, but Dauphine Street in the Faubourg Marigny and through the Old Quarter is on the highest ground. After the storm, the area was not flooded. However, if you migrated towards Saint Claude Avenue, only three blocks parallel, the water was at our knees.

Like a responsible tenant, I was in touch with my landlord to offer her a report on the property, but that exchange did not go well. She began demanding rent for September, October, and November—the three months after the storm. The federal government had suspended the paying of mortgages for those three months, and I let her know that I was not going to pay rent for an apartment I could not live in because the city was severely crippled. In addition, we were not allowed to stay, and I can't even recall if we stayed the night there because the electricity was still out in the entire area. Nonetheless, she literally screamed at me, as if possessed, "THE LANDLORD DECIDES WHEN THE TENANT PAYS THE RENT!!"

Again, I let her know there was no paying of mortgages for property owners because of the federal disaster declarations to suspend mortgages, and that I could not pay rent for an apartment with no electricity that was uninhabitable in a broken city that we were not allowed to even re-inhabit then. She threatened to evict me and throw all my artworks and belongings to the streets. This was truly alarming, but like other landlords in the severely gentrified Marigny, she had morphed into what I called a "property piranha." My nearby neighbor, the one and only Margarita Bergen, a celebrated and premiere New Orleans personality and arts patron, hosted a much needed social gathering of artists and friends at her nearby Marigny Street condominium, and I believe she had a generator at her place.

Since Katrina's floodwaters marked three-quarters of the city uninhabitable, a new culture of evictions, spawned from the devastation and opportunistic landlords, became even more ubiquitous than the putrid mold impeding our health and mental well-being. Rampant and unfettered greed was on exhibit in a vile manner, and many landlords began evicting artists and other tenants—throwing their art and belongings onto the streets or raising our rents to unimaginable prices. In the face of such a catastrophe, when we could have all used more exemplary acts of human kindness, compassion, and community solidarity, many landlords added to the social calamity and exacted inhumane practices that can only be described as racial, cultural, and economical cleansing.

This was the culture of fear and threats that we returned to. In order to properly "bring back New Orleans," its artists, writers, and musicians needed decent and affordable places to live, but we all faced a tidal wave of evictions crashing through our homes with the same force as Katrina's flood waters crashing through the levees. We were being displaced all over again, and there was a cultural exodus to nearby cities such as Atlanta, Austin, and Houston. They all welcomed New Orleans musicians and artists with open arms instead of eviction notices.

These small-minded, reptilian capitalist landlords further displaced our creative human resources, and very little has been written about the added trauma that these property piranhas inflicted on many who lived in neighborhoods close to the old Quarter. It was obvious that they couldn't have cared less for the art and culture-bearers that uniquely define this city, and they were obviously only interested in bloating their bellies with more greenbacks in the wake of this human tragedy. Many of these landlords were collecting rents for months when our apartments were legally uninhabitable while simultaneously collecting loss-of-rent claims for these months from insurance companies and FEMA. Those landlords were one of the biggest "obstacles" that artists in these neighborhoods encountered in our return to the ravaged city.

As an artist deeply invested in my community, I was engaged in the rebuilding of our wounded metropolis with other artists, and art was a vital quotient and ingredient in this process. Artists were part of the cultural renaissance of our ruined town. In one of the follow-up essays sent to presenters and folks receiving my cultural newsletter on the recovery process, I stated, "We will not have our voices silenced—especially by property-owning piranhas abusing our rights." This was sent via a piece titled "How Can Artists Return to a Culture of Evictions in Post-Katrina New Orleans?" At the Margarita gathering, my good friend and lawyer Gordon Patton was appalled that my landlord would take such action to demand rent. My odious landlord had sent me a notice of immediate eviction, and she must have been surprised when Gordon, who took on my case pro bono, sent her a letter saying that he was representing me and suing her for wrongful collection of rent for an uninhabitable property in post-Katrina New Orleans. Her threats stopped, and all I can say is that it's good to have "lawyer friends." As soon as I could get back to stay longer, I began looking for a new place to rent. As I've noted before, I'm an undying optimist and am engaged in cultural activism. This personal drama was happening as I was in the process of touring and developing the new *Cone of Uncertainty* solo show.

I noted this property piranhas problem in my show then, and I engaged in telling a personal story to address universal concerns. Artists and working-class people living in the Faubourg Marigny and Tremé neighborhoods were all affected by this perverse greed. Let's dare to remember that property became more priceless than people, and Katrina easily revealed that flawed fissure in this capitalist matrix.

5. *Returning to Ecuador in December 2005 to January 2006 / A Wedding Proposal in Quito*

I forget how it happened and what initiated the decision to make the geographical leap back to the home of my birth in Guayaquil, Ecuador, by the end of 2005. Claudia and I worked well under crisis, and it became obvious that we had to take our relationship to another level after surviving Katrina together and escaping the social chaos that followed on a stolen school bus. I loved living in "sin" for the few years before we made the leap to get married. It was an inevitable direction we were moving towards. I returned to Ecuador for the first time in some fifteen years, and it was magic to re-discover the home of my birth with Claudia, my newfound love, to introduce her to my extended family there of aunts and uncles, and cousins and second cousins—lots of family who had been worried for my survival because they all knew I was living in New Orleans when Katrina hit.

It was a magical part of my post-Katrina resurrection to reconnect with my many family members still in Ecuador. One of the few memories that I still have from my childhood days in Guayaquil is of the joyous and loud New Year's Eve celebrations that take place all over town and across the petite country. Ecuador is positioned between Peru to the south and Colombia to the north, with the Pacific Ocean as its coastal waters. Ecuador derives its name from that imaginary, globally-defined line called the equator. In the 1960s and 1970s, the US began recruiting waves of immigrants from these three countries to come and work in the textile industries of New York. This was a period when Manhattan was the capital of the garment industry, and clothing was actually manufactured in Big Apple Gotham. On TV up north in New Jersey and New York, commercials of the Union Label were quite common to promote the then thriving manufacturing industry, and they needed immigrants to fill these jobs, which were often low paying and had long hours.

The Immigrant Crosses . . .

El emigrante cruza por varias razones
por necesidad económica.
The immigrant crosses for various reasons
for economical necessity
por el sueño de otra vida mejor
por evitar percusión política,
for the dream of a better life
to avoid political persecution
por libertad social y religiosa
porque el acto de cruzar es un poema físico
for social and religious freedoms

because the act of crossing is a physical poem
y un grito rebelde y un ejercicio mítico
porque a veces hay que cruzar simplemente
because the act of crossing is a rebellious scream
a mythic undertaking because sometimes
you simply have to cross
y porque a veces nos cruzan a nosotros mismos
y por eso no hay solución
mas que cruzar y el otro lado es una línea quebrada
and for that there is no solution other than to cross
and sometimes the border crosses you
and the other side is a broken line
where dreams can become nightmares
because the immigrant lives in between spaces always
in between the country they left and the new one
where they inhabit precarious conditions

I invite you to become a conceptual tourist in my loaded performance landscape the same way I accepted the challenges of an epic migration, a new language, and a new country when I crossed into the unknown as a child of seven. That was a performance of faith, but one in which I had no choice. El primer choque cultural fue cuando me cortaron mi nombre natural de nacimiento, mis dos apellidos de mis raíces Latina. The first cultural car crash and new-reality jolt came when my two last names, which are part of my Latino familial identity, were severed from each other because of a rather incomprehensible appetite for abbreviation in this Anglican world dominated by monosyllabic name combinations such as John Smith, Bill King, and Tom Jones. My full and more melodic birth name of José Eduardo Torres Tama was reduced to José Torres, and for that, there was no solution at the time. I witnessed the indifferent scalping of my heritage, the butchering of a metaphoric umbilical cord connecting me to the ghosts of all my dead relatives. My ties to South America were abruptly and unexpectedly cut by the pen of US border officials, and without much warning, this dream quest began with a name change—simplifying my new, official North American ID into a combination as common as Joe Brown. It would take me another eleven years to begin undoing that unnecessary act perpetrated by those customs officers in Miami and a lifetime of creative endeavors to challenge the dominant cultural matrix with its own language for the imperial posture it chooses, as it marginalizes all others outside of its Eurocentric and Anglican paradigms. It was in college that I first reclaimed my two last names and began signing my drawings and paintings and poems as José Eduardo Torres Tama. Some GrinGo teachers thought that there were two people occupying one seat. ¡Ay, caramba!

On that day of September 9, as I passed the Miami US customs inspection, I emerged another immigrant child along the yellow brick road, with only mi madre querida to offer the necessary love and protection to combat the many racial confrontations that were just beginning. My mother was witness to the slashing of our names, but, like many immigrants who arrive on these shores, she did not have much of a vocabulary to protest these actions. Perhaps it was best to accept this dramatic imposition upon our identities for entry into the land of opportunity. As any immigrant undergoing inspection by customs officials to cross a border would suggest, be flexible and offer the least amount of resistance because these guards can be the most brutal and temperamental of authority figures, and the objective is to be allowed passage, to cross al otro lado and begin dreaming in Spanglish.

My mother emigrated from Ecuador in the late 1960s with a suitcase full of hope, her only child at the time (me), and barely any words in English to negotiate our passage. Here I was, returning decades later to Ecuador after having been there during my college years, when I was twenty. I still had an Ecuadorian passport back then, and I had to go through a labyrinth of paperwork and official documents to be allowed to leave four weeks later. Fortunately, I had family lawyers there who helped me negotiate all of that, because the local authorities wanted to know why I had not done my required military service, and they even wanted to charge me for taxes. That I had not lived in Ecuador since I was seven did not matter, but after some money was paid and with my lawyer uncle's support, we negotiated my eventual release. Crossing borders has always been a challenge for me—especially when I traveled with an Ecuadorian passport. Such travels are easier now with a passport from the "Empire" of GrinGolandia.

Back in my homeland, I knew that I wanted to propose to Claudia there, and when we made it to the beautiful capital city of Quito, with its handsome and well-preserved Spanish colonial architecture, I intuited this was the site for an epic proposal. Our bus entered the historic center of Quito, and I could clearly see El Panecillo that holds the impactful 135-feet statue of a Winged Virgin Mary, which is referred to as the Virgin of Quito. In my twenties, when I was last back in Quito, I had climbed to El Panecillo on foot from the old town area, and I knew this was the perfect setting for a proposal, the first and only such proposal I ever threw down as a performance ritual to any woman I had been involved with. Now, I had to buy an engagement ring, and there's a section in the old town of Quito with numerous jewelry stores.

Quito is actually known for having a great many petite stores for purchasing high-quality jewelry. During a bit of a rainy day before heading to El Panecillo, I had to figure out how to sneak away to buy an engagement ring from one of those stores, and that was not an easy task because Claudia and I were always together. I was also on the hunt for a leather jacket, and Quito is also known for having many stores that sell the fabulous leather coats that are made in the nearby indigenous town of Otavalo. In Quito, like in Rio Bamba, which we had visited a few days earlier, indigenous Quechua people who are part of my Ecuadorian heritage are everywhere—especially at all the open-air markets. We located one store that had some sweet-looking leather jackets, and we began looking for any that I could consider.

Claudia was looking at leather sandals, and being near the door, I snuck out and ran to a jewelry store I spotted a few doors down. It was half a block over and across the street. In Spanish, I asked the Quechua male attendant for an engagement ring. He went immediately to a set of diamond rings, and I expressed that I was not into diamonds because of their blood-stained origins. We spotted a silver sapphire ring that was perfect, and I bought it in what I believed to be a quick minute. Maybe five minutes in all had passed, and I ran back to the corner leather store—where a very agitated Claudia was waiting while the light rain mist increased. She was super upset and questioned why I had abandoned her at that store in the middle of town. The excuse I offered was that I'd seen a cool leather jacket that drew my eye a few stores down and had just wanted to check it out, assuming that she was engaged with the leather sandals. She was not buying any of it and remained mad until I suggested we get some ice cream at a nearby confectionary store with sweet, locally made pastries and coffee for sale. We bought some tasty ice cream treats that saved me, and I was prepared with an engagement ring in a little black box hiding in my pocket.

The next morning we took a bus to El Panecillo, and below the feet of the large winged Virgin Mary, which could be seen from any point in the city, there was museum cloister dedicated to the *Encuentro*—where a mural in the round dome depicted the indigenous Yavirac people meeting the Spanish conquistadors. *Encuentro* is used as the historical term for the "encounter" of our indigenous ancestors with the conquistadors. This was indeed a "sacred place," and it was even more so because we were under the huge statue of the Virgin of Quito. Claudia was inspired and began singing, in her majestic, operatic voice, "Stella Splendens," a fourteenth-century Spanish pilgrimage song offered to the Black Madonna of Montserrat. When I first traveled to Spain and made it to Barcelona back in the mid-1980s, I made it to Montserrat via cable car. It's about fifty minutes from the Catalan capital, and it so happened that when I arrived at the mountainous terrain, there was a festival procession celebrating the Black Madonna. The holy statue was being paraded, and the magical chorus was singing "Stella Splendens." So, I have had a deep connection to this medieval song, and just then, as Claudia was finishing the last verse, I went down on one knee and proposed with the sapphire ring, shining in its silver splendor, inside the handsome black velvet box.

I asked the inevitable and iconic question: "Will you marry me?"

Claudia began to cry, and tears began streaming from my eyes as well. She said, "Yes!"

Later, when she asked where I bought the ring, I mentioned the previous day and my disappearing act in the old town to sneak away and purchase it. We laughed about it at the nearby tourist café in El Panecillo's landscape, and the view of the city was absolutely breathtaking from such glorious heights. I am a big believer in the Goddess of Serendipity, and I believe in living a life of magic—as much as possible. This proposal ritual was "live art" magic. It was one of the great moments of my life and a pure post-Katrina blessing. We took the bus back to our hotel in town, and we were now riding back as an engaged couple.

Before heading to Quito and after our final November trip back to our critically wounded New Orleans, I had shaved my head and asked Claudia to assist me. In many cultures, the shaving of one's head is performed as a ritual of mourning, and the storm had marked me. I was still deep in a mourning period for my devastated adopted home—barely recovering from the collective trauma of the great flood. Also, in my touring travels as an artist in exile, I kept seeing groups of Tibetan monks at the many airports I was traversing. They were traveling across the country, and their saffron robes and shaved heads intrigued and inspired me. I traveled back to Ecuador sporting a shaved head, and as we were performing this ritual in Gainesville, Florida, I experienced a transformation. I actually looked younger, and the final result of a clean-shaven head with no hairs at all was a release of a previous persona. I was free to become the new, post-storm me and to reinvent myself for this new chapter of my mythic journey. Returning back to Ecuador was part of that process—as was proposing to Claudia and being engaged.

6. NPR's *Latino USA* Radio Commentaries: Hard Living in the Big Easy for Immigrant Reconstruction Workers

For five years, from 2006 to 2011, I contributed radio commentaries to NPR's *Latino USA*. Those commentaries explored the many challenges of life in the immediate months and years after the storm. I addressed the myriad human rights violations immigrants were subjected to while rebuilding a once crippled and flooded city. I love New Orleans, but the "city that care forgot" has not cared much about the most valuable and dedicated work force to have aided in its speedy recovery. This French and Spanish colonial Catholic port city has a long legacy of labor exploitation, and it's been abetted by the most abhorrent of crimes against humanity: the selling of enslaved African men, women, and children. Let's dare to remember that New Orleans was the premiere port city for the distribution of enslaved Africans into the "land of the free," and the Catholic Church was a major accomplice to such crimes and brutal commerce.

The Crescent City has been cruel to my Latin American immigrant brethren. We must not forget that New Orleans, like the rest of this settler colonial system founded on the near genocide and extermination of indigenous First Peoples, with its empire built on the bloodied backs of enslaved African people, is seriously addicted to enslaved labor. "Undocumented" immigrants serve the empire's wanton addiction for cheap labor abuse.

Note that I refrain from using the term "slave" and prefer to use the term "enslaved." Employing "slave" is a careless act that lends itself to a belief that African people were "just slaves" accepting of this abominable condition. African people in GrinGoLandia were enslaved, and New Orleans was a premiere port for distributing such enchained human cargo into the rest of the South. The "selling of flesh" was the big business that put New Orleans on the map, and by 1850, it was one of the most prosperous cities in the Union because it also bred enslaved peoples. Believe that, baby, darling, boo-hoo you. As a poet, language is as vital to me as breathing, and if we are to liberate ourselves from the colonial conditions that have been imposed upon us, we must check the colonizer's language and resist using it to further their damage on our spirits, our psyches, and our bodies. I'm just saying.

Maria Hinojosa, the award-winning journalist and host of *Latino USA*, introduced many of these three-minute commentaries I scripted for them,

INSIDE THE CONE OF UNCERTAINTY:
BETWEEN THE DARK & THE LIGHT

and I am most grateful to have been a constant voice from ground zero here in New Orleans as the reconstruction developed. One radio commentary was titled "Hard Living In the Big Easy," and I explored the rising rents that followed for those of us who dared to return. Also, this commentary noted that Latin American immigrants were facing severe challenges while rebuilding the flooded city. At best, I offered three to four commentaries to their weekly news journal per year. These commentaries aired nationally, and most were recorded at WWNO 89.9 FM, our local NPR station. For the fifth anniversary of the storm in August 2010, I contributed a piece titled "Los Invisibles / The Invisible Ones." I addressed how Latin American immigrants were everywhere on reconstruction sites all over the city, but while they were physically ubiquitous, they were rendered invisible because the city and media turned a blind eye to their suffering. If you Google my name and *Latino USA*, they have archived this four-minute piece on their site. Google it, because Latinos, we love to Google.

It was as if our immigrant community was trapped in a bizarre science-fiction reality—where they were ubiquitous but invisible simultaneously. I dared to expose the wage theft many reconstruction workers experienced after laboring arduously in the immediate, punishing heat that followed the storm to rebuild the city for twelve-hour days—but often, they were not paid the promised wages by contractors, who threatened to call immigration agents and have them deported. National and local contractors exploited the "undocumented status" of many workers and have cheated the people who have rebuilt this city out of millions, maybe billions, since the storm. That's a truth that most want to turn a blind eye to, but it has been my prime directive to shine a big light on the mistreatment of immigrant reconstruction workers and their families who have brought back this city from the dead. Immigrant workers repaired hotels, hospitals, and government buildings. They salvaged hotels before they were declared uninhabitable to help reignite the engines of the viable tourist industry.

For a decade, from 2010 to 2019, I have engaged in a "docu-theater" process of filmed interviews with immigrant laborers and undocumented people, and this development strategy has informed three solo performances and numerous writings published on platforms such as the PBS blog, *HowlRound Journal*, Alternate ROOTS narratives, and others. The Taco Truck Theater was a radical theater on wheels ensemble project, also informed by the docu-theater process I cultivated. When our diverse Taco Truck Theater ensemble debuted in January 2017, our thematic thrust was that "Black Lives

Matter" and "No Human Being Is Illegal!" We addressed the parallel struggles of African Americans seen as "less than human" historically by "white police," who have killed Black people with impunity, and the dehumanization of immigrants as "illegal aliens" akin to terrorists—with no human rights afforded to them because of being "undocumented." This was back in 2017, before the May 25, 2020, murder of George Floyd in Minneapolis by a white cop who extinguished George's last breath with a knee to his neck for nearly nine minutes.

As a performance artist, my life experiences inform my work, and when I returned a month later, on October 1, 2005, I was witness to a remarkable and unexpected sight. Thousands of Latin American immigrant workers were covering all neighborhoods of the devastated Crescent City—like a host of reconstruction angels engaged in the epic recovery. Immigrant reconstruction workers were on hundreds of rooftops, laying down many miles of plastic blue tarps to cover water damages. They were on every construction site across the city. Immediately, I began documenting their stories through informal Spanish language conversations on the streets, and trying to understand how they managed to inhabit a city that was under a state of martial law—where you couldn't get in or out. Immigrant workers were actually smuggled in on purpose to assist with the massive rebuilding efforts, and because most were "undocumented," they became victims of wage theft at the hands of abusive contractors.

This is the dark and dirty secret in the open air of the post-Katrina reconstruction, and I have been very loud about telling this story across the country and internationally. The *Latino USA* commentaries on NPR offered me access to an audience of millions across the land via radio magic. My first commentary aired during Mardi Gras 2006, recounting a cold night when the infamous Krewe du Vieux rolled with their forever irreverence, and I addressed the importance of our communities being able to costume, parade, and dance in the streets to exorcise our collective trauma. Cuban collaborator and brilliant filmmaker William Sabourin O'Reilly and I used the recording for a short film titled *Mardi Gras as a Public Healing Ritual for Wounded New Orleans*. Our short ran at national film festivals in a series called *Below Sea Level Stories*, organized by multimedia artist Courtney Egan.

7. The Cone of Uncertainty Performance at the ATHE Conference
In 2007, the Association of Theater in Higher Education (ATHE) Conference took place in New Orleans. Then LSU theater professor Les Wade,

who knew my work, recommended me as a local performer to be featured at the conference, and I threw down a fifty-five minute *Cone* performance. Some three hundred-plus theater scholars in attendance were moved to their feet, and it introduced my work to numerous theater professors. A number of national and international performance projects developed from that showcase.

The ATHE performance of *The Cone of Uncertainty* launched me across the Atlantic, and Professor Joshua Abrams, a performance art scholar who saw that show, engaged the Roehampton University Theater Department, where he taught, to bring me in for a May 2009 visiting-artist residency. For a week, I guided a committed group of about seven theater students, and they wrote their own performance about witnessing the storm through media news coverage. The Roehampton students opened for me with a thirty-minute original ensemble performance piece before my *Cone* show. It was a memorable experience to inspire students to create an original performance about the storm that recounted what they'd witnessed on television.

Inspired by the many filmed interviews I've conducted of undocumented immigrants, my other docu-theater performance is titled *Aliens, Immigrants & Other Evildoers*, and I am still touring this show, which was first developed for the stage back in September of 2010. Locally, it was commissioned by the Ashé Cultural Arts Center and through a Creation Fund Award from the NPN. Our co-commissioning partners were MECA in Houston and GALA Hispanic Theatre in DC. For a decade, from 2010 to 2019, I conducted filmed interviews with undocumented immigrants in the cities of Houston, Minneapolis, New Orleans, Tulsa, and Washington, DC. It has been a big part of my creative strategy and mission to bring efficacy to my work and to stage the lives of real people who have been dehumanized with the insidious and hateful moniker of "illegal aliens."

In the immediate months after the storm, I sneaked back into town a number of times and was able to develop trust with workers simply because I communicated in Spanish. I am completely bilingual and often begin the scripting of my performances with spoken word poems written in Spanish. Later, I translate them into English, but Spanish is a sensual language for poetry. Yes, it is the Spanish colonizers' language, but I am a South American artist from Ecuador. Spanish is my first language, and serves as my "metaphoric umbilical cord" that keeps me connected to my Latin American roots. I developed relationships with this imported Spanish-speaking Latin labor force, and later, with their approval, I began filming those interviews. I photographed and filmed the many public protests reconstruction workers staged on the streets of New Orleans.

The Congress of Day Laborers/Congreso de Jornaleros is the organization of immigrant activists that organized many public protests, especially every May 1, for International Workers' Day. Congreso activists exposed a plethora of human rights abuses and health risks that reconstruction workers were subjected to in the toxic waters of the flooded city. They have exposed the disappearances of immigrants in local jails, while others were often held indefinitely in New Orleans prisons for pure profit, in a city and state that thrive on the incarceration of Black and Brown people as one of their biggest businesses. The general public is often misled to believe that tourism, music, and food drive the engines of this economy, but the state of Louisiana is an incarceration state. Louisiana jails more people than the entire country of China. ICE detention centers are plentiful in rural, faraway towns such as Jenna, LaSalle, and Pine Prairie. Louisiana is only second to Texas in the thousands of "undocumented" immigrants it incarcerates in these private-for-profit ICE prisons. We should be outraged!

In July of 2010, the Congress of Day Laborers challenged the so-called "suicide" of a Salvadoran immigrant who was picked up by the NOPD and turned over to ICE agents. The NOPD had no legal right to contact ICE, but, as immigrant activists have exposed, they operate as "poli-migra" units. This means the NOPD actively engages in racially profiling immigrants, Brown immigrants especially, and reports any individual they apprehend and consider to be "illegal" to local ICE agents. They have no official authority to do this, but the New Orleans Police Department is one of the most corrupt policing systems nationwide.

José Nelson Reyes-Zelaya died within twenty-four hours in ICE custody, and they claimed he committed suicide. ICE representatives offered no further evidence to the Salvadoran consulate or his family. Immigrants die in ICE detention centers often, and their deaths are generally mysterious and proclaimed as "suicides." According to the Congress of Day Laborers, he was the eighth immigrant who had died in ICE detention custody by that summer of 2010. Reyes-Zelaya was twenty-eight years young and the father of two US-born children. The moving public protest and vigil organized by the Day Laborer activists across from City Hall inspired me to take further action. I began using all of my creative strategies to bring greater attention to such fatal violations against my immigrant people. The photo retablos/assemblages I constructed were exhibited as part of 2010's PhotoNOLA, the citywide festival of photography established post-Katrina by the New Orleans Photo Alliance.

The *Advocate* newspaper featured my open studio exhibition with a cover story in their arts & entertainment insert, Beaucoup. Written by Dean Shapiro, the feature was titled "Welcome to America." I was photographed inside my Saint Roch Avenue studio holding one of the photo assemblages I constructed to house the black-and-white photos from the vigil of the fallen Salvadoran immigrant father. The photos I captured also inspired a series of large mixed-media works-on-paper, titled *Hard Living in the Big Easy: Immigrants & the Rebirth of New Orleans*. In September 2018, the University of New Orleans St. Claude Gallery exhibited this series of twenty art works, including new photo retablos of other public protests. Two hundred-plus visitors attended the opening of that exhibition. The many photos I captured of numerous street protests organized by the Congress of Day Laborers inspired these large mixed-media works-on-paper.

My prime directive was simply to honor their valiant efforts to fight for the rights of reconstruction workers and to have them "see themselves" as worthy subjects to illustrate the human condition of a marginalized labor force. For many immigrants in attendance, there was a great sense of pride in "being seen." They saw themselves as important enough to have an art show dedicated to them, and one that chronicled their years of public protests. We had a number of Congreso members attend the exhibition, and the UNO St. Claude Gallery walls were covered with Spanish and English narratives of the show. The undocumented immigrant community "saw themselves" on the walls of this regal gallery on Saint Claude Avenue. I am grateful to Cheryl Hayes, who was the UNO Fine Arts department chair at the time. Two years prior, she'd invited me to open the 2008 fall season with an exhibition that featured the large mixed-media artworks created to honor our immigrant reconstruction workers.

In the Latin American tradition, it's the job of the artist to remember and speak the people's truth against the "official lies" of governments. My exhibition was a creative response to honor our immigrant community, and beyond being labeled as simply Latino, our immigrant community is Honduran, Mexican, Salvadoran, Peruvian Mexican, Peruvian, and even Brazilian. Many are descendants of indigenous peoples such as the Maya, Mixtec, and Zapotec, and some Black Hondurans are Garifuna as well.

I cannot bask in a privilege that I'm not afforded to make art for art's sake when the attacks on my Brown body and my immigrant community are more than abstract. Our immigrant people have given of their blood, labor, and love to rebuild a city that has exploited their labor and ignored their human suffering.

This is an excerpt from my artist's statement on the UNO St. Claude Gallery walls, and it was translated into Spanish. On a universal level, these artworks celebrated the humanity of a people dehumanized as "illegal aliens" and challenged the raging anti-immigrant hysteria gripping the land in 2018, with a POTUS who campaigned to vilify immigrants as easy scapegoats for everything that was failing in the "Empire." My aim was to forge pictorial narratives that documented the epic struggles of immigrants during a time of perpetual persecution. Latin American immigrants have been a big part of the rebirth of New Orleans, but they faced a clear and present danger during the four years from 2016 to 2020, with a hostile administration in the White House. In the twenty years since the storm, the *Hard Living in the Big Easy* show is the only such visual arts exhibition with works created by a Latin American immigrant, and one branded as a real-life "storm refugee." I dared to depict the "live art" protests that brought national media attention to the despicable labor abuses our New Orleans immigrant community has endured—while rebuilding a city that exploited their labor to rise from the post-Katrina flood waters.

> The workers and families who helped rebuild New Orleans live in terror today. [...] If they leave their homes to walk their children to school, if they go to the laundromat or the barber shop or the grocery store, they will be targeted for nothing more than looking Latino, and their families might never see them again.[47]
> — Bill Quigley, professor of law, Loyola University

As part of the exhibition texts, Mr. Quigley's quote was blazoned on the walls for the 2018 UNO St. Claude Gallery exhibition. I have the greatest

---

47 Bill Quigley, "Why I stand with the immigrant workers who rebuilt New Orleans: Bill Quigley," *NOLA.com* (New Orleans, LA), November 13, 2013, https://www.nola.com/opinions/why-i-stand-with-the-immigrant-workers-who-rebuilt-new-orleans-bill-quigley/article_df32c34d-93fd-5fae-aa98-80d08172bd31.html.

respect for this gentleman, who was always there to bear witness to the many public protests staged by the Congress of Day Laborers.

8. The Louisiana Endowment for the Humanities Disappears Immigrants In Their 2018 Tri-centennial Anthology

For two decades, I have worked feverishly to employ a variety of genres from performance art solos to experimental theater ensembles; from the visual arts to photography; from NPR commentaries to a debut poetry publication; and scripting essays like this one to have our immigrant community recognized, honored, and not forgotten. It broke my heart to immeasurable fractions to see how easily we could be erased and disappeared by "white scholars" in their myopic chronicles of current history. It was one of the darkest moments of the post-Katrina years for me.

The Louisiana Endowment for the Humanities (LEH) published *New Orleans & the World: 1718–2018 Tricentennial Anthology*, and the book's table of contents clearly illustrates how the LEH has brutally disappeared our immigrant community and our heroic reconstruction workers from any mention in their two hundred-plus-page coffee-table publication. The LEH has exhibited "unchallenged power" to disappear us—as if we did not even exist. This is another immense post-Katrina trauma I have carried in my heart and in my body. Within this group of heralded writers and scholars, not one was of Latin descent, and not one person spoke for us. It's not surprising, because there was obviously no one of Latin/Hispanic heritage at that table of LEH decision-makers.

This celebrated anthology fills public and school libraries across the city and state. Are we that insignificant a people that we merit such easy disappearance in a book that will live for the next three hundred years as "the official chronicle" of New Orleans history from 1718 to 2018? This is not a matter of maligning the LEH for some benign oversight, as it was put by one white woman writer whose writing is included in this book. This is about holding the LEH accountable on a national and international level for a historiographical crime against our immigrant people. During an era of raging anti-immigrant hysteria, it's beyond disgraceful when an organization with "humanities" in their moniker acts as a privileged gatekeeper—making editorial decisions on who shall be remembered and who shall be forgotten. The LEH needs to rebrand itself as the Louisiana Endowment for the Inhumanities for their brutal cultural deportation of our Latin American immigrant people from their anthology.

9. My Post-Storm Sons Are the Premiere Light That Offers Me Hope

New Orleans is my mythic muse, my eternal mistress, and I have loved her and continue to love her like no other. I owe the cultivation of my many creative practices to its moist and mysterious tropical terrain. At times, I am critical of her, the way one is critical of a lover because of mad devotion, and I want her to measure up and do the right thing for her diverse people. I have come back to her time and time again because there is no other city in these Divided States that I can consider living in. She has burrowed her charms, elixirs, and supernatural juju deep into my skin and across my psyche. I am her devotee. I take refuge in New Orleans from the rest of this insane and sometimes soulless system. I will surely die here, and intrinsically intuit and know that I have died and lived here many times before. I want my ashes distributed across the mighty muddy Mississippi River on a Mardi Gras Day, delivered by my two handsome hybrid boys, mis bellos carnalitos/mis vatos guapos.

My two sons, Darius Amancio and Diego Arjuna, were both conceived here. They are Ecuadorian-German-Irish and Quechua Native Latino gringitos of the new millennium. They exemplify the epitome of multiracial possibilities that inspires some belief in this experiment called the US. They are both my true post-Katrina light.

I was afraid of having children because my biological father was an "invisible man" in my life. My boy's mama, Dr. Claudia Copeland, wanted children, and we actually broke up three times while living in sin together before the storm. I was simply resistant to the idea because I had a lingering pain in my psyche from not having had a father in my life. My two boys have served as the magical cure and natural elixir to heal this mythic wound that made Father's Day a time for me to hide. I have been in the process of becoming the father I never had, and Darius and Diego have been extremely patient with me.

Darius was born in exile while in Gainesville, Florida, but in April of 2006, he was conceived on the night of a New Orleans-style funky and ceremonial wedding, with a brass band leading our friends and family in a second line from my Marigny barrio to the river, where we were led by our neighborhood Yoruba priestess, Sula Evans (aka Sula Spirit), and a poet friend, Andy Young, in a petition to Yemaya and Oshun for their blessings. While we had the wedding vows and party take place in the luscious backyard of the Dauphine Street apartment we were renting then, we were spiritually united at the river with African chants and our respective families and wedding guests,

INSIDE THE CONE OF UNCERTAINTY: BETWEEN THE DARK & THE LIGHT

amigos/amigas y familia, holding small, glass-encased white votive candles that lit their smiling faces as our witnesses against the majestic dusk of an April night in New Orleans.

In April of 2006, New Orleans was still critically wounded and fragile, but our hearts were collectively strong and joyful on that glorious wedding day. I escaped with Darius's mama on that stolen school bus back in September 2005, and we married on April 22, 2006. It was Earth Day, and we were grounding our fertile terrain for children to grow. We have been divorced some many years since, but this does not take away from a wedding that was enacted as a "loving ritual" back then. We remain co-parents committed to our big teen boys, now ages eighteen and fifteen. I've let both boys know that they were born when Mama and Papa's love was at its blessed peak.

Diego was born in September of 2009 at Touro Hospital, a year after our final return from another period of exile, where, from fall 2007 to the summer of 2008, we spent some time in Leipzig, Germany, a far cry from the Louisiana swamp. Claudia had accepted a postdoctoral position in Leipzig, former East German territory. I followed devotedly to take care of baby Darius—not even a year old yet. When Hurricane Katrina hit, I experienced a paradigm shift, and maybe it was something to do with facing mortality that changed my mind. I can't say that I thought too much about it, but I was just ready for children after our great escape on the stolen school bus.

For six months of every year, we live with the threat of hurricanes wiping us off the map at the mouth of the mighty and muddy Mississippi River. New Orleans contends with what I have often perceived as the karmic vengeance of hurricanes originating their threats on the African continental shores from whence ships of enslaved humans departed centuries before. Perhaps these storms are the amassed screams of enchained Africans reincarnated as violent "water furies" from one century to another, furious water balls of human horror from the Middle Passage, and natural punishment for a port city's participation in the most abhorrent of mortal sins: the enslavement of other sentient beings.

This aging Dixie Madame has survived fires and storms, slavery and Civil War, yellow fever plagues and segregation, eroding wetlands and urban neglect, as a geographical exile from the rest of the Union. Our survival is dependent on some precious amnesty from the river, and a few times a week, I bicycle to the river to offer my obeisances.

My greatest belief in the future of this system lies in the hybrid make-up of my two boys, Darius Amancio and Diego Arjuna. Both conceived in New

Orleans post-Katrina, my hope is that their future is one where hybrid people are celebrated and everyone recognizes diversity in all its forms, and no one is forced or conscripted to point at one group or another to employ as scapegoats and to demonize.

My hope is that their future is one where the country lives up to its greatest promises and manifests a more inclusive and progressive "American Dream." In September 2024, Diego reached fifteen years of age, and I end with this poem that commemorates his birth and joining his big brother Darius to complete our petite family. Bearing witness to their mama's giving birth to both of my sons was simply a testament to the Pachamama powers of the Divine Feminine. There is no other experience on this planet that can match such a live art manifestation. I was grateful to be present and bear witness to the miracle of life twice.

Waiting for Diego with Baby Boy Darius

Son quince años ya de una esperanza divina
de los gran milagros de una vida entregada a la magia
y tu hermanito Darius ni tres añitos todavía
también esperando con gran alegría y entusiasmo
for his baby brother to arrive
y tu mama sagrada con el coraje
de entregarte a esta vida loca
sin la intervención de drogas
pero con un grito hondo y desesperado
"He's coming inside this dirty car!"
while I was driving us at 7 a.m. to Touro
making mistake of holding your screaming mama's hand
she almost crushed mine and had read that was possible
Diego on the edge of your Virgo birth
like a petit prince arrived on your projected due date
because it's intrinsic to the mythos of your being
with such medical science riding your back
like melodic classical sweet music
charmed from your wooden violin
and your smile lights a path to your glorious voyage
and we waited because Baby Diego completed the family
when I caught you dropping from your mama's womb

INSIDE THE CONE OF UNCERTAINTY: BETWEEN THE DARK & THE LIGHT

onto my hands like a newborn miracle
my skin receiving you because we're connected that way
second time I witnessed such
"live art" because Baby Darius nearly three years before
arrived through your brave mama's courage
also without drugs ala natural but with big screams
transformed into bigger joy when Darius finally joined us
two weeks late made us parents the first time
it was surreal to see a baby bald head crown
between your mama's legs eventually crawling
birthday boy naked on that early morning cold January
in our Gainesville exile and lessons began
when I sang to sleep your fragile body with froggy limbs
porcelain wobbly head to hold while my heart expanded
like I've never loved before with infinite care
Katrina in Greek means pure and cleansing for a new chapter
and psychic pain of not having a father present
began vanishing like a benign nagging tumor
I was free from that haunting
deep in crevices of my heart that longed
for a greater meaning to Father's Day
and both your arrivals were life-affirming rituals
because every future father should embrace the glory
of their child's entrance into this mortal realm
Darius and Diego have grown my heart
Grand Canyon-wide and it's a wild ride
I am still digging with you
Vatos Guapos as teens today
I'm just saying!

Ashé y Adelante!
Si Se Puede!

BLESSED BY GOD'S GRACE AND FAMILIES' FAITH
DWIGHT & TRUDELL WEBSTER

This story is a bit complex and does not lend itself to being recounted on a straightforward linear trajectory, in that our movements as a family diverged and converged as necessity dictated, due to my position as a pastor trying to minister to a flock spread out over a wide swath of the country, though mainly in the Southern states. Trudell's situation evolved as well, with a California return home of sorts, but to something far different than the home she'd left. This Berkeley High School and San Francisco State University graduate had to juggle working and child- and family-care with self-care.

Where my family is now is in stark contrast to where we were before the Cat Five Hurricane Katrina came barreling out of the Gulf of Mexico and made landfall on its coast. The youngest and oldest sons, Amir Anane Augustine (Brooke) and Dwight Nathaniel (Sandra), currently live in New Orleans, as does a granddaughter, Aubrey Gail, her mother, Traci (Tonian), and a bonus grandson, TJ. One son, Toussaint Idell (LeAndria), lives in Washington, DC, and one son, Kwame Ammon (Crystal), lives in Vancouver, British Columbia, Canada, with our two other grandchildren, Zora Wynn Audrey and Mercer Eugene.

August 27, 2005
Due to my misgivings, Trudell and I were not in agreement on how and with what our oldest son, Dwight Nathaniel, was to return to Florida A&M University after having taken a break. Thanks to a family friend, Brother Al Mims, Trudell rented a Penske truck to help Dwight Nathaniel return to school in Tallahassee, Florida, with the intention of bringing household items to Florida and returning the truck to New Orleans within a day.

Somehow, between the administrations of New Orleans Mayor C. Ray Nagin and Louisiana Governor Kathleen Blanco, a determination was made that a contraflow evacuation would be implemented so that more people could escape the hurricane's potentially devastating effects. This meant that all highway traffic was to go only east or west—but on both sides of the highways, in one direction out of the city and its suburbs, for the evacuation of 1.2–1.4 million people out of the New Orleans metro area.

By the evening on Saturday, the day before Katrina was to make landfall, it became clear that not only would we at Christian Unity Baptist Church (CUBC) have to cancel one of our two morning services, but that folks had decided to evacuate ahead of Sunday altogether. I figured that I would have to go to the church anyway. So, with the pressure of the coming storm, Deacon Chair Felix Johnson Jr. had come to the church to tie up some loose ends and leave as well. He told me to go ahead and leave since there was no one there to hold service for anyway. Besides, Trudell had already told me that though I was, as pastor, Christian Unity's "captain," under no circumstances was I to try to "go down with the ship!" She said, "Bring my boys to Florida!"

With our two younger sons, Kwame and Amir, in tow, we headed east out to the interstate, I-10, toward Tallahassee. So far, so good. But in the brief time it took to stop in Slidell to gas up and get snacks, the road had become so congested that it took ten hours to get to Tallahassee—twice the time it would normally take. It took us literally an hour to pass through or by each city: Gulfport, Biloxi, Mobile, and Pensacola. One of the blessings was that we got decent mileage on our 2005 Ford Freestyle.

Considering the changing scene, I had asked Trudell to book a room in Tallahassee for two nights. Though not many people had come as far as Tallahassee, we were clear that the storm's landfall would preclude the possibility of returning the truck on Sunday. And when we reviewed Google Earth aerial photos of our cul-de-sac and home in the 9th Ward's New Orleans East, where water had stacked cars on top of cars and the level was just below the eaves of the roofs, the reality began to sink in that we were not likely to be able to return home any time soon.

While in Florida, when Trudell contacted Penske of Tallahassee, they directed her to bring the truck to them on Monday. They said because Trudell had rented it from New Orleans and come to that part of Florida, it was the only fleet vehicle they were able to save.

There was another blessing in that we had originally planned to attend a wedding over Labor Day weekend in the Atlanta, Georgia, area. On Tuesday,

August 30, we drove from Florida to Atlanta for the wedding I was to officiate on the Saturday of that weekend. The bride, one of Trudell's best friends, and the groom, realizing that we were actually "homeless," booked a room for us earlier than planned in the Atlanta metro area.

The bride gave Trudell one of her dresses to wear to her wedding, because we had left New Orleans with clothes only for a few days, as we'd planned to return before the wedding. And Trudell still has that dress to this day.

Our second-eldest son, Toussaint, was at Morehouse College, so we were able to see him while in the Atlanta area.

After the wedding, we stayed with dear friends, Drs. Walter E. and Sharon W. Fluker and sons, until September 13. Their express desire was to provide us with enough time and space to sort out things without enduring an indignity that so many others we knew and heard of were experiencing. People who'd evacuated elsewhere, near to and far from New Orleans, had been welcomed at first. But shortly thereafter, it became clear that, given the citywide devastation, with around 80 percent of it being covered with water, a projected two- or three-day—or even a week's—stay was likely to last much longer. Folks—friends and family—were unceremoniously asked to leave or ushered out with whatever it was they'd brought with them for the evacuation. Folks were forced to crowd into emergency centers if they did not have enough money both to pay for lodging and to eat.

Not only did the Fluker elders welcome us with open arms, but their sons, Hampton Sterling and Clinton, did too. While with the Flukers, we did not want for anything—material, financial, or spiritual. They, in addition to Drs. George and Sadie McCalep and Rev. Dr. Michael N. and Sylvia Harris, were living examples of "salt of the earth" and "light of the world" as they shared with our family and our congregation, CUBC, their friendship, generous finances, and the possibilities for a fresh start in other facilities.

Trudell and I both had nieces who came to our aid. For me, it was the daughter of one of my older sisters, Florence Epps. Her daughter, my niece, Lisa, had moved to Scotland for a year for her husband's job, and they, at the urging of my sister, offered their house in Conyers, Georgia, for that length of time.

We did not know that there were others in the Atlanta area who were making preparations to assist this preacher, wife, and two of four sons. One had gone to the extent of preparing a living space and researching schooling for the boys, while the other investigated making a church facility available for planting a start-up.

Trudell's niece, denise brown (niecy), who was more like a sister, was a Berkeley High School vice principal. As a solution to where we would land, she offered her home and to assist us by getting the two boys into school in California. For all of us, it was paramount that neither the eighth-grader, Amir, nor the high school senior, Kwame, would have to endure more trauma by missing school, as was the case with many other school-aged evacuees.

A family meeting was held with all the sons weighing in on the decision of what would be done, where we should go, and what would be the best course of action for the family. I had been away from the Philadelphia area so long that it was far less of an option. Staying in the Atlanta area with the one vehicle with which we had evacuated while going to and from Conyers, so far from our friends and family spread out in the somewhat unfamiliar Atlanta metro area, suggested more struggle than we might be able to manage well. So, the boys voted to go to California, back to Trudell's home, a more familiar locale due to our treks back and forth over the years.

Even though we did not evacuate to the Philadelphia area, several of my family members blessed us with gift items, material and monetary. Members from the churches that we had been a part of across the country sent us support, including Jerusalem Baptist Church in Washington, DC, where I'd answered my call to preach and started my ministry.

At first, the plan was to live with niecy. But Trudell's elder sister, Alma, who also loaned us her minivan for a while, contacted Trudell's former high school teacher, Rev. Dr. Robert McKnight, who was Alma's former classmate, about teaching possibilities for both of us. He had become a well-known, respected pastor while continuing to teach.

His parishioner, Gwynth Arnold, whose husband, Bob, had recently passed, and her adult only-child, Carla Foster, wanted to do something impactful to assist internally displaced persons who had become a part of the newly extended New Orleans diaspora. They let us live in their available house and made it our home by stocking and completely furnishing it down to a waterbed for which they apologized, not knowing that we had lost our master bedroom's waterbed in New Orleans.

After accepting their offer and upon flying from Atlanta (where we'd parked the car with the Flukers), we came to the house in a very safe North Oakland area. Gwyn, Carla, Rev. McKnight, and his wife, Venus, were at the house waiting for us to arrive. We also met Carla's husband, Michael, and their two children, Mercer and Maya. They had cleaned and stocked up the two-bedroom with a multiplicity of things to meet our needs.

The story with the Foster–Arnold family did not stop there! Carla had two friends and work colleagues, Karen Nickel and Pamela Hopkins, who were about to travel overseas when they heard of our situation. They were so kind and generous that they loaned us their SUV until they returned weeks later. The Flukers had allowed us to keep our Ford Freestyle parked at their place until we could arrange to get it shipped across the country. That blessing came through Daniel, the nephew of a CUBC minister and his wife, the Lanes. Daniel helped us to ship the vehicle through his business. We consider our Webster–Foster–Arnold families to be blessings in each other's lives. In the nearly twenty years since this elected kinship was initiated, we continue to thank God for family-by-choice as we share and enjoy mutual support as Gwyn, and all of us, advance in age.

In 2006, Kwame graduated from his mother Trudell's alma mater, Berkeley High School, one of the nation's most progressive secondary institutions. Two of Kwame's classmates from New Orleans also ended up in the Bay Area, which provided him with welcomed camaraderie.

The blessings continued as the El Cerrito NAACP provided Kwame with a scholarship. Kwame had earned admission to Benjamin Franklin High School, one of Louisiana's premier public secondary schools, before being displaced by the hurricane. Through the advocacy of Mrs. Elmettra Patterson and her son, Reginald, a trustee at historic abolitionist, coed-pioneering Oberlin College and Conservatory, Kwame was able to build on his academically solid senior year at Berkeley High by matriculating at the Ohio liberal arts college. Professor Rev. Dr. A. G. Miller and his wife, Dean and Minister Brenda Grier-Miller—also the pastor and first lady of the Oberlin House of the Lord Fellowship—were referred to us by Walter and Sharon Fluker. Ironically, they both met us at the school's orientation and kept a weathered eye out for Kwame for his entire four years at Oberlin. Kwame graduated in 2010.

Amir was to attend Willard Middle School in Berkeley, not far from the house we were living in in North Oakland. But Carla Foster was a trustee board member of the K–12 Head-Royce School, one of the best private schools in the United States, when they decided to offer nearly full scholarship aid to five students in the Bay Area who'd evacuated in the wake of Katrina. Carla and Michael's children attended Head-Royce, and thanks to the whole family, Amir made it through his first year. Over time, the other four selected students opted not to continue at Head-Royce, and Amir became the sole beneficiary of the largess of that school and was able to graduate from there and go to college in 2010.

Both Amir and Kwame, while in high school, found jobs in the Bay Area and were each able to build a work ethic that still serves them.

We met so many people who poured out so much and poured into us such love that it sometimes seemed a little overwhelming as we received cash, gift cards, and understanding ears and hearts from people everywhere, including those who had lost all they had in the Oakland Hills fires of over a decade earlier.

The blessings continued to flow. Unplanned and orchestrated meetings with connections and various kinds of assistance abounded. Trudell's brother Wayne, sister Verta, and Verta's husband, Calvin Walker, were exceedingly generous and supportive with their time and resources. A person who had suffered a tremendous loss overheard our brother-in-law talking about us being displaced from New Orleans. She was kind enough to offer Trudell the complimentary support of massage therapy.

Trudell was also able to find a Katrina support group in Berkeley where she was able to get free counseling for a year. We were blessed by Tzu Chi, a Buddhist nonprofit organization, with material and collegial support. Community-minded and Afro-sensitive St. Columba Catholic Church in Oakland hosted us and gifted us with a beautiful quilt.

Pre-Katrina and not far from our home back in New Orleans East, Trudell had become an entrepreneur and successful businesswoman as the owner of the Simple Tranquility Wholistic Massage Spa and Salon. Though everything had been lost on the first floor, a few things would eventually be salvaged from the second floor by myself and Toussaint.

In California, Trudell was able to work in several different venues. Trudell broadened her horizons post-Katrina while in the Bay from 2005 to 2008, working as the assistant to the dean of student services/assistant registrar at the Starr King School for the Ministry, part of the Graduate Theological Union in Berkeley, California. Later, she landed a promotion as the administrative assistant to the president of Starr King in 2008.

2008 was a busy year. By virtue of my community work and the fact that Trudell had been an entrepreneur, we were invited to accompany New Orleans Mayor Nagin on a friendship and trade excursion to South Africa. It was also the year our first granddaughter, Aubrey, was born.

As she had already become nationally board certified and was a licensed massage therapist, Trudell was able to land a teaching position with the National Holistic Institute (NHI) College of Massage Therapy Emeryville & San Francisco Bay Area. There, she touched the lives of numerous students, who, when she'd encounter them from time to time in the Bay Area, would thank her for not only instructing but mentoring them. From 2008 to 2010, she taught over sixty classes on massage therapy and health education and was responsible for seeing classes through completion of 720-hour curricula at NHI.

Members of Christian Unity Baptist Church were so spread out across the country in the aftermath that, to this day, many of us reckon time as either pre-Katrina or after- or post-Katrina. So, post-Katrina, after seeing that Trudell, Kwame, and Amir were more or less settled in the Rockridge section of North Oakland, I set my sights on trying to see about the welfare of our members. I had started a kind of Baptist itineracy while in the Atlanta area and later extended it by visiting members in Baton Rouge, Houston, Dallas, and the greater metropolitan area of Atlanta. I was even able to get into New Orleans while in Atlanta to check on the house, the church, and the condition of the neighborhoods by connecting with members of the New Orleans Police Department and the Health Department, which was headed by Rev. Dr. Kevin U. Stephens, who, as assistant to the pastor, would eventually succeed me as CUBC's senior pastor.

It was in City Hall, in a meeting room provided by Dr. Stephens, that we—several ministers and denomination figures—met with civil rights veteran Rev. Dr. C. T. Vivian. When he read about the destruction that wreaked havoc on the city by way of the catastrophic failure of the levee and flood-wall system, he reached out to the activist church community with a plan to help bring back the city by building up the people through strategically located churches.

Because I had been in and out of the city and some of my colleagues were between New Orleans and Baton Rouge, I reached out to Rev. Donald Boutte to help make contact with other pastors. That is when Churches Supporting Churches was born. With Dr. Vivian's contacts and seemingly indefatigable energy and spirit, we were able to rally resources sufficient to spark recovery by putting finances into the hands of pastors for their churches and their own support, as well as sponsor reflection retreats for pastors and their spouses, where there could be a space of trust and confidentiality for venting, sharing, self-care, healing, and non-directive spiritual guidance.

Our home was flooded twice. Once through Hurricane Katrina, where the high-water mark was 7.2 feet of water. Shortly after that, Hurricane Rita flooded the house again, and we were not able to salvage anything from it. I literally had to shovel and wheelbarrow out my mud-ladened work and destroyed sources. In fact, I had spent considerable time and money amassing all of the books, articles, and such that I'd needed to complete my dissertation on gospel music for my PhD in Religion, Theology and the Arts and its defense at the Graduate Theological Union (GTU).

Rev. Dr. Archie Smith Jr. had agreed to be my committee chair, and with the patience of Job, he shepherded me through the fits and starts of the research, writing, and defense of my doctoral journey. He even literally pleaded with one of my committee members on the eve of my defense to relent and remain on the committee after all of the work had been completed. Post-Katrina, Archie took me around from office to office at the GTU. And to my great appreciation and benefit, thanks to their tremendously awesome act of grace, I was able to continue and complete my work and graduate. But it was not before a sister-colleague, a former GTU program director and professor, came to my rescue and replaced the aforementioned dissertation defense committee member. The Rev. Dr. Cheryl Kirk-Duggan stepped in and agreed to serve on the committee, though my defense had to be postponed from 2010 to 2011.

In the meantime, I continued my itinerancy and commuted between the West and Gulf Coasts, with less travel to the other cities to meet members. Some had decided to stay where they were. Some moved back to New Orleans, and yet others moved to other places.

Blessings continued to pile up for us as a family and for our church. Under the leadership of Esben Just, jazz- and gospel-loving tourist friends who'd visited our church services many times pre-Katrina from Copenhagen, Denmark, held a benefit concert and sent us tens of thousands of dollars to assist Christian Unity in its recovery. Another Dane whom we had not known previously also sent us thousands. We received funds from World Vision. Money came from the Caribbean and across the country.

My ministerial mentors, colleagues, well-wishers, friends, and friends of friends with whom I'd been connected around the country invited me to come and preach. It was not because I was so great a preacher, but rather it gave them a chance to contribute to the post-Katrina recovery of someone they knew directly, and they believed I would be accountable and see to it that contributed funds would bless my family, while funds raised for the church and entrusted to me would go directly to Christian Unity. We received funds from the Bush–Clinton Katrina Fund after my competent young professionals, such Ashleigh Gilbert (Gardere), put together the required qualifying documents to receive the grant and help account for the disbursement. I traveled anywhere and everywhere when someone said they wanted to assist in our recovery from the hurricane and the epic failure of the levee and flood-wall "protection" of the city. We even received books from all over the country to help replace those that many of us had lost.

As a result, when we marched back into the church on First Sunday, March 2006. We first marched around the city blocks of Conti, N. Claibourne, Bienville, and N. Derbigny with a New Orleans brass band. We then entered the building, a former bowling alley that had been built in the 1960s by Catholic laywoman Margaret Lauer as part of a would-be entertainment complex, because Black folk had not been allowed to attend performance venues on Canal Street. Major Lanes had also once been PPP Skating Rink, a bingo parlor, a reception hall, and, before we acquired it, a venue for a Bobby "Blue" Bland blues concert.

We had worship, baptism, communion/The Lord's Supper, and Brother Richard Winder, our in-house real estate broker for the original building acquisition deal, burned the mortgage note on the building because we, by the grace of God, had received enough tithes, offerings, contributions, grants, and gifts to retire the debt on the building.

We were further blessed to have our house in New Orleans cleaned, gutted, and rebuilt (twice, because of contaminated drywall), by the grace of God and many, many other good and gracious hands, including volunteers from organizations and denominations from around the country, including the Progressive National Baptist Convention, Trinity Episcopal Church - New Orleans, the Mississippi Delta Grassroots Caucus, the Baptist Peace Fellowship of North America, Every Church A Peace Church, and the Mennonite Disaster Service and Mennonite Central Committee. We had the added assistance of the Church of the Brethren, through which I found a fast friend in David Jensen of the Institute for Human Rights and Responsibilities, whereby he and Dr. Vivian conducted numerous sessions with us on Kingian nonviolence philosophy.

For the last seven years, Dwight and Trudell Webster have been a bicoastal commuter couple. Trudell (née Brown) and Dwight live between Gulf Coast's New Orleans East and Emeryville of the West Coast's San Francisco East Bay Area.

Trudell Webster is a practicing licensed massage therapist in both New Orleans and the Bay Area. Before the hurricane hit, Trudell was owner of the successful Simple Tranquility Wholistic Spa and Salon in New Orleans East.

Dwight Webster has been serving for seven years as senior pastor of the historic 134-year-old Beth Eden Baptist Church in West Oakland, California. It is the "Mother Church" and oldest Black Baptist church in Alameda County. This fall will mark my seven-year anniversary as senior pastor, after I also served there some forty years ago as minister of youth and young adults. After having been referred there by the Rev. Dr. J. Alfred Smith Sr., Beth Eden is where I met Trudell and where we later married in 1982.

I am honored to be an affiliated faculty member and an advisory committee elder at the Sankofa Institute of the Oblate School of Theology in San Antonio, Texas. In the Bay Area, I serve as vice chair of the Berkeley School of Theology board of trustees, secretary of the board of directors of the Seafarers Ministry of the Golden Gate at The International Maritime Center, and as a member of the board of directors of the Leadership Institute at Allen Temple. Trudell is currently training as a lay counseling therapist of the Friendship Bench-New Orleans, an evidence-based bridge mental health service project that originated in Harare, Zimbabwe.

> *Though the storms keep on raging in my life*
> *And sometimes, it's hard to tell my night from day*
> *Still, that hope that lies within is reassured*
> *As I keep my eyes upon the distant shore;*
> *I know He'll lead me safely to that*
> *Blessed place He has prepared*
>
> *But if the storms don't cease*
> *And if the wind keeps on blowing,*
> *My soul has been anchored in the Lord*
>
> — "My Soul's Been Anchored in the Lord,"
> as sung by Douglas Miller

Curtis Mitchell and Rev. Cathy Hall Johnson mandated the song above to be sung at their wedding on May 4, 2019, at Triumph Baptist Church in Philadelphia, Pennsylvania. I took it to be a reprise of a rendering that I'd shared with that church upon being invited to preach in the aftermath of Hurricane Katrina, in 2009 or 2010. Rev. Cathy and Triumph financially blessed us tremendously that day, which went a long way toward our recovery.

Curtis was one of the first musicians to accompany my efforts as a vocalist at the historic Jerusalem Baptist Church in Georgetown, Washington, DC, where I started my ministry as a Howard University student, under the leadership of Rev. Dr. R. Clinton Washington. Cathy was a schoolmate of mine at Colgate Rochester Crozer Divinity School in Rochester, New York.

This gospel music favorite is an anthem of testimony to many of us who survived the ravages of Hurricane Katrina. Another Gospel standard is Margaret Pleasant Douroux's "If It Had Not Been for the Lord on My [Our] Side." Drawn from Psalm 146:1, it is the often sung sentiment of so many of us who experienced one of the most powerful storms this country has seen: "*Where would I—where would we be?*"

FROM NEW ORLEANS TO BIRMINGHAM:
A Journey of Resilience After Hurricane Katrina

KYSHUN WEBSTER SR.

It's impossible to put into words the fear and uncertainty that consumed me when we realized Hurricane Katrina was going to hit New Orleans in August 2005. I can still remember the weight of the moment—knowing that my life, my family, and my city were about to be forever changed. I had just married Taralyn, the love of my life, and we had my four-year-old daughter, Treshor, and a beautiful newborn son, my junior, in our arms. We were still fresh in our marriage, full of plans, hopes, and dreams. But everything felt precarious as the storm loomed large on the horizon.

The decision to leave New Orleans was one of haste, as there was only a short window to evacuate. We had family and friends we'd grown up with, memories woven into every corner of the city. But the storm was coming, and we knew we had to get out. Two days before the winds arrived, we packed up our little family and joined my extended family in a mass exodus as we voyaged to Texas. As we made our way out of the city, the realization of what we were leaving behind began to hit. We didn't know then that we wouldn't return for months, that New Orleans would never be the same.

Now we arrived in Dallas, Texas, where my sister resided. We all packed into just a couple of hotel rooms to save on the costs. It wasn't long after our departure that we became fixated on the news coverage and binge-watched the news for hours. The images on the television screen seemed unreal at first, almost as if we were watching a disaster movie that we could pause or turn off. But as the scenes of devastation flashed by—flooded streets, rooftops barely visible above the waterline, people clinging to debris—the weight of reality began to settle in, heavy and merciless. We were crowded together in a small hotel room in Dallas, a fragile refuge from the storm that was annihilating our home. No one spoke. It felt as if the air itself had stilled, as if the whole world was watching in collective disbelief.

The camera panned across familiar neighborhoods, now unrecognizable under murky water and shattered remains. Places we'd walked, streets we'd driven, and landmarks we'd known all our lives had become nothing but wreckage swept away or drowned in muddy currents. The French Quarter was now a ghostly echo, and places we'd once called home seemed worlds away. It was like watching the Acropolis crumble, a great civilization collapsing, and all we could do was sit there, frozen, staring at the screen, our hearts breaking with every passing second.

My wife, normally so steady, sat silent yet uneasy, clutching our newborn close to her chest. There was a rawness in her eyes, an aching sorrow that words couldn't reach. Our son stirred in her arms, unaware of the calamity unfolding on the screen, blissfully ignorant of the world that had forever changed around him. I glanced at her and saw the weight she carried, an unspoken urge to rush back, to be with the others who had stayed behind, to stand shoulder to shoulder with her colleagues in what felt like an apocalyptic scene. But we both knew she couldn't go, not now. And the helplessness of it nearly consumed us.

As the coverage continued, I felt my pulse quicken. The thought of our future—our home, our city—was a hollow ache in my chest. New Orleans wasn't just a place: it was a heartbeat, the soul of our lives, and now it lay in ruin. We could only imagine the fates of those who had stayed, those who couldn't leave or wouldn't, each one a loved one or friend or stranger who shared our city, now left to face the unimaginable. We mourned for them even as we tried to reckon with our own escape, grateful yet haunted by guilt for having the means to evacuate in the face of so many not having the resources to flee for their lives.

The scenes on that screen held us captive, and for those moments, we felt like shadows caught between the life we had known and the uncertainty of what lay ahead.

The Shero's Battle

Watching my wife grapple with everything felt like a second storm tearing through our lives. She sat by the window, staring off into a blur of loss and longing, holding our tiny, six-week-old son in her arms. I could see the battle inside her—a profound ache to return to New Orleans, to stand with her fellow officers, who were facing unimaginable devastation. As a seven-year

FROM NEW ORLEANS TO BIRMINGHAM:
A JOURNEY OF RESILIENCE AFTER HURRICANE KATRINA

veteran of the New Orleans Police Department, she had dedicated her life to service, to running toward danger instead of away from it. Now, stranded with us in Dallas, guilt weighed heavy on her, and it cut deep.

She was still on medical leave, recovering from childbirth, but the pull to be out there, back with her team, seemed unbearable to her. Her colleagues were fighting just to survive, losing their own homes and their own sanity, some barely able to distinguish between the lives they were trying to save and the lives they were losing. And then there were those who'd left the force, abandoning their posts to stay with their families, a choice she could understand yet found so difficult to accept. She saw it as a betrayal of their oath, a violation of the very spirit of first responders.

More than once, she turned to me, her face full of pain and tears, pleading to return. Her eyes held a fire, fierce and desperate, as if only by going back could she silence the gnawing guilt and helplessness. I knew she was willing to push through her own physical and emotional exhaustion to be there, to stand alongside her comrades. But I held her close, reminding her of our son, of this fragile new family. I reminded her that even the strongest warriors need time to heal. Each time I spoke, I watched her resolve waver, a mix of relief and heartbreak settling over her face. I knew how much it cost her to stay.

In those moments, I understood more than ever the weight she carried and the sacrifice she was making by staying with us. I could only try to be her anchor as she grieved, as she yearned to be a protector and partner for her fellow officers even from miles away. The battle inside her was a testament to her strength, and yet it left her feeling utterly helpless. I held her tight, hoping that, somehow, I could offer her the peace she so desperately needed, knowing that her heart was still with those she'd vowed to protect.

After days of watching the destruction and death and feeling paralysis, we knew our evacuation would not be a turnaround trip. Like most New Orleanians used to the hurricane party drill, we'd brought limited resources: clothes for two to three days and a couple of Igloos filled with drinks and cold cuts for survival.

Days later, when our limited supply of food was up, we had to go on a hunt, realizing that our ATM cards, connected to New Orleans-based banks, were not able to function. Hence, we had no access to money and were in dire need to replenish food supplies. So, we left the hotel and tried to navigate the sprawling city. The heat was relentless, pressing down on us like it had no intention of letting up. We saw a food giveaway line, and there I stood, holding my son close, feeling his tiny, warm body against my chest as we anxiously waited to see what the giveaway line, which seemed to stretch endlessly, was distributing. Dallas felt foreign and expansive, so far from the comforts of New Orleans, and nothing around me felt familiar or steady. My son's cries pierced the heavy air, each one striking a deeper pang of guilt and regret within me. Only six weeks old, barely beginning his life, and already here he was, held by his father in a line for handouts. I looked down, and his wide, searching eyes met mine, so fragile, so trusting. Tears blurred my vision.

I had just defended my dissertation and earned my PhD. This was supposed to be a season of new beginnings—Taralyn and I had celebrated our first wedding anniversary just a month before Katrina tore our world apart. And now, here I was, barely able to provide a meal for my family. Pride, dignity, everything felt stripped away as I stood there, feeling like a beggar, desperate and hollowed out.

My wife stood nearby, quiet, holding herself together with a strength I couldn't find in myself at that moment as quiet tears streamed down my face. I knew she was hurting, too. We hadn't calculated for this—a life uprooted, a city lost, loved ones scattered and gone. I wanted to tell my son that I was sorry, that I would fix this, that things would get better, but I didn't know how or when. In those moments, everything felt unbearably fragile, like our whole new life might slip away with just one more gust of wind. Given that our first stop was Dallas, Texas, we realized after a couple of months that it was vast—too vast, in fact, to feel a sense of community and belonging. The sprawling cityscape felt so distant, both physically and emotionally. It lacked the intimate, community-based vibe and effervescent culture we were used to in New Orleans. The people were nice, but it didn't feel like home. After two months of trying to adjust, we knew we needed something different. Dallas was too big, too impersonal for what we needed during this uncertain time. So, with a mix of hope and hesitation, we decided to move again.

That's when Karin and Noah Hopkins intervened in our lives in the most meaningful way. Karin and Noah had lived in New Orleans for decades but had decided to sell their New Orleans East home and move to Alabama just about a year before Katrina. It was as if they knew in advance a storm was coming and evacuated earlier than most. They had always been dear friends of mine, and when they heard we were struggling, Karin insisted that we move to Birmingham, Alabama. They had a warmth and sincerity about them that made it hard to say no. They had built their own lives there and were thriving, and they believed that we could, too. Birmingham was smaller, quainter, and, in their eyes, a place where we could build a new foundation for our family.

Halfheartedly, we packed up and headed for Birmingham with the hope that this was the right decision, leaving our extended family behind in Dallas. Upon arriving, we realized that they were right. The smaller, tight-knit community felt like a safe haven for us. It wasn't New Orleans, but it offered a chance to breathe, to heal, and to start over. Karin and Noah were pivotal in helping us settle in. They introduced us to other displaced New Orleanians, who would become lifelong friends, along with their network, which helped us tap into opportunities that we might not have found on our own. The bond between the displaced New Orleanians in Birmingham deepened. It was as if we all carried this shared understanding of loss, but also of resilience. Together, we formed a small but powerful community of people who were determined to rise from the rubble and return to New Orleans to make our city a proud place to live again.

The gumbo gathering in Birmingham

It was a warm, muggy night in Birmingham, and we were still trying to get our bearings in this new city. Karin and Noah were absolutely thrilled to introduce the small group of New Orleanians to whom she played host to "someone special." This wasn't just any official in Birmingham; she was a respected architect with a deep admiration for New Orleans. Karin described her with glowing enthusiasm, so I figured we'd be in for a good time.

We arrived at her beautiful home, a modern masterpiece that looked like it had been plucked right out of an architecture magazine. As soon as we stepped inside, we caught a whiff of something simmering on the stove. A few steps further in, I got a clear look at the pot. It was gumbo—or, at least, that's what we were told. I shot a look at Taralyn, who raised an eyebrow. Now, if you know anything about New Orleanians, you'll know that our gumbo is a sacred thing. It's not a recipe; it's a legacy, an art form, a birthright. And right off the bat, the aroma of this "gumbo" wasn't quite passing the test.

"Y'all, I am so excited for you to try my gumbo," the host announced with pride, ladling generous portions into our bowls.

Her grin was big, but the gumbo—well, let's just say that it wasn't what we'd expect. Where was the dark, rich roux? The smoky andouille sausage? The shrimp, the crab, or the okra? Instead, we spotted a few chopped carrots and Owens breakfast sausage floating around, some dark tasteless liquid, and—was that . . . corn?

Karin, bless her heart, was trying to mask her expression, knowing full well what was coming. Noah gave me a slight nudge, his eyes widening as he looked down at his bowl. Taralyn gave me a soft kick under the table, as if to warn me to behave myself. I'd like to think I'm a polite guest, but this was asking a lot.

"So," the host said, looking straight at us, her face bright and expectant. "What do y'all think? Does it taste like the gumbo you remember?"

You could have heard a mouse tap-dance on cotton. We exchanged glances, each of us trying to muster a smile that said, *Well, it's . . . something.*

Karin, our saving grace, took a small spoonful, smiled, and nodded thoughtfully. "It's . . . different," she said, clearly working hard to find a compliment without telling a lie.

Our host beamed. "It's my special recipe!" she said, fishing for compliments like a pro. "I did my best with what I could find here in Birmingham."

I couldn't help myself—I cleared my throat, then said as diplomatically as possible, "It's definitely a . . . creative twist." Karin gave me a look, half-horrified and half-amused, knowing exactly what was going through our heads.

When we finally left, Karin let out a laugh. "I probably should've warned her about serving gumbo to a group of New Orleanians," she admitted, chuckling.

Noah grinned and added, "Next time, maybe we bring a pot of real gumbo for her to try." Taralyn and I nodded vigorously. We may have been far from home, but some things you just can't replicate. Lesson learned: as a New Orleanian, never let a non-native host invite you over for gumbo; instead, delight the host by cooking it for them.

Mobilizing my inner strengths to mobilize others

I knew that New Orleans had been devastated, and while I was grateful for the refuge Birmingham provided, my heart was still tethered to my city, to the place that had shaped me. I realized that my purpose wasn't just to survive this crisis but to do something about it. I needed to act, to help others who were displaced, and to help New Orleans recover.

In the months after earning my PhD, a milestone I had poured years of effort into, and returning from Minneapolis, I thought I would feel unstoppable, ready to step into a role that would help shape the future of New Orleans. But the reality was far more sobering. At just twenty-something years old, I often felt like my ideas and vision for improving education and youth engagement in the civic culture were dismissed by the leadership circles that

FROM NEW ORLEANS TO BIRMINGHAM:
A JOURNEY OF RESILIENCE AFTER HURRICANE KATRINA

held the reins of decision-making. There was a pervasive sense that youth equated to inexperience, and while I saw opportunity and innovation in my generation, the old-money status quo leadership seemed blind to it. It was as if the weight of rebuilding was a club, and I along with other people of color weren't on the guest list, and conscious efforts were at play to exclude us.

This internal conflict grew louder as I debated whether to stay in New Orleans or use this exodus opportunity to seek opportunities elsewhere. I loved the city—its culture, its people, its soul—but the lack of acknowledgment of what I could bring to the table made me question whether it was worth staying. I felt like a tree trying to grow in rocky soil. I wanted to help rebuild, but how could I contribute meaningfully if no one was willing to listen?

Enter Linetta Gilbert. A longtime friend and mentor, Linetta had been a guiding light in my life for years. When Katrina struck, she was just a few years into her tenure serving as a senior program officer at the Ford Foundation in New York. From her post, she had a bird's-eye view of the city's challenges and the broader social issues that Katrina had laid bare. More importantly, she had an unwavering belief in the power of young leaders to drive change.

When I expressed my frustrations and doubts to her, she listened intently, her calm and wise demeanor both comforting and challenging. "This is your city," she said firmly. "You have the right to shape its future. Don't let anyone tell you otherwise. The rebuilding of New Orleans isn't just about structures—it's about people like you, with the vision and energy to reimagine something better and more equitable."

Linetta didn't just offer words of encouragement; she put her influence behind her belief in me. She connected me to networks, opened doors to funders, and advocated for the inclusion of younger voices in conversations about the city's recovery. Her support was a lifeline, a reminder that while some might not yet see the value in my contributions, others did. More importantly, her faith in me helped me find faith in myself.

Through her guidance, I began to see my role in the recovery effort not as someone waiting to be invited to the table, but as someone who could build a table of my own. I realized that staying in New Orleans wasn't just about enduring the challenges—it was about proving that my generation had the creativity, resilience, and resolve to drive the city's transformation.

Linetta's mentorship became a cornerstone of my journey. She taught me that leadership isn't always about being the loudest voice in the room—it's about staying true to your vision and finding the people who will amplify it with you. With her support, I found the strength to stay, to fight for the future of my city, and to know that my contributions mattered, even if not everyone was ready to see them yet.

So, in the depths of despair, feeling helpless as I watched my city struggle in the wake of Hurricane Katrina, I realized that there was something I could do. I didn't have to sit on the sidelines, overwhelmed by loss and longing. Before the storm, I had run a nonprofit called Operation REACH, a youth development organization focused on strengthening communities by empowering young people. Even though our foundation had been shaken, I knew that Operation REACH could be a part of the solution, a way to help rebuild New Orleans and give families hope for a future. So, I founded the Gulfsouth Youth Action Corps, an initiative designed to help the youth of New Orleans and beyond, particularly those impacted by the storm. It became my way of honoring the city's resilience, its history, and the generation of young people who had been deeply affected by the devastation. Through the corps, I worked to create programs that would bring hope, empowerment, and resources to the city's youth. It was my attempt to serve the future while trying to heal from the past.

With this clarity, I launched the Gulfsouth Youth Action Corps, a bold initiative to bring summer programming to New Orleans. My vision was simple but ambitious: to mobilize college students from across the nation, inviting them to lend their energy and talents to support children in our city. These programs would not only provide kids with a safe, nurturing environment, but they would also help families feel supported enough to return home, to rebuild and reclaim their lives.

I knew I couldn't do it alone. As if the universe was aligning, I got another call that seemed to seal my path. Zakenya Perry, one of my employees, who was living in the 9th Ward before the storm—the area most ravaged by the storm—had lost everything, but her spirit was unbroken. She was just as committed to rebuilding her life as I was to rebuilding New Orleans. I knew that it wasn't enough for me to stay in Birmingham and help from afar—I needed to bring more people into the fold, more people who could help restore our community.

One person immediately came to mind: Zakenya, affectionately called Zee. She had been a new hire, barely two weeks on the job at Operation Reach before Katrina hit. A single mother living in the 9th Ward, Zee had to evacuate to Houston ahead of the storm, leaving behind nearly everything. Months later, when this inspiration to act struck, I called Zee with

FROM NEW ORLEANS TO BIRMINGHAM:
A JOURNEY OF RESILIENCE AFTER HURRICANE KATRINA

an urgent request: to relocate once again, this time to Birmingham, to help relaunch Operation REACH from there. Without hesitation, Zee agreed. So, I moved her to Birmingham, where she, too, would find the support she needed to rebuild.

Within days, she had packed her things and arrived, ready to do whatever it took to make the Gulfsouth Youth Action Corps a reality. I helped her settle in, securing her an apartment and some basic furnishings, but more importantly, we leaned on each other. Our relationship transformed from employer-employee into a family bond. We helped each other babysit, shared meals, and celebrated holidays together and small victories. In this new chapter, we were no longer just colleagues; we were a team, connected by purpose and a shared determination to rebuild our lives.

Our first summer of programming was a success, providing children with safe, enriching activities while their families pieced together their lives and homes. The sight of kids laughing and learning amidst the ruins was a symbol of the city's rebirth, and for the families returning, it was a lifeline. I remember thinking as I watched the youth in our programs—youth who had lost their homes, their schools, their sense of stability—that this was the true battle. The rebuilding of New Orleans was not just about bricks and mortar, but about restoring the physical city. It was about restoring the spirit of the people who called that place home. We had to invest in the next generation and ensure they had the tools, opportunities, and hope to rebuild their own lives and their own futures.

I hadn't realized the scale of what we had accomplished until I received an unexpected call from the White House after the first year of this demonstration launch. They saw the potential to expand our efforts across the Gulf Coast, reaching communities that were equally devastated but often forgotten. The call to action wasn't something I ever anticipated, but when your community and country need you, you rise to the challenge. I saluted, so to speak, and prepared to take our grassroots organization to new heights. A little homegrown nonprofit that I started in college had now been tapped by the Corporation for National and Community Service, at the request of the US president, to scale and expand across the Gulf Coast region.

Fifteen years have passed, and Zee is still by my side, and we have an enduring friendship. She is my "sister," and her boys call me uncle. Together, we transformed a moment of hopelessness into a lifelong mission of service and resilience, finding family and purpose in the process.

Moreover, the sense of connection I found in Birmingham, particularly among the displaced New Orleans citizens, was like nothing I had experienced before. In our collective despair, we found strength. In our grief, we found purpose. We were all doing our part to help each other move forward, and every small victory felt like a win for the entire city of New Orleans. We were no longer just victims of a storm—we were agents of change, committed to rebuilding not just our own lives but the lives of everyone who had been affected.

Reflecting back, the journey from New Orleans to Dallas and then Birmingham was never easy, and at times, it felt like we were in limbo, unsure of what our next step would be. But what I learned throughout this journey is that it's possible to survive and thrive in the most uncertain circumstances. We learned to make new friends, to create new communities, and to find our way back to purpose.

Eventually, we returned to New Orleans. The city wasn't the same, and neither were we. But in the process of rebuilding our lives, we discovered a deeper sense of purpose. We had learned how to survive in a new place, and in doing so, we felt a profound responsibility to return, not just as displaced citizens but as leaders who could help heal the wounds of our city.

When we returned, it wasn't just about rebuilding what had been lost—it was about rebuilding with intention. We didn't just want New Orleans to return to what it had been. We wanted it to be better. More inclusive. More resilient. More unified. Through the Gulfsouth Youth Action Corps, we worked to create a better future for the youth of New Orleans, giving them the tools to create a city they could be proud of.

Looking back, I realize that this journey was never just about one person, one family, or even one city. It was about all of us, displaced but determined, coming together to rebuild, to reimagine, and to rise above the devastation. We didn't just survive the storm—we grew from it. And in doing so, we learned the true meaning of community and resilience.

My journey from New Orleans to Birmingham wasn't a straight line, but it was one that taught me lessons I carry with me every day. It taught me that no matter how far you are from home, no matter how much you've lost, there's always a way to start over, rebuild, and to find hope. And it reminded me that no matter where life takes you, your roots, your community, and your purpose will always lead you back home.

The devastation of Hurricane Katrina marked a turning point in my life, a moment that shaped not only who I am but also what I could accomplish for

FROM NEW ORLEANS TO BIRMINGHAM:
A JOURNEY OF RESILIENCE AFTER HURRICANE KATRINA

my community and beyond. Out of the darkness and displacement, I discovered a resilience and purpose I hadn't fully tapped into before. In launching the Gulfsouth Youth Action Corps from a small office shared with Karin and Noah's business operation in Birmingham, we successfully rallied hundreds of college students from across the country to help us rebuild New Orleans. It was a remarkable sight: students arriving from universities everywhere, bringing hope, energy, and hands ready to work.

From this tragedy, I learned how to be strategic under intense pressure, to scale a homegrown vision to something greater than I ever imagined, and to embrace opportunities that stretched my limits. My PhD, earned just before the storm, became more than an academic achievement: it was a training ground that readied me for this profound mission. I was no longer just a "young visionary" with ambitious ideas—I was a leader guiding an effort that would impact over ten thousand youth across the Gulf Coast, helping them find stability in a turbulent time.

By Christmas 2005, we returned to New Orleans, our home on the west bank side of Algiers mercifully unscathed. It became a refuge for our family, a place for them to stay as they made short trips to the city to rebuild their lives. This time, we played the role of hosts, just as Karin and Noah had done for us in Birmingham. It was a full-circle moment, and we were grateful to be a place of strength and comfort for those we loved.

My wife returned to the New Orleans Police Department, stepping back into her role with unwavering resolve, ready to serve the city she loved. She also partnered with me to lead an effort to bring back early childcare facilities for families. In addition to her day job of protecting and serving as one of NOPD's finest, she also helped to launch the Knowledge Garden Child Development Center at a time when childcare facilities had been decimated and childcare facilities were scarce. With her support, I continued leading Operation REACH and the Gulfsouth Youth Action Corps, which had grown into a symbol of resilience and hope. In our own ways, Taralyn and I had become heroes to our community—not through grand gestures, but by embracing our duty to rebuild, protect, and serve. The storm had torn through our lives, but it also unveiled a strength within us to help our city heal and find new life amid the ruins.

REFLECTIONS
MK WEGMANN

Hurricanes for a New Orleanian are familiar and regular occurrences. When Katrina was heading to New Orleans in 2005, I was on vacation at the beach in North Carolina. I was president and CEO of the National Performance Network (NPN), from which I retired in 2017.

As a native and lifelong New Orleans citizen, I was concerned but not alarmed by the news reports that Katrina was heading towards New Orleans. Over the years, I'd experienced many dangerous hurricanes and was well aware of the devastation they can cause. Growing up in the Broadmoor neighborhood, our house was a raised basement structure built in the 1930s after the devastating floods of 1927. Broadmoor is deep in the bowl of New Orleans. Building codes in New Orleans after those floods meant that houses were raised at least three feet above sea level. In Broadmoor, unfinished basements in houses raised them even higher than those codes. Ironically, those codes were forgotten after World War II, when the suburbs around New Orleans exploded with slab-on-grade houses on the drained swamplands, one of the reasons so many houses were lost in Katrina.

Our house was the one where our neighbors came when a storm was coming, and I have many memories of long nights with a house full of neighbors, waiting for a hurricane to approach and pass. I have memories of standing on the porch with my daddy in the calm as the eye passed, Daddy pointing out the shifts in wind direction at the passing of the eye.

My father, Joseph Anthony Wegmann, was the middle child among the eleven Wegmann brothers, sons of John X. Wegmann and Sophie Bonhage. My father was vice president of the Lafayette Insurance Company, and my uncle George was president of the company. This was in the days when many businesses and companies were locally based, not part of a larger corporation, before corporate mergers and acquisitions sucked away ownership of so many local businesses. Lafayette knew their customers, the people whose homes they insured; they had personal relationships with them. And, of course, in New Orleans, insurance companies knew all about hurricanes.

I was a senior in high school when Hurricane Betsy struck New Orleans and the levees in the Lower 9 were deliberately breached.

I am a thirteen-year graduate of Ursuline Academy, kindergarten through high school. I was privileged to have been taught by this order of nuns during an era of deep social justice activism in the Catholic church. At the time, Ursuline was both a day school and a boarding school, both for elementary and high school students. Many of the boarders were from Latin American countries, including Cuba, who were sent to Ursuline for a few years to learn English and experience US culture; Ursuline also had a school in Cuba, as it did in other US cities.

My parents used to let us board at Ursuline on long weekends when they went to insurance conventions, which was exciting for me. We were taught French from kindergarten through high school, so boarding was an opportunity to learn rudimentary Spanish by playing games with the Latin American boarders. One early lesson about hardship came for me after Castro took over Cuba; some of the same Cuban students who'd been boarders for a few years as privileged children came back to be taken in by Ursuline as refugees. I remember Mother Damian Aycock, an Ursuline nun, talking to us and encouraging us to be understanding of the trauma that our classmates were experiencing and encouraging compassion and generosity in our behavior. We had known these girls as privileged borders experiencing a year or two in New Orleans; now, they had returned with nothing as immigrants.

Ursuline was also at the forefront when Catholic schools were racially integrating in New Orleans. In 1962, Ursuline enrolled Black students in high school and kindergarten at the start of my freshman year of high school. My memories are that the preparation our teachers gave our class started much earlier. We were told that we were a special class, that we were privileged to be a part of an historic moment. We were taught the legacy of Ursuline nuns who came to New Orleans in 1727 and their history of teaching Indian children and enslaved girls. I remember being told to stand up as an individual, to not "follow the crowd," to be true to myself when hard moments came. One of those hard moments came during the summer after eighth grade. Rumors flew about the three Black girls who would be joining our class as freshmen. Many of my classmates, girls who had been in our class since kindergarten, were pulled out of

Ursuline because their parents didn't want them to be in the same school with Black children.

My education did teach me about the evils and horrors of slavery; I was not shielded from the pictures of the children who integrated New Orleans public schools and the vitriol that was hurled at them; I knew about Emmett Till. I was taught the importance of stepping up and speaking up. Later, in my freshman year of college, the first thing I signed up for at orientation was the NAACP.

In 1965, when Hurricane Betsy struck, my father was inundated with work, since every building in New Orleans had damage. I'd previously worked summer jobs at Lafayette Insurance, which was located at 2123 Magazine Street. I was asked to come and work after Betsy. There was no electricity, but the phone lines were working, though they did not ring; I just picked up the receiver and someone was there: "Tell Mr. Joe my roof is gone. Please tell me what to do." Most of the callers knew my father by name and expected that he would personally respond, and he did.

One of my father's employees lived in the 9th Ward and lost their house and everything the family owned. My parents took them in to live in our house until they were able to find a new place to live. Hurricane Betsy ultimately led to the necessity of selling Lafayette Insurance. Like many independent companies, it did not have the re-insurance to withstand such devastating losses. But the lesson I learned, that those with privilege should share it, has stuck with me my whole life.

Following my graduation from high school, I attended Spring Hill College, a Jesuit school in Mobile, Alabama. I chose Spring Hill because Mobile has Mardi Gras, which meant I could come home to New Orleans for Carnival.

From a young age, I was involved in theater; Ursuline had a strong program. In my bios in theater programs, I used to say that I made my stage debut as the baby Jesus in a Christmas pageant at Ursuline, and in addition to a love of horses and volleyball, I was in every play I could be in throughout my years of education at both Ursuline and Spring Hill, though I never majored in theater.

My love of New Orleans brought me back after college, rather than going to New York; I knew that meant that I was giving up the possibility of working in the theater. I received my MA in English from LSUNO (now UNO) while participating in theater at La Mise en Scène, including the infamous production of *Marat/Sade*. I was working for an art gallery in 1976 when the impetus to found the Contemporary Arts Center arose after an exhibit of Bob

Tannen's work. I volunteered for its early projects that year. In 1977, I joined Don Marshall as the second staff person, and I have been deeply involved with it ever since; I am now an emeritus board member. In 1992 I became managing director of Junebug Productions and in 1999 was appointed President and CEO of NPN. NPN moved to New Orleans because it was a condition of my taking the position. I've never wanted to live anywhere else. Though I did not have a career as an artist in New Orleans, I found my place as a cultural organizer. Making New Orleans a place where artists can thrive has motivated me. Supporting social and racial justice is the frame in which I work.

Thus, when Hurricane Katrina struck and the levees failed and then every system failed, leading to the Superdome and Convention Center horrors—and there are still one hundred thousand people who can't or won't come back—I realized I could sink into depression. Or, I could step up and speak up and notice the incredible and generous help given by so many, many people.

Artists were among the earliest responders to the people of New Orleans; both local and national artists flocked to New Orleans to add their creative skills and resources to our recovery. The number and scope of projects initiated by artists, many of which lasted for years beyond 2005, have had a lasting impact. Some examples include:

- The I-10 Witness Project, a media-based effort by Mondo Bizarro, a community-based story project documenting the myriad of tales in the aftermath of Hurricane Katrina. Starting in the fall of 2005, it provided a safe space to express the impact of the storm on people's lives. The artists traveled throughout Louisiana and surrounding states to interview people in shelters, relief workers, community organizers, artists, medical staff, city planners, and government workers. All participants were given a copy of their story.

- *The Portrait Project* by Lisa Silvestri (another Ursuline graduate), which used photographic narrative to capture the images and stories of people who lost everything, including their family photographs.

- Cherice Harrison-Nelson used her grant-writing skills to write as many as a hundred grant proposals for other members of Mardi Gras Indian groups to purchase beads and feathers and other materials so that they could sew their suits and replace pieces of suits that were lost in the floods in the aftermath of Katrina.

- Paul Chan's *Waiting for Godot* in New Orleans, which created four site-specific outdoor performances in the Lower 9th Ward, produced by New York-based Creative Time. It evolved into a larger production of free art seminars, educational programs, theater workshops, and conversations in the community.

- The Colton School Project, organized by the Create Alliance of New Orleans (CANO) under the leadership of Jeanne Nathan, which took over the damaged Colton School to provide free studio and exhibition space for seventy-eight artists, cultural workers, culinary artists, and small organizations.

- Transforma Projects, a collective of artists and creative professionals who organized to support creative practices that impacted other sectors such as education, health, and community development. It supported three pilot projects: *Home, New Orleans?*, developed with four neighborhood community centers and Dillard, Tulane, and Xavier Universities; Operation Paydirt/Fundred Dollar Bill Project, by artist Mel Chin; and Plessy Park, initiated by the Crescent City Peace Alliance. Transforma also administered a Creative Recovery Mini-Grants program, which gave small grants to more than forty artists and organizations. The work of Transforma was documented in a publication that can be found at transformaprojects.org.

My work in the aftermath of the hurricane and floods was through my role as the president and CEO of The National Performance Network (known as NPN), which moved its offices to New Orleans in 2000. NPN was originally founded as a project of Dance Theater Workshop in New York City. Formed as a network, its purpose was to support the creation of new performing arts for touring in a context of community engagement. At the time of Katrina, NPN was composed of sixty organizations from across the US, including nineteen organizations in the US South. This was unusually high Southern representation for a national organization at the time. The three NPN partners (as members are called) in New Orleans were Ashé Cultural Arts Center, Junebug Productions, and the Contemporary Arts Center, which was one of the founding members of NPN. NPN's values match my own: to contribute to a healthy, just, and sustainable world.

NPN's strategy was to provide subsidies and support to enable artists to tour their work and receive a fair wage. Its structure was intentionally designed to share resources equitably among its members. It was artist-focused, and its subsidies were matched by NPN partners to directly provide financial support to artists for their work. The touring model allowed artists to be in residency in a community for a minimum of a week, including direct opportunities to engage with the local community beyond public performances, in direct contrast to then prevailing touring models in which artists arrived in a place, loaded into the theater, performed, loaded out, and left, never engaging with the people there beyond those in the audience. Many of the artists in NPN's network are activist-artists whose work addresses the concerns and issues of communities.

Among New Orleans artists whose work has been supported by NPN are John O'Neal, José Torres-Tama, Kathy Randels/Art Spot Productions, Mondo Bizarro, Scott Heron, Cherice Harrison-Nelson, and Saddi Kahli, among many others. Upon moving its offices to New Orleans, NPN made a commitment to create and sustain programs based in Louisiana by sharing NPN's resources with the local community. NPN's commitment to establishing visibility and connections locally grows out of the expectation that NPN partners engage locally while participating nationally, with a focus on convening, partnerships, and regranting. As an intermediary organization, NPN is able to provide access to national resources to which local artists and organizations would not otherwise have connections.

NPN's offices were housed in the Arts Business Center that was operated at the time by the Arts Council of New Orleans at 225 Baronne Street. Katrina severely damaged that building, and NPN lost its offices, as did everyone else in the building. I also had my own office there, predating NPN's move to New Orleans. Fortunately, though windows were blown in on the seventeenth floor, our files and archives and office furniture were not lost, and we were able to retrieve them in November of 2005. The staff was dispersed across every time zone in the US during the months after Katrina.

Two factors enabled NPN to continue its work while we were displaced from New Orleans:

- Our sources of funding were national; we were financially secure and did not have to lay off staff.

- Thérèse Wegmann, NPN operations manager (and my sister), made a backup of our QuickBooks data and took it with her when she evacuated from New Orleans.

NPN was able to work virtually for the next six months, returning to New Orleans in January of 2006. NPN, along with Junebug Productions, whose offices had also been part of the Arts Business Center, were given free office space at the Contemporary Arts Center.

Our national funding partners, within days after Katrina, got in touch with NPN and provided support to aid us. Specifically, the late Claudine Brown of the Nathan Cummings Foundation provided funding to allow us to get laptops and cell phones to all of our staff as well as a home office allowance to help support them. Our national NPN partners, other colleague organizations, and funders, each in different ways, came to the support of the New Orleans and Gulf Coast communities that were affected by Katrina. We were privileged. We used our privilege to leverage support for our community in New Orleans.

After returning our offices to New Orleans in 2006, we hosted a series of convenings for arts and cultural organizations to provide information about resources such as those from FEMA, the Small Business Administration, foundations, and others. Under the leadership of NPN's chief operating officer, June Wilson, we worked closely with Ashé and others to write a cultural plan to supplement the Bring New Orleans Back commission's plans for the future of New Orleans, which had not comprehensively included the arts and culture communities in its work. Despite the fact that none of those plans went anywhere, the process of convening helped us to help each other.

Through NPN's national visibility, we were able to act as a fiscal sponsor and as an intermediary partner for individual artists and organizations in New Orleans on behalf of recovery efforts for our city. My appreciation for, literally, the world, which stepped up to aid New Orleans and its cultural community in recovering from the devastation that followed Hurricane Katrina, erased my cynicism and restored my faith in my fellow human beings. In the years that followed, everywhere I went, I met people who, when I said I was from New Orleans, said, "Oh, yes. I went there and volunteered." The projects described above are just a small sample of the ways that artists and culture-bearers aided us in our recovery.

I've lived in the Marigny neighborhood, at the corner of Frenchmen and Chartres, since 1983, in the "sliver by the river" where the city did not flood during Katrina, and though I had some wind damage, I didn't lose my home as so many others did. I was vacationing on the beach and had my car, my computer, and my dogs with me. Had I been there, I probably would not have evacuated—I never had before. My neighbor Kenny Claiborne, who lived in the building, had keys to my apartment, and he, knowing I would approve, invited other neighbors who had not evacuated to move into my place. They cleared everything off of my balcony before the storm; after it, after the floods came, he and others roamed the neighborhood, boarding up windows and taking down signs to protect businesses from looting.

They emptied my refrigerator and freezer and defended my property. Kenny famously operated "Radio Marigny," using a generator to return music to the silent street that Frenchmen had become. On a personal level and on a world level, the lesson of Katrina is in how we take care of one another.

After I returned to New Orleans right before Christmas 2005, and in the months and years afterward, I watched the groups of folks, from young to old, that walked from downtown to the French Quarter after gutting and rebuilding houses. Businesses of every stripe marshaled volunteers to help restore the city. My colleagues from NPN came in groups to volunteer, as did groups from businesses as conventions returned.

One last personal anecdote: In December of 2006, my sister left her dog in the care of a friend in the Bywater neighborhood while she went to Virginia to celebrate the holidays with family. Miss Hattie was an elderly, thirteen-inch Beagle missing some toes on one foot. She'd been lost for more than two weeks when I got a phone message on my landline (those phones still worked after the storm; cell phones did not). Some folks living in the Common Ground encampment in the 9th Ward had come across Miss Hattie. She had crossed Saint Claude and she had crossed Claiborne Avenue, both large, four-lane thoroughfares—she had gone through three neighborhoods seeking her way back home to my sister's house in Metairie. These volunteers who were cleaning up houses and streets found the phone numbers on Miss Hattie's collar and called until we got their message and were able to pick her up. It was a small act of kindness in the midst of their giant efforts to help us in the city of New Orleans.

THE FINANCIAL PART
LYNNETTE WHITE-COLIN

It's 2:00 a.m. I just finished making sandwiches: ham and turkey with mayo and mustard, and a baked chicken breast for my picky-eater son. Fruit, snacks, and drinks are neatly stacked in the ice chest as I pull it into the living room near the front door. Everything is finally packed; the suitcases, books, magazines, CDs, and games for my eight-year-old are at the front door. I'm tired and feeling very anxious. The smooth jazz on The Weather Channel continued to play in my head as I brushed my teeth, showered, and finally got into my bed with my husband snoring loudly. I pushed on him a bit to temporarily stop his gargling noises so that I could fall asleep.

It felt as if I had only been asleep for ten minutes when the alarm blared at 5:00 a.m. I hit the snooze, turned over on my side, and tried to close my eyes again. The sheer anxiety I felt kept them from shutting. My husband yawned loudly as he got up and made his way into the bathroom. Once he was in the shower, I was up and at 'em. I quickly washed my face and brushed my teeth, put on a little make-up, and threw on a pair of shorts and a white T-shirt. I slipped my feet into my favorite flip flops and went in to wake the boys.

I had already laid out clothes for them, so it didn't take them long to get ready. Juney, the oldest (eighteen years old), a freshman at Dillard University, brought out his own bag of goodies to bring with him. I told him to put it with everything else at the front door. It seemed like a pretty large bag for a few days, but I didn't question it. I dropped two packages of strawberry Pop-Tarts in the toaster for them and made two glasses of chocolate milk. Lane, my baby boy, sat down at the table and began to eat. He had questions about where we were going and how long it would take and when we were coming back and what about school, which he had started just a couple of weeks prior. I answered his questions, gave him a kiss on the head, and assured him everything would be fine, and we would be back in a few days.

THE FINANCIAL PART

We finally got the bags loaded into the SUV; Hubby did a once-over through the house while the boys and I got into the car. Just as we were about to pull out of the driveway, Juney pulled out the cage with Snake in it!

Snake was the name of his pet snake, a bald python. The plastic cage was the same one that we'd brought Snake home in when we purchased him, which he had now outgrown! Juney reasoned with us that Snake would not be OK in his aquarium for the few days that we would be gone. I had taken him on Saturday to purchase a mouse to feed Snake. His dad told him Snake would be OK because he had just eaten. Juney persisted in his argument that Snake had to come with us. The disciplinarian in me came out, and we brought Snake back into the house, turned on the light in his aquarium to keep him warm, and hit the road with an angry Juney in the backseat.

We were headed to Houston, where the rest of my family were going, or so I thought. Hubby, who managed ATMs for a big, national bank, had other plans. Dallas would be a better location for him to work from.

That change turned out to be a blessing. It took us eleven hours to make it to Dallas, instead of the seven hours it would have taken otherwise. My other family members didn't make out so well. It took them twenty-four hours to drive to Houston!

We checked into the hotel at 6:30 p.m., relaxed for just a bit, and went out to get dinner. We all were exhausted from the long drive. We showered and settled in for a good night's rest.

I kept the television on overnight and listened to The Weather Channel in between napping, the channel's smooth jazz background music still stuck in my head.

On Monday morning, we woke to the kids wanting to go out to the pool. Hubby took them to get breakfast and then to swim. I stayed in and kept watch on The Weather Channel, CNN, NBC, and WDSU, a New Orleans news station, on Hubby's laptop. The video coming out of downtown New Orleans didn't look so bad. CNN showed live video from Canal Street; it appeared we had skirted the worst of another hurricane—again. I was thinking that maybe we should pack up and head out to get ahead of the traffic going back to New Orleans. Hubby thought differently, that we should wait. That turned out to be good advice.

On the local news on the computer, I watched a well-known reporter drive near the Superdome; he stopped to speak with a pedestrian walking in the rain toward the Dome. They asked him where he was going. The man in turn asked the reporter if the station knew about all the water in the 9th Ward.

That scared me. It brought back memories of what I knew had happened after Hurricane Betsy in 1965. By 4:00 in the afternoon, there was water in the streets of downtown New Orleans that had not been there earlier in the day.

By the next day, cell phone service was sporadic at best. It was difficult getting through to my family. I tried desperately to reach my staff at the credit union I managed. After so many attempts, I tried texting for the first time on my flip phone. It took some doing, but I reached Jony, the member services representative via a text message.

The news was not good. She had been notified that her and her mother's home in New Orleans East was underwater. I got through to the other employees and it was the same story; they had lost everything too!

The cable networks were showing the rooftop rescues and the complete devastation in the city, but I hadn't heard anything about the west bank of the city, where I lived.

It turned out that the Westbank had been spared of flooding. We had wind damage, but nothing too serious. We would need a new roof, and the ceiling in the garage had fallen in onto Juney's car, but that was it.

After panic set in at the news that we would not be able to return home, we relocated to a hotel in Lafayette, Louisiana, on Thursday, thanks to Hubby's employer. We got there just in time to get both sons registered in school, Juney at the University of Lafayette and Lane at Live Oak Elementary School. The registration process for Lane was a bit chaotic. There was one location exclusively for Katrina evacuees, and there were a lot of us. I was told by our hotel manager to ask for a specific school that he said was one of the best in Lafayette. When it was our turn, I asked about the good school. When the woman at registration informed us that Lane would have to attend Live Oak School because we were "homeless," my knees buckled, and I nearly hit the floor. But we got through it. School started on Monday. Hubby went to a bank branch to work; I was left at the hotel by myself. It was the first time that I allowed myself to cry.

Meanwhile, the CEO of the credit union quickly went to work contacting funders and investors. He was able to access a one million-dollar grant from the Ford Foundation. We quickly set up a loan fund for New Orleans residents who were evacuated to help them get into housing and purchase things they needed. The fund was set up to deploy small-dollar loans up to five thousand dollars, with very little regard for credit history or current employment. Recipients would not be required to begin paying the loans back for six months, when they would be in a much more stable place. Checking accounts with debit cards were opened to allow for digital access to the funds. The loan fund would also help Hurricane Katrina victims to purchase cars to replace those lost in the floods.

I didn't have a laptop. I used the hotel's business center as my office and maintained a consistent watch over the fax machine, where I was receiving loan applications. Hubby allowed me to use his laptop when he could.

On Monday, two weeks after the hurricane, I went to a shelter at the Lafayette Cajundome. It was set up to be a FEMA center. They allowed me to sit at a table to speak with individuals about opening accounts, helping them to set up direct deposit for their federal funds and apply for our disaster recovery loans. Many of the people I spoke with were receiving their federal checks by mail to their homes. They usually received payments at the end of the month or on the third of each month. The storm had happened on August 29, which meant they had missed those payments. Setting up direct deposit allowed them to have their payments sent electronically to their new credit union accounts.

I went to the Cajundome site for three days. I met some great people from Lafayette who came to help evacuees at the Cajundome. Churches came with food, clothing, toys, and books. Ms. Mary, a spirited Black woman who spoke very loudly, came to the Cajundome each day I was there. She was an usher at her church. She thanked me for the work I was doing and invited me to come to her church soon, where they were also helping New Orleans evacuees. I was scheduled to go to the church on September 23. Ms. Mary insisted on picking me up from my hotel to drive to the church. I called her at 8:00 on the morning of September 22 to reconfirm our appointment.

In her loud voice, she said, "No, dawlin', Hurricane Rita is headed to Lafayette, and we have to evacuate!" I hadn't been watching the news. We now had to evacuate for the third time! We ended up in a vacant apartment in Monroe, Louisiana, thanks again to Hubby's employer. The drive there was somber; nobody talked. Lane didn't have his usual thousand questions. We were exasperated!

My employer set up an office for me to work in Baton Rouge, Louisiana. They also assigned a staff person to look for housing for my family in Baton Rouge, where they had an existing office. They wanted to make sure I could and would return to New Orleans, although I had no plans to move my family to Baton Rouge. Nonetheless, I drove to Baton Rouge Monday through Thursday for the next two weeks, contacting the credit union's customers to see how I could help and accepting and processing loan applications.

One of the clients I called was Mr. Moore. A week before the storm, I closed a loan for him for a new dump truck. After asking how he and his family were, I inquired as to whether he had taken the truck (for which I had not yet received the title) out of St. Bernard Parish, where he lived. Unfortunately, he had not. The truck was under water. I assured him that we would get things on track to get him another truck because the recovery in New Orleans would provide a plethora of opportunities for him.

While I was still working in Baton Rouge, I contacted Carol, a good friend and former colleague. She had found an apartment in Baton Rouge for herself and her mother. They lived in Central City. Her mother had recently had a stroke, which is why she didn't evacuate when the storm came. In the days after the storm, when things got really bad in the city, she packed, got her mom into her Honda Civic, and they began driving through the water in the street. She was near the Walmart on Tchoupitoulas Street, which had been looted, when the car stopped. It couldn't make it through the water.

Before long, a police officer pulled up to the car. He was in a black Lincoln town car; he told her to get out of the car. She explained that her mother was in the back and could not get out. She told him she was just trying to get to Baton Rouge, where they could find a place to stay. He helped her to get her mom out of the car, put her in the town car, and gave Carol the keys. He then gave her directions to get to Interstate 10 and told her to just go. A couple weeks later, when I met her for lunch in Baton Rouge, she was still driving the Lincoln town car; we later learned the police had to commandeer cars from car dealerships to get around the city. Carol eventually turned the car in when she made it back to New Orleans.

We managed to make it back to New Orleans a couple of times to check on our house and to get clothes for all of us. We drove Juney's car back to Lafayette so he would have transportation to get to the university and to pick up his little brother from the bus stop. Jessica, Juney's girlfriend (now his wife), was in Rayne, Louisiana, with her family, an hour's drive from Lafayette. We drove up to see her, and she came to spend time with us too at the hotel. We also brought Snake back to Lafayette. We had to sneak him into the hotel, as it was a no-pets property. We put clothes over his cage to hide him from housekeeping.

We left Lafayette to return home on Saturday, October 1. It was a good thing because the day before we left, the housekeeper found Snake! She went screaming through the hotel. We bought pizza for the hotel staff, thanked them for their hospitality, and got on the road.

THE FINANCIAL PART

On our way home in three cars, it was a bit eerie. Lane rode with hubby. Juney and I drove our cars behind them in a caravan. There was hardly any traffic on the interstate. As we got closer to home, it was emotional seeing billboards along the interstate welcoming us back home.

Home was not easy. Only one supermarket was open near where we lived, and they only allowed twenty customers in at a time to shop for limited food and supplies. Raising Cane's and the Big Easy Deli were the only restaurants open. Whenever another restaurant or retail shop opened, it made the local news.

Lane's school opened one of their two campuses. Dillard University held classes at the Hilton Hotel downtown. On Monday, we left for school and work, almost like usual. Hubby worked from home until he found a bank branch on the Westbank to work out of. The lights were back on in Central City, where the credit union is located; armed national guardsmen were still guarding the streets, and helicopters were still flying around.

As meetings started to take place in the city, I made the rounds. FEMA centers were open; local and state government agencies held meetings at downtown hotels, and several important meetings were held at Ashé Cultural Arts Center, which was next door to the credit union.

I had a system: I went out to the centers and meetings Monday to Wednesday, to let people know about the recovery and car loans. On Thursday and Friday, I processed and closed loans by appointment.

Word got around, and soon I was overwhelmed with loan applications. I worked in the credit union until nine, sometimes ten o'clock at night. Douglas Redd, one of the proprietors of Ashé Cultural Arts Center, would walk with me to my car at night. I did that for nearly four months until we were able to hire a staff person in January.

There were elderly people who didn't have computers to get through to FEMA, and trying to get through on the phone was nearly impossible. I dedicated one of the computers in the credit union to allow people to submit their FEMA applications and to use our phones to make calls. I learned as much as I could about FEMA's processes so I could instruct people on what to do.

I heard so many horror stories. We all shared our Katrina stories with everyone we met. I can still remember the faces of people recounting their nightmares.

I won't ever forget the beautiful young woman who told me how she and her four-year-old daughter made it to the roof of their townhouse in Metairie when the water started rising at 8:30 in the morning. They stayed on the roof for three days. They both had third-degree burns from the sun and insect bites all over their bodies. When they were rescued, they were first to get on one of the buses headed to Houston because of the burns. Upon their arrival, emergency medical services were waiting to take them to a hospital. She came back to New Orleans to attend the state's meeting at Ashé Cultural Arts Center that provided information about the state's grant programs. It was such a comfort to me to be able to provide her with capital to help her to get an apartment for her and her little girl.

The credit union used some of the funding from the Ford Foundation to provide grants to individuals and organizations. Ashé Cultural Arts Center was provided with twenty thousand dollars to re-grant to culture-bearers. Before the storm, Carol, one of the founders of Ashé, had asked me to speak with some of the culture-bearers to see if we could develop financial products that could help them. After an initial meeting with a few of them, we scheduled a larger meeting that was to take place on August 29. Of course, that meeting didn't happen. The twenty thousand dollars was awarded to many of the creatives who would have attended that meeting.

The credit union awarded grants to first responders and pump operators who stayed during the storm. We also found teachers, who had all lost their jobs, to provide grants to.

The city of Hammond, Louisiana, asked me to come out to speak with officials there about our programs. There were a lot of New Orleans evacuees in Hammond. The credit union allowed me to provide thousand-dollar grants to twenty evacuees in Hammond. The city officials worked with us to help find people who needed to open accounts and apply for recovery loans. I'll never forget that one of the grants was to Betty, a woman I had worked with years ago at a community action agency. Betty had a large presence; she was over six feet tall. I was so glad to see her! We hugged each other for a long time. The minute I saw her, my heart began to ache. I remembered her telling me the story of how she'd lost her three kids in the flood during Hurricane Betsy in 1965. I could only imagine how emotionally distressing this had been for her. It was cathartic for me to provide some relief for her and the other nineteen people who received our grants that day.

The Jewish Funds for Justice (JFSJ), an organization out of New York City, contacted me. They wanted to come to New Orleans and meet with pastors from local churches. I arranged a tour bus and invited twelve local clergymen who all sponsored charitable programming (food, housing, and other services) within their churches. JFSJ requested that the pastors write a summary of what it would take to get their programming back up and running. Before they left New Orleans, JFSJ provided grants to each of the pastors to restore their programming. One pastor in particular stood out for me. I spoke at his little corner church in Central City a couple of times. He frequently walked over formerly incarcerated men and women to open accounts at the credit union. He used his grant to purchase a van for the church. He continued to bring individuals to the credit union, but now he could drive them there.

Mr. Moore, whose dump truck was flooded in St. Bernard Parish, made his way back to New Orleans. I had contacted his insurance company; they agreed to pay off the loan despite not having the title. I told Mr. Moore to complete an application so that we could get him another truck. He had other plans. He had already shopped and found two trucks and a trailer with all the bells and whistles. Somehow, we made it happen! Mr. Moore became the first Black contractor in New Orleans to receive a Level One contract with the Corps of Engineers.

I met up with Laverne Toombs at a public meeting. She worked for a well-known elected official. She later came by the credit union to apply for a recovery loan to purchase clothing, as she had lost everything she owned in the flood and she needed to be out in public representing her employer. Additionally, her car had flooded. I was able to help her to get the clothing she needed and to purchase a car. When she saw that I had been working by myself in the credit union, she came back several times to help me to answer the phones, make some calls, and to get some of the filing under control. Laverne and I are still friends today.

In late October, I attended the annual conference of Opportunity Finance Network, the trade association for community development financial institutions. I participated on a panel to discuss what my credit union was doing to help people in New Orleans. I was so surprised at the number of people who wanted to speak with me. Many of them gave me checks to help support the credit union's work. I remember a very small woman who spoke very softly. She was Jewish, and she gave me a check for eighteen dollars. She said that the number eight represented infinity. She said the work I was doing would continue to help into infinity. I kept a copy of her check. I believed it would bring me luck in the future.

During the year after the storm, Entergy, the power company, partnered with the credit union and the Foundation for the Mid South to provide grants to households affected by the storm. The grants were put into checking accounts; debit cards were mailed to the recipients. More than four thousand individual and family grants were awarded throughout the affected area, totaling $3.6 million.

Shortly before I left Lafayette, Jarvis DeBerry, a local newspaper reporter, contacted me about a car loan. We got an application underway for him, but he was more interested in learning about what I had been doing to help individuals after the storm. He said that several people had told him about me, which is how he came to call me on my cell phone. A few months later, he called to let me know that he was submitting an article about women in New Orleans who had gone above and beyond to assist individuals and families after the storm. I was excited when an article, albeit small, was written about the work I had done in *Essence* magazine.

In November 2005, the Louisiana Disaster Recovery Foundation was formed. Months later, it invested in a consortium of nonprofit organizations and community development financial institutions, forming the Center for Enterprise Development (CED). This group's mission was to help bring back and sustain minority-owned small businesses in New Orleans. It was a four million-dollar investment over three years that assisted countless small businesses. Subsequently, New Orleans realized a boom in Black entrepreneurship.

By the end of December 2006, I had almost single-handedly processed and deployed more than one million dollars in small recovery loans and grants. The credit union grew by six hundred percent in the year after Hurricane Katrina. Countless small business owners, individuals, culture-bearers, and nonprofit organizations were assisted in staying in and/or returning to their homes and places of business.

As devastating as Hurricane Katrina and its aftermath were, there were some pretty amazing things that happened also, as demonstrated by this publication. New Orleans is resilient. Our culture, our community, our people have been tested many times over; we fought back then and will always fight for this city and our place in it.

MY SILVER LINING
FREDDI WILLIAMS EVANS

Prior to the landfall of Hurricane Katrina, my daily schedule was full and complex. Professionally, I worked as an artist facilitator in the Jefferson Parish Public School System and was a children's book author with an active list of engagements. Personally, I was a mother of two children in college, and passionately, I was a relentless researcher of the history and significance of New Orleans' Congo Square. My ultimate goal was to provide the general public with a comprehensive study of the historic landmark that focused on the people who'd gathered there, highlighting their contributions to our society and their influence on our culture.

Two weeks before the hurricane's landfall, I declared that my years of research and writing were finished and began to prepare my manuscript for submission. Runagate Press, a local publishing company founded by Kalalmu ya Salaam and Kysha Brown Robinson, had agreed to publish it. Although I didn't know it at that time, the manuscript was far from finished. Had it not been for the storm, my studies on Congo Square may have ended there, and the extent of my contribution to the understanding of New Orleans history and culture may not have been realized. While Hurricane Katrina itself was not a blessing, many circumstances that resulted benefited some of its victims. In my case, conditions that followed the storm tremendously elevated my work. Like a silver lining in a dark cloud, good fortune appeared in the midst of tragedy and despair.

My study of Congo Square began in the early 1990s, several years before I became a member of NOMMO Literary Society, a creative writing workshop for Black writers directed by Salaam. My initial research resulted in a multi-disciplinary, site-specific performance for children that involved a storyteller, drummers, and dancers, entitled *I Hear the Drums*. The Africana Studies Department of the Orleans Parish Public School System sponsored the children who attended. However, due to inclement weather, the location for the performance was changed from Congo Square to nearby Christian Unity Baptist Church. With funding from a grant for regional projects coordinated by the Contemporary Arts Center, the performance was duplicated in Jackson, Mississippi, at the Smith Robertson Museum, with artists from that area. The research for *I Hear the Drums* provided the foundation for the manuscript that members of NOMMO critiqued during weekly sessions. My editor for the project, Dr. Paulette Richards, also a member of NOMMO, was an associate professor of English at Loyola University in New Orleans.

With both of my children away during the years preceding the hurricane, I was able to focus on my work, spending many after-school hours at local university libraries. With my having a full-time job and being neither a college student nor college faculty member, conducting such intensive research was challenging. I was not able to check out books from most libraries and archives or access online search engines and research sources from my home. Documents and other source materials were not digitized as they are now, which demanded that I work on-site on weekends, holidays, and during summer breaks. I had to copy large sections of books, use every available collection or library, search for rare and out-of-print editions, and purchase quite a few texts. Richards, who was fluent in French and read Spanish, assisted in translating documents and traveled with me to most archives out of town.

On Saturday, August 27, 2005, the two of us met at our scheduled time to discuss the remaining steps for the manuscript. Aware of the approaching storm and the need to evacuate, I invited her to come with me to my brother and sister-in-law's home in Madison, Mississippi. We decided to take note cards and work on the book's index while there. Salaam sent messages and made phone calls to NOMMO members, telling us to take all our jump drives and hard drives. I also packed boxes of files. By the time we left New Orleans that afternoon, three other people had requested to join us: AumRa and Ettie Frezel and their daughter Shemsi, who attended Ben Franklin High School. AumRa attended NOMMO regularly, and Ettie attended occasionally, meaning that the four of us formed the largest group of NOMMO members who evacuated together.

We all lived with my brother and sister-in-law, Ray and Diane Williams, and quickly received food, visits, and support from other family and community members. Diane announced via emails that we were all vegetarians, and deliveries of food items arrived from across the country almost daily for several weeks. The first Tuesday that we were there, the day of our weekly NOMMO meetings, Salaam gave Richards, who was also NOMMO's associate director, permission to lead the last meeting of the NOMMO Workshop, ending ten years of a New Orleans literary tradition. Having to hold that last session in exile underscored the anxiety that we all felt about the plight of our city and the uncertainty of its future. Documenting and preserving its history became of utmost importance. When discussing the status of the book with Salaam, he said, "This is bigger than Runagate now. We need to send the book to Marie Brown," a trailblazing African American editor and literary agent based in New York.

With Salaam's endorsement, Brown agreed to receive my work and consider representing it. Over the course of months, she discussed it with editors as well as supporters and advocates of New Orleans history and culture like Ed Bradley and Wynton Marsalis, who provided a blurb for the back of the book when it was eventually published.

Hope swelled inside of me at the thought of a New York publisher, but frankly, the manuscript wasn't ready. It needed much more work. I eventually queried editors myself and found someone who recognized the manuscript's value and potential. James Wilson at the University of Louisiana at Lafayette Press decided to send it out for peer reviews. The resulting critiques offered a path forward, but it was a high order that came with a lot of additional work. Wilson was not sure that I would accept the challenge, but I did. It recognized it as my silver lining in the dark cloud.

Although the additional work was painstaking, it was important. While a couple of articles on Congo Square had been published in historical journals, they were not accessible to the general public. Moreover, they failed to focus on the people—who they were, where they'd originated, what they contributed to this land beyond physical labor, and how they continued to influence today's popular culture. The task before me was daunting, but I pursued it with purpose and passion.

Although Marie Brown did not secure the publisher for the book, she did negotiate my contract for *Congo Square: African Roots in New Orleans* as well as the contract for my subsequent book, *Come Sunday: A Young Reader's History of Congo Square*, also published by University of Louisiana at Lafayette Press. *Come Sunday* received the 2018 Independent Publisher Book Awards Bronze Medal and was a finalist for the 2018 Next Generation Indie Book Awards. I was also invited to write the foreword for the children's picture book *Freedom in Congo Square*, written by Carole Boston Weatherford and illustrated by R. Gregory Christie.

Today, I am internationally recognized for my work on Congo Square, including books, essays, and a website (CongoSquareConnection.org). *Congo Square: African Roots in New Orleans*, published in 2011, the first comprehensive study of the historic location, received the Louisiana Endowment for the Humanities (LEH) Humanities Book of the Year award in 2012. My research and advocacy for the historic landmark influenced the passing of the 2011 New Orleans City Council Ordinance Calendar No. 28,411, which officially changed the name of the location from Beauregard Square, named after Confederate General P. G. T. Beauregard in 1893, to Congo Square, the popular name before and after the Civil War.

In 2012, I was invited to speak at UNESCO's (United Nations Educational, Scientific and Cultural Organization) inaugural International Jazz Day in Congo Square. Upon the release of the book's French edition in 2012, the American embassy in Paris, France, sponsored my presentations there. In 2014, the American embassy in Senegal sponsored my presentations in Dakar and Saint Louis, in conjunction with a tribute to jazz musician John Coltrane and in celebration of International Jazz Day. Other international engagements include presentations at the Bordeaux Congo Square Festival in Bordeaux, France, in 2013 and the keynote lecturer at the 100 Years of Beat Festival, Haus der Kulturen der Welt, Berlin, Germany, in 2018. In 2024, the Louisiana Endowment for the Humanities presented me with the Lifetime Contributions to the Humanities Award for my work on Congo Square and historical markers about the Louisiana slave trade.

These accomplishments and others may not have come to pass had it not been for the storm that wreaked havoc on our city on August 29, 2005. Breaches in the levee system that protected us from Lake Pontchartrain contributed to heavy and extensive flooding that impacted roughly 80 percent of the city. Rescue efforts and the security of New Orleans required the full evacuation of the city's approximately 480,000 residents—the majority of whom were African Americans.

Damage from the flooding was augmented by destruction from heavy rain and strong winds, the latter of which damaged my home on the west bank of the city. The extensive ruins qualified me for a FEMA (Federal Emergency Management Agency) trailer, where I lived while navigating the repairs. An anchor for me during that time was my job. The Jefferson Parish Public School System fully reopened the first week of October, without laying off any of its employees. Although strong winds and heavy rain had damaged some of the schools in the district, none received devastating flood waters. Students and staff at the schools that did experience extensive damage held classes at undamaged schools on staggered schedules. Perhaps the building that received the worst damage was the administration building, which housed my office. Those of us who worked there set up offices in a nearby warehouse until FEMA constructed a more suitable, yet temporary, facility.

My stable employment in Jefferson Parish was indeed a blessing, but it conflicted with the slow recovery in Orleans Parish, where I lived. When I returned for my job, my neighborhood was still blocked off and none of my immediate neighbors were back in their homes. Major parts of the infrastructure, like stoplights and streetlights, had not been repaired, making it unsafe to be there. The opportunity to live in FEMA trailers that the school system offered was not preferable, and my close acquaintances in Orleans Parish were still evacuated. So, with early mold and mildew remediation, I lived in the undamaged section of my house until my FEMA trailer arrived. After using it for a couple of weeks, I moved back into my house so that two Dillard University students from South Africa could live in the trailer.

Around the same time that I returned to New Orleans, Richards' brother picked her up and took her to Atlanta, where she still lives. The Frezels drove to Delaware to live with Ettie's brother and remained there until Shemsi graduated from Sanford School in Hockessin, an elite, private school that opened its doors to her because of Hurricane Katrina.

Despite the hardships and inconveniences that I experienced upon returning to the city, I recognized and focused on the silver lining that the storm had ushered my way. The recovery period following the storm allowed me to settle down and take a break from my full and complex schedule. It enabled me to spend more time reading, researching, cross-referencing, and processing the sources that I'd found. It placed in my path what I needed to conduct a more comprehensive study of Congo Square, secure a publisher that would present my work in a scholarly manner, and make a more significant contribution to understanding the landmark's powerful history, widespread influence, and rich legacy.

CONTRIBUTORS

ORISSA AREND

Orissa Arend is a mediator, freelance journalist, and psychotherapist in New Orleans. She is author of *Showdown in Desire: The Black Panthers Take a Stand in New Orleans*. She is a pillar with a justice-seeking coalition called Justice & Beyond and a longtime ally of the People's Institute for Survival and Beyond.

Currently, she is involved in a church-based project for reparations for slavery, Jim Crow, and the aftermath. This is an attempt to begin a small process of making amends for the complicity of her church—Episcopal—in the egregious sin of espousing white supremacy socially, theologically, and politically.

She enjoys reading, playing tennis, learning something new, sitting by the Wolf River in Mississippi, and trying to glimpse the future through her two children and eight grandchildren.

STEVEN BINGLER

Steven Bingler is the founder and CEO of Concordia, a community-centered engagement, planning, and architectural co-design studio in New Orleans, Louisiana. Concordia, from the Latin word meaning "agreement between people and harmony among things," is also the firm's one-word mission statement.

The Concordia studio explores its mission in several ways, including research collaborations with universities (Stanford University's Global Projects Center, MIT's Media Lab, Harvard's Project Zero, and University of California Berkeley's Center for Cities + Schools) and governmental agencies (US Department of Education and National Aeronautics and Space Administration), and through a diverse network of collaborations with community-based organizations.

Steven is included in Wikipedia's roster of internationally acclaimed urban planners. His manuscripts and research papers have been published in books and journals on urban planning, architectural design, education, public health, and smart growth. His work has received support from the Ford, Rockefeller, Gates, Wallace, Prudential, George Lucas, Irvine, and William Penn Foundations and the Philadelphia Education Fund. Concordia's award-winning education, cultural, housing, and recreation projects have appeared in *Newsweek*, *The New York Times*, *Los Angeles Times*, *USA Today*, *The Wall Street Journal*, *Metropolis*, *Architecture*, and *Architectural Digest*.

Steven is also a musician and naturalist who grew up in a working-class family in Charlottesville, Virginia, where he was one of the first in his family to graduate from high school. He received his architectural training at the University of Virginia, where he is a member of the school's prestigious Raven Society and a recipient of the School of Architecture's Distinguished Alumni Award. In 2014, he co-authored an op-ed for *The New York Times* with architectural critic Martin Pedersen, advocating for a realignment of contemporary planning and design practices around more design equity and inclusionary practices, which led to the creation of the Common Edge Collaborative (commonedge.org).

CAROL BEBELLE

Carol Bebelle is a native New Orleanian. She holds a bachelor's degree from Loyola University in sociology, a master's degree from Tulane University in education administration, and has a twenty-year career in the public sector as an administrator and planner of human service programs. She is also a published poet and essayist. Her written works can be found in various anthologies, reports, and journals.

J. B. BORDERS

James B. Borders IV is the author of *Marking Time, Making Place: An Essential Chronology of Blacks in New Orleans Since 1718* (Beckham, 2015). Borders is also a consultant specializing in organizational development and capacity-building for small and emerging cultural and social-service nonprofit corporations. He has previously served as executive director of the Louisiana Division of the Arts; managing director of the National Black Arts Festival; managing director of Junebug Productions (an outgrowth of the legendary Free Southern Theater); founding editor of *The New Orleans Tribune*; editor of *The Black Collegian Magazine*; coordinator of major events at the University of Rhode Island; and co-founder of the Black

Theatre Group, which evolved into Rites and Reason Theatre at Brown University. Borders is a graduate of Brown University (AB 1971, AM 1978).

ANDREA CHEN

Andrea Chen is a pioneering social impact leader with over two decades of experience driving systemic change through inclusive entrepreneurship and racial justice initiatives. As the CEO, co-CEO, and co-founder of Propeller: A Force for Social Innovation in New Orleans, she built a nationally recognized economic justice incubator that partners with hundreds of entrepreneurs, business owners, and social justice changemakers to transform their visions into thriving ventures. A certified leadership coach and Stanford graduate, she balances her work with meditation, yoga, and hiking. She divides her time between New Orleans and the Bay Area, where she lives with her husband, Kevin, and daughter, Magnolia.

FLOZELL DANIELS

As chief executive officer of the Mary Reynolds Babcock Foundation (MRBF), Flozell Daniels Jr. leads the overall operations of the Foundation, from grantmaking to investing, communications, and strategy, providing both organizational and field leadership. Flozell represents MRBF's programs and vision for change to its grantee and philanthropic partners as well as to the general public. Flozell previously served as CEO and president of the Foundation for Louisiana (FFL), which launched in 2005 as the Louisiana Disaster Recovery Foundation to foster an equitable recovery from Hurricanes Katrina and Rita. It has since grown to become a "catalyst for justice," supporting communities statewide through grantmaking and loan products, leadership development programs, and advocating on myriad issues facing Louisianians, including climate justice, economic justice, criminal justice reform, and racial and gender justice. Prior to his fourteen-plus years leading FFL, Flozell was assistant vice president and executive director of state and local affairs for Tulane University and served in the mayor's office during Marc Morial's tenure as public policy specialist in the division of Federal and State Programs.

CONTRIBUTORS

Flozell has always worked with the understanding that the fates of all Southern people are tied together. From his early work on the Equity and Inclusion Campaign covering Louisiana, Mississippi, and Alabama to his co-founding of Grantmakers for Southern Progress, Flozell holds a longstanding commitment to building the South's infrastructure for justice for all.

JARVIS DEBERRY

Veteran journalist Jarvis DeBerry is an opinion editor at MSNBC.com. His previous roles include founding editor of the Louisiana Illuminator, columnist and editorial board member for cleveland.com, and deputy opinions editor, columnist, and editorial writer at *The Times-Picayune | NOLA.com*. He was on the team of journalists awarded the Pulitzer Prize for Public Service for its coverage of Hurricane Katrina and the deadly flood that followed. His columns have won awards from the New Orleans Press Club, the Louisiana–Mississippi Associated Press, and the National Association of Black Journalists. *I Feel to Believe*, a collection of DeBerry's *Times-Picayune* columns, was published in 2020 by the University of New Orleans Press and was selected as One Book One New Orleans' 2022 book of the year. He and his wife, Kelly, have one daughter, Naomi.

LLOYD DENNIS

After working for the historic Free Southern Theater and becoming the first Black person to do craft work for the Bell phone system, Lloyd escaped the Army and served in the Air Force as an electronic technician.

Then he continued work as a Black pioneer, servicing electronics on tugboats and ships and then as a computer technician at the local Federal Reserve branch.

Self-taught as a photographer, over forty years he and his wife grew their photography and video business.

He served as president of the New Orleans Multicultural Tourism Network for two years and as board president for Ashé Cultural Arts Center/ Efforts of Grace for thirteen.

He contributed to conversations about education in New Orleans by producing several films, including *A History of Public Education in New Orleans* with historian Al Kennedy.

Committed to young people all his adult life, in 2007 he co-founded the Silverback Society, which coordinates and trains mentors for adolescent boys in public schools.

He is a W. K. Kellogg Foundation Community Leadership fellow.

In 2020, he accepted Mayor Cantrell's appointment and still serves as board chair for the New Orleans Tourism and Cultural Fund.

Married for fifty-four years, he has three children and three grandchildren.

LUCAS DÍAZ

Lucas is a Dominican-born immigrant to the United States who has lived in the New Orleans area since the 1970s. A father of three, he completed his PhD in sociology from Tulane University's City + Culture + Community program in 2022 after working twenty years in the local nonprofit and government sector. Since 2000, Lucas has worked on nonprofit management, community engagement and organizing, government-based public participation programs and policies, leadership development, and nonprofit fundraising. In 2007, he co-founded Puentes New Orleans, a New Orleans-based community organization serving the Latinx community, then served as the first director of the mayor's Neighborhood Engagement Office for the city of New Orleans from 2011 to 2013.

While pursuing his PhD in sociology, Lucas continued to work in the public sector, coordinating a community engagement program for the SELA Drainage program with the New Orleans Sewerage and Water Board; working with the Foundation for Louisiana, helping their effort to revamp their LEAD the Coast civic leadership program; and working with Allegany Franciscan Ministries (in Florida), co-developing and implementing a twelve-month leadership fellowship program that completed its last cohort in September 2023. Today, he continues to work with communities, where possible, while serving as the assistant director for research and evaluation at Tulane's Center for Public Service and advancing projects that promote public leadership development. He published his first academic book, *The Know-How of Public Leaders in Collective Politics*, in July 2024.

ASHLEIGH GARDERE

Ashleigh Gardere is a leader dedicated to a future where everyone in the nation can thrive, and she has remained committed to making that future real in partnership with common and uncommon partners. Throughout her twenty-plus year career, she has witnessed the power of collaboration to deliver meaningful change as she helped accelerate systems transformation and equity through executive roles in government, business, and the nonprofit sector. Now, Ashleigh serves as president of PolicyLink, a research and action institute where she is focused on redesigning the nation to work for all. She understands that realizing a multiracial democracy requires new values and governing standards in the service of our collective flourishing; new ways of working between government and community; and new ways of being, both individually and as part of institutions.

Ashleigh has raised over $350 million to support social innovation and institution-building towards this future of collective liberation. She was also recognized by Living Cities as one of the nation's Top 25 "Disruptive Leaders" working to close racial opportunity gaps. Before joining PolicyLink, Ashleigh served as executive vice president and chief operating officer of the New Orleans Business Alliance; vice president of Community Relations at Chase Bank for Louisiana; and a senior advisor to former New Orleans Mayor Mitch Landrieu, where she was the chief strategist of the mayor's Economic Opportunity Strategy.

Ashleigh is the board chair of the Mary Reynolds Babcock Foundation, which partners with organizations and networks to alleviate poverty and increase social and economic justice in eleven Southern states. She holds a bachelor's degree in urban studies from New York University and a master's degree in public policy from Harvard University's Kennedy School of Government, where she was a Public Policy and International Affairs Fellow. She is proud to be from New Orleans, where she lives with her husband and two sons.

CONTRIBUTORS

LINETTA GILBERT

Linetta J. Gilbert serves as managing partner of Gilbert & Associates. A respected leader in the philanthropic community, her areas of practice include strategy development/planning; technical assistance to advance organizational culture and community-wide racial equity outcomes; board development; leadership development; and group facilitation.

Linetta has held leadership positions with several notable foundations, including the Greater New Orleans Foundation, Foundation for the Mid South, the Annie E. Casey Foundation, and the Ford Foundation. As senior program officer for social justice philanthropy with the Ford Foundation, over nearly a decade, she invested, monitored, and leveraged one billion dollars in resources dedicated to transforming and strengthening community-based philanthropic organizations worldwide. In the wake of Hurricanes Katrina and Rita, Linetta helped guide decisions on philanthropic investments that would help to rebuild infrastructure and increase capacity in government, resident leadership, nonprofit organizations, and the business community to transition the region from recovery to transformation.

Linetta uses her years of development experience through her service on governing boards of Agenda for Children, the Amistad Research Center, the Old Algiers Main Street Corporation (vice chair), and The Solutions Project, a national funding intermediary that amplifies climate justice solutions created by frontline communities building power for equitable and regenerative economies. She has served as chairman and founding member of the Board of Directors for the Foundation for Louisiana.

In 2019, she was recognized for her achievements in philanthropy by being selected as the twenty-ninth James A. Joseph Lecturer by the Association of Black Foundation Executives. In that same year, the Community Investment Network, a national group of young adult donors, established a Linetta J. Gilbert Service Award to be awarded annually to persons with distinguished service in community philanthropy. In 2018, the city of New Orleans recognized Linetta as one of three hundred individuals who made significant impact during the city's three hundred years of existence.

CONTRIBUTORS

KELLY HARRIS-DEBERRY

Kelly Harris-DeBerry is an award-winning poet and author of *Freedom Knows My Name* and the chapbook *Home Girl*. She has received fellowships from Cave Canem, the Fine Arts Work Center, and more. Her poems have been published in various publications, including a poetry translation displayed in Germany. A writer of poetry and Black culture, Kelly has written for the Louisiana Endowment for Humanities and other cultural platforms and organizations. She received degrees from Kent State and Lesley Universities. She is the wife of Jarvis DeBerry and the mother of Naomi. kellyhd.com

HERREAST J. HARRISON

Herreast J. Harrison, 9th Ward resident since 1965, successfully owned and operated three nursery schools in the area for over thirty-two years. The mother of Cherice Harrison-Nelson, Donald Harrison Jr., Michele Harrison, and Cara Harrison Daniels, she is a fifth-generation quilter, an accomplished beadwork and quilt artist and curator, and co-founder of Guardians Institute (GI), a New Orleans nonprofit. Mrs. Harrison holds an MA in museum studies, has exhibited and curated exhibits globally, and has won several honors, including the City of New Orleans' Living Legend Award and the Louisiana Endowment for the Humanities' Light Up for Literacy Award, both for GI's book program.

GI was conceived by Mrs. Harrison to promote the arts as well as reading and fiscal literacy programs; other youth activities included a sewing school, music programs, and African diaspora drumming and dance. The Big Chief Donald Harrison Sr. Book Club is the cornerstone program of Guardians Institute. Through the book club, Mrs. Harrison has gifted over forty thousand new books to area children to establish or replace lost personal libraries and enhance academic achievement. Mrs. Harrison remains active at eighty-four years old: she is currently curating an exhibition featuring women and girls' ceremonial attire.

CHERICE HARRISON-NELSON

Cherice Harrison-Nelson is an educator, narrative beadwork, visual, and performance artist, and arts administrator. She is the co-founder of the Mardi Gras Indian Hall of Fame (now DBA UNOLA) and co-editor of eleven publications. She has coordinated numerous exhibitions and panels on African retentive cultural expressions from New Orleans. Her creative expressions have been performed and presented locally and internationally. She is the recipient of several honors: a Fulbright Scholarship to study in West Africa, the Louisiana Endowment for the Humanities Teacher of the Year Award, a 2016 United States Artist Fellowship, and a Joan Mitchell Artist-in-Residency.

She approaches her art as a cognitive provocateur, with the specific intent to engage observers through imagery and performance that explore gender roles, classism, and other limiting/confining norms. Her work is primarily autobiographical as well as simultaneously ancient and contemporary. Using imagery from her family history, ancestral homeland, and life experiences, she is her own muse. To quote: "I am not masking when I debut my ceremonial attire on Carnival morning; I am revealing my authentic self, naked and rooted in the strength of my personal history. I cannot mask as myself." She is currently appearing throughout the city of New Orleans as a contemporary Plague Doctor character in performance installations focused on the Black Lives Matter movement, environmental injustice, gentrification, and contemporary colonial paradigms.

SHARON HOWARD

Sharon G. Howard retired on July 29, 2011 as the deputy assistant secretary for the Louisiana Department of Health and Hospitals Office of Public Health (OPH). Mrs. Howard was appointed assistant secretary for OPH in 2002 by Governor Murphy J. (Mike) Foster and appointed again in 2004 by Governor Kathleen Blanco.

Mrs. Howard began her service in state government in 1970. She began employment with OPH in 1988 in the Policy Planning and Evaluation section as a health planner before managing the Child Health and Maternity Program. She left OPH in 1992 to work as the Louisiana KIDMED outreach manager and provider relations manager. When Mrs. Howard returned to OPH in 1994, she served as the state director of the Family Planning Program until August 1999 and as the division director for the Division of Health Services between August 1999 and her appointment as assistant secretary for OPH. Her experience also includes employment as a social worker with the Orleans Parish School Board and the Office of Family Support.

Mrs. Howard has over thirty-five years' experience in the areas of management, program development, policy making in public health, Medicaid, public assistance, and social service agencies.

Mrs. Howard received a BA in sociology from Loyola University and a MSW in health/mental health from Southern University's School of Social Work and is currently the CEO of Howard-Henry LLC.

Howard-Henry LLC provides contracted consulting services in the areas of advocacy, policy development, fundraising, medical/business services, and provider–business relations.

PAMELA JENKINS

Pamela Jenkins is a research professor of sociology at the University of New Orleans (emerita). She is a faculty member of UNO's Center for Hazards, Assessment, Response, and Technology. Her latest book with Steve Kroll-Smith and Vern Baxter, *Left to Chance*, documents the recovery of two African American neighborhoods after Hurricane Katrina. Since retirement, she has been part of research projects analyzing impacts of sea level rise and the Louisiana coast, including *View from the Coast* and *Making Sense of a Place at Risk*. She is currently working on her second book about the recovery efforts from Hurricane Katrina, tentatively titled *Sundays at Pam and Ed's*.

CONTRIBUTORS

CHARLIE JOHNSON

Charlie T. Johnson Jr. is a native of New Orleans who describes himself as an artist, art educator, and art advocate who enjoys working in many visual art media. He received a BA in art education from Southern University at New Orleans and both a Master of Fine Arts and a PhD in urban studies from the University of New Orleans. Charlie taught public school children in New Orleans and Washington, DC before accepting a Southern University at New Orleans professorship—from which he retired in 2019. He has published numerous art-related catalogs and articles in newspapers and journals. In 2016, Charlie and his wife Louise authored a book titled *Didn't Wash Us Away: Transformative Stories of Post-Katrina Cultural Resilience*, an anthology of stories by culture-bearers who returned to rebuild New Orleans after Hurricane Katrina.

Charlie prefers painting realistic portraits and African textile-inspired mixed media compositions. His artwork has been exhibited in the United States, Africa, Europe, and Canada. He has curated art exhibitions of South African and Haitian art at the New Orleans Convention Center, along with other curatorial activities. He serves on the National Conference of Artists' Board of Directors and, for more than twenty-nine years, has been the coordinator of the National Conference of Artists Martin Luther King Jr. Commemorative Art Exhibition. Charlie has received honors, awards, and recognitions for artistic creativity, tireless advocacy for artists, and African American art recognition.

CHAKULA CHA JUA

From 1971 to 1976, was a staff member of the legendary Free Southern Theater. ✦ From 1978 to 1980, was technical director, actor, and playwright for the Ethiopian Theater. ✦ In 1979 and 1980, was creative dramatics specialist for the New Orleans Recreation Department. ✦ In the early to late 1970s, was one half of Chakula and Chink, billed as New Orleans' Only Professional Black Comedy Team. ✦ In 1978, directed the world premier of Tom Dent's probing drama *Ritual Murder*, which dealt with the theme of Black-on-Black violence, which his own Chakula cha Jua Theater continues to perform to this day. ✦ In 1998, he received the prestigious Big Easy Award for the twentieth-anniversary production of *Ritual Murder*. ✦ In 1985, founded the Chakula cha Jua Theater Company and began writing and producing critically acclaimed plays on African American history, teen pregnancy, substance abuse, respect, and violence. ✦ His poetry and plays have been published in such renowned literary journals as *Nkombo*, *African American Review*, and *Callaloo* and in the anthologies *A Bend in the River* and *Word Up*. ✦ For the past twenty years, worked in the New Orleans Public Schools as drama instructor in the Arts Connection and the Talented Arts Theatre/Drama programs. ✦ Until his death in 2025, he continued to work with adults and children, using theater as a tool to speak the truth to the people and bring about some positive social changes.

DAMIA KHANBOUBI

Damia Khanboubi is a creative producer, digital marketing strategist, graphic designer, and program officer with a fierce dedication to amplifying marginalized voices and dismantling systems of oppression. With a distinctive blend of artistry, strategic thinking, and leadership, she uses her diverse skill set to craft powerful narratives and develop impactful programs and events that inspire action and advance justice, equity, and liberation.

Born in Casablanca, Morocco, and raised in New Orleans, Damia's upbringing in two vibrant and very different cultures has instilled in her a unique perspective on the intersectionality of identity and community. This cultural duality informs her work and ensures that she approaches every project with a deep sense of cultural sensitivity and inclusivity.

Outside of work, Damia finds joy in crossword puzzles, game nights, and traveling with loved ones.

DWANA MAKEBA

Dwana Makeba is a passionate author, writer, and advocate for self-empowerment through storytelling. Known for her compelling narratives and deep cultural insights, Dwana's work often explores themes of identity, resilience, and personal growth. She is the author of *Didn't Wash Us Away*, a poignant novel that delves into the complexities of African American life, exploring the strength and endurance required to overcome life's challenges. The book captures both the painful and uplifting moments of a community's journey, weaving together stories of love, loss, and survival.

Her second book, *Gems and Juice*, is a collection of empowering essays and life lessons written with a mix of humor and wisdom. It touches on various aspects of life, from relationships to self-love, offering readers the tools to navigate their own journeys with confidence and grace.

In *Makeba's Guide to Natural Hair*, Dwana combines her personal experience with a deep understanding of cultural significance, offering readers practical advice and inspiration on embracing their natural beauty. The guide addresses the unique challenges of caring for natural hair while celebrating the joy of self-acceptance and cultural pride.

Dwana Makeba's work has resonated with readers across diverse communities as she continues to use her writing as a means of empowerment, healing, and celebration of one's true self. With a unique voice and perspective, Dwana is quickly becoming a respected author and thought leader in the literary world.

ED MORRIS

Ed Morris was born at Charity Hospital in New Orleans. He is a poet, preacher, servant leader, lawyer, and family griot.

CONTRIBUTORS

LOUISE MOUTON JOHNSON

Louise Mouton Johnson, visual artist and arts educator, was born and educated in New Orleans, Louisiana. After graduating from Xavier in 1976 with a BFA, she went to Cranbrook Academy of Art in Michigan and earned her MFA in 1980, specializing in printmaking. She taught visual arts in the New Orleans public school system for thirty-three years, fourteen of which were spent at NOCCA, while at the same time continuing to practice professionally, exhibiting and selling her prints, drawings, and quilts. In the spring of 2018, Johnson was selected as an Artist-in-Residence at the Joan Mitchell Center, where she was able to use the time and assigned studio space to plan and complete a body of artwork, including a major collaborative mixed-media commission.

Louise Mouton Johnson recently participated in a group exhibit entitled *Unthinkable Imagination: A Creative Response to the Juvenile Justice Crisis* at the Newcomb Art Museum of Tulane University. In the fall of 2023, she received a Take Notice grant from the National Performance Network. Louise Mouton Johnson has been an active member of the National Conference of Artists, New Orleans Chapter, since 1993, serving as recording secretary for more than ten years, assisting with the NCA Martin Luther King Jr. Annual Commemorative Exhibition, and chairing the annual Margaret Burroughs Symposium.

MINISTER WILLIE MUHAMMAD

Student Minister Willie Muhammad has served as the representative of the Honorable Minister Louis Farrakhan in New Orleans, Louisiana, at Muhammad Mosque No. 46 for nearly twenty years. A New Orleans native, he graduated from Walter L. Cohen High School and earned a bachelor's degree in secondary education from Xavier University. He is married to Sister Michelle Muhammad, with whom he shares two daughters.

A gifted playwright, Mr. Muhammad has received the August Wilson Award, with works like *A Forced Family Tradition* and *Color Me Dead* performed on stage. He was also a fellow in the Norman C. Francis Leadership Institute. Currently, he teaches history and social studies at Eleanor McMain High School.

Mr. Muhammad is a community leader and host of the nationally recognized online show *I HAVE A TESTIMONY*, featuring notable figures such as Rock Newman and Doug E. Fresh. He spearheaded the Nation of Islam's conflict resolution program, presented in over twenty-five cities, and has published materials promoting family and economic empowerment.

His outreach initiatives include Friendships in All Walks of Life, hosting community leaders like Big Chief Tyrone Casby. Honored by the Shriners of New Orleans, he became their first Honorary Lecturer. Mr. Muhammad also contributed to Hurricane Katrina recovery efforts and worked to hold law enforcement accountable in the Danziger Bridge case.

Passionate about youth development, he remains active in education, arts, and community empowerment, believing the future lies in nurturing young minds.

JAMILAH PETERS-MUHAMMAD

Jamilah Yejide Peters-Muhammad, known by her community as Mama Jamilah, describes herself as a born, bred, and deep-fried New Orleanian. She is a lifelong culture-bearer who cannot remember a time in her life when she was not immersed in the cultural gumbo that is New Orleans.She strongly believes that if we teach our youth who they are, no one can tell them who they are not. She is dedicated to preserving and promoting the wellness and cultural traditions of her African ancestors. She is co-founder of the Congo Square Preservation Society, Kumbuka African Drum & Dance collective, and Bamboula 2000. Mama Jamilah has performed and taught African dance and culture for over forty years. She is a gifted healer, dancer, singer, percussionist, and choreographer. Mama Jamilah is a member of Guardians of the Flame Maroon Society and, in the truth of the tradition, now has a fourth generation in the Black Masking Mardi Gras tradition.

Mama Jamilah works as the community outreach nurse of the New Orleans Musicians' Clinic and Assistance Foundation, health and wellness specialist at Ashé Cultural Arts Center, Health Ministry lead at the Christian Unity Baptist Church, and ministerial lead of Christian Unity's dance ministry, Mawasi. She currently serves locally and internationally around the work of spirituality, health, community, and culture. She is the founder of Shade Tree Ministries, dedicated as a place of solace and refuge to ALL.

Under Shade Tree, she has taken groups to share her love of travel and ROOTED Cultural Tours, a performing company. "Preserving the past to strengthen the future" is a mantra that guides her mission. She is blessed to be a mother, grandmother, and great-grandmother and serve as Mama Jamilah to her community.

VALENTINE PIERCE

Valentine Pierce explores all forms of writing: poetry, essays, playwriting, one-woman shows, short stories, journalism. Her debut book is *Geometry of the Heart* and her second book is *Up Decatur: Second Edition*.

As a visual artist, Pierce focuses on photography and graphic design work, which include poetry. She took her first tentative steps in 2000 for the *Inspirations* exhibit. She returned to New Orleans in February 2000, where her work was part of the *Future Reflections/Past Predictions* exhibit at the Isaac Delgado Fine Arts Gallery.

Pierce was the June 2006 writer-in-residence at A Studio in the Woods. Her writing has been published throughout the US. She has been featured on cable television and radio stations, including WWNO's *The Reading Life*. She co-hosted the Rhythm & Muse open mic at the Berkeley Museum, hosted WRBH's *The Writer's Forum*, and produced shows, including *It's Personal*, for which she received a New Orleans Jazz & Heritage Foundation grant.

In its review of the anthology *From a Bend in the River*, which includes Pierce's poem "Rivers of My Soul," the *Times-Picayune* called her a stalwart of the New Orleans poetry scene. The poem was choreographed by Newcomb College for Women's dance department for the inauguration of Tulane University's president. Spoken word presentations include the 2023 New Orleans Words and Music Festival as well as the 2017 and 2024 Louisiana Book Festivals.

Venues include WWOZ, City Park, community theaters and centers, universities, libraries, cafés, barroom patios, backyards, and varied cities.

CONTRIBUTORS

LOYCE PIERCE-WRIGHT

Loyce Pierce-Wright, a "champion of the common good," has lived a life of service to community and church. She earned a BS in French and Spanish education from Southern University in Baton Rouge, Louisiana, and a master's degree in educational administration and urban studies from the University of New Orleans. Her journey began as a foreign language teacher. She later served as deputy director of Human Resources Policy and Planning for the city of New Orleans and as assistant vice chancellor for Academic Affairs at Southern University at New Orleans. She was then tapped sequentially, by three governors, to serve as the executive director of the Louisiana Commission on Human Rights for nearly seventeen years, championing fairness and equality.

Her church service spans decades. She is a lector at St. Raymond & St. Leo the Great Catholic Church and has served as pastoral council president, chairperson of the Planning Committee, and co-author of a history of the church entitled *Rising to Greatness*. She currently serves as president of the Board of Directors of the YWCA Greater New Orleans and EXCELth Primary Health Care. She is a member of the Louisiana Civil Rights Museum Advisory Board, Malcolm Jenkins Foundation, New Orleans Alumnae Chapter Delta Sigma Theta Sorority, Inc. and the Crescent City (LA) Chapter of The Links, Inc. Loyce finds her greatest joy in family. She is the loving widow of Louis C. Wright Jr. and devoted mother of Dr. Kiana Wright. Her personal mantra is, "There are Blessings in the midst of the storm, and God is . . . ."

GREGORY RATTLER SR.

Until recently, Greg Rattler was a managing director in the Government Banking segment of JPMorgan. He retired with over thirty-two years of government banking experience with governmental clients in Louisiana and Arkansas. Spanning his career, he was directly involved in financing over $1.2 billion in government credit transactions throughout the state of Louisiana. He has also participated in numerous leadership roles on various internal initiatives of the bank.

Greg previously served as deputy director and director of finance for the city of New Orleans in the administration of Mayor Ernest Morial and as first assistant state treasurer for the state of Louisiana in the State Treasurer Mary Landrieu administration.

He holds a BA in public administration (1981) and an MBA (1985), both from Loyola University of New Orleans. He is a proud 1978 honors graduate of St. Augustine High School in New Orleans. He is a fellow of the University of New Orleans' Institute of Public Policy, the American Society for Public Administration, and the Louisiana chapter of the Government Finance Officers Association. He is also a fellow of Leadership Louisiana, Inc. (1998), the New Orleans Regional Leadership Institute (2003), and the Loyola University Institute of Politics (2008).

His current civic commitments include board membership on the Trustee Board of Loyola University New Orleans, the Xavier Ochsner College of Medicine, Community Sailing New Orleans, Inc., and the Finance Advisory Committee of St. Augustine High School. Greg is a member of the Silverback Society, which mentors at-risk eighth grade males in schools throughout New Orleans. He is active in the Zulu Social Aid & Pleasure Club and is a member of the Krewe of Bacchus. Greg is a lifelong member of the Blessed Sacrament/St. Joan of Arc Catholic Church, serving on the Marriage Ministry, the Parish Finance Council, and the Men's Ministry. Greg is married to Twyla Rattler and is the proud father of four sons and a grandparent to three grandchildren.

ASANTE SALAAM

Asante Salaam is a multidisciplinary artist, cultural alchemist, and visionary leader who transforms the ordinary into the extraordinary through artistry and collaboration. Rooted in New Orleans' rich cultural landscape and a legacy of Black arts activism, she combines timeless principles with innovative approaches to create experiences that inspire and reimagine.

Her work transcends boundaries, bridging local heritage with global perspectives, amplifying voices, and honoring traditions. From launching The Helis Foundation John Scott Center to producing cultural festivals and convening indigenous community workers across continents—including in New Zealand, Mexico, and the United Kingdom—Asante curates transformative projects that spark collective growth.

With over three decades of creative leadership, Asante has led initiatives in regenerative hospitality consulting for Beloved Community, family-focused programs for TrainingGrounds, and sustainable cultural practices for diverse organizations. During her eight-year tenure with the city of New Orleans' Office of Cultural Economy, she produced arts, cultural, and economic development programs.

Her art, influenced by personal growth and holistic healing practices, includes visual chronicles of transformation, immersive installations, and imaginative portraits. Asante has held residencies at A Studio in the Woods and the Joan Mitchell Center and holds a Bachelor of Fine Arts from the School of the Art Institute of Chicago.

Asante's creative journey spans the globe, blending artistry, cultural diplomacy, and innovation to elevate humanity. Rooted in New Orleans—a city of cultural richness, indomitable spirit, and boundless creativity—she invites us to embrace transformation and the limitless power within us to shape new, empowered realities.

MATHEW SCHWARZMAN

My name is Mathew "Mat" Schwarzman, and I was born in 1960. I am Jewish, male, heterosexual, middle class, a Sagittarius. I have lived on all three coasts: the East Coast (southern New Jersey) for my first twenty-six years, the West Coast (San Francisco/Oakland) for the next fourteen years, and the Gulf Coast (New Orleans) for the last twenty-three years. This is the place I want to stay. The amazing Mimi Zarsky and I have been married since 1991, no kids. In college, I was trained as a theater artist and transformative learning educator. My proudest work accomplishments are creating educational programs for adults, like the Arts & Social Change Program at New College of California, and for youth, like the Creative Forces Teen Theater Group at New Orleans Charter Science and Mathematics High School. I co-authored *The Beginner's Guide to Community-Based Arts* with cartoonist Keith Knight. Currently, I am co-leader of the Trinity City Comics project, which engages young people in reading, writing, talking, and making art about the future of New Orleans.

CONTRIBUTORS

JULIE MENHATI SINGLETON

Julie Menhati Kherita Singleton, owner of The Breath Is Life Spa LLC, is a mother, native of New Orleans, Louisiana, and community wellness advocate. Her healing journey began as a young mother with two children (Tracy and Charlene Tantira Bridges), when she intuitively understood the important trifecta formed by health, wellness, and the spiritual connection of self.

This sparked inspiration to begin a full journey of study and practices, which garnered certification as a licensed massage therapist, HTAP, and labor companion (doula).

Leaning into her soul's work, Menhati exemplifies incredible compassion and the deep integrity in her being and in her healing work. She's a loving force of keen intuition, demonstrating great empathy toward all people.

Her passionate mission is to awaken her clients, community, and students to the importance of feeling alive and well by opening their hearts and minds to self-love.

NICK SLIE

Nick Slie is a New Orleans-born performer, director, producer, and cultural organizer. He is the co-founding artistic director of Mondo Bizarro and a professor of theater at Nunez Community College. His creative endeavors range from interdisciplinary solo performances to intimate community gatherings, from innovative digital storytelling projects to large-scale site-responsive productions. Since 2002, Nick's wide array of imaginative projects have toured to art centers, universities, and outdoor locations in forty states across the country and abroad.

Nick's family has loved and listened to the mysteries of Southeast Louisiana for ten generations. For over two decades, he has been passionately engaged in his hometown of Bulbancha/New Orleans, collaborating across sectors on a vast array of local performance and arts-based civic engagement endeavors. Interdisciplinary projects like the I-10 Witness Project, *Loup Garou*, *Race Peace*, *Cry You One*, the Gulf Coast Climate Justice Convening, and, most recently, *Invisible Rivers* have effectively catalyzed emotional engagement in the pressing issues of his home and, in so doing, created space for transformative action across race, class, and sector.

From 2004 to 2008, Nick served on the executive committee of Alternate ROOTS. He is the former board chair for the Network of Ensemble Theaters, was co-director of the Art and Survival Gathering, and currently serves on the boards of Goat in the Road and the North American Cultural Laboratory. He recently directed the seven-state tour of Clear Creek Creative's *Ezell: Ballad of a Land Man* and is deep in the dream space for Mondo Bizarro's current interdisciplinary project, *Invisible Rivers*.

KAREL SLOANE-BOEKBINDER

This family was guided by fate. Karel was introduced twice to Leo by two different friends. Neither of the friends knew each other, and each had different connections to Leo: one had been in a marching krewe with him, the other was a co-worker—two different friends from two completely different social circles. At the time of both introductions, Karel was dating someone else. When Katrina happened and the levee failures flooded the city, Karel began commuting weekly between Memphis and New Orleans and couch surfing. Out in New Orleans with Juliet Pazera, Leo's co-worker, they ran into him, and Juliet asked if Leo might have room for Karel to stay in the future. Karel being a houseguest led to long conversations, laughter, and the opportunity to get to know one another. That was twenty years ago—Leo and Karel were married April 14, 2007. Ted was born August 17, 2009.

Karel is an Equity Member Candidate and a SAG-Eligible actor represented by King Watts Talent; she has been an artist with Community Visions Unlimited since the Utility Box Project's inception in 2012. Since 2022, she has been a featured singer every Tuesday at Café Negril on the world famous Frenchman Street in New Orleans; all performances are available on the Café Negril YouTube page. In 2006, she received Maybelline's Women Who Inspire Confidence Through Education Award and, in 2011, the Big Easy Award for Arts Education. In 2011, Microsoft chose Karel as one of twenty-nine teachers for its Innovative Education Forum. Karel's master's thesis, *The Physiology of Creative Expression: Research and Practical Applications*, is available on Amazon.com.

CONTRIBUTORS

JOSÉ TORRES-TAMA

José Torres-Tama is an Ecuadorian-born interdisciplinary provocateur of Quechua indigenous descent. He's an award-winning performance and visual artist; published playwright and poet; photographer and journalist; arts educator with the Ogden Museum of Southern Art; and director of ArteFuturo Productions in New Orleans. Since 1995, he has toured nationally and internationally and performed at theater festivals in Slovenia, Poland, Mexico City, and Toronto. Brown, Duke, Cornell, Vanderbilt, and Louisiana State Universities and other academic institutions have presented his genre-bending performances.

He has received three National Performance Network Creation Fund Awards, two NALAC Fund for the Arts grants, two NEFA Project Capacity Building Grants, and a MAP grant for his radical *Taco Truck Theater* on-wheels ensemble project. In 2020, he was nominated for a prestigious Herb Alpert Award in the Arts, and in 2021, he finished a four-month studio residency at the Joan Mitchell Center in New Orleans and created a new large painting.

From 2006 to 2011, he contributed post-Katrina commentaries to NPR's *Latino USA* and exposed the myriad human rights violations Latin American immigrant reconstruction workers endured while heroically contributing to the epic rebirth of New Orleans. *ALIENS, IMMIGRANTS & OTHER EVILDOERS* is his critically acclaimed show, and it has sold out theaters in Houston, Minneapolis, New Orleans, and Los Angeles.

Northwestern University Press published the full one-man play script of *ALIENS* in *Encuentro: Latinx Performances for the New American Theater*, an anthology of six contemporary Latinx playwrights. Diálogos, an imprint of Lavender Ink inNew Orleans, published *Immigrant Dreams & Alien Nightmares*, his debut poetry collection of socially conscious verse. *Hard Living in the Big Easy: Immigrants & Photography of Post-Katrina Protests 2010–2019* is his forthcoming book. www.torrestama.com

CONTRIBUTORS

LISA USDIN

Dr. Usdin is the president of Swamplily, LLC. In this capacity, she has helped match the strategic interests of philanthropic organizations with the needs and capacities of local nonprofits and governmental agencies in diverse areas. In the last fifteen years, she has worked with the Ford, Open Society, Conrad N. Hilton, David and Lucille Packard, and Greater New Orleans Foundations and the Foundation for Louisiana. She has served on expert advisory panels on community resiliency for the National Academy of Medicine, the RAND Corporation, and the Robert Wood Johnson Foundation. In addition, she has taught courses on building community engagement in public health efforts for the Region 6 Public Health Leadership Institute, the Centers for Disease Control and Prevention, and Tulane University School of Public Health and Tropical Medicine and has facilitated strategic planning processes for groups such as the city of New Orleans, National Network of Public Health Institutes, and Montefiore Einstein Medical Center in the Bronx.

Dr. Usdin was awarded a Bellagio fellowship from the Rockefeller Foundation. She graduated magna cum laude with a BA in psychology from Duke University and has a master's degree in public health from the University of California at Berkeley and a DrPH from the international health department at Tulane School of Public Health and Tropical Medicine. She has served on the Joan Mitchell Foundation, Second Harvest Food Bank, WWNO, Propeller, and Louisiana Public Health Institute.

KYSHUN WEBSTER SR.

Dr. Kyshun Webster, artist, author, activist, and academician, is an award-winning, maverick scholar and social innovator who, since his teenage years, as an applied social scientist, has used the community as his laboratory for social innovation and change. A native of New Orleans, Webster has more than twenty-five years of experience working with youth across the educational and juvenile justice spectrum—from cradle to careers. Dr. Webster once led a national youth organization, the Gulfsouth Youth Action Corps, with a bodacious vision that boldly proclaimed, "One day, no one would have to ask the proverbial question, 'Where will our next generation of leaders come from?'" The organization funded youth-led, youth-driven solutions to community problems affecting youth. Webster is a two-time recipient of the coveted Open Society Equality Fellowship Award. Currently, Dr. Webster is the executive producer of *Children of The Dream*, a docu-series film in production that tells the story of how civil rights icons in the 1980s developed the 21st Century Youth Leadership Movement, in which he participated, to prepare youth to lead at this very moment in time.

TRUDELL & DWIGHT WEBSTER

Trudell Webster is nationally certified in massage therapy and bodywork, with more than twenty-four years dedicated to the disciplines of massage therapy, the healing arts, and health education, having completed the Blue Cliff College massage therapy diploma program. Prior to that, she graduated from San Francisco State University, San Francisco, California, with a BA in broadcast communication arts/journalism and pursued graduate studies toward the master of theology degree at Xavier University, New Orleans, Louisiana.

Trudell's mission and ministry in the field of holistic health and wellness is to make a difference on the planet—one muscle at a time.

Dwight Webster is the senior pastor of the 134-year-old Beth Eden Baptist Church in Oakland, California and is pastor emeritus of Christian Unity Baptist Church in New Orleans, having served for over twenty-seven years as its senior and founding Pastor.

He is the co-founder of the Jeremiah Group, a broad-based community coalition; Churches Supporting Churches, a post-Katrina recovery group; and Justice and Beyond, an intersectional forum and advocacy platform in New Orleans.

He served as interim director and interim dean of the Program of Black Church Studies at Colgate Rochester Divinity School/Bexley Hall/Crozer Theological Seminary (CRDS/BH/CTS) in Rochester, New York, and as director of the Center for African and African American Studies at Southern University at New Orleans.

Rev. Webster graduated from Howard University and CRDS/BH/CTS, receiving a BS and MDiv, respectively, and completed his PhD at the Graduate Theological Union in Berkeley, California.

Trudell and Dwight have four sons and four grandchildren.

MK WEGMANN

MK Wegmann is a lifelong New Orleanian who has been active in the arts and culture community throughout her life and work. She has fifty-plus years of experience in presenting and producing for nonprofit visual and performing arts organizations and is an advocate for social and racial justice.

Her thirteen years as a student at Ursuline Academy anchored her dedication to the arts and to the values of courtesy, loyalty, courage, and service. Upon graduating from Spring Hill College, Wegmann returned to New Orleans and completed the Master of Arts degree from LSUNO. She served as director of the Contemporary Arts Center for its first fourteen years and continues to volunteer. From 1992 to 1999, she served as the managing director of Junebug Productions, producing the Ec(h)o Arts Festival: People Gathering for Environmental Justice in 1998. In 2000, the National Performance Network (NPN) moved its offices to New Orleans, and she served as president and CEO until her retirement in 2016; NPN supports the national and international touring and commissioning of original work by community-engaged contemporary artists.

Since retiring, she consults with arts organizations in the visual and performing arts. Among her recent clients are Dance/USA, Antenna, National Assembly of State Arts Agencies, and Guardians of the Flame. She is one of the founders of the Louisiana Presenters Network and a past board chair of Alternate ROOTS and was founding president of the National Association of Artists' Organizations (NAAO). She received the Community Arts Award from the Arts Council of New Orleans and the Fan Taylor Distinguished Service Award from the Association of Performing Arts Professionals. Board service includes the Creative Alliance of New Orleans (CANO), Alternate ROOTS, Ursuline Academy Board of Trustees, and the Contemporary Arts Center's Emeritus Board.

MK lives on Frenchmen Street, loves cooking for big parties, and is known for her Mardi Gras Day open house. She shares her life with Lisa Mount, and they both live in New Orleans and in Sautee Nacoochee, Georgia.

LYNNETTE WHITE-COLIN

Lynnette White-Colin is an independent consultant specializing in public and private sector projects related to economic development. She previously held the position of senior vice president of Business Growth & Strategy at the New Orleans Business Alliance (NOLABA), a public–private partnership with the city of New Orleans. During her tenure, Ms. White-Colin secured over four million dollars for the organization and led small business programming focused on alleviating growth barriers for underrepresented founders. She established InvestNOLA, a business growth accelerator aimed at scaling high-growth potential businesses owned by ethnic minorities. Furthermore, she managed relationships within the local private sector, anchor institutions, and public agencies to foster procurement contract opportunities for business owners of color.

Prior to her role at NOLABA, Lynnette directed economic development programming at the Urban League of Louisiana, where she oversaw a high-performing Women's Business Center and founded the Contractors Resource Center and the Women-In-Business Challenge Accelerator. These programs continue to support Black-owned construction firms and women business owners.

As executive director of the Oretha Castle Haley Boulevard Merchants & Business Association and the Main Street Initiative, she led a revitalization strategy for the historic commercial corridor and cultural district of Oretha Castle Haley Boulevard, resulting in over $200 million in development projects. Additionally, she initiated the first commercially-focused urban land trust in the country.

Previously, as vice president with Hope Enterprise Corporation, Ms. White-Colin served as regional director of retail operations for Hope Credit Union. In this role, she worked extensively with small and micro businesses to facilitate financing access. She also directed consumer lending, deposit and retail operations, and managed the organization's socially responsible investment and philanthropic relationships, leveraging over eight years of diverse banking experience.

Lynnette holds a bachelor's degree in business administration from the University of New Orleans and was awarded a Certified Credit Union Executive certificate from the National Federation of Community Development Credit Unions at Southern New Hampshire University. She serves on the boards of the International Business Innovation Association and New Orleans Redevelopment Unlimited, an agency of the city of New Orleans. Her former board memberships include Ashé Cultural Arts Center, the New Orleans Regional Black Chamber of Commerce, and the East New Orleans Business Development District.

FREDDI WILLIAMS EVANS

Freddi Williams Evans is internationally recognized for her scholarship on New Orleans' Congo Square. Her book *Congo Square: African Roots in New Orleans* received the 2012 Louisiana Humanities Book of the Year Award and has been published in French. Her research and advocacy influenced the New Orleans City Council ordinance that changed the name of the historic location from Beauregard Square, named after Confederate General P. G. T. Beauregard in 1893, to Congo Square in 2011. She has presented in France and Senegal, sponsored by American embassies, as well as in Berlin, Germany, and Bordeaux, France.

Evans is the founder of CongoSquareConnection.org, an online resource for the study of the landmark. She co-chaired the New Orleans Committee to Erect Historic Markers on the Slave Trade to Louisiana and helped to erect the UNESCO Site of Memory Middle Passage Marker. As an arts educator, she implemented and administered programs in public and private organizations and initiated the first New Orleans Teaching Artist Institute.

Her books for young readers include *Passing It On: The Art of John T. Scott*, *Come Sunday: A Young Reader's History of Congo Square*, *Hush Harbor: Praying in Secret*, *The Battle of New Orleans: The Drummer's Story*, and *A Bus of Our Own*.

Evans received the 2024 Lifetime Contributions to the Humanities award from the Louisiana Endowment for the Humanities. She is a native of Madison, Mississippi, and a graduate of Tougaloo College, in Tougaloo, Mississippi, and Hahnemann Medical College (now Drexel University) in Philadelphia, Pennsylvania.